Web Design:
The Complete Reference
Second Edition

About the Author

An Internet professional for numerous years prior to the introduction of the Web, Thomas Powell brings an interesting combination of networking and technical expertise to the Web design community. In 1994 he founded PINT, Inc. (www.pint.com), a web development firm with headquarters in San Diego, which serves numerous corporate clients around the country.

Powell is also the author of numerous other Web development books, including the bestsellers: *HTML: The Complete Reference*, *JavaScript: The Complete Reference*, and *Web Site Engineering*. He also writes frequently about Web technologies for *Network World* magazine.

Mr. Powell teaches Web design and development classes for the University of California, San Diego Computer Science and Engineering Department, as well as the Information Technologies program at the UCSD Extension. He holds a B.S. from UCLA and an M.S. in Computer Science from UCSD.

About the Technical Editor

Fritz Schneider is a software engineer at a major Internet search engine. He is co-author of JavaScript: The Complete Reference and served as the technical editor for HTML: The Complete Reference. Schneider holds a B.S. in Computer Engineering from Columbia University and an M.S. in Computer Science from UC San Diego.

Web Design:
The Complete Reference
Second Edition

Thomas Powell

McGraw-Hill/Osborne

New York   Chicago   San Francisco
Lisbon   London   Madrid   Mexico City
Milan   New Delhi   San Juan
Seoul   Singapore   Sydney   Toronto

McGraw-Hill/Osborne
2600 Tenth Street
Berkeley, California 94710
U.S.A.

To arrange bulk purchase discounts for sales promotions, premiums, or fund-raisers, please contact **McGraw-Hill/Osborne** at the above address. For information on translations or book distributors outside the U.S.A., please see the International Contact Information page immediately following the index of this book.

Web Design: The Complete Reference Second Edition

1234567890 DOC DOC 0198765432

ISBN 0-07-222422-8

Publisher
  Brandon A. Nordin

Vice President & Associate Publisher
  Scott Rogers

Acquisitions Editor
  Megg Morin

Project Editor
  Julie M. Smith

Acquisitions Coordinator
  Tana Allen

Technical Editor
  Fritz Schneider

Copy Editor
  Carl Wikander

Proofreaders
  Linda Medoff, Paul Medoff

Indexer
  Jack Lewis

Computer Designers
  Carie Abrew, George Toma Charbak

Illustrator
  Michael Muller, Lyssa Wald

This book was composed with Corel VENTURA™ Publisher.

Contents at a Glance

Contents

Part I

Foundation

Part II

Site Organization and Navigation

Part III

Elements of Page Design

Part IV

Technology and Web Design

Part V

Appendixes

Acknowledgments

When you take the time out of your life to write a doorstop-sized book like this one, you tend to rely on a lot of people's assistance. I'll mention only a few of them here to avoid adding any more pages to this already massive tome.

First, as always, the folks at Osborne were a pleasure to work with. Megg Morin somehow puts up with me year after year and the books keep getting done. Without Megg, I probably wouldn't be a prolific author. Tana Allen also provided great assistance in editing and project management, while Carl Wikander provided rigorous copy editing. Finally, thanks to Julie Smith for enduring the ghastly long phone calls necessary to help ferret out proof problems.

My technical editor Fritz Schneider did an excellent job. Having seen the other side of the fence as my co-author on the *JavaScript: The Complete Reference*, he didn't let me get away with much.

My employees at PINT provided dozens of right hands for me and deserve special mention. First, Mine Okano has helped run another book project and done an excellent job at it. I am not sure she expected this when she came to work for me, but she's done a great job. Dan Whitworth also continues to tackle book projects, and probably wonders what he did in a previous life to deserve fixing my poor grammar. Catrin Walsh and Kim Smith lent some valuable assistance in the site production, usability, and site testing content. Other PINT employees, including Jimmy Tam, Rob McFarlane, Maria

Defante, Eric Raether, Cathleen Ryan, Meredith Hodge, Nigel Paxton, David Sanchez, Dave Andrews, Melinda Serrato, Michele Bedard, Candice Fong, Cory Ducker, Anh Gross, Kun Puparussanon, Huijuan Yin, Marcus Richard, Kevin Griffith, Christine Lawson, and numerous others, helped out directly on edits or just kept the projects rolling while I was busy. Joe Lima, Allan Pister, Christie Kennedy, and Jared Ashlock deserve some praise for getting some of my outside software project duties taken care of as well.

The students in my undergraduate and extension classes always make good points and many of their ideas are incorporated into new editions. Daisy Bhonsle deserves to be singled out for always helping with my books by catching errors and making suggestions for improvements.

Somehow I find a way to have time outside of the Web for friends, family, and home. My wife Sylvia made sure I didn't work all day on the weekends, and our Schnauzer puppy Tucker kept both of us very busy with his antics. However, now that I'm finished with the book and the dog is housebroken, with any luck a restful Wakaya visit or other trip will be up next.

Finally, the most thanks go to the thousands of readers around the world who have purchased my various Web technology and design books. It is really a great pleasure to get such positive feedback and see folks putting this information to good use.

Introduction

A thick Web design book without glossy paper and pictures! Who would have thought it would be published? That's exactly what I set out to do a few years back and it seemed to make sense to enough readers that now it has even been massively updated. Why engage in such a fool's errand? Simply because there are plenty of Web design books out there that provide color snapshots of well-implemented sites or short discussions of the cool features in today's trendy sites. However, given the fluid nature of the Web, the interesting sites have often changed by the time the ink has dried on the pages, leaving only a paper record of what the site used to be like. Worse yet, what *is* left only tells part of the story. It often hides the usability problems, the technical execution problems, and the slow loading pages. Even so, I often turn to such resources as they provide a great deal of visual inspiration. But they tell only half the story—and I will try to tell the other half in this book.

The goal here is to talk about what makes sites work beyond the trends of the latest font or visual treatment. Usability will certainly be a major concern, but so will correct construction. I'll try to speak from the experience I gained from building hundreds of sites over the years with my firm. Some of the projects worked well and others didn't, and I found that I learned not only from my successes, but also from the failures of both my own projects and those I have observed or rescued. Experience is truly the best teacher in an industry as young as Web design. I'll try to make sure to teach the fine balance between designer wants and user needs, between form and function, and between uniqueness and consistency, all while respecting what is possible to execute in the chaotic medium known as the Web.

After reading this book, you'll truly appreciate how Web design is a fluid mixture of art and science, inspiration and execution, and ultimately, of frustration and elation. You may excel on the visual side of a site only to fail in the technology or delivery aspects. Web design is all-encompassing and the investment in understanding deeper medium and technical issues will pay huge dividends in future projects.

Yet as you read this book, you might not always agree with what I have to say. You may even find that some of the rules and suggestions are not perfectly consistent. However, that may be the point—to get you to think and not dismiss something out of hand. Instead, ponder why such rules and suggestions were developed before you throw caution to the wind. Great designers, regardless of medium, bend or break established rules on purpose. Real breakthroughs rarely come due to ignorance or arrogance.

Unfortunately, I won't be able to guarantee a proven step-by-step process that ensures a great Web site. Some things really do take practice. Building numerous sites and browsing even more sites is required to excel at Web design. However, I can say that if you do read this book, you'll have at least half of what you need to make great sites. The rest will be up to you and your creativity. So get out there and show the Web what you can do!

Using This Book

The book is used as a textbook for a course in Web design theories and practices as well as a reference book. The first section provides foundation information about common Web design principles, usability issues, core Web technologies, and development practices. The second section focuses primarily on site organization, navigation, and usability concerns. The final section addresses execution issues with focus on best practices. The appendices of the book provide compact reference material on HTML, CSS, fonts, colors, and other Web issues. Such an organization should make this book not only useful to understand major Web design issues, but to keep around for future consultation. The Web site at www.webdesignref.com provides support for the book including examples, reference materials, related links, and of course errata. More novice Web designers should read the book sequentially as chapters build on one another. However, experienced designers may find that single chapters or sections can be read safely in isolation if they are familiarizing themselves with a particular topic or attempting to fill in knowledge gaps.

The text does assume that readers are fairly fluent in core Web technologies like HTML, CSS, and JavaScript and can use basic graphics manipulation tools like PhotoShop or Fireworks. Readers interested in better understanding the core Web technologies may find *HTML: The Complete Reference* (www.htmlref.com) and

JavaScript: The Complete Reference (www.javascriptref.com) also useful. The three books together provide a complete discussion of the theory and execution of the popular client-side Web technologies that are not tied into the use of a particular Web tool. Tutorial books on the various editors and other Web tools can of course be utilized in conjunction with any of the books.

Good luck to you!

Thomas A. Powell
tpowell@pint.com
Summer 2002

The
Complete
Reference

Part I

Foundation

Chapter 1

What Is Web Design?

3

Most discussions of Web design get off track in short order, because what people mean by the expression varies so dramatically. While everyone has some sense of what Web design is, few seem able to define it exactly. Certain components, such as graphic design or programming, are a part of any discussion, but their importance in the construction of sites varies from person to person and from site to site. Some consider the creation and organization of content—or, more formally, the *information architecture*—as the most important aspect of Web design. Other factors—ease of use, the value and function of the site within an organization's overall operations, and site delivery, among many others—remain firmly within the realm of Web design. With influences from library science, graphic design, programming, networking, user interface design, usability, and a variety of other sources, Web design is truly a multidisciplinary field.

Defining Web Design

There are five areas that cover the major facets of Web design:

- **Content**   This includes the form and organization of a site's content. This can range from the way text is written to how it is organized, presented, and structured using a markup technology such as HTML.

- **Visuals**   This refers to the screen layout used in a site. The layout is usually created using HTML, CSS, or even Flash and may include graphic elements either as decoration or for navigation. The visual aspect of the site is the most obvious aspect of Web design, but it is not the sole, or most important, aspect of the discipline.

- **Technology**   While the use of various core Web technologies such as HTML or CSS fall into this category, technology in this context more commonly refers to the various interactive elements of a site, particularly those built using programming techniques. Such elements range from client-side scripting languages like JavaScript to server-side applications such as Java servlets.

- **Delivery**   The speed and reliability of a site's delivery over the Internet or an internal corporate network are related to the server hardware/software used and to the network architecture employed.

- **Purpose**   The reason the site exists, often related to an economic issue, is arguably the most important part of Web design. This element should be considered in all decisions involving the other areas.

Of course, the amount each aspect of Web design influences a site may vary according to the type of site being built. A personal home page generally doesn't have the economic considerations of a shopping site. An intranet for a manufacturing company may not have the visual considerations of a public Web site promoting an action movie. Precisely what is meant by the expression "Web design" seems to be fluid; our discussion must take this into account, but at the same time provide ideas concise enough for the designer to keep in mind at all times. We'll start first with abstract definitions and get more concrete as we move on.

The Web Design Pyramid

One way to think of all the components of Web design is through the metaphor of the Web pyramid shown in Figure 1-1. Content provides the bricks that build the pyramid, but the foundation rests solidly on both visuals and technology, with a heavy reliance on economics to make our project worth doing.

As Web designers, we try to plan our sites carefully, but construction is difficult. The shifting sands of Web technology make it challenging to build our site; construction requires teamwork and a firm understanding of the Web medium. Even if we are experts able to construct a beautiful and functional Web site, our users may look at our beautiful construction with puzzlement. Designers, or their employers, often spend more time considering their own needs and wants than those of the site's visitors. Our conceptual Web pyramids may become too much like brick-and-mortar pyramids—impenetrable

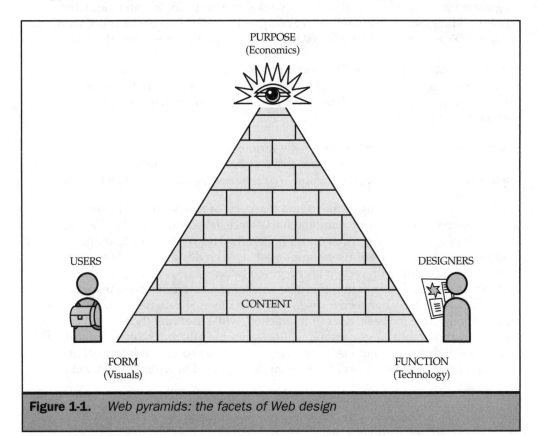

Figure 1-1. *Web pyramids: the facets of Web design*

tombs that leave us wondering if the users who strike out over the Web to reach our monuments can even find the door. Do they even understand the point of the site?

While Web development challenges aren't quite on the level of those faced by the ancient Egyptians, building a functional, pleasing Web site that can stand the test of Internet time is certainly not easy. The pyramid provides a simple way for designers to think of all aspects of Web design in interplay, but does little to provide a deeper understanding of the Web medium.

The Medium of the Web

While the Web pyramid analogy is a very abstract way of describing Web design, it is a useful tool for showing the interplay of the various components of Web building. A more practical way to discuss Web design is to think of the various components of the Web medium, as shown in Figure 1-2.

Today's Web sites are primarily a basic client-server network programming model with three common elements:

The server-side   This includes the Web server hardware and software as well as programming elements and built in technologies. The technologies can range from simple CGI programs written in PERL to complex multi-tier Java based applications and include backend technologies such as database servers that may support the Web site.

The client-side   The client-side is concerned with the Web browser and its supported technologies, such as HTML, CSS, and JavaScript languages and ActiveX controls or Netscape plug-ins, which are utilized to create the presentation of a page or provide interactive features.

The network   The network describes the various connectivity elements utilized to deliver the Web site to a user. Such elements may be the various networks on the public Internet or the private connections within a corporation—often dubbed an *intranet*.

Complete understanding of the technical aspects of the Web medium, including the network component, is of paramount importance in becoming a great Web designer, and much of this book will focus on these details. The Web pyramid diagram again reminds us of the important user component, as Web design really is a networked programming pursuit with certain user-focused issues.

Web sites are used as a communication mechanism between a site's owners and its users, and occasionally between its users and each other. Site owners usually set the message and define the basic rules of interaction, while users are those who visit the site and attempt to use the content or facilities presented there. The communication path between site owner and visitor can vary. Site owners often set information for users to consume, in somewhat of a one-way interaction. Other times users can post

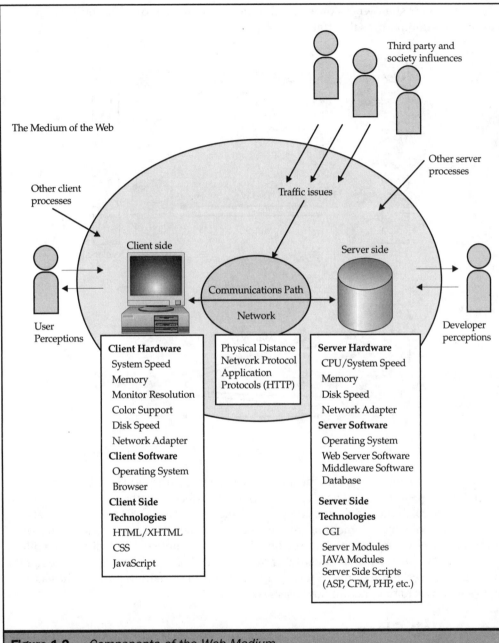

Figure 1-2. *Components of the Web Medium*

information for site owners or even other users, creating more of a multi-way communication path, as illustrated here:

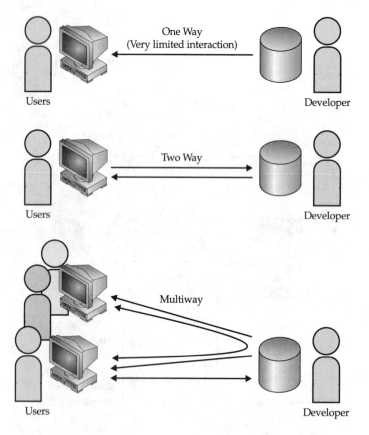

During any communication, most users are generally unaware of the medium when things are working correctly. While users are affected by the medium, they often do not distinguish the individual components such as network, HTML, style sheets, and JavaScript—unless something goes wrong. In the negative case of a slow site, or one that causes visual or functional errors, the user may notice the medium but still may not distinguish which aspect of it is causing the problem. Users tend to see not the parts themselves, but the sum of them. This makes it important to think of sites as a whole, in order to understand how users see them.

Types of Web Sites

Users tend to view Web sites, and thus Web site design, by the function of the site or by its visual appearance. It is important to be able to describe sites this way; however, there are many more ways to categorize them. While the possible categories of sites may appear endless, we can safely group sites in a few general ways. We'll start first with the abstract and then move to visual categorizations.

Abstract Groupings

First, consider if a site is information focused or task focused. Sometimes we may describe this distinction as one between a site that is *document-centered* and one that is *application-centered*. Document-centered or informational sites provide information for users, but they provide very limited interactivity (other than allowing the user to browse, search, or sort the information presented). Sites that are task or applications oriented allow the user to interact with information or accomplish some task, such as transferring funds from a bank account or buying a new sweater. Hybrid sites do a little of both; these are becoming more common as the line between information and application blurs. Figure 1-3 plots the continuum from a simple static document-oriented site

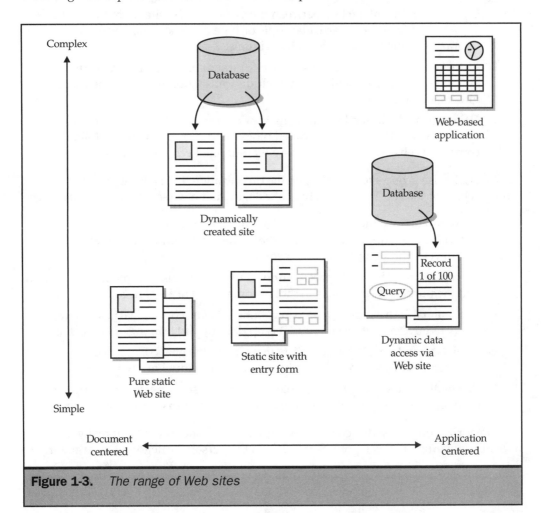

Figure 1-3.   *The range of Web sites*

(often called a "brochureware" site) to full-blown software applications. This abstract grouping suggests that there is a transition from more document- or print-oriented Web sites to more interactive programmatic Web sites. This is indeed true; the intersection between the two philosophical camps is a source for much of the contention—and innovation—in the Web design community.

Another way we might group sites is within the following broad categories:

- **Informational sites**   These sites provide information about a particular subject or organization (the "brochureware" sites). These are the most common Web sites on the Internet and often take on aspects of the other site categories over time.

- **Transactional sites**   This type of site can be used to conduct some transaction or task. E-commerce sites fall into this category.

- **Community sites**   These provide information or transaction-related facilities, but focus on the interaction between the visitors of the site. Community-based sites tend to focus on a particular topic or type of person and encourage interaction between likeminded individuals.

- **Entertainment sites**   These sites are for game playing or some form of amusing interaction, which may include transactional, community, and informational elements.

- **Other sites**   Included here are artistic or experimental sites, personal Web spaces such as Web logs (also called blogs), and sites that may not follow common Web conventions or have a well-defined economic purpose.

We might also group sites based upon the organization that is running, or in some sense paying for, the site. Within this type of categorization we see five major groupings:

- **Commercial**   A site in this group is built and run by an organization or individual for commercial gain, either directly through e-commerce or indirectly through promotion for some off-line purchase of goods or services.

- **Government**   This site's parent entity is ultimately a government organization, and the purpose of the site is to satisfy some social or legal need.

- **Educational**   This type of site's parent entity is some educational institution (perhaps government related), and it is used to support learning or research goals.

- **Charitable**   A charitable site exists to promote the goals of a nonprofit organization or the charitable activities of an individual or organization.

- **Personal**   The site exists at the sole discretion of some person or group for any number of reasons, usually as a creative outlet or form of personal expression.

Categorization can be difficult. For example, educational sites might really fall under the governmental category. Some sites in the personal category may arguably belong in the charitable or commercial group, depending on the reason for the person putting the site together. Now we turn to the more visual characteristics of sites, with a few sample categories of sites commonly seen on the Web.

Visual Groupings

As we group sites visually, we may see a range from those which rely more heavily on text and those which focus more on graphic presentation or imagery. The four most common design schools on the Web are:

- **Text oriented**   These are sites designed with a focus on textual content. Such sites, as shown in Figure 1-4, are relatively lightweight, download-wise, and often somewhat minimalist in design.

- **GUI style**   These are sites that follow certain graphical user interface (GUI) conventions from software design, such as top-oriented menu bars, icons, and pop-up windows. GUI-oriented sites range from simple GUI devices added to a primarily text-oriented site to full-blown Web applications with customized user interface widgets. Figure 1-5 shows some examples of GUI style Web sites.

Figure 1-4.   *Text-oriented sites*

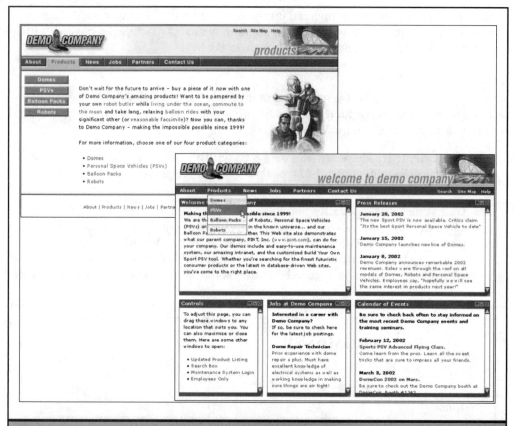

Figure 1-5.   *Web Designs with a little GUI or a lot of GUI*

■ **Metaphorical**   Metaphor sites borrow ideas from "real life." For example, a site about cars might employ a dashboard and steering wheel in design and navigation. A metaphor-designed site, as shown in Figure 1-6, tends to be extremely visual or interactive. This may be frustrating to some users and engaging to others.

■ **Experimental**   Experimental designs attempt to do things a little differently than the norm. Creativity, unpredictability, innovation and even randomness are often employed in sites following the experimental design style, as shown in Figure 1-7.

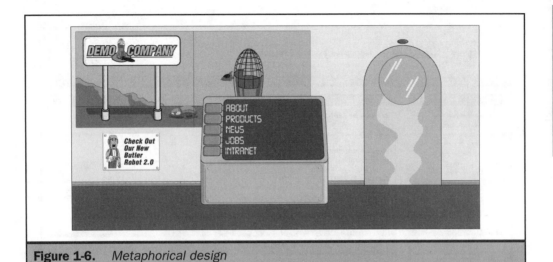

Figure 1-6.   *Metaphorical design*

Figure 1-7.   *Experimental design*

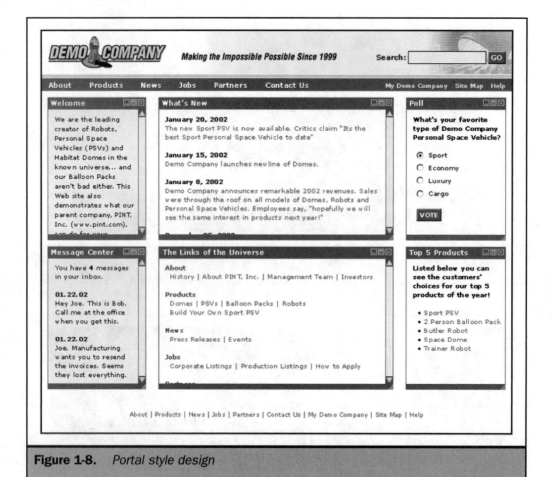

Figure 1-8.   *Portal style design*

Of course, on the Web we find mixtures of form or potential new categorization of sites. For example, how would you categorize a *portal site*, such as the one shown in Figure 1-8, that provides a wealth of content, navigation choices, and even community related-facilities in a single page? This is certainly a design style that is used in a great deal of sites. We see the potential rise of other design categories when we look at Web site genres such as e-commerce sites, particularly strict "catalog and cart" sites, as well as online personal journal sites called "Weblogs" or "blogs." We'll take a closer look at these design ideas in later chapters.

A Clearer Definition of Web Design

So, after all this discussion, what exactly is Web design? It is obviously a very user-centered multidisciplinary design pursuit that includes influences from visual arts, technology, content, and business. A succinct definition follows.

Web Design: A multidisciplinary pursuit pertaining to the planning and production of Web sites, including, but not limited to, technical development, information structure, visual design, and networked delivery.

Because Web design is so multidisciplinary, it is often appropriate to pull ideas and theories from related fields. Indeed, we've been doing that even in the very first pages of this book. Some people, however, take this approach a little too far, developing their sites in a manner similar to print pieces or adopting so many software GUI interface conventions that the user becomes confused. While Web design borrows heavily from other design pursuits, there are significant differences. For example, the medium is very different than print because more function is provided—not unlike software. Delivery issues and content effects make Web sites different from traditional software applications as well. Web design isn't just adoption of old ideas. It's something altogether new.

We shouldn't say the Web is totally different either. There are plenty of people who do that as well. The Web is so revolutionary, they say, that none of the old rules hold. This is complete nonsense. Despite the proclamations of pundits, new media forms have always adopted conventions from other forms and invented new ones of their own. Furthermore, no new form has completely eliminated any other. Radio, magazines, newspapers, television, and other entertainment media all continue to exist in some form or other despite emerging technologies and new media forms. The Web certainly isn't so new that we should throw out any valuable concepts we learned before. It does, however, have its own principles. We should strive to understand other media design concepts and modify them to fit the Web. The rest of the introduction will present some of the themes of Web design and conclude with a "roadmap" for the rest of the book.

Web Design Themes

When discussing Web design, we see similar themes come up over and over again. Whether it's the political struggle between a corporation's marketing department and information technology group over site ownership, or a graphic designer trying to convince a client of the appropriateness of a particular look or multimedia technology, these themes are at the heart of the matter. These issues often result in rather heated discussions among designers, as well as between designers and their clients both inside and outside corporate Web teams. While there is no simple answer to some of these issues, they are relatively easy to describe.

Generally the major themes behind modern Web design include:

- Designer needs versus user needs
- The balance of form and function
- The quality of execution
- The interplay between convention and innovation

In the abstract sense, these themes are not at all unique to the Web medium. Artists like Leonardo DaVinci certainly struggled at times to balance the desires of patrons and even his viewing public with his own needs. Commercial artists producing something like a magazine advertisement or billboard have to balance the demands of visual look with successful and clear communication. Execution varies in any discipline, but in one as young as Web design, the effects are more evident. Lastly, the rules of convention and the desires of innovation are as common as the struggle of a young person rebelling against convention, the middle age designer discovering the wisdom of the masters, and the old designer trying to rediscover his or her innovative youth. Despite the general nature of these themes, their specific details vary with each medium. It will be valuable to introduce each here before we encounter them later on. We start with the most important issue first: user-centered versus designer-centered site design.

User-Focused Design

A common theme of Web design is the focus on users. Unfortunately, a common mistake made in Web development is that, far too often, sites are built more for designers and their needs than for the site's actual users. Always remember this important tenet of Web design:

> **Rule: YOU are NOT the USER.**

What you understand is not what a user will understand. As a designer, you have intimate knowledge of a Web site. You understand where information is. You understand how to install plug-ins. You have the optimal screen resolution, browser setup, and so on. When you build your site around your own visual characteristics and skill levels, you often will confuse the actual users of the site. You must accept the fact that many users will not necessarily have intimate knowledge of the site you have so carefully crafted. They may not even have the same interests as you.

Given the importance of the users' interests and desires, it might seem appropriate to simply ask the users to design the site the way they want. This seems to be a good idea until you consider another basic Web design tenet:

> **Rule: USERS are NOT DESIGNERS.**

Not everyone is or should be a Web designer. Just as it would seem foolish to let moviegoers attempt to direct a major motion picture on the basis of their having viewed numerous movies, we should not expect users to be able to design Web sites just because they have browsed a multitude of sites. Users often have unrealistic requirements and expectations for sites. Users will not think carefully about the individual components of a Web site. In summary, users are not going to have the sophisticated understanding of the Web that a designer will have.

That said, the key to successful, usable Web site design is always trying to think from the point of view of the user. *User-centered design* is the term given to design that always puts the user first. But what can we say about users? Is there a typical user? Does a "Joe Average Internet" exist that we should design our sites for? Probably not, but we certainly should consider certain traits, such as reaction times, memory, and other cognitive or physical abilities, as we design sites. An overview of cognitive science helps us understand basic user capabilities; we will discuss this topic further in the next chapter. Remember, however, that while users may have similar basic characteristics, they are also individuals. What may seem easy to one user will be hard for another. Sites that are built for a "common" user may not meet the needs of all users. Power users may find a site restrictive, while novice users find it too difficult. Users are individuals with certain shared capacities and characteristics. Sites should take account of the relevant differences while focusing on the commonalities, as stated by the following Web design tenet:

Rule: Design for the common user, but account for differences.

Lastly, we can see that the differing needs of the user and the designer raise an issue of control. Control over a visit to a site is an unwritten contract between the designer and the visitor to how the experience will unfold. Often, sites provide little user control, forcing the user to view content in a predetermined order with little control over presentation or technology. Rarely do we find the exact opposite occurs, where the site gives users ultimate control over visitation, allowing them to choose what to see and how to see it and even allowing them to add to or modify the site's contents. However, most sites do allow the user some choices and the ability to control experience, but always under the influence of the designer's requirements. We'll revisit some of the general ideas of control and user experience throughout the book.

Form and Function

A key problem with Web design is that sites often do not balance form and function. Under the influence of modernism, many designers have long held that the form of something should follow its function. Consider that the form is one base of our Web design pyramid analogy, while function is the other. Function without form would be boring: while the site may work, it won't inspire the user. Conversely, even if the form is impressive, if the function is limited, the user will be disappointed. There needs to be a clear and continuous relationship between form and function. Put simply, the form of a site should directly relate to its purpose. If the site is marketing-driven, it might be very visual and even incorporate heavy amounts of multimedia if it helps to accomplish our goals. However, if the site is clearly a task-based one, such as an online banking site, it might have a much more utilitarian form. Of course, determining the appropriate form for a site requires that the function of the site be clearly defined. Unfortunately, for many Web sites the ultimate function of the site isn't always clearly conveyed. Even worse, the relationship of form and function for the site is not always clearly established.

Rule: Make sure the visual form of a site relates to its function.

It is likely that there will be a continual struggle between form and function, despite the fact that in nearly all cases the only side the designers should be on is that of their users. In fact, there really need be no disagreement. Form and function do not always have to fight; they complement each other nearly all of the time. A nice-looking design makes a functional site much better, while great functionality will make up for a deficiency in "look and feel" over time.

Seasoned designers understand this balance and practice the idea of holistic design by following the rule that the correct execution and integration of all facets of the site will outweigh the value of a single component. In fact, the real difference between a Web designer and a mere Web builder is that the former is capable of not only executing the individual parts of a site correctly but can also breathe extra "life" into the project as a whole.

Execution: The Easy Part?

HTML, XML, CSS, JavaScript, Java, Flash, browser compatibility, server capacity, and all the other components of Web development are the easy part of Web design. While learning a new technology might take some time and effort, it is generally quite easy to say whether some HTML or other technology is used correctly or not. However, today's sites are riddled with execution problems, ranging from simple typos to significant technical compatibility, delivery, and usability problems.

A Web site should only be considered excellent if it is useful, usable, correct, and pleasing. The meaning of each of these considerations is somewhat subjective, except in the case of correctness. For a site to be well designed, its execution must be excellent. This means that the site must not *break* in any way. The HTML must be correct and the images saved properly so that the page renders itself as the designer intended. Any interactive elements, whether in the form of client-side scripts in JavaScript or server-executed CGI programs, must function properly and not result in error messages. The navigation of the site must work at all times. Broken links accompanied by the all too familiar "404: Not Found" message are not the sign of a well-executed site. Errors, in fact, should be handled, and the site should fail gracefully, if at all. While execution seems like an obvious requirement for excellence, too many sites exhibit execution problems to let this consideration go unmentioned:

Rule: A site's execution must be close to flawless.

Why are execution problems rampant in Web sites? Simple: this is a young industry with changing standards. Consider state-of-the-art Web design from a few years ago and you'll see the difference. Further, most Web professionals often didn't have the background in computer science, networking, hypertext theory, cognitive science, and all the other disciplines that might affect the quality of the produced site. Some naïve designers even ignore the inherent differences in the emerging Web medium by not addressing problems of varying resolutions, color reproduction, bandwidth limitations, and so on. A Web designer who overlooks these types of technical characteristics of the Web is like the print designer who will not admit that ink bleeds on paper—great Web designers must know and respect the medium, which includes everything from browsers and bandwidth to programming and protocols.

Rule: Know and respect the Web and Internet medium constraints.

So, given the environment of Web design, we end up with today's assortment of sites, from those that are standards-compliant, lightweight, user-friendly, informational, and task-rich to those that are browser-specific, unusable, or multimedia bandwidth hogs touted as "next generation" designs. Yet does this comparison suggest that all good sites are the same? Not necessarily.

Conformity versus Innovation

Many Web designers feel that design theories and site design categorization increase conformity and stifle innovation. It is true that rigidly following design templates such as "top-left-bottom" layout or adhering to such common practices as putting organizational logos in the left corner of a Web page will limit some page design choices; designers have misunderstood the reason for these conventions. Consider that, while it might be possible to design books with triangular pages, few books are done this way. The cost of production, the awkwardness, and the reader's unfamiliarity with such a shape could make a triangular book a risky proposition. Most books are square or rectangular and have a distinct cover, title page, table of contents, chapter breaks, and so on. Are these conventions stifling to the book designer? Few would say they are; a great deal of creativity is still possible within the given constraints of a modern book. The same should be said for Web design. Graphical User Interface (GUI) design for software programs has influenced what is considered standard for Web user interfaces, but new ideas have also emerged. Designers need to respect conventions of navigation choices, navigation placement, colors, and so on. These ideas do not limit design; they simply constrain sites to recognizable forms so that users do not find the sites they visit to be completely different.

Rule: Appropriately respect GUI and Web interface conventions.

All these general "designing theories" set the stage for learning Web design, but when you apply them to a real site the theories will become much more specific. In short, we have a lot of ground to cover, so let's get started.

Learning Web Design

Reading a book like this is useful in uncovering the theories and commonly held practices of Web design, but more is required if you are to ever achieve mastery of Web design. Always remember that learning the basics of Web site development is not necessarily difficult, but do not underestimate the time and effort it will take to become an accomplished designer. This is no different from carpentry, painting, writing, illustration, or just about any skill you can think of. So make sure you set reasonable expectations for yourself as you learn.

One useful approach to learning Web design is by evaluating the efforts of others. We can look at what is done right and what is done wrong and try to emulate the good and fix the bad. Beware, however: it is not always easy to evaluate and compare site designs. Far too often people compare that which is not comparable. You would never compare a video game with a word processor, yet both are software programs. Why, then, do we compare experimental sites with corporate sites, or e-commerce sites with Web design agency portfolio sites? Far too often, this type of comparison is done in the Web design community. Sites and books put forward a variety of sites as absolute yardsticks of great design. Yet, obviously, not all sites will have the same issues as those that the "excellent design" rules were derived from. What is cool or clever for one site may be an absolute disaster for another. A great example is the splash page shown in Figure 1-9. A *splash page* is the term used to describe an entry page to a site—one that comes before the actual home or core page of the site.

Figure 1-9. *A splash page*

A splash page is often used to set the tone for the site and may consist of an interesting animation, preloading sequence, or some form of "installation" information in regards to what technology is required or what the user's expectations should be. While splash pages can be effective, very often they are not. The mere mention of the phrase "skip intro" results in hearty chuckles among many designers. Yet the much maligned splash page may just happen to have some uses. Some movie and entertainment sites have found such sequences to be an integral aspect of their sites. Just like a movie without opening credits, these sites would be incomplete without a splash page. This simple example illustrates the most dangerous problem facing those learning Web design—namely, assuming there is only one form of good Web design. Often, it seems that the only absolute in a fluid discipline like Web design is that there is no absolute.

Rule: There is no form of "correct" Web design that fits every site.

As you read this book, you'll notice that various rules and suggestions are presented. These are fairly safe and well thought out, but their real value comes from understanding the motivation for them, not from blindly applying them. The importance of this distinction will become apparent once you see that many of the "rules" seem at odds with other rules. Exhibiting good judgment that strikes a balance between conflicts is a key attribute of a great Web designer.

A discussion of site evaluations that attempts to cover all aspects of Web design from taste to technical implementation can be found in Chapter 5, and a checklist useful during such site evaluations is presented in Appendix B. Yet do not fall into the trap of becoming a professional critic. Certainly it is important to point out what not to do by finding flaws in sites or criticizing what is bad, but spending too much time discussing bad Web design may not be fruitful, particularly when you consider that there is no accounting for poor taste. It is easy to criticize, but it is much more difficult to take your acquired knowledge and apply it to a site of your own.

In the final analysis, the best approach to learning Web design is obviously by doing. Reading about site design theory or reviewing sites simply isn't a replacement for building sites of your own. Yet before you set out constructing a site, learn the core principles of Web design as well as the building and evaluation procedures that will help you construct your Web sites well.

Summary

Pinning down exactly what is meant by the term Web design can be difficult. At best we can see that Web design is a multidisciplinary pursuit that consists of five primary components: content, visuals, technology, delivery, and purpose. However, theories of exactly how these components should mix together vary from person to person as well as project to project. Striking a fine balance between form and function, user and designer, content and task, and convention and innovation is the lofty goal of the Web designer. The good designer knows that scales should not tip too far one way or another and tries to avoid the absolutisms of "correct" Web design. Yet not everything in the field of Web design is so abstract—many specifics can be found. Correct mastery of the technical medium and knowledge of various details and conventions are mandatory for aspiring Web practitioners. We begin the discussion of the core aspects of Web design in the next chapter, which focuses on user-centered design.

Chapter 2

User-Centered Design

As discussed in Chapter 1, Web sites are often developed from one particular philosophical reference point. Sometimes this point of reference is content-centered; other times, it is technology-centered. Even more frequently, it is graphics-centered. However, the real emphasis when building sites should always be the user. Keeping users in mind and always trying to meet their needs should be the key focus of user-centered design.

Understanding users needs isn't easy. While users may share common capabilities such as memory or reaction time, each user is still a distinct individual. Sites should be built for common user capabilities, rather than for the extreme novice or power user. Sites should be accessible to all and be able to account for the differences exhibited by individuals. Building a usable Web site is challenging, since what is usable to one person may be problematic for another. The likelihood of building a user-centered site is greatly improved through user interviews, testing, or even iterative design. Always be wary, though, of falling into the "user trap." While a site should always be built for users, the desires of the site's creators must also be met, even though these may be somewhat at odds with the desires of the site's users. The fine balance of power between user and designer is not always easily achieved.

Usability

Everyone has a vague idea of what it means for something to be *usable*. People will talk at length about how Web sites are supposedly user friendly, intuitive to use, or simply "usable." What, exactly, does it mean for something to be usable? First, consider the concept of *utility* in connection with two e-commerce sites that sell books and offer the same basic features. Both allow the user to search or browse for books, read information on books, purchase books, and track their orders. If both sites have basically the same features, they have the same utility—meaning they can do the same thing. Given that the sites have a few basic functions, you may find it easier to perform the same task on one site than the other. In this case, we can say that one site is more usable (has greater utility) than the other. Unfortunately, it is difficult to agree on what is usable. Plenty of people have attempted to characterize what usability is. Consider the following definition adopted from an ISO standard definition of *usability*:

> **Definition: Usability is the extent to which a site can be used by a specified group of users to achieve specified goals with effectiveness, efficiency, and satisfaction in a specified context of use.**

Consider each piece of the definition. First, note that we should limit the group of users when talking about usability. Recall that usability will vary greatly depending on the user.

Next, usability should be related to a task. You should not consider a site to be usable in some general sense. Instead, discuss usability within the context of performing some task, such as finding a telephone number for contact, purchasing a product, and so on. Usability is then judged by the effectiveness, efficiency, and satisfaction the user experiences trying to achieve these goals.

Effectiveness describes whether or not users are able to actually achieve their goals. If users are unable to, or only partially able to, complete a task they set out to perform at a site, the site really isn't usable. Next, usability is related to efficiency. If users make a great number of mistakes or have to do things in a roundabout way when they visit a site, the site isn't terribly usable. Last, the user must be satisfied with the performance of the task.

Many other definitions of usability exist. Some usability professionals suggest that usability can be concretely defined. Maybe it could be computed as some combination of the completion time for a typical visit and the number of errors made during the visit. From the user's point of view, that might not mean much. Users might just be concerned with how satisfied they were after performing a task. Many usability experts, such as Jakob Nielsen (http://www.useit.com), tend to have similar definitions more in line with the ISO one. For example, Nielsen suggests that the following five ideas determine the usability of a site:

- Learnability
- Rememberability
- Efficiency of use
- Reliability in use
- User satisfaction

By this definition, a site is usable if it is easy to learn, easy to remember how to use, efficient to use (doesn't require a lot of work on the part of the user), reliable in that it works correctly and helps users perform tasks correctly, and results in the user being generally satisfied using the site. This still seems fuzzy in some ways, and conflicts arise easily in the usability area. For example, a site that is easily learnable by a novice user may be laborious to use for a power user. Because people are different and come with different levels of capabilities and Web knowledge, not everyone is going to agree on what is supposedly usable. A site that is easy to one user may be hard for another.

Rule: There is no absolute description of what constitutes a usable site.

Even without considering user differences, we may find that usability varies according to how a single user interacts with a site. Usability also often depends on the medium of consumption—textual content viewed on the screen may be more usable in a large size, but when it is consumed on paper, it might be better smaller. If you have tried to read large amounts of small-size content online, you know it can be difficult. People tend to find that it is much easier to read it on paper. Some experts have suggested that people read much slower onscreen and tend to scan more than read content online. In this case, the medium of consumption—screen or print—has affected the usability of the content. In the case of the Web, the medium, which includes networks, browsers, screen sizes, and technologies like HTML, often contributes in a large way to usability problems. Throughout this book, the mantra of "know thy medium" should be repeated over and over.

Rule: Usability depends on the medium of consumption.

What is considered usable often varies between sites. An entertainment site would have different usability constraints than a commercial one. Further, the user's familiarity with a site—as well as how often the user accesses the site and for what purpose—will affect the site's perceived user friendliness. Consider how people may feel about the usability of a site that they have never been to before and are only marginally interested in, as opposed to one that they frequently visit or must use. They may be much more forgiving of errors in the site they need to use or have come to use than in the one they are just casually interested in. In short, a "throwaway" single-time-visit site has different usability constraints than a site a user relies on day to day.

Rule: Usability depends on the type of site as well as the user's familiarity with it.

This idea might seem a tad unusual, but it shouldn't. People often come to believe inefficient ways of doing things are perfectly acceptable. Be careful about getting too scientific when talking about usability (measuring page clicks, mouse travel, errors rates, and the like). How users "feel" about the experience when they come away—their satisfaction with the site or the task performed—is really the most important thing. For some people, how they feel may not always be logical or even totally related to what happened during the site visit. Consider how many people gain satisfaction from performing difficult tasks; they may feel that way about some sites as well. Also, people let organizations that they are familiar with outside the Web get away with things at their sites that a new company can't, simply because they trust the name brand of the older firm. On the other hand, don't assume that the occasionally illogical user can be used as an excuse to produce a site that is hard to use. A site that requires the user to learn a new way of doing things, is inflexible, results in errors, or just doesn't work will generally result in poor user satisfaction. Improve usability and users will be happier.

Rule: Usability and user satisfaction are directly related.

To understand how to make something usable, you must understand users. The next few sections will discuss usability in light of user capabilities and tendencies. The conclusion of the chapter will revisit these subjects and present a few rules of thumb that can be applied during Web site design to improve a site's usability.

Who Are Web Users?

Site designers often make the common mistake of oversimplifying or completely ignoring the capabilities and desires of users. In some cases, concerns about designing the site with a particular browser or bandwidth in mind replace any serious thought of the user. Don't design your site for Netscape—design for people who happen to use the Netscape browser. Always remember the following very important Web design rule:

Rule: Browsers don't use sites, people do.

Fortunately, most designers don't go the extreme of completely forgetting the user, but often they do oversimplify who the site's users are. Far too often, sites are built for some elusive stereotypical Web user—the modem user accessing via AOL, perhaps. This user is just a nameless person surfing the Internet to be enticed into visiting the site and performing whatever task the designer desires. The reality is that users are not automatons with the same capabilities and desires, but individuals with a wide range of physical capabilities, needs, wants, expectations, and goals. Real Web users have bad days or can't always figure things out sometimes, just like the rest of us.

Suggestion: There are no generic people. Always try to envision a real person visiting your site.

While it may not be possible to create a perfect stereotypical user to design Web sites for, there are some general things that can be said about users. The first thing is to think about how today's typical user interacts with a Web site. Until alternative browsing environments such as cell phones or PDAs become much more commonplace, a user of your site is almost certainly sitting at a desk or table with a computer. Users sit at most a few feet from a monitor and generally use a keyboard and a mouse to interact with a Web site shown on the monitor. Primarily, they are using their eyes to access the information on the screen, though sound may also come into play. The stimulus from the site is filtered, and choice items may be consumed or, more accurately, committed to short- or long-term memory. The information they consume then may cause them to react by, for instance, clicking a link or entering data into a form. This simplified view of a user interacting with a site is shown in Figure 2-1.

| Note | *Adding in the constraint of mobility, the user's environment can really change usability. If you consider a user who is walking while browsing on a PDA or cell phone, you can see how the environment can affect usability.* |

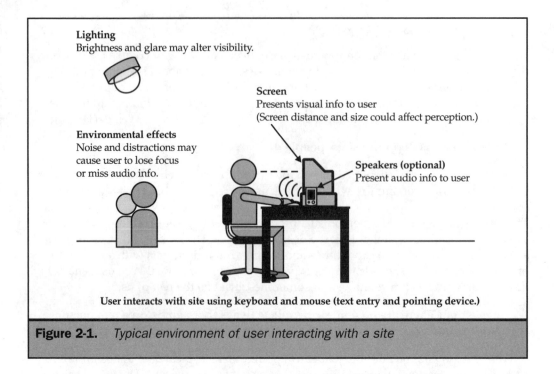

Figure 2-1.   *Typical environment of user interacting with a site*

You can describe how people tend to react to the world around them, including Web sites, in the following way. First, they encounter some sensation that is stored in memory. Then they try to understand the sensation, which is filtered both consciously and unconsciously. Information from past experiences may be called into action, influencing how they perceive things and possibly helping them decide what to do. From this perception, they may perform an action—or possibly take no action—that will later result in more sensations to be interpreted. This simplified action/reaction/ action loop is shown here:

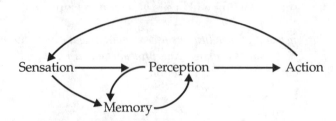

Do not think that people can be simplified to a formula where a stimulus is provided that results in an action. People are more complicated than that. People are capable of learning things, and information they encounter is committed to memory that can be used to modify what they do. Further, people aren't perfect. Problems may occur, such as not remembering things properly. Different people perceive stimuli differently. Not everyone sees color quite the same way, for instance. Despite its simplification, the model does force designers to consider how people interact with the world—which includes their Web site. Common user characteristics such as sensation and memory need to be well considered, at least in a general sense, when building sites.

Common User Characteristics

There are no generic people, but people tend to have similar physical characteristics. Most people tend see about the same, are capable of remembering things, and react to stimuli in about the same way. However, remember that people are individuals. There will be some users who will be able to see much better than others. There will be people who can memorize hundreds of links and be able to quickly filter them, and others who will be overwhelmed when presented with more than two choices. There will also be a few users who react much faster or much slower to information than the average user. However, as with all aspects of Web design, we should aim first for the common user and make sure to account for differences. Let's first consider common user characteristics such as vision, memory, and stimulus reaction.

Vision

The first aspect to consider about users is how they receive information from a Web site. The primary way most users consume data from Web sites is visually. They look at a screen and consume information in the form of text, color, graphics, or animation. The user's ability to see is obviously very important. Consider, for example, users with poor eyesight. Unless the text is very large and the contrast between foreground and background elements very distinct, they may not be able to effectively interact with the content of the site. Unfortunately, many sites seem to assume that users have nearly superhuman vision, as text is sized very small, or a minor degree of contrast is used between foreground and background elements. A simple example of some of contrast and sizing problems can be found at http://www.webdesignref.com/visionissues.htm.

In order to avoid troublesome color combinations, designers should be aware of how color is perceived by the human eye. Three factors affect how color is perceived:

- **Hue**   the degree to which a color is similar to the basic colors—red, green, and blue—or some combination of these colors.
- **Saturation**   the degree to which a color differs from achromatic (white, gray, or black).
- **Lightness**   the degree to which a color appears lighter or darker than another under the same viewing conditions.

Users with vision that is somewhat color deficient are often unable to differentiate between colors of similar hue when those colors are of the same lightness and saturation. For example, someone with the most common color deficiency—red-green color blindness—has trouble distinguishing between red and green when the red and green are close in saturation and lightness. Such color vision issues can be troublesome when you consider the difficulty in distinguishing between red and green traffic lights. Does the color-deficient user really know when to stop or go? In the real world, probably so, since the red light is always the top light— but on the Web, things aren't always so cut and dried. If links are similar in hue, lightness, and saturation, it might be difficult for someone to determine which links have been clicked and which have not.

Web page designers can avoid vision issues for users if they follow a few simple rules. First, make sure not to use text or graphic combinations that have a similar hue. Instead of using light blue on dark blue, use blue on yellow or white instead.

Suggestion: Avoid using text, graphics, and backgrounds of similar hue.

It is possible to get in trouble when using colored text on backgrounds with similar saturation. For example, instead of using a grayish blue text on a rose color background, where both colors are close to achromatic gray, use white text on a rose background, or vice versa.

Suggestion: Avoid combining text, graphics, and backgrounds of similar saturation.

The most obvious problem is when contrast is not great enough. Designers need to consider that dark text on a dark background or bright text on a bright background just may not be readable on all monitors or by people with color or vision deficiency. Instead of using a light blue text on a pale yellow background, use blue text on a white background. Or, black text on a white background is always a safe bet. Yellow and black contrast very well, and, therefore, they are used on road signs that are very important to read. However, before changing your Web site to this color combination, consider that design shouldn't be thrown completely out the window just because of usability concerns.

Rule: Keep contrast high. Avoid using text, graphics, and background of similar lightness.

A very important use of color in a Web page is link color. In general, you should really avoid modifying link colors in any way. However, if you do modify link colors, make sure to avoid using link state colors of similar hue, similar saturation, or similar lightness to the background or to one another. For example, avoid links that change from red to pink. For some reason, designers seem to favor such types of combinations. Instead, consider using links that change from dark blue to pink, similar to the normal link state. Be careful with the background color, as it may interfere with link readability. Because of this, white is a good background color. However, if a sacrifice has to be made with color contrast, make the visited state color the one with the contrast problem, since these are links the user would generally be less interested in.

Links, as well as normal text, often have problems with backgrounds. In particular, avoid patterned backgrounds with multiple hues, saturations, or levels of lightness.

Backgrounds like speckles or texture patterns tend to make poor backgrounds; instead, choose a subtle pattern or simple color.

Suggestion: Avoid using busy background tiles.

To make pages more readable and to deal with users who might have some color or vision deficiency, Web designers should make sure colors that are meant to distinguish items are significantly different in two areas (for example, hue and lightness). By following this rule, if the user is color deficient in one area (for example, red-green hue), he or she can still distinguish the item by another attribute, such as its lightness or saturation.

Rule: Make sure colors that are meant to distinguish items like links are significantly different in two ways, such as hue and lightness.

For more in-depth discussions of vision, color, and imagery on the Web, refer to Chapters 12, 13, and 14.

Memory

Memory is critical to a user being able to utilize a site. If users are unable to remember anything about a site as they browse it, they will become hopelessly lost, since they will not be able to recall if they have been someplace before. However, any user's memory is far from perfect, and users don't consciously spend time trying to memorize things. Users tend to always follow a simple rule: try to do minimal work for maximal gain. Simple human nature suggests that a user is not going to spend a great deal of time to figure something out unless there is a potentially good payoff.

Rule: Users try to maximize gain and minimize work.

Of course, what is considered a good payoff will vary from person to person. Some people like to solve complex puzzles just for personal satisfaction. For them, the payoff is an intense feeling of accomplishment from solving a problem. However, let's assume that users are generally not going to exhibit such behavior; rather, they will only work hard if they know they need to or if there is a really good payoff that will result. If you want a blunt or somewhat negative way to remember this idea, just assume users are lazy! More general rules of thumb about how users tend to act will be presented later in the chapter. The previous rule is simply presented to tie in with a few ideas about memory.

Now, assuming users will not like or even avoid Web sites that require them to work too hard, forcing them to memorize things is not a good idea. To illustrate this idea in practice, consider the interface of an automated telephone banking system. When you call the bank, you are prompted for your account number and then read a list of items and corresponding keys to press—"Press 1 for balance, press 2 for transfer, press 3 for payments... ." If you encounter such a system and are unfamiliar with all the choices, using the system can be difficult. You may find that you will try to remember a choice presented in your mind until all the choices have been presented. If too many choices are presented, you might not be able to recall the range of choices or you might even forget which item you chose and have to listen to the choices again. Now, if the same information were presented on a small text menu, it would be much easier to find the item. You would just look over the list and pick the appropriate one. The voice example requires you to recall the choices, which is very difficult. In general, it is easier for users to recognize choices than to recall them. Because users who make mistakes will then tend to favor easier-to-use systems, we should always try to rely on recognition over recall.

Rule: Recognition is easier than recall.

There are plenty of examples of how recognition is easier than recall. Students generally consider a multiple-choice test to be easier than a fill-in test. You must study, of course, for each (assuming the tests are created correctly), but the amount of memorization required is much higher for the fill-in test. The multiple-choice test doesn't require the depth of memory because you will see the answer and recognize it (hopefully) with only a minimal amount of "recall effort."

It turns out that many of the rules and suggestions presented in this book ultimately are related to this idea of recognition being easier than recall. For example, consider the idea of modifying link color. If we turn off link coloring so that links never look visited, we are forcing users to recall whether they have selected a certain link before. If the links do change color, users simply have to recognize the different color to know they have been there before.

Rule: Do not make visited links the same style or color as unvisited ones.

Another important aspect of memory to consider is that it isn't perfect. Users are not going to memorize things easily and often will have only partial memory or a flawed memory of something. Just as in real life, repetition will lead to improved memory. For example, frequent users or power users may actually rely on memorization of the location of objects on the screen, but most users will have only vague memories of how link choices or pages are organized. However, when people are memorizing things, it is known that image memory is one of our most robust forms of memory. It is far easier to retrieve pictures or even words or ideas that evoke pictures than it is to retrieve abstract ideas without visual cues from memory. It is often far easier to remember a person's face than it is to remember the person's name. Given that users will generally find it easier to remember visuals, it would be wise to make pages that should be remembered visually different from the rest. For example, in site navigation, a home page serves as a safe zone for a user. Using a distinct image or a different color is important in making the home page memorable. However, do not assume the user to have perfect memory—don't make the home page only subtly different from the other pages or expect the user to notice or memorize text items.

Suggestion: Make pages that should be remembered visually different from the rest.

Another aspect of memory that is important to the usability of Web pages is the amount of information a person can recall from short-term memory. Let's return to the automated phone banking system example. When users hear the choices, they have to memorize them. If too many choices are presented, they might forget an item. This is an example of short-term working memory. In a sense, we need a little scratch space in our brain to remember something for a few moments. This memory does not hold a great number of items and is highly volatile. Cognitive scientists have long been interested in short-term memory and have conducted many experiments where participants are presented random objects or words and asked to quickly look at them or to make choices from them to test short-term memory. What is found is that participants are able to recall a range of seven items, plus or minus two, from short-term memory. What this means is that when given five to nine items, the user will be able to recall all the items for a short period of time and have them equally present in mind for choosing among them.

The implication of users being able to remember quickly 7 ($\pm$2) items on Web design may or may not be profound. If you present a user with a set of links, shouldn't you limit the choices to from five to nine? It would seem you should—if you want the user to choose from the choices "fairly." For example, if you present a list of dozens of what may appear to be randomly ordered links to a user, you will find that the user will have a tough time picking from them. You may notice that users will tend to favor extremes. In practice, the author has seen this happen on Web sites. For example, a large music site faced a problem in that bands listed in the site having names beginning with A or Z had a much higher download rate than anything else. What was happening is that users had little knowledge of the bands, so they would scan the lists and— unless something jumped out at them—they tended to choose the first or last items in the list to see what happened. They really couldn't remember all the names of the bands that were interesting as they went along—there were just too many of them. If you want users to easily choose from a list of things that are equally important, you should limit your set of choices to between five and nine items.

Suggestion: Limit groups of similar choices such as links to between five and nine items.

However, do not go overboard with the five to nine items idea. Some usability experts, in fact, believe this rule has no place on the Web. This seems unwarranted, given the support for the rule both from long-term human capabilities studies and from GUI practices, which tend not to put 100+ choices on a single screen. However, there is some merit to the idea of not putting too much stock in the 7 ($\pm$2) rule. Consider that some designers might be tempted to use this rule to suggest that pages should have only five to nine links on them. However, this could be rather limiting if you have a lot of content. Users can focus on items progressively. Consider, for example, being presented five to nine distinctly different clusters of links on a page. Maybe the clusters are labeled and colored so the user chooses a cluster after looking at each. Once in the cluster, there are five to nine links. In this sense, there might be as many as 81 links on a screen, and the user will still be able to use them easily. When looking at well-designed pages with numerous links, you hopefully will see fewer than 100 links and notice that the clustering used an organization method, such as alphabetical, to avoid memorization.

Memory rules of thumb can also be applied to clicks. It appears that users are able to remember about three pages presented sequentially. Anything more than that and there tend to be gaps in memory. For example, as users click through dozens of pages, they will probably remember a variety of pages but not all sequentially. The memorable pages may be visually different enough to trigger recall. Usually, such distinguishable pages are termed *landmarks*—the most obvious landmark page in a site being, of course, the home page. However, if you want users to remember a path, they tend to remember only about three page views sequentially—and maybe fewer if the pages look nearly identical. Therefore, you should not expect a user to memorize a sequence or path longer than three items without repeated use. The number of markers showing location and path in today's sites and the user's continual reliance on the Back button and browser's history mechanism demonstrate how tenuous sequential memory tends to be. Because of these memory constraints, we tend to see many sites trying to reach content within three clicks or complete transactions in as few screens as possible.

Suggestion: Aim for memorization of only three items or pages sequentially.

This is by no means a complete discussion of memory, but it does serve to remind Web designers that, in order to make a site easy to use, we need to limit the amount of memorization going on. The less effort the users expend trying to recall what sequence of buttons they pressed or what choices they may have seen, the better.

Response and Reaction Times

If you have watched people browse around Web sites, it is obvious that some people are faster than others. Some users appear to cut quickly through page content and make choices rapidly, and are frustrated with even the slightest download delay. Others struggle to keep up and seem to have the patience of Job when it comes to waiting for pages to load. However, over time you'll come to find that people's patience for Web page loading will go away, particularly as they become more frequent users. Consider, for example, how long it takes for users to become annoyed at an automated teller machine that has not returned their money to them. The entire transaction may only take a few seconds, but customers are quickly annoyed. But when automated tellers first came out, a wait of even 30 seconds to a minute seemed tolerable compared to waiting in a long bank line.

Tip: Users tend to be more patient with something they are unfamiliar with or that is a novelty.

We see this novelty/patience dynamic on the Web all the time. Sites that could be considered single-visit sites, like movie promotion sites or designer portfolios, get away with huge download times. These sites could be termed single-visit or "throwaway" sites, since the user is unlikely to return. Splash pages, excessive animations, and long downloads are less annoying to a user who hasn't seen them before, but patience wears thin on return visitation. Consider that even when a splash page has a "skip intro" button, a return visitor will still be frustrated with having to even make such a choice. The very fast loading design of successful, heavily frequented sites, such as portals or e-commerce sites, shows that patience wears thin. The needs and desires of the first-time visitor, who in some sense could be considered a novice user of the site, are different than the frequent or expert user of a site. However, users do not have infinite patience, and they are getting more and more impatient as they get used to what facilities the Web, or a particular site, provides. In general, we find the following rule to hold true:

Rule: The amount of time a user will wait is proportional to the payoff.

The better the payoff, the longer the user will wait. Users who get something for free or who are stealing some desirable piece of software or music seem to be willing to wait an eternity. Consider users who illegally download software, songs, and movies from the Internet with a modem. They'll literally spend hours searching for and downloading songs when they could have gone out, worked at a near-minimum-wage job, and earned enough to purchase an entire CD in a similar period of time. Of course, this imbalance will certainly change with the increase in bandwidth—much to the annoyance of the music industry. But it remains true that if you are going to expect a user to wait for a page to load, there better be something useful there.

The amount of time users will wait will vary based on the individual user, his or her personality, and the potential benefit of waiting. However, there are some things we can say about response and reaction times for users in general. Some usability experts (for example, Jakob Nielsen, www.useit.com) relate that studies about response times report similar results. Common response times and user reactions are summarized in Table 2-1.

Time Elapsed	Probable User Reaction
0.1 second	When something operates this fast or faster, it appears instantaneous or nearly instantaneous to the user. Unfortunately, due to bandwidth and technology constraints, few Web pages will exhibit this level of responsiveness in the near future.

Table 2-1. *Response Time and User Reactions*

Time Elapsed	Probable User Reaction
1.0 second	When something reacts in around a second, there is no major potential for interrupt. The user is relatively engaged and not easily distracted from what is happening on the screen.
10 seconds	This is suggested to be the limit for keeping the user's attention focused on the page. Some feedback showing that progress is being made is required, though browser feedback such as a progress bar may be adequate. However, do not be surprised if the user becomes bored and decides to move on to something else.
> 10 seconds	With a delay this long, the user may actually go about other business, look at sites in other windows, talk on the phone, and so on. If you want users to continue to pay attention, you will have to give them constant feedback about progress made and some sense of when the page will be finished (as when downloading software, the browser lets users know how much time is left to complete the download).

Table 2-1.   *Response Time and User Reactions* (continued)

When it comes to the Web, there is generally little chance of going too fast for the user. Most of the time, it takes more than a few seconds even on a broadband connection to download something. However, be careful once something like a Flash file is downloaded. If the user has a faster processor than you, the program may end up running much faster on their system than expected, so much so that the user might not be able to keep up. On occasion, you may notice how animations used in some Web pages appear to travel at a rate only a superhuman could read.

Tip: Be careful with overly fast response times of downloaded objects.

In most cases, a Web site will probably not outpace the user; in fact, it may be much too slow for the user's liking. Because users may get impatient, you need to make sure that they are given some indication of the progress being made. The browser itself actually gives a great deal of feedback about the progress being made. When loading a page, a browser will generally convert a cursor to a wait indicator (such as an hour glass), spin or pulsate a logo (generally in the upper-right corner of the browser), provide a progress meter towards the bottom of the screen, and display messages about objects being loaded in the status bar at the bottom of the screen. The Web designer will design pages to provide even more feedback. For example, the designer may build pages so text loads first or pieces of the page are loaded one at a time. Often, designers will cut images up into multiple pieces, so the user will see a little bit loaded at a time. Also, designers often use images that load in a progressive fashion from an unclear one to a sharp one so that the user is able to get a general sense of a complete fuzzy picture early on and watch its loading progress, if necessary. Figure 2-2 illustrates all these progress indicators in action.

For page loads that only take 10–20 seconds, the feedback given by the browser and incremental loading of a page should be enough to let the user know something is going on. However, when loading takes longer, you should give the user more information. For example, many sites that use binary technologies like Flash use a special loading page complete with a status bar showing progress. Such progress meters can also be created using technologies like JavaScript. However, don't bother with a progress bar

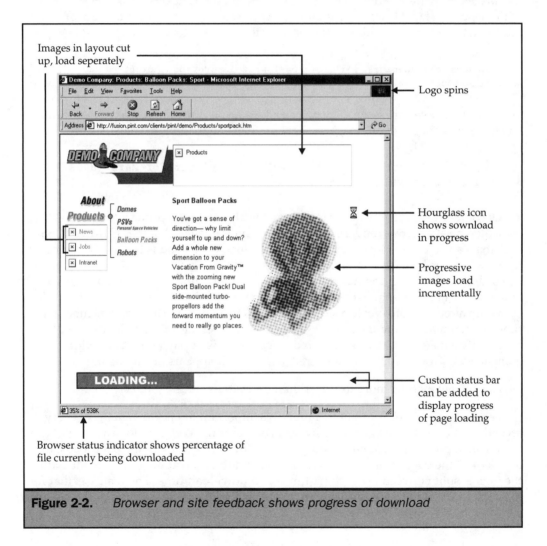

Figure 2-2.   *Browser and site feedback shows progress of download*

or other forms of feedback unless load times are around 30 seconds or more. (With the proliferation of broadband Internet access, this time will certainly diminish; even now, many broadband users are likely to get impatient around 20 seconds or less, and in due time even 10 seconds may seem like a long wait.)

Rule: When response times such as page loads take more than 30 seconds, try to provide your own feedback to the user, such as a load-time progress bar.

If you are building a static site, there are some simple tricks to let the user know about a longer wait for an object. For a very large image download, besides interlacing the image or having it show up progressively sharper, it is also possible to use a trick with the **<img>** tag's **lowsrc** attribute. You could load a low-resolution version of an image first, or even a graphic message stating the image is loading, like so:

```
<img src="hirezpicture.jpg" lowsrc="lowrezpicture.jpg" height="1000"
width="1000" />
```

Or, you might have a message display instead. Some designers have even experimented using the **alt** attribute of an image to show file size or a loading message, like so:

```
<img src="hirezpicture.jpg" alt="Loading picture of Mars (800K)"
height="1000" width="1000" />
```

Of course, it is probably better to reserve the **alt** text for its primary purpose—providing an alternative rendering for users without images. Another HTML or CSS trick that can be used to let a user know about a long download is to use a background image with a message on it that says a page is loading, which is eventually covered up by content that is being downloaded. Other forms of loading screens can be created in both JavaScript and Flash. An example using these techniques is shown in Figure 2-3.

When attempting to create a site that appears responsive to a user, remember that time is what matters the most. How users actually perceive a page loading will not necessarily equate to the bytes delivered. A user who isn't paying for bandwidth isn't going to care if 1K or 100MB is delivered, as long as it appears fast to them.

Rule: Time matters more to a user than bytes delivered.

Because time is so important to a user, it is important to take advantage of every second. Consider that the general way users navigate the Web is to look at a page scan to find an appropriate link, click, and then wait for the page. Once the page loads, they then look at the page to find the next link or spend time consuming the content. Notice the time is split between user "think time" and download time. The reality is that for most users, the think time for navigation pages is pretty small compared to the wait

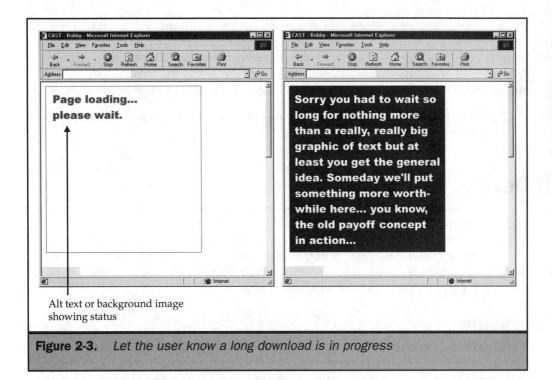

Figure 2-3.   *Let the user know a long download is in progress*

time. For content pages, however, the user may spend a great deal of time looking at the page. One way to improve responsiveness is to take advantage of the thinking time by downloading information to be used later on. This is often called *preloading* or *precaching*. Assuming you are able to preload most or all of the next thing to be looked at by the user during the think time, the next page load time could be significantly reduced. Somewhat like the magician who has the result of a trick set up in advances, downloading during idle moments can produce a nearly mystical appearance of speed.

Suggestion: Improve Web page response time by taking advantage of user "think time" with preloading.

A variety of browser accelerator tools have been built in an attempt to improve Web responsiveness by preloading pages linked from the current page. The only problem with this approach is that many pages have so many outbound links that it is difficult for the browser to predict the page the user will load next. The best way to improve the odds of caching the correct "next page" is to look at the common paths users take through a site by examining a log file and then putting in code to preload pages along these paths. However, this just improves the odds. The only time you can really guarantee that preloading will improve things is when the user is navigating a linear progression of pages.

The responsiveness of a Web site is a key aspect of a user's feeling of the site's usability. Beyond loading of pages, consider that time is important to a user even after a page has loaded. For example, if a page loads quickly but users can't figure out what is going on in the page within about ten seconds, they can become just as frustrated as waiting for a simple page to download. Aim for what might be called the "ten-second Web page." A ten-second Web page is one where the user gets the gist of the page in about one minute and can decide after that whether to consume the content more seriously or not.

> **Tip: Aim for a ten-second limit for the user to determine the basic gist of a page's content or purpose after loading.**

Dealing with Stimulus

Users are constantly being bombarded by stimuli from our sites. The text, the links, the graphics, animation, even sound all create a cacophony of information that the user tries to distill meaning from. Because of the continual stimulation, we need to filter out some of the data, and we do this both unconsciously and consciously. Three primary ways it is thought that people filter sensation data include thresholds, something dubbed the "cocktail party effect," and sensory adaptation.

Thresholds

Rather than deal with every minute change that happens, we tend to notice only something that exceeds a particular threshold. For example, if on a Web page an object moves very slowly—say a pixel every few seconds—we may not notice at first because the speed of its movement is below our absolute threshold. However, over time we may notice the movement. Thresholds are tough to predict. Depending on their psychological state, users may be able to detect something under normal conditions; but, if they are tired or distracted, they may not be able to notice the difference between two similar but different colors or fonts that have been used to separate navigation forms.

When designing pages, designers should always consider thresholds. Thresholds suggest making objects or pages noticeably different from each other so that users will be easily able to understand their difference. For example, consider if link and text color in a page are too similar. The user may have to carefully inspect underlined text to make sure that it is a link and not just underlined text, because text colors are only subtly different. In other words, they might not always be sure what's a link and what isn't without putting in at least some degree of effort. Designers should strive not to force the user to spend time and effort trying to interpret the differences between objects on a page, since it both is frustrating and takes time away from the main goal of getting the user to consume the content or perform a task. Consider the threshold effect when trying to differentiate objects on a page.

> **Suggestion: Make page elements obviously different if they are different.**

Things need to be just different enough for the user to notice. If the designer is too subtle, however, the user may not be able to tell. And if you go overboard, the design may backfire. It would be easy enough to always put site buttons in bright colors and content in dark colors, but this could be annoying to the user. The next two ideas show how users tend to filter out information when being bombarded with excessive stimuli.

Cocktail Party Effect

The cocktail party effect describes how people are able to concentrate on important data when being bombarded by nonessential stimuli. People at a cocktail party can concentrate on their own conversation despite being in a room filled with numerous other conversations. Don't dismiss the other conversations as background noise. If the listener stopped and focused on another conversation, he or she probably could hear certain parts of it. However, the threshold effect is also in play during a cocktail party. If the person you are trying to listen to speaks too softly, if the proximity of other conversations is too close, or if the volume of other conversations is too loud, the listener will be overwhelmed by the outside stimuli.

Web page designers should consider that, as in cocktail party conversations, the user might want to concentrate on only a small portion of the information on a page. The rest is background noise that has to be filtered out. If there is too much going on, users will not be able to effectively concentrate on what they want and become frustrated. Therefore, we should try to section things off just as in a cocktail party, so the user can effectively concentrate. A good site has lots of choices but provides the visitors the ability to focus on what they want to see. Toward this end, we might consider grouping similar items together and separating groups of items with a lot of white space. Also, within text, we might convey important points in a bullet list or a pull quote, or highlight them with a background color. Always strive to limit noise—namely, competing objects on a page. If you don't, and the site is like the cocktail party that gets too loud, users won't be able to filter out information that isn't important to them.

> **Suggestion: Limit page noise and segment page objects so that they don't compete so much visually that users are unable to focus on what they are interested in.**

Thresholds and the cocktail party effect present a balance between having too little of a difference and too much. Don't become so concerned with trying to get an absolutely perfect balance of stimuli—just try to get it about right. You may consider erring in favor of a little too much, since people are very adaptable, as shown by the next cognitive science idea.

Sensory Adaptation

Sensory adaptation occurs when users become so used to a particular stimulus that they no longer respond to it—at least not consciously. Think of the watch on your wrist. You probably don't notice it normally. Take the watch and put it on your other wrist and you'll notice it for a while, but eventually you'll get used to it. That's sensory adaptation. Life is filled with things that people adapt to: the ticking of an alarm clock, the clothes you wear, the loudness of the music coming from your car stereo, and so on. Life on the Web is no different. Users adapt to Web stimuli quickly. That continually animated GIF that grabbed the user's attention once or twice quickly fades into the background.

Probably the most interesting sensory adaptation is the rise of so-called "banner blindness." People are becoming so used to the shape and location of banners that they are just tuning them out. Experiments as well as click rate studies show that people don't look at banners terribly attentively. Animation added to the mix improved things, but it, too, has succumbed to sensory adaptation. Rich banner ads complete with sound and complex interaction are being experimented with to see if they can regain user attention. And we have pop-ups that are quickly swatted away by users as fast as they spawn. The bottom line is that users will decide what they want to focus on. Designers may want users to focus on something such as a banner ad or a download button, but in order to grab their attention, they will have to continue coming up with new tricks as users adapt to stimuli over time.

> **Rule: Sensory adaptation does occur on the Web. If you want a user's full attention, you'll have to vary things significantly and often.**

Sensory adaptation suggests that the numerous fonts, animations, and colored regions on a page may go unnoticed over time. This doesn't mean that we should completely avoid using things to stimulate the user, but we should not be as reliant on them, since they lose strength with use. Sensory adaptation really suggests that, in order to get a user's full attention, we have to "wake them up" with something different. A little bit of surprise can be useful to make the user pay attention. However, be careful with this idea. In general, users will want to peacefully go about their business and will expect pages to look and act consistently. We shouldn't disturb them, but should let them focus on the task or content at hand. If you bombard the user all the time, they will feel uncomfortable because of the lack of consistency, and they may become so annoyed that they leave.

Movement Capabilities

Once the user has absorbed information they have been provided, they will eventually react to it and make some choice. While someday voice interfaces may become commonplace, today's Web sites are generally manipulated using the keyboard or mouse. Therefore, we should always attempt to minimize user efforts using these devices. Few sites consider that users may prefer using the keyboard or arrow keys, instead of a mouse, to move through choices in a page. While many form pages are optimized for quick navigation via the keyboard, other pages may not be.

Rule: Try to optimize keyboard access for all pages in a site, not just form pages.

Consider also the work users perform moving their mouse around the screen. Moving the pointer around the screen takes effort, and a button or link press may take up to a few seconds if a user has to move a long distance or focus on clicking a very small button. In fact, the time it takes a user to press a button is governed by something called Fitt's law (Fitts, 1954). Fitt's law basically states that the smaller the button to press and the farther away it is, the longer it will take to perform the action. This seems logical, since users tend either to overshoot small click targets because they moved too fast or to take extra time to clock the button more carefully.

Fitt's law would suggest that to improve speed of use and thus efficiency, we should first bring things closer together. First, we might consider reducing the amount of mouse travel between successive clicks. Notice how efficient a wizard-style interface is, since after clicking "Next" the successive "Next" button tends to be directly under or very close to the current mouse position. There is no reason we couldn't apply this to navigation elements. Try to keep successively clicked buttons close together. Navigation bars tend to encourage following this plan, anyway.

Rule: Minimize mouse travel distance between successive choices.

However, with the Web, we can't always be sure that the user will press another button within the page as their next choice. In fact, quite often the user may move to a browser button such as the Back button rather than rely on internal site navigation nearby. Given some users' preference for the browser Back button, designers should try to minimize the mouse travel to the Back button. The question is, travel from where? We should assume that the user will probably hover over the navigation bar or near the scroll bars most of the time. While we can't decrease the distance from the scroll bars, which will tend to be far away from the Back button in the upper left of the screen, there is no reason that we should not consider putting primary navigation buttons on the left or top portions of the screen. Doing so will minimize the distance from a primary selection area and the heavily used Back button, thus reducing mouse travel and increasing the speed at which the site can be used.

Rule: Minimize mouse travel between primary page hover locations and the browser's Back button.

Fitt's law would also suggest that we make clicking targets larger, particularly if they are far away. Some designers find this design suggestion troublesome because it suggests making big huge buttons, which would take up a great deal of screen real estate as well as potentially making the site look like it was designed primarily for novice users. Big buttons also bring too much attention to the interface. However, buttons should be made big enough for users to mouse to them relatively quickly—and spaced out well enough so they are able to click them without accidentally click an adjacent choice.

Rule: Make clickable regions large enough for users to move to them quickly and press them accurately.

General user capabilities are not all that we need to consider when discussing what ideas affect usable Web design. We must also consider the world the user inhabits and the user's general and unique characteristics and experiences.

The User's World

People truly are the centers of their own universe, in the sense that they perceive everything initially from their own point of view. Consider the idea of how a user might perceive the Web site shown in Figure 2-4. The user lives in the real world.

Users are affected by their environment: the physical conditions of their location, the noise around them, the visual quality of the monitor they are using, and so on. From their world, they access your Web site via the medium of the Internet and the Web, which includes things like network connections, servers, browsers, and so on. Once on the Web, they navigate about and visit sites. If they decide to actually interact with a site, they finally begin to consume or react to the content presented.

The presentation and navigation layers in Figure 2-4 could be interchanged considering that a user's ability to navigate Web space is greatly affected by the way it is presented.

Suggestion: Always remember that you need to bring a site into the user's world, not the other way around.

The preceding suggestion is an important one. Designers will naturally believe that they have set the rules for their sites and that users are just visitors. While this may be true, users tend to interpret things from their own perspective. Each user will have his or her own opinions, capabilities, environment, and experiences, all of which will influence how the site is interpreted. A fine balance between what the user thinks and

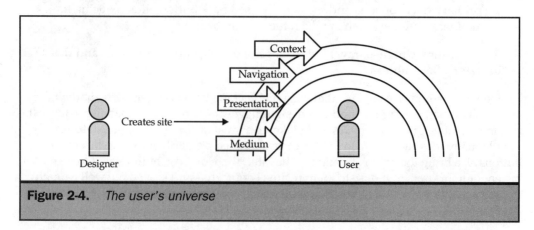

Figure 2-4.   *The user's universe*

wants and what the designer thinks and wants has to be struck. This will be discussed in more depth later in this chapter.

User Environments

The user is heavily influenced by what could be called their *environment of consumption*. For example, consider a user in a public place such as an airport using a public Internet kiosk to remotely access their e-mail. The user is standing up—it might be crowded and noisy—waiting to dash off to the plane. Because of this environment, the user may not be tolerant of long waits, excessive menus, or anything that slows down the task at hand. Further, due to the noise, the user may not be able to always hear sound cues. Last, because the user is standing up, the amount of time they might spent during the whole online session will certainly be significantly less than a normal session at the office. When designing for users, always think about where the user is accessing the site from. Table 2-2 details some of the possibilities.

The environment will greatly affect the user's view of what is "usable." For example, color combinations that contrast acceptably indoors might be troublesome outdoors. Designers must take into account the environment of consumption.

Location	Characteristics
Office	Generally computer-based access Single user Relatively quie Should be primarily work or task focused, at least during primary work hours Often high speed
Home office or bedroom	Generally computer-based access Single user Noise level variable, but often quiet Purpose may be work or play Access could be anytime Speed of access varies dramatically from modem to high speed
Home living room	Access may be from set-top box or video game console Distance from device may be farther Use may be less input oriented (reduced typing) Noise level variable May be group-oriented access or single user Access probably more entertainment related Printing may not be an end result

Table 2-2.   *Common User Environments Characteristics*

Location	Characteristics
Cybercafe	Probably computer-based access Cost may influence usage Noise level variable Use is probably entertainment or research Speed of access probably high May be group-oriented access or single user Security or privacy may be a concern
Public kiosk	Cost may influence usage Noise level variable User may be standing Use will be less input oriented (reduced typing) Use is probably task oriented, focused on e-mail or access to very important information Access to location-related information may be a high priority Security or privacy may be a concern
Car	Probably noncomputer-based access (PDA or smart phone) Use will be less input oriented (reduced typing) Focus will not be primarily on the access if user is the driver Use is probably task oriented or limited to very important information Access to location-related information may be a high priority Speed and quality of access is probably low
Mass transit or plane	Probably either noncomputer-based access (PDA or smart phone) or a laptop User may be standing or sitting Use could be entertainment or work Access to location or time-sensitive information may be a high priority Speed and quality of access is probably low Security or privacy may be a concern
Outside	Probably noncomputer-based access (PDA or smart phone) Screen glare could be a significant problem Use will be less input oriented (reduced typing) User may be standing or moving Noise level variable Use is probably task oriented or limited to very important information Access to location-related information may be a high priority Speed and quality of access is probably low

Table 2-2.   *Common User Environments Characteristics* (continued)

Rule: Account for the characteristics of the probable environment in which the user will access a site if possible.

General Types of Users

There are three levels into which users can be classified to reflect their knowledge of how to use a Web site: novices, intermediates, and experts or power users.

A novice user is one who may have little knowledge of a site or even of how the Web works. A novice user will need extra assistance and may prefer extra clicks with extra feedback to accomplish a simple task. An example of an interface tuned to novices would be a wizard that automates some common task.

At the other end, power users are those users who understand the Web or a site very well. Power users should be considered in two distinct categories: frequent and infrequent visitors to the site. A power user who frequently visits a site to utilize advanced features such as sophisticated searching, may directly form their own URLs, and memorize the position of objects within a page or the site. A power user who is an infrequent visitor to a site may not be familiar with the site's structure but will expect certain facilities, such as search, to be available to navigate a site. Power users will need relatively little handholding and will desire to click less and consume more. Obviously, the distance between a power user and novice user is great. A site geared too much toward one audience or the other will certainly annoy—the power user if the site has been dumbed down, or the novice user if the site is geared mostly toward power users.

The third group of users, the infrequent intermediate user, is actually the largest category of users on the Web. Most users are infrequent intermediate users because they pretty much understand how the Web works, but may not know how to navigate a particular site in a very efficient manner. Infrequent intermediate users do not continually revisit the site; if they do, they will probably eventually become a power user. Because site usage tends to be dominated by intermediate users, you may consider designing the site for the capabilities of these users. However, doing so may lock out novice users and bore or restrict advanced users.

The best approach to building a site for basic user groups is to build a site that provides features that cater to all users. Software applications do this, so there is no reason a Web site cannot. A software application may provides keyboard shortcuts and other features, such as customizable interfaces, for power users while also providing icons and menu systems for intermediate and novice users. Help systems and wizards are other features mostly geared toward the novice user. A Web site could provide features like a clean URL system, advanced search facility, and personalization features for an advanced user. A site with consistent navigation bars that have button labels similar to other sites (About, Products, Careers, and so on) is very friendly to novice and intermediate users, and it can also have dynamically built "bread crumb"–style navigation lines, popular with advanced users. Last, a Web site could provide help systems, maps, and alternative forms of access such as simple text links for the novice.

> **Suggestion: Aim to create an adaptive Web site that meets the requirements of novices, intermediates, and advanced users.**

In the perfect world, there is no reason that a Web site can't be built to meet the needs of all general user groups. However, time and cost constraints may limit the number of features that can be added to some Web sites. In such cases, it is probably best to aim for the largest group of users: the intermediate. This may lock out some novice users unable to figure the site out. There is an argument to be made for aiming at the lowest common denominator in a user. The problem with this is that if you start building only for the complete novice, you can quickly alienate users who know what they are doing.

> **Suggestion: Design for the intermediate user if an adaptive Web interface is not possible.**

Even if an adaptive interface is built, there is bound to be a user who doesn't understand or like the site we have built.

> **Tip: Remember there will always be users who don't like or get a site, no matter how good it is.**

Users are individuals with different tastes and opinions. They will have different experiences, capabilities, personalities, age, gender issues, and cultural issues. Some individuals may have disabilities that prohibit them from using a Web site that most users find easy to use. Users bring what they know from the real world and from other Web sites to your site. They may expect to use symbols from the real world, such as those for navigation. However, they may also bring knowledge of how Web sites work that they gained from visits to many other sites. Knowledge of how traditional software applications work may also be brought into play. Remember, as mentioned early in the chapter, that users bring the site into their world—they don't visit the universe of your Web site. Your site is just a speck in an overall universe of Web sites. In fact, it could be said that most of the time users are not at your site. Some call this the 99 percent rule, since 99 percent of the time, users are probably not using your site. You should, therefore, make sure that your site follows any conventions and meets expectations set up by other sites.

> **Rule: Users bring past experiences with the world, software, and the Web to your site. Make sure your site meets their expectations.**

You need to make sure that your site acts like other sites or software users have used and meets their general expectations. Remember the rule of consistency: if you do things differently from how everybody else does, you can't rely on a user's past knowledge and you force the user to learn something new. Of course, the challenge with real users is that expectations will vary greatly based on their experience. However, try to understand that there are some common conventions from GUI design or Web sites that users are probably familiar with.

GUI Conventions

Graphical user interface (GUI) design has long followed a variety of standards developed by operating system vendors such as Microsoft and Apple, or industry groups like The Open Group (http://www.opengroup.org). These conventions are obvious in most software applications. Consider the screen snapshot of Microsoft Word shown in Figure 2-5.

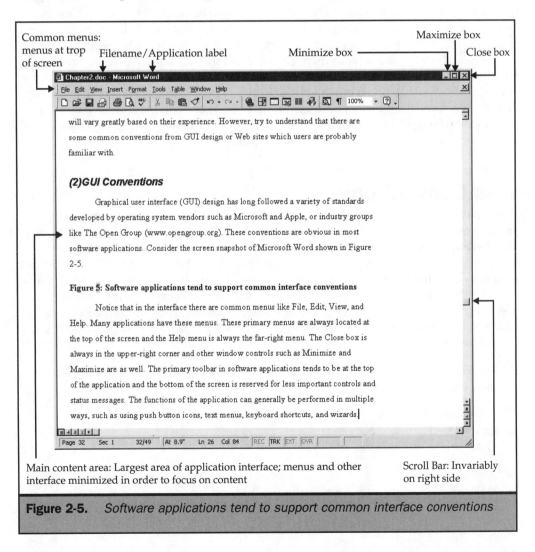

Figure 2-5. *Software applications tend to support common interface conventions*

Notice that in the interface in Figrue 2-5 there are common menus like File, Edit, View, and Help. Many applications have these menus. These primary menus are always located at the top of the screen, and the Help menu is always the far-right menu. The Close box is always in the upper-right corner, and other window controls such as Minimize and Maximize are there as well. The primary toolbar in software applications tends to be at the top of the application, and the bottom of the screen is reserved for less important controls and status messages. The functions of the application can generally be performed in multiple ways, such as using push button icons, text menus, keyboard shortcuts, and wizards.

GUI conventions are very useful to know, particularly when designing forms and other interactive elements of a site. In later chapters on implementation, we'll discuss the use of GUI widgets and the difference between Web and GUI interfaces. The Web has not been able to develop conventions that are as well understood as those for software applications. There are two main reasons for this. First, software applications are often defined significantly by the operating system they are written for. Microsoft has great influence on how applications written for Windows should work. Apple can dictate conventions for Macintosh software. Second, the ability to author and distribute software applications is restricted to a much smaller group of people than in Web design. Many Web designers lack any formal understanding of GUI conventions and may actually shun them in favor of artistic freedom. This struggle is fortunately changing, as the focus on user-oriented site design becomes more popular.

Web Conventions

While Web sites may not exactly follow GUI usability conventions, they do have a loose set of conventions. Straying from the way that most Web sites work is a dangerous idea. Unless you happen to be running an important day-to-day use site like an internal site, a heavily trafficked site like Amazon, or a portal like Yahoo!, you will probably not be able to introduce any conventions of your own. In fact, if users come to expect that a company logo in the upper left-hand corner of the screen will return them to the home page, you had better do this in your site. If you don't do this, you may surprise the user, which could cause a negative reaction. Forcing the user to learn a new idea also could cause a negative feeling.

Rule: Do not stray from the common interface conventions established by heavily used sites.

Web conventions, unfortunately, are difficult to pinpoint. A few well-known ones are summarized in Table 2-3.

Convention	Description
Upper-left corner logo signals home page return.	Users tend to expect a corporate logo to return them to the home page. Most sites put this in the upper-left corner. An explicit Home button, as well as a ToolTip, is a good idea.
Text links are repeated at the bottom of a page.	Most sites like to repeat text navigation at the bottom of a page, particularly if top or side navigation is a graphical form.
Back-to-top link used on long pages.	While sites will provide text navigation to move to the next page, a back-to-top link or arrow is generally included at the bottom of the page to quickly jump the user up the page.
Special print forms used for heavily printed pages.	Increasingly, sites are providing special printer-friendly versions either in a stripped HTML form or even in an Acrobat form. This is most commonly found on sites that distribute large volumes of content.
Shopping cart in the upper right.	Typically, the shopping cart icon or link is found in the upper-right corner of the screen.
Clickable items are blue and underlined.	Fight it all you want, but most text links are blue and underlined. While many users may be able to understand nonunderlined links or different colors, the best way to signify that something is pressable is making it blue and underlined. Be careful with creating logos or other content that are blue, as users may actually try to click on it.
Secondary navigation elements such as a site map or search are presented separately from sectional navigation.	Because site maps, site indexes, help systems, and search facilities are navigation aids, most sites have tended to put less emphasis on links to them. However, given the rise in popularity of search features, content-rich sites may emphasize search facilities.

Table 2-3.   *Some Common Web Conventions*

Figure 2-6 illustrates some of the common Web conventions used in a page within the DemoCompany site.

Logo links to home page

Text links are blue and underlined

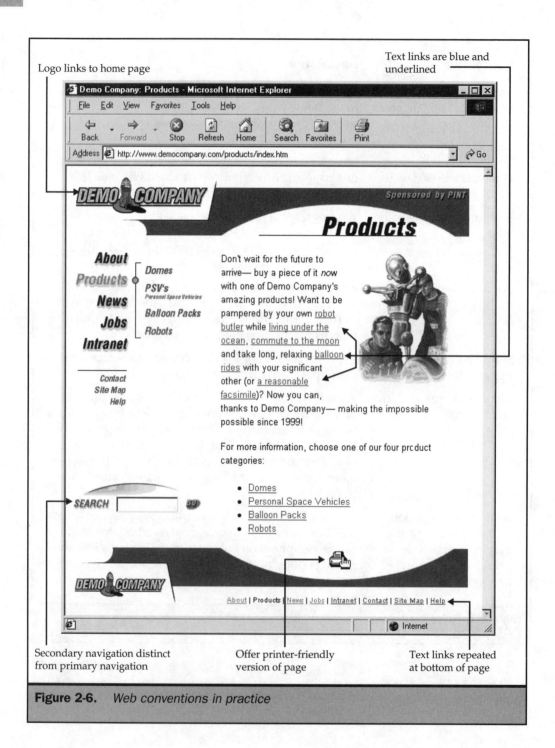

Secondary navigation distinct from primary navigation

Offer printer-friendly version of page

Text links repeated at bottom of page

Figure 2-6.   *Web conventions in practice*

The problem with Web conventions is that they are moving targets. New conventions may be invented and sweep across the Web like fads. For example, frames and splash pages used to be popular, but they have somewhat fallen out of favor. Conventions are not always well considered and may often have more to do with novelty than usability. However, this shouldn't lead you to invent new conventions or avoid those that are current. The best way to keep up with current conventions is to simply browse the well-trafficked e-commerce and content sites often and look for common features. If users are exposed to features there, such as single-click ordering, it isn't going to be difficult to explain to them how it works on your site. Don't assume that everyone understands common conventions or that all users will be able to use current conventions. Some users will have special needs.

Accessibility

There is no way to account for all the small differences between people. In fact, we only aim to create sites that *most* people like. This may lead us to stereotype groups of users (like casual female surfers under 18, and so on), but this may be an approach we have to make. Yet, this does not mean that you should go out and build a site catering to the largest demographic group of users hitting your site. Try to please as many distinct groups as possible by making your site as accessible as possible. Don't forget that some people may have difficulty if you assume that all users have perfect physical and technical capabilities.

Providing accessibility for people who may have deficiencies involving sight, hearing, or other physical capabilities isn't just a nice idea anymore—it may actually be required for some organizations, particularly government agencies—and many companies could incur serious liability if they do not account for all users. For example, Section 508 of the 1986 Federal Rehabilitation Act requires that the federal government include solutions for employees with disabilities when awarding contract proposals. This would also eventually apply to systems such as intranets, extranets, and most likely public Web sites. Also, the 1992 Americans with Disabilities Act (ADA) states that firms with 15 or more employees provide reasonable accommodation for employees with disabilities. This could apply to intranets or extranet creation!

But making a Web site accessible is something that should be done, not because of some law or to avoid future litigation, but because doing so could result in a much better Web site for everyone. Very often, creating systems that are accessible to all users also creates benefits for all users, regardless of capability. For example, the so-called talking books, initially considered for the blind, fostered books on tape. Also consider that easy ramps to access buildings, and curb cutouts made for wheelchairs, make walking easier for all and tend to reduce the number of people falling flat on their face after crossing the street or severely twisting their ankles as they step off the curb.

The W3C (http://www.w3.org) has long advocated designing sites for maximum accessibility and promotes the Web Accessibility Initiative (http://www.w3.org/wai). The WAI is concerned not only with creating sites that are accessible to people with disabilities, but also with making sites that are accessible by anyone who might be operating in a different environment than what a designer considers "normal." Remember that users will not necessarily be using a fast connection and a large monitor like yours—or if you aren't using a fast connection with the latest and greatest, your users just might be! From the W3C guides, you should always consider that users may have different operating constraints:

- They may not be able to see, hear, or move easily, or may not be able to process some types of information easily (or even at all).

- They may have difficulty reading or comprehending text because of language problems.

- They may not be able to use a keyboard or mouse because of access method (such as a cell phone) or physical disability.

- They may have a less-than-ideal access environment, such as a text-only screen, a small screen, a screen without color, or a slow Internet connection.

- They may be accessing the site in a nonstandard environment where they may be affected by environmental factors—accessing the Web in a noisy cybercafe or as they drive a car, for instance.

- They may have an older browser or a nonstandard browser or operating system or use an alternative form of user interface, such as voice access.

To deal with these issues, the W3C has issued a few suggestions to improve the accessibility of a site. These are summarized here:

- **Provide equivalent alternatives to auditory and visual content**   In other words, don't rely solely on one form of communication. If you use picture buttons, provide text links. If audio is used, provide a text transcript of the message, and so on.

- **Don't rely on color alone**   As discussed earlier in the chapter, not everyone will be able to view colors properly; so if color alone is used to convey information, such as what constitutes a link, people who cannot differentiate between certain colors and users with devices that have noncolor or nonvisual displays will not be able to figure out what is being presented. In general, you need to consider avoiding color combinations with similar hues or not enough contrast—particularly if they are likely to be viewed on monochrome displays or by people with different types of color vision deficits.

- **Use markup and style sheets, and do so properly**   Basically, make sure to use HTML for structure and CSS for presentation. Especially avoid using proprietary markup or presentation elements and avoid using technology that may not render the same way in different browsers.

■ **Clarify natural language usage**   Make sure to define terms and use markup that indicates acroymns, definitions, quotations, and so on. In other words, use more logical markup. Further, make sure to clearly indicate the language being used in the document so that a browser may be able to switch to another language.

■ **Create tables that transform gracefully**   In short, don't use tables for layout— use them for presenting tabular data such as a spreadsheet. When tables are used, provide a clear caption, column headings, and other indicators of the meaning of cell contents.

■ **Ensure that pages featuring new technologies transform gracefully**   This is a key idea discussed throughout the book. Basically, make sure that, if you are going to push the limit of design, any new technologies degrade gracefully under older browsers. For example, if you are relying on JavaScript, does the page still work without it on? Or at least evor gracefully?

■ **Ensure user control of time-sensitive content changes**   Make sure that moving, blinking, scrolling, or autoupdating objects or pages may be paused or stopped by the user. Besides being highly annoying, such distractions may actually make it difficult for users to focus on the site.

■ **Ensure direct accessibility of embedded user interfaces**   If you use an interface within the page—for example, a Java applet that has its own internal interface— make sure that it, too, is accessible.

■ **Design for device independence**   Try to build interfaces that can work in multiple devices, including those with different screen sizes, different viewing devices (cell phones as well as computers), and different manipulation devices (keyboard or mouse and keyboard). A particularly important consideration is just making sure that a site doesn't rely solely on the mouse for navigation. Some users may find mouse movement difficult, and power users may actually prefer to use the keyboard for navigation.

■ **Use interim solutions**   Because not all browsers will support the same technologies or standards completely, make sure to provide alternatives in the short term for noncompliant browsers.

■ **Use W3C technologies and guidelines**   A somewhat self-evident but occasionally troublesome suggestion. Of course you should always try to follow the W3C guidelines, at least in spirit. However, be careful because many W3C guidelines are no more than proposed ideas, and browsers may lack significant or consistent support for a defined specification.

■ **Provide context and orientation information**   In some sense, this just means to explain things or provide instructions for complex areas. You should design pages so that the meaning of links is clear through the use of ToolTips or scope notes. Further, forms should be designed that explain what is required. In the most basic way, a site should provide a help system.

- **Provide clear navigation mechanisms** Basically, you should provide obvious navigation that is easy to understand and at a consistent location on the screen. Navigational aids such as search engines, site maps, and site indexes should also be provided.

- **Ensure that documents are clear and simple** Yet another fairly obvious suggestion, but powerful nonetheless, is that simplicity will lead to greater accessibility. Given that not everyone will be able to read a language well, and usability is directly related to simplicity and consistency, try to make your documents simple.

Besides manual inspection of a site, it is easy enough to evaluate it for accessibility using a tool such as Bobby (http://www.cast.org/bobby), as shown in Figure 2-7. Bobby

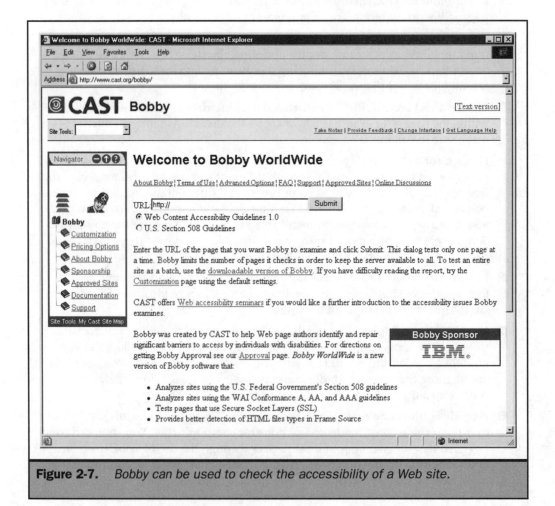

Figure 2-7. *Bobby can be used to check the accessibility of a Web site.*

will analyze a Web page and see if it meets certain basic accessibility criteria, such as the use of **alt** text.

Building a Usable Site

One of the keys to usable Web site development is to focus from the beginning on the users of the application. Remember that the user's goal is not to use computers or to use your Web site. The user's goal is to accomplish some task—purchase a product, find a bill payment center, register a complaint, and so on. You should try to make direct contact with users, and you must listen to them. Do not fall into the trap of thinking that you should just simply ask users what they want and then they will design your site for you. Users are not designers, and they make illogical or unrealistic requests. Because of this, you may be tempted to implement your own idea of a great site instead, without regard for user requests. However, the core idea of user-centered design is to always remember we are designing for users and not ourselves. Recall again the following very important Web design rules:

Rule: You are NOT the user.

Rule: Users are NOT designers.

Although not all user input will be valuable, you should solicit information from your intended audience. You might consider interviewing them or giving a survey. Whatever you do, make sure to let users talk—and listen to them. While this may seem like JAD (Joint Application Design), which will be discussed in Chapter 4, we will not let users control the project; rather, they will be used as a source of ideas and a way to verify the execution of implemented features. From interviews, you should build a profile of stereotypical types of users. While this may seem to be a bad idea, consider that unless you have a very small audience, it is virtually impossible to build a site that will conform perfectly to all the preferences and task requirements that all possible users might have. Even if it were possible, it would be prohibitively expensive.

From your discussions with users, build a prototype site, or just a set of simple diagrams on paper of how pages might look, and test it out with users. Make sure you test your site with users as early as possible in the development cycle so as not to build a site that users can't figure out.

Suggestion: Perform user testing early and often.

There are many ways to verify usability. Tests might include

- Casual observation of users
- Surveys and interviews
- Focus groups

- Lab testing
- Heuristic evaluations by developers or usability experts

The results of the tests can include more quantitative measurements, such as the number of mistakes made during a task, the amount of mouse travel, the time it takes to perform a task, and so on. Tests will certainly also have to include qualitative measures of what feature the users liked or didn't like. Before you don a white coat and rent lab time in a room with a two-way mirror to observe users, consider that formal testing may be overkill for most sites because of the cost and trouble of performing user tests in a formal fashion. Simple observations might do the trick, and opinions tend to be free from many users, though not always well founded. Collect a few users, or even your friends and neighbors, and sit them down at the site, and have them perform a few tasks. What's interesting is that even an informal test will uncover the major problems with a site. However, informal tests only work if you let them. Designers seem far too proud of their sites and tend to act as co-pilots, showing a user the interesting aspects of a site. Talking too much during a test or guiding the user in any way keeps the user from making his or her own decisions and may actually steer the user away from mistakes.

Suggestion: When performing even an informal usability test, avoid talking too much or guiding the user.

Before running off to round up your friends to ask them what they think, first consider that far too often users will tell you what you want to hear or what they *think* they would do in certain situations. Or they simply may not want to admit their misunderstandings. It is better to observe users' behavior than to rely on statements from them. However, if this is not possible, user input is acceptable, particularly if it is coupled with your own ad hoc usability analysis of a site. For instance, see whether the site follows the basic usability criteria that have been described in this chapter. Table 2-4 presents some guidelines you should use for judging a site.

When evaluating a site, the rules of thumb here cover the basic aspects of usability. However, don't assume just because the site meets most of these basic ideas that it is a good site. There are plenty of other ways for a site to fall down. For example, a site might not contain excellent content, its technology may be unreliable, or its graphics may be hideous to look at. Chapter 5 presents a more in-depth evaluation procedure that accounts for many other aspects of Web design. Remember that usability isn't the only part of a positive Web experience.

Guideline	Explanation
Be consistent	Consistency is the key to an easy-to-use interface. If something is consistent, the user only has to learn it once. Within your own site, don't change the position of buttons or the way things act.
Don't violate a user's expectations, and make sure to follow Web and GUI conventions	Consistency can go beyond the contents of a site. Users will have expectations about how things work shaped by visits to other sites. Make sure your site is consistent with what they expect. In short, follow any conventions used in GUI or site design that the user is familiar with.
Support the ways people use Web pages	Users use the Web pages in a few basic ways. They load a page, they unload a page, they print the page, they save the page (either by bookmarking the address or saving the file to a local drive), they read the page, or they interact with the page (such as by filling in forms or manipulating content objects within the page). As with the previous guideline, make sure users can do all the things they expect to be able to do. If users expect to print or bookmark a page and they can't, they may consider the site unusable.
Use surprise properly and sparingly	Occasionally, being inconsistent is useful. If you want to "wake a user up," it might be OK to dramatically change the way a page looks or acts. Just make sure you don't do this often, since users may never become comfortable with the site and may even become frustrated with the ever-changing interface.
Simplify the site and individual pages as much as possible	Simplicity makes it easy for users to understand a site. Try to pare a site or page down to its bare essentials. Look at statistical logs to determine what pages are not needed from a site. On a page level, remove clutter from layouts and try to reduce visual noise.

Table 2-4.   *Common Web Usability Guidelines*

Guideline	Explanation
Rely on recognition, not recall	Memorization is difficult. Don't expect the user to memorize the structure of your site or the position of your buttons. Minimize what the user has to remember by exposing available choices. Even something as simple as hiding a menu when it isn't in use increases the cognitive load on a user, since they have to memorize what items are on what menus.
Do not assume users will read instructions	You may not get a chance to hold a training class for every user who visits your site. Generally, users will read help files only when they are in trouble. Make sure that they don't need to be trained. Avoid introducing features in a site that would require training or documentation for proper use.
Prevent or correct user errors	Don't let users make mistakes that are unnecessary. For example, validate form entries and limit users to doing only what they should. Don't provide a choice that is not easily undone by the user. If errors do occur, let the user know about the error and its possible solution.
Provide feedback	Let users know what's happening. Don't be imprecise with feedback. If there is going to be a delay, let them how long it is going to take. If an error has occurred, provide a clear error message.
Support different interaction styles	Try to provide multiple ways of doing the same thing to deal with different approaches to problems. For example, some users may prefer to use a site map rather than a search engine when looking for something. Don't limit users, but do account for a range of interaction styles, from novice users to power users.
Minimize mouse travel and keystrokes	Typing and moving the mouse around the screen is work for the user, so try to minimize it. This means successive button choices should be nearby. Try to minimize the distance from primary navigation to the Back button, which is certainly the most commonly pressed button in a browser. Navigation should probably be toward the top of the screen.

Table 2-4.   *Common Web Usability Guidelines* (continued)

Guideline	Explanation
Consider medium of consumption.	Make sure to understand where the user will consume the content—on screen or on paper. If users print pages to consume them, shouldn't the usability test be performed on the paper document as well?
Consider environment of use.	If known, consider where a user will interact with a page. Where users interact with a page will affect how usable they perceive it. For example, relying on sound in a noisy environment isn't a wise idea.
Focus on speed.	Users dread slow-loading sites. Make sure pages are fast-loading by practicing minimal design. This doesn't mean eliminating graphics, only that a page should be no slower than it needs to be to deliver its message.

Table 2-4. *Common Web Usability Guidelines* (continued)

Usability Above All Else

One problem with usability discussions is that it is easy to use usability concerns as a way to squash any other reasonable value. For example, some people have gone so far as to discuss how banner ads contribute to poor site usability because they are animated or increase the download time. However, consider that without the banner ads the site may not be economically viable. Pleasing graphics also are a common target for usability experts. It is interesting to note how boring most usability gurus' sites actually are. While a site without much graphics may be usable, it might not do much to improve the brand identity of the organization running the site; in fact, without graphics, it may undermine brand identity built through other mediums. In some situations, it may be important to let the user endure a slightly longer download in order to see the corporate logo and new advertising look.

Advanced technology also is a common enemy of good site usability. The truth is that while advanced technology may lock out some users, what is provided may be worth it. If we always designed for the lowest common denominator, we'd still have text-only Web pages. Don't let usability completely stifle innovation. Usability is certainly very important, but there are often other considerations in a Web site's design. Always remember that while we design for users, we are ultimately in control of our site.

Suggestion: Do not use usability concerns as a way to avoid or eliminate visual, technological, or economic aspects of a site.

Who's in Control of the Experience?

While it is true that we must give the people what they want, the masters of sites—meaning those who pay for them—may have desires that are not congruent with the desires of the site's users. Do not become a slave to the user; remember that, in some sense, we are the masters of our own sites. How we want to treat our visitors is going to influence greatly how they feel about visiting our sites. Do you want to be a dictator, forcing the user to download certain plug-ins or resize a window? Conversely, you could be very democratic and let users pick their own path through your site. You may even allow users to modify content on the site or influence other users with indicators of link popularity. Last, you could aim for a middle ground and maybe act as a benevolent dictator, trying to help users along the way and giving them freedom within certain constraints, but always trying to guide them along.

The issue of control during a site visit is somewhat of an unwritten contract between the site user and the developer. There is give and take in the relationship. While one of the main tenets of user-centered design is to put the user in control, users are imperfect like everyone else; if we give them complete control, they may make serious errors. Developers will want to keep users from making mistakes. However, the role of the benevolent dictator of the online experience is difficult. If you control things too much and users notice that they can't resize their window or press certain buttons, they may become angry or frustrated. The key is to provide an illusion of control.

Users should be able to do everything they need to do and nothing more. People need to feel like they are in control, but the control should have limits. Good interfaces exhibit this control. Consider, for example, the famous adventure game *Myst*™. In *Myst*, the user can click objects onscreen and move in a direction simply by clicking in the appropriate direction. The interface is very simple and also very restrictive, though game players rarely notice this. In *Myst*, as in many well-designed video games, the progression is very controlled by the game designer, but the illusion of control is always preserved. A great Web site would follow the cue of a video game by trying to guide someone to a conclusion like purchasing a product, but in a manner that the user doesn't really notice.

The best example of the balance of control in an experience is probably Las Vegas. Casinos create a complete experience of visiting an ancient land, tropical paradise, or foreign country. A gimmick outside the casino like an exploding volcano or pirate battle attracts hordes of visitors. The intent is that some of these visitors will step onto the nearby conveyor belt to be quickly whisked into the casino. Inside the casino, temperature, lighting, and oxygen level are carefully controlled in an attempt to create a pleasant environment. The passage of time becomes difficult to determine because windows are few and tinted, and clocks are nonexistent. Assistance is plentiful from dealers and waitresses who will provide free drinks. If you get hungry, cheap food is nearby at an all-you-can-eat buffet. Want to stay overnight? Rooms are reasonably priced—and if you spend enough, they might even be free. But when you come to your senses as your wallet begins to empty, notice how difficult it is to find the exit! Good

Las Vegas casinos practice the ultimate in experience design, second only (maybe) to Disneyland. The experience is always controlled; the point is to maximize the money the casino takes in. If you step out of line, get irate and loud when you lose, or try to do something to win back control in gambling by card counting, you'll find that you are quickly escorted outside. The experience is fun and you can win, but the control is there and the house always has the edge. It's pure math. If you plan to run a commercial site, learn from Las Vegas.

> **Suggestion: Practice "Las Vegas" Web design. Provide the user with a pleasant experience, complete with perks and the illusion of unlimited choices, but control the situation strictly at all times.**

Summary

Usability is about the aspects of a site that aren't always noticeable but yet seriously influence the ease in which a user is able to accomplish a task using the site. Usable sites should be easy to learn, easy to use, and easy to remember. They should also result in few errors and be satisfying to the user. While some ways to improve usability, such as consistency and simplicity of design, are easy to formulate, sometimes it is difficult to satisfy the needs of every user. One reason is that users have different Web skill levels—novice, intermediate, and advanced (power users)—that will affect site usability. Another is that, while users generally share certain capabilities for accessing a site, such as vision and memory, users are also individuals, with unique characteristics, opinions, and experiences. They will also tend to view your site as a mere island in a big ocean of sites, and it is best to assume that they won't want to learn your special rules.

With so many varieties of users, you probably won't be able to perfectly accommodate every user's unique tastes and requirements. However, if you create an adaptive interface that can be used by the three broad categories of users and make sure to test your site carefully with real users, you stand a good chance of making a site that is usable by most users. Be particularly careful not to lock users out, particularly those who may be disabled or slightly different from your average user.

Finally, a site should always be built to meet the needs of its users within the constraints or the desires of its creators. However, never use the quest for a usable site as a way to avoid difficult problems or as an excuse not to use graphics or technology or introduce new features that a user might want. An overzealous Web professional waving the usability banner can easily stifle innovation. Balance is always the key to great Web design.

Chapter 3

The Web Medium

While the human element may be the most critical aspect of Web-based communication, effective Web design is also extremely dependent on correct technical execution. If a site is poorly constructed or error ridden, visitors may lose sight of its message or function. To excel at Web design, practitioners should have a complete understanding of the elements of the Web medium.

The Web medium is composed of three major components: client, server, and network. We will briefly overview each component and its subcomponents here in order to provide designers with a complete vocabulary of modern Web technology—and possibly provoke further study. We will also provide links about the activities of the various standards bodies, particularly the World Wide Web Consortium (W3C), which defines Web technologies, and the IETF, which sets many of the network, related protocols. Later chapters will focus on correct site execution and the effects of Web technologies on design decisions.

Core Web Technologies

As described in Chapter 1, the Web is implemented as a client-server system over a vast public network called the Internet. The three components of any client-server system are the client side, the server side, and the network. A visualization of the basic components that make up the Web is shown in Figure 3-1. We will now survey each of the primary components in turn, starting with the client side, which is primarily defined by the browser.

Web Browsers

The Web browser is the interpreter of our Web sites. It is very important to understand the Web browser being supported and what capabilities it has. The two most common browsers at the time of this book's publication are Microsoft's Internet Explorer (which accounts for the majority of browser users) and Netscape's Communicator (Navigator). While these two browsers account for most users accessing public Web sites, there are numerous other versions of browsers in use.

Note   *The exact figures for browser usage at public Web sites are continually changing and are tracked by various statistics sites as well as browser-related sites such as http://www.upsdell.com/BrowserNews/.*

The problem with published browser usage reports is that they don't necessarily reflect your browsing audience. Consider a site that publishes Macintosh software—its browser usage pattern might actually show a fair number of users with OmniWeb, a Macintosh-specific browser that has a notable number of rabid followers. However, most sites probably wouldn't consider OmniWeb something to even think about. Depending on your users, the types of browsers will vary. From statistics showing that surveyed

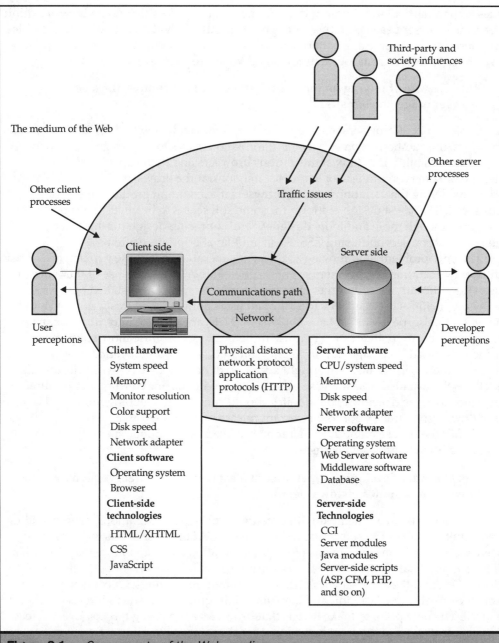

Figure 3-1. *Components of the Web medium*

sites favor a particular browser, it does not necessarily follow that your site will exhibit the same browser usage patterns—though it is pretty likely. Look at your own log files to determine browser usage patterns. If you are building an intranet site, you might not even have to look at your logs to understand what browsers are in use.

> **Rule: Beware of relying on published browser usage figures; track actual browser usage on *your* site.**

Given a mix of browsers made up of the top two vendors with a smattering of other browsers, the question becomes how this information relates to site design and technology use. One possibility is to look at the various browsers and their capabilities, and then design for some common set of features. First, look at the browsers listed in Table 3-1.

Considering the variations among browsers, the common ground isn't terribly advanced. The safest design platform for some still seems to be what Netscape 3.*x* supports, though more and more designers are embracing design for the 4.*x* and 5.*x* generation browsers and using CSS, Flash, and JavaScript more often.

The only problem with moving to the next generation is that the gap between what different generations of browsers support can be rather large. Because of this, sites (and users) significantly favor Internet Explorer over Netscape. (The installed base for IE browsers includes between 85% to 90% of all users at the time of this writing.) With the advent of Netscape's Mozilla-based browsers (Netscape 6 and 7, and Mozilla 1.0), things may get more interesting because these browsers promise more support for standards-based Web page development than Netscape's 4.*x* generation browsers. Even so, there will not be an overnight adoption of new, non-IE browsers around the Web. As the installed base increases, the longer it will take for consumers to embrace new technologies. Therefore, public sites should consider developing for at least one, if not two, generations prior to the current release of a browser. Even more than six years after the release of the 2.*x* generation browsers, some public sites still support that generation of browsers perfectly.

> **Tip: Consider developing for at least the last two, if not three, versions of a browser to account for slow upgrades.**

It is easy to be overwhelmed with potential browser considerations, even if dealing just with the major browsers' most recent versions. At the time of this writing, there were more than 20 major versions of the 4.*x* generation alone and more than 400 other different potential Netscape variations—primarily older versions or beta releases—floating around the Web, all with different capabilities and bugs. Of course, Netscape isn't the only browser vendor, and there are slight upgrades made to Internet Explorer as well. The only point to make here is that browsers are moving targets. Every release has new features and different bugs. Just because someone is using a 4.*x* generation browser doesn't guarantee a site will work the same under the same version on another platform or under an interim release. Sorry, but Netscape 4 or Internet Explorer 4 on Windows won't work the same on Macintosh and NT. Even different interim releases like 4.03 and 4.5 may have significant differences in page rendering and bugs. Add in

Browser	Version	HTML Version Support	JavaScript	CSS	Programming	Comments
Internet Explorer	3	HTML 3.2 + extras	JavaScript 1.0	Somewhat	Helper apps, ActiveX controls, Netscape plug-in compatibility, Java, VBScript	Some corporate and slow upgraders still use this version. Good possibility to target this browser for a fall-back version of a site.
Internet Explorer	4	HTML 4 + extras	JavaScript 1.1 + extras. Note that the browser supports more advanced JavaScript features, but its **language** attribute support indicates 1.1 as the maximum supported JavaScript.	Partial CSS1	Helper apps, ActiveX controls, Netscape plug-in compatibility, Java, VBScript	IE 4's main advances were in CSS support and improved JavaScript. IE 4 was the first browser to support pages that could be significantly manipulated after page-load using JavaScript and relying on the Document Object Model (DOM).
Internet Explorer	5	HTML 4 + extras	JavaScript 1.2 + extras. Note that the browser supports more advanced JavaScript features, but its **language** attribute support indicates 1.2 as the maximum supported JavaScript.	Most of CSS1 + some extensions	Helper apps, ActiveX controls, Netscape plug-in compatibility, Java, VBScript	IE 5 mostly refines the features provided in HTML 4, though it does begin the use of client-side XML.

Table 3-1. *Common Browser Versions and Characteristics*

Browser	Version	HTML Version Support	JavaScript	CSS	Programming	Comments
Internet Explorer	5.5	HTML 4 + extras	JavaScript 1.2 + extras. The same conformance issue as previous browsers hold; IE 5.5 supports more advanced JavaScript but may not report it properly using some scripting techniques.	Most of CSS1 + some extensions	Helper apps, ActiveX controls, Netscape plug-in compatibility, Java, VBScript	IE 5.5 continues to refine the basic ideas presented in IE 4 and 5 with enhancements to style sheet support and XML.
Internet Explorer	6.0	HTML 4 + extras, XHTML 1.0	JavaScript 1.3 + extras. Note that the browser supports more advanced JavaScript features but its **language** attribute support indicates 1.3 as the maximum supported JavaScript.	CSS1 + extensions	Helper apps, ActiveX controls, Netscape plug-in compatibility, and VBScript. Note that IE 6 does not initially ship with Java, though many users add it.	IE 6 continues to refine the basic ideas presented in IE 4 and 5.x with enhancements to standards support and XML. DOM Level 1 compliance is close to full.
Netscape	1.x	HTML 2 + extras	No	No	Helper apps	No frames (good example of a worst-case graphical browser). Generally not considered in design decisions.
Netscape	2.x	HTML 2 + extras	JavaScript 1.0	No	Helper apps, plug-ins, Java	No background color on table cells, Java implementation buggy, JavaScript limited to simple form validation. Rarely considered in design decisions.

Table 3-1. *Common Browser Versions and Characteristics (continued)*

Browser	Version	HTML Version Support	JavaScript	CSS	Programming	Comments
Netscape	3.x	HTML 3.2	JavaScript 1.1	No	Helper apps, plug-ins, Java	Rollover buttons become possible, Java more stable. Occasionally considered as a fall-back browser in design decisions.
Netscape	4.x	HTML 4 + extras	JavaScript 1.2, 1.3	Some CSS1 + CSS-P	Helper apps, plug-ins, Java	Limited DHTML support, primarily object movement and visibility; CSS support buggy, suppressed JavaScript error messages, automatic installation of plug-ins introduced. Still considered by some designers because of slow Netscape upgrades.
Mozilla/ Netscape	Netscape 6.x/ Mozilla 1.x	HTML 4.01, XHTML 1.0	JavaScript 1.5	Full CSS1, partial CSS2	Helper apps, plug-ins, Java	Great standards support for XHTML, CSS, XML, PNG, and other W3C approved standards. Not widely used at time of this edition's publication.

Table 3-1. *Common Browser Versions and Characteristics (continued)*

the continual use of half-done beta browsers, and you have a recipe for disaster. Pages often won't render correctly, and errors will ensue. Users unfortunately won't always place blame correctly. A small layout problem may be interpreted as the designer screwing up, not the browser vendor releasing a poorly tested product.

Rule: Users often don't blame browsers for simple errors—they blame sites.

So what's a developer to do? First, make sure you know what's going on. Keep up with the latest news in browsers at sites like http://www.upsdell.com/BrowserNews/. In particular, watch out for beta and interim releases. They are often the most dangerous, and users will not consider a 6.1 and 6.2 to be significantly different.

Tip: Be careful of features in beta and interim releases of browsers.

The next thing to consider is exactly what browsers you need to be aware of. This requires that you know the browsers used by the site's audience, so look to your log files. In general, public sites should be as browser agnostic as possible, while private sites like intranets may be designed specifically for a single browser. Designers should

Browser	URL	Comments
Internet Explorer	http://www.microsoft.com/ie	Consider having the last three versions of this popular browser. Note that this may require having multiple systems or boot options to run numerous versions of IE.
Netscape	http://browsers.netscape.com/ browsers	With so many versions available, consider using the last version of each major release: 6.2, 6.1, 6.0, 4.7, 4.6, 4.5, 4.0x, 3.x, and 2.x
Mozilla	http://www.mozilla.org	The browser behind Netscape's project to build a 6.x generation browser should always be followed as a preview to what's coming soon and to test Web standards.

Table 3-2. *Useful Browsers for Testing Purposes*

FOUNDATION

Browser	URL	Comments
Opera	http://www.opera.com	This fast, standards-aware browser is becoming very popular and may be a strong third choice for some users.
America Online	http://webmaster.info.aol.com/	Not a Web browser per se, but the use of Web browsers under AOL and associated AOL TV is often very troublesome. Developers should look at public sites under AOL very carefully.
Lynx	http://lynx.browser.org	It is useful to test with Lynx, a text-only browser, to understand how a page renders without any graphics.
Amaya	http://www.w3.org/Amaya/	Not a realistic browser for users, but the W3C's test browser often implements interesting standards-related features before commercial browsers. Useful for experimenting with specifications. Avoid for realistic testing.

Table 3-2. *Useful Browsers for Testing Purposes* (continued)

be aware of the browser families listed in Table 3-2. Users interested in development for non-PC platforms may also find Palm (http://www.palmos.com/dev/), television (http://www.developers.aoltv.com/ and http://developer.msntv.com/), and cell phone simulators (http://developer.openwave.com/) very useful tools for testing sites.

Tip: Beyond the leading browsers, consider testing with standards-oriented browsers as well as text-only or alternative-environment-access browsers.

Given the number of browsers available and the significant difficulties involved in testing dozens of different configurations just to ensure a site renders under common viewing environments, some authors decide to write for a particular browser version or indicate that a particular vendor's browser is the preferred viewing platform. Many sites that do this exhibit a browser badge on the site. If a particular browser is required, do not blatantly advertise it on the home page as many sites do. It simply announces that you practice exclusionary development.

Tip: Do not advertise favored browsers blatantly on a home page.

Markup Languages

The foundation of any Web page is markup. Markup technologies such as HTML, XHTML, and XML define the structure and possible meaning of page content. Despite the common belief that markup languages define the look of Web pages, and the equally common use of HTML in this manner, page appearance should really be accomplished using other technologies, particularly style sheets.

HTML

HTML (HyperText Markup Language) is the primary markup technology used in Web pages. Traditional HTML is defined by a SGML (Standardized General Markup Language) DTD (Document Type Definition—see the upcoming section "XML") and comes in three primary versions (HTML 2, HTML 3.2, and HTML 4). HTML 4 comes in three varieties: transitional, strict, and frameset, with most document authors using the transitional variant. HTML 4.01 is the most current and final version of HTML. An example of an HTML document showing common structures is presented in Figure 3-2.

While the various tags and rules of HTML are fairly well defined, most browser vendors provide extensions to the language beyond the W3C definition. Further, the browsers themselves do little to enforce the markup language rules, leading to sloppy usage of the technology. Also, while HTML should be used primarily for structuring a document, many developers use it to format the document for display as well. HTML's formatting duties should eventually be completely supplanted by Cascading Style Sheets (CSS). However, even with adequate style sheet support in browsers, many developers continue to use HTML tables and even proprietary HTML tags in their page design. There are no plans for further development of HTML by the W3C and browser vendors, and developers are encouraged to embrace XHTML.

The HTML 4.0 specification is available at the following URL:

- http://www.w3.org/TR/html401/

```
<!DOCTYPE HTML PUBLIC "-//W3C//DTD HTML 4.01 Transitional//EN">
<html>

<head>

<title>Sample HTML Document</title>

<!-- Just an HTML comment -->

<meta http-equiv="Content-Type" content="text/html; charset=iso-8859-1">
<meta name="description" content="Another sample meta item">
</head>

<body>

<h1>Sample Heading</h1>
<hr>
<p id="firstParagraph">Just a sample paragraph of text with some
<strong>logical</strong> and <b>physical</b> formating elements. We
may also find both named character entities like &copy; and numeric
entities like &#92; in HTML documents.</p>

<p>Tags may <em>nest <strong>deeply</strong></em> and complex tags like
<a href="http://www.yahoo.com" id="link1" class="externalLink">links</a> may
have attributes.</p>

</body>
</html>
```

Figure 3-2.   *Sample Document with common HTML structures*

XHTML

XHTML is a reformulation of HTML using XML (extensible Markup Language) rather than SGML. XHTML solves two primary problems with HTML. First, XHTML continues to force designers to separate the look of the document from its structure, by putting more emphasis on the use of style sheets. Second, XHTML brings much stricter enforcement of markup rules to Web pages. For example, XHTML documents must contain only lowercase tags, always have quotes on attributes, and basically follow all the rules as defined in the specification. Figure 3-3 shows an example document in HTML and its equivalent in XHTML.

A rigorous discussion of HTML and XHTML that covers all the requirements of XHTML can be found in Appendix C as well as in the companion book, *HTML: The Complete Reference* (www.htmlref.com).

```
Original HTML document

<html>
<head>
<!-- note the forgotten DTD -->
<title>HTML Document</title>
</head>

<body>
<H1>Traditional HTML is not case sensitive</H1>
<hr>
<p align=center>Many tags may have optional
close tags and often HTML authors do not
quote their attributes
<br>
<p>Tags may <i><b>Cross</i></b> and physical
tags may be used instead of logical ones.</P>

</body>
</html>
```

```
Modified XHTML document

<?xml version="1.0" encoding="iso-8859-1"?>
<!DOCTYPE html PUBLIC "-//W3C//DTD XHTML 1.0
Transitional//EN" "http://www.w3.org/TR/xhtml11/
DTD/xhtml11-transitional.dtd">
<html xmlns="http://www.w3.org/1999/xhtml">
<head>
<!-- DTD now in place -->
<title>HTML Document</title>
<meta http-equiv="Content-Type"
content="text/html; charset=iso-8859-1" />
</head>

<body>
<h1>XHTML is all in lowercase</h1>
<hr />
<p align="center">All tags are closed and tags
with no close tag become self-describing empty
tags.</p>
<p>Tags may <strong><em>not</em></strong> and
logical tags and OSS should be used.</p>

</body>
</html>
```

Figure 3-3. *Moving from HTML to XHTML requires syntactical strictness*

XHTML's syntactical strictness is both its biggest benefit and biggest weakness. Well-formed pages may be easier to manipulate and exchange by a program but are harder to create for a human. Uptake of XHTML has been slow because of this strictness. XHTML's extra rigor makes it less accessible than HTML, which is much more forgiving to beginners. So, until more tools that generate correct XHTML become available, the language will probably continue its slow uptake in the Web community at large.

The following URLs provide important information about XHTML:

- XHTML 1.0 Specification: http://www.w3.org/TR/xhtml1/

- XHTML Basic Specification: http://www.w3.org/TR/xhtml-basic/

- XHTML 1.1 Module XHTML: http://www.w3.org/TR/xhtml11/

XML

Extensible Markup Language (XML) is being touted by many as a revolutionary markup technology that will change the face of the Web. Yet, despite the hype, few understand exactly what XML actually is. In short, XML is a form of SGML modified for the Web;

thus, it allows developers to define their own markup language. So, if you want to invent YML (Your Markup Language) with XML, you can. To do this we would define the rules of our invented language by writing a *document type definition*, or *DTD*. A DTD defines how a language can be used by indicating what elements can contain what other elements, the values of attributes, and so on. A simple DTD to define a grading language for elementary school children is defined here:

```
<!--Grades DTD-->
<!ELEMENT  grades  (student+)>
<!ELEMENT  student (course+)>
<!ATTLIST  student  name  CDATA   #REQUIRED
           sex  (M|F)  #REQUIRED
           level  (1|2|3|4|5|6)  #REQUIRED>

<!ELEMENT   course EMPTY>
<!ATTLIST  course title  CDATA   #REQUIRED
           grade  (PASS|FAIL)  #REQUIRED>
```

This DTD file named grades.dtd would be referenced by an XML file such as the one shown here:

```
<?xml version="1.0"?>
<!DOCTYPE GRADES SYSTEM "grades.dtd">
<!-- the document instance -->
<grades>
<student name="Thomas" sex="M" level="3">
   <course title="Math" grade="PASS" />
   <course title="English"  grade="FAIL" />
</student>

<student name="Sylvia" sex="F"  level="1">
   <course title="Math" grade="PASS" />
   <course title="Art" grade="PASS" />
</student>
</grades>
```

The example would not only be syntactically checked, but we could check the validity of the document against the DTD, a process known as *validation*. Yet, regardless of correctness, without a defined presentation you will not see much of a result, as shown in Figure 3-4. Presentation will eventually be handled by applying style rules to the XML document using one of the technologies discussed in the next section.

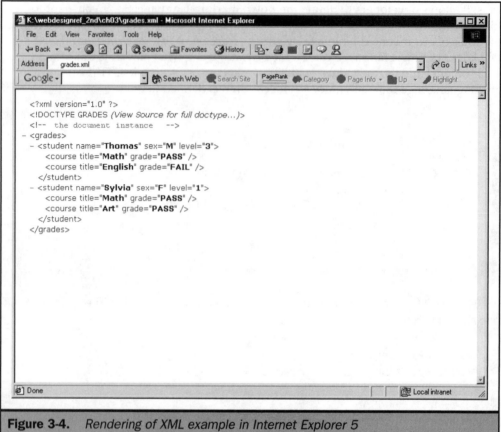

Figure 3-4. *Rendering of XML example in Internet Explorer 5*

Many readers may now be wondering about the value of developers defining their own individual markup languages. Why not just use XHTML or HTML? Wouldn't inventing new languages be the equivalent of creating a markup Tower of Babel on the Internet? Maybe, or it just may enable a whole new range of possibilities for markup. So far, the negative impact of inventing too many custom XML-based languages has been limited, and most Web developers are content using a commonly defined language like XHTML, WML (Wireless Markup Language), SVG (Scalable Vector Graphics), and numerous other XML-based languages. The precision and self-description properties of XML documents should enable a new class of Web technologies called *Web Services* that really could change the Web by allowing sites and programs to talk with each other more easily.

The XML Specification can be found online at http://www.w3.org/TR/REC-xml.

Style Sheet Technologies

Markup languages like HTML do not excel at presentation. This is not a shortcoming of the technology, but simply that HTML was not designed for this task. In reality, the look of the page should be controlled by the design elements provided by CSS (Cascading Style Sheets). In some cases, particularly when using an XML language, markup transformation may also be required to create the appropriate presentation format, so XSL (eXtensible Style Language) will be used as well.

CSS

CSS (Cascading Style Sheets) is used to specify the look of a Web page. This technology has been present at least partially in browsers as old as Internet Explorer 3.0, but it has long been overlooked in favor of HTML-based layout for a variety of reasons, including lack of consistent browser and tool support, as well as simple developer ignorance. With the rise of the 6.*x* generations of browsers, CSS is finally becoming a viable prospect for page layout.

CSS-based style sheets specify rules that define the presentation of a type of a type (for example, **<h1>**)—a group or, more correctly, class of tags—or a single tag as indicated by its **id** attribute. Style sheet rules can be used to define a variety of visual aspects of page objects, including color, size, and position. The various style rules can be combined depending on tag usage—thus the "cascading" moniker for the technology. An example of CSS in use is shown in Figure 3-5.

These URLs provide more information about CSS:

- CSS1 Specification: http://www.w3.org/TR/REC-CSS1/
- CSS2 Specification: http://www.w3.org/TR/REC-CSS2/

XSL

XSL is another style sheet technology used on the Web. It is primarily used to style XML languages. This is usually accomplished through XSL Transformation (XSLT), which is often used to convert XML markup into other markup, often XHTML or HTML plus CSS. It is possible to also use XSL Formatting Objects to style content, but, so far, this does not seem to be a commonly employed aspect of XSL. Thus, when developers

CSS files can be linked externally

different style sheets can be used for different situations

```
<!DOCTYPE html PUBLIC "-//W3C//DTD XHTML 1.0 Transitional//EN"
"http://www.w3.org/TR/xhtml1/DTD/xhtml1-transitional.dtd">

<html xmlns="http://www.w3.org/1999/xhtml">
<head>
<title>CSS Example</title>
<link rel="stylesheet" href="printstyle.css" media="printer" />
<style type="text/css">
<!--
   h1 {text-align: center; color: red; font-size: 48pt;}
   p  {color: red; font-size: 16pt; line-height: 150%;}
   #idTest {background-color: orange;}
   .classTest {font-style: italic; background-color: yellow;}
   div {background-color: yellow; border-style: dashed;}
-->
</style>
</head>
<body>

<h1>CSS can style tags</h1>
<hr />
<p style="color: green">Inline style can be applied and
may override some rules as suggested by the cascade.
Tags can have <span id="idTest">ids</span> to set
style as well as <span class="classTest">classes</span> that can
occur <span class="classTest">multiple</span> times.
</p>

<div style="position: absolute; top:300px; left:300px;">
CSS provides perfect positioning and layout when it is
working correctly</div>

</body>
</html>
```

CSS rules also can be placed document wide in a <style> tag

comments ued to mask CSS from non-style aware browsers →

tag rules

rule for a single tag named by id attribute

rule for group of tags named by a class

inline style may also be used but does not provide separation of structure and style

CSS affrds pixel perfect layout

Figure 3-5. *An example of CSS*

speak of XSL, they often are speaking of XSLT. An example of XSL Transformation is shown in Figure 3-6.

The relationship is set on the second line in the grades.xml file. The grades.xsl file specifies the transformations that would result in the HTML output as shown in Figure 3-7.

Note *Generally, the XSL transformation occurs on the server side, but XSL may become more prevalent on the client side as browsers continue to advance.*

```
<?xml version="1.0"?>
<?xml-stylesheet type="text/xsl"
href="grades.xsl"?>
<grades>

<student>Thomas</student>

 <course>
  <title>Math</title>
  <grade>B</grade>
 </course>

 <course>
  <title>History</title>
  <grade>A</grade>
 </course>


 <course>
  <title>Art</title>
  <grade>D+</grade>
 </course>

</grades>
```

```
<?xml version='1.0'?>
<xsl:stylesheet xmlns:xsl="http://www.w3.org/
TR/WD-xsl">
<xsl:template match="/">

<!DOCTYPE HTML PUBLIC "-//W3C//DTD HTML 4.01
Transitional//EN">
<html>
<head>
<title>Grade Sheet</title>
</head>
<body>
<table border="1">
<caption><xsl:value-of select="grades/student"/>
</caption>
<tr>
   <th>Course</th>
   <th>Grade</th>
</tr>

<xsl:for-each select="grades/course">
   <tr>
    <td><xsl:value-of select="title"/></td>
    <td><xsl:value-of select="grade"/></td>
   </tr>
</xsl:for-each>

</table>
</body>
</html>
</xsl:template>
</xsl:stylesheet>
```

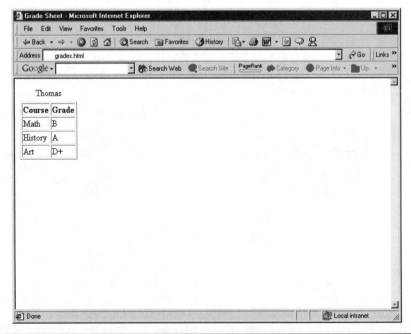

Figure 3-6.   *XSLT in action*

Information about XSL can be found at these URLs:

- XSL Transformations 1.0 Specification: http://www.w3.org/TR/xslt
- XSL Activity at W3C: http://www.w3.org/Style/XSL/

Images

Most Web browsers support either directly or through extension a variety of image formats, such as GIF, JPEG, Flash, and PNG. The image formats can be separated into two general categories: *bitmap* (or *raster*) images and *vector* images. Raster images describe each individual pixel and its color, while vector images describe an image generally as a collection of mathematical directions used to draw—or more precisely, *render*—the image. Regardless of storage format, all images become bitmaps onscreen. The fundamental difference between the two general image formats is shown here:

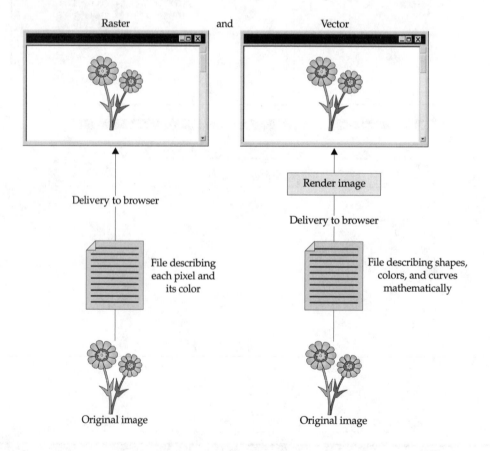

Some designers speak of the value of one general format over the other, but, in reality, both have their problems. Vector images tend to be compact in description and can be scaled mathematically, but they suffer in potential rendering time and realism. Bitmap images can be very detailed but do not scale up well and tend to be very large in terms of file size. We will examine the specific types of the images in the following sections. A complete discussion of their usage is presented in Chapter 14.

GIF

GIF (Graphics Interchange Format) is a bitmap format that does not provide a great degree of compression or color support, being limited to 8-bit or 256 simultaneous colors. However, the GIF format is relatively versatile and supports transparency, animation, and interlacing. It is commonly used in Web pages for logos, graphical navigation elements, and photos that do not require high-quality reproduction.
Information about the GIF Specification can be found at this URL:

- http://www.w3.org/Graphics/GIF/spec-gif89a.txt

JPEG

JPEG (Joint Photographic Experts Group) images support up to 24-bit color and are well suited for reproduction of photographs. Despite being a raster format, JPEG images allow designers to balance file size with image quality and support an impressive lossy compression algorithm that can significantly shrink image size with little discernable quality loss to the casual viewer. JPEG images do support progressive loading, but are not quite as versatile as GIF images because they lack transparency and animation features.
Information about JPEGs can be found at these URLs:

- JPEG Activity at the W3C: http://www.w3.org/Graphics/JPEG/
- JPEG Specification: http://www.jpeg.org/

The JPEG 2000 standard aims to eliminate many of the problems with JPEG and provide an even greater degree of quality and compression than standard JPEG files. However, so far, JPEG 2000 is not available in Web browsers.

PNG

PNG (Portable Network Graphics) images provide an advanced image format designed to replace GIF as the dominant form of graphics on the Web. PNG images provide three primary advantages over GIF: alpha transparency, which provides variable degrees of transparency (versus GIF, which has a single degree of transparency); gamma correction to help improve image brightness across systems; and improved interlacing and compression. While PNG provides numerous benefits, many of its advanced features are not properly implemented in the latest browsers, so the rush to embrace the format has yet to materialize.

Information about PNG can be found at these URLs:

■ PNG Activity at the W3C: http://www.w3.org/Graphics/PNG/

■ PNG Resources and Specifications: http://www.libpng.org/pub/png/

Flash

Macromedia's Flash is a vector image format that supports still images, animations, and complex interactivity using a built-in scripting language similar to JavaScript, called ActionScript. The format, defined in the form of an SWF file, is arguably the most popular multimedia format on the Web. It is used for implementation of navigation systems, animations, and presentations, as well as full-blown Web sites. The biggest complaint made about the format is that it is proprietary; thus, Macromedia has opened the format to the public, though it is not blessed by the W3C (which backs a rival standard called SVG). It could be further said that Flash, which was first popularized as an alternative to Macromedia's complex and sometimes clunky CD-ROM development environment Director, has become amost exactly what it sought to augment.

Information about Flash can be found at these URLs:

■ Macromedia's Flash Homepage: http://www.flash.com

■ SWF File Format Page: http://www.openswf.org

SVG

SVG (Scalable Vector Graphics) is an XML language for describing simple two-dimensional images. Because the language is XML based, scripting interaction is straightforward using standard JavaScript in conjunction with the Document Object Model. While the SVG format is an open standard, it has been slow to be adopted by the Web development community and will be unlikely to overtake Flash in the near term.

Information about SVG can be found at these URLs:

■ SVG Activity at the W3C: http://www.w3.org/Graphics/SVG

■ SVG 1.0 Specification: http://www.w3.org/TR/SVG/

VML

VML (Vector Markup Language) is yet another vector image used in Web pages. It is relatively unnoticed by most Web developers, despite the fact that it has been natively supported in Microsoft Internet Explorer since the 5.0 version. It was briefly introduced to the W3C for standardization, but SVG is being pushed over VML, and Flash is currently the popular vector format for the masses. However, Microsoft-oriented developers should be well aware of this format, since it is found in pages exported from Microsoft products.

Information about VML can be found at these URLs:

- W3C VML Note: http://www.w3.org/TR/NOTE-VML
- Microsoft VML Info:
  http://msdn.microsoft.com/library/default.asp?url=/workshop/author/vml/

Other Image Formats

The previously discussed image formats are the primary standard for well-supported image formats on the Web. However, other images are supported in some browsers, and, in theory, the **<img>** tag does not discriminate among the type, of images included in a Web page. The most important other format is probably BMP, which is supported by Microsoft's Internet Explorer. A variant called Wireless BMP (WBMP) is also noteworthy and is supported in some wireless browsers. Many browsers, particularly older browsers or those with a UNIX release, support Xbitmaps. Using plug-ins or helper applications, everything from PostScript files to TIFFs can be viewed in a browser.

Animation

A little animation can spice up a Web page a great deal. Animation on the Web is used for many things: active logos, animated icons, demonstrations, and short cartoons. There are a variety of animation technologies available to Web designers. Some of the most common animation approaches include animated GIFs, Flash and Shockwave, and JavaScript animations (also called DHTML). Other animation possibilities also exist: Java-based animations and older animation techniques such as "server push" are still possible. However, the field has narrowed significantly, and very few older or propriety animation formats are actually worth exploring. Table 3-3 details the animation choices commonly used and provides some facts about each.

Sound

Audio technologies on the Internet cover a lot of ground, from traditional download-and-play systems in a variety of formats such as WAV and MP3 to *streaming audio,* which attempts to play data as it is downloaded over a connection. Surprisingly, the most advanced technologies, and the most popular, may not be the best solution for Web sites. For example, MP3 files, while of high quality, tend to take too long to download, and streaming technologies might not provide reliable playback in all situations because of the unpredictable delivery conditions on the Internet. Fortunately, much has improved since the simple days of adding a WAV or MIDI file for background music, but there is still a long way to go before sounds will become commonplace, primarily because of the large size of audio files.

Audio files can be compressed to reduce the amount of data being sent. The software on the serving side compresses the data, which is decompressed and played back on

Animation Technology	Comments
Animated GIFs	Animated GIFs (GIF89a) are the simplest form of animation and are supported natively by most browsers. Looping and minimal timing information can be set in an animated GIF, but complex animation is beyond this format's capabilities.
JavaScript/DHTML	JavaScript can be used to move objects around the screen. This type of use of JavaScript is often described as dynamic HTML, or DHTML. Regardless of the name, this form of animation tends to be choppy and is not suggested for anything beyond simple button rollover and scrolling text effects.
Flash	Macromedia Flash, introduced earlier in the chapter, is the leading format for sophisticated Web, based animations. Flash files are very compact, and most Web users have Flash preinstalled on their system. Flash supports a growing programming facility based upon JavaScript.
Shockwave	Shockwave files are compressed Macromedia Director files. Their main benefit over Flash is simply that they support complex scripting. However, with the growing features of Flash, Shockwave files are falling quickly out of favor.

Table 3-3.   *Common Web Animation Choices*

the receiving end. The compression/decompression software is known together as a *codec*. Just like image formats, audio compression methods are either lossy or lossless. Typically, audio codecs are lossy because of size considerations. Common audio delivery approaches for Web pages are shown in Table 3-4.

Video

The holy grail of Internet multimedia is certainly high-quality, 30-frames-per-second, real-time video. The main challenge to delivering video over the Internet is its extreme size. Digital video is measured by the number of frames per second of video and by the size and resolution of these frames. A 640 × 480 image with 24 bits color and a frame

File Format	Description
WAV	Waveform (or simply *wave*) files is the most common sound format on Windows platforms. WAVs may also be played on Macs and other systems with player software.
MPEG (MP3)	*Motion Pictures Experts Group* format is a standard format that has significant compression capabilities. MPEG Level 3 or MP3 files are very commonly used for distribution of music on the Web. However, due to their size, MPEG files can be unwieldy for direct Web page playback unless streamed over a fast connection.
RealAudio (.rm)	*RealAudio* (http://www.real.com) is the predominant streaming technology currently in use on the Web. It requires a proprietary player, but basic versions of the player are available free.
MIDI	*Musical Instrument Digital Interface* format is not a digitized audio format. It represents notes and other information so that music can be synthesized. MIDI is well supported and files are very small, but it is useful for only certain applications due to its sound quality on PC hardware.
Windows Media Audio (WMA)	Windows Media Technologies (http://www.microsoft.com/windows/windowsmedia) offers a suite of utilities for creating, serving up, and viewing streamed multimedia, including high-quality audio. This is a serious competitor to the Real platform.
SWF	While it is not a music format per se, many sites opt to embed sound within Flash files. Flash files typically import either WAV or MP3 files.

Table 3-4. *Common Web Audio Choices*

rate of 30 frames per second takes up a staggering 27MB per second—and that's without sound. Add CD-quality audio (705,600 bits of data for each second of data; for stereo, double that amount to 1.4 Mbps) and the file size increases proportionately. Granted, these are uncompressed frames and audio, but the point is that a lot of compression as well as bandwidth is needed for high-quality, large-size video.

As with audio, numerous formats are supported for Web-based video, including AVI, QuickTime, MPEG, RealVideo, and ASF. Table 3-5 presents a brief overview of the various Web video formats.

Even with improvements in network and compression technology, audio and video services have a long way to go on the Web if they are to approach the quality and reliability that users are familiar with from radio and television. Until that time, developers should always proceed with caution with real time media technologies. Further, just because audio and video can be delivered over the Web doesn't mean that it should be. Always pick the best media format for the message to be delivered and remember that if you have nothing to say, whether it is in Flash or not isn't going to help. We now switch gears and turn our attention to the programming aspects of the Web medium.

Video Format	Description
AVI	*Audio Video Interleave.* The Video for Windows file format for digital video and audio is very common and easy to specify. AVI files tend to be too large for streaming directly but are often used for small download-and-play clips.
MOV (QuickTime)	MOV is the extension that indicates the use of Apple's QuickTime format (http://www.apple.com/quicktime/). A very common digital video format, it continues its popularity on the Internet.
Windows Media Video (WMV)	The Windows Media platform (http://www.microsoft.com/windows/windowsmedia) also supports streaming video, and, because of the ubiquity of the Windows Media player, this format has become one of the most popular video platforms on the Web.
Real Platform (RM)	The only major challenger to the Windows Media platform, the Real platform delivers surprisingly reliable video at various quality levels depending on end-user bandwidth availability.
Flash (SWF)	Like audio, some developers prefer to avoid the headache of multiple technologies in a page and embed video in Flash or even convert the individual video frames to Flash frames. While not always the best solution for straight streaming, for interactive video clips, Flash is hard to beat.

Table 3-5.   *Common Web Video Formats*

Programming Technologies

Understanding the basic idea of adding programming to a site isn't hard, but it's easy to get overwhelmed by the number of technologies to choose from, particularly if you assume that each is very different. The reality is that Web programming technologies can be placed into two basic groups: client side and server-side. Client side technologies are those that are run on the client, generally within the context of the browser, though some technologies like Java applets or ActiveX controls may actually appear to run, or may truly run, beyond the browser, and Helper applications do so implicitly. Of course, programs can and do run instead on the server and thus are appropriately termed server-side programming. Table 3-6 presents the general programming choices available to Web developers; Figure 3-7 shows the relationship of all programming technologies.

The challenge of Web-based programming is making sure to choose the right technology for the job. More often than not, designers are quick to pick a favorite technology, whether it is JavaScript, ColdFusion, or ASP and use it in all situations. The reality is that each technology has its pros and cons. In general, client-side and server-side programming technologies have characteristics that make them complimentary rather than adversarial. For example, when adding a form to a Web site to collect data to save in a database, it is obvious that it would make sense to check the form on the client side to make sure that the user entered the correct information, since it would not force a network round-trip to the server just to check the input data. Client-side programming would make the form validation more responsive and frustrate the user less. On the other hand, putting the data in the database would be best handled by a server-side technology, given that the database would be located on the server side of the equation. Each general type of programming has its place, and a mixture is often the best solution.

Client Side	Server Side
Helper applications	CGI scripts and programs
Browser API programs	Server API programs
—Netscape plug-ins	—Apache modules
—ActiveX Controls	—ISAPI extensions and filters
—Java applets	—Java servlets
Scripting languages	Server-side scripting
—JavaScript	—Active Server Pages (ASP/ASP.NET)
—VBScript	—ColdFusion
	—PHP

Table 3-6. *Web Client-Side and Server-Side Programming Options*

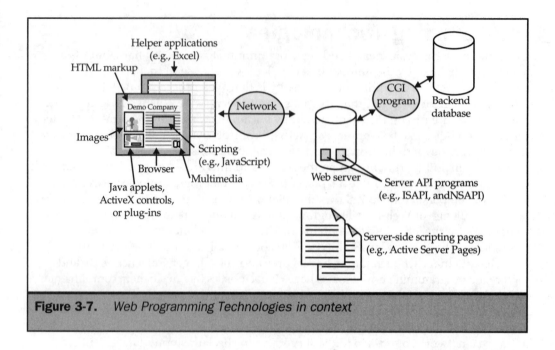

Figure 3-7.   *Web Programming Technologies in context*

Rule: Consider using both client-side and server-side technologies in a site, rather than one or the other.

Client-side Programming

The first group of programming facilities we discuss are client-side technologies. Client-side programming technologies run the gamut from simple helper applications—launched upon download of media types like Zip files or of Word documents—to scripts built in browser-based scripting languages, such as JavaScript.

Helpers

One approach to client-side programming comes in the form of programmed solutions, like helper applications. In the early days of the Web, around the time of Mosaic or Netscape 1.*x*, browsers had limited functionality and support for media beyond HTML. If new media types or binary forms were encountered, they had to be passed to an external program called a "helper application." Helper applications generally run outside the browser window. An example of a helper application would be a compression or archive tool like WinZip, which would be launched automatically when a compressed file was downloaded from the Web. Helpers are often problematic because they are not well integrated with the browser and lack methods to communicate back to the Web browser. Because the helper was not integrated within the Web browser, external media types and binaries could not be easily embedded within the Web page. Last, helper applications generally had to be downloaded and installed by the user, which kept many people from using them.

The idea of a helper application is rather simple: it is a program that the browser calls upon for help. Any program can be a helper application for a Web browser, assuming that a MIME type can be associated with the helper. When an object is delivered on the Web, HTTP header information is added to the object, indicating its type. This information is in the form of a MIME type. For example, every Acrobat file should have a content-type of *application/pdf* associated with it. When a browser receives a file with such a MIME type, it will look in its preferences to determine how to handle the file. These options may include saving the file to disk, deleting the file, or handing the file off to another program, such as a helper or browser plug-in. With MIME types and helpers, a developer can put Microsoft Word files on their Web site; users may be able to download them and read them automatically, assuming they have the appropriate helper application. Figure 3-8 overviews the basic way helper applications operate.

Oddly, helper applications are not used as much as they could be. Consider, for example, the use of HTML on an intranet. Within an organization, data may often be created in Microsoft Word or Excel format. While it is possible to easily translate such information into HTML, why would one want to? HTML is relatively expensive to create and, often difficult to update, and may limit the quality of the document's presentation. The main reason that documents are put in HTML is that they can ubiquitously read, meaning we don't have to rely on users having a particular application to read our document, other than a Web browser. However, in an intranet, this probably isn't an issue. In fact, it might be easier to create helper mappings on every system within a corporation rather than to reformat documents in HTML.

> **Suggestion: Rely on helper applications when translation to a native Web form is impractical.**

Netscape Plug-Ins

Plug-ins were introduced by Netscape in Navigator 2 and have limited support in other browsers, like Opera or Internet Explorer. Internet Explorer favors ActiveX controls, which are described in the next section. Using plug-ins addresses the communication and integration issues that plagued helper applications. Recall that helper applications are not integrated into the design of a Web page, but rather appear in a separate window and may not be able to communicate well with the browser. However, plug-ins are components that run within the context of the browser itself and, thus, can easily be integrated into the design of a page and can communicate with the browser through technologies like JavaScript (which will be introduced in a moment).

The plug-in approach of extending a browser's feature set has its drawbacks. Users must locate and download plug-ins, install them, and even restart their browsers. Many users find this rather complicated. Netscape 4 offers some installation relief with

1. Browser
checks lookup
table mapping
MIME to action.

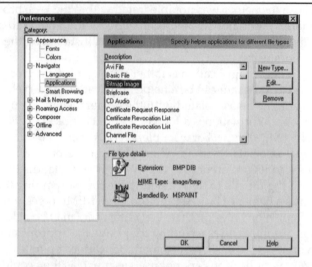

2. If no cation,
browser prompts
user.

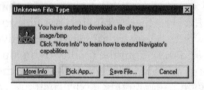

3. Pass to helper
application if set
up to do so.

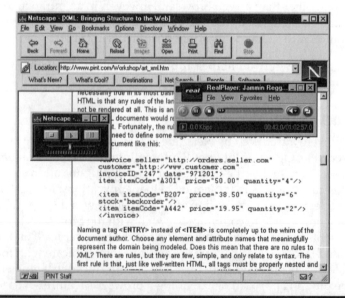

Figure 3-8.   *Overview of helper use*

self-installing (somewhat) plug-ins and other features, but plug-ins remain troublesome. To further combat this problem, many of the most commonly requested plug-ins, such as Macromedia's Flash, are included as a standard feature with Netscape browsers. The standard plug-ins are primarily geared towards media handling and include Macromedia Flash and Shockwave, Adobe Acrobat, and Real player (audio and video). If plug-ins are used, make sure to focus on the popular ones first, given the installation hassle you'll put the user through.

Suggestion: Focus on using only the more popular plug-in technologies unless automatic installation can be performed.

Note *Even if installation were not such a problem, plug-ins are not available on every machine. An executable program, or binary, must be created for each particular operating system; thus, most plug-ins work on Windows systems, though a few of the more popular ones have versions that work on Macintosh and UNIX systems as well.*

The main benefit of plug-ins is that they can be well integrated into Web pages. They may be included by using the **<embed>** or **<object>** tags, though **<embed>** is nearly always favored. For example, to embed a short Flash movie called welcome.swf that can be viewed by a Flash player plug-in, you would use the following HTML fragment:

```
<embed src="welcome.swf" quality="high"
       type="application/x-shockwave-flash" scale="exactfit"
       width="406" height="59" bgcolor="#FFFF00">
</embed>
```

The **<embed>** element displays the plug-in (in this case, a Flash animation) as part of the HTML document. Of course, always remember that the main downside of plug-ins is the barrier to entry they create because of installation and system requirements. If installation can be improved, designers will be able to rely on the technologies provided more and more.

ActiveX

ActiveX (http://www.microsoft.com/activex), which is the Internet portion of the Component Object Model (COM), is Microsoft's component technology for creating small components, or controls, within a Web page. ActiveX distributes these controls via the Internet, adding new functionality to Internet Explorer. Microsoft maintains that ActiveX controls are more similar to generalized components than to plug-ins because ActiveX controls can reside beyond the browser, even within container programs such as Microsoft Office. ActiveX controls are similar to Netscape plug-ins in that they are persistent and machine-specific. Although this makes resource use a problem, installation is not an issue: the components download and install automatically.

Security is a big concern for ActiveX controls. Because these small pieces of code potentially have full access to a user's system, they could cause serious damage. This capability, combined with automatic installation, creates a serious problem with ActiveX. End users may be quick to click a button to install new functionality, only to have it do something malicious, like erase an important system file. The potentially unrestricted functionality of ActiveX controls creates a gaping security hole. To address this problem, Microsoft provides authentication information to indicate who wrote a control, in the form of code signed by a certificate, as shown by the various dialogs in Figure 3-9.

Certificates only provide some indication that the control creator is reputable; they do nothing to prevent a control from actually doing something malicious—that's up to the user to prevent. Safe Web browsing should be practiced by accepting controls only from reputable sources.

Adding an ActiveX control to a Web page requires the use of the **<object>** tag. For example, this markup is used to add a Flash file to a page.

```
<object classid="clsid:D27CDB6E-AE6D-11cf-96B8-444553540000"
        codebase="http://download.macromedia.com/pub/shockwave/
        cabs/flash/swflash.cab#version=5,0,0,0"
        width="406" height="59">
    <param name="movie" value="welcome.swf" />
    <param name="quality" value="high" />
    <param name="scale" value="exactfit" />
    <strong>Sorry, no ActiveX in this browser!</strong>
</object>
```

What appears in a browser with no ActiveX? Just a short message indicating the user doesn't have ActiveX. The reality is that the page should allow alternative technologies, such as plug-ins using the **<embed>** tag or even images, before giving a failure message.

Suggestion: If ActiveX controls are used on a public site, make sure to provide alternatives for Netscape or other browsers.

Java

The main downside of component technologies like Netscape plug-ins and Microsoft ActiveX controls is that they are fairly operating system specific. Not every user runs on Windows or even Macintosh, so how do you deal with such a heterogeneous world? One solution is to create a common environment and port it to all systems—this is the intent of Java.

Sun Microsystems' Java technology (http://www.javasoft.com) is an attractive, revolutionary approach to cross-platform, Internet-based development. Java promises a platform-neutral development language, somewhat similar in syntax to C++, that allows programs to be written once and deployed on any machine, browser, or operating

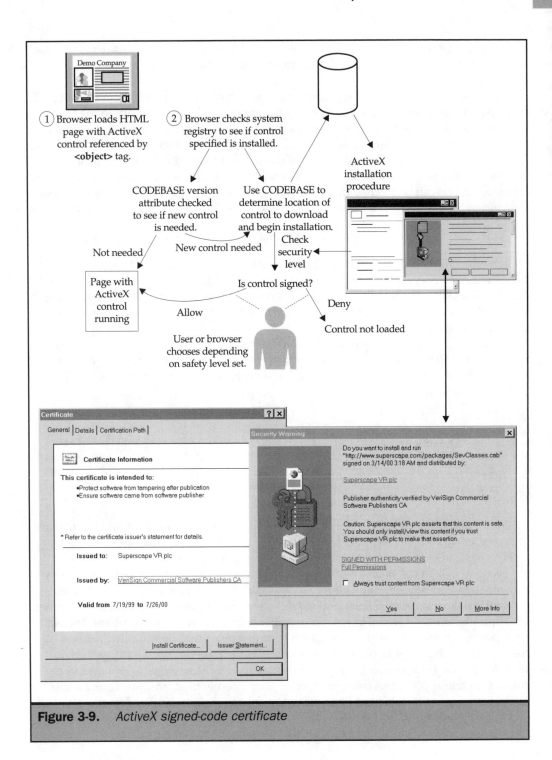

Figure 3-9. *ActiveX signed-code certificate*

system that supports the Java virtual machine (JVM). Web pages use small Java programs, called *applets*, that are downloaded and run directly within a browser to provide new functionality.

Applets are written in the Java language and compiled to a machine-independent byte code in the form of a .class file, which is downloaded automatically to the Java-capable browser and run within the browser environment. But even with a fast processor, the end system may appear to run the byte code slowly compared to a natively compiled application because the byte code must be interpreted by the JVM. This leads to the common perception that Java is slow. The reality is that Java isn't necessarily slow, but its interpretation can be. Even with recent Just-In-Time (JIT) compilers in newer browsers, Java often doesn't deliver performance equal to natively compiled applications.

Rule: Consider end-user system performance carefully when using Java.

Even if compilation weren't an issue, current Java applets generally aren't persistent; they may have to be downloaded again and again. Java-enabled browsers act like thin-client applications because they add code only when they need it. In this sense, the browser doesn't become bloated with added features, but expands and contracts upon use.

Adding a Java applet to a Web page is relatively easy and can be done using the **<applet>** or **<object>** tag, though **<applet>** is preferred for backward compatibility. If, for example, we had a .class file called helloworld, we might reference it with the following markup:

```
<applet code="helloworld.class"
        height="50"
        width="175">
<h1>Hello World for you non-Java-aware browsers</h1>
</applet>
```

In the preceding code, between **<applet>** and **</applet>** is an alternative rendering for browsers that do not support Java or that have Java support disabled.

The basic idea of how Java is utilized is shown in Figure 3-10.

Security in Java has been a serious concern from the outset. Because programs are downloaded and run automatically, a malicious program could be downloaded and run without the user being able to stop it. Under the first implementation of the technology, Java applets had little access to resources outside the browser's environment. Within Web pages, applets can't write to local disks or perform other potentially harmful functions. This framework has been referred to as the *Java sandbox*. Developers who want to provide Java functions outside of the sandbox must write Java applications that run as separate applications from browsers. Other Internet programming technologies (Netscape plug-ins and ActiveX) provide less safety from damaging programs.

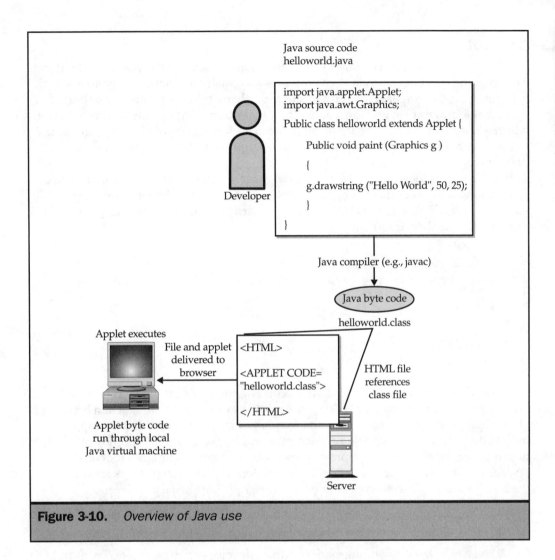

Java source code
helloworld.java

```
import java.applet.Applet;
import java.awt.Graphics;

Public class helloworld extends Applet {

    Public void paint (Graphics g )

    {

        g.drawstring ("Hello World", 50, 25);

    }

}
```

Developer

Java compiler (e.g., javac)

Java byte code

helloworld.class

Applet executes

File and applet
delivered to
browser

```
<HTML>

<APPLET CODE=
"helloworld.class">

</HTML>
```

HTML file
references
class file

Applet byte code
run through local
Java virtual machine

Server

Figure 3-10. *Overview of Java use*

The reality of Java, as far as a Web designer is concerned, is that it really isn't useful on public sites. There are so many different Java Virtual Machines in browsers that the idea of "write once, run everywhere" has been turned into "write once, debug everywhere." The major benefit of Java applets just isn't there. Designers should need no proof other than the fact that major sites that relied on Java applets have in most cases long since removed them. However, within intranets or on the server side in the form of Java servlets, we have seen Java achieve significant success.

JavaScript

JavaScript, which is of no relation to Java other than in name, is the premiere client-side scripting language used in Web browsers. Originally developed by Netscape for Navigator 2.0, the language has grown significantly over the years and is supported by all major browsers in one form or another. For example, Microsoft, supports Jscript, which is their take on the JavaScript language. Standardization of the language came in the form of ECMAScript, but the name JavaScript continues to be used by most developers.

JavaScript is a loosely typed scripting language that has simple uses for tasks like form data validation or minor page embellishments, such as rollover buttons. The inclusion of JavaScript in an HTML page is primarily handled by the **<script>** tag. For example, in this short fragment,

```
<h1>About to leave HTML</h1>
<script type="text/javascript">
<!--
   alert("Hello from JavaScript!");
//-->
</script>
<h1>Welcome back to HTML</h1>
```

we see a statement printed in an HTML document, then an alert dialog is created by JavaScript, and finally another HTML statement in executed. The interaction between HTML and JavaScript is significant, and mastery of markup is required to reap the most benefits from this technology. JavaScript will be presented in this book in small, hopefully palatable, doses to improve page usability. Some techniques for correct JavaScript use will also be presented. For an in-depth discussion, readers should see the links provided or the companion book, *JavaScript: The Complete Reference*.

Information about ECMAScript and JavaScript can be found at these URLs:

- ECMAScript Spec: http://www.ecma.ch/ecma1/STAND/ECMA-262.HTM
- Netscape JavaScript Information: http://developer.netscape.com/javascript/
- Microsoft Scripting Information: http://msdn.microsoft.com/scripting

Document Object Model

With the rise of the standardized *document object model*, or *DOM*, JavaScript is poised to become nearly as important as HTML or CSS for Web developers, because it will provide the ability to manipulate any aspect of an HTML document. In the past, page manipulations were possible using browser and document objects defined by each browser vendor. Browser differences made all but the simplest scripts difficult to implement. The W3C DOM specification promises to help ease cross-browser scripting because it specifies a language-neutral interface that allows programs and scripts to dynamically access and update the content, markup, and style of Web documents.

Since the DOM is used via JavaScript to manipulate HTML documents, this usage is often referred to as *dynamic HTML*, or *DHTML*. However, the term really is deceptive and its usage is not encouraged. The DOM comes in two primary variants at the moment: DOM Level 1, which provides access and manipulation facilities for basic markup elements and bindings to manipulate HTML tags, and DOM Level 2, which extends the interface to allow manipulation of CSS properties and provides a richer event interface.

Online information about the DOM can be found at these URLs:

- DOM Level 1 Spec: http://www.w3.org/TR/REC-DOM-Level-1/
- DOM Level 2 Core Spec: http://www.w3.org/TR/DOM-Level-2-Core/
- DOM Level 2 Events Spec: http://www.w3.org/TR/DOM-Level-2-Events/
- DOM Level 2 Style Spec: http://www.w3.org/TR/DOM-Level-2-Style/

Server-Side Technologies

The Web server handles the server side of the Web communications medium, responding to the various HTTP requests made to it. Servers may directly return various file objects, such as HTML documents, images, multimedia files, scripts, or style sheets, or they may run executable programs, which return a similar result. In this sense, the Web server acts both as a file server and as an application server. We will survey the basic components of the server side here before addressing the network components of the medium.

Web Servers

Like the Web browser, the Web server frames the environment of each Web transaction. The term "Web server" is usually understood to mean both the hardware and software. The major issue with hardware is whether the Web server is capable of handling the memory, disk, and network input/output requirements resulting from site traffic. The interplay of operating systems, such as UNIX or Windows 2000, and Web server software also is closely related to performance, as is security.

From Apache to Zeus, all Web server software platforms handle basic HTTP transactions, but all tend to offer more than basic file serving facilities. Most Web server platforms provide basic security and authentication services, logging, and programming facilities. An in-depth discussion of the popular servers and their facilities is presented in Chapter 17; here, we will focus only on the programming aspects of sites.

CGI

The oldest of the server-side programming technologies, CGI (Common Gateway Interface) programs can be written in nearly any programming language, though commonly Perl is associated with CGI applications. CGI is not a language or program, but in fact just a way to program—unlike other server-side programming environments, which define both language and style. CGI defines the basic input and output methods for server-side programs launched by a Web server, as illustrated in Figure 3-12. While assumed by some to be slow and insecure, CGI is adequate for many Web development projects when correctly understood and used.

Online information about CGI can be found at these URLs:

- CGI Overview and Documentation:
  http://hoohoo.ncsa.uiuc.edu/cgi/overview.html

- CGI Resource Index: http://cgi.resourceindex.com/

Server-Side Scripting

Server-side scripting technologies, such as Microsoft's Active Server Pages (ASP) or Macromedia's ColdFusion, allow dynamic pages to be created easily. All server-side scripting languages, including the popular ASP, ColdFusion, JSP, and PHP languages, work fairly similarly. The idea is that script templates that contain a combination of HTML and scripting language are executed server side to build a resulting Web page. Usually, some form of server engine intercepts page requests, and when files with certain extensions—such as .asp, .cfm, .jsp, .php, or .shtml—are encountered, the script elements in the page are replaced with the resulting markup output. The process is illustrated in Figure 3-13.

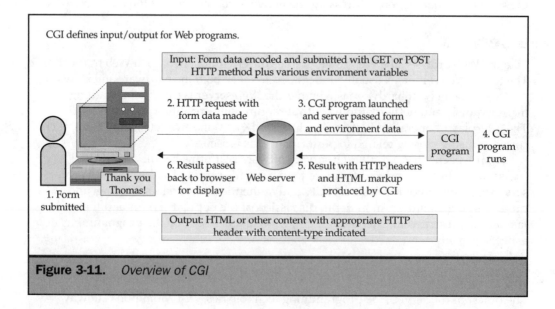

Figure 3-11.   *Overview of CGI*

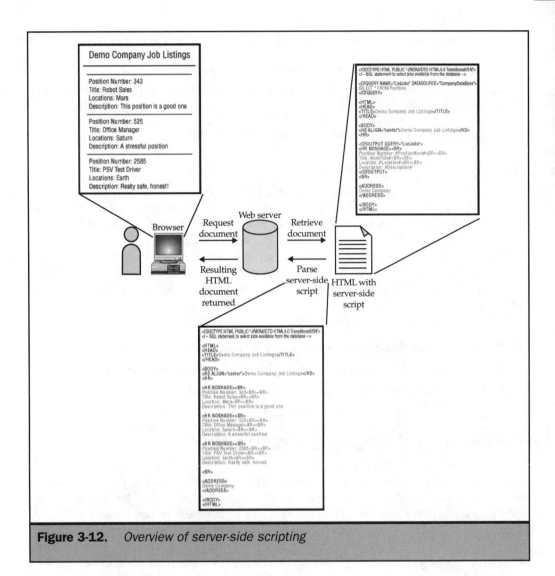

Figure 3-12.   *Overview of server-side scripting*

Server-side scripting languages are often used to build dynamic pages from databases, personalize content for users, or generate reusable components in pages. The syntax for each language is different, and many developers are somewhat religious about the merits of one language over the next, but the fact of the matter is that none of them scales well for extremely high-volume sites. Such sites usually require server API programs, which are discussed next.

Online information about server-side scripting can be found at these URLs:

- ASP Information: http://msdn.microsoft.com/asp
- ColdFusion Information: http://www.macromedia.com/software/coldfusion/
- PHP Information: http://www.php.net/
- JSP Information: http://java.sun.com/products/jsp

Server APIs

Server API (Application Programming Interfaces) programs are special server-side programs built to interact closely with the Web server. A simple way to think of server API programs is as plug-ins to a Web server. Common APIs include ISAPI for Microsoft's IIS server, NSAPI for the Netscape/IPlanet/Sun server, Apache Modules for Apache, and Java servlets for Java-enabled Web servers. The benefit of server API programs is that their close interaction with the Web server generally translates into high performance. The downside, of course, is the complexity of writing such a program and the possibility that an errant server module may actually crash the entire server.

Information about server APIs can be found at these URLs:

- Apache Module Information: http://modules.apache.org/
- ISAPI Filters/Extension Information: http://msdn.microsoft.com
- Java Servlet Information: http://java.sun.com/products/servlet

Network and Related Protocols

The underlying protocols of the Web include the TCP/IP suite of networking protocols. Not a single protocol but a group of protocols, TCP/IP is what makes all services on the Internet possible. Individually, IP (Internet Protocol) provides the basic addressing and routing information necessary to deliver data across the Internet. However, TCP (Transport Control Protocol) provides the facilities that make communications reliable, such as correction and retransmission. Together, in conjunction with the Domain Name Service (or DNS), which is the process of translating fully qualified domain names like www.webdesignref.com into their underlying IP addresses (66.45.42.235), we have the ability to build higher-level services, such as e-mail or Web sites, on the Internet. Knowledge of lower-level protocols may seem pointless to many Web designers, but it is particularly helpful to understand networking details when designing extremely scalable Web sites. However, regardless of site aims, the next protocol discussed should be understood by every Web designer.

HTTP

HTTP (Hypertext Transport Protocol) is the application-level protocol that handles the discussion between a user-agent, generally a Web browser, and a Web server. The protocol is simple and defines eight basic commands (GET, POST, HEAD, PUT, DELETE, OPTIONS, TRACE, and CONNECT) that can be made by a user-agent to request or manipulate data. Responses may contain both numeric and textual codes (for example, 404 Not Found) and associated data.

The simplicity of the HTTP protocol is both a blessing and a curse. It is simple to implement, but its lack of state management and its performance problems plague Web developers. The HTTP 1.1 specification as defined in RFC 2616 addressed many of the performance problems, but state management still has to be resolved using cookies, hidden data variables, or extended URLs. An overview of HTTP can be found in Chapter 17, while Appendix G details its request and response format.

Information about HTTP can be found at these URLs:

- W3C HTTP Activity: http://www.w3.org/Protocols/
- HTTP 1.1 Specification: ftp://ftp.isi.edu/in-notes/rfc2616.txt

MIME

MIME (Multipurpose Internet Mail Extensions), the unsung hero of Web protocols, is used by browsers to determine what kind of data they have received from a server. Specifically, an HTTP header called Content-type contains a MIME value, which is looked up by a browser to understand what type of data it is receiving and what to do with it. Servers append MIME types to HTTP headers either by generating them from a program or by mapping a file extension (for example, .html) to an appropriate MIME type (for example, text/html). MIME allows Web sites to deliver any type of data, not just the common Web formats like HTML.

Information about MIME can be found at this URL:

- MIME Specification: http://www.ietf.org/rfc/rfc2045.txt

Addressing: URL/URI/URNs/URCs

To request and link to Web pages, it is necessary to use an addressing scheme. Web users are familiar with *URLs (Uniform Resource Locator)*, like http://www.webdesignref.com/, which specify protocol and location. In specifications, *URI (Uniform Resource Identifier)* is the more commonly accepted term for short names or address strings that refer to a resource on the Web. Yet, whatever the name, URI or URLs do not provide all that may be required on the Web in the future, since they specify only location. *Uniform Resource Names (URNs)* and *Uniform Resource Characteristics (URCs)* may eventually be implemented to provide non-location-dependent addressing and extra information about resources, respectively. However, resource characteristics are more commonly specified using a form of meta data, as described next.

Online information about addressing can be found at this URL:

- W3C Addressing Activity: http://www.w3.org/Addressing/

Meta Data

Meta data is defined as data about data. Web developers may be familiar with putting meta data in a Web page using the **<meta>** tag. Often, this is used to specify keywords and descriptions for search engines. For example,

```
<meta name="keywords" content="robots,androids, bots">
<meta name="description" content="Demo Company makes the best
       robots in the Solar System!">
```

Meta data is also used in Web pages to control page characteristics, particularly those related to HTTP headers. For example,

```
<meta http-equiv="Expires" content="Wed, 15 May 2002 08:21:57 GMT" />
```

would set an expiration date for a Web page using the HTTP expires header.

The key to meta data is having a consistent and descriptive enough vocabulary for describing data. The Resource Description Framework (RDF) provides a standard way for using XML to represent meta data in the form of statements about properties and relationships of items on the Web. However, RDF itself is just a framework and needs a vocabulary. A popular vocabulary called Dublin Core initially has started to gain some traction. However, at the time of this edition's writing, the use of meta data vocabulary beyond the simple **<meta>** tag for keywords and descriptions is not common practice on the Web, though it is prevalent in many large sites and very common in large intranets.

Online information about meta data can be found at these URLs:

■ W3C RDF Information: http://www.w3.org/RDF/

■ Dublin Core Metadata Initiative: http://dublincore.org/

Web Services

Finally, the latest wrinkle in the Web medium is the rise of Web Services. The basic concept of Web Services is that Web sites may interact directly with each other, exchanging information or even running programs remotely. Web Services allow for complex distributed applications to be built using the pieces of various Web sites. For example, imagine running a small travel site and offering flight, hotel, and car rental booking services directly from your site through a large travel partner's Web site without the user being aware. Web Services would provide the facilities for your site to talk to others and seamlessly make such a service possible.

The key to Web Services is the use of standardized message formats, typically specified in XML. A protocol called SOAP (Simple Object Access Protocol) appears to be the leading candidate for Web Services. However, others do exist, and Web Services are not prevalent enough yet to assume victory for SOAP. Beyond messaging protocols,

FOUNDATION

Web Services also require a facility for service providers to describe their offered services, and for users to discover the services they require. So far, service description is being handled by a protocol called WSDL (Web Service Description Language), while service discovery is handled by UDDI (Universal Description, Discovery, and Integration). As mentioned, these protocols may not necessarily become standard; but regardless of what protocol is adopted, Web Services will provide for a much richer Web experience, which is coming to be known as the *semantic Web*.

Information about Web Services can be found at these URLs:

- W3C Web Services Activity: http://www.w3.org/2002/ws/
- W3C Semantic Web Activity: http://www.w3.org/2001/sw/

Note *A good portion of the activity in the Web Services space revolves around Microsoft's .NET technology, which also provides SOAP as well as a sophisticated Web programming environment. However, what .NET actually means to Web Services and what it includes are still very fluid. The best source of information on the Microsoft variant of Web Services can be found at http://www.microsoft.com/net/.*

Summary

Understanding the various aspects of the Web medium is mandatory for aspiring Web designers. Even if the focus is only on front-end interface creation, designers should have at least passing knowledge of the various components of the Web sites, ranging from addressing systems to XML-based Web Services. While it might be said that architects often make lousy carpenters, it can also be assumed that they generally have some sense of the properties of the building materials their projects use, and so should Web architects. Some of these "building materials," such as Web browsers, HTML/ XHTML, CSS, JavaScript, and media formats, should already be very familiar, while others, like XML and networking protocols, may seem of little use to visual designers. However, with the transition away from simple print-oriented Web design to more interactive software-focused Web sites, designers would be well advised to become more proficient in programming and networking technologies. The next chapter explores just how Web sites are built and provides a useful overview of the processes that can be employed to guide complex Web projects.

Chapter 4

The Web Design
Process

B uilding a great Web site can be challenging. With so many different components, ranging from visual design to database integration, there is plenty of room for things to go wrong. In order to minimize the risk of a Web project failing, we need a process to guide us. Unfortunately, some Web designers utilize what might be called the "NIKE" method of Web development—they *just do it*, often with little forethought or planning. Building a site this way is not methodical. The site's goals tend to be loosely defined, the process more intuitive than procedural, and the end result highly unpredictable. Sites developed this way are like plants. They grow organically—sometimes into a beautiful flower, but more often into a tangled mess. Complex Web sites require careful planning. A process or methodology should always be employed to help guide our Web design and development efforts.

The Need for Process

Today, Web development finds itself in a crisis similar to the "software crisis" of the late 1960s. A few years ago most Web sites were little more than digital brochures, or "brochureware." Creating such a site didn't require a great deal of planning—often, it was sufficient simply to develop an interface and then to populate the site with content. Since then, sites have become much larger and more complex. With the introduction of interactivity and e-commerce, sites have clearly moved away from brochureware to become full-fledged software applications. Despite this, many developers have yet to adopt a robust site-building methodology, but continue to rely on ad hoc methods.

Note   *The "software crisis" refers to a time in the software development field when increasing hardware capabilities allowed for significantly more complex programs to be built. It was challenging to build and maintain such new programs because little methodology had been used in the past, resulting in numerous project failures. Methodology such as structured or top-down design was introduced to combat this crisis.*

Evidence of the crisis in Web development practices is everywhere. Unlike the in-house client/server software projects of the past, the dirty laundry of many failed Web projects is often aired for all to see. The number of pages that seem to be forever "under construction" or "coming soon" suggests that many Web sites are poorly planned. Some sites have been in a state of construction for years, judging by their content or date of last modification. These online ghost towns are cluttered with old content, old-style HTML, dated technologies, broken links, and malfunctioning scripts. Don't discount some of these problems as mere typos or slight oversights. A broken link is a catastrophic failure, like a software program with menus that just don't go anywhere!

The reason why sites exhibit problems certainly vary. Some sites may deteriorate simply because their builders got bored or moved on. Other sites may fall apart because the site wasn't considered useful, or funding was withdrawn. Still other sites probably just couldn't be completed because the sites overwhelmed the developers—they may not have understood the tools they were working with, or were not versed well enough in the medium's restrictions. The almost countless dead sites on the Web suggest that Web development projects are risky and often fail.

Ad Hoc Web Process

Often the process to build a Web site is to simply implement the site, perform a brief visual test in a browser, and then release it to the world. This is similar to the "by the seat of your pants" code-and-test process used in small software projects. The numerous problems in Web sites built using informal methods show the problem with this overly simplistic approach. Today's process for the Web is so fast that the process almost boils down to two steps: implement and then release. Visual Web design tools encourage this design-on-the-fly approach. Some tools encourage the developer to immediately mock up an interface and later use wizards to add functionality, while others can create huge amounts of code but have an interface added later on. There is no doubt that a speedy approach to development, given the time demands of the Web, is important. Releasing a shoddy, poorly thought-out site, however, may backfire when users become frustrated with the site's problems.

In the software industry, most professionals tend to agree that such informal or "design as you go along" methods are only good for small projects, generally with only one programmer, and where future maintenance is not expected to be great. Often, programs built with such little planning exhibit convoluted programming logic—often called "spaghetti code," which is very difficult to maintain because nobody besides the initial developer can untangle the mess. Even the initial developer may forget the meaning of the code over time.

Web sites exhibit similar patterns. Small Web sites that have short expected life spans are often built by one person using little methodology. Inspection of the site's underlying HTML, JavaScript, and navigation structure will frequently show that "spaghetti code" is being served, complete with a side dish of "markup salad."

Planning can help offset some of the problems that may be encountered during a Web development project. Unfortunately, in the ad hoc Web process, planning is often limited to a few brief meetings, a brief but incomplete collection of potential content, and maybe a hastily conceived flow diagram. The amount of time spent planning is generally negligible next to the amount of time spent during implementation. Of course, it is always possible to plan too much and suffer from a form of "analysis paralysis," which keeps a site from ever getting built, but this is relatively uncommon. Always have the amount of planning be proportional to the complexity of the project. The key to dealing with project management challenges is to create a formal process by which to plan, implement, test, and deploy a site in a structured manner.

Basic Web Process Model

To help reduce the difficulty in constructing sites, we should adopt a *process model* that describes the various phases involved in Web site development. Each step can then be carefully performed by the developer, using guidelines and documentation along the way telling the developer how to do things and ensuring that each step is carried out properly. An ideal process model for the Web would help the developer address the complexity of the site, minimize the risk of project failure, deal with the near certainty of change during the project, and deliver the site quickly with adequate feedback for management during the process. Of course, the ideal process model would also have to be easy to learn and execute. This is a pretty tall order, and it is unlikely that any single process model is always going to fit all the particular requirements of every project.

The most basic process model used in Web site development should be familiar to most people, as it is deductive. The basic model starts with the big picture and narrows down to the specific steps necessary to complete the site. In software engineering, this model is often called the *waterfall model*—or sometimes the *software lifecycle model*, because it describes the phases in the lifetime of software. The stages in the waterfall model proceed one after another until conclusion. The model starts first with a planning stage, then a design phase, then implementation and testing, and ends with a maintenance phase. The phases may appear to be distinct steps, and the progress from one stage to another may not always be obvious. Further, progress isn't always toward a conclusion; on occasion, previous steps may be revisited if the project encounters unforeseen changes. The actual number of steps and their names varies from person to person, but a general idea of the waterfall model is shown in Figure 4-1.

Note   *While this model of Web development is probably the most common, many Web designers seem to think they invented a special form of it; then they publish it on their Web site as their patent-pending design process. There really isn't anything new here, whether there are five steps or seven steps or whether the names are complex sounding or simple. Always remember that what matters is that the model helps the site's production and improves the final result.*

The good thing about the pure waterfall approach is that it makes developers plan everything up front. That is also its biggest weakness. There is often a great deal of uncertainty as to what is required to accomplish a Web project, particularly if the developer has not had a great deal of Web development experience. Another problem with this process model is that each step is supposed to be distinct. The reality is that in Web development, as in software, steps tend to overlap, influence previous and future steps, and occasionally need to be repeated. Unfortunately, the waterfall approach can be fairly rigid and may require the developer to stop the project and redo many steps if too many changes occur. In short, the process doesn't deal well with change. Even so,

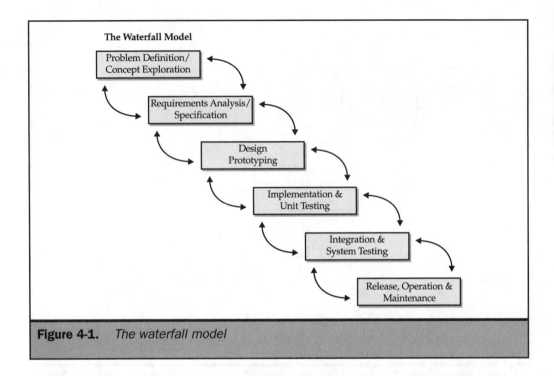

Figure 4-1.   *The waterfall model*

the waterfall model for site design continues to be very popular because it is both easy to understand and easy to follow. Further, the distinct steps in the process appeal to management, as they can be easily monitored and serve as project milestones.

Modified Waterfall

One important aspect of the waterfall model is that it forces developers to plan up front. However, because of all the steps required in the process, many developers tend to rush through the early stages and end up repeating them again later on or building a site based upon flawed ideas. The process is so rigid that it doesn't support much exploration, and it may cause unnecessary risk. One possible improvement is to spend more time in the first few stages of the waterfall and iterate a few times, exploring the goals and requirements of the site before entering into the design and implementation phase. Because of the cyclical nature of this process, it has been dubbed the "modified waterfall with whirlpool" (similar to the small whirlpools that are often found near a waterfall in nature). When approaching a project with a high degree of uncertainty, the modified waterfall with whirlpool approach, as illustrated in Figure 4-2, is a good idea.

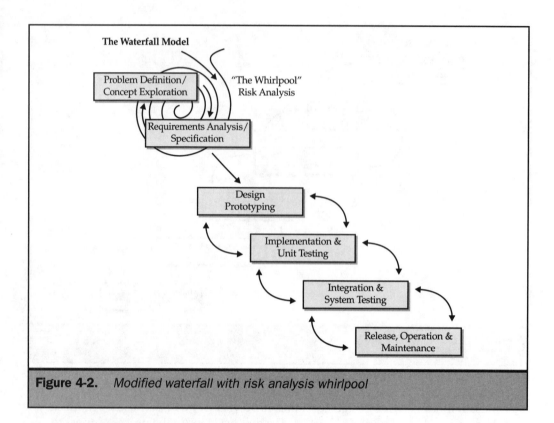

Figure 4-2.   *Modified waterfall with risk analysis whirlpool*

Joint Application Development

The last software development process model that makes sense for Web site development is called *joint application design*, or JAD. It is also called *evolutionary prototyping* because it involves evolving a prototype site to its final form in a series of steps. Rather than creating a mock site to test a theory, a prototype is built and shown to the client or potentially the end user. The concerned party then provides direct feedback that is used to guide the next version of the prototype, and so on until the final form is developed. The basic concept of JAD is shown in Figure 4-3.

Many aspects of the JAD process model seem appropriate for Web development, particularly when it is difficult to determine the specifics of a project. The process is very incremental, as compared to the large release approach of the waterfall model, so it also appears to be faster. However, JAD can have some serious drawbacks. First, letting users see an unfinished site could harm the relationship between the users and developer. Even when users want to actively participate in guiding the project, we must always remember that users are not designers. This guiding Web design principle should always be remembered, as users may steer development off course with

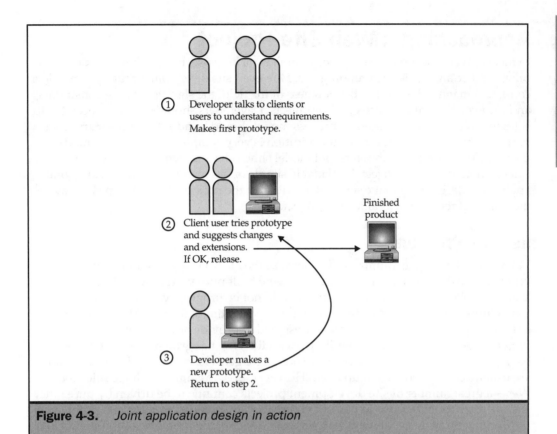

Figure 4-3.   *Joint application design in action*

unrealistic demands. Budgeting a project run in a JAD style is also difficult, since the number of revisions can't be predicted. If users are fickle, costs can quickly spiral out of control. Remember that the core concept behind JAD is to build the wrong site numerous times until the correct site falls out. Despite its drawbacks, JAD has its place in Web development, particularly in maintenance projects. However, for initial project development, JAD is best left to experienced developers—particularly those who are capable of communicating with users well.

A few possible candidates for guiding a Web project have been discussed. Numerous others exist and might serve a developer equally well. Remember that the act of building a site is to clearly identify a problem to solve or a goal to reach and then attempt to arrive at an outcome in a consistent and enlightened manner. Site development should be approached critically and deliberately rather than casually or passively. A critical approach doesn't necessarily rule out chance or sudden inspiration, and it does offer the opportunity to direct it. Designers should not look at the use of Web site engineering concepts as limiting factors, but rather as something that can guide design.

Approaching a Web Site Project

In theory, Web site engineering process models make sense, but do they work in practice? The answer is a resounding *Yes*. However, site development rarely works in a consistent manner, because of the newness of the field, the significant time constraints, and the ever-changing nature of Web projects. Developers should always proceed with caution. To guide development, a process model should be adopted at the start of the project. If the site is brand new or the addition is very complex, the waterfall model or the modified waterfall with whirlpool model should be adopted. If the project is an extension maintenance project, is relatively simple or has many unknown factors, joint application design may make sense. Regardless of the project, the first step is always the same: set the overall goal for the project.

Goals and Problems

Many Web site projects ultimately fail because they lack clear goals. In the first few years of Web design, many corporate sites were built purely to show that the firm had a site. Somehow, without a site the firm would not be progressive or a market leader; competitors with sites were considered a threat. Many times, the resulting site provided of little benefit because it wasn't really designed to provide anything other than a presence for the company. As familiarity with the Web has grown, the reasons for having Web sites have become clearer. Today, site goals have become important and are usually clearly articulated up front. However, don't assume that logic rules the Web—a great number of site development projects continue to be driven by pure fancy and are often more reactive to perceived threats than intended to solve real problems.

Coming up with a goal for a Web site isn't difficult; the problem is refining it. Be wary of vague goals like "provide better customer service" or "make more money by opening up an online market." These may serve as a good sound bite or mission statement for a project, but details are required. Good goal statements might include something like:

- Build a customer support site that will improve customer satisfaction by providing 24/7 access to common questions and result in a 25 percent decrease in telephone support.

- Create an online automobile parts store that will sell at least $10,000/month of products directly to the consumer.

- Develop a Japanese food restaurant site that will inform potential customers of critical information such as hours, menu, atmosphere, and prices, as well as encourage them to order by phone or visit the location.

Notice that two of the three goal statements have measurable goals. This is very important, as it provides a way to easily determine success or failure, as well as assign a realistic budget to the project. The third goal statement does not provide an obviously measurable goal. This can be dangerous because it is difficult to convince others that the site is successful or to even place a value on the site. In the case of the restaurant site, a goal for number of viewers of the site or a way to measure customer visits using a coupon would help. Consider a revised goal statement like this:

■ Develop a Japanese food restaurant site that will inform at least 300 potential customers per month of critical information such as hours, menu, atmosphere, and prices as well as encourage them to order by phone or visit the location.

The simple addition of a particular number of visitors makes the goal statement work. By stating a number of desired visitors, the restaurant owner could compare the cost of placing advertisements in print or on the radio versus the cost of running the site to provide the same effective inquiry rate.

Brainstorming

In general, coming up with a goal statement is fairly straightforward. The largest problem is keeping the statement concise and realistic. In many Web projects there is a desire to include everything in the site. Remember, the site can't be everything to everyone; there must be a specific audience and set of tasks in mind. To determine goals, a brainstorming session is often required. The purpose of a brainstorming session is simply to bring out as many potential ideas about the site as possible. A white board and Post-it notes are useful during a brainstorming session to quickly write down or modify any possible ideas for the site.

Oftentimes, brainstorming sessions get off track because participants jump ahead or bring too much philosophy about site design to the table. In such cases, it is best to focus the group by talking about site issues they should all agree on. Attempt to find a common design philosophy by having people discuss what they don't want to see in the site. Getting meeting participants to agree they don't want the site to be slow, difficult to use, and so on is usually easy. Once you obtain a common goal in the group, even if it is just that they all believe that the site shouldn't be slow, future exploration and statements of what the site should do seem to go smoother.

Note *When conducting a project to redo a site, be careful not to run brainstorm meetings by berating the existing site, unless no participant in the project has any ownership stake in the site. A surefire way to derail a site overhaul project is to get the original designers on the defensive because of criticism of their work. Remember, people have to build sites, so building a positive team is very important.*

Narrowing the Goal

During the brainstorming session, all ideas are great. The point of the session is to develop what might be called the *wish list*. A wish list is a document that describes all possible ideas for inclusion in a site regardless of price, feasibility, or applicability. It is important not to stifle any ideas during brainstorming, lest this take away the creative aspect of site development. However, eventually the wish list will have to be narrowed down to what is reasonable and appropriate for the site. This can be a significant challenge with a site that may have many possible goals. Consider a corporate site that contains product information, investor information, press releases, job postings, and technical support sections. Each person with ownership stakes in a particular section will think his or her section is most important. Everyone literally wants a big link to his or her section to be on the home page. Getting compromise with so many stakeholders can be challenging!

One possibility for narrowing the goal is to use small sheets of papers or a deck of 3 × 5 cards. Have each one of the ideas written on a card and put them in a large pile. Now go around the room and have each person pull out one card at a time to include in the site on the basis of importance. Of course, make sure to limit the number of cards pulled from the pile. By performing a procedure like this, it's more likely that all of the most important ideas will surface. Unfortunately, this exercise may fail—particularly if the participants place a great deal of ownership in their respective areas.

Audience

The best way to narrow a goal is to make sure that the audience is always considered. What a brainstorming group wants and what a user wants don't always correspond. The first thing to do is to accurately describe the site's audience and their reason for visiting the site. However, don't look for a generic Joe Enduser with a modem who happened upon your site by chance. It is unlikely such a user could be identified for most sites, and most users will probably have a particular goal in mind. First, think about what kind of people your end users are. Consider asking some basic questions about the site's users, such as these:

- Where are they located?
- How old are they?
- What is their gender?
- What language do they speak?
- How technically and Web proficient are they?
- Are the users disabled (sight, movement, and so on) in any manner?
- What kind of connection would they have to the Internet?
- What kind of computer would they use?
- What kind of browser would they probably use?

Next, consider what the users are doing at the site:

- How did they get to the site?
- What do they want to accomplish at the site?

- When will they visit the site?
- How long will they stay during a particular visit?
- From what page(s) will they leave the site?
- When will they return to the site, if ever?
- How often do they return?

While you might be able to describe the user from these questions, you should quickly determine that your site would probably not have one single type of user with a single goal. For most sites, there are many types of users, each with different characteristics and goals.

Stats Logs

If the site has been running for some time, you have a gold mine of information about your audience—your stats logs. Far too often designers don't really look at logs for anything other than basic trends such as number of page views. However, from looking at logs you should be able to determine useful information, such as the types of browsers commonly accessing the site, the general pattern of when and how visitors use the site, the current delivery and server requirements, and a variety of other valuable ideas. Of course, stats logs won't tell you much about user satisfaction and specific details of site usage.

User Profiling

The best way to understand users is to actually talk to them. If at all possible, you should interview users directly to resolve any questions you may have about their wants and characteristics. A survey may also be appropriate, but live interviews provide the possibility to explore ideas beyond predetermined questions. Unfortunately, interviewing or even surveying users can be very time consuming and will not account for every single type of user characteristic or desire. From user interviews and surveys or even from just thinking about generic users, you should attempt to create stereotypical but detailed profiles of common users.

Consider developing at least three named users. For most sites, the three stereotypical users should correspond roughly to an inexperienced user, a user who has Web experience but doesn't visit your site often, and a power user who understands the Web and may visit the site frequently. Most sites will have these classes of users, with the intermediate infrequent visitor most often being the largest group. Make sure to assign percentages to each of the generic groups so that you give each the appropriate weight. Now name each person. You may want to name each after a particular real user you interviewed, or use generic names like Bob Beginner, Irene Intermediate, and Paul Poweruser.

Now work up very specific profiles for each stereotypical user using the questions from the previous section. Try to make sure that the answers correspond roughly to the average answers for each group. So, if there were a few intermediate users interviewed who had fast connections, but most have slow connections, assume the more common case. Chapter 2 discussed the concept of general user characteristics versus individual traits in more detail.

Once your profiles for each generic site visitor are complete, you should begin to create visit scenarios. What exactly would Bob Beginner do when he visits your site? What are the tasks he wishes to perform? What is his goal? Scenario planning should help you focus on what each user will actually want to do. From this exercise, you may find that your goal statements are not in line with what the users are probably interested in doing. If so, you are still in the risk analysis whirlpool. Return to the initial step and modify the goal statement based on your new information.

Site Requirements

Based on the goals of the site and what the audience is like, the site's requirements should begin to present themselves. These requirements should be roughly broken up along visual, technical, content, and delivery requirements. To determine requirements, you might ask questions like these:

- What kind of content will be required?
- What kind of look should the site have?
- What types of programs will have to be built?
- How many servers will be required to service the site's visitors?
- What kind of restrictions will users place on the site with respect to bandwidth, screen-size, the browser, and so on?

Requirements will begin to show site costs and potential implementation problems. The requirements will suggest how many developers are required and show what content is lacking. If the requirements seem excessive in view of the potential gain, it is time to revisit the goal stage or question if the audience was accurately defined. The first three steps of the process may be repeated numerous times until a site plan or specification is thrown out of the whirlpool.

The Site Plan

Once a goal, audience, and site requirements have been discussed and documented, a formal site plan should be drawn up. The site plan should contain the following sections:

- **Short goal statement**   This section would contain a brief discussion to explain the overall purpose of the site and its basic success measurements.
- **Detailed goal discussion**   This section would discuss the site's goals in detail and provide measurable goals to verify the benefit of the site.

■ **Audience discussion** This section would profile the users who would visit the site. The section would describe both audience characteristics and the tasks the audience would want to accomplish at the site.

■ **Usage discussion** This section discusses the various task/visit scenarios for the site's users. Start first with how the user will arrive at the site and then follow the visit to its conclusion. This section may also include a discussion of usage measurements, such as number of downloads, page accesses per visit, form being filled out, and so on as they relate to the detailed goal discussion.

■ **Content requirements** The content requirements section should provide a laundry list of all text, images, and other media required in the site. A matrix showing the required content, form, existence, and potential owner or creator is useful, as it shows how much content may be outstanding. A simple matrix is shown in Table 4-1.

Content Name	Description	Content Type	Content Format	Exists?	Owner
Butler Robot Press Release	Press release for new Butler 7 series robot that ran in *Robots Today*.	Text	Microsoft Word	Yes	Jennifer Tuggle
Software Agreement Form	Brief description of legal liability of using trial robot personality software	Text	Paper	Yes	John P. Lawyer
Handheld Super-computer Screen Shot	Picture of the new Demo Company Cray-9000 handheld palm size computer	Image	GIF	No	Pascal Wirth

Table 4-1. *Content Matrix*

Content Name	Description	Content Type	Content Format	Exists?	Owner
Welcome from President Message	Brief introduction letter from President to welcome user to site	Text	Microsoft Word	No	President's Executive Assistant

Table 4-2.   *Content Matrix* (continued)

- **Technical requirements**   This section should provide an overview of the types of technology the site will employ, such as HTML, JavaScript, CGI, Java, plug-ins, and so on. It should cover any technical constraints such as performance requirements, security requirements, multi-device or multi-platform considerations, and any other technical requirements that are related to the visitor's capabilities.

- **Visual requirements**   The visual requirements section should outline basic considerations for interface design. The section should indicate in broad strokes how the site should relate to any existing marketing materials and provide an indication of user constraints for graphics and multimedia, such as screen size, color depth, bandwidth, and so on. The section may outline some specifics, such as organizational logo usage limitations, fonts required, or color use; however, many of the details of the site's visuals will be determined later in the development process.

- **Delivery requirements**   This section should indicate the delivery requirements, particularly any hosting considerations. A basic discussion of how many users will visit the site, how many pages will be consumed on a typical day, and the size of a typical page should be included in this section. Even if these are just guesses, it is possible to provide a brief analysis of the server and bandwidth required to deliver the site.

- **Miscellaneous requirements**   There may be other requirements that need to be detailed in the site plan, such as language requirements, legal issues, industry standards, and other similar considerations. They may not necessarily require their own separate discussion, but instead may be addressed throughout the other sections of the document.

- **Site structure diagram**   This section should provide a site structure or flow diagram detailing the various sections within a site. Appropriate labels for sections and general ideas for each section should be developed based on the various user scenarios explored in earlier project phases. Organization of the various sections of the site is important and may have to be refined over time. Often a site diagram will look something like the one shown in Figure 4-4.

- **Staffing**   This section should detail the resources required to execute the site. Measurements can be in simple man-hours and should relate to each of the four staffing areas: content, technology, visual design, and management.

- **Time line**   The time line should show how the project would proceed using the staffing estimates from the preceding section combined with the typical waterfall process outlined earlier in the chapter.

- **Budget**   A budget is primarily determined from the staffing requirements and the delivery requirements. However, marketing costs or other issues such as content licensing could be addressed in the budget.

The actual organization and content of the site plan is up to the developer. Remember, the purpose of the plan is to communicate the site's goals to the various people working on the project and help guide the project towards a positive conclusion. Don't skip writing the plan even though it may seem daunting, as without such a document you can only develop a project in an evolutionary or JAD fashion. Furthermore, it will be nearly impossible to obtain any realistic bids from outside vendors on a Web site without a specification.

A finished plan doesn't allow you to immediately proceed to implementation. Once the specification is developed, it should be questioned one last time. The completed

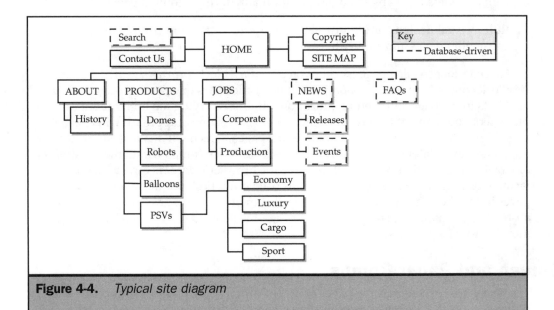

Figure 4-4.   *Typical site diagram*

specification may reveal unrealistic estimates that will throw you back in the whirlpool of questioning initial goals or audience. If it survives, it may be time to actually continue the process and fall over the waterfall into the design and prototyping stage.

Design Phase Dissected

The design or prototyping stage is the most fun for most Web designers, as it starts to bring form to the project. During this phase, both technical and visual prototypes should be developed. However, before prototypes are built, consider collecting as much content as possible. The content itself will influence the site and help guide its form. If the content is written in a very serious tone but the visuals are fun and carefree, the site will seem very strange to the user. Seeing the content up front would allow the designer to integrate the design and content. Also, consider that content collection can be one of the slowest aspects of site design. Many participants in a Web project are quick to attend brainstorming meetings but are difficult to find once their content contributions are required. Lack of content is by far the biggest problem in Web projects. Deal with this potential problem early.

> **Suggestion: Always collect content as soon as possible**.

Block Composites

Design should proceed top-down. Think first about how the user will enter the site and conclude with about how they will leave. In most cases, this means designing the home page first, followed by subsection pages, and finally form or content pages.

> **Rule: Visual design should proceed in a top-down fashion from home page to subsection pages and finally to content pages.**

First consider creating page mockups on paper in a block form, as shown in Figure 4-5. Block comps (or more commonly *wireframes*) allow designers to focus on the types of objects in the page and their organization without worrying too much about precise placement and detail of the layout itself. The block sectioning approach will also help the designer to consider making templates for pages, which will make it easier to implement them later on. Make sure to create your block comps within the constraints of a Web browser window. The influence of the browser's borders can be a significant factor. Once the home page block comp has been built, flesh out the other types of pages in the site in a similar fashion. Once a complete scenario has been detailed in this abstract sense, make sure that the path through the blocked screen is logical. If it is, move on to the next phase.

Screen and Paper Comps

The next phase of design is the paper or screen prototyping phase. In this phase, the designer can either sketch or create a digital composite that shows a much more

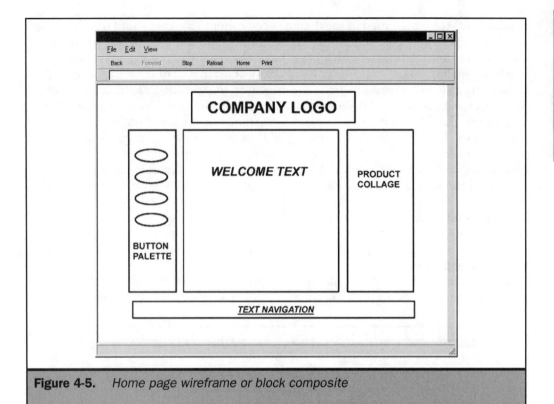

Figure 4-5.   *Home page wireframe or block composite*

detailed visual example of a typical page in the site. Make sure that, whether you do the composite on paper or screen, a browser window is assumed and that screen dimensions are considered. A piece of paper with a browser window outline as used in the block comp stage can be used for sketches.

Suggestion: Always consider the bordering effect of the browser window when developing visual composites.

Sketch the various buttons, headings, and features within the page. Make sure to provide some indication of text in the page—either a form of "greeked" text or real content, if possible.

Note   *Many designers appear to use only temporary "lorem ipsum" or greeking text within screen composites. This approach does bring focus to the designed page elements, but if real content is available—use it! This more closely simulates what the final result will be like.*

The comping stage provides the most room for creativity, but designers are warned to be creative within the constraints of what is possible on the Web and what visual requirements were presented in the design specification. Thinking about file size, color support, and browser capabilities may seem limiting, but doing so usually prevents the designer from coming up with a page that looks visually stunning but is nearly impossible to implement or download in a reasonable amount of time. In particular, resist the urge to become so artistic as to reinvent an organization's look in a Web site. Remember, the site plan will have spelled out visual requirements, including marketing constraints. The difficult balance between form, function, purpose, and content, as discussed in Chapter 1, should become readily apparent as designers grapple with satisfying their creative urges within the constraints of Web technology, user capabilities, and site requirements. A typical paper comp is shown in Figure 4-6.

In the case of a digital prototype, create a single image that shows the entire intended screen, including all buttons, images, and text. Save the image as a GIF or JPEG and load it into the Web browser to test how it would look within a typical environment. At this stage, resist the urge to fully implement your page design with HTML. You may end up having to scrap the design, and it would be wasteful to fully implement at this stage.

Once your paper or digital prototype is complete, it should be tested with users. Ask a few users to indicate which sections on the screen are clickable and what buttons

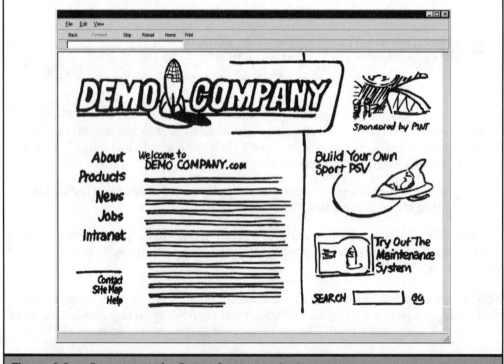

Figure 4-6.   *Paper comp for Demo Company site home page*

they would select in order to accomplish a particular task. Make sure to show the prototype to more than one user, as individual taste may be a significant factor in prototype acceptance. If the user has too many negative comments about the page, consider starting over. During prototyping, you can't get too attached to your children, so to speak. If you do, the site will no longer be user focused, but developer focused. Remember the following design rule:

> **Rule: Don't marry your design prototypes. Listen to your users and refine your designs.**

Once you come up with an acceptable home page design, continue the process with subpages and content pages. A typical subpage composite is shown in Figure 4-7.

In highly interactive sites, you may have to develop prototype pages for each step within a particular task, such as purchasing or download. Prototype pages for such steps may have to be more fully fleshed out and include form field labels and other details to be truly useful. A sample paper composite for a more interactive page is shown in Figure 4-8.

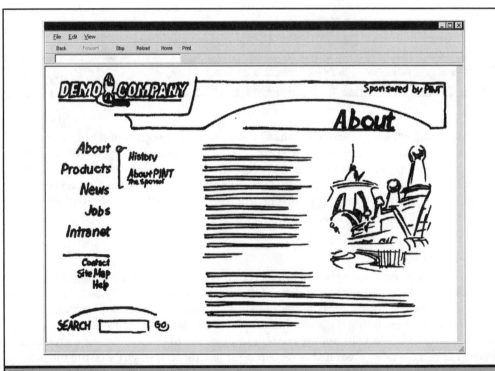

Figure 4-7.   *Subpage paper composite for Demo Company*

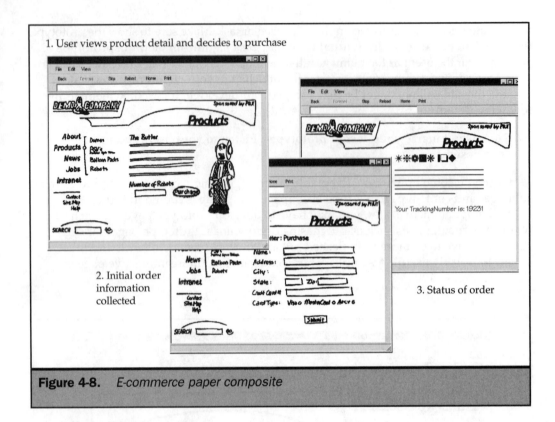

Figure 4-8. *E-commerce paper composite*

While not all sites will require technical prototypes, developers of highly interactive sites should consider not only interface prototypes but also working proof of concept prototypes, showing how technological aspects work, such as database query, personalization, e-commerce, and so on. Unfortunately, what tends to happen is that technical prototypes are not built until a nearly complete interface is put in place, which may result in a heavy amount of rework.

The Mock Site

After all design prototypes have been finalized, it is time to create what might be called the mock, or alpha, site. Implementation of the mock site starts first by cutting a digital comp into its pieces, assembling the pages using HTML, and, potentially, cascading style sheets. Try assembling the site with templates so that the entire site can be quickly assembled. However, do not put the content in place during this phase. Use greeking text on most pages unless real text is required for testing scenarios. Once the mock site is assembled, the site should be fully navigable—but with no content and only canned or basic interactivity.

It is important not to go through too much trouble implementing technical features that may change. For example, in an e-commerce site, you may want to make only one or two products purchasable. In that situation, it is a good idea to have a few users try the mock site. Observe if the site is easy to navigate and responsive. Have users attempt to complete real tasks with faked results in place. If the users have difficultly performing the tasks, you may have to consider scrapping the design and returning to a previous step in the development process. Generally, this won't happen unless the site was overdesigned or little user feedback was considered until that point.

Beta Site Implementation

Once the mock site is acceptable, it is time to actually implement the real site. Real content should be placed in pages, and back-end components and interactive elements should be integrated with the final visual design. Implementation and technology considerations are too numerous to discuss here and are presented individually in Chapters 11–17. While implementation would seem to be the most time-consuming aspect of a project, in reality, if all the components have been collected and prototypes built previous to this stage, the actual site implementation might occur relatively rapidly.

Testing

For most developers, testing is probably the least favorite aspect of the Web development process. After all the hard work of specification, design, and implementation, most people are ready to just launch the site. Resist the urge. Testing is key to a positive user takeaway value. Don't force your users to test your site after its release. If they encounter bugs with what is considered a production site, they won't be forgiving. Always remember the following design rule:

Rule: Sites always have bugs, so test your site well.

Unfortunately, testing on the Web is generally relegated to a quick look at the site using a few browsers and maybe checking the links in the site. Bugs will exist in Web sites, no matter what. Unfortunately, most developers consider that if the site looks right, it is right. Remember from Chapter 1 that site design doesn't just include visual design: you must test all the other aspects of site design as well, as expressed in the design rule presented here:

Rule: Testing should address all aspects of a site, including content, visuals, function, and purpose.

The next chapter will discuss evaluation and testing of sites in detail, particularly when looking at a completed site, but the basic aspects of Web testing are overviewed here.

Visual Acceptance Testing

Visual acceptance testing ensures the site looks the way it was intended to look. View each of the pages in the site and make sure that they are consistent in layout, color, and style. Look at the site under different browsers, resolutions, and viewing environments equivalent to those of a real user. Browse the site very quickly and see if the layouts jump slightly. Consider looking at the pages while squinting to notice abstract irregularities in layout. Visual acceptance testing may also require each page to be printed. Remember not to focus on print testing pages that are designed for online consumption.

Functionality Testing

Functionality testing and visual testing do overlap in the sense that the most basic function of a page is to simply render onscreen. However, most sites contain at least basic functions such as navigation. Make sure to check every link in a site and rectify any broken links. Broken links should be considered catastrophic functional errors. Make sure to test all interactive elements such as forms, shopping carts, search engines, and so on. Use both realistic test situations and extreme cases. Try to break your forms by providing obviously bad data such as typing in a search query that would not return a result or one that would return a very large number of matching pages. Remember: users won't think and act as you do, so prepare for the unexpected.

Content Proofing

The content details of a site are very important. Make sure content is all in place and that grammar and word usage is consistent. Check details like product names, copyright dates, and trademarks—and always remember to check the spelling! Clients and users may often regard an entire site as being poor just on the basis of one small typo; the importance of this cannot be stressed enough. The best way to perform this test is to print each page and read literally every single word for accuracy.

System and Browser Compatibility Testing

Though system and browser restrictions should have been respected during development, you should verify this during testing. Make sure to browse the site with the same types of systems and browsers the site's users will have. Unfortunately, it often seems that designers check compatibility on systems far more powerful than the typical user's. The project plan should have detailed browser requirements, so make sure the site works under the specified browsers.

Delivery Testing

Check to make sure the site is delivered adequately. Try browsing the site under real user conditions. If the site was designed for modem users, set up a dial-up account to test delivery speed. To simulate site traffic, consider using testing software to create virtual users clicking on the site. This will simulate how the site will react under real conditions. Make sure that you test the site on the actual production server to be used or a system equivalent to it. Be careful not to underestimate delivery influences. The whole project may be derailed if this was not adequately thought about during specification. For further information on delivery conditions, see Chapter 17.

User Acceptance Testing

User acceptance testing should be performed after the site appears to work correctly. In software, this form of testing is often called *beta* testing. Let the users actually try the working site and comment on it one last time. Do not perform this type of testing until the more obvious bugs have been rectified.

> **Rule: User testing is the most important form of testing.**

User testing is the most important form of testing because it most closely simulates real use. If problems are uncovered during this phase of testing, you may not be able to correct them right away. If the problems are not dramatic, you may still release the site and correct the problems later. However, if any significant issues are uncovered, it is wise to delay release until they can be corrected.

Release and Beyond

Once the site is ready to be released, don't relax—you are not done. In fact, your work has just begun. It is now time to observe the site in action. Does the site meet user expectations? Were the site development goals satisfied? Are any small corrections required? The bottom line is that the site must live on. New features will be required. Upgrades to deal with technology changes are inevitable. Visual changes to meet marketing demands are very likely. The initial development signifies the start of a continual development process most call *maintenance*. Once over the waterfall, it is time to climb back to the top, as stated in the following design rule:

> **Rule: Site development is an ongoing process—plan, design, develop, release, repeat.**

Welcome to the Real World

While the site development process appears to be a very straightforward cycle, it doesn't always go so smoothly. There are just too many variables to account for in the real world. For example, consider the effects of building a site for another person such as boss or client. If someone else is paying for a site to be built, you may still need to indulge their desire, whether or not the requests make sense or satisfy user wants. Because of this possibility, make sure you attempt to persuade others that decisions should always be made with the user in mind. Try showing the benefits of design theories rather than preaching rules. Be prepared to show examples of your ideas that are fully fleshed out. However, accept that they often may be shot down.

Most Web projects tend to have political problems. Don't expect everyone to agree. Departments in a company will wrestle for control, often with battle lines being drawn between the marketing department and the technology groups. To stir up even more trouble, there may be numerous self-proclaimed Web experts nearby ready to give advice. Don't be surprised when someone's brother's friend turns out to be a Web "expert" who claims you can build the whole site with the latest Web development tool in one hour. The only way to combat political problems is to be patient and attempt to educate. Not everyone will understand the purpose of the site; without a clear specification in place, developers may find themselves in a precarious position open to attack from all sides.

Another challenge in building Web sites is dealing with the degree of change in a project. Quite often new stakeholders arrive during the middle of the project, new technologies are adopted during development, features are added or removed at a moment's notice, visuals are changed to conform to new branding, and even the focus of the project changes just before launch. The process model that we adopt will likely help us bring order to a project, but it won't solve every problem, particularly when the scope changes too much. If there is too much change, a project will get off track and you'll have to revisit aspects of development you had thought were finished.

Finally, always remember that the purpose of following a process model like the one discussed in this chapter is to minimize the problems that occur during a Web project. However, no process model will account for every real-world problem, particularly those involving people. Experience is the only teacher for dealing with many problems. Developers lacking experience in Web projects are always encouraged to roll with the punches and consider all obstacles as learning experiences.

Summary

Building a modern Web site can be challenging, so site builders should adopt a methodology or process model. This process model should help guide the development process, as well as minimize risk, manage complexity, and generally improve the end result. Software engineering process models such as the modified waterfall can be applied easily to most Web projects. However, when project management experience is lacking or there are no clear goal statements, a prototype-driven or joint application process should be employed. It will be difficult to plan for what is unknown, and, if the process can't be hammered down, it is probably best to try something quickly, fail, and learn from it.

While iterative prototype-based development would seem to easily fit with the organic nature of many sites, it can produce needless risk and result in building the wrong site numerous times before building the right one. Planning during the early stages of a site's development minimizes risk and should improve the end result. A design document that usually includes site goals, audience and task analysis, content requirements, site structure, technical requirements, and management considerations should always be developed. The design document guides the production of the Web site. During the design phase of site production, use block diagrams, paper mock-ups, storyboards, and even mock sites to reduce the likelihood of having to redesign the site later on. If a plan is well thought out and the design phase prototypes are built, implementation should proceed rapidly and require little rework. However, once it's finished, be careful not to rush the site online—adequate testing is required. Maintenance and continued vigilance will be required, or your finely crafted site will begin to degrade.

The Complete Reference

Web Design

Chapter 5

Evaluating Web Sites

Often, developers are faced with upgrading an existing Web site rather than starting from scratch. Being able to fully evaluate the execution of a Web site is an important skill that all developers should strive to master. Site evaluation is also a great way to learn from others. Looking at sites that are well executed may inspire designers, while evaluating those that are broken may show them how to avoid errors. Yet site evaluations are not always easy to conduct. Often, developers focus on what they are familiar with or focus only on surface aspects of sites, such as visual design. As in building a site, an evaluation of a site must focus not only on visuals but also on technology, content, purpose, and delivery. Even when keeping all aspects of Web design in mind, a developer looking at a site may not understand either the initial design considerations or the decisions made that result in what is being evaluated. In this sense, evaluators may have to act as archeologists and try to uncover deeper meaning from basic site characteristics.

The primary method for site evaluation we present in this chapter is often termed *expert evaluation*. The goal is to study a site as informed developers and try to find common execution and usability problems. However, the problem with this type of site evaluation is that developers may not think like users and may assume that things are usable when they are not. Expert evaluation is simply no substitute for real user interviews and testing. Yet don't quickly dismiss expert analysis in favor of usability studies. User testing does little to uncover execution flaws, so we should make sure that sites pass the execution part of our evaluation first before wasting valuable user testing time. Further, many common usability problems are easily observable and user testing simply verifies what a skilled developer may already know to be true through experience. Given these considerations, we will proceed with an overview of expert evaluation first, followed by a discussion of conducting user testing.

The Goals of Expert Evaluation

There are two goals when conducting expert evaluations of Web sites. The first is to uncover obvious execution flaws with sites, such as poor HTML markup, error prone JavaScript, broken links, and other problems (which should be caught during quality assurance but often are not). The second goal is to find obvious usability problems with a site before conducting user testing.

While the use of quality assurance tools and practical knowledge of the various aspects of the Web medium will help us find execution gaffes, usability problems can be more difficult to ferret out. We need to be mindful of how users think when conducting this part of testing. We need to be particularly careful when making assumptions about purpose, audience, creation method, and so on. If these assumptions are incorrect, the associated conclusions could be equally incorrect.

Conducting an Evaluation

When starting an evaluation, it is important to stop and record some basic information. For example, note the URL of the site you are to evaluate, the date, the time, the person conducting the evaluation, and the reason for the evaluation. When you begin the evaluation, you should block out some time to do the evaluation continuously; otherwise, your impressions could be adversely affected. Consider recording your end time to get an idea of how long it took to reach your conclusions. In general, the evaluation will be broken into the following steps:

1. First impression
2. Home page pretesting
3. Sub-page pretesting
4. Navigation pretesting
5. Task analysis
6. Execution Analysis
7. Final Impression

When we have finished with the evaluation, any required supplementary materials should be prepared, and an evaluation summary developed. Appendix B provides a sample form for conducting a site evaluation. Reading the following sections will help you understand the motivation for the various tests and how to conduct them.

First Impression

The first thing to do before you start the detailed evaluation is to stop and write down your first reaction to the site's home page. Just load the home page and look at it for at most five to ten seconds, and write down whatever comes to mind. Ideally, you will not be too familiar with the site, so the first impression will not be tainted. (Be sure to clear your browser's temporary files and cookies to make certain that your results are not skewed by the site already being cached.) If you are very familiar with the site, you might want to get a few other people, show them the site, and ask what they think on a scale from 1 to 5 (where 1 is a negative feeling and 5 is positive). The point here is to gauge a user's initial feeling for a site—remember, people aren't always rational. Unfortunately, a first impression is only just that if it is truly the first time you are looking at a site. Don't discount this part of the test. Even though a first impression may be an emotional reaction heavily influenced by visuals or environment considerations, record it and try to understand what causes your feeling. If users coming to a site have a very positive or negative first impression, it could certainly affect their desire to go further.

Home Page Pretests

The first few pretests conducted will give you a basic sense of the usability of the home page. Some of the pretests will require you to make some logical assumptions that you will later verify to show usability of the site, so don't start using the site yet or you'll spoil this part of the evaluation. Just keep the home page onscreen and your hands off the mouse and keyboard.

Identity Pretest

The first pretest to be conducted could be called the identity test. To conduct this test, look at the home page for between 30 seconds to a minute, and see if you can figure out the organization's name, the topic of the home page, and any sense of what the site is about. It would seem obvious that a site should clearly communicate its goals and purpose right away, but often that just isn't the case. Consider the two home pages in Figure 5-1—which passes the home page identity test for you?

Now ask yourself what users are supposed to accomplish at the site. More important—who is the site actually built for? For some sites—particularly those that you may not have much involvement in—performing a site evaluation may be much like an archaeologist looking at an ancient civilization's ruins. The purpose, use, and users of a particular aspect of a Web site will be almost as difficult to discern by a site evaluator as the significance of a few stones from a larger structure by an archaeologist.

Navigation Pretests

The next and probably the most telling is the navigation pretest. In this test, before you use the site, look at the home page and attempt to guess which areas of the screen are clickable. You may consider printing the page and circling the hot spots, conducting what is called a *paper test*. However, given that many pages may not be designed for printing or will remove navigation features in print, it is best just to do a screen test and run your finger, not the mouse, around the screen trying to determine if something is clickable or not. Once you have evaluated the whole page, go back and check your intuition. You will probably find that some clickable areas of the page do not obviously look like they are for purposes of navigation, while other things that *look* clickable actually aren't. Common reasons for failure include inconsistent color usage such as using blue text for labels and logos, removing underlines on links, and trying to make images and supporting materials link together. Note the number of believed links and actual links, determine an accuracy ratio, and record any notable problems for your final report.

The second navigation pretest requires determining the purpose of each clickable zone on the page. Once the links have been identified, record each and write a brief statement about what will happen when the link is pressed. Once finished, check your record by visiting each link and noting whether your guess was correct or not. Surprisingly, this test fails quite often because of poor labels. Often, failed link labels use a metaphor, jargon, or acronym, so make sure that your wording is plain and simple.

What do they do?

BRINGING THE FUTURE TO YOU TODAY!

Making the impossible possible since 1999! We are the leading creator of Robots, Personal Space Vehicles (PSV's) and Habitat Domes in the known universe... and our Balloon Packs aren't bad either!

Check out our new robot line-up!

New DOME Special

»Find out more

Robot   Trainer   Security   Male/Female Friend

Figure 5-1. *Looks can be deceiving*

Once finished with these basic tests, you might want to scan link labels for style and consistency. Make sure that the labels are of similar length, wording, and style, both textually and visually. Observe the rules of the page for what is clickable and what is not, and note any inconsistency in visual style in clickable regions, regardless of whether any such region passed the initial clickable pretest.

Sub-Page Pretests

The primary sub-pages of the site—namely, those that are directly accessible from the home page—should be tested using the same pretests described in the previous two sections. However, for the identity pretest, focus more on the purpose of the page than on the organization. The navigation pretests should proceed normally. While this may seem like a lot of work for an average size site, it should proceed rather quickly if the sub-pages follow a consistent design and navigation pattern. If they do vary greatly, you are probably facing a site that has a high degree of design and navigation inconsistency and deserves significant analysis.

Site Navigation Testing

Once the first layers of the site have been examined, it is time to perform simple tests to probe the quality of the global site navigation. Good sites will provide consistent, well-executed navigation and should provide alternative navigation schemes, such as site maps, indexes, and search engines. First, look to make sure that placement of navigation is consistent from page to page. Subtle shifting may occur, so try browsing the site extremely fast and notice whether the menu items bounce or jump position slightly from page to page. Even this minor variation can break the perceived stability of a site. Next, look to see how robust the navigation is and whether multiple forms of site navigation are supported. Numerous navigation execution questions should be asked during this phase. Is the current location clearly indicated with labels or link path indicators? Does the site have text links at the bottoms of pages? Is alternative text used for graphical navigation buttons? Does the site require excessive scrolling? Are back-to-top links used on longer pages? Does the site have a map or index? The questionnaire in Appendix B presents many of the questions you should be asking during the navigation analysis phase.

One form of navigation that deserves special attention, if present, is the search facility. Very often, search is poorly implemented in a site, despite the fact that more and more users are coming to rely on it. Chapter 9 presents a thorough discussion of how search should be implemented in a site; but for now, focus on how the search is accessed, how it deals with errors, and how both positive and negative results are presented. Search facilities should be clearly marked and easily accessible from every page. A well-implemented search should correct errors or at least clearly indicate them when they occur. Once a positive query is returned, the results should be easy to navigate and refine. All these issues are covered in the sample evaluation; but if you evaluate sites on your own, make sure to enter nonsense queries and "extreme positive" queries, like the organization name, in the search field, to see how the extreme cases are handled.

FOUNDATION

Task Analysis

The testing so far has concentrated on general navigation of a site, but the goal of navigation is to help a user accomplish some task. Generally, on the Web, users are doing one of three general tasks:

1. Reading
2. Looking for something
3. Performing some interaction

The third task covers user activities like interacting with menus, filling out forms, or other mechanical tasks. Our testing should make sure that the site supports all three of these general task groups. Once we have verified that, we should consider the specific tasks unique to a particular site.

Testing Readability

When thinking about reading Web content, you have to consider both when and how the user will read the content. A user may read content immediately, may print it to read offline, or may bookmark it to read or print at a later date. Web content should be readable both onscreen and on paper.

Testing printing is easy: just print each page in the site. Be careful, though; some pages may purposely not be designed for printing. Also, you may have special print buttons or Adobe Acrobat files for printing. If this is the case, make sure to note the approach and whether it is effective.

Testing the screen readability of content is a little more difficult. Of course, reading content is the best test, but it tends to take a long time. You will almost certainly find, as you perform this test, that content is too long or complex to be easily read onscreen. Even when content is written for screen use, page layout and contrast may make it difficult to read. One way to test page layouts and contrast is to perform what the author dubs the "fuzzy eye" test. In this test, squint and look at the page. If you can still discern the general sense of the page structure easily, the layout and contrast is probably adequate; if you cannot, the items may be too close together or contrast may not be strong enough.

Testing Findability

Of course, information is only useful if site visitors can find it. In order to test the findability of information in a site, you first need to have at least some familiarity with the content in the site before attempting to find an item likely to be there. The simplest findability test would be to look for something required in just about any site—for example, contact information. Once a generic item has been determined, try to find the information from an arbitrary point in the site. You may find that even this test requires numerous clicks once beyond the home page. You can also try the same test using the site's secondary navigation facilities, such as the site map and search facility.

The other findability tests are similar to the simple one just described, but they require that you find a particular item that is very specific to the site. For example, if products are sold, try to find the price of a particular product, the cheapest product, and the most expensive product. If the organization is a corporation, try to find information about the management team or, if it is publicly traded, its current stock price or last reported revenue figure. There are many possible information tasks, and you may want to record not only whether the task was successful or not, but also the time it takes or the number of clicks required to find something—as well as your feelings about the ease of use and adequacy of results.

Testing Interactivity

The final task-related test concerns the various interactive features of the site. This testing is primarily related to filling out forms for performing tasks such as ordering products, making contacts, creating memberships, and so on. Each primary feature of the site should be tested in three ways: correct usage, extreme negative, and extreme positive. Correct usage means following the steps—filling out a form and so on—to buy a product in the basic, obviously correct manner. You may find that it is difficult to figure out what to do during this test. If so, make sure to note down frustrations. Extreme negative and extreme positive tests make mistakes on purpose during interactive tasks. In extreme negative testing, obviously false or blank answers are provided to see if the site handles these properly. Extreme positive testing goes in the opposite direction and tests for out-of-range values and things that would be obviously beyond the capacity of the site. Well-designed sites should limit errors, so, ideally, interactive tests will cause frustration rather than raise execution issues. Unfortunately, given the state of Web development procedures (as discussed in Chapter 4), many execution errors may exist in tested sites. We will discuss a few things to look for in the next section.

Execution Analysis

Execution testing focuses on trying to make sure the site is built correctly. Execution includes issues with content, visuals, technology, and delivery. For example, with content, you might look to see if site content is up-to-date or if there are spelling and grammar errors in pages. Technical execution would focus on whether the site follows standards for HTML, CSS, XML, and other technologies. Visual execution would be concerned with image quality and file size. Delivery would be focused on speed and server capacity. The next few sections detail a few of the things to keep in mind as you evaluate each area, with the Appendix B checklist providing a set of specific questions to try to answer.

Content Execution

The quality of a site is heavily influenced by the freshness and quality of the content presented. A site's content should be appropriate in quantity—not too much that it is difficult to find appropriate information easily, but not so little that the user is left wanting more. The content should also be up-to-date and accurate. Execution issues, such as spelling, grammar, and tone, should also be well considered. Last, the details of the site should be very carefully examined. Truly, with Web sites, the devil is in the details. Copyright dates, trademarks, product names, and very small formatting errors are often glaring to the user and may ruin an otherwise excellent experience.

A good way to evaluate content is to do a careful screen and paper walk-through. Printing pages and going over each one very carefully is probably the best way to find typos and consistency issues. However, many Web maintenance tools and even page editors can be used to spell-check pages. When looking for details, it is tough to spot everything; fortunately, some Web site maintenance tools can be used to evaluate consistency of terminology through the use of custom rules that look for the inclusion of certain key phrases.

Visual Execution

Evaluating the look and feel of a site can be difficult because doing so is, to a great degree, a matter of personal taste. However, execution of images and layout should be evaluated regardless of your personal take on a site's aesthetics. Images may not be used properly or optimized correctly. There may be color problems in the site, font sizing issues, and page layout problems. In many cases, the page layout may not even fit the screen resolution or print correctly. Pay particular attention to tests of the site under less than ideal conditions, such as lower resolution. In many cases, a site layout will completely fall apart when images are turned off or font sizes modified. When doing the visual portion of a site evaluation, it is important to print out a screen capture of the evaluated page, as it may change over time. Screen printouts can be marked up to draw attention to problem areas as well as interesting features. Figure 5-2 shows an example of a marked-up page with visual and navigation execution notes.

Technical Execution

Web design relies heavily on technology, ranging from simple markup languages to complex programming approaches. When evaluating a site you have full access to, it is possible not only to look at client-side technologies, such as HTML, but also to examine server-side technologies, such as CGI programs or databases. Unfortunately, when examining sites externally, you may be limited to looking only at technology easily viewed at the browser or the effect of technology executed on a server. For some evaluators, it may be appropriate to call in a professional programmer to evaluate the quality of examined code, as glaring errors may escape those who know CGI or JavaScript only just enough to use provided scripts. We overview a few of the more common technologies here for evaluation and leave the rest for Appendix B.

HTML/XHTML   Because HTML serves as the bedrock of a Web site, particular attention should be paid to the accuracy and quality of HTML. With the rise of XHTML, use of the doctype indicator and strict compliance are becoming particularly critical. Compliance with the various HTML or XHTML standards should be examined by validating key pages in the site. Online validators, such as http://validator.w3.org, can be used, but readers may

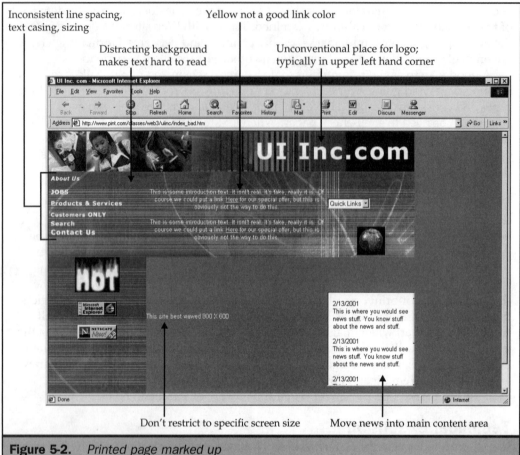

Inconsistent line spacing, text casing, sizing

Yellow not a good link color

Distracting background makes text hard to read

Unconventional place for logo; typically in upper left hand corner

Don't restrict to specific screen size

Move news into main content area

Figure 5-2.   *Printed page marked up*

find stand alone validation tools like CSE Validator (http://www.htmlvalidator.com) to be superior. Figure 5-3 shows this validator in action.

Proprietary tag usage or trick HTML should be carefully noted. Inspection **<meta>** tags, comments, and other small signs such as consistent page formats should be noted to help determine how HTML was created—such as with a tool or by hand. In some cases, telltale signs like indentation patterns of markup may indicate creation by a particular HTML editor; but if it is possible to directly query the developer, ask which tools were used and what standards were followed if any.

CSS   Cascading Style Sheets are rapidly becoming an important technology for presenting Web pages. CSS use provides a major benefit in allowing separation of document structure from presentation. However, unless the site uses external style sheets, this benefit is reduced. Document-wide style sheets or inline styles are adequate,

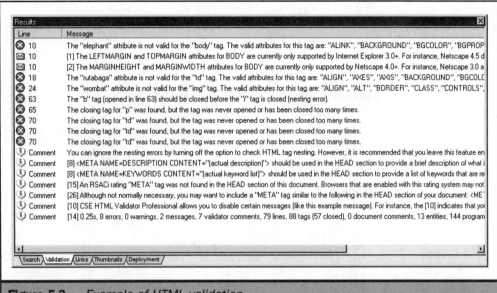

Figure 5-3. *Example of HTML validation*

but their use should be considered less than ideal. Regardless of the method of including style rules, extreme care must be taken with CSS because of all the browser bugs and rendering differences. Compliance with the CSS1 and CSS2 standards may not be as important as making sure the various CSS properties work under common browsers. However, a CSS checker, such as http://jigsaw.w3.org/css-validator/, should be used. Close attention should also be paid to the types of rules used and whether or not there is any problem with browsers that do not support CSS. Testing with an older browser or with the CSS facilities turned off should be performed.

JavaScript   JavaScript is a very important part of many Web pages, but far too often it is not used in a reliable manner. Well-executed JavaScript-laden pages will employ the **<noscript>** tag to address scripting being turned off, and may even restrict usage without script enabled. Scripts also should be able to address browser incompatibilities and should not throw error messages like the one shown here:

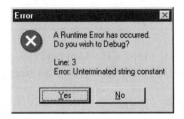

Fortunately for Web site visitors, most browsers are shipped with the default to turn off JavaScript error notifications, since otherwise you would probably see a great number of them. Set your browser's preferences to show errors, as shown here in Internet Explorer.

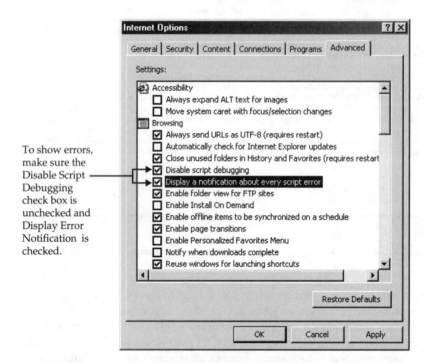

To show errors, make sure the Disable Script Debugging check box is unchecked and Display Error Notification is checked.

In Netscape, you should check the JavaScript console for the error message shown here:

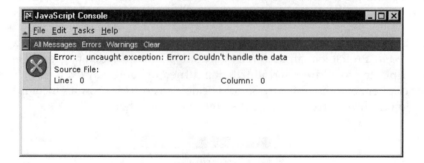

Cookies   For many, the use of cookies is an invasion of personal privacy. The reality is that cookies are very useful to get around programming limitations caused mainly by HTTP protocol limitations. However, regardless of your personal take on cookies, it is important to know whether a site uses cookies and what they are used for. Some sites may even issue multiple cookies per visit, each with a different purpose. Careful inspection of cookie data can yield valuable clues to how a site works. If cookies are used, it is important to verify the site still works with cookies off. Also, if cookies are used, a statement indicating what they are used for should be available on the site.

Browser Support   Probably the most well-known aspect of site testing is browser support. Many site testing protocols simply advise designers to test in as many browsers as possible. The reality is that you should attempt to create a matrix of the various browsers and perform the technology and layout tests within each browser individually. Oddly, you may find that there are subtle rendering differences in each browser, as well as numerous bugs. A large matrix showing all the different versions of each browser and operating system is the best way to conduct a browser test. Unfortunately, you may find that there are literally dozens of versions of just the 4.*x* generation of Netscape. Because of the difficulty of testing so many combinations, you may want to focus on those browsers that are known to use your site. In some cases, such as with an intranet, the browser being used may be obvious; but before guessing what browsers a site's users commonly use, consider accessing the log files to make sure.

Delivery Execution

How the site is delivered is extremely important to understanding the site's usability. Users appreciate fast downloads, but, as will be discussed in Chapter 17, speed of delivery is often influenced by many factors beyond the size of files being delivered. It is important to understand the server resources used to deliver a site, including both hardware and software used. It is also important to understand how the site is hosted. How the site eventually connects to the Internet can impact performance greatly. Using even simple network tools like "ping," it is possible to determine the responsiveness of a server. Many operating systems provide this tool; for example, under Windows, access the DOS prompt and type **ping** and a host name. If you typed **ping www.webdesignref.com**, you might see something like this:

```
C:\WINDOWS>ping www.webdesignref.com

Pinging www.webdesignref.com [66.45.42.235] with 32 bytes of data:

Reply from 66.45.42.235: bytes=32 time=32ms TTL=114
Reply from 66.45.42.235: bytes=32 time=66ms TTL=114
Reply from 66.45.42.235: bytes=32 time=27ms TTL=114
Reply from 66.45.42.235: bytes=32 time=95ms TTL=114

Ping statistics for 66.45.42.235:
    Packets: Sent = 4, Received = 4, Lost = 0 (0% loss),
Approximate round trip times in milli-seconds:
    Minimum = 27ms, Maximum = 95ms, Average = 55ms
```

The round-trip time of data can be used to get a general sense of the responsiveness of the server. It is also possible to acquire other server and network information using tools like WHOIS, traceroute, nslookup, and others. On Windows, most of these tools are included in the operating system, can be found in the public domain, or are nicely packaged in network tools like WS_Ping ProPack (http://www.ipswitch.com/).

After server and network issues, the size of the pages delivered should be considered. Most site analysis tools will identify pages that are considered large. You can set the threshold for what is considered large, byte-wise, in most of the programs, but some consider anything over 30–50K (including any graphics in the page) as a large page, despite the rising popularity of faster Internet access. Theoretical download times under a variety of line speeds can also be determined with a site analysis tool, and most Web page editors like Dreamweaver even provide facilities to determine page weight and download speed. However, do not rely solely on theoretical times; test the site under actual conditions, if possible. Since network conditions are always changing site delivery, test results may vary greatly from moment to moment.

The Final Question

Now that you have evaluated many aspects of a site, consider what you would give the site as a final score. You don't have to be very scientific about your final rating. Given how much you know now about the site, do you think it is a great site or not? Were you able to accomplish the tests easily? Would you take away a positive, neutral, or negative feeling about the site? Consider listing a few of the reasons that made you skew one way or another.

Evaluation Reports

After finishing your evaluation, you should put together a report summarizing your findings. Make sure to illustrate your findings with as many frame grabs and diagrams as possible. Also, try to provide as many specific details as possible, as well as indications of where the errors are in the site and how they might be fixed. Complete reports should include a detailed analysis of a site, including the number of pages, the page weights, broken links, technology usage, and so on. Because of the tedious nature of compiling such information, we leave this part of the evaluation to tools. Consider using a maintenance or quality assurance tool to analyze the basic characteristics of the site. Quality maintenance tools such as Coast Webmaster (http://www.coast.com) can produce high-quality reports like the one shown in Figure 5-4. However, do not substitute tool use for a real expert evaluation because tools will miss many usability and execution errors.

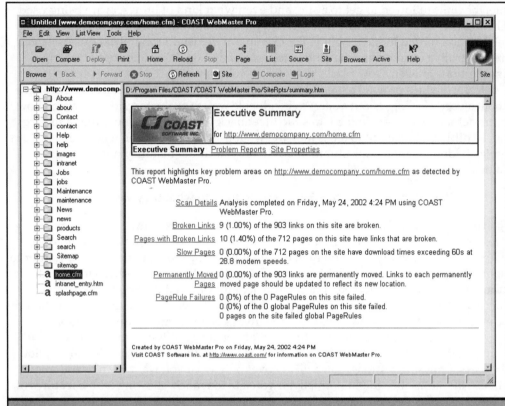

Figure 5-4.   *Site Quality Report from a maintenance tool*

User Testing

While the evaluation process just described is useful to uncover many types of site problems, it is important not to limit evaluations just to inspection. Developers may focus on certain things and completely miss problems commonly encountered by users. Further, this form of evaluation does not adequately reflect how users actually use a site.

Looking at log files can provide valuable insight into how a site is used. Log files will show who is looking at a site (by IP address or domain name, mostly), what pages users commonly look at, when they look at these pages, the paths users take through a site, the links followed to get to a site, and even what kind of browsers are being used. The log file really does show if content is popular and may provide a great deal of information related to site usability. For example, a tremendous number of users leaving the site from a certain page may indicate a problem. Log files can be used to verify assumptions or even show places to look for problems.

While log files provide a great deal of useful information, they really say very little about a user's feelings about a site. An invaluable way to evaluate a site is to watch how users actually use a site and try to solicit feedback from them. Conducting a user test can be difficult. Be careful to focus more on what users do and not on what the say. Users typically don't want to look stupid and will often indicate that they understand something when they don't.

Rule: Pay attention more to what users do than to what they say.

The best way to deal with this problem is not to let users know that they are taking a test; you might even try to casually watch them without their knowledge. If you ask users to take a usability test, you may find that they pay more attention or try harder to figure things out than they might usually. The assumption almost seems to be that test administrators will be pleased at how proficient they are. At the opposite end of spectrum, on occasion testers will purposefully look for errors. In either case, it should be evident that testing conditions may not always be the same as user conditions.

A very important aspect of testing is making sure not to get too involved. For example, if you ask users to evaluate a site, don't guide them through it. If you co-pilot the users' browsing sessions, they will uncover only what you want them to and maybe not use the site as they might normally. If you talk too much, showing off the features of the site, you may not give users a chance to say what they think. User testing can be very difficult for site designers who want to put their work in the best light possible, and they may be very unwilling to listen to user criticisms.

Suggestion: Consider having a person not involved in the site design process conduct a user test.

You can certainly be very scientific about user testing: using two-way mirrors, recording mouse travel and keystrokes, and even monitoring pauses or mistakes made by the user during a typical task. Some might go so far as to watch facial expressions or even monitor the blood pressure of the test subject. However, the end result is often really the most important aspect of the test. Remember that, in the final analysis, probably the only real important things to users are whether they were successful in their mission and enjoyed the visit. This does not mean that the study of usability lacks reasonably measurable characteristics; it just suggests that, as imperfect creatures, humans may not always act logically and may even quickly forget the difficulty of performing a task if there is a wonderful reward at the end. Readers interested in understanding more about user testing and usability, particularly the theory and practice of conducting usability tests, should visit http://www.useit.com and http://www.usableweb.com.

Summary

Site evaluations serve both to provide quality assurance and to increase the skills and knowledge of developers. This chapter provided an overview of designer-directed evaluation, while focusing on execution and usability. The tips provided here in conjunction with the detailed checklist presented in Appendix B should uncover many of the common problems in Web sites. However, users may uncover more, and user evaluations should always be performed if possible because, in the end, the acceptability of the site will be determined by the users. However, do not discount developer evaluation, since it makes no sense to have users evaluate a site that is obviously built incorrectly or that exhibits known usability problems.

The Complete Reference

Web Design

Part II

Site Organization and Navigation

Chapter 6

Site Types and Architectures

Just as there are many types of software—from games to business applications—there are many types of Web sites. Sites can be grouped generally in categories like intranet or extranet sites, as well as specific-purpose sites like portals, entertainment sites, or personal home pages. Each type of site will have different design constraints related to the site's purpose. Organizing the site appropriately will help the site achieve its purpose. Numerous site structures—from simple linear organizations to complex mixed hierarchies—exist. Conventions, as well as heuristics from cognitive science and traditional GUI conventions, provide some clues as to which structures work well. However, the structure of a well-designed site isn't always apparent to the user—nor should it be.

Site Types

We begin by breaking sites into various groupings to understand the specific requirements of each group. Obviously there are numerous ways to categorize Web sites. Possible groupings include audience, level of interactivity, frequency of change, size, type of technology used, visual style applied, and of course the purpose of the site. The following three general categories of Web sites are universally accepted: *public Web sites*, *extranets*, and *intranets*.

> **Definition: A public Web site, an Internet Web site, an external Web site, or simply a Web site is one that is not explicitly restricted to a particular class of users.**

An *external Web site* is, in a sense, a public place available to anyone on the Internet at large to visit. Not every user in the world may want to visit the site—the site shouldn't be designed for such a wide range of users—but there is no set limitation as to who can visit the site. At the opposite end of the spectrum would be an intranet Web site, generally called simply an intranet. An intranet site is generally very private, and is often available only to users on a particular private network.

> **Definition: An intranet Web site is a site that is private to a particular organization, generally run within a private network rather than on the Internet at large.**

In between these extremes—an external Web site and intranet—would be a semiprivate site. An extranet is the most common example of a semiprivate site. An example of an extranet would be a site catering to company partners or resellers.

> **Definition: An extranet site is a Web site that is available to a limited class of users, but is available via the public Internet.**

The major difference between the three basic site categorizations is audience. Public Web sites are completely open, while intranets and extranets are more exclusive. The more private the site, the greater understanding the designer will have about its potential users. As mentioned numerous times up to this point, understanding a site's users is crucial when designing a site. Consider that for a private intranet, a designer may actually be able to physically meet each and every potential user of the site. The designer may know the capabilities all the users, from their sophistication as computer users to the equipment or browser they use. On the opposite end of the spectrum is the public Web site. Designers of public sites often know relatively little about their users. They may rarely get to interact with their users directly and often will have little knowledge about the range of user capabilities. The design considerations will vary dramatically between the general Web sites, as illustrated in the following table:

	Intranets	Extranets	Public Sites
Info About Users	High	Medium	Low
Capacity Planning	Possible	Usually possible	Difficult to impossible
Bandwidth	High	Varies	Varies greatly
Ability to Set Technology	Yes	Sometimes	Rarely

This grouping of sites is the most generic partitioning by audience. We could go further and talk about sites geared for basic demographics like age groups (children, teens, adults, or senior-citizens) or gender (male or female). We could even further talk about specific characteristics such as ethnicity, socio-economic status, political orientation, and so on. However, these groupings begin to cross over too much into purpose issues and veer away from general characteristics common to all sites, so let's continue the discussion with more general groupings.

Grouping by Interactivity

Another way to classify sites is by how interactive they are. Many sites are not particularly interactive, but consist primarily of static content that a user may browse or search through. Such sites are often dubbed *static* sites because the user is unable to alter the site in a direct manner.

> **Definition: A static site is one where content is relatively fixed, and users are unable to affect the look or scope of the data they view. In short, the visitor has minimal ability to interact with the site's content other than choosing the order in which to view content.**

Accessing a static site is like reading a paper magazine. A user can choose to flip back and forth between pages and read articles in a different order, but the presentation is relatively rigid. There is really no ability to do anything with the content of a static site other than read it onscreen, print it out to read on paper, or copy chunks of content for use somewhere else.

On the other hand many sites, particularly community related sites, allow users to contribute or modify content to some degree—such sites might be dubbed *interactive*. The degree of interaction the user may have with the site's content may range from the simple ability to comment to the creation of content either with or without further editing by the site's owner or other users.

> **Definition: An interactive site is one where the users of the site are able to interact directly with the content on the site or with other users of the site.**

Of course to some degree, all sites have some interactivity in that users can choose how they want to browse content. However, truly interactive sites allow users to manipulate the content itself, and in some cases even add their own content. A site that allows a user to post technical support questions for other users to view would be considered interactive, while a site that only allows users to browse preexisting answers to questions would be considered static.

Grouping by Frequency of Change

Another dimension of site categorization is the frequency that content changes. Sites that never change might again be dubbed *static*; those that do change could be thought of as *dynamic*. "Dynamic" is used in this context in terms of page content and not page generation, which is a separate issue we'll discuss shortly. Most sites aren't absolutely static; changes are usually made to pages gradually over time. The more frequently the site changes, the more dynamic it could be thought to be. Content may change on a regular basis, like daily, weekly, and so on, or it may change in a less scheduled manner.

Sites may also change on a continual basis. For example, a personalized site is one that changes per visitor, often in response to either current or past visitor activities. A common example is an e-commerce site that may offer "specials" or suggest products based upon previous buying habits of the visitor or even the buying habits of other visitors to the page being accessed. Other examples of personalized pages are those for portals (my.yahoo.com) that provide so-called "my" style pages configured by users to suit their own particular interests.

> **Definition: A personalized site is one where content is directly geared towards a particular user, and the user generally can explicitly determine the content, look, or technology contained within a page.**

Indicating to users when site content has changed is very important in dynamic sites. Often a small statement with the date of the last change is put on a page to show how fresh its content is. Often this is just a text line that is modified by the page maintainer or is output from a small JavaScript. Users may also look to copyright information on a page or other apparently trivial items to get a clue about page freshness.

While modification dates may vary from page to page, sites may also exhibit more consistent update statements beyond just copyright information. For example, some sites include statements about the current day, week, month, or year in the page design to indicate how often the page is changing.

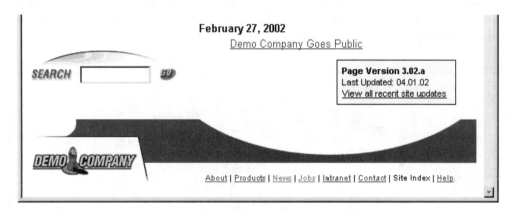

Grouping by Time of Page Creation

When considering time in site designs, it's important to clearly state when pages are actually built for visitors. In many cases pages are static, in that they are created ahead of time for the user and change very little. In other cases pages may be built at a scheduled time as their content is created or altered. Finally a page may be generated just as a user requests them, often termed a *dynamically generated* page.

> **Definition: A dynamically generated page is created at request or view time for the user.**

There are numerous benefits to dynamically generated pages. First the content can be customized to suit what the user may be looking for. Search result pages are a common form of dynamic page. Dynamic pages can also be created to take into account browsing conditions or technology restrictions. For example, a static site has only one form of presentation that all users must deal with, while a dynamic site may have multiple forms optimized for different browsers or bandwidth levels. The downside is that dynamically generated sites are significantly more complicated to create and often are very server intensive, as each page must be generated for users when they visit. Yet another benefit is that dynamically generated pages are often easier to maintain. For example, in dynamic sites, "page look" can be maintained in common templates, footers can be added to all pages, navigation held in common files, and so on.

Dynamically generated sites often use a database to store site content. In these sites, pages are constructed from content merged into page templates at request time to create the final page for delivery. Given the complexity and potential serving costs, pages should be dynamically generated only if necessary. For example, even if pages are stored in a database, unless they change per visit, they should not be uniquely created for each visitor. Doing so would be plainly wasteful, and caching such page content in the form of static pages outputted from the database will result in a much more responsive and scalable site. Conversely, though, if content does change often or per visitor, there is no value to trying to pre-generate pages, so don't try. More information on site serving considerations will be given in Chapter 17. A comparison between static and dynamically generated sites is shown in Figure 6-1.

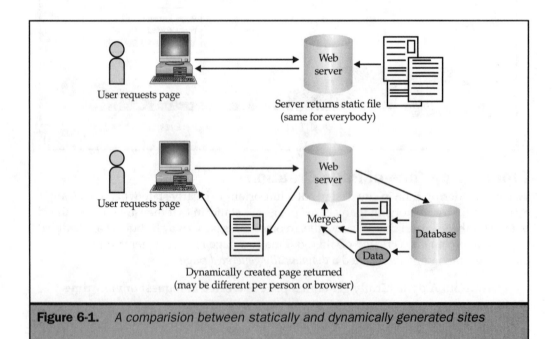

Figure 6-1. *A comparision between statically and dynamically generated sites*

Grouping by Size

Another possible consideration when grouping Web sites is to consider their size. Size doesn't mean much in many sites, particularly when they are generated from database-stored content; however, regardless of this fact, the number of pages continues to be used as a classification metric. While there are no precise breakdowns of what constitutes a large site or a small site, the following groupings seem useful:

< 10 pages	Very small site
10–100 pages	Small site
100–1000 pages	Mid-size site
1000–10,000 pages	Large site
> 10,000 pages	Very large site

The value of these groupings is that they reflect the effort and people involved. Very small and small sites are generally tended by very few people and often have limited technological considerations. Mid-size and large sites may be maintained by a small group of people and have more complex technology behind them. Finally, large and very large sites may have a considerable number of individuals maintaining them, given their complex technical and delivery requirements. Given the growing volume of Web-based documents, we could certainly shift the previous groupings and add breakdowns for sites in the hundreds of thousands and millions of documents range.

Grouping by Technology Usage

Grouping sites by their size or degree of interactivity often directly intersects with technical considerations. In general, we might consider technology in sites when we plot how document-centric or application-centric a site is. Recalling the discussion from Chapter 1, we see that many sites are not much more than simply brochures and thus are very *document-centric*. Other sites, such as online banking or shopping sites, might provide a great deal of interactivity, making them more *application-centric*. The continuum of sites grouped by their general technology use, from simple documents to full-blown Web-based software applications, is shown in Figure 6-2.

We can further classify sites by the specific type of technology used, such as HTML with presentation determined by tables or XHTML with presentation using style sheets. In particular, we might want to group sites that embrace standard technologies defined by the W3C versus those that continue to embrace older browser or vendor-specific technologies. However, further grouping sites by whether they use Java, ASP, ColdFusion, XML, or some other technology at this point adds little value to our discussion. We will return to these ideas later on when we look at the execution of sites.

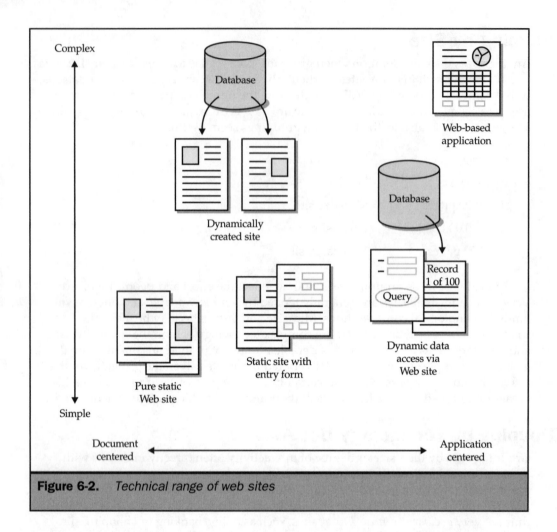

Figure 6-2. *Technical range of web sites*

Grouping by Look

We may also group sites by the visual design style used. Simple grouping might discuss how visual the site is. Does it rely on images or not? Are colors used? However, we probably don't have to be so simple—instead, we can categorize sites in four visual groups:

- **Text-focused**   Focusing on text content with limited design and graphics
- **GUI style**   Following graphical interface conventions
- **Metaphorical**   Providing a rich interface often based upon a metaphor from the real world
- **Experimental**   Breaking conventions and presenting content and site navigation in a new or surprising manner

Examples of each style are presented in Figure 6-3.

Grouping by Purpose

As we have seen there are numerous ways to characterize sites, including their audience, their frequency of change, their technology, or their look. However, these characterizations may seem too abstract at times. There are numerous genres of sites that use these abstract forms. We need to focus more on the reason for a site, namely its purpose. We'll focus in this discussion only on public Web sites, but characterizations of private intranet sites could also be made. One very general way to categorize public sites would be as *commercial, entertainment, informational, navigational, artistic,* or *personal.* The general goals, audience, and features of each type of site vary dramatically. Because of this, be cautious not to apply the same design philosophy to each form.

Commercial Sites

Commercial sites are those sites that are built primarily to support the business of some organization. Generally, the primary audience of a commercial site is made up of potential and current customers of the organization. A secondary audience often includes potential and current investors, potential employees, and interested third parties such as the news media or even competitors. Given such an audience mix, common purposes for commercial sites include

- **Basic information distribution**   The site is used to disseminate information about products and services provided by the organization. Other basic information provided generally includes how to contact the firm via methods other than the Web.
- **Support**   Portions of the site might be built to provide information to help existing customers effectively use products or services provided by the organization.

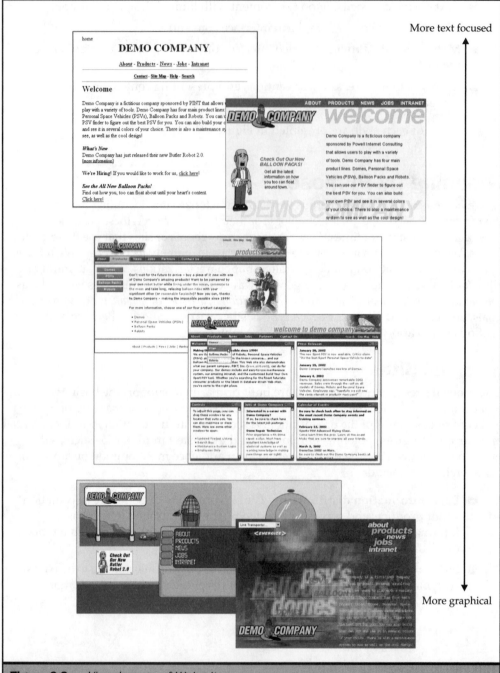

Figure 6-3. *Visual range of Web sites*

- **Investor relations**   A public company or one seeking outside investment might build a site or a section within a site to disseminate information about the current financial situation of the company, as well as future opportunities for investment.

- **Public relations**   Many firms use their Web sites to distribute information to various news gathering organizations, as well as to provide general goodwill information to the community.

- **Employee recruiting**   A Web site is often used to post information about employment opportunities and benefits of working for a company.

- **E-commerce**   A growing number of commercial Web sites allow a visitor, whether an end consumer or a business partner like a reseller, to conduct business directly on the Web site. Common facilities supported by e-commerce sites include transactions like ordering, order status inquiries, and account balance inquiries. Therefore, we might break out e-commerce-focused commercial sites. Such sites are usually termed *transactional* sites.

Look at all the potential purposes of a commercial site, and you'll see that the following premise follows directly:

Premise: The overriding purpose of any commercial site is to serve the user in a way that will benefit the company either directly or indirectly.

Given this premise, consider that the purpose of information dissemination is to try to get people to purchase a product or service from the company. Whether the method is a direct approach trying to persuade the user or an indirect approach of providing helpful information intended to foster a trusting relationship between the organization and the potential customer, the purpose is always the same—try to encourage a business transaction to take place.

Informational

Informational sites are different from commercial sites in that their main purpose is information distribution. Informational sites often have to do with government, education, news, nonprofit organizations, religious groups, or various social-oriented organizations. While the sites may be driven by some commercial factors, the primary purpose is to inform rather than cause a transaction to happen. Understanding the audience mix of an informational site is difficult, since it depends highly on the type of information being provided. About all that can be said is that the audience of the site is someone who has an interest in or is required to view the information provided.

The purposes of informational sites vary dramatically. A site at a university for a class might help educate visitors on a certain topic like American History. An informational site for some particular religious, social, or political group might have a primary purpose of convincing people to join or donate something to the organization.

SITE ORGANIZATION AND NAVIGATION

News sites might have a primary purpose of informing people of current events in a helpful manner so that people rely on the resource enough to sell their attention to various advertisers. A government site might have a purpose of informing citizens of various law changes, convincing them to join civil or military service, or even getting them to vote a particular way. The crossover between commercial and informational sites can be great, but always remember that the main difference is that commercial sites are much more economic-driven than informational sites. Informational sites may be built to meet design criteria that may not make fiscal sense. A commercial site always has an underlying goal of trying to increase the profits of the firm, and its purpose is often more predictable.

Entertainment

Entertainment sites are generally commercial, but they have special considerations. The purpose of an entertainment site is simply to entertain the site's visitors—in some sense they are selling entertainment. In other words, they are trying to sell an enjoyable experience. While commercial sites such as e-commerce sites do want the site visitor to have a positive or even entertaining experience, entertainment is really a secondary objective. While a site selling clothes might have a jungle explorer theme and entertain the visitor with tales of visiting far-off lands, the bottom line is that the experience is to help sell clothes. If the clothes don't sell, the site doesn't work. In the case of an entertainment site, the purpose is to sell the experience itself.

Creating an entertaining experience—whether it be visiting a Web site, playing a video game, or watching a movie—isn't something that is easily engineered. Keeping the viewer occupied and happy can be difficult and isn't always as formulaic a task as people might believe. For example, Hollywood continually struggles to understand why some blockbuster movies bomb while an unknown independent movie succeeds. Novelty is about the only thing that seems to continually sell. If a story is too much like something a person has experienced before, it often seems boring or formulaic. Web sites that are built to entertain are often required to break with convention to be successful.

> **Premise: Entertainment sites may find novelty or surprise in design more useful than structure or consistency.**

Navigational

A navigational site is one whose focus is on helping people find their way on the Internet. Oftentimes these sites are called *portals*, since the sites serve as major hubs pointing to other destinations.

> **Definition: A portal is a site that is generally a primary starting point for a user's online journey and serves to help people find information. Portals often attempt to provide as much information and serve as many tasks for the user as possible in order to encourage them stay or to at least continually revisit the site.**

Navigational sites would also include search engines or site directories, which, coincidentally, are often the backbone of many portal sites.

Community

A community site is one whose purpose is to create a central location for members or a particular community to congregate and interact. Visitors come to the site, which is often very informational in nature, not just to find content that is interesting to them but also to interact with other like-minded individuals. Community sites are very interactive and are often dynamically generated and personalized. The content of a community site varies as greatly as with that of an informational site. Some communities may be very general in their membership, focusing on a broad demographic, such as women. Other communities may be very focused and target a select group of individuals, such as Asian American college students in southern California.

Community sites and informational or commercial sites often cross over. The main distinction between pure information or commercial sites and community sites is simply the ability for a site's visitors to interact with each other. If, over time, the ability to interact with other site visitors becomes commonplace on commercial and informational site, the special distinction of community sites will be lost.

> **Definition: A community site is any site that allows easy interaction between site visitors and serves as a meeting area for site visitors rather than simply a viewing area for visitors to view canned content.**

Artistic

An artistic site is a site that is purely the expression of the individual or artist. The purpose of the site would be to inspire, enlighten, or entertain its viewers. In some cases, the site may simply be the product of the artist just trying to express his or her feelings. The site's creator may not really care what the viewer thinks of the site. As long as the site makes the artist happy, it is successful. Artistic sites may be user driven only in that they encourage thought and may go out of their way to avoid convention or logic.

> **Premise: The design of artistic sites may purposefully defy common Web conventions.**

Personal

Like an artistic site, a personal site—often called a *personal home page* or just a *home page*—is often an expression of its creator. Personal pages may be built to inform friends or family, or they might just be built as a way to learn a new skill, like knowing HTML. Some personal pages appear to be literal shrines to their creators in some vain attempt to become famous through the Web. Other personal pages are mere résumé sites, useful to show to potential employers during job searches. A new form of personal page serving as an online journal or diary, dubbed a *blog*, has also become popular. Like artistic sites, personal sites will not be discussed to any major degree in this book, because often their main purpose is simply to make their creators happy. However, you would do well to consider that many personal sites could certainly improve their look, structure, usability, or technology.

The social implications of personal Web sites warrant a short aside before we move on. In some sense, the purpose of the personal page is to personify the individual on the Web. Unfortunately, this can be a rather dangerous concept. While it would seem obvious not to post your credit card number, social security number, bank account numbers, and so on to your personal page, the degree of details posted on many personal pages is frightening. Many people post intimate details of their lives, from pictures of friends and family to literally their daily diary. While such online exhibitionism might seem harmless, consider the possibility of stalking or profiling. Users should consider that stating all your likes and dislikes online in the form of a personal page is a direct marketer's dream. Profiles are easy to build from such information and may result in highly targeted and potentially intrusive junk email. Far worse might be the possibility for stalking or even identity theft from personal Web site-related information. Just remember that posting a personal Web page isn't too different from posting information on a local bulletin board in a town square. You never know who is going to look at the information and what they might do with it.

Site Structure

Given the type of site and other information, we can begin to apply structure to it. We find that there are two structural aspects to any Web site—logical structure and physical structure. A logical structure will describe documents that are related to other documents. The logical structure defines the links between documents. However, the logical location of documents within a site may not relate to the actual physical location of a document. A physical structure describes where a document actually lives, showing, for example, the document's directory path on a Web server or its location in a database.

> **Premise: A Web site's logical structure is more important to a user than its physical structure.**

Users generally don't care where information comes from as long as they can find it. A user doesn't need to know what disk drives contain what data and how you have decided to organize your file tree. For example, a particular file might live in a deep directory on a file system, with a path like D:\WebSite\DemoCompany\Assets\Product\RobotButler\index.htm. However, from a user perspective, the URL might appear as http://www.democompany.com/RobotButler/. Resist the urge to expose paths to users. As the maintainer of the site, you will have to have explicit knowledge of the site's physical structure, but a user should not have to.

Rule: Do not expose physical site file structure, if possible.

The benefit of not showing real paths should be clear. By abstracting away paths, you are free to change the location of files freely as long as they map to the appropriate URL known to users. Fortunately, all modern Web servers support mapping facilities to create virtual paths, so there is no requirement to directly mimic your logical structure in a physical file system.

Rule: A site's logical document structure does not have to map to directly match physical structure.

From a programming point of view, think of your site's URLs as your public interface. Every URL exposed is a potential address to access your site that will have to be maintained. If you are able to avoid exposing all URLs, using anything from frames to dynamic pages, you increase your ability to change the implementation of the site underneath.

Site Organization Models

There are four main organizational forms used in Web sites: *linear, grid, hierarchy,* and *web.* Variations on some of the schemas are common, as are combinations of each within a larger site. Choosing the correct site organization is important in making a site usable. For example, an online sales pitch would benefit from a linear form where slide two follows slide one. In some sense, the user is almost forced to see the content in the order the designer wants. If the presentation were organized in another fashion, such as a tree form, it might encourage users to access slides out of order, possibly reducing the impact of the sales pitch. Other information, such as answers to technical support questions, might be better suited to a non-sequential access form, because forcing the user to wade through pages of needless information would be extremely frustrating. The goal is to pick the most appropriate organization form for the content, so complex content can be made clear.

Linear

A *linear* form is the most familiar of all site structures because traditional print media tends to follow this style of organization. For example, books are generally written so that one page follows another in a linear order. Presenting information in a linear fashion is often very useful when discussing a step-by-step procedure or completing a process such as checkout in an e-commerce site, but there are times when supplementary information may be required. Linear forms can be modified slightly to provide more flexibility, but will eventually result in a grid, hierarchical, or pure web form when extended too much.

Pure Linear

A *pure linear* organization facilitates an orderly progression through a body of information, as shown by the illustration here.

Pure linear

On the Web, this form might be good for a presentation like a "slide show" to give new visitors an overview of a company and its products. By using a controlled sequential organization like a linear form, the designer can ensure that the user receives the information in the intended order.

The linear style of organization provides a great deal of predictability because the designer knows exactly where the user will go next. Because of this knowledge, it may be possible to *preload* or *prefetch* the next bit of information to improve perceived performance of the site. For example, while the user is reading the information on one screen, the images for the next screen can be loaded into the browser's cache. When the user advances to the next screen, the page is loaded from the cache, giving the user the illusion that the page downloads very quickly. Preloading is not a viable solution unless the user's next path can be anticipated, as is the case with a linear organization.

Because there is really no choice but to move forward or back, a user may find a linear form to be very restrictive. Because of this, it is often important to let a user know how far they are in a linear structure, and what is previous and what is behind the page being viewed. Indicating that a user is on a page in a series could be as simple as putting a label on the page, like "Page X of Y" where X is the current page number and Y is the total number of pages.

 A pure forward linear form can be difficult to implement on a Web site because of the browser's backtrack feature, so it is generally assumed that all linear forms are bidirectional unless the site is programmed to act otherwise.

Linear with Alternatives

While a linear organization is useful to present information in a predetermined order, it may provide little room for the user to interact with the information. A *linear with alternatives* organization simulates interactivity by providing two or more ways to leave a page, which eventually ends up pointing the user back to another page within the sequence, as illustrated here.

Linear with alternatives

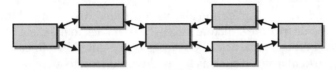

The uses of this form are numerous. Imagine a quiz site that prompts the user for a Yes or No answer to a question on each page and then advances the user to the next page based on the answer. Though it might appear to the user that there is some back-end technology at work, in reality the two tracks are already established, and the user is just presented with an illusion of interactivity. A health care site might use a general health quiz to attract people's interest. The quiz might begin with a question such as, "Do you smoke?" Users who answer "yes" advance to a page that describes the hazards of smoking while users who answer "no" see a message congratulating them on their to decision to abstain from cigarettes. Regardless of their answers the first question, both users advance to question two. Though the pages are static and there is no dynamic generation of pages, to the user it appears that there is some interactivity. Despite its appearance of choice, the linear with alternatives structure preserves the general linear path through a document collection.

Linear with Options

A *linear with options* structure is good when the general path must be preserved, but slight variations must also be accommodated, such as skipping particular pages. This type of hypertext organization might be useful for an online survey in which some users might skip certain inapplicable questions. Given that the linear with options structure generally provides a way to skip ahead in a linear structure, this organization is often called *linear with skip-aheads*. An example of this structure in action might be a bicycle presentation. While some core pages may be common to all bikes, certain pages may be skipped based on a user's particular interest in mountain bikes or road bikes. In paper documentation, a survey that asks the taker to skip to a particular question based on some criterion matches the linear with options form. The basic idea of this site structure is shown here.

Linear with options

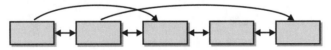

Again, this organization simulates an intelligent system even though it is often nothing more than static files in a well-designed hypertext structure.

Linear with Side Trips

A *linear with side trips* site organization allows controlled diversions. Although the user might take a short side trip, the structure forces the user back to the main path, preserving the original flow. Perhaps an article about frogs is presented in a linear fashion. A hyperlink on a particular word such as lily pad would lead to a tangential page with the definition of the word and maybe a short series of pages discussing how frogs and lily pads are related. Eventually the side trip dead-ends or returns the viewer back to the main path. A side trip to a linear progression is like a sidebar to a magazine article. Rather than distracting the user too much from the main path, this bit of information enhances the experience. Making the side note part of the main linear progression would dilute the continuity of the primary message. However, when many side trips are added into the linear progression, the structure begins to look like the common tree or hierarchy form discussed later in the chapter.

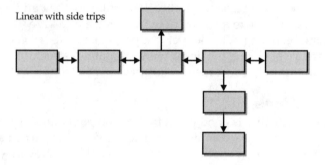

Linear with side trips

Grid

A *grid* is a dual linear structure that presents both a horizontal and a vertical relationship between items. Because a grid has a spatial organization, it is good for collections of related items; however, a pure grid structure is (so far) uncommon on the Web. When designed properly, a grid provides horizontal and vertical orientation so the user will not feel lost within the site. For example, items in a clothing catalog might be organized into categories like shirts, pants, and jackets. Another way to organize information would be by price. A grid style would allow a user to look across a price category, as well as within a particular line of clothing very easily.

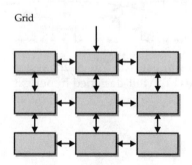

Grid

While a grid structure is highly regular and may be easy for a user to navigate, not many types of information are uniform enough to lend themselves well to this organization style. One notable exception is product catalogs.

Hierarchy

The most common hypertext structure on the Web is the tree or hierarchy form. While a hierarchy may not provide the spatial structure of a grid or the predictability and control of a linear structure, the hierarchy is very important because it can be modified to hide or expose as much information as is necessary. Hierarchies start with a root page that is often the home page of the site or section. The home or root page of the site tree serves as a "landmark" page and as such often looks much different than other pages in the site. Site landmarks such as home pages are key to successful user navigation. This is further discussed in the next chapter. From the home page, various choices are presented. As the user clicks deeper into the site, the choices tend to get more and more specific, until eventually a destination, or leaf page, in the tree is reached. Because of this arrangement, trees tend to be described by their depth and breadth.

Narrow Trees

A *narrow tree* presents only a few choices but may require many mouse clicks to get to the final destination; this organization emphasizes depth over breadth.

Narrow hierarchy

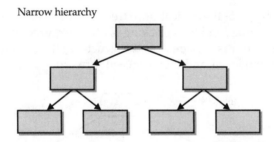

A narrow tree may require the user to make many choices to reach a leaf page, but for some sites this is a very effective way of quickly funneling users into the correct category. For example, a Web site for an employment service generally has two main audiences: job seekers and employers looking to hire. Making this distinction obvious on the home page and requiring the user to choose a category facilitates quick and easy access to relevant sections of the site. Expanding the top-level choices to include the specific options for job seekers and for employers could be distracting. Using a narrow hierarchy as a means of progressive disclosure can help keep the user focused. However, it may increase the number of clicks required for the user to get to the ultimate destination. It is important to balance these two factors and to avoid putting up unnecessary barriers between users and the information they desire. One indication that a site hierarchy is too narrow is when there are many pages that are purely navigational beyond the home page. Remember that users want "payoff"—clicking endlessly through pages provides little more than frustration.

Wide Trees

A *wide tree* or *wide hierarchy* is based on a breadth of choices. Its main disadvantage is that it may present too many options as pages have numerous choices emanating from them.

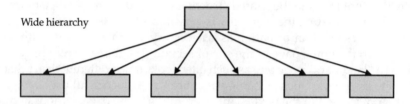

While the user only has to click once or twice to reach the content, the time spent hunting through all the initial choices may be counterproductive. Many people think that everything important must go on the home page. However, if everything gets a link from the home page, then the hierarchy is not preserved and information may lose its effectiveness—in some sense becoming lost in a crowd. Choosing the appropriate balance between site depth and breadth will be discussed later in the chapter.

Web Trees

The reality of the Web is that the typical pure tree structures are rarely used. In a pure tree, there are no cross-links, and backtracking is often required to reach other parts of the tree. Imagine that a user is at page A in the structure shown here; to reach page B, they have to back up two levels and then proceed forward.

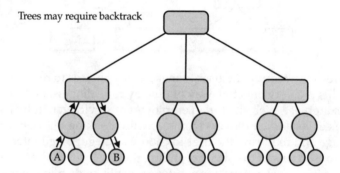

While backtracking on the Web is possible using the browser's Back button, links going backward are often added to pages so that users who reach a page not through its primary path can navigate the site. In many cases, pages are cross-linked by means of a navigation bar or explicit back-links to help users quickly navigate the site structure. Consider the site diagram shown in Figure 6-4.

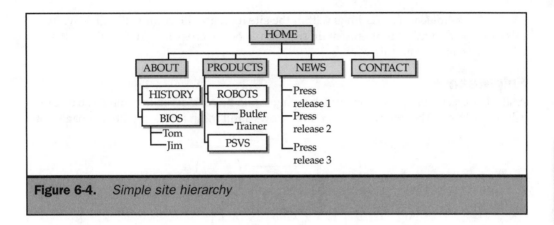

Figure 6-4. *Simple site hierarchy*

It would be common to create a navigation bar for such a site that contained the main sections of the site such as Home, About, Products, News, and Contact, like so.

With such a navigation bar, it would be much easier to jump from section to section without a significant degree of backtracking. However, the site diagram would be much more complex and look something like the one in Figure 6-5.

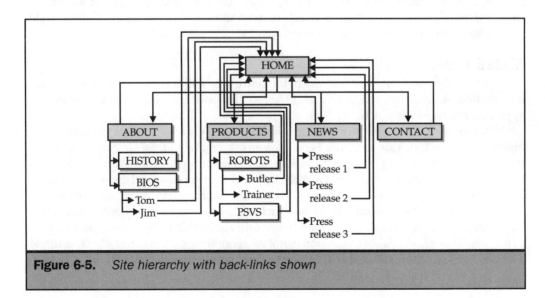

Figure 6-5. *Site hierarchy with back-links shown*

The back-links and cross-links within the site increase the complexity greatly. In this case, keep in mind that only main section pages are cross-linked. Imagine if the whole site were linked this way.

Full Mesh

A site that links every page to every other page could be considered to exhibit a structure called a *full mesh*. The following illustration shows a full mesh for a site with five pages.

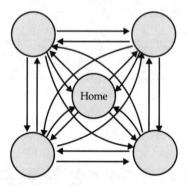

In a full mesh, the number of links is equal to the number of pages multiplied by the number of pages minus one (links = $p \times p - 1$, where p is the number of pages). This means for a 5-page site, there are 20 links. For a 10-page site, there are 90 links. For a 100-page site, there are 9,900 links (100 × 99), and for a 1,000-page site, there are nearly one million links! A full mesh doesn't really work out that well from a usability perspective, especially considering the 7 +/– 2 discussion presented in Chapter 2, nor from a visual design perspective. In practice, most sites tend to use a partial mesh style with cross-links to only the most important pages.

Mixed Forms

While a wide tree may present too much, too narrow of a hierarchy will hide too much information. A linear approach may provide too little user control, while a pure Web approach provides too much.

In some cases, there will be a need to augment the hierarchy to allow choices to bubble up to the top. This structure is called a *mixed form* or a *mixed hierarchy*, as the tree is the dominant form of the structure. A mixed form is probably the most common form of site organization used on the Web. Linear devices, skips, and even grids may be contained within a mixed form. Consider a site that contains Download Now or similar buttons that skip deep into a site structure. This is somewhat like a linear-with-skips structure. Other sites may contain linear tours available only from certain pages in the site. Though spatial organization is not as pronounced as in other site structures, a hierarchy is still generally evident in most mixed sites.

Mixed hierarchy

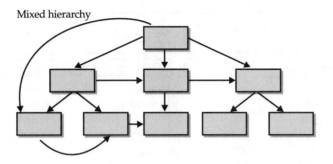

One common mixed style is the use of a linear structure to enter a site with a tree once the real home page is reached. Sites or sections of sites that have splash pages, installation procedures, or other linear constructs leading up to a central page that a user can explore from use this type of structure. A structural diagram of this form is shown here:

Tree with linear entry

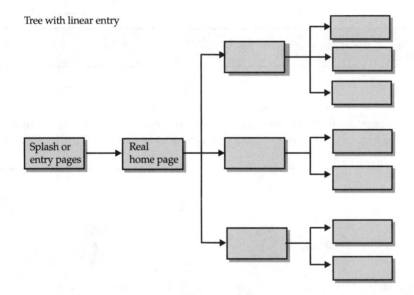

Another style, which is not really unique, is termed the *hub and spoke* structure. Many sites consist of main pages called hubs and then subpages that are reached via spokes. To visit other pages in the site, the user is forced to return to the hub page. Many portals use this style to encourage page revisits. However, there is really no difference between the hub and spoke model and a typical tree as shown in Figure 6-6.

One benefit of hub and spoke is that it may provide an easy way to conceptualize a site: central sections of content (the hub), with spokes of related content that the user briefly visits before returning to the hub. Another, related reason that designers may like to think in terms of hub and spoke designs rather than simple trees is that it may

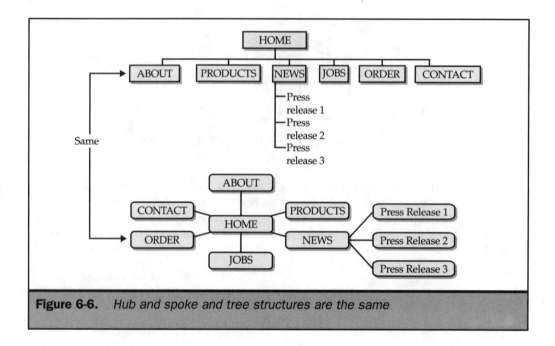

Figure 6-6. *Hub and spoke and tree structures are the same*

provide a good way to visualize site content. For example, some site-mapping tools present site diagrams in this style because they are easier to lay out than a tree structure. See Figure 6-7 for an example of a hub-and-spoke visualization of a site.

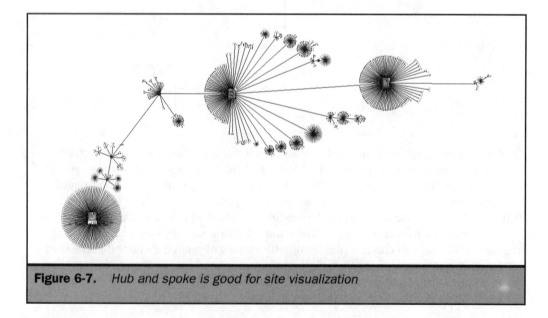

Figure 6-7. *Hub and spoke is good for site visualization*

Web Style

When too many cross-links, skip-aheads, and other augmentations are made to a structured documentation collection, the form will become unclear to the user. When a collection of documents appears to have no discernible structure, it is called a *pure web*, as shown in the illustration here.

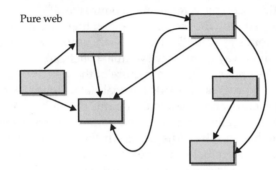

Pure web

A pure web structure can be difficult to use because it lacks a clear spatial orientation. Though information can be accessed quickly if the correct choice is made, it may be difficult to orient oneself in a Web site with an unclear structure. If a site's structure is unclear or unfamiliar to the user, they may resort to a home-page-based navigation, always returning to a top level when beginning a new task.

The benefit of a less structured form is that it provides a great deal of expressiveness. For example, a technical paper might provide links to related diagrams, supporting statements, and papers, and even excerpts from outside resources. The organization of the site may not easily fit any one of the more structured forms. While some might argue that the confusing pure web structure may cause the user to lose focus and make it difficult for participants to form a mental map of the site, this may actually not be a problem when the information or task is properly designed.

Usability and Site Structures

While a linear structure may be easier for users to comprehend than a mixed tree or pure web, users do not necessarily memorize the layout of a site or visualize a flowchart in their head of pages as they move around. In some sense, information structure may not matter if the user's focus can be retained. Whether something is back, next, or up from a current page in the site should not be the user's focus. The important things are what the users are doing and what information they are accessing. If users are content and accomplishing their goals, they really aren't lost. When organizing a site, always attempt to retain the perspective of the user visiting the site. Many, if not most, of the visitors will be relatively unfamiliar with the site and its structure. Don't assume that the organization will be clear to them, and remember that underlying organization may not have to be clear if the site is providing satisfactory utility to the user.

Consider that a user really goes through three phases upon reaching a site. Phase 1 is entry to the site. In phase 2, the user moves around the site, which could be termed the "visit phase." Phase 3 is the conclusion of the visit, in which the user exits from the site either happy, having reached a successful conclusion, or unhappy or neutral, having failed or given up on the task. Figure 6-8 shows a conceptual overview of how this might work for a site with a single entry point and single primary conclusion page, such as an order confirmation message in an e-commerce site.

In reality, sites are generally not so simple. Often there are many entry points to a site, and many exit points as well. During the visit, users may make a variety of moves both towards and away from their eventual conclusion. They are probably not completely aware of the underlying site structure of the visit and are happy as long as they feel they are making progress towards the goal state. Figure 6-9 shows a conceptual overview of a site's structure and possible user paths through the site structure.

Of course things aren't really ever as simple as the structures we've described so far. Another consideration that must be addressed is whether a visit is standalone or part of a much larger continuous session that nearly seamlessly covers multiple different sites. For example, consider a user trying to book a vacation online. Users may visit a single site trying to accomplish their goal or they may visit a search engine or portal site and

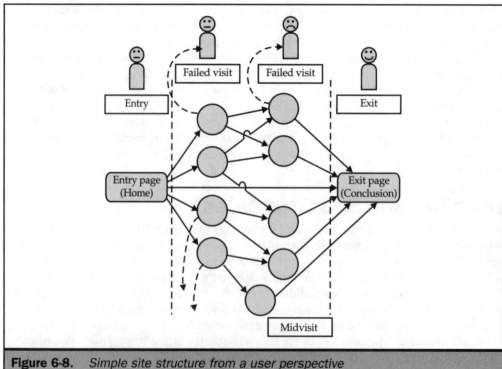

Figure 6-8. *Simple site structure from a user perspective*

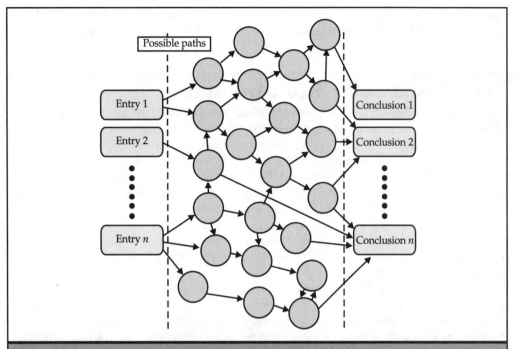

Figure 6-9.   *Actual site path can be complex*

begin to bounce over numerous sites comparing prices and destinations, entering and exiting numerous sites while trying to reach their final goal. How users perceive site structures in these different navigation scenarios is important and is shown in Figure 6-10.

Even though users may not focus heavily on site structure, don't throw out logical information structuring like linear, grids, and hierarchies in favor of a pure web structure that gives up spatial information. Remember that people are spatially oriented and

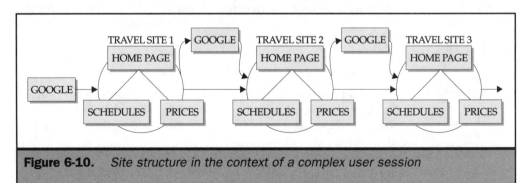

Figure 6-10.   *Site structure in the context of a complex user session*

prefer to navigate in terms of location. Web sites are locations. People generally talk about "visiting" sites, not about reading them. We'll study navigation issues in depth in the next chapter.

Porous and Solid Site Structure

The previous discussion suggests that entry and exit are really the key milestones for the user. Therefore, another way to categorize Web sites would be on the number of entry points to a site. Using exit points isn't realistic because every page in a site can be considered an exit if the user just decides to quit. When a site exposes all documents with public URLs, it could be said to exhibit a "porous" structure. A porous site does not force users to enter through common points such as the home page, major section pages, and so on. Most users will probably enter through such pages, but theoretically any URL, however deep in the site structure, could be an entry point. In contrast, a site with a "solid" structure would be one that severely limits the entry points to the site to a few URLs or even a single URL. Figure 6-11 presents a graphical representation of porous and solid site structures.

The advantage of a solid site structure is that it does not expose all the inner workings of the site. By hiding such information, the underlying site content can be changed easily. Another advantage of a solid site is that by forcing users to enter through known points, their experience can be controlled much better. Users entering through known points can be exposed to important announcements, setup tasks can be performed more easily, and they can be oriented to the site in a consistent manner. However, the downside is that the user will not be able to directly enter any particular URL in the site. Power users may be extremely frustrated by the inability to save their place within a large structure.

The table below summarizes the basic pros and cons of the two site forms:

Site Type	Pros	Cons
Porous form	+Puts user in control +Allows the user to enter any URL directly or enter by bookmark	−Decreases ability to change deep pages without addressing outside linking −Does not easily provide a common entry point for announcement, setup, or orientation information
Solid form	+Does not expose site structure, making modification and maintenance easier +Forces user to enter through known points +Makes tracking of users more predictable	−Removes user from control. −May limit the effectiveness of outside search engines

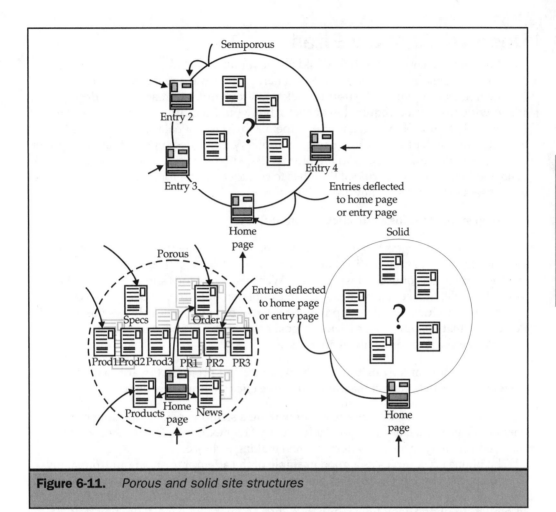

Figure 6-11. *Porous and solid site structures*

Some readers may wonder why sites should be made solid or semisolid and how this may be accomplished. First of all, understand that sections of sites have long been made this way. Consider, for example, a shopping cart checkout procedure. Letting users bookmark deep pages during a procedure does not make sense. While the user may bookmark the location, the site will apply some form of session management to expire pages or deny users from entering a process midstream. We could also check page requests to see what the referring page is and limit access. Other examples of less porous site structures include some types of dynamic content and secured sections of sites that require login. Over time, the use of defined access points to site content will have to take off if sites are to be easily changed.

Deep vs. Shallow Sites

Another way to characterize sites would be the number of clicks required to reach a destination. Consider the choice between a narrow tree and a wide tree structure. A narrow tree would require the user to click numerous times to reach pages deep in the site. A wide tree would require fewer clicks, but would require users to look among numerous links for the one that interests them. Obviously, a balance between link breadth and site depth is the best choice. Various Web studies suggest that users prefer sites that require fewer clicks and are more satisfied with a wide selection of choices. A good and highly advisable rule of thumb is to consider aiming for a depth of three clicks to get users to the content they are looking for.

Suggestion: Aim for a site click depth of three.

The three-click suggestion makes sense when considering the limited number of locations for different navigation bars on pages, traditional GUI conventions, and memory limitations of users. Inspection of Web site access logs should back up the three-click rule. In fact, many sites seem to exhibit bailouts in only one or two clicks.

Of course reducing a site's depth to three clicks or fewer is not always possible. Remember that *progress* towards an end goal must be made and shown to the user within three clicks (and ideally every click).

Suggestion: Aim for positive feedback indicating progress towards a destination with every click, with a maximum of three clicks without feedback.

Consider, however, that as a result of making a shallower site by putting numerous links on the pages, the design may inadvertently favor extremes. When faced with many choices, users may focus on extremes when making a choice.

The phone book serves as a good example of the attempt to stand out from many competing choices. For example, in alphabetical listings of non-preferential choices, observationally the letter A and Z sections are often selected. Notice how in the Plumbing section of the phone book how many firms have names like AAA Plumbing or Z-1 plumbing. To combat the effects of first choice and last choice in a large listing such as the phone book, boldfacing, color, and display-style advertisements are used to help choices stand out from the crowd.

Similarly, Web designers try to call attention to certain areas with larger sizes, bolder color, animation, or blinking—the digital equivalent of shouting. While at first these persuasion techniques may work, they may also cancel each other out or leave the user feeling annoyed. Over time a user will become accustomed to any extra stimulation and the attention-grabbing techniques lose their power; this is what is called *sensory adaptation*. Ideally, users should be given the ability to distinguish what is important from what is not and to be able to easily find the choice they are looking for.

Given that a breadth-oriented site structure seems best to reduce clicks, would the 7 +/– 2 idea related to short-term memory recall of choices make sense? Probably not, given that five to nine choices is far too few choices for many sites, consider instead five to nine clusters. Each of the clusters of links will use a different attractive technique like a color, animation, or graphic. With a maximum of five to nine clusters and five to nine items per cluster, a page could hold anywhere from 25 to 81 links.

> **Suggestion: Even for wide site structures, consider a range of 25–81 links per page when page links are ideally clustered.**

Unfortunately, with dozens of links, users are bound to make mistakes, and important links may be lost in the clutter. Because of this potential for user mistakes, many sites favor a redundant link approach, in which numerous links lead to the same conclusions. Convention suggests that the number of links to a particular page is proportional to its importance.

> **Premise: The more important the page, the more redundant links should be provided to it.**

Consider how many links in a site point to a home page—or to software download pages or a purchase page—and it becomes apparent that redundant links are commonplace within many sites. Increasing the number of links pointing to successful conclusions just increases the odds of the user hitting the right link. Be careful not to add too many redundant links, though, lest the users feel they are being pushed towards a particular page. Again, the control issue becomes apparent. If nearly every link in a page pushes a user towards a particular conclusion, the user may feel frustrated with the lack of control.

> **Suggestion: Redundant links in a site should be no more than 10 to 20 percent of a page's total exit links.**

Despite the likelihood that users are better able to deal with flat site structures, many sites completely avoid building sites this way. Certainly some of the reason could be attributed to developers being unaware of the idea, but many times the rules of thumb are avoided on purpose. Consider a site whose revenue is primarily from banner advertisements. For such a site, the more banners viewed by the user per visit, the better. In the mind of the owner of such a site, a design that gets users quickly to their destinations is one that takes money out of the site's own pocket. Many banner-driven sites favor hub and spoke site design or deep tree structures as a way of forcing the user to click through numerous pages and view more banners.

Of course, there is a limit to the "click more, view more ads" approach, in that unsatisfied users won't continue to click if they get frustrated. In some situations, site designers will design to reduce clicks to the lowest tolerance level without overly confusing a user with too many choices. In other situations, they will want to increase clicks to the maximum tolerance level without frustrating the user. Oftentimes the specific type of site being built drives the type structure used.

Picking a Site Structure and Type

The idea of picking the correct structure for a Web site by organizing information into a collection of pages is often called *information architecture*. Choosing the correct structure for a site is complex and can be influenced by many factors. For example, the data itself may suggest a particular method of organization. This could be considered a bottom-up approach. For example, a slide show really should be organized in a linear fashion, since the logical order of the presentation would be lost if the information were presented in another form, such as a tree.

Another way to consider organizing information would be more top-down, based upon the use of the data. This approach would give priority to who is using the site and how the data it provided is consumed. For example, linear structures will provide little control for the user and limited expressiveness, but they will be very predictable. Novice users will prefer simple structures such as linear structures or deep trees, since the choices to be made in such structures are relatively easy.

> **Premise: Novice users prefer sites with predictable structure and may put up with extra clicks or a lack of control to achieve a comfortable balance.**

Of course, a power user will often find a site with a very rigid structure or one that requires a large number of clicks to be very restrictive. Spatial feedback is not as important to the power user as control or flexibility of navigation.

> **Premise: Power users or frequent site users want control and will favor structures that provide more navigation choices.**

Each site structure style has its own pros and cons. Figure 6-12 shows the relationship between the expressiveness and predictability of the different site structures. While linear is very predictable, it provides a limited relational view. While a pure web form is very expressive, it can be confusing. The hierarchy and mixed structures share the middle ground, allowing users to move progressively closer to end results in a predictable manner. When building sites that are not dynamic, aiming for the middle ground is the best bet. Given this observation, it is no wonder that most sites tend to exhibit some form of hierarchy.

Proper information design is key to the development of a successful Web site. If a site has great content and a great interface, but poor information architecture, it may be relatively useless. If the user cannot easily find the information, the site loses its effectiveness. Most sites now use a mixed hierarchy approach that is familiar to many Web users. Depending on the goals of the site, several types of structures might be combined. For example, while the overall structure of a site might be a hierarchy, a pure linear structure could be used to provide an introduction to a company, and a narrow hierarchy or even a grid could be used in the technical support section.

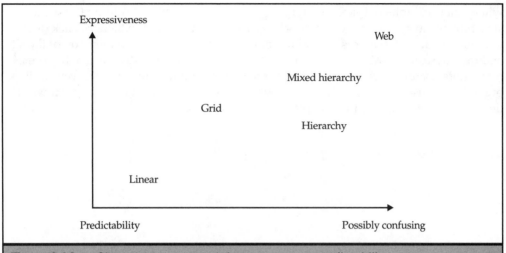

Figure 6-12. *Site structure: expressiveness versus predictability*

The key point of site structure is to make the site easier for the user to navigate. Always remember that users are not going to intimately understand the underlying site structure—nor should they have to. Remember that from the user's point of view, they enter the site, move around the site trying to accomplish their goal, and then eventually leave. Users will not care about structure as long as they achieve what they want in a positive way. So, any structure that we choose for a site should help users navigate around and improve their likelihood of success. The next chapter focuses on site navigation and organization.

Summary

One way to categorize Web sites is by their audiences. Public Web sites tend to have loosely defined audiences, while a private intranet's audience may be very well known to the site creator. Audience considerations greatly affect the design considerations of a site. Sites can also be categorized by size, technology, and visual designs, but the most important grouping is related to the purpose of the site. Obviously, all sites do not have the same purpose and thus do not necessarily share the same design considerations. Commerce pages have much different considerations than entertainment pages. Designers should always be careful not to apply the same design criteria to a site regardless of audience or purpose. However, despite audience or purpose, most sites share similar organizations. Some sites have simple architectures, like a linear progression of pages, while others exhibit complex hierarchies or mixed forms. When building the site's structure, always consider cognitive science issues and attempt to balance click depth with link breadth. Designers should understand that the logical organization of the site and the physical organization do not have to match. In fact, the structure of the site is often more useful to the designer than to the user. While structure can improve a site's organization, users may not always be aware of a site's form as they navigate toward desired content or attempt to complete a particular task.

The Complete Reference

Chapter 7

Navigation Theory

N avigation is the art of getting people or things from one place to another. We navigate the real world when we take a trip to a far-off land or walk down the hall to get a glass of water. While the Web is not a physical place, users utilize navigational cues to move around the information space. Many ideas from real-world navigation can be adapted to the Web. However, site designers are cautioned to remember that the Web is not the real world: direct translation doesn't always work. Web navigation should help users understand where they are, where they can go, and how they can get somewhere else. The visibility, labeling, and placement of navigational elements go a long way toward making things clear to the user. Since navigation is such a complex subject, this chapter will focus primarily on the basic theory and core practices such as navigation placement onscreen. The following chapters will focus on implementation details such as link usage, frames, search engines, site maps, and other navigation aids.

Navigation

In real life, we often need to get from point A to point B. Maybe we need to pick up a package at the post office, drop off our dry cleaning, or just get out for some fresh air. We want to reach our intended destination quickly and efficiently and not get lost along the way. That's the focus of navigation. Navigation is concerned with helping people find their way.

When navigating, people often ask the following questions:

- Where am I?
- Where can I go?
- How do I get where I want to go?

They also tend to ask secondary questions that are related to the primary questions. For example, lost people often ask

- Have I been here before?
- How can I get back to where I was?

Sometimes, if a trip is long, or simply if the individual is a child in the back seat of a car, the question is

- How long will it take to get there?

All these questions are valid. Unfortunately, on the Web it isn't always easy to answer these questions with any precision. Always remember that, at least in its current form, the Web lacks the physicality of the real world. In fact, given the lack of physicality, the exact location on the Web may not be as important as you think; users may be much more concerned about possible future directions and a general sense of how to get where they are going.

Some experts suggest that users act somewhat like animals foraging for food when navigating the Web. The users, as information omnivores, sniff the scent of the information they are looking for or the task they are trying to complete. Once on the trail, they keep on it until the scent dies. If they begin to get lost, they back up until the scent is strong again. If they get completely lost, they may quickly retreat to a known safe place such as a home page or move to another mode of navigation such as searching for more specific content. The context switch between searching and foraging can be blurry. The idea of information foraging suggests that the particular navigation strategy may not be quite as important as the users' sense that they are on the right track and basically know where they are. Good navigation should always try to answer users' navigation questions by providing cues to show the users they are on the right path. This is done with navigational aids such as URLs, page labels, landmark pages, and navigation menus.

Where Am I?

It is often difficult for users to know where they are, since the Web lacks central points of reference. In the world of naval navigation, longitude and latitude can be used to chart a course. However, these concepts rely on a finite earth and the convention of starting measurement from Greenwich, England, for longitude and the earth's equator for latitude. Does the Web contain an absolute center? Let's say Yahoo! is the center of the Web. How many clicks are we away from Yahoo! at any given moment? The answer is, paradoxically, both one click and many. It really depends on if you allow people to access something directly or if they must follow a path. URLs can give a precise location, but may say little about a document's physical location relative to other documents (and users do not always understand URLs). Users may instead come to rely not only on URLs, but page labels, colors, and even document styles to understand where they are.

Precise Location on the Web: URLs

Today, the URL (Uniform Resource Locator) defines location on the Web. A user's browser may identify the current page as http://www.democompany.com/products/trainer.htm. The URL precisely answers the user's "Where am I?" question. Unfortunately, the answer may not be useful or understood by the user. Consider the previous URL. The address states that the user is accessing a page called trainer.htm in the products directory on a machine named www.democompany.com. Of course, this address may not tell us much as far as our location relative to other pages. Relationships between pages, both within and outside a Web site, are not easy to judge from a URL. This page may be a single click away from a page on a server in a foreign country halfway around the world—for instance, there could be a link to http://www.robotparts.co.nz/robots/bodyparts.htm, a fictitious robot parts vendor in New Zealand. Users can glean some information from a URL like this link including the basic physical location from a geographic domain (in this case, "nz"), a server name, and maybe a directory or document name. However, don't expect the URLs to always show where people are. Many dynamically generated sites have URLs like

```
http://www.robotsforsale.com/store/showprod.cfm?&DID=7&User_ID=6185
1&st=1985&st2=-78872300&st3=211170630&CATID=3&ObjectGroup_ID=18
```

This is not exactly something users can easily use to tell where they are! While it won't always be possible, you should always strive to make URLs easy to understand.

Rule: Use simple and memorable URLs to improve navigation.

Because a URL specifies a location, you should not hide it or make it unclear unless you are trying to prevent users from reusing the link, which may be appropriate if you are trying to produce a site with a solid or semi-solid structure (see Chapter 6). However, often designers will inadvertently remove URLs—for example, when using frames or opening new windows without the location bar.

Rule: Do not hide or obscure URLs unless you are trying to keep people from direct linking.

Page and Site Labels

Beyond the specificity of a URL, users may get a somewhat less precise location through various labels on the page. Explicit labels that indicate the current site, site section, and page are usually found toward the top of every page. The typical convention in Web site design is to provide an organizational logo or label in the upper-left corner to indicate a site, and then various textual or graphical labels below or to the right to indicate a section or page.

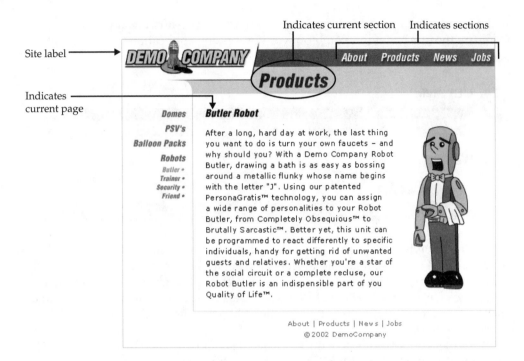

Indicates current section   Indicates sections

Site label

Indicates current page

Most pages contain a page label that may indicate the contents of the page as well as provide some sense of location within a site. Generally, the page label is located at the top of the page and is set off on its own. Designers should make sure to make page labels look different from navigation or content. Generally, this means labels are larger, are in a different font or color, or are grouped alone. The position of page labels should also be consistent from page to page.

Rule: Use consistent and explicit page labels for all pages in a site.

It is not only important to indicate the particular page users are on, but sometimes the site (or even sub-site or subsection) they are in as well. The most common way to do this is to use the corporate or organization logo or name throughout the site. The position of the site label varies, but probably the most common location is the upper-left corner of the screen. Given that this is the primary scan path of the user, it will reinforce to the user that they are indeed on the same site. Some sites put it on the right, but Web conventions appear to favor the upper left, which is consistent with the location of program icons in the title bar of most software applications. Compare the title bar of this common word processing application to the Web site shown here.

GUI Style

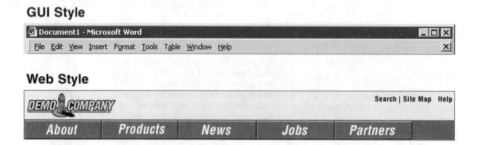

Web Style

Notice that while the Web site does lack the typical Minimize, Maximize, and Close boxes of a GUI application, it has an icon showing the current site, as well as a label showing the current document. Of course, the Web site is highly stylized compared to the application, but the labeling of Web sites tends to be consistent: navigation aids, shopping cart icons, and help buttons to the right, with site, section, and page labels generally to the left.

Regardless of the position of the site label, it should always return the user back to the home page of the site. Think of this as a panic button for the lost user—an instant way to get back to the main page. Though many users will know this Web convention, you should also consider using the **title** attribute so that when the mouse passes over the logo, it indicates that it will return them to the site's home page. (This idea is discussed in detail in the next chapter.) Also, remember that you do not have to limit yourself to only a logo to return home. Many sites provide more explicit "Back to Home" buttons within the page, particularly at the bottom.

Rule: Site-wide labeling icons or words such as the organization name or logo should always return a user to the home page of the site when clicked.

While logo clicking to the home page is a common convention, you may want to consider extremely explicit "home" button links in your site to address users who may be unfamiliar with this convention.

Another way to indicate location is through an *implied page label*. When using graphical buttons, the current button will be indicated with a different style. Sometimes, designers will make the selected state of the button bright in order to let users know they are on that particular page. However, this is the role of the page label itself, not the selected button statement. In fact, such buttons should no longer be selectable. Putting it in a bright color would suggest that it is more important than other buttons, rather than less. This common mistake is illustrated in Figure 7-1.

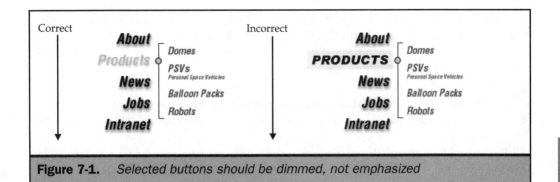

Figure 7-1.   *Selected buttons should be dimmed, not emphasized*

Also, recall that the convention of a typical graphical user interface is to gray out a selection that is no longer selectable—users will expect buttons to act this way.

> **Suggestion: Button states should be considered a secondary form of page labeling, and the selected state should always be subdued, not prominent.**

A more advanced form of page labeling adds more information about location. This style could often be called a *depth gauge*, since it shows the user's depth in the site, as shown here.

Home > Products > Robots > **Trainer**

Notice in this case that the first three links in the label are selectable while the fourth is bold, showing that it is the current page we are on. Some people like to use the pipe (|) symbol rather than the greater than (>) sign.

Home | Products | Robots | **Trainer**

The difference between the separators may seem subtle, but notice that the first style suggests progression. In fact, many people mistakenly view this form of page label as path information. While it is true that it shows a path from the home page, in this case, to the Trainer robot, the path is not necessarily how the user ended up at this page. This confusion leads some people to refer to this form of page labeling as a *path indicator*, but *depth gauge* seems more accurate, since it really shows the distance from the main page—not path.

The last way to label a page is not a common technique, but it is easy to implement. The browser status bar normally does not display any information unless the user is rolling over a link. During the default time, it could display the current page label as well as URL information. Consider putting information about the current page as well as its URL in the status bar so that users can see it when they are focusing towards the bottom of the page. Using a short script within the **<body>** tag triggered by the **onload** event is an easy way to set this up. If the browser doesn't understand JavaScript, it will simply ignore this statement:

```
<body onload="window.defaultStatus='Current page: Robot Trainer
(http://www.democompany.com/products/robot/trainer.htm)';return true;">
```

The only downsides to the default status bar message is that it may be overlooked by the user or the user may not easily notice that it changes between the default message and the URL destinations when the mouse passes over links. More information on such specific usability practices with links is presented in the next chapter. All the forms of page labeling, including the status bar message, are shown in action in Figure 7-2.

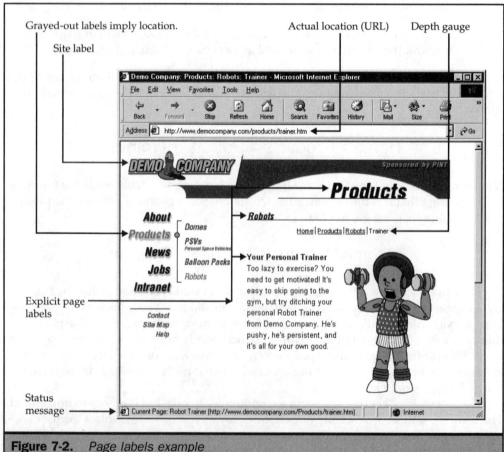

Figure 7-2.   *Page labels example*

Page and Site Style and Location

Another way to let the users know where they are is by the look of the page relative to other pages. This form of feedback is not exact, but it will give the user a relative idea of where they are in a site.

Many sites use color-coding to imply location. With this method, each section of the site has a different primary color for its buttons and graphic flourishes. For example, the site may use red for products, green for investor relations, blue for technical support, and so on. Each page in the section would use this primary color to reinforce where the user is. The only limitation to the use of color to identify location is that the colors of each section must be different enough to be noticeable to all users. Given that people may perceive color differently or have limited color-viewing environments, you may be limited to primary colors like black, red, yellow, green, cyan, blue, and magenta. Even if you push it and add colors like orange, you may find that you are limited to around 10 or 12 colors. Because of the significant difference between colors needed to achieve the required distinctiveness, sites with many different sections may find this approach limiting.

Suggestion: When using color-coding to imply section location, make sure the colors used are significantly different from each other.

Note *Some designers despise the color-coding approach to section identification because it often results in a garish rainbow-style site, particularly if the buttons on the Navigation palette are colored to represent their section. Despite this criticism, this design style is very commonly used.*

Another approach to implying location is through theme. Consider how, in the real world, many neighborhoods may utilize a theme like trees (Elm St., Birch St., Pine St.) or planets (Venus Ct., Neptune Way, Mars Place) for street names to bind the various locations together. They may use common street sign designs or other flourishes to distinguish the neighborhood from adjacent ones. Web sites can use themes as well. Some sites may use certain forms of illustration or pictures on all pages within a section as a device to let people know they are in the same section. For example, in the products section, they may have a picture of a salesperson on all the pages; in the investor relations area, a picture of a broker watching a stock ticker; in the tech support area, a picture of a technical support operator, and so on. The theme concept works well, but often designers go crazy with the theme and begin naming sections "Tech Support Garage" or even "The Garage" instead of just "Technical Support." If you're not careful, it is easy to take the theme so far that it becomes a metaphor-based design. This may work out in some cases, but consider what happens if the user just doesn't get it. In general, metaphors tend to be difficult to pull off.

Suggestion: Do not go so overboard with theme-based location hints that you fall into a designer-defined metaphor.

As with color, the key to using thematic hints to indicate location is making sure that the hints or page styles are different enough for the user to notice. This can be difficult because usability suggests that pages be consistent in form. Variation should be just noticeably different, but not so different that each page appears unique. This is particularly important if we are to take advantage of landmark pages, discussed further on in the "Landmarks" section.

Where Have I Been?

When you get lost, you might worry about how to get back to where you once were. Also, if you feel that you are traveling around in circles, you may wonder if you have already seen this page or the current links. One important aspect of letting the users know where they have been is changing link colors once a link has been visited. This is often called *breadcrumbing*, after the famous fairy tale *Hansel and Gretel*, in which the children drop bread crumbs to find their way back out of the forest. Typically, unvisited links are blue while visited links are purple. Because a user may rely on the link colors to determine if they have tried a choice or not in the past, it is unwise to modify link colors. Doing so could be almost as detrimental to a site visitor as the forest animals eating all the kids' breadcrumbs.

History

Besides coloring links, a Web browser also keeps track of where users have been with a mechanism called *history*. The reference to each page visited is stored in a browser's history list, and the user can use the Back and Forward buttons to traverse the entries in the list. In this sense, Back and Forward are really temporal back and forward. Some sites use link labels like "Back" on the site and utilize a JavaScript to provide the same function as the history mechanism, as shown here:

```
<a href="javascript:window.history.back()">Back</a>
```

Using a script like this is not a good idea, since the page that the back link sends users to will vary according to where they just came from. Users do not expect a site link to act like a browser Back button. Despite the poor label, a user would expect a link labeled "Back" to send the user one back in the site structure, not perform a back as in the browser history—which may even send them outside the site. Except in a few cases when using complex framed sites, designers should not use the history mechanism with normal site links.

Suggestion: Do not attempt to mimic the browser history mechanism with links.

To avoid any unnecessary confusion about the meaning of back links, designers are always encouraged to explicitly label their back links. For example, "Back to Products" or "Back to Robot Butler" is always preferred to simply "Back."

Rule: Avoid links named simply "Back." Always explicitly indicate where a back link will go.

Do not underestimate the user's focus on the history. Certainly the favorite button of novice users is the Back button. When some novice users become lost, they like to click the Back button faster than a hungry monkey hitting a food dispenser bar in a behavioral study. While users should certainly try to use the browser's Go menu to quickly traverse the history list, the reliance on the Back button should not be overlooked. Some sites use redirection to send users to another page or site, perhaps to take them to a browser-specific site version, or to deal with an outdated URL. Regardless of the reason, the method employed often has no delay and creates a page that the user is unable to back out of using the browser's standard Back button. In this situation, when the Back button is clicked, it takes the user back to the page with the redirect, which promptly returns them to the page they are trying to back out of.

Rule: Do not hijack a user's Back button unless the site's functionality requires it.

Such looped pages caused by redirection can be highly annoying to a user who has to shut down his or her browser and open a new window, or figure out how to use the Go menu to jump over the redirection page.

The reason for the loop often has to do with the misuse of the **<meta>** tag. Using a script like the following can minimize this problem in JavaScript-aware browsers.

```
<!DOCTYPE HTML PUBLIC "-//W3C//DTD HTML 4.0 Transitional//EN">
<html>
<head>
<script type= "text/javascript">
<!--
location.replace("redirectpage.html");
//-->
</script>
<noscript>
<meta http-equiv="Refresh" content="0; URL=redirectpage.html">
</noscript>
</head>
<body>
This page has moved <a href="redirectpage.html">to URL here</a>.
</body>
</html>
```

Note   *Some programmed Web sites may purposefully try to disable Back buttons with immediate redirects or quickly expire pages that users back into to avoid user errors. Such practices, which may be considered bad in terms of usability, are often necessary.*

Indicating Past Visits with Cookies

Probably the most advanced form of indicating to a user they have visited a site before is using a cookie.

> **Definition: A *cookie* is a small bit of textual information handed out by a site that is stored on the user's system.**

In some sense, a cookie is like a laundry ticket. When you visit a site, you are given a cookie that is then saved on your system, assuming you allow it. Any preferences you set could be stored to the cookie and reread every time you visit the same site. The basic use of cookies is to save state information in order to provide advanced Web facilities, such as site personalization. A full discussion of programming cookies for user tracking is beyond the scope of this book. For now, just consider that a cookie can be used to track a user and provide some assistance in navigation.

Beyond link color, there is really little information to let users know they have been some place before. A user's own memory—both short-term and long-term—is the main way that the user will know whether he or she has been some place before. Given the imprecise nature of human memory, users probably won't be able to remember specifics, such as a document's URL or detailed contents, but they may remember general characteristics of a page or site. For example, users may be able to remember the color or even layout of a site or page, particularly if it is significantly different from that of other sites or pages they have visited. Pages that are easily remembered in such ways could be considered landmark pages.

Landmarks

In the offline world, we utilize many techniques to find our way—probably the most basic is the landmark. A landmark is a prominent identifying feature of a landscape, basically something unique enough that it is easily noticed and remembered. People use landmarks as points of reference for navigation all the time. For example, when giving someone directions, you might say "my house is just past the flag pole" or "turn right when you get to the Burger Shack." Since we use a landmark to fix our position relative to other objects, a landmark must be easily identifiable and memorable.

On the Web, users tend to identify two major landmarks. The first is the page they enter the Web with; this could be called the user's home page or start page. Often, this page is set to the user's personal home page or company's home page or to a portal page such as Yahoo!. This landmark doesn't change very often. However, the second form of landmark on the Web is a little more transitory. When a user enters a site for exploration, the home page of the site is often used as a temporary landmark. The key to a landmark is that the page must look different enough from other pages visited for the user to identify it is a landmark. If it looks too similar, the user may not be able to recall whether the page he or she is currently on is the landmark or not.

However, don't go overboard with the idea of using differences to improve memorability. Consider an actual consumer goods site that used a randomization script to make its home page look significantly different every time the page was loaded. The idea was to make the site look dynamic. However, during a site visit, users who became lost often returned to the home page to begin again, but, in this case, home wasn't how they left it. The randomization caused disorientation. The comfortable landmark of the site's home page changed, and the users were confused as to where they were. Even worse, the URL bar in the browser had been hidden, and many users truly had no idea where they were and just gave up. Landmarks must be different, but they also must be stable if they are to be used as points of reference for the lost visitor.

> **Rule: Users remember their start page as a permanent landmark and the home page of a visited Web site as a semi-permanent landmark. Therefore, these pages should be stable in their presentation but look noticeably different than other pages visited.**

Where Can I Go?

Often, the most important question users have is about where they can go. The various links and labels on a page indicate the places that the user can go. Users will generally select a destination by the choices presented to them, unless they have some previous knowledge of some potential destination or have been to the site before and bypass what is shown. Presentation of the various choices available to the user is important. The first thing to consider is to make sure the choices available are obvious. Some sites aim to hide choices behind pull-down menus or place them offscreen with some slide-off menu. Users may not notice such choices, so they are less likely to be selected.

> **Suggestion: Don't hide a destination choice from a user unless the link is not important or clutter would result.**

Placing Navigation

The position of navigation elements is not only a question of taste; it also brings up numerous usability issues. Looking at a screen, there are really only five general areas for navigational elements in a Web page: top, bottom, left, right, and center. Each of these locations has its pros and cons.

Top Navigation

Many sites put navigation choices toward the top of the screen. This makes sense given that it is fairly likely that all the navigation choices will show up immediately. Also, traditionally in graphical user interfaces, the top of the screen is home to the primary menus of a program—so why not on a Web site? Given that the most common scanning direction of a typical Web page is left to right and top to bottom, this is a good location for navigation.

An obvious navigation problem is that users may scroll the navigational elements off the screen as they travel down the page. When users hit the bottom of the page, they may be ready to move on; but with a top-only form of navigation, they would have to scroll back up to the top of the page in order to continue. To combat this problem, many sites adopt one or more of the following solutions.

Fix Navigational Elements in Top Portion of the Screen

Generally, this is accomplished with frames, which results in some usability problems (discussed in the next chapter on navigation practices). It is also possible to use JavaScript to create a floating navigation palette that sticks to the top of screens, but this is only supported in the more recent browsers. Last, under CSS2, it is possible to use the position property with a value of Fixed to peg information at a particular location. Unfortunately, this extremely useful property is not commonly implemented in browsers at the time of this book's writing.

Use a Back-to-Top Link

Some sites use a back-to-top link that jumps the user back to the top of the page where the Navigation palette is. This has the downside of requiring an extra click before the user can navigate away from the page. The upside to a back-to-top link is that the user may just simply want to return to the top of the page. This type of link avoids a great deal of scrolling. The opposite, the go-to-bottom link, is not common, because the user has no idea really of what is at the bottom—so why would one want to go there? In the case of the top-of-page link, the user has been to the top or knows the navigation to be there, so there is reason to select the link. One downside to the go-to-top link is that some users may be surprised that the link scrolls the page up. Using a good label, like "Return to top of page" or simply "Top of page," is favored over the shorter "Top." Some designers prefer to use upward-pointing arrows. In such a case, make sure that at least the **alt** or **title** text reveals the purpose of the link.

Top ↑

Back to Top ⇧

Return to top of page

A few implementation points about back-to-top should be addressed now to get them out of the way. The issues with back-to-top links concern when and where they should appear. One thought is they should appear only at the very bottom of the page. However, some people might argue that, for users who scroll half-way down a page and want to return to the top, such link help doesn't help. It would be possible to address this by having a back-to-top link appear dynamically as a user scrolls, floating in the bottom of the page. Another issue concerns on which side of the screen the back-to-top link should appear. Some argue for the right since users may finish reading text on the right. Some argue for the left since often there is a natural empty margin for the link. No clear convention exists, so the choice will be left up to designers and what feels right for a particular site.

Provide Text Links at Bottom of Page

Text links that mimic the top links are often added to the bottom of a page, usually below a horizontal rule. Often, the text links are separated by brackets ([ ]) or pipe symbols (|) to distinguish them as navigation links.

The style of navigation of mimicking top links on the bottom of a page is often termed a *header-footer design*. This form is so common that many users tired of waiting for a page's graphical buttons to load will quickly scroll to the bottom of the page to utilize the backup text links.

Prominence of Navigational Elements

Another aspect of top navigation that can be troublesome is that labeling and site branding, such as a corporate logo, can be lost among the navigation elements. For example, look at this navigation bar:

Notice how the logo, the page label indicating location, and the buttons all compete for user attention. It has been exaggerated here purposely, but the point still holds—with top navigation, make sure not to let your buttons drown out the rest of the information presented at the top of the page. Consider the use of menu bars within typical software applications—generally they are very thin and take up no more than 10 percent of the vertical screen real estate. However, in many Web sites, the navigation bars can get quite large, making it less likely that the user will see much content without having to scroll, and potentially putting more focus on navigation than content.

Tip *When using top navigation, be careful not to overwhelm page labeling and site identity information with navigational elements.*

Bottom Navigation

In most cases, bottom navigation doesn't seem to make much sense, as it would probably force scrolling. This is because navigation elements would probably not show up in the first screen region unless page content is limited or the user has a very tall screen. Of course, with frames or other technologies, it is possible to fix navigation at the bottom of the screen that appears onscreen. (This will be touched upon later in this chapter with a complete implementation discussion in the following chapter.) However, even without frames, an upside of placing navigation at the bottom of the screen is that it leaves the top free for page labeling and corporate branding.

A potential problem with navigation placed at the bottom of a page is that the navigation is not in the primary scan path of the user. However, if the user did scan the whole page, he or she would eventually reach the bottom of the page where the navigation resides, just as they were ready to move to the next page. Because of this usage pattern, many sites provide text links on the bottom of the page (as mentioned in the previous section). However, putting the primary navigation forms, such as a graphical button, at the bottom of the screen is not suggested and does not fit with where software traditionally places controls.

 Avoid placing primary navigation at the bottom of the screen; instead, reserve this area for secondary or reinforcement navigation.

Left Navigation

The left portion of a page is a very common position for navigation elements. Since English and other Western language readers will scan information left to right, this puts the navigation directly in the reading path of the user. Also, the left of the screen is a common location for navigation in many programs and has also become somewhat of a convention in Web design. Even in print design, left-side navigation is common—for example, most tables of content feature content description to the left, with page locations to the right.

A navigation bar on the left of the page creates a type of "navigation fence" that the user must jump over to read content. This can serve as a distraction, or as a limiting region for the page, which improves design. Consider also that left navigation creates a margin for content that would be absent without a navigation bar. The main problem is that the navigation bar consumes precious screen real estate that limits how much content can be shown on a typical page. Say, for example, the user has a limited screen resolution, like 640 pixels by 480 pixels. Given browser chrome and the fact that the user may not immediately maximize the browser to take up the full screen, there may be as little as 570–580 pixels available for content. Even with a liberal assumption of 600 pixels or more for content, there still may be little room for content once the buttons are added in, as shown in Figure 7-3.

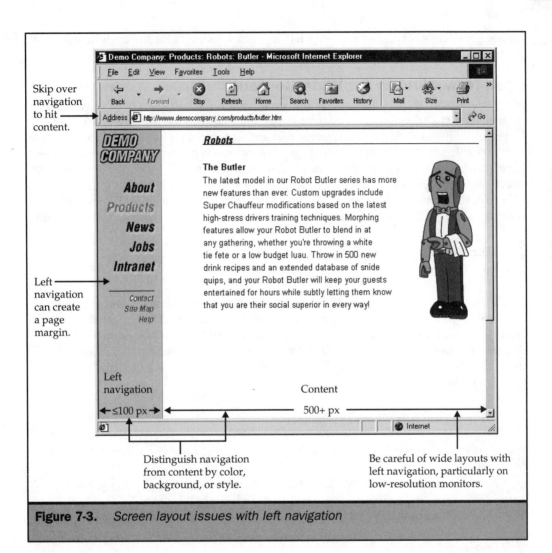

Figure 7-3. Screen layout issues with left navigation

| Tip |

When using left navigation, make sure to reformat content to fit a narrow screen.

Unfortunately, it may be impossible to reformat all content to deal with left navigation screen limitations. There are only three approaches to this problem, as discussed next.

Let User Scroll If Necessary

While the number of low-resolution systems is rapidly diminishing on the desktop, with the rise of Web appliances and mobile access this may change dramatically in the future. Users are not comfortable with left-to-right scrolling, and site designers should not format content so that it forces this.

Open New Window for Wide Content

Many sites opt to open a window without left navigation when users need to view wide content such as a table that can't be reformatted and requires the full screen width at low resolution. Removing the navigation and letting content go full-screen is also common with sites that format content for printing. While opening a new window does have drawbacks, it may be a necessary workaround in a limited-resolution environment. There are two ways to open a new window for the wide content. The first relies on the use of the **target** attribute in HTML, while the other uses JavaScript. To open a new window using HTML, simply set the **target** attribute on a link to **_blank,** as shown here:

```
<a href="widepage.htm" target="_blank">Product Table (new
window)</a>
```

Of course, it might be a good idea to let the user know you are about to open a new window by explicitly stating this. The downside to the HTML approach is that while it generally works, it does create a window with full browser controls. Many designers prefer to open a special window to display wide content. For example, the HTML here shows how a JavaScript could be used to create a link that opens a special maximized window:

```
<script language="text/javascript">
<!--
function createWindow(filename, width, height)
{
 var newWindow = window.open(filename, "","toolbar=0, location=0,
        directories=0,status=0,menubar=0,scrollbars=1,
        resizable=1,copyhistory=0,width="+width+",height="+height);
 }
//-->
</script>

<a href="http://www.yahoo.com"
onclick="createWindow('http://www.yahoo.com', 640,460); return
false">Yahoo!</a>
```

In this case, we pass the desired size of the window to the **createWindow** function. We gave it something equivalent to about the maximum resolution under 640 × 480. We use only 460 because the window taskbar may take up some room. It is also possible to use JavaScript to sense for screen resolution and open up to the size of the screen.

It is even possible to go to full-screen and take over the entire desktop, but this is not suggested.

The main downside to using new windows without browser chrome and navigation is that some users may be confused by the new window and not know how to use or close the window. Because of this potential confusion, an explicit Close button or even a frameset should be used to indicate the use of an external window. Some sites even use this approach when opening links to outside sites. Figure 7-4 shows some examples of how this might work.

Hide Left Navigation

Some sites have begun to use JavaScript to hide left navigation and show it only if required. This form of slide-out or pull-out navigation does save screen real estate, but exchanges the space issue for usability problems related to hiding the navigation from the user. Hiding the navigation limits the users' awareness of the range of choices they have (until they access the navigation). On the other hand, a slide-out navigation does place the majority of the focus on the content. An example of a hidden menu in practice is shown in Figure 7-5.

Right Navigation

Recently, placing navigational elements on the right has become popular. Some argue that right navigation places the navigation out of the way of the content and allows the user to immediately dive in and read the content. Right navigation supporters also note that the navigation buttons will be near the scroll bar, thus limiting mouse travel for the user.

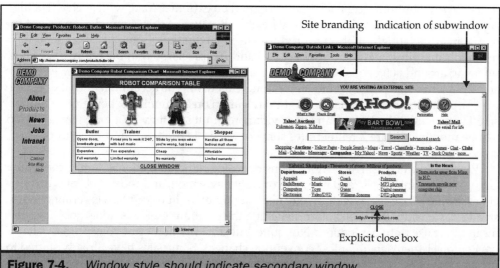

Figure 7-4. *Window style should indicate secondary window.*

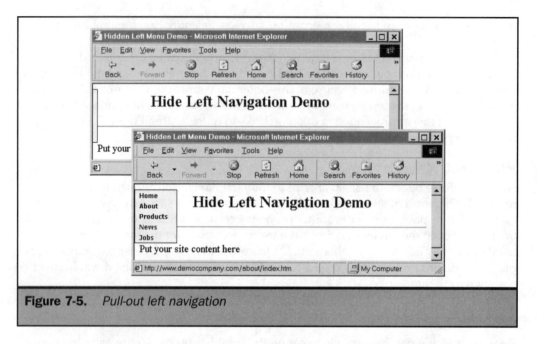

Figure 7-5.   *Pull-out left navigation*

Despite its potential upside, right navigation has some potentially serious drawbacks. First, consider a simple question: Where exactly is the right? Depending on a user's monitor and browser size, the distance from the left to the right of the screen may vary greatly. On a very large monitor, the navigation could be very far from the left edge of the screen, and the mouse travel between the navigational elements and the users' favorite button—the Back button—could be extreme. Also, with such a flexible right side, screen design has to be very flexible. Because of this, some designers opt to create an artificial right margin for right-focused navigation. Generally, they tend to make this margin somewhere between 600 and 700 pixels, so that the entire page ends up being around 800 pixels wide, which is approximately equivalent to the width of standard letter-size paper on most monitors. This would be acceptable, but it does not really obtain the second benefit of right navigation on all monitors: being close to the scroll bars. Sure, it is closer than left navigation, but it still may be a long way away on a huge monitor. Figure 7-6 illustrates some of the basic problems and benefits of right-oriented navigation.

Probably the biggest reason not to consider using right navigation is simple convention. Graphical user interfaces tend not to favor right navigation, and most Web sites do not either. While left-style navigation may not be optimal, right navigation is certainly not standard. Consider this well before switching the position of a site's doorknob! Does this mean never use right navigation? Not quite, but certainly don't put your primary site navigation elements there unless convention changes. Some sites have already started to put advertisements, cross-links, and secondary forms of the navigation on the right.

Suggestion: Avoid placing primary navigation on the far right of the screen.

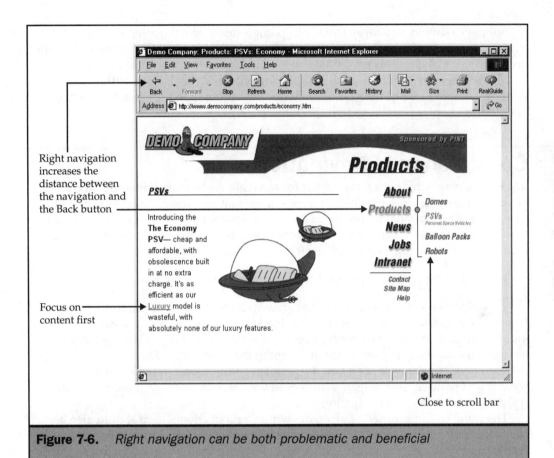

Figure 7-6. *Right navigation can be both problematic and beneficial*

Center Navigation

The last choice for navigational elements within a window is the center. Generally, putting heavy navigational elements such as graphical buttons or image maps in the center of the page is only done on the home page. Navigation-in-the-center designs tend to be heavy and don't leave much room for content, since the navigation is in the user's primary focus region. However, for home pages, this may not be a problem. Considering that the main purpose of a home page is to help the user to decide where to go, putting a site's initial navigation in the middle makes sense. This design also allows a home page to be visually different from subpages, making it easier to establish it as a landmark page.

> **Suggestion: For home pages or other landmark pages, consider using center-oriented navigation to distinguish them from other pages in a site.**

Subpages should stay away from using center-oriented navigation regions, other than for simple text links. Content should appear in the center of the screen so that the only navigational elements presented there would be cross-links within content.

There is one final choice for navigation elements, and that is outside the current window. A discussion of frames and subwindows, often called *remotes*, is presented later in this chapter (see the section "Subwindows").

Consistency of Navigation

Regardless of which position is selected for navigation—or even if literally all the positions are used, just with different types of navigation—everything must be consistent. If primary navigation is on the top and secondary navigation is on the left, then keep those there. Variation of navigation may be possible between landmark and other pages, but the following Web design rule should always be considered.

Rule: Placement of navigation should be consistent within a page layout.

The importance of the stability of navigation cannot be overstated. It is known from numerous studies that consistency is the key to usability, and navigation that jumps around the screen may confuse or disorient the user. Even if the placement of navigation is basically the same, subtle jumping may still occur. The easiest way to spot this is to do a "fast browse" of a site. To perform a fast browse, quickly click between screens and notice if the navigation moves or you have to move your mouse greatly to reach the next choice in a navigation bar.

The number and position of elements within a navigation region should also be stable from screen to screen. Many sites add and remove buttons from navigational regions as the user moves around. Imagine if an application like your favorite word processor suddenly added primary menu items or deleted them as you worked. Do not even be tempted to remove a navigation choice just because it is the one the user selected; instead, make it unselectable or gray it out. Simply removing it will cause all the buttons to shift. Consider the menus choices shown in Figure 7-7. Notice that removing an item as it is selected from the navigation changes the size of the region, breaking the stability, and that the menu are obviously not the same.

Look carefully and you'll see that one of the menus actually has a slight button change in it. It is obvious in the picture, but if you try browsing a site that uses varying buttons, it may be difficult to discern the difference from page to page. Understand that users *will* find the movement of buttons and the addition of choices in this manner highly disorienting.

Rule: Navigation should be consistent, and elements should exhibit stability in position, order, and content.

The previous rule doesn't preclude the addition of navigational elements. However, if we do add them, we must certainly let the user know we are about to do

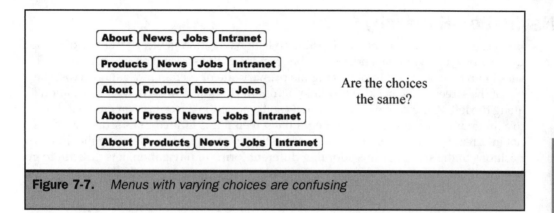

Figure 7-7.   *Menus with varying choices are confusing*

that and make it obvious what was added. For example, in a tree navigational control, the user can expand or contract navigation to show or hide navigational choices. This type of control indicates that navigation will change and differentiates the added navigational items. For example, in the unexpanded and expanded tree control shown in Figure 7-8, the exposed navigational choices in the expanded tree are indicated by indentation as well as a different style.

Tree controls are by no means perfect. Often, the tree control will expand too far down or to the right. In fact, after expanding three or four levels, tree controls for most sites get somewhat unwieldy.

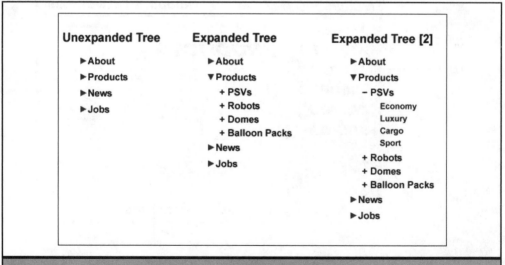

Figure 7-8.   *Tree navigation allows navigation flexibility*

Navigation Hierarchy

Besides using an expandable/collapsible style of navigation device, designers often opt to show new navigational choices in other regions of the screen. For example, many sites follow the convention of placing the primary site or section navigation across the top of the screen, with backup text links across the bottom and secondary navigation along the left. A third level of navigation can be added in a tree fashion on the left or, to a limited degree, toward the center of the screen if it is limited in its scope and does not interfere with the content. What's interesting to see is that, while using the different positions of the screen means adopting different forms of navigation, it is difficult to go beyond three or four levels of site navigation.

> **Suggestion: When separating navigation choices by position onscreen, four locations present a hard barrier to go beyond.**

Usually, this common navigation form, which some designers refer to as TLB or "top-left-bottom" navigation, includes text links backing up the primary navigation. In this form, the primary navigation is laid across the top of the page, with secondary navigation along the left side of the page. Generally, the subnavigation is also less prominent than the primary navigation. A simple TLB block diagram is shown in Figure 7-9.

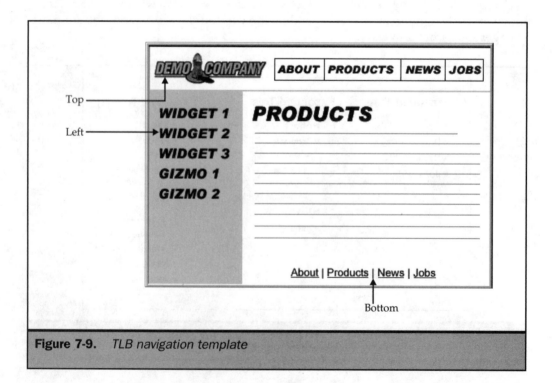

Figure 7-9. *TLB navigation template*

The TLB approach to setting navigation meaning by screen position makes good sense if you consider the user's scan path. If users look first to the top of the screen, they will read across the primary navigation choices. Once they return to the left to begin looking down the screen, they will see secondary choices. If they scroll the page to look through the content or choices, they will eventually reach the bottom of the page, where they are greeted with the text form of the main navigation. TLB design may not seem creative to many designers, but it is a convention and it does work.

Navigation and Scrolling

A contentious issue for some is whether or not pages should scroll, particularly when navigational elements are involved. No scrolling advocates feel that keeping pages a fixed size makes things consistent, and thus more predictable for the user. This may be true considering that with variable page sizes, users really don't have any idea of the volume of information they are about to receive after a typical button click. Of course, there are numerous drawbacks to the fixed-page-length concept. The page size issue is discussed thoroughly in Chapter 11. For now, consider that pages that are just used to navigate to other pages probably shouldn't scroll. You should always strive to minimize the user's effort in selecting the next page, and scrolling offscreen to see choices both adds movement and forces the user to recall any choices not visible. This idea leads to the following Web design suggestion.

> **Suggestion: Navigation-oriented pages should fit vertically within the screen whenever possible, as should primary navigation in all other types of pages.**

This rule suggests, in particular, that pages that simply lead to others should be on the screen region that does not scroll or be, as they say, "above the fold." It is impossible to guess an exact height that is available because browsers have different amounts of surrounding chrome and users may minimize their browser window at their own discretion. However, using scripting, it is possible to determine screen height on page load, as discussed in Chapter 11—although the user is always free to change things at will. In all cases—particularly when dealing with low screen resolutions such as 640 × 480—designers should always be conservative in their estimates. Many sites fit the entire navigation within the first 300 or 400 pixels, regardless of screen resolution. The first screen is considered the prime screen real estate, since any navigation outside this region may require the user to scroll to activate it.

Navigation and Mouse Travel

Besides striving to limit scrolling to navigational elements, designers should always attempt to limit mouse travel between navigational choices. First, always consider the distance between the navigation elements and the Back button, which is the most common browser button used by the user. While advanced users may use a right-click or a similar navigational shortcut to avoid moving the pointer to the upper-left corner of the screen, many users will not do this. Therefore, the distance between navigation items and the Back button should be minimized when possible.

Suggestion: Minimize the distance between primary site navigation buttons and the Back button.

The mouse-distance rule applies generally to mouse selections made navigating a site. The selections may be either to the Back button or to another button within the screen if the user is going to stay within the site. If users are moving away from the site, they may move to invoke a window in which to type a new URL or move to the address bar to do the same thing. It is advisable to limit the amount of mouse travel a user must make between choices. If this distance is limited, with the next choice appearing close to the button just pressed, navigation will appear effortless.

Suggestion: Always attempt to limit mouse movement between navigation items.

Limiting mouse distance isn't just a common sense method to improve navigation. Consider again Fitt's law, as discussed in Chapter 2, which indicates that the time it takes for a user to click a button is inversely proportional to the button's size and distance from the current mouse position. Basically, if the button is small, the user can't get to it quickly if it is far away. If you keep buttons big and right next to the previous selection, Fitt's law says the user will be able to use the interface quickly. If you consider how easy it would be to press big red buttons that appear right next to each other, you can see that Fitt's law may state the obvious. Then why are small buttons jumping up all over Web pages? To benefit from Fitt's law, bring choices closer together and make choices that are farther away larger. Notice that many interfaces, such as installers and Wizard-style interfaces, already limit mouse travel by making the screens similar, with the next button to click near the position of the last one clicked.

Frames

One navigation device that can be used to improve stability and possibly reduce scrolling—and maybe even mouse travel—is the frame. Frames, unfortunately, have somewhat of a bad name on the Web, primarily due to some early implementation problems and some vocal critics, such as usability expert Jakob Nielsen (http://www.useit.com). The reality is that frames are generally misused, but they actually do have some redeeming features that should be considered before dismissing them out of hand.

The biggest problem with frames is a misunderstanding of their purpose. Many designers accidentally use frames as a page layout tool. The truth is that frames are navigation devices. The idea of a frame is to divide the screen into multiple regions, panes, or windows. The benefit of breaking the browser window into multiple independent regions is that doing so allows the viewer to see more than one document at a time. In fact, even with a simple two-frame design, as shown in Figure 7-10, there are actually three documents being used—a document setting up the frames, a document for the left frame, and a document for the right frame.

Frameset Document:

```
<!DOCTYPE html PUBLIC "-//W3C//DTD XHTML 1.0 Frameset//EN">

<html>
<head>
    <title>Simple Frame Example</title>
</head>

<frameset cols="250,*">

<frame src="fileone.htm" name="1" />
<frame src="filetwo.htm" name="2" />

</frameset>
</html>
```

Browser Rendering:

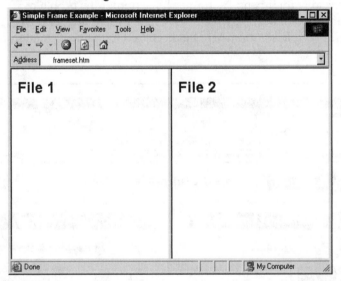

File 1 Code:

```
<html>
<head>
    <title>File One</title>
</head>

<body>

<h2>File 1</h2>

</body>
</html>
```

File 2 Code:

```
<html>
<head>
    <title>File Two</title>
</head>

<body>

<h2>File 2</h2>

</body>
</html>
```

Figure 7-10.   *Overview of frames*

The benefits of using frames can be great. First, frames make it possible to fix navigation onscreen at all times. Whether navigation buttons are placed in a frame at the top, left, bottom, or even right of the screen, the buttons can be fixed to never scroll away.

Another benefit of frames is that they can create an appearance of speed. Consider the case of the fixed navigation shown in the previous example. If you click the various links in the navigation bar, only the right portion of the screen updates while the left stays onscreen. Because there is less screen repainting, the site appears fast to the user. If the frameset is much larger, the illusion is more noticeable.

Frames also allow multiple documents to be shown within the window at once. For example, if you want to compare various items, it might be possible to build a framed environment so that the user could click buttons and bring up pages with products to compare, as shown in Figure 7-11. This example also suggests that using frames can result in very complex navigation.

However, despite their benefits, frames have numerous problems involving search engines, printing, bookmarking, screen real-estate availability, and URL hiding. These issues and their possible solutions will be discussed in the next chapter, on navigation practices.

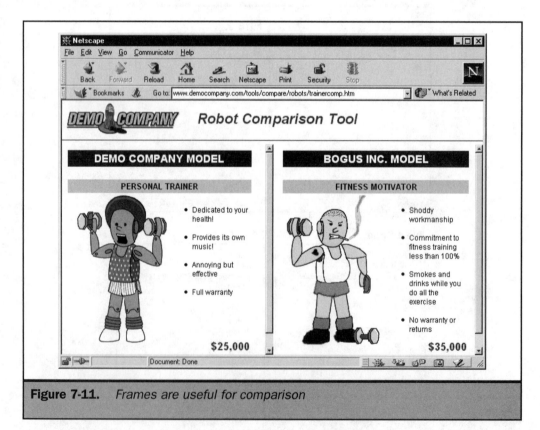

Figure 7-11.   *Frames are useful for comparison*

Subwindows

Another navigation scheme—less popular than frames—is the use of pop-ups. Pop-up windows are used for a variety of reasons, from navigation remote controls to banner advertisements. Unfortunately, very often it is not obvious to users when pop-ups are being launched, and, in some cases, they spring up unexpectedly. An example of the particularly annoying "last chance" pop-up is shown in Figure 7-12. These annoying pop-ups are so troubling that users may install software that kills windows of a certain size, so be careful of using pop-ups for important information.

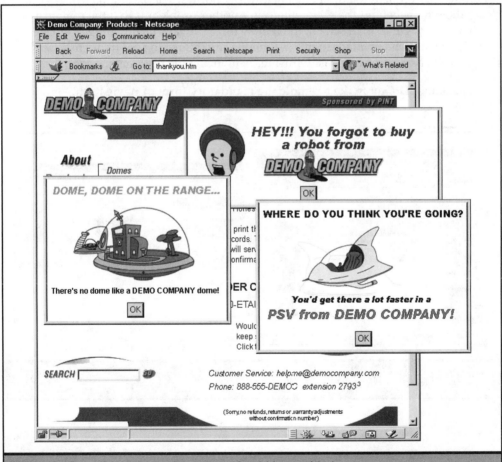

Figure 7-12.   *"Last chance" pop-ups should be avoided*

Navigation Remotes

A special type of pop-up window known as a "remote" may be valuable in some instances. Basically, a remote is a small subwindow that is detached from the browser and can be used to load content into the main window. An example of a remote is shown in Figure 7-13.

In some sense, a remote is like a frame in that it is always available—though it isn't attached to the main window. Remotes could also be considered equivalent to a tear-off menu or floating palette in a traditional software application.

The main problem with remotes is that they can get lost. Some people set their operating environment to automatically lower windows. This could make it easy to "lose" the remote behind the main window. Another problem is that the remote just gets in the way. On a small screen, the remote might always be hovering over content, since there would be no place to put it. Remotes are interesting for frequently used sites, but other sites should consider using them in an only optional manner.

Suggestion: Do not make a remote the mandatory form of navigation.

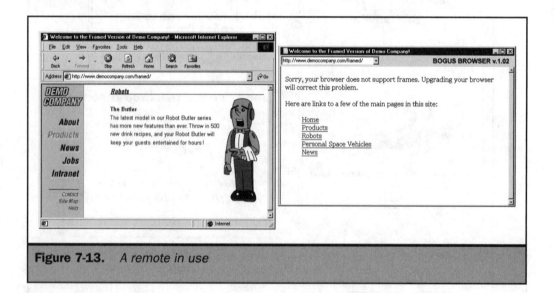

Figure 7-13.   *A remote in use*

Bookmarking

Bookmarking is an important aspect of navigation. Often, the user will bookmark a page to return to it in the future. In some browsers, the user may even bookmark the page so that it is downloaded for offline viewing or is checked on a regular basis automatically for changes. Traditionally, designers could do little to affect bookmarking other than make it difficult for a user to bookmark a page by using a frame. However, under Internet Explorer 5 and beyond, it is possible to somewhat customize bookmarks or, as they are called in Microsoft parlance, "favorites."

The simplest customization is to create a custom icon to be associated with a bookmark. First, create a small icon you wish users to see in a graphics tool. The icon file must be saved as the .ico type and must have the dimensions 16 pixels by 16 pixels; otherwise, the browser will ignore it. Next, copy the icon to the root directory of your Web server handling pages for a particular domain (for example, http://www.democompany.com/favicon.ico). Internet Explorer will automatically use this icon any time a user sets a favorite or quick link for your site, as shown here.

> ● RealPlayer Home Page

Note   *Some people express concern that a potential privacy risk occurs with a standard bookmark file. A request for a standard graphic like favicon.ico can be filtered from a log file and used to indicate that the user has bookmarked the page.*

One important consideration with bookmarking is making sure to deal with dynamic data. For example, you may have a special URL where you store the latest press release (http://www.democompany.com/latestnews). After a particular item is no longer the latest item, it is moved to an archive and replaced by a new item. Imagine a user's frustration if the user bookmarks a particular piece of content only to have it change—which leads us to a brief discussion on navigation practices to avoid.

Navigation No-No's

Before concluding this chapter, let's take a look at a brief list of navigational no-no's, some of which we have touched on already. None of these problems will necessarily completely ruin a site's navigation, but all can frustrate the user greatly.

Back-Button Hijacking

The user's favorite browser button, particularly the novice user's, is the Back button. Unfortunately, some sites turn this off through the use of redirection. Be careful in making special pages that just redirect a user to another page instantly. Often, this is done to sense for a particular browser using JavaScript. It is much wiser instead to sense the browser on the server side and build the page to fit. With this model, the user will be able to back out of the page as if it were a regular page.

Link Color Tricks

Modifying link colors so users don't know where they have been can be very confusing, as can suggesting to users that they have been to certain places by setting a link color to appear as though it had been clicked. Changing the link color away from the common blue/red/purple scheme might be acceptable, but avoid doing so if you can.

Heavy Use of Pop-Up Windows

Many sites have begun to spawn windows as users begin to leave a site. Often, these windows contain advertisements for other sites or attempt somehow to keep the user from leaving. Very unscrupulous designers might even attempt to override the user and send them back to the site they are trying to leave. Don't beg. Just let users go if they want to.

Unique Navigation

Users navigate the Web all day, and they don't have a great deal of patience for sites that deviate too much from the norm. Some designers bemoan the rise of navigation sameness that results when people utilize existing conventions. They argue that site navigation has begun to look so similar that users can't tell the difference between sites and that there is little room for creative flexibility. However, the consistency of site navigation plays to usability. Users have come to understand designs like Amazon or Yahoo!. Why deviate too far from such designs when you can reap the benefit of previous user experience? People know how these sites work, just as they understand basic Web conventions such as blue as a link color and standard GUI conventions. Further, consider that most word processors and spreadsheets work the same, so why shouldn't most e-commerce sites follow suit? Remember, you aren't selling navigation to the user!

Heavily Branded Buttons

Overemphasis on navigation elements over content is often due to the designer's attempt to "brand with the buttons" and make the navigation be the design. The idea here is to attempt to build brand through a visually distinctive navigation look. A distinctive-looking button *may* be memorable to a user, but the odds are against it. Consider the last time you really sat and admired buttons in an elevator. Well, maybe as a designer you might, but ask the person in the elevator with you what they think and they may consider you a little odd. Again, remember that users use navigation only to accomplish a task they have set out to perform.

Reliance on Back Button

If you rely primarily on the Back button for navigation—particularly on content pages—you may create an orphan page lacking outgoing links. If a user has followed a particular path through the site, the Back button will work fine. However, users may not enter the site the way you think. If the user bookmarks a page accessed from outside the site and then returns another day—the Back button won't get the user out.

Making Users Work Too Hard

Like it or not, people can be somewhat lazy and will generally prefer sites that don't require much effort to use. This becomes more and more important as the user continues to use the site. The buttons should be placed obviously and be legible. Don't force the user to strain visually, mentally, or physically to use your navigation. Users should not have to recall information about buttons to choose—they should simply have to recognize the choices. Last, don't make the user work physically to move around the site. Navigation should always be as effortless as possible. Consider checking the amount of mouse travel by focusing carefully on the distance between subsequent choices.

> **Rule: Limit scrolling and mouse travel in navigation as much as possible.**

Also, consider measuring the number of clicks it takes to reach a destination page. We often consider three to be the maximum number of clicks, but you should not focus solely on clicks. It may be more the page-load time, often due to the network round-trip time, that frustrates the user. Consider limiting your navigation depth to three page loads.

> **Rule: Consider a maximum of three page loads before a result.**

It is easy to build bad navigation, but it is sometimes hard for designers to detect what is bad. The reason is that, as a designer, you are probably going to know how to navigate your own site. Take to heart any complaints you receive from users about site navigation problems. If you suspect a problem, conduct a quick site evaluation focusing on navigation, as discussed in Appendix B.

Summary

In the real world, people take different approaches to navigation, depending on the circumstance. For example, people act differently during a museum visit than during a park visit, or a store visit, or when looking for a friend's house. Depending on the task at hand, the navigation techniques vary. Regardless of the site type, the goal of navigation should be simply to help users find their way. Good navigation should help a user answer location questions, such as "Where am I?" or "Where can I go?" or "How do I get where I want to go?" or "Have I been here before?" or "How can I get back to someplace I was?" The use of page labels, URLs, landmark pages, page style, and color can help users identify location. Navigation elements can be added to help users make choices about future destinations.

The placement and stability of navigation items should be well thought out. While advanced techniques such as hidden menus, frames, and remotes can address some problems, they may also introduce problems that should be considered before implementation. Last, always remember that navigation is a means to an end, not the end itself. Generally, users are not going to marvel at the beauty of your navigation system; in fact, they will probably consider your site a small stop on a much larger journey they are taking on the Web. Sites should not focus on bringing undue attention to their navigation. In fact, if the user notices it too much, we are probably not doing a good job. The next chapters discuss the actual use of various navigational elements, such as links, search engines, and navigational aids such as site maps.

The
Complete
Reference

Web
Design

Chapter 8

Basic Navigation Practices

221

Now that we have covered basic navigation principles, it is time to examine how to correctly build navigation systems in Web sites. Starting with basic links, we will survey the use and styles of links in sites—including text links, buttons, icons, and image maps. We will also look at the use of more complex navigational devices, such as menu systems, frames, and external windows. Such related topics as search systems, system maps, and indexes will be presented in following chapters. Details and best practices for navigation are examined throughout, with a focus on managing user expectations and helping users find their way to desired content.

Link Types

The core of Web-based navigation is the *hypertext link*. The Web's linking model is relatively simple, as links are traditionally unidirectional and, in the absence of special programming, will cause a single page to load. Yet even with such simple links, we can categorize links used in Web sites in a variety of ways.

The most common way to categorize links is by the address or URL of the document to load. *Internal links* connect to another page or URL within a site. Internal links would also include *intrapage links*. These are links that jump a user around a single file. An example of an intrapage link is the "back to top" link that is frequently found in lengthy pages. An *external link* points to a page outside the current site.

Another way to categorize links is by how predictable they are. For example, links within a navigation bar tend to be fairly consistent in position, style, and even destination from page to page. We could call these links *structured links*, because their use often aligns very closely with the hierarchical structure common to most Web sites. Structured links are beneficial to users who are on a planned mission to find something or accomplish a particular task.

Unstructured links, on the other hand, are those that may appear somewhat random to the user. For example, contextual links within the body of text could be considered unstructured links. If I were suddenly to suggest in the middle of a sentence that you see the Robot Butler at http://www.democompany.com/products/butler.htm (as indeed I just did), you'd get a firsthand example of how baffling an unstructured link might appear to a user who encounters one on a Web page. Why, exactly, did I give you a link to the Robot Butler then and there, inviting you to drop the thread of my argument entirely? Unstructured links do not necessarily follow the structure of a Web site and may jump across a site structure or outside a site at any time. However, do not assume that unstructured links should never be used. On the contrary: a site with only consistent navigation links will feel stale. Consider adding a few contextual jumps and "exploration" links to your pages—primarily to important words and phrases within the body of text. These tangential links might just encourage a visitor to stay and look around. Not everyone is going to be on a precise mission; letting people wander a bit can be useful.

Suggestion: Occasionally provide some unstructured links within document text to promote exploration and thinking.

Be careful with unstructured links, however; as discussed in the previous chapter, logical navigation within a site is central to its usability. Links that appear random to the visitor may confuse users, as will too many cross-links.

Another way to categorize links on a Web site is in terms of how they are created. Are the links permanently pointing to the same content, or are the links created dynamically based upon content? We call these two link types *static links* and *dynamic links*.

Definition: A static link is one where the destination file is hard-coded into the anchor by the document author.

Most Web sites use predominantly static links. A dynamic link that could change based upon environment, time, or condition is usually best suited to interactive Web sites. For example, a dynamic link might link to a site of the day or something that changes all the time. A simple example of a dynamic link would be a link labeled "You might also like" in an e-commerce site that takes users to a page or destination based upon buying habits, sales promotions, and so on.

Definition: A dynamic link does not have a fixed destination. Instead, the destination document is computed at page view time according to the environment and needs of the viewer.

Dynamic links offer two significant advantages over static links. First, dynamic links react to user conditions, so they may present different destinations based upon user skill, browser capabilities, user preference, or other environment conditions. Second, dynamic links provide the potential for improved maintenance. A common problem with Web sites is an excess of broken links. A site where links are dynamically determined could avoid this problem, since links can be automatically recalculated as pages are added or removed. As discussed later in this chapter, dynamic links could remove the major burden Web designers face in maintaining sites.

A Taxonomy of Link Forms

Given the basic types of links, their execution can come in many forms, ranging from basic HTML text links to complex images with irregularly shaped hotspots (called *image maps*). Each form of link has its uses and will be examined in turn. Designers are strongly cautioned to make linked content obvious. Remember: running a mouse all over the screen in an attempt to find the active click regions is a tedious and frustrating task for users. After each form of link is discussed, the techniques for ensuring usable links will be presented.

Text Links

The most basic form of link in a Web page is the *text link*, specified by plain text within an <a> tag, as shown here:

```
<a href="http://www.democompany.com">Visit Demo Company --
                Makers of the Robot Butler</a>
```

These forms of links are very versatile; they are used both for primary navigation links and as contextual links within large amounts of textual material.

A common position for text links within a site is at the bottom of a page. These backup links are often used to mimic the links on top of a page or to provide alternative link forms in place of heavy graphical links such as image maps. Many advanced users instinctively scroll down to the bottom of slow-loading, graphics-laden pages, looking for text links to use instead.

> **Suggestion: Always provide textual links at the bottom of pages when using long pages or pages with graphical buttons.**

Examples of all the previously discussed text link forms are shown in Figure 8-1.

Text links are very useful because their download time is minimal and it is easy to update them or even make them completely dynamic. The major downside to text links is that they are often difficult to spot, particularly when designers change link feedback, such as color or underlining (discussed later in the chapter). While fixed navigation links may be relatively easy to spot, text links buried within content will become nearly invisible when link decoration is modified dramatically.

Graphic Text Links

Because text links are rather basic looking and may not support the marketing goals of Web sites, some designers opt to use graphic text links. Up until the release of 4.0-generation browsers, the only way to accurately control text appearance on the Web was to use graphics. For significant navigation links, designers would often create graphical text buttons.

To ensure that these graphic text items appear pressable, designers often choose a different font for the text buttons, change their color, increase their size, set the text away from other content, or use an effect such as a drop shadow. Figure 8-2 shows a variety of text treatments used to make graphic text buttons.

A major downside of graphic text buttons is that, even when optimized, they can result in significant download times, particularly when combined with rollover states. No matter how much optimization is employed, the word "About" in plain text will always use fewer bytes than a GIF image containing the same word. Further, image buttons may limit accessibility in many cases. Without alternative text, they cannot

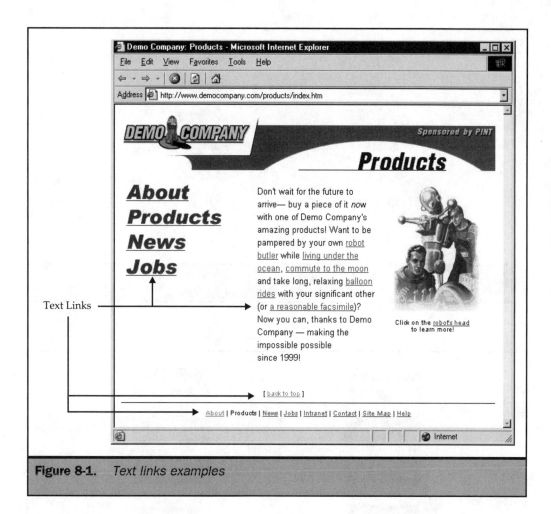

Figure 8-1.   *Text links examples*

be translated to nonvisual environments; even within a graphics environment, they may not change to fit the resolution of the viewing environment. With the rise of style sheets, graphically styled text should eventually become unnecessary.

Buttons

Stylizing a link to make it look like a button is a good way to improve the usability of site links. It is possible to make custom buttons with graphics or utilize HTML form buttons. For example, putting a stroke around a button and giving it some relief is an easy way to make a region look pressable. There are a variety of button styles that can be employed, as shown in Figure 8-3.

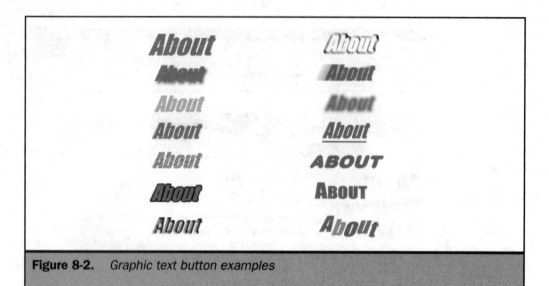

Figure 8-2. Graphic text button examples

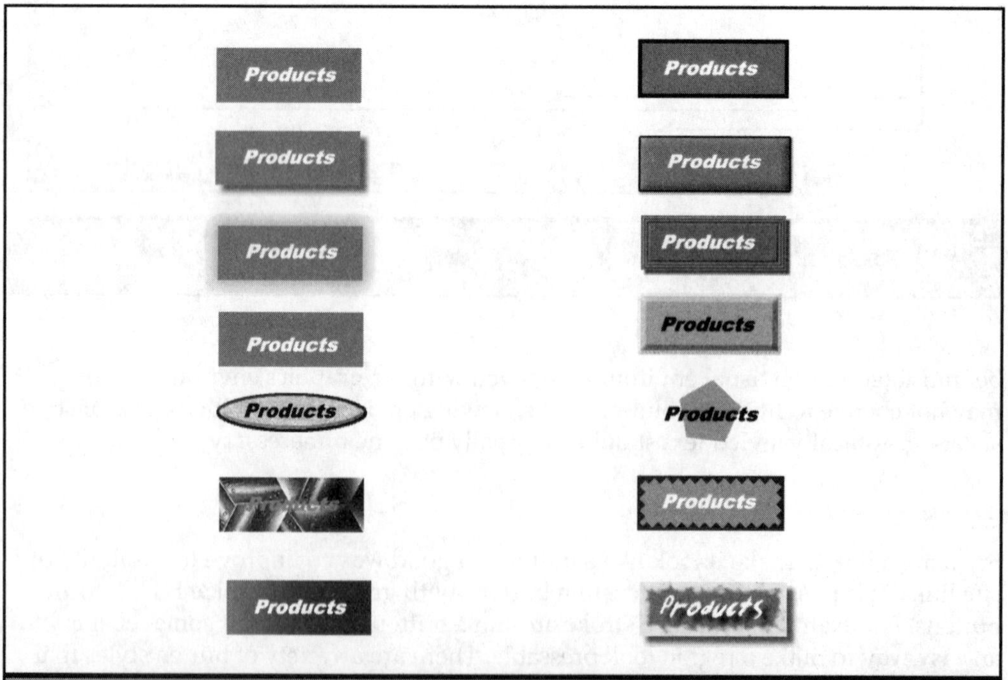

Figure 8-3. Examples of button styles

Icons

An icon is a small picture used onscreen to represent some action or content. Icons can be used alone or with words. By themselves, icons can save space. A very visual icon can often say more in a few pixels than even a few words can. Consider the following icons and their equivalent words.

 HOME

 E-MAIL

 PRINT

An icon can easily become as decipherable as ancient Egyptian hieroglyphics. Consider the meaning of the following common Windows system icons.

**Icons Without
Labels**   **Match with Meaning**

Internet options   World time

Add/Remove programs   Tools

Regional settings   Directory assistance

ODBC data sources (32 bit)

Without labels, it is very difficult to decipher the meanings of icons unless the idea is very simple. Without their associated text labels, it is somewhat difficult to understand some icons. The icon of the earth may be well understood, but its meaning within the context of a page might vary from a button that accesses some multinational corporation's global home page to a link about geography. A label brings clarity to the meaning of an icon. Consider the same icons now with their labels. They are far easier to deal with.

Add/Remove
Programs

Internet
Options

ODBC Data
Sources (32bit)

Regional
Settings

Unfortunately, with their labels showing, icons lose their space advantage. By using the **title** attribute like so,

```
<img src="printericon.gif" alt="print" title="Print this page" />
```

it is possible to hide icon labels until a user puts the pointer over the icon.

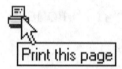

While tool tips improve icon usability, site designers should try to show labels wherever possible to avoid users having to hold their mouse over an icon to determine what it means.

Regardless of label usage, icons may retain some advantages over text links. Icons are often easier for users to recognize than words. Even when icons are difficult for people to decipher, people may still be able to recall their meaning over time more easily than words. Think how people often remember faces but not names. (This issue relates to the discussion of recognition and recall and visual memory in Chapter 2.) Consider the Paste icon common to many desktop applications:

Does the clipboard really say "paste," when you think about it? Can you even tell this is a clipboard at such a small size? Over time, it may not matter what icons represent—users simply know that when they press the picture of the magnifying glass over the paper, they get a print preview. In this sense, many common desktop icons have become somewhat idiomatic for the user. As the Web grows, some icons will certainly become commonplace and their meaning fairly well understood. Most of these icons will probably owe some heritage to desktop applications, but some may be new. Table 8-1 presents a few common icons used on the Web and their typical meanings.

Note *The particular style for the icon is inconsequential. Consider the shape to be the primary focus of the icon.*

Be careful not to fall into the trap of assuming that icons make it possible to provide perfectly transparent site navigation without having the user actually need to read anything. While it may be true that users don't have to be able to read to decipher an icon, consider what happens next. If an illiterate user or non-native speaker can decipher an icon's meaning, they still will typically end up at content that they may not be able to consume because of their language skills. In summary, don't think that use of icons will solve all localization issues.

Task Icon

Email / Contact

Print

Post (message to discussion board)

Download or save

Access shopping cart

Edit

Delete

Close

Attach

Navigation Icon

Home

Back

Forward

Table 8-1.   *Common Icons Found on Web Sites*

Navigation Icon *(continued)*

Scroll Up

Scroll Down

New Window

Help

Search

External link

Content Icon

Audio

Video

Picture blowup

Acrobat file

New information

Table 8-1. *Common Icons Found on Web Sites* (continued)

Image Maps

Many visual Web interfaces use image maps or large images with clickable regions called *hotspots*. Image maps are very popular because they allow designers to make arbitrary click shapes. In the case of buttons or icons, the clicking region is square or rectangular. With an image map, rectangles, circles, and arbitrary polygon shapes are possible.

Image maps as defined in HTML come in two forms: client-side and server-side. Server-side image maps are defined by the inclusion of the **ismap** attribute and a link to a map file on a remote server, as illustrated by this simple example:

```
<a href="shapes.map">
<img src="shapes.gif" ismap border="0" width="400" height="200" />
</a>
```

The map file would contain coordinates indicating the hotspots as well as the URL to fetch when a particular hotspot is selected. A sample map file might look like this:

```
rect rectangle.htm 6,50 140,143
circle circle.htm 195,100 144,86
poly polygon.htm 256,120 306,52 333,58 336,0 386,
73 372,119 322,172 256,120 256,119 256,119 258,118

default defaultreg.htm
```

The problem with server-side image maps is twofold. First, decoding where a user should go based on where they clicked requires a visit to the server, where the server interprets the map file. The network round-trip could slow the user down. Second, as the user mouses over the various parts of the image, coordinates—rather than a URL—are shown in the status bar.

http://www.pint.com/html/Chapter5/shapes.map?117,110

Coordinates of the pointer position are less than ideal feedback for users who often consult the URL for information about link destination. Fortunately, server-side image maps are primarily a thing of the past. All modern browsers support client-side image maps. A client-side image is defined using the **usemap** attribute for the **<img>** element. The **usemap** is set to reference a **<map>** element somewhere else in the file that indicates the hotspots in the image. The following simple example illustrates the HTML markup required for a basic client-side image map:

```
<?xml version="1.0" encoding="iso-8859-1"?>
<!DOCTYPE html PUBLIC "-//W3C//DTD XHTML 1.0 Transitional//EN"
"http://www.w3.org/TR/xhtml1/DTD/xhtml1-transitional.dtd">
<html xmlns="http://www.w3.org/1999/xhtml">
<head>
<title>Client-side Image map</title>
<meta http-equiv="Content-Type" content="text/html; charset=iso-8859-1"
/>
</head>
<body>

<h1 align="center">Client-side Image map Test</h1>
<div align="center">
<img src="shapes.gif" usemap="#shapes" alt="shapes test"
    border="0" width="400" height="200" />
</div>

<map name="shapes" id="shapes">
  <area shape="rect" coords="6,50,140,143"
    href="rectangle.htm" alt="Rectangle" />
  <area shape="circle" coords="195,100,50"
    href="circle.htm" alt="Circle" />
  <area shape="poly"
    coords="255,122,306,53,334,62,338,0,388,
            77,374,116,323,171,255,122"
    href="polygon.htm" alt="Polygon" />
  <area shape="default" href="defaultreg.htm" />
</map>

</body>
</html>
```

Despite the daunting markup involved in specifying active regions in an image, creating an image map doesn't have to be difficult. A variety of image-mapping tools exist for creating maps. Popular editors such as Macromedia's Dreamweaver provide tools for simple editing of image maps, as shown in Figure 8-4.

Before defining an image map, make sure you are not going to modify the image. If you resize an image or move things around, the hotspots will not be adjusted and may not relate. Making an image map is generally the last part of a layout.

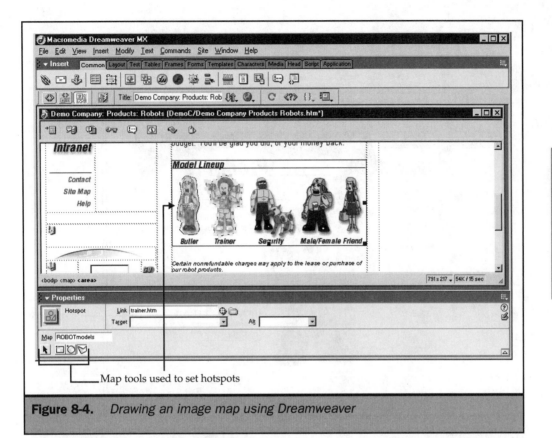

Figure 8-4. *Drawing an image map using Dreamweaver*

The primary benefit of image maps is that they allow irregular hotspots, which can be used to create interesting interfaces, such as the one shown in Figure 8-5. In this example, rolling over the various parts on the robot reveals information about its features.

A secondary benefit of image maps is that they may reduce the number of requests to a server. Designers will often cut up menu bars into multiple images, particularly when trying to create rollover images. Always remember that file size isn't everything; with a page laden with many small changes, the increased number of connections to a server may slow page loading significantly. Because a single image map may include many hotspots, a large navigation bar with multiple image requests can be reduced to a single request—although the resulting image map may be quite large.

The main problem with image maps is that they tend to encourage very lush layouts that may result in significant download time. Further, image maps tend to be less accessible than standard link forms, particularly for nonvisual-rendering environments.

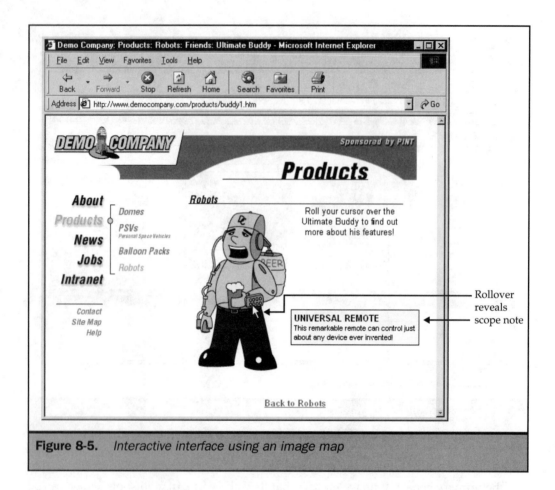

Figure 8-5. *Interactive interface using an image map*

Therefore, designers are always encouraged to provide secondary navigation links for image maps, as shown in Figure 8-6.

> **Suggestion: When using image maps, always provide a secondary navigation form, such as text links.**

Other Link Forms

Besides text links, buttons, and image maps, there are many other objects that can trigger a page load or action. The most common are a special form of advertising button called a *banner ad* and modified form elements. However, with HTML 4.0 and XHTML, it is possible to make anything trigger a page load.

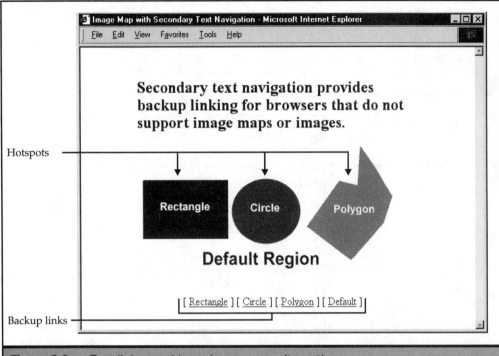

Figure 8-6. *Text links provide an image map alternative*

Banners

Given the commercial nature of many Web sites, banner ads are a common occurrence. Banner ads come in many sizes and are often animated. Clicking the ad will generally take the user to the advertiser's site. The effectiveness of the advertisement is often measured by its click-through rate, meaning the percentage of people who see the ad who actually click it. Unfortunately, over the years, the click-through rate for banners has plummeted. Some experts attribute this to a phenomenon dubbed "banner blindness." Basically, banner blindness suggests that users have become so accustomed to the size, shape, and placement of banners that they can easily ignore them. Here we see sensory adaptation at work. Because of this trend, advertisers have adopted a variety of new shapes and sizes. The Internet Advertising Bureau (http://www.iab.net) specifies the standard banner sizes shown in Figure 8-7.

Banner forms other than those shown in Figure 8-7 may be available, depending on the site. Further, the size of the banner in kilobytes and the possibility for animation may vary from site to site. For example, one banner network had a limit of 10KB for

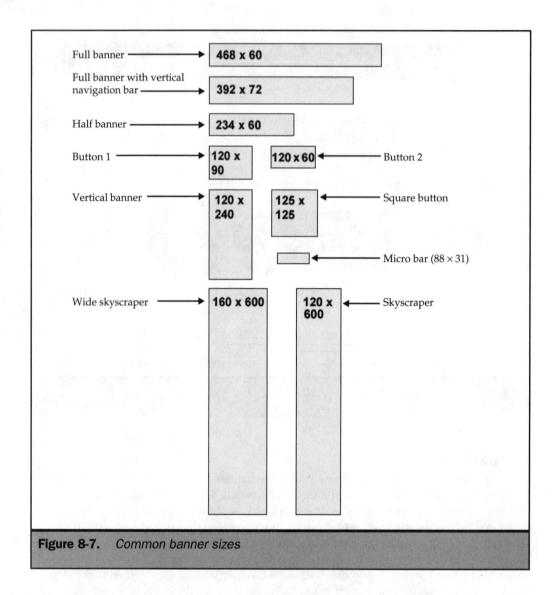

Figure 8-7.   *Common banner sizes*

banner ads and seven seconds of animation without looping. Make sure to check the specifications of your banner network before creating banners.

Even if you are not interested in designing or hosting advertisements, you should be aware of these standards. If a user thinks something is a banner, it will be treated as such. Designers are warned to avoid making non-advertising links in a similar style as banner ads.

Tip *Avoid making your buttons similar in size or style to banner advertisements.*

Regardless of your particular take on the usefulness of banners, they are a common link form and it is important to understand their conventions.

Using GUI Widgets for Link Triggering

Many sites have come to rely on using various form widgets for navigation in a site. Probably the most common form element used to trigger links is the pull-down menu. Many sites utilize a menu as a quick-jump facility to move from page to page, as shown here.

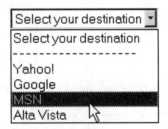

The markup and JavaScript presented below illustrates how a pull-down could be used to create a simple portal selection menu:

```
<!DOCTYPE html PUBLIC "-//W3C//DTD XHTML 1.0 Transitional//EN"
"http://www.w3.org/TR/xhtml1/DTD/xhtml1-transitional.dtd">

<html xmlns="http://www.w3.org/1999/xhtml">
<head>
<title>Menu Redirection</title>
<script type="text/javascript">
<!--
function redirect(menu)
{
   var selected = menu.selectedIndex;
   var destination = menu.options[selected].value;
   if (destination.length > 0)
    window.location = destination;
}
//-->
</script>
</head>
<body>
<form action="redirection.cgi">
```

```
<select onchange="redirect(this)">
<option value="" selected>Select your destination</option>
<option value="">- - - - - - - - - - - - - - - - -</option>
<option value="http://www.yahoo.com">Yahoo!</option>
<option value="http://www.google.com">Google</option>
<option value="http://www.msn.com">MSN</option>
<option value="http://www.altavista.com">Alta Vista</option>
</select>
<noscript>
<input type="submit" value="go" />
</noscript>
</form>
</body>
</html>
```

Weblink: See this and other code online at http://www.webdesignref.com/.

To utilize this navigation device, simply copy the code, substitute the **value** attribute for each **<option>** tag for your destination URL, and label the **<option>** appropriately. For menu choices that don't go anywhere, make sure to provide a blank value.

Before using pull-downs in a site, consider two issues. First, notice that the script relies on JavaScript. In many versions of this code, if the script isn't on, the **onchange** attribute is ignored and thus the menu doesn't work. The code in the previous example instead puts in a submit button when script is off and sets the form **action** attribute to a CGI program called redirection.cgi, which could be written to do the same things as the short JavaScript. Site designers are encouraged either to avoid adding a pull-down if JavaScript is disabled or to provide a backup CGI program.

While the pull-down has become commonplace and appears to be fairly well understood by users, the use of other form elements for navigation purposes should be avoided. In particular, neither radio buttons nor check boxes should ever be used in this manner.

Menus

While it is easy enough to provide simple graphical button palettes that look like menus, traditionally, a page reload was required to expand menu choices. Simple GUI menus using the **<select>** tag improved upon that; and by using Flash or JavaScript in conjunction with CSS, it is possible to create sophisticated navigation bars. It is even possible to create cascading menus to allow for deep navigation into a site. A navigation menu in use is shown in Figure 8-8.

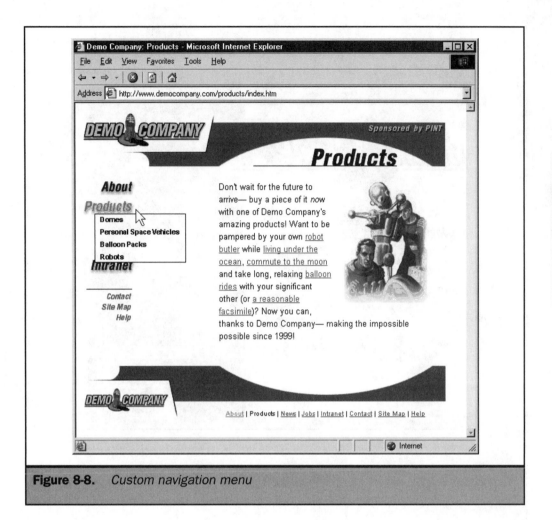

Figure 8-8.   *Custom navigation menu*

The form of the menu is arbitrary and may include standard GUI-style menus, pop-up menus, outline style menus, or even tree controls. A few examples are shown in Figure 8-9.

Given the amount of JavaScript logic necessary to make complex menus work in most browsers, we avoid its presentation here and direct readers to the book's support site (http://www.webdesignref.com) for help. However, be aware that serious browser compatibility problems may result from using complex menus, so proceed with caution.

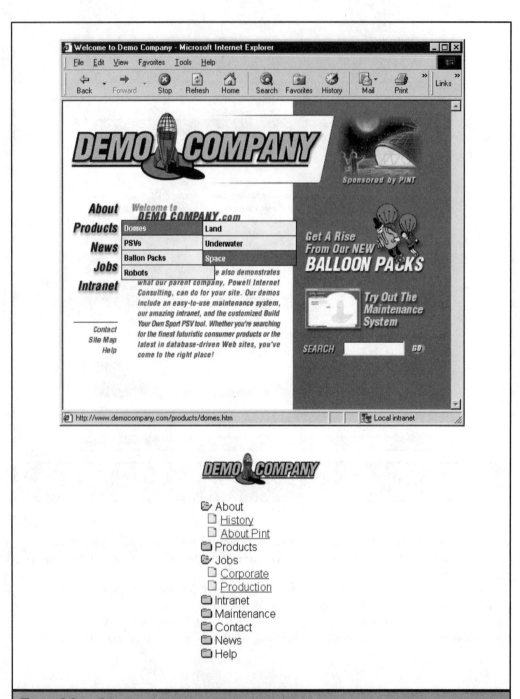

Figure 8-9. Other navigation menus

Hotspots Everywhere?

Finally, with the introduction of HTML 4 and XHTML, it is now possible to make nearly every HTML element clickable using the **onclick** core event handler and attaching it to JavaScript. For example, try the following HTML markup with a small JavaScript attached to the **onclick** attribute:

```
<p onclick="window.location='http://www.yahoo.com';">
Is this a link? Maybe or maybe not.</p>
```

If you are using a standards-compliant browser (Internet Explorer 4+ or Netscape 6+), clicking the paragraph will actually load a new page. However, if your scripting support is off or you are using an older browser, nothing will happen. Regardless of browser support, the potential for problems should be obvious. With the ability to make anything clickable, the possibility of confusing the user becomes great. The next section deals with how to ensure it is obvious what is clickable in a page and what is not.

Usable Links

No matter what link form or combination of link forms a site employs, when it comes to the actual implementation of links on a site, certain interface design considerations will always apply: Links should enhance rather than detract from a site's overall usability. They should provide adequate feedback to the user about what they signify, and they should be an adequately supported feature of the site rather than being left to bear the entire burden of site navigation on their own. The next section addresses these general implementation issues by taking up a series of specific topics that relate to them: link usability; rollovers; user expectations; the use of scope notes; and, finally, keyboard support for links.

Link Conventions

Like it or not, users expect links to be blue and underlined. Further, they expect buttons to literally look pressable, which often means using hackneyed effects like bevels or drop shadows. Unfortunately, some designers do not find these conventions conducive to appealing layout and often just ignore them. Before deviating from such conventions for some aesthetic reason, it is important to understand the usability of links. Always remember that it won't matter how good the site looks if the user can't figure it out.

Link Colors

The default link colors on the Web are blue for non-visited links, red for links that are being activated (pressed), and purple for visited links. It is also possible under the CSS2 specification to modify the color of a link when a pointing device is hovering over or about to select a link. There is no standard defined color for this, but it appears that red is the most common color for the hover state.

Link colors can easily be overridden using HTML or CSS. Changing link colors in HTML requires modifying attributes for the **<body>** element, while CSS relies on pseudoclass rules for the **<a>** element. Table 8-2 shows the link types, colors, and modification syntax.

> **Note**   *Some consideration of the position of the CSS rules for link colors should be made. The order of definition within a global or linked style sheet should be unvisited; visited; hover; and, finally, active. Any other order may produce incorrect results, considering that cascade will cause style rules to be potentially overriding.*

Changing link colors significantly from their blue/red/purple settings is dangerous. For better or worse, users have come to understand that blue is the color of links and purple is the color of links they have already pressed. The differences in link color are important because they show users where they have been. This is often called *breadcrumbing,* in the spirit of the *Hansel and Gretel* story, where the children drop bread crumbs to find their way out of the forest. Unfortunately, site designers occasionally feel that it is useful to override breadcrumbing for marketing reasons. The idea might be that if the user can't tell they have been to a certain page before, they might be encouraged to revisit. While it might seem a good idea at first to encourage multiple page views, consider the frustration of a user going around in circles revisiting pages they already saw before.

Rule: Never completely remove a visited-link indication.

Link Type	Standard Color	HTML Tag	CSS Pseudoclass Rule
Unvisited	Blue	**<body link="*colorvalue*">**	a:link {color: *colorvalue;*}
Visited	Purple	**<body vlink="*colorvalue*">**	a:visited {color: *colorvalue;*}
Hover	N/A	N/A	a:hover {color: *colorvalue;*}
Active	Red	**<body alink="*colorvalue*">**	a:active {color: *colorvalue;*}

Table 8-2.   *Link Types and Colors*

Another reason for changing link colors might be for aesthetics. The blue or purple color combination just might not fit with corporate colors. Of course, once changed, the visited links may look better to some, but the end user might not recognize links or know which links they have visited before.

Rule: Avoid changing link colors.

If link colors must be changed for some reason, always make sure there is a great contrast between unvisited and visited links. Also, make sure that link colors contrast enough with background colors to easily be seen. Poor color choices can make a site difficult to use for most people and impossible for those with any vision impairment. For a more in-depth discussion of color use on the Web, see Chapter 13.

Link Decoration

Under common browsers, links are often indicated not only by color but also by underlining. The second form of feedback is useful particularly when users are not sensitive to color changes. Therefore, designers should be sensitive to the use of underlines in design. The HTML **<u>** tag and the CSS **text-decoration** property both can be used to create underlines, like so:

```
<u>This looks like a link</u><br />
<span style="text-decoration: underline">
This also looks like a link</span>
```

Unfortunately, this type of text can confuse a user who attempts to click it thinking that it is a link, which inspires the following design rule:

Rule: Avoid underlining non-linked text in Web documents—use italics or bold instead.

While underlining is useful to provide a second form of link feedback beyond color, a page filled with underlined text often does not look terribly pleasing. Because of this, many people opt to turn off link underlining in their browser preferences. Users who do this should not be a primary concern, but they do provide an additional reason not to alter link color significantly. However, with CSS, it is now possible for designers to turn off text link decoration themselves with the **text-decoration** property, as shown by the following rule:

```
a    {text-decoration: none;}
```

Of course, this could make it very difficult for users to determine what is linked text. Another form of feedback should be added to linked text, such as changing its font family, size, style, or background color. For example, after turning underlines off, linked text could be indicated by using slightly larger text, bold text, italic text, a varied text style such as small caps, changing background colors, or even changing the font family in use. Some designers believe that it will help to set the hover state like so:

```
a     {text-decoration: none;}
a:hover {text-decoration: underline; color: red;}
```

However, it really doesn't help. While links will change as users move around the page, they will have to find what is hot and what is not.

As discussed in Chapter 12, when using text it is important to set up a clear type hierarchy and provide enough of a difference between font size, style, and family for a user to clearly distinguish differences. When the changes are subtle, the link text will look too similar to the normal text and confuse the user.

Suggestion: Avoid automatically turning off link underlining. If you do, add another link indicator form.

Link Feedback: Cursors

Often, browsers will indicate that something is a link or is pressable by changing the cursor. In most GUI systems, the typical cursor is an arrow or pointer that changes to a hand when something can be clicked or an I-beam when something can be typed into (such as a form field). CSS2 introduced the ability to change the cursor for an element using the **cursor** property.

For example, to set the cursor when a user moves over a **<b>** tag to make it appear pressable, you might use a style rule like the following:

```
<b style="cursor: hand">Can you press me?</b>
```

CSS2 defines a variety of cursors, as shown in Table 8-3.

 *The common value **hand** is actually not CSS2 defined but is supported in Internet Explorer.*

The CSS3 specification proposes a variety of new cursor property values, as shown in Table 8-4.

 Typical renderings for CSS3 cursor values were not possible, since no browser supported these values at the time of this edition's writing.

CSS Cursor Property Values	Description	Typical Rendering
auto	The browser determines the cursor to display based on the current context	N/A
crosshair	A simple crosshair generally resembles a plus symbol.	
default	The browser's default cursor is generally an arrow.	
hand	This displays the cursor as a hand (Not standard but commonly supported).	
move	This indicates something is to be moved; usually rendered as four arrows together.	
e-resize	This indicates resizing as a double arrow pointing east–west (left–right).	
ne-resize	This indicates resizing as a double arrow pointing northeast–southwest.	
nw-resize	This indicates resizing as a double arrow pointing northwest-southeast.	
n-resize	This indicates resizing as a double arrow pointing north–south.	
se-resize	This indicates resizing as a double arrow pointing southeast–northwest.	
sw-resize	This indicates resizing as a double arrow pointing southwest–northeast.	
s-resize	This indicates resizing as a double arrow pointing north–south.	
w-resize	This indicates resizing as a double arrow pointing west–east.	
text	This indicates text that may be selected or entered; generally rendered as an I-bar.	
wait	This indicates that the page is busy; generally rendered as an hourglass.	
help	This indicates that Help is available; the cursor is generally rendered as an arrow and a question mark.	

Table 8-3. *CSS2 Cursors and Typical Renderings*

CSS3 Cursor Property	Meaning
copy	Indicates something is to be copied. Could be rendered as an arrow with a small plus sign next to it.
alias	Indicates an alias or shortcut to something. Often rendered as an arrow with a small curved arrow next to it.
context menu	This cursor shows a context menu, usually selected with a secondary mouse button available for the object. Often rendered as an arrow with a small menu graphic next to it.
cell	Indicates that a cell or set of cells may be selected. Should be rendered as a thick plus sign.
grab	Indicates that the object could be grabbed. Should be rendered as an open hand.
grabbing	Indicates that the object has been grabbed. Should be rendered as a closed hand.
spinning	Indicates that the program is performing a task. Similar to the **wait** property, but the user may still be able to interact with the program. A variety of renderings, including a spinning beach ball, are possible.
count-up	Indicates that the system is performing a counting up operation. Could be rendered as finger counting.
count-down	Indicates that the program is performing a count down operation. Like count up, could be rendered as fingers.
count-up-down	Indicates that the program is alternately counting up and then counting down.

Table 8-4.   *CSS3 Cursor Properties*

Custom Cursors

CSS2 defines the ability to define a custom cursor. On a Windows system, cursors are defined using a .cur file, which is a 32 × 32 or smaller bitmap—generally with 16 colors. Cursors are also occasionally animated, and in such cases may have an .ani file extension. According to the CSS2 specification, a browser should retrieve a cursor file from a specified URL—similar to retrieving a font. The property takes a list of cursor values separated by commas. So the CSS rule,

```
#specialcursor   {cursor: url("robot.cur"),
                   url("robot.csr"), default;}
```

would specify to set the cursor to either robot.cur, robot.csr, or the default cursor when the user's mouse passes over the element whose **id** attribute is set to **specialcursor**. Internet Explorer 6 supports custom cursors, as demonstrated here:

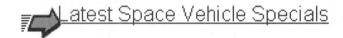

  Comet Systems (http://www.cometsystems.com and http://www.cometzone.com) supports both an ActiveX control as well as a Netscape plug-in that can provide custom cursors for older browsers.

However, be aware that, as with changing link color, changing the cursor may leave some users confused about the meaning of a pressable region.

Links and Ellipses

In graphical interfaces, ellipses (…) are often used to indicate that something more will happen when a user selects a particular command—usually that more input is required. However, this idea does not translate well to the Web. Consider that nearly all links have something behind them, and the user expects this. Probably the only time you should use ellipses is when the page will simply open another page that contains a large number of choices and little content. Today, few sites use ellipses, except occasionally when using teaser excerpts that lead to more information, as shown here.

Gravity Defeated

Today the DemoCorporation announced that gravity has been defeated.

Dr. R. Smart boasted that his anti-Newton drive would turn the

Personal space craft industry on its head. [More...]

Conventions may change, but for now ellipses should be avoided in most cases.

Suggestion: Avoid using ellipses in links, as they are generally redundant.

Rollovers

A very common link feedback mechanism to show something is active is called the *rollover*. A rollover link is a link that activates in some fashion, usually with a color or shape change, when the user's mouse is positioned over it. While the use of rollovers is so common on the Web that they have become a cliché, they can be useful to provide more feedback to a user, add a little spice to a page, and— in very well-done cases— provide more information about a link's purpose.

The simplest way to make a rollover link is to activate text links using the CSS2 **a:hover** pseudoclass in a **<style>** tag, as shown here:

```
<style type="text/css">
<!--
a:hover {color: #ff0000;}
-->
</style>
```

In this case, any text link will turn red when users place their mouse over the linked text. Using a style sheet rule, it is possible to change the link to show a variety of changes, such as text size or style. Designers are cautioned to avoid too dramatic of a roll effect, as the browser may have to repaint the page in a very obvious way as the user rolls on the link.

It is also possible to create basic text rollovers for graphical buttons using JavaScript. These types of rollovers work basically in the following fashion.

1. Create a regular graphic button.

2. Next, create an activated version of the button about the same size.

3. Finally, add a JavaScript that swaps the normal image button for its activated image when the user's mouse passes over it and changes it back to the normal state when the user passes off the button.

The JavaScript code is relatively simple to write, and requires only that the images be loaded in first and that support for the JavaScript Image object be determined. The following code illustrates the basic rollover:

```
<!DOCTYPE html PUBLIC "-//W3C//DTD XHTML 1.0 Transitional//EN"
"http://www.w3.org/TR/xhtml1/DTD/xhtml1-transitional.dtd">
<html xmlns="http://www.w3.org/1999/xhtml">
<head>
<title>Simple Rollover</title>
<script type="text/javascript">
```

```
<!--
/* Preload the images */

if (document.images)
  {
    abouton = new Image(85, 48);
    abouton.src = "images/abouton.gif";
    aboutoff = new Image(85, 48);
    aboutoff.src = "images/about.gif";
  }

function rollOn(imgName)
{
   if (document.images)
        document [imgName].src = eval(imgName + "on.src");
}

function rollOff(imgName)
{
   if (document.images)
        document [imgName].src = eval(imgName + "off.src");
}

// -->
</script>
</head>
<body>

<a href="about.htm"
   onmouseover="rollOn('about')"
   onmouseout="rollOff('about')">
<img src="images/about.gif" width="85" height="48"
     border="0" alt="About" name="about" id="about" />
</a>

</body>
</html>
```

To use the code, simply add a new **<img>** tag with proper **height** and **width** attributes. Make sure to name your **<img>** element. Then add the preloading code

SITE ORGANIZATION AND NAVIGATION

to load the *on* state for the image. So, to add another button for a "products" button, you would add

```
producton = new Image(85, 48);
producton.src = "images/producton.gif";
productoff = new Image(85, 48);
productoff.src = "images/product.gif";
```

in the preloading section of the JavaScript. Within the **<body>**, add another link to an image, like this:

```
   <a href="products.htm"
onmouseover="rollOn('products')"
onmouseout="rollOff('products')">
   <img src="images/product.gif"
width="85" height="48" border="0" alt="Products"
name="products" id="products">
   </a>
```

The script should work in Netscape 3.0 versions and beyond and Internet Explorer 4.0 versions and beyond. The only problem with using the script is making sure to name the images properly. If you are not interested in adding this type of script by hand to your document, many Web editors, including Macromedia Dreamweaver, support the addition of such scripts, and it's often just a matter of running a command like "Insert Rollover Image" and selecting the appropriate image states. Figure 8-10 shows the Dreamweaver dialog box using similar data from the previous example.

Graphic button states should be the same as text link states—unvisited, active, visited, and the new state—hover. Despite this, many sites lack all the states for their buttons. The main reason for this is that for graphical buttons, each extra state causes more images to be downloaded. Because of this, consider the following design suggestion:

> **Suggestion: Graphical buttons should have at a minimum an unselected and a selected state. Mouseover states and active press states should be considered optional.**

When used properly, rollovers are useful because they further let the user know that the object is active. Most of the time, rollovers are somewhat gimmicky—just making text glow or a button change shape. However, in some situations, rollovers can

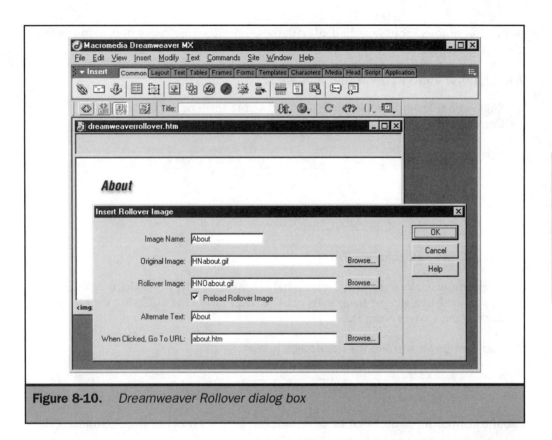

Figure 8-10. *Dreamweaver Rollover dialog box*

be used to let a user know what is about to load by revealing some descriptive text. When used in this fashion, a rollover effect can actually make buttons more usable.

Understanding User Expectations

For users, possibly one of the most annoying aspects of using a Web site (beyond slow-loading pages) is choosing a page and then not getting the information expected. From a user's perspective, each link represents a door, and the link label is supposed to indicate what is beyond each door. When users aren't sure what is behind a link, they are forced to try the link—and potentially return back if it wasn't what they were looking for. At first, this might sound somewhat fun—almost like exploring, but after a while it can become very frustrating.

Site designers should always strive to let the user know what they will see when they press a link. When faced with a link, the user might ask the questions shown next.

A few suggestions about how to deal with these questions are presented, along with illustrated examples.

What kind of content does this link load?

Suggestion: Provide good labels indicating the form of the content. Consider using icons to show content types.

Datasheet – robot235.pdf (Adobe Acrobat Format)

 Robot Datasheet

Where will the link take me?

Suggestion: Make sure to indicate whether the link will jump them within a page, within a site, or to an external site. Don't hide the URL; the user may deduce the answer from it.

Use up and down arrows for intrapage jumps.

Back to Top ↲ | Spec Sheet ↴

Label external links as such or use an icon. Leave all other links alone so the user assumes they are normal internal site links.

Demo Company Partners [outside link]

Demo Company 🌐

Will it mean a long download?

Suggestion: Indicate an external link by exposing the URL or using an icon. Indicate file size if triggering a download.

Specification.pdf (854K)

Will it cost money?

Suggestion: Use an icon or symbols, or issue an Alert dialog before the link.

$ sign-up today $

Specification **(payment required)**

Is the linked content fresh?

Suggestion: Avoid changing visited link colors. Add the last modification date, where necessary. Use a "New" icon.

Printer drivers [Updated 1/6/02]

NEW Specifications

Is the link going to take them to a secure or password-restricted area?

🔒 Login

Is the content potentially offensive?

Suggestion: Use an alert, or warn with an obvious label.

The key to most of these questions is to label a link properly. While links themselves sometimes have to be short—using the **title** attribute, a text rollover or extra scope notes information can be provided to the user. The status bar also presents a place for informing the user of a link's destination. Each of these approaches will be discussed in turn.

Using Scope Notes

One of the best ways to let users know about the meaning of a link, beyond good labeling, is through the use of *scope notes*. Scope notes provide a description of what a link means as well as other contextual information. Consider a link label like "About." We could add scope notes to clarify the meaning of the label, as shown here:

About

Information about Demo Company including corporate history, press releases, and self congratulating biographies.

Make sure to set your scope notes in a smaller font or a different style, so as not to overwhelm the primary link.

It is possible to increase the benefits of scope notes by providing skip-ahead links within the description text, like so:

> About
>
> Information about Demo Company including corporate history,
> press releases, and self congratulating biographies.

The only major downside to scope notes is that they may clutter up a layout or take focus away from important items on a page. In some sense, the scope notes are like help information. They really are the most use to those who are looking for more information. Because of the potential drawbacks, many designers decide to hide scope notes and reveal them only when a user passes over or invokes a link.

In general, you should avoid putting skip-ahead links in scope notes that are revealed. It is very annoying for a user to try to ensure their mouse does not make the scope note disappear as the user moves to click the newly revealed link. So, if you are including skip-ahead links in your rollovers, ensure that the scope note stays revealed once users pass their mouse over it.

title Attribute

The simplest form of revealed scope note is the ToolTip information provided by the **title** attribute. Set the **title** attribute for a link to any desired text, as shown here:

```
<a href="about.htm" title="Information about Demo Company including
corporate history, press releases, and self congratulating
biographies.">About</a>
```

When the user holds his or her mouse over the link, the extra link information should appear like so:

The link titles should provide more information about what the link will do, but should not be so verbose as to be ignored. Try to make link titles short and scannable—maybe 10 to 15 words, or around 60 to 80 characters maximum.

Be careful with long link titles, as some older browsers will not wrap title information, and scope information could be clipped.

When using graphical text buttons, there may be some question as to whether **alt** or **title** attribute text will show. In a well-behaved browser, the alternative text defined by **alt** is shown when images are loading or when the images are off, or while the **title** is shown on mouseover. Of course, not all browsers may follow this specified meaning, so you may consider making the **title** and **alt** attribute information the same, if necessary.

Rollover Messages

It is possible using rollovers to reveal text or imagery someplace else on the screen as the user mouses over a link. A script can be written to reveal a scope note as well as change the state of the link, as shown in Figure 8-11.

Generally, designers are encouraged to use rollovers that reveal extra information; but always remember that, like multiple state rollovers, rollover messages can be

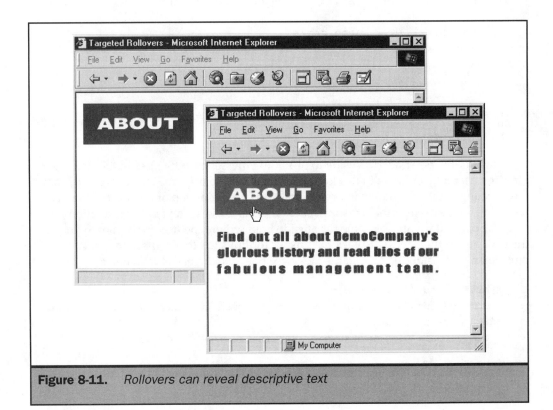

Figure 8-11.   *Rollovers can reveal descriptive text*

troublesome because they require numerous images. Fortunately, using style sheets, lightweight rollover messages can be built.

Status Bar Messages

It is possible to show link results in the status bar at the bottom of the browser window. Generally, a browser will display the destination URL in the status bar, but it is possible to customize this using a short JavaScript to have a custom message when a user passes his or her mouse over the link, as shown here.

A few sample links showing how to do this are given next; just change the string in single quotes to the appropriate message:

```
<a href="http://www.democompany.com/"
    onmouseover="window.status='Visit Demo Company, home of the
Robot Butler!'; return true;"
    onMouseout="window.status='';return true;">Demo Company</a><br>

<a href="http://www.yahoo.com/"
    onmouseover="window.status='Have you been to Yahoo! today?';
return true;"
    onmouseout="window.status='';return true;">Yahoo!</a><br>
```

Note *The **onmouseover** code must return a **true** value; otherwise, the status message will not display.*

Consider the potential downside to providing messages to the user in the status bar. First, the user may not look in this location. Second, if the user does look here, they may be expecting URL information in order to make a determination of link destination. Far too often, the status information shown here repeats the basic text link information. This could be particularly troublesome for outside links, where the user may want to know the URL before they decide to click the link, or for links to other content forms. With outside links, consider using a status message style, like the one shown here:

```
<a href="http://www.yahoo.com/"
    onmouseover="window.status='Have you been to Yahoo! (www.yahoo.com)
today?'; return true;"
    onmouseout="window.status='';return true;">Yahoo!</a>
```

Suggestion: When using status bar messages, consider providing URL information with the text when linking externally.

In many ways, providing status bar messages is redundant, because the same information could be provided in a **title** attribute, as shown here:

```
<a href="http://www.yahoo.com/"
    title="Have you been to Yahoo! (www.yahoo.com) today?">Yahoo!</a>
```

In this particular example, the ToolTip will even show the destination URL directly where the user's mouse is focused, as well as in the user's status bar. Of course, such redundancy may become annoying to users. Probably the only real upside to the status bar message is that it will work on older JavaScript-aware browsers that do not support the **title** attribute.

Keyboard Support for Links

Designers should always strive to make sites usable and accessible by all. Remember that some users may find the mouse difficult to use or prefer to use a keyboard. Links should be easily invoked using keyboard commands. Most browsers support tabbing of links, and some already support accelerator keys.

The HTML 4.0 specification adds the **accesskey** attribute to the **<a>** tag as well as to various form elements. With this attribute, it is possible to set a key to invoke an anchor without requiring a pointing device to select the link. The link is activated with the combination of the accelerator key, usually ALT, and the key specified by the attribute. Therefore,

```
<a href="http://www.yahoo.com" accesskey="Y">Yahoo!</a>
```

makes a link to Yahoo!, which can be activated by pressing ALT-Y under compliant browsers like Internet Explorer 4.*x* and greater and Netscape 6.*x* and greater.

Note *You may find that the primary browser window has to be selected before accelerator keys become active.*

While adding keyboard access to a Web page would seem a dramatic improvement, HTML authors are cautioned to be aware of access key bindings in the browsing environment. Assuming the major browsers support the **accesskey** attribute, page authors would be cautioned to stay away from accelerators using the keys for the common menus in browsers presented in Table 8-5.

One other problem with accelerator keys is how to show them in the page. Generally, in software, the letter of the accelerator key is indicated by underlining. Of course, links are generally underlined in browsers, so this approach is not feasible. It is possible with

SITE ORGANIZATION AND NAVIGATION

Key	Description
F	File menu
E	Edit menu
V	View menu
N	Navigation menu (Opera 6)
G	Go menu (Netscape/Mozilla) Messaging menu (Opera 6)
B	Bookmarks menu (Netscape/Mozilla only)
A	Favorites menu (Internet Explorer Only)
T	Tools or Tasks menu
M	E-mail menu (Opera 6)
S	Search menu (Netscape 6), News menu (Opera 6)
W	Window menu (Netscape 7/Mozilla)
A	Favorites menu (Internet Explorer Only)
H	Help

Table 8-5.   *Browser Reserved Accelerator Keys*

style sheets to change link direction, so underlining the first letter is possible, but then the user may be disoriented because they expect links to be fully underlined. Another approach to indicating the accelerator key might be to set the access key letter of a text link in bold or slightly larger size. Designers are encouraged to adopt whatever notation becomes standard on Web pages.

It is possible to use the **tabindex** attribute of the **<a>** tag to define the order that links will be tabbed through in a browser that supports keyboard navigation. The value of **tabindex** is typically a positive number. A browser will tab through links with increasing **tabindex** values, but will generally skip over those with negative values. So, **<a href="about.htm" tabindex="1">** sets this link to be the first thing tabbed to. If the **tabindex** attribute is undefined, the browser will tend to tab through links in the order in which they are found within an HTML document.

Advanced Web Linking Models

Today, the Web exhibits a very simple linking model; however, that may change in the future. HTML 4.0 introduces the **<link>** element, which can be used to define linking relationships between documents. The most common way that the **<link>** element is used is when associating a style sheet to a Web page, as shown in this example:

```
<link rel="stylesheet" href="corporate.css" />
```

A **<link>** element like this is found in the **<head>** of an HTML document.

It is possible, however, to specify any arbitrary relationship using the **rel** attributes. For example, using **<link>,** we might define which document is likely to be clicked next, like so:

```
<link rel="next" href="nextpage.htm" />
```

Some newer browsers, notably Mozilla, have begun to support **<link>** either natively or through add-ons. However, until browsers support more link types, the simple linking model will have to suffice.

Link Maintenance

Even when links are used correctly within a site and a user understands the meaning of each link perfectly, links will require maintenance. One approach is not to let broken links enter a site in the first place. A site that uses dynamic links can avoid broken links because, as pages are added, all links are adjusted. However, most sites do not employ dynamic links, so invariably, over time, content changes and internal links may break. More commonly, links to external sites will break as other sites move their pages without considering outside linkage.

Ferreting out the broken links within a site can be tedious, but doing so should be a top priority. A broken link should be considered a serious problem. Users clicking a broken link are on the road to nowhere, eventually to receive the now infamous "404 Not Found" message or something similar. Imagine if a menu on a software application triggered a message saying "Sorry—spell check not found!" Such failures would not be tolerated in software and should be considered as serious a problem in a site.

Rule: Broken links should be considered catastrophic failures.

Fortunately, identifying and fixing broken links isn't terribly difficult. Armed with a maintenance tool, finding broken links is a simple matter. However, if you have

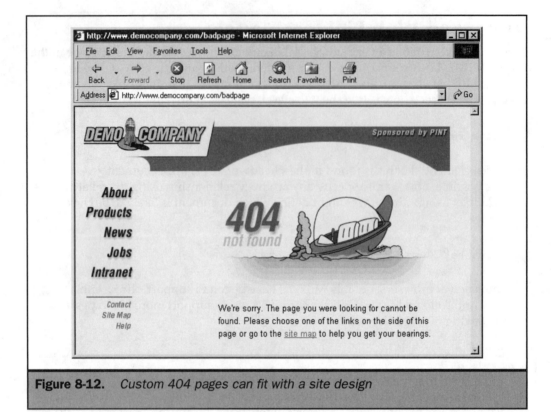

Figure 8-12. *Custom 404 pages can fit with a site design*

external links within a site, even constant monitoring isn't going to keep broken links out of the site at all times. To account for the unforeseen broken link, consider installing a custom 404 page. Then, put information such as a link to a site map or a method to contact the site's administrator in the custom error page. An example custom 404 page is shown in Figure 8-12.

 Installation of a custom 404 error page depends on the server being utilized and may require special configuration.

Redirection Pages

Rather than show errors, many sites prefer to redirect users to new pages. If the content at a URL has moved to a new location, it is best to install a page that points people to the new page or even quickly redirects them there. Some site maintainers prefer to send people directly to the new page while others will install a temporary page informing visitors of the page change, like the one shown in Figure 8-13.

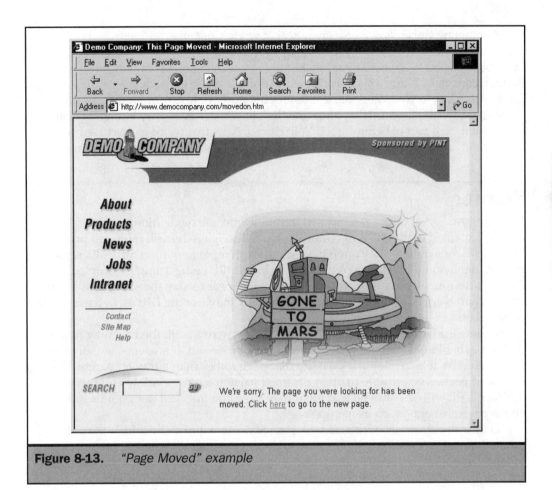

Figure 8-13.   *"Page Moved" example*

Sending people directly to the new page may be seamless, but it does take some control away from the user. For example, if the user requests a particular page on, say, robotic dogs, and a redirect takes them to a different page, the user will become very frustrated. Always make sure that the new page is related to the moved page.

Redirection and 404s

Some sites prefer to send users directly to the home page of the site if they request a page that no longer exists. This is not a recommended approach, since it may confuse users. Errors are inevitable, and users will make them. A goal of a site designer should be to soften the blow and help users avoid making errors—not take control away from them. Further, instant redirection for bad page requests will not encourage a site maintainer to address the reason behind the errors.

Suggestion: Avoid automatic redirects for 404 errors.

Maintaining site links can be a great deal of work. Custom error pages and redirection pages can help, but Web managers will have to be ever vigilant in link monitoring. Good Web sites should make sure to watch log files for referring sites. Further, consider visiting a search engine and doing a reverse search. Specifically, search for sites that link to yours and make sure they are up-to-date on any significant site changes made. Making sure that other sites link to you correctly may be a great deal of work, but it is all part of being a good Web citizen. Now that we have discussed basic linking and its management fully, let's turn to a wrinkle in Web navigation: frames.

Frames

The much-maligned frame can introduce trouble into site navigation, particularly if not implemented correctly. While frames may reduce page refresh rates and provide for complex navigation, they often have significant implementation difficulties. Also, they fundamentally break the Web rule of a single URL being a single document. In fact, in most framed environments, the URL will appear to stay the same. This can be a serious problem when you consider that the user may use the URL to determine his or her location.

Because the URL does not change in a framed environment, the user may find it difficult to bookmark interior pages. This may be by design, but users generally feel they should be able to bookmark a particular page rather than a framed parent. Even advanced users who are able to open a framed page in a new window and bookmark the deep URL will be annoyed that what they have bookmarked does not include all the page elements, such as navigation.

Because the browser window is split, framed documents can be difficult to print. To print a framed page, the user must know to click in the framed region before printing. Many sites that use frames do not make the various regions of the frames obvious, so the user may have problems knowing what region to click in order to print.

Last, many designers have found out the hard way that search engines do not work well with frame designs and may not be able to index site contents or follow links. Because of these limitations, some designers have abandoned frames altogether. This is unfortunate, since it is possible to deal with most of the problems presented. In fact, the real problem with frames is that they are difficult to implement properly, particularly if you want to address all their shortcomings. When using frames, it is easy to screw up your site.

While frames can be difficult for some users, people—both designers and users— are becoming more used to frames, and common forms of frame have begun to appear. Further, it is possible to get around many of the limitations of frames mentioned in the preceding paragraphs, such as bookmarking and fixed URLs. Unfortunately, the solution often comes at the loss of frame benefits, such as the decrease in screen refreshes, or with an increased reliance on scripting. Improvement in Web browsers will also solve some frame problems. Already, Internet Explorer provides much better support for printing frames. However, despite all the potential advances in frame technology, the main problem continues to be sloppy execution.

Using Frames

This section will discuss frame use as, well as some techniques to avoid problems. However, for a full discussion of frame syntax, readers are directed to the companion book, *HTML: The Complete Reference*. The first thing to consider is whether you even need to use frames. Remember, frames are navigation devices, so you should only be using them when you are trying to create regions such as control bars that load other portions of the screen—not when you are attempting to create some sophisticated layout.

> **Suggestion: Avoid using frames for layout. Use them for navigation.**

If it makes sense to use frames, stick to the styles shown in Figure 8-14. It is likely that a user will have encountered one of these common styles; thus, many of the negative effects of not knowing what will update when things are clicked will be alleviated by plain experience.

The common feature of all these frame layouts is that the little regions control the big regions. This makes sense, considering navigation should always be smaller than the content presented. Also, the regions tend to control regions that are adjacent or below them.

> **Suggestion: When using frames, make smaller frames control larger adjacent frames.**

Besides the two-, three-, and four-frame layouts, many designers opt for a fixed-frame layout style similar to a picture frame, with the content fixed in the middle of the screen. This is often done more for its dramatic layout than for navigation. Unfortunately, despite its potential for a unique layout, such a design can be problematic—particularly given subtle layout problems with frames under the various browsers. While future browsers may solve such problems, do not underestimate the not-so-subtle frame-rendering differences in browsers. In reality, frames should not be used for layout—CSS should be.

Printing Frames

The best suggestion with printing frames is to make a design obvious enough so a user knows what region of the screen is in what frame. Users should be able to pick up on the problem and click in the region when printing. It is also possible to add a print button to a framed page.

Bookmarking Issues

Because frames show the URL of the frameset document and not the actual contents, it is often difficult for the user to bookmark the page. First, consider that you may not want people to bookmark some pages. Many complex e-commerce sites frame internal pages on purpose because they are often dynamically generated and may have very difficult URLs.

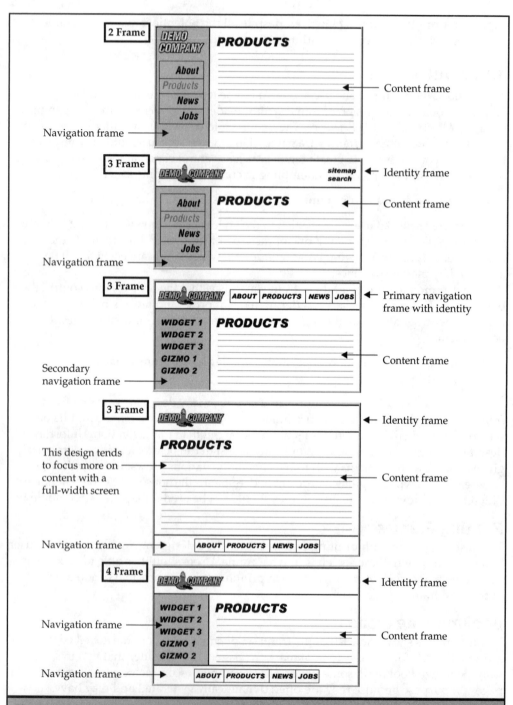

Figure 8-14.   *Common frame designs*

However, users often will try to bookmark a framed page and the browser will not show the correct page. For example, as shown in Figure 8-15, when users bookmark the page on the left, leave, and then return, they see the initial frameset on the right. Notice how the URL is the same in both the screens.

Fortunately, some of the newer browsers like Internet Explorer are able to deal with frame bookmarking problems and will not exhibit this problem. Of course, a more sophisticated user will figure out how to bookmark just the framed page. Unfortunately, they will find that they lose any contextual information, such as navigation, when they return, and that they have inadvertently created an orphan page where the user is unable to navigate without splicing the URL, as shown in Figure 8-16.

There are two approaches to get around the frame bookmark problem. The first is to create multiple framesets, each with a different URL that is bookmarkable. The problem with this approach is that you lose the reduced screen refresh benefit of frames and you are forced to create multiple documents. A better approach to the bookmarking problem is to use a scripting language to detect whether if the user is entering in an unframed page and dynamically rebuild the appropriate frameset, if necessary. For example, if you define your frameset for a section of the site with the file frameset.htm, you can use JavaScript to see if a page is within a frameset defined by that file. If it isn't, you can then

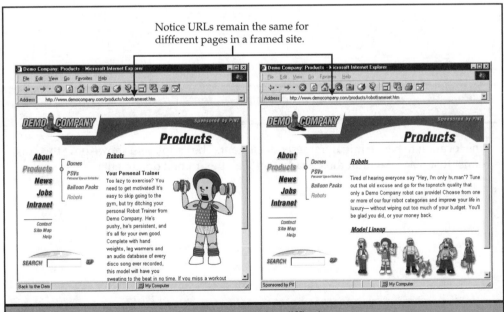

Figure 8-15.   *Bookmarking framesets may be difficult*

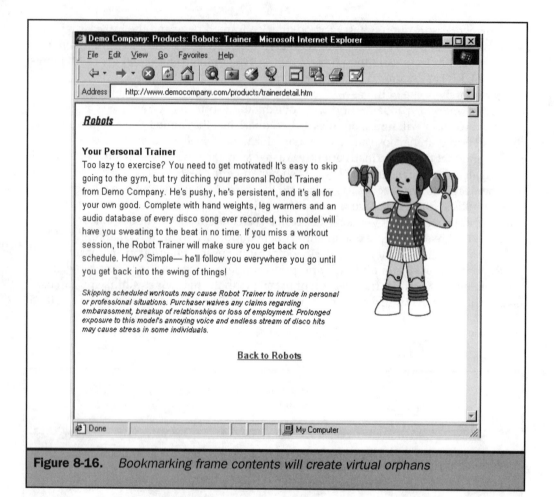

Figure 8-16.   *Bookmarking frame contents will create virtual orphans*

set the location to be the initial frameset document. The script here shows how this might be done. Just place it within the **<head>** tag of all the framed documents.

```
<script type="text/javascript">
<!--
 var containingwindow =
top.location.pathname.substring((top.location.pathname.lastIndexOf("/"))+1).
toLowerCase();

  if (containingwindow!="frameset.htm")
    top.location.replace("frameset.htm");

//-->
</script>
```

This script will not work if the user has gone deep into a frameset, since the regenerated frameset will point to the initial document in the frameset. What we would have to do instead is dynamically generate the frameset itself, based on the page that was not within its frames. The following files illustrate how this is done. Make sure that you run this example from a live Web server. If you don't, it generally won't work because the URL will not be formed normally.

File: frameset.htm

```
<!DOCTYPE html PUBLIC "-//W3C//DTD XHTML 1.0 Frameset//EN">
<html xmlns="http://www.w3.org/1999/xhtml">
<head>
<title>Dynamic Frames Demo</title>
</head>
<script>
<!--
  function getPage()
  {
   return unescape( window.location.search.substring(window.location.search.
indexOf("=")+1));
  }

  document.write('<frameset cols="100,*">');
  document.write('<frame src="controls.htm" name="controls">');
  if (window.location.search=="")
    document.write('<frame name="display" src="page1.htm">');
  else
    document.write('<frame name="display" src="'+getPage()+' ">');
  document.write("</frameset>");
// -->
</script>
</html>
```

File: controls.htm

```
<!DOCTYPE html PUBLIC "-//W3C//DTD XHTML 1.0 Transitional//EN"
"http://www.w3.org/TR/xhtml1/DTD/xhtml1-transitional.dtd">

<html xmlns="http://www.w3.org/1999/xhtml">
<head>
<title>Control Frame</title>
</head>
<body>
<a href="page1.htm" target="display">Page 1</a><br>
```

```
<a href="page2.htm" target="display">Page 2</a><br>
<a href="page3.htm" target="display">Page 3</a><br>
</body>
</html>
```

File: Page1.htm

```
<!DOCTYPE html PUBLIC "-//W3C//DTD XHTML 1.0 Transitional//EN"
"http://www.w3.org/TR/xhtml1/DTD/xhtml1-transitional.dtd">
<html xmlns="http://www.w3.org/1999/xhtml">
<head>
<title>Page 1</title>
<script>
<!--
var container = "frameset.htm";
var wname = top.location.pathname.substring((top.location.pathname.
lastIndexOf("/"))+1).toLowerCase();
if (wname!=container)
    parent.location.replace(container +

"?display="+escape(this.location));
// -->
</script>
</head>
<body>
<h1 align="center">Page 1</h1>
</body>
</html>
```

The other files, page2.htm and page3.htm, are exactly the same as page1.htm. Just change their titles and headings so you can tell the difference. The key to this demonstration is bookmarking an individual framed page. Select a framed page like page1.htm and directly bookmark it. Now, when you return to the page, it should automatically generate the surrounding frameset, so the page is not orphaned. The only downside to this technique, which can also be accomplished using a server-side technology, is that it causes an extra round-trip to the server to rebuild the frameset.

> **Weblink: For a live example of the dynamic frameset, see the examples at http://www.webdesignref.com/.**

Layout Issues

When using frames for layout or for navigation, it is important not to be too restrictive. Many designers turn off frame borders, turn off scrolling for all frames except the content frame, and restrict resizing of the frames by the user. While doing all this may create a nice-looking layout, consider what happens for a user whose screen isn't large enough to hold the frameset in its entirety. If you are not using screen resolution sensing, you should be careful when turning off frame resizing and scrolling. About the only time you should do this is when you set the size of a navigation frame exactly equal to the minimum size of its buttons.

Suggestion: Do not turn off frame resizing and scrolling unless resolution is very well accounted for.

Frame borders are another issue. Keeping the borders on a framed environment may make it more obvious where the frames are, but could result in a less than optimal layout, as shown by the examples in Figure 8-17. However, if the user will have to resize frames, it is a good idea to keep the frame's borders on.

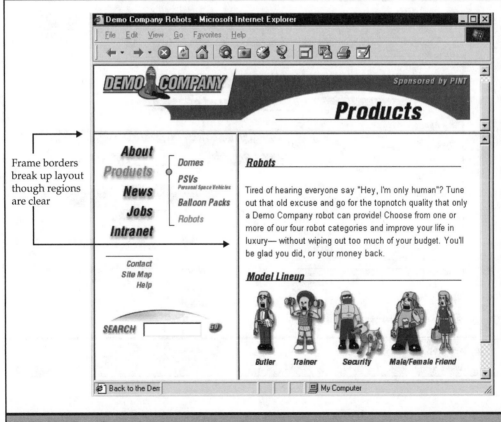

Figure 8-17.   *Frame borders can be ugly*

Frame Busting

A common problem with frames occurs when a frameset starts to appear within an existing frameset. Sometimes this is done on purpose by outside sites trying to capture the user. Other times, it is simply a mistake, and the frames begin to appear within themselves. This developer's mistake could be dubbed the "Russian dolls problem," after the famous Russian dolls that contain smaller and smaller identical dolls, as shown in Figure 8-18.

While you can clearly deal with the problem when caused by designer error, you might wonder how to keep users from framing your site. A simple way if you are not using frames in your own site is just to write your HTML to make sure that every link in your site has its **target** attribute set to **_top**, as shown here:

```
<a href="robots.htm" target="_top">Robots</a>
```

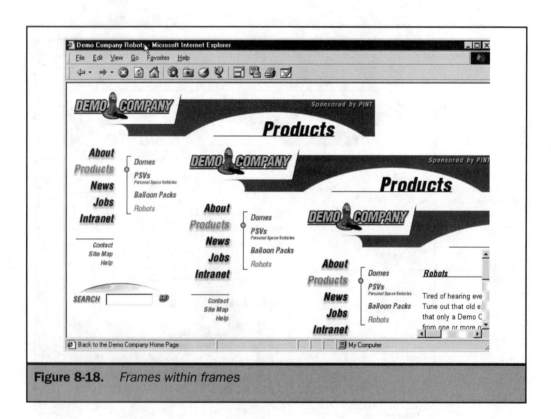

Figure 8-18.   *Frames within frames*

With this approach, any time a user is within a frameset, the next link loaded will load over the top of the existing frameset. This technique is often called "frame busting." Another approach is to use a short JavaScript to detect whether the page is framed and then bust out of the frames. This could be used even within a frameset document of your own, so you can use frames in your own site safely.

```
<script type="text/javascript">
<!--
if (window != top)
  top.location.href = location.href;
//-->
</script>
```

However, be careful with frame busting. While it may be true that the extra real estate gained will improve the layout, the user may want the framed environment. Consider that maybe the user was just taking a side trip to your site and wanted to keep the other site's navigation around in order to return easily to the old site. Again, the control issue rears its head. You could certainly write the script to check with the user whether or not they want to kill the frames, but this may annoy the user.

```
<script type="text/javascript">
<!--
if (window != top)
  if (confirm("Remove framing document?"))
    top.location.href = location.href;
//-->
</script>
```

\<noframes\>

A potentially serious problem with frames is that not all browsers support frames. Very old browsers, such as early versions of Netscape or Mosaic, as well as browsers found on network appliances or handheld devices, generally have limitations associated with frame pages. Further, many search engines will not index sites with frames. This could severely limit the site's ability to be listed with public search engines, as discussed in Chapter 9. If frames are used, make sure that at least some content is presented using the **\<noframes\>** tag within a frameset document. Users without frame support, as well as search engines, will be able to see this content, while typical users will see the framed site, as illustrated in Figure 8-19.

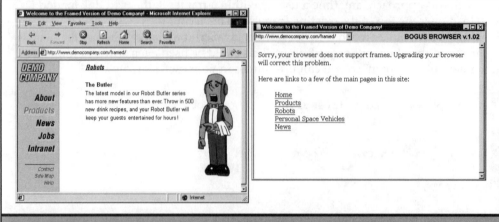

Figure 8-19.   *Users who don't support frames see a much different site*

Of course, dealing with both frame-supporting browsers and browsers that don't support frames may mean creating two versions of every page. Though this can be done dynamically, it may be expensive. However, before simply creating a **<noframes>** page that tells users to upgrade their browser, consider that the numerous users who seem to dislike frames with a serious passion might appreciate an unframed site.

Multiple Windows and Navigation

Using multiple windows onscreen can introduce some interesting navigation considerations. For example, consider the following link, which spawns another window:

```
<a href="http://www.yahoo.com"
onclick="newWindow=window.open('http://www.yahoo.com', 'subWindow1',
'height=200,width=300');return false;">Open Yahoo window</a>
```

In the case where JavaScript is on, you will get a pop-up window like the one shown in Figure 8-20.

Pop-ups can be useful for displaying status information, picture blow-ups, and a variety of other useful items. It is even possible for multiple spawned windows to load content into each other, as shown in Figure 8-21. In this case, we see that multiple windows really are the same thing as frames; they even use the **target** attribute on links. The only major difference is that bookmarking and printing might not be quite as difficult.

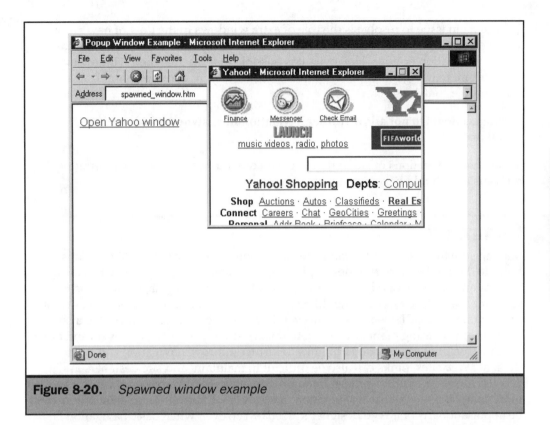

Figure 8-20.   *Spawned window example*

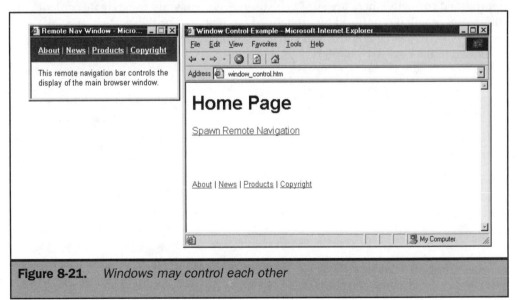

Figure 8-21.   *Windows may control each other*

The main issue to resolve is the role of extra windows in the flow of navigation. When designed correctly, a pop-up window must be dismissed and will have no further navigation options. However, it is possible that the spawned window may allow for more navigation or may even include history; in either case, navigation may become confusing.

Suggestion: Do not allow further navigation in spawned windows if at all possible.

Beyond navigation considerations, spawned windows may also be frustrating for users and should be avoided in most cases.

Summary

Making sure that users understand site navigation, particularly what the various links do, is an integral part of developing a usable site. There are many ways to add navigational links in a Web site, including text links, buttons, image maps, and even arbitrary hotspots. Designers should respect common link conventions such as color, underlining, and URL feedback. However, it is possible to change link styles in an aesthetically pleasing manner using both images and style sheets. Rollovers and other dynamic facilities can be added to links to further improve navigation and create dynamic Web sites. Links can also be difficult to maintain, and site designers are encouraged to account for broken links and moved pages. Frames and windows add more complexity to the basic navigation model but, with careful implementation, can be important parts of a Web designer's arsenal. Yet, even when basic navigation is approached correctly, there are sure to be users who will want to navigate content differently or will be confused by predefined navigation. For those users, special facilities such as search engines and site maps should be provided, and these are discussed in the next two chapters.

Chapter 9

Search

Many users will find browser-oriented navigation systems an inefficient way to find what they are looking for. Often, a user knows something exists and just needs to find it within a site. Search functions appeal to power users, frequent visitors, and the plain impatient, who are all looking to find a result quickly. A well-executed search facility is one major advantage a Web site has over printed media, as it gives users greater control over a site's content, allowing them to filter it to just what they want to see. Larger Web sites, especially those with complex data, must provide search facilities—and may consider making it the central navigation method. Searching facilities, however, must be designed with the user in mind. Before adding search to a site, give careful consideration to how users expect a search to work, the type of search required, the design of the search page, the help system, and the types of search-result listings.

How Users Search

Before getting into the theory of how search systems work and how to utilize both external and local search engines to improve site design, consider first how people actually use search facilities. People search for a variety of reasons. A big reason to search is to look for something known to exist. An example of known-item searching is when a user is looking for a particular part, like "RBA-4456." In this case, it is usually easy for the person to locate the item in question, assuming that the search facility has seen it before and particularly if the item is fairly uncommon.

Oftentimes, however, users may not know if the item they are searching for exists or not—in fact, they might just be searching to see *if* such an item exists. A query like "Robot shops" might be used for a general search that could have as its object the existence of a shop that repairs robots. Other times, a user may perform an exploratory search to get a sense of the extent of something. For example, a query for "Robot Butler" might be done not only for the existence of such a device, but to see the extent of sites offering information on a metallic servant. It would seem that known-item searching is what users would generally use search engines for, but, oddly, existence and exploratory searching are commonly employed.

Regardless of the reason for a search, users go through four basic steps.

Formulate a Query   Depending on the search facility being used, the query formed by the user may vary greatly. A simple query might include only keywords, like "Robot Butler." More complex queries might include Boolean queries like "Robot AND Butler." Many search engines utilize queries filled with symbols, such as "+Robot +Butler –Jeeves." The search facility may even support a natural language interface where the user can ask something like "Where can I buy a robot butler?" The query formulation might not just include the selection of various search words, but also may offer refinements to search criteria, such as indicating the areas to search, a date range to query, data types to search, and so on. Users may also at this point specify how they would like their results returned— say, for example, ten at a time, sorted by last update. However, further criteria beyond keywords are usually part of an advanced search and are usually performed only by more experienced users.

Execute the Search and Wait for the Result   The second step of searching usually consists of a simple button click, followed by a short wait for network round-trip time plus time required for the search engine to run the query and list the result. While there isn't much going on interactively during this phase, don't ignore it. The user views this as a discrete step in the process and will not wait around forever for results to appear.

Review the Results   Once the results have been listed onscreen, the user will peruse them to see if there is anything interesting in the list. During the review stage, the user will rely greatly on supplementary information, such as relevancy ranking and a description of the results including summaries, modification dates, and file sizes. During the review stage, the user may sort or filter the results in order to help them determine what to do. However, the actual decision concerning results will be influenced highly by what is actually returned by the query. Results will vary from the so-called negative result that contains no matches to the huge volumes of data when every document in a collection is returned. Most cases will be somewhere in between these extremes.

Decide What to Do with the Result   On the basis of the results, the user decides what to do. For example, if there are no results, the user may search again with a new query or may simply give up. If the search didn't appear to provide the correct answer, the user may also search again. When the search provides too many results, the user may try to refine the search. Maybe the user selects a few of the choices in the search results to examine. While there may be numerous variations, basically the user decides to explore some of the results, redo or refine the search, or just quit.

This basic overview is important to keep in mind when designing a search facility. Later in the chapter we'll present theory and practical design suggestions that deal with each step the user takes during the search process. However, before doing this we'll present an overview of how search engines function.

How Search Engines Work

So how do search engines work? First, a large number of pages are gathered off a Web site (or the Web at large, in the case of public search engines) using a process often called *spidering*. Next, the collected pages are indexed to determine what they are about. Finally, a search page is built where users can enter queries in and get results related to their queries. The best analogy for the process is that the search engine builds as big a haystack as possible, then tries to organize the haystack somehow, and finally lets the user try to find the proverbial needle in the resulting haystack of information by entering a query on a search page.

Gathering Pages

Every day the Web is growing by leaps and bounds. The true size of the Web is unknown, and it will undoubtedly increase even as you read this sentence. At any given moment numerous documents are added and others are removed. Gathering all the pages and keeping things up-to-date is certainly a significant chore. Users always want to know which search engine covers the most of the Web, but the truth is that today even the largest search engines index maybe only a third of the documents online. Some index only a few percent. This may change in the future, but for now be happy that not everything is indexed. The resulting mess of information to wade through would be even worse. In the case of local site search engines, the index might also not cover the entire site nor be updated often.

Most search engines use programs called *spiders*, *robots*, or *gathers* to collect pages of the Web for indexing. We'll use the term "spider" to mean any program that is used to gather Web pages. Spiders start their gathering process with a certain number of starting point URLs and work from there by following links. In the case of a public search engine, starting URLs are either submitted by people looking to get listed or built by forming URLs from domain names listed in the domain name registry. Local search engines work in the same way, but may be given a very small number of starting points if the site is well connected.

As the spider visits the various addresses in the list, it saves the pages or portions of the pages for analysis and looks for links to follow. For example, if a spider were visiting the URL http://www.democompany.com, it might see links emanating from this page and then decide to follow them. Not all search engines necessarily index pages deeply into a site, but most tend to follow links—particularly from pages that are well linked themselves or contain a great deal of content.

Indexing Pages

The next step search engines take is attempting to determine what a page is about. This is usually called *indexing*. The method each search engine uses varies, but basically an indexer looks at various components of a page, including possibly its **<title>**, the contents of its **<meta>** tags, comment text, link titles, text in headings, and body text. From this information it will try to distill the meaning of the page. Each aspect of a page might have different relevance, and within the actual text, the position or frequency of different words will be taken into account as well. However, not all content within a page matters to a search engine. For example, *stop words* are words that a search engine ignores, normally because they are assumed to be so common as to carry little useful information. Examples of stop words might be "the," "a," "an," and so on. Most search engines have some stop words, but some engines like AltaVista claim to even index common stop words like "the."

While the use of stop words may improve a search engine by limiting the size of the index file and focusing it on more content words, it may not match how users think about queries. Novice users may feel "The Best Butler Robot" is a better query than

"Best Butler Robot." Sometimes the stop word may be important to the search. Consider searching for a song title like "Rock the Town." "The" is an integral part of the term and without it many other songs may come up. However, if the search were for "Rock the Casbah," it would be easier to throw out the noise word "the," given that "Rock" and "Casbah" rarely occur near each other. Deciding what stop words should be used can be very problematic given the broad topic domain of many Web sites.

Once a page has been analyzed for the various keywords, it is ranked in relation to other pages with similar keywords and stored in a database. Ranking is the very secret part of search engine operation. How a particular search engine decides one page should be ranked higher than another is what search engine promotion specialists are always trying to figure out. A very popular way to rank pages today is based upon determined site landmarks. Home pages and major section pages may be given higher weight than other pages in a site. Pages that have numerous incoming links will also be given extremely high ranking.

Providing a Search Mechanism

The final aspect of a search engine is the search page itself. A search page is the interface the user makes their query from, and it generally contains a primary query text box as well as other search fields for advanced users who may want to modify a query. The degree of complexity of the search page varies greatly in public search engines. Consider the difference in interfaces between basic and advanced search pages for various public search engines shown in Figure 9-1.

Users can enter queries as simple natural language questions—like, "Why is the sky blue?" (as encouraged by sites like www.ask.com)—or as complex Boolean expressions using advanced filters. Once queried, the search engine will retrieve the pages that meet the criteria and present them on a result page. Figure 9-2 shows a result page for the search engine Google (www.google.com).

From the result page, users can pick some results to explore, further refine the search with a new query, or just give up and try another method to locate what they were hunting for. The general function of search engines is illustrated in Figure 9-3.

Understanding what people expect Web-wide search engines to do is important, because users will bring their past experiences with searching to bear when using your local site search. Labeling, form layout, and result pages should somewhat mimic what users have come to expect from the public search engines. However, be careful not to directly imitate what public engines do. Public search sites aim primarily to get users to starting points for searching, while local search facilities on a site aim to provide a high degree of search accuracy. In fact, public search engines aren't always terribly accurate. They are often geared towards the needs of advertisers and the demands of dealing with the numerous tricks people employ to try to improve their site's ranking.

> **Rule: Utilize past user experience with public search engines by using similar layout and labeling in local search facility design, but avoid imitating aspects of public search engines that deal with the uncontrollable nature of public Web sites.**

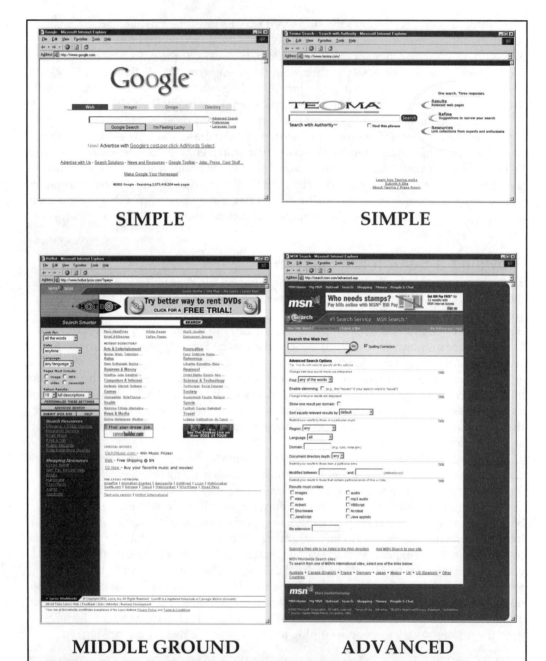

Figure 9-1. *Search interfaces may vary dramatically*

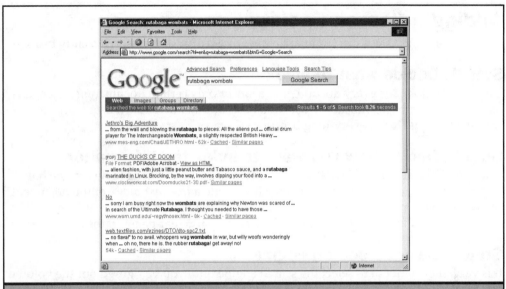

Figure 9-2.   *Google's result page is clean and simple*

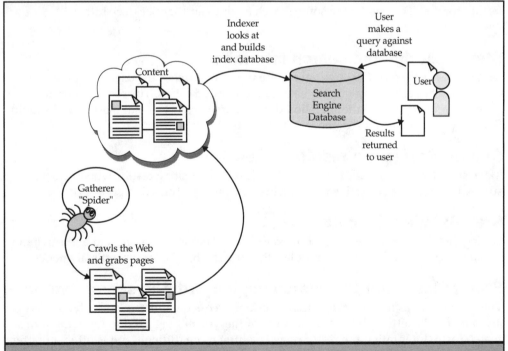

Figure 9-3.   *Overview of search engines*

Adding a Search Facility

The following eight steps can summarize the process of adding a search facility to a site.

Step 1: Decide what to index

Do you want to index every document in a site or only certain documents? Often, it is only a parts catalog, technical support database, or other area that a user wants to search. Don't just index everything because you can.

Step 2: Decide how you want to index the information

Once you have determined what you should index, you will need to determine how it will be indexed. Should the search engine just create a free text index of the document set, where every non stop-word is recorded, or would it be better to create a special search term vocabulary and relate search terms to particular pages in the site?

Step 3: Select a search engine

It is very important not to select the search engine until you've figured out the volume and type of information you wish to search, as well as how it will be indexed. There are numerous search engines available, both free and commercial. Search engines can be installed locally on your system or outsourced to third parties, who will run the search facility for you. For pointers to some search engines and services, see http://www.searchtools.com.

Step 4: Design the search interface

Design the search screen to account for the types of searches the user may perform. Often, searches are separated into basic and advanced forms. The search interface should be integrated into the site, should meet the search needs of the users, and should fit the type of data being searched.

Step 5: Design the results pages

Make sure to consider building pages that deal with positive results when a query is successful, as well as negative results when nothing is returned.

Step 6: Index the data

During this step, the search engine is used to *crawl* all or part of the site and build an index. You may actually be forced to manipulate the index by hand to create optimal queries.

Step 7: Integrate the search engine with the search interface

This step involves making the search interface access the index. Generally, this is just a matter of setting the *action* attribute of the <form> tag used to implement the search form. Integrating the result page is a little more difficult, but is often a matter of taking the designed result page and making it into a special template the search engine can read.

Step 8: Test and monitor

A key aspect of implementing a search engine is making sure to test that it gives back the correct results for important queries. Search engines should also be monitored and common queries identified. Users also should be allowed to rate the value of the individual search results so that refinements can be made.

It is also very important for dynamic sites to re-index their search features on a regular basis. Such sites could be re-indexed manually by webmasters or editors when new content is added to the site or be automatically set up for regularly scheduled re-indexing.

The focus of the next few pages is not on how to actually create an index, which will vary greatly by the data being indexed, as well as the search engine being used, but to show how to design the various aspects of a search interface.

Designing the Search Interface

Assuming that a search facility is needed, a designer should first and foremost consider what the user wants to search for. Far too often, search engines are added to a site and set to index everything using a free text search. Similar to a Web-wide search, users pound their heads as they search for a particular part number like KF-456 only to be shown every single document the part number occurs in, ranging from press releases to technical notes. To the user, the ordering of the documents from this type of search may seem arbitrary, with the most important document not appearing first in the list. What's interesting is why this form of search was used. Designers assume that since public search engines work like this, so should their local search engine. This seems like a good idea—users are familiar with formulating search strings at public sites and bring this knowledge with them to your site. However, global search engines are not very accurate for a variety of reasons, including the fact that numerous sites try to fight their way to the top of returned results. Public search engine results don't always seem to make sense, and the ordering often seems more random than systematic.

Consider that in your own site, if you want a particular page to be shown when a user types in "Robot Butler," you can cause that page to be shown. Remember, when building a local search facility, to copy the style, syntax, and interface of public Web search engines, but don't imitate their imprecise functionality.

The main advantage of local searching is that you can utilize controlled vocabularies to deal with what users will probably want to search for. Besides relating keywords with certain pages in a more precise manner, you may even suggest common queries for users to run. Remember, local search engines provide designers with a much greater degree of control than public search engines.

Accessing Search

You should consider how your users will access the search facility. Some sites create a special button labeled "Search" that, when selected, takes the user to a special search page. Other sites utilize a search field within all pages. A visual comparison of the two approaches is shown in Figure 9-4.

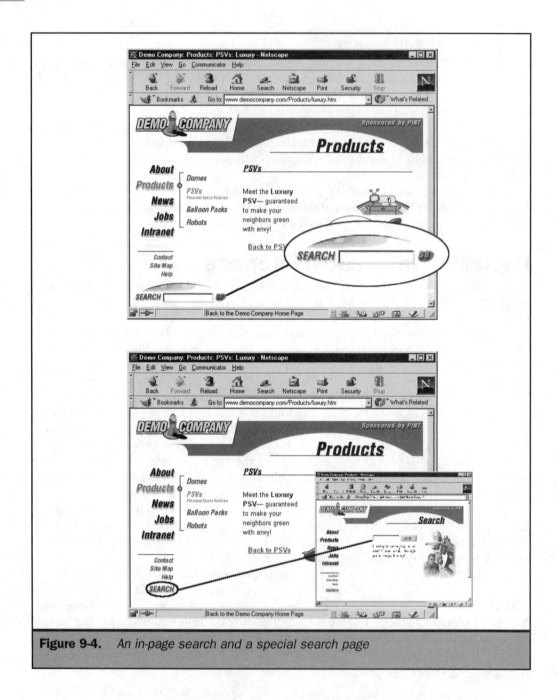

Figure 9-4. An in-page search and a special search page

While putting the search directly on the page eliminates one click for the user, a search field within a content page must be very basic. There still may be a need for a special search page if more complex queries are to be formed. It really isn't possible to put advanced search mechanisms within every page, as it tends to make the search facility too prominent and takes away from the page's primary purpose of delivering content. So the question is really to expose a simple search facility on content pages or provide it on a special search page. Regardless of the choice, search should be easily found from every page in a site.

Suggestion: When search is available in a site, include a search button or field on all pages.

Designing a Basic Search Interface

The search facility of a site should look the same as the rest of the site. Often it is not the same because it is added by technical staff, who may not be concerned when setting up the search templates to match the site's look and feel. Users who utilize such search engines may feel they have left the site if the look changes greatly. Look at the two search facilities shown in Figure 9-5; the need for integration should be obvious.

Rule: Search forms and result pages must match the look and feel of a site.

Also, the search form should fit the type of data being searched. For example, if users are searching for objects that are colored, shouldn't the search form provide a way to specify by color? The example search interface in Figure 9-6 for searching for personal space vehicles shows how search forms should match the content that is being searched.

Consider the golden rule of designing a search facility for a site—the more we know about what users are looking for, the better able we'll be to help them find it. One way to do this is to analyze what people search for by looking at the queries they enter. No matter how we figure out what users search for, we need to help users narrow down their search properly. For example, if we are searching for names, try to help people enter in last names or first names into individual text boxes rather than just letting them type names into a single text box. If part numbers are being searched in a range from 1 to 10,000, then let people know that that is the range, limit them to the range, and alert them if they are out of range. A ToolTip set using the **title** attribute in HTML or a simple JavaScript is an easy way to let people know about ranges without explicitly printing them onscreen. A few search forms that fit the data being searched are shown here:

SITE ORGANIZATION AND NAVIGATION

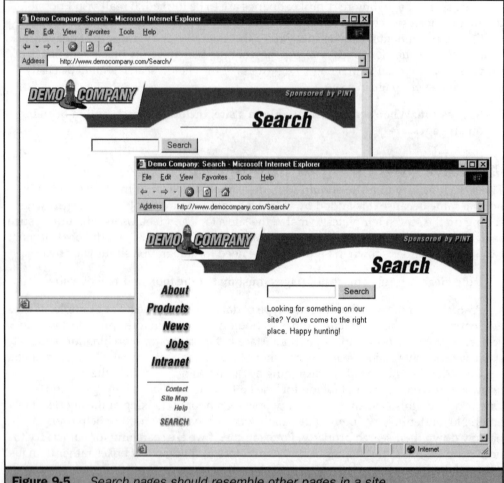

Figure 9-5. *Search pages should resemble other pages in a site*

Rule: A search form should match the content being searched.

The primary element of a search form is the actual search query field. A big question is how long should the search field be. The query text field should be large enough to hold at least a few search terms without scrolling. On average, users type two keywords in search fields.

The size of the search field also is related to the emphasis of the search task for the page. If search is the primary emphasis of the page and users are going to form complex searches, an input size in the range of 30 to 40 characters is common. A survey of the public search engines shows that most use a size of 30, 35, or 40 characters for their

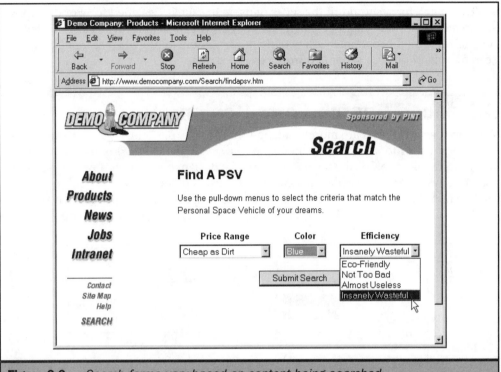

Figure 9-6. *Search forms vary based on content being searched*

primary search field, though Google is much larger at 55 characters. This size makes the search field a fairly large element, width-wise, on a typical page. When search is a secondary aspect of a page, the size should be about half the size—usually from 15 to 18 characters, which should allow a few keywords for a simple query. Of course, the size of the search box should always be designed with the search terms and the page layout in mind.

> **Suggestion: Primary search text boxes should be about twice as big as secondary search text boxes.**

The second aspect of the search form is the button to execute the search. Sometimes a form button is used, while other times a custom button is used. The use of a form button is probably slightly more intuitive for users. The label of the button also varies. Some favor "Search," others "Find," and some even something as simple as "Go." A lot of this depends on the context of the search. If the word "search" is used to label the field, labeling the button "search" seems a little redundant.

SITE ORGANIZATION AND NAVIGATION

The search form should fit the types of users the site is designed for. For example, a search facility for kids might be playful and have few instructions, while a search facility for engineers might contain a variety of fields for visitors to tune their searching. Simple search forms should be separated from advanced ones.

Advanced Search Form Design

Advanced search forms are more challenging to design, particularly if there are many ways for the user to tune the search. First, if the search is to allow Boolean searching using AND, OR, or NOT, the form must either be designed with pull-downs to separate search terms or provide explicit instructions for users on how to build Boolean queries, as shown in Figure 9-7. However, creating Boolean expressions can be a serious problem for many users. Try to avoid suggesting their use in basic searches where possible.

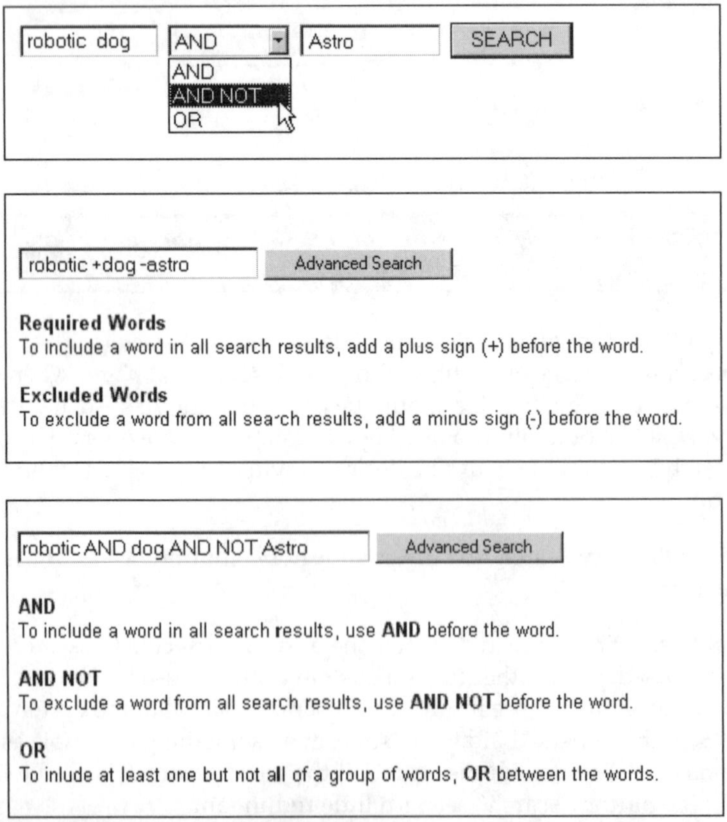

Figure 9-7.   *Boolean search query interfaces*

Advanced search forms often include various fields to limit the time of search. For example, forms may allow users to specify a date range to search when looking for time-sensitive information. They may also be able to limit the type of data to search by format (image, PDF, sound, and so on), as well as by content type (for example, press releases or specifications). Some search facilities allow the user to search only certain parts of a site. This may be called a *scoped* search. Unfortunately, users may not understand a site's sectioning, so it may be better to allow limits on topics, categories, or ideas rather than on sections of a site. A common way to do either form of scoped search is using a pull-down as shown here:

Search | Products ▼ | for | robot butler | GO |

Suggestion: It is generally better to limit a scoped search to a topic, category, or idea rather than a section of a site.

Other possibilities for an advanced search facility include allowing users to limit the number of results to be returned, to set the way results should be returned, and to search for meta information, such as document authors. Figure 9-8 shows an example of an advanced search form.

A very important part of advanced search forms is the instructions. Not all search engines work alike, and you should provide explicit instructions for the user, either directly on the search screen or using pop-up windows. Do not use a separate page for your search instructions, as it forces the user to either print out the instructions or quickly memorize the information. Besides instructions, example queries and field usage should also be provided in an advanced search page.

Rule: Advanced search facilities must provide instructions and examples.

Result Page Design

Designing result pages must take into account two extreme possibilities: no results and way too much information. Even when just about the right information is returned, a well-designed result page should help the user discern what is relevant. The rule of thumb for a result page: the more information the better—often people can't determine the value of one result over another. A well-designed result page should include the items shown in Table 9-1.

Not all types of search engines are able to provide all of these items—particularly advanced relevancy and matching indication. However, designers should strive to include all elements in a result page.

Rule: Result pages should provide as much information as possible so users can decide what items to peruse further.

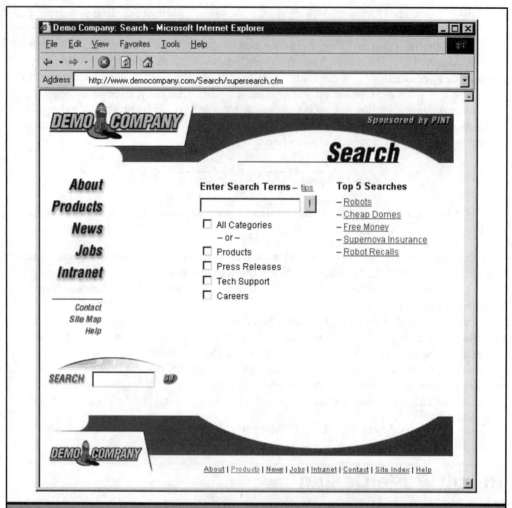

Figure 9-8.   *Advanced search forms should be carefully designed*

Result Page Element	Description
Original query	The original query string used should be prominently displayed on all result pages so the users don't have to recall what search string they used.

Table 9-1.   *Common Result Page Elements*

Result Page Element	Description
The scope of the search and the results found	The total number of documents searched and returned should be indicated (for example, 10,000 documents searched, 20 matches).
Context of current results	There should be some indication as to what part of the result list the user is looking at (for example, page 2 out of 10, or items 30–40 out of 200).
Page or document titles	Each item returned should be clearly titled.
URL of returned page	The actual URL of the individual documents should be shown, as it may provide useful information to the user.
Page summaries	A brief summary of a returned page's contents should be shown. This is often picked up either from the **<meta name="DESCRIPTION">** element or the first few lines of text in a document. A user may have the option to show or hide the page descriptions.
Date or time information of results	Minimally, the create date or date of last update of a returned document should be shown. Some search facilities also provide an indication of the time the index was last built, the time it took to search the index, and the time the query was performed.
Size of returned pages	The file size of the document returned should be indicated. This is especially important if the files being searched are large binaries.
Type of result	In some searches, other forms of data such as Adobe Acrobat, Microsoft Word, or multimedia data may be returned. Make sure to indicate the format of data with a label or icon.

Table 9-1.   *Common Result Page Elements* (continued)

Result Page Element	Description
Relevancy of results	A relevancy ranking should be clearly indicated. Usually, search results are ranked from highest to lowest. A percentage score or bar should be used to show the difference between items.
Keyword matches	Since users are highly annoyed when they are unable to figure out why a particular page is returned for a query, show the keywords matched and, if possible, highlight these words in context in the summary. If possible, when the user selects a document, the query terms should also be clearly highlighted.
Navigation	Navigation to move through the result set should be provided. Common buttons include "Next 10 documents" or "Previous 10 documents," where the step value changes depending on the user's preference. Navigation to see the first or last page in a result set is also sometimes used.
Refinement options	The ability to refine the query should be present. Users may be able to search against the result set or even perform a brand-new query.
Help	Help information explaining the format of the results should be available.

Table 9-1.   *Common Result Page Elements* (continued)

Search result pages often lack any provision for site navigation. When users access a results page, they are not just searching—they may also want to switch back to a browsing mode to investigate results. Remember, users are just looking for an answer, and they may move in and out of approaches in their hunt, so provide browsing facilities on search results when possible in case the user wants to leave the result page easily. Figure 9-9 presents a search results page that includes most of the elements listed in Table 9-1.

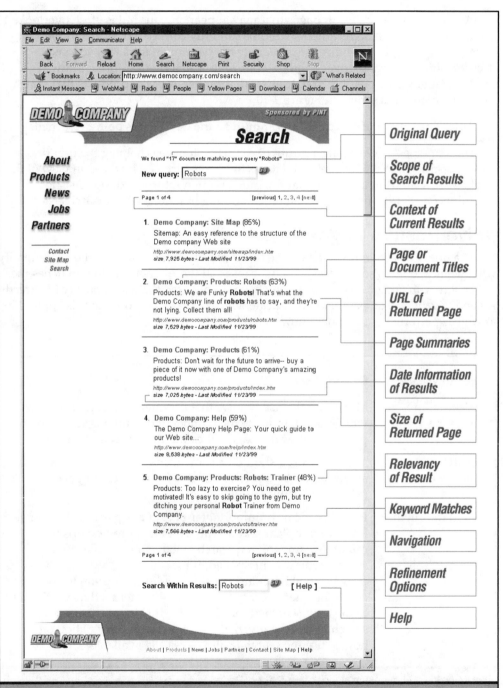

Figure 9-9. *Example search result page*

One aspect of search result pages that may appear obvious but is often overlooked is that the format of data returned should be carefully considered. For example, just listing a page title, URL, and description may not be enough for a user to make a decision about one choice over another. For example, if a user performs a search of products, it might be possible to output small thumbnails of the products that match the user's criteria, as shown in Figure 9-10.

Rule: The format of search results should fit the data that is being returned.

The key aspect of designing a positive search result page is helping the user find and make a decision about which returned items to pursue further. However, in view of the public Web search engines where far too much is often returned, designers should carefully consider the negative result when nothing has met a user's search criteria.

Negative Results Page

When a query results in no matches, the result page should try to help the user identify what went wrong. In some cases, it may be just that there is nothing that matches the search terms. In other cases, the user may have simply used the search facility incorrectly. A good negative result page should indicate which of these two conditions is applicable as well as perform the functions shown in Table 9-2.

Feature	Description
Clear failure message	Make sure the user knows that the query failed and perhaps why it failed. Indicate the number of documents searched and provide a clear message indicating that the search failed.
Search again mechanism	The query used should be shown, and the option to search again should be directly available from the result page (as with a positive results page).
Help information	Probably the most important aspect of a negative results page is to provide clear and useful help. First, provide tips that might explain why the search failed. For example, often search terms are misspelled. If the search engine doesn't provide spell checking, consider adding an option to spell check the query string. If possible, show terms that are similar to the term searched for. Consider showing the common search terms. Finally, make sure that help information on how to use the search facility is readily available.

Table 9-2. *Features of a Negative Result Page*

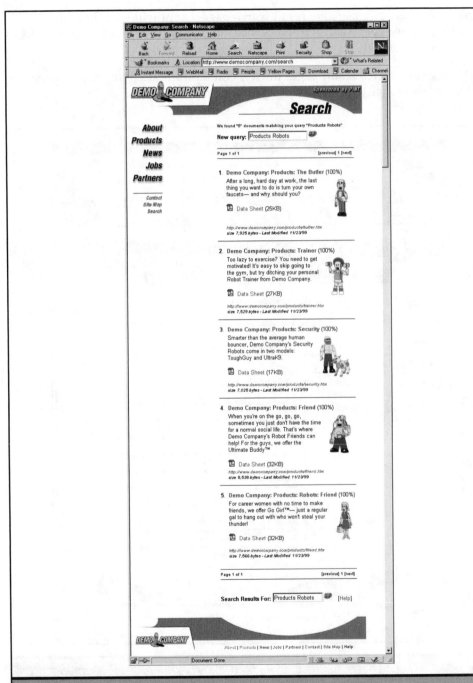

Figure 9-10.   *Search results vary based on the data searched*

Figure 9-11 presents a negative result search page that provides all the features useful to help the user get back on track. Notice that the negative result page also fits with the design of the site.

Rule: Negative search result pages must include information on why a query failed and potentially how to fix the query.

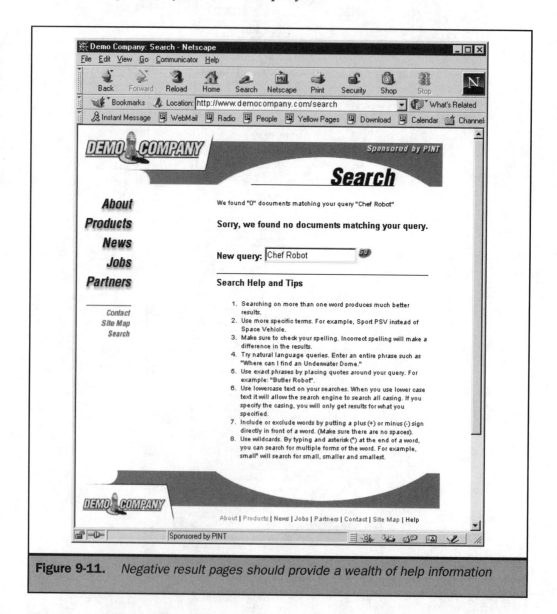

Figure 9-11. *Negative result pages should provide a wealth of help information*

Similar to broken link pages, negative result pages probably come up more than we would like. Make sure to monitor the negative queries to determine the usefulness of a search facility. Measure the percentage of negative queries and try to identify common bad queries. If your site is missing something, the negative queries may reveal the items that users are really looking for. Negative query monitoring is only one way to improve search facilities, so let's take a look at a few other strategies.

Improving Local Search

Despite our best efforts, local searching of Web site contents often fails. Why? Usually it is due to one of the following four problems:

- Search item not found on site
- Keyword mismatch
- Misspelled words and other near hits
- Search interface problem

The first problem really isn't solvable. If a user believes an item exists in the site and it doesn't, all we can really do is fail nicely. The other problems, however, can be addressed.

Addressing Near Hits

Keyword mismatch often has to do with the fact that how a user searches for something might not be exactly the way that the item is indexed. The basic problem has to do with vocabulary. For example, a user may enter "automobile" as a search term when the relevant pages were indexed under "car." Obviously, the two words are synonyms, so the search should not have failed. To solve this problem a site designer should come up with a controlled vocabulary of search terms, including related words. Generally termed a *thesaurus*, such a cross-reference of keywords can be generated uniquely, or for certain knowledge domains, a predefined set of words can be adopted.

Similar to keyword problems are searches that include misspelled words or words that run together. Particular attention should be paid to alternative spellings of words related to regional language differences—for example, color and colour. If possible, the search system should provide a "Did you mean?" facility to get users to the items they were actually looking for.

SITE ORGANIZATION AND NAVIGATION

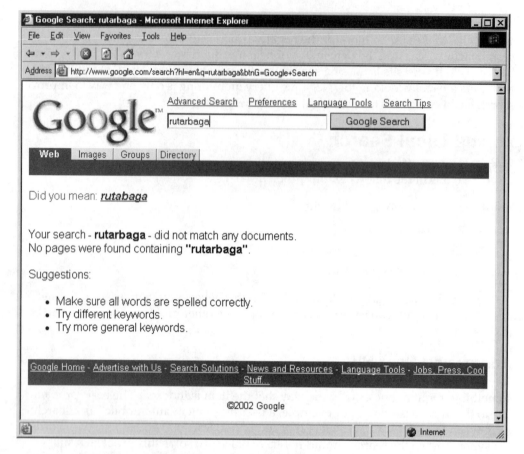

Any search-fixing facility might also try to address run-together search terms, like "spaceship" and "space ship."

Show Common Queries

Local search engines obviously are not as user-focused as they could be, considering that few of them address the fact that most users will enter the same simple one- or two-word queries. Since this is the case, it is wise to ensure that such queries match up with their intended result. Understanding what these special keywords are does not require a detailed analysis of site contents; the search engine itself should be able to tell you what people are searching for. You may then consider showing the popular searches that have been fixed to return correct results right on the search interface, as shown here.

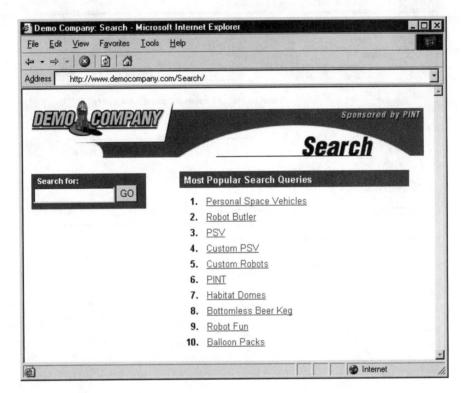

Scope Properly

When advanced searching facilities are provided, scoped searches are one of the best ways to improve the chances of search success. The first task is to limit the scoping. As mentioned earlier in the chapter, avoid scoping sites by hierarchical sections of site data but focus more on topics. Further scoping possibilities include limiting the search to a particular file type (such as PDF, GIF, HTML), date range, author, and so on.

Regardless of the scoping method used, make sure to allow the user to broaden or narrow the scope at will. For example, on the result page you might have a link that allows the search to be expanded to the whole site or to research within the set of results.

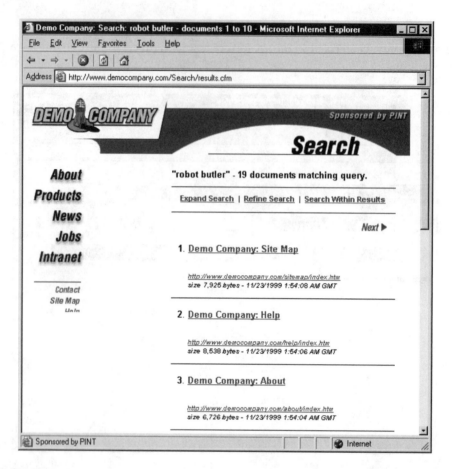

Add Polish

Search interfaces often suffer from a lack of usability and interface polish. For example, most local search sites will allow a user to enter in a blank query, only to have the query spit out an error message. If a blank search query is not allowed, try to address it right away using a simple JavaScript error message.

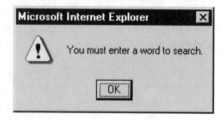

In some cases a blank query might return all pages in a given search space, but if it does not, allowing an obviously bad query is pointless.

Suggestion: Disallow blank search queries unless they return a complete page set.

Monitor and Maintain

Be as user-focused with search design and maintenance as with other areas of a site. Be sure to track your search logs so you can see why and how your site visitors are having problems with search. Watch searches that find zero matches and do your best to add new synonyms, terms and information that address these issues. For common searches, make sure the intended results come up.

Go Beyond Search

Finally, remember that users will move back and forth between browsing and searching. It isn't all-or-nothing when it comes to site navigation strategies. Try providing access to topic categories and browse facilities within a search interface, if possible, as shown in Figure 9-12.

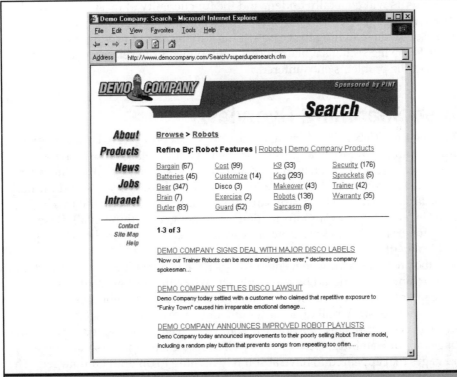

Figure 9-12. *Combine Search and Browse for Powerful Navigation*

The next chapter will explore other navigation facilities beyond search, but before we conclude let's turn our attention to how designers try to utilize search engines and other facilities to promote and drive traffic to their site.

Public Searching

As previously mentioned, site designers must be especially careful not to fall into the familiar trap of exactly imitating search on the Web at large. The needs of Web-wide searching are very different than those of a single site, or even a group of controlled sites. Unfortunately, users often expect site-search facilities to act similarly to public search engines like Google or Lycos. Public search engines have to deal with the extremely difficult task of gathering and indexing the enormous and ever-changing Web, which has numbers of documents that are purposely filled with misleading information. Then, from all this information, the user is supposed to quickly and easily retrieve a useful result using a simple query. In summary—finding a needle in a haystack is a much easier task than searching the Web. Regardless of the difficulty, users do rely on public search engines a great deal and their searches do work more often than not. Designers should consider a user's experience with Webwide search engines, since users will generally understand the functionality of these engines and apply that knowledge when they use a local search engine. Further, we need to understand Web-wide searching to see how it fits into the task of driving users to our Web site. The following sections will explore the components of Web searching and explore some of the problems encountered.

Full Web Searching Overview

The requirements for Webwide searching are daunting. Users expect to be able to quickly type in a simple search phrase at a global search engine like AltaVista or Google and end up with a realistic result. Consider the chances of walking into a public library and finding a particular passage in a book in a few seconds and you'll understand the near futility of the task. When searching, users are often overwhelmed with too much information, are shown irrelevant information, or do not get anything at all. Despite the resulting frustration, users keep pounding away at search engines, hoping to get a good result in a matter of minutes.

Many of the problems with search engine usage have to do with users not searching correctly. Searching really should be used only when looking for known items or for very specific topics. Consider searching for a general term like "hamburgers." Search engines may not necessarily pull up sites about hamburgers or even large hamburger restaurant chains. In fact, testing this query in some search engines resulted in numerous links to pages about Hamburg, Germany, as well as recipe sites for personal home pages and pages that appeared to have absolutely nothing to do with hamburgers. The problem is that the search term isn't specific enough. If you search for something like "White Castle Slyders"—a regionally famous hamburger in the United States—you may find a more useful list of results.

When looking for general information on a subject, users usually turn to a directory rather than a search engine. The main difference between a search engine and a directory is that a directory usually involves some human editing and usually contains a very limited number of links. Yahoo! is probably the most famous directory around, but it now provides search engine features as well. In fact, most of the search engines have begun to offer directory links as well as searching. Many popular search engines now focus more on delivering users to sites that focus on a particular topic rather than trying to get users to a very specific site. Directories like www.about.com or www.dmoz.org are organized by individuals who are responsible for a particular type of content. The benefit of a directory is that having a site organized by people can result in limiting content to just the "good sites." While automatic gathering and categorization of content can be a powerful tool, until Artificial Intelligence is vastly improved the value of human editing and categorization should not be underestimated.

> **Definition: A Web directory is a human-edited and organized collection of site links and associated information such as descriptions and reviews.**

In comparison to a directory, a pure search engine is more like the phone book that you can only search. This is similar to calling your information service and asking for a phone number, except you ask for something related to a particular topic. Consider using a phone information service such as 411 in the United States and asking for the phone number of a "Chinese restaurant" rather than asking about a particular Chinese restaurant. If you ask for a particular restaurant, chances are you're going to get a good result. However, when asking for general information you'll be very lucky if the operator actually spends some time to give you a particular restaurant they know about, or even returns one that looks reputable based upon its ad in the print directory. In many cases, directory assistance might just give you the first one or even a random one from a list. Search engines tend to act the same way. They are good at returning specific answers, but results vary otherwise.

Search engines always attempt to be comprehensive and may list numerous sites without regard to content quality or freshness. Search engines are primarily automated in the collection and organization of links, though today some human editing as well as directory-oriented results are being used. This is due partly to the massive amount of search engine trickery going on, as well as a desire to improve the result sets for users. The reason for the trickery is a desire by Web site owners to use search sites to drive as much traffic to their sites as possible.

Search Engine Promotion

Site owners always want to be number one in search engines. Consider if you are a small travel agent. You probably would love it if people could go to a search engine, type **travel**, and have a link to your site show up as the first one. You'd get a large number of visits for sure. Unfortunately, there are probably a lot of other people who would like to be number one, and being ranked 4,036th isn't going be worth much. In fact, if you are outside the first 20 sites or so returned, you probably aren't going to get many clicks at all. Because of this, page designers are always trying to determine how search engines categorize pages and then building their page with keywords in such a way to get a high ranking. In some ways, this idea is similar to how people name their company something like AAATravel in order to get listed first in the phone book. Unfortunately, consider how many travel agents in the world want their site to be in the top ten in search engines and you'll see a potential problem. The Web is not as geographically specific as the phone book. Imagine that there is only a single phone book for the United States. There would probably be dozen of pages filled with companies, all starting with AAA. The Web already has this problem, and that's one of the reasons you get so many results when you run a query for a competitive industry like discount travel.

The war to be first in the search engine has an obvious result—the rise of "pay for position." Consider that the tricks to be at the top of the search engine list spread rapidly. For common search phrases, it is nearly impossible to stay at the top of the list for long since other sites use the same search engine promotion techniques. Already search engines such as Overture (www.overture.com) are opting to push people to the top of the list that are willing to pay for position. Priority placement is also being made for banner ads triggered to correspond to particular search phrases. Just as with the phone book, naming your company AAATravel might put you at the top of the line listings, but readers may opt instead to look at the large display ads. Search engines will eventually adopt the same model. Further, as end users become more sophisticated, they will begin to rely more on directory listings for generic topics and use search engines only for very specific or complex lookups. The eventual outcome of the search engine war will almost certainly be a return to traditional models of information retrieval methods used in other advertising forms where you pay for audience relevancy and position. For now, designers should consider not taking advantage of search engine positioning methods, regardless of their long-term viability.

Adding to the Engines

Getting a site's pages gathered by a search engine is the first step in making a site findable on the Web. The easiest way to do this is simply to tell search engines that your site exists. Most search engines will allow you to add a URL to be indexed. For example, Google allows you to add a site for gathering by using a simple form (http://www.google.com/addurl.html). Of course, adding your site to every single search engine could be a tedious task, so many vendors (http://www.submitit.com) are eager to provide developers with a way to bulk-submit to numerous search engines. Most Web site promotion software, such as WebPosition Gold (http://www.webposition.com), also includes automated submission utilities. Today you may find that the simple guaranteed submission to a search engine costs money. Undoubtedly, this trend will continue.

You should consider how many search engines you'll want to submit your site to. Some people favor only adding few links to the important top ten engines, especially Yahoo! Numerous studies, as well as this author's experience, suggest that big search sites, particularly Yahoo, account for most search engine traffic. However, some site promotion experts feel this is not correct and believe it is best to create as many links to sites as possible. In fact, a whole class of link sites—"Free For All" links or FFA sites (not to be confused with anything related to the Future Farmers of America)—have sprung up to service people who believe that "all links should lead to me" works. The reality is that most of these link services are pretty much worthless and often generate worthless Traffic and spam messages. Further, consider that even if you do get back links and e-mail, it is mostly from people who are doing the same thing you're doing—trying to get links.

Robot Exclusion

Before getting too involved putting yourself in every search engine, remember that it isn't always a good idea to have a robot index your entire site, whether it is your own internal search engine or a public search engine. First, some pages such as programs in your cgi-bin directory don't need to be indexed. Second, many pages may be transitory, and having them indexed may result in users seeing 404 errors if they enter from a search engine. Finally, you may just not want people to enter on every single page—particularly those pages deep within a site. So-called "deep linking" can be confusing for users entering from public search engines. Because these users start out deep in a site, they are not exposed to the home or entry page information that is often used to orient site visitors.

Probably the most troublesome aspect of search engines and automated site gathering tools such as offline browsers is that they can be used to stage a denial of service attack on a site. The basic idea of most spiders is to read pages and follow pages as fast as they can. If you tell a spider to crawl a single site as fast as it possibly can, all the requests to the crawled server may very quickly overwhelm it, causing the site to be unable to fulfill requests—thus denying services to legitimate site visitors. Fortunately, most people are not malicious in spidering, but it does happen inadvertently when a spider keeps reindexing the same dynamically generated page.

Robots.txt

To deal with limiting robot access, the Robot Exclusion protocol was adopted. The basic idea is to use a special file called robots.txt that should be found in the root directory of a Web site. For example, if a spider was indexing http://www.democompany.com, it would first look for a file at http://www.democompany.com/robots.txt. If it finds a file, it would analyze the file first before proceeding to index the site.

> **Note**   *You will find that many spiders will ignore a robots.txt file with a URL like http://
> www.bigfakehostingvendor.com/~customer/robots.txt, where the robots.txt file is not
> located in the root directory. Unfortunately, you will have to ask the vendor to place an
> entry for you in their robots.txt file.*

The basic format of the robots.txt file is a listing of the particular spider or user agent you are looking to limit and statements including which directory paths to disallow. For example,

```
User-agent: *
Disallow: /cgi-bin/
Disallow: /temp/
Disallow: /archive/
```

In this case, we have denied access for all robots to the cgi-bin directory, the temp directory, and an archive directory—possibly where we would move files that are very old but still need to be online. You should be very careful with what you put in your robots.txt. Consider this file:

```
User-agent: *
Disallow: /cgi-bin/
Disallow: /images/
Disallow: /subscribers-only/
Disallow: /resellers.html
```

In this file, a special subscribers-only and resellers file has been disallowed for indexing. However, you have just let people know this is sensitive. If you have content that is hidden unless someone pays to receive a URL via e-mail, you will certainly not want to list it in the robots.txt file. Just letting people know the file or directory exists is a problem. Consider that malicious visitors will actually look carefully at a robots.txt file to see just what it is you don't want people to see. That's very easy to do: just type in the URL like this: **http://www.*companytolookat*.com/robots.txt**.

Be aware that the robot exclusion standard assumes that spidering programs will abide by it. A malicious spider will, of course, simply ignore this file, and you may be forced to set up your server to block particular IP addresses or user agents if someone has decided to attack your site.

Robot Control with <meta>

An alternative method to the robots.txt file that is useful particularly for those users who have no access to the root directory of their domain is to use a **<meta>** tag to control indexing. To disallow indexing of a particular page, use this **<meta>** tag in the **<head>** section of the HTML document:

```
<meta name="robots" content="noindex" />
```

You can also inform a spider not to follow any links coming out of the page:

```
<meta name="robots" content="noindex, nofollow" />
```

When using this type of exclusion, just make sure not to confuse the robot with contradictory information like

```
<meta name="robots" content="index, noindex" />
```

or

```
<meta name="robots" content="index, nofollow, follow " />
```

as the spider may either ignore the information entirely or maybe even index anyway. The other downside to the **<meta>** tag approach is that fewer search engines support it than do robots.txt.

SITE ORGANIZATION AND NAVIGATION

Optimizing for Search Engines

Optimizing your site for a search engine is not difficult. The first thing to do is to start to think like a search engine—in other words, don't really think at all. Search engines literally look at pages and make educated guesses about what pages are about by following a set of rules to try to understand what the page is about. For example, search engines look for word frequency, **<meta>** tags, and a variety of other things. However, they really can't tell the difference between a page about the Miami Dolphins football team and a dolphin show in Miami. The reason is that search engines generally rely on keyword matching in conjunction with some criterion such as the placement of words in a page or the number of linking sites. So if a designer knows what a search engine is looking for, it is easy enough to optimize a page for the search engine to rank it highly. The next few sections provide a brief overview of some of the things search engines look for as well as some tricks people have employed to improve their search ranking.

<meta> Tags

Many search engines look at the **<meta>** tags for keywords and descriptions of a page's content. A **<meta>** tag like

```
<meta name="Keywords" content=" Butler-1000, Robot butler, Robot butler
specifications, where to buy a robot butler, Metallic Man Servant, Demo
Company, robot, butler" />
```

could be used in our example page about robot butlers. Notice how the content started with the most specific keywords and phrases and ended with generic keywords. This should play into how most users approach search engines.

Once a search engine looks at the **<meta>** tag, it may rate one site higher than another based upon the frequency of keywords in the **content** attribute. Because of this, some designers load their **<meta>** tags with redundant keywords:

```
<meta name="Keywords" content=" Robot butler, Robot butler, Robot
butler, Robot butler, Robot butler, Robot butler, Robot butler,
Robot butler, Robot butler, Robot butler" />
```

However, many search engines consider this to be keyword loading and may drop the page from their index. If the keyword loading is a little less obvious and combinations of words and phrases are repeated,

```
<meta name="Keywords" content=" Robot butler, Butler-1000, Metallic
Man Servant, Robot butler, Butler-1000, Metallic Man Servant, Robot
butler, Butler-1000, Metallic Man Servant, Robot butler,
Butler-1000, Metallic Man Servant " />
```

the search engine may not consider this improper. An even better approach is to make sure the pattern of repeating words isn't quite as obvious, as shown here:

```
<meta name="Keywords" content=" Butler-1000, Robot butler, Metallic
Man Servant, Robot butler, Butler-1000, robot, Robot butler,
Democompany, Metallic Man Servant, Butler-1000, robot, butler,
Robot butler, Butler-1000" />
```

However, be aware that search engines may still notice the heavy use of certain words or phrases and consider this spamming, potentially reducing the page's ranking or dropping it from the index completely.

Search engines also look at the description value for the **<meta>** tag. For example,

```
<meta name="Description" content="The DemoCompany Robot Butler is
the most outstanding metallic man servant on the market. The
Butler-1000 comes complete with multiple personalities and voice
modules including the ever-popular faux-British accent." />
```

would be included on the robot butler page and could be examined by the search engine, as well as returned by the search engine on the result page. Because the **<meta>** tag description may be output for the user to see, provide some valuable information in the description that will help users determine if they want to visit your site. Preferably, keep the description to a sentence or two and, at most, three or four sentences.

Titles and File Naming

One important aspect of search engine ranking is making sure your page has a very good title. For example,

```
<title>Robot Butler</title>
```

is a bad title as far as search engine ranking goes. A better title might be:

```
<title>Butler-1000: Specification of Demo Company's Robot Butler,
the leading metallic man servant on the market</title>
```

Remember that people also look at page titles, and they are used for bookmarking, so a really long title may be more appropriate for search engines than for users.

The name of a file can also be important for search engines. Rather than naming a file "butler.htm," use "butler1000robotbutler.htm." If you have a good domain name and directory structure, you may create a URL that almost makes sense. For example, if we named our server democompany.com, as well as www.democompany.com, we may have a URL like this:

```
http://democompany.com/products/robots/butler1000robotbutler.htm
```

Notice how this almost includes the same information as the title. This provides the secondary benefit of letting users know where they are, rather than resorting to cryptic URLs like this:

```
http://democompany.com/products.exe?prod=robots&mod=butler1000
```

Relevant Text Content

One of the best ways to get indexed is to have the keywords and phrases actually within the content of the page. Many search engines will look at text within a page, particularly if it is either towards the top of the page or within heading tags like **<h1>** or **<h2>**. Search engines may also look at the contents of link text. Thus,

```
<a href="specifications.htm">Specifications</a>
```

is not as search engine friendly as

```
<a href="specifications.htm">Robot Butler Specification</a>
```

One problem with search engines focusing on page text is that designers often create home pages that are primarily graphic. Search engines accessing such pages may have little to go on besides the **<meta>** tag and page title and thus rank the page lower. Consider using the **alt** attribute for the **<img>** tag to provide some extra information; for example,

```
<img src="robot.gif" alt="Butler-1000: Demo Company's industry
leading robot butler" />
```

Of course, putting the actual text in the page would be better. Some designers resort to either making text very small, or in a color similar to the background, or both, so that users won't see it but search engines may pick it up; for example,

```
<font size="1" color="white">The Demo Company Butler1000 is the
best robot butler. The Demo Company Butler1000 is the best robot
butler. The Demo Company Butler1000 is the best robot butler.</font>
```

Be careful with the small or invisible text trick. Many search engines will consider this to be spamming and may drop the page from the search engine.

Links and Entry Points

Another aspect of search engine ranking has to do with the number of links leaving a page, as well as the number of pages that link to a page. Landmark pages such as home pages tend to have a lot of outgoing and incoming links. Search engines would prefer to rank landmark pages highly, so it is important that key pages in your site have links to them from nearly every page. Some search engines also favor sites that have many sites pointing to them. Because of this, people are already starting to create sites solely for the purpose of pointing to other sites.

Another approach to improving search engine ranking is to submit many pages in a site, or even off a site, to a search engine. All of these entry pages, often called *doorway pages*, point to important content within your site. Unfortunately, doorway pages are more like decoy pages, as they can be loaded with false content to attract the visitor and eventually deposit the user at a page they didn't really want to see. The problem with search engine promotion is that the distance from simple logical keyword loading to various tricks is a short one—particularly if designers obsess with top-ten ranking.

Tricky Business

The tricks employed by search engine specialists are numerous and change all the time. Many ideas are simple add-ons to normal Web design techniques. For example, many designers rely on invisible pixel shims to force layout. Search engine promoters might say, "Why not put **alt** attributes on these images to improve things." Imagine, for instance, having the following all over your page:

```
<img src="pixel.gif" alt="robot butler robot butler robot butler" />
```

Pity the user who pauses on top of one of these invisible pixels only to have a ToolTip pop up screaming about whatever the page is promoting. Spamming pages with invisible text, small text, and multiple images, or just loading the **<meta>** or **<title>** tags, are not the most sophisticated tricks, but they often work.

Other tricks include the infamous "bait and switch," where a special search engine page is created and then posted to a search engine. Once the ranking is high, the bait page is replaced with a real page built for users. A more complicated version of this could be dubbed "feeding the dogs"(or page or site cloaking). In this scenario, you write a program that senses when a search engine hits the site, and then the program "feeds" the engine the page that it wants to see. Like a ravenous dog, it gobbles up the food with no idea it just ate the equivalent of informational pig snouts. As real users hit the site, they aren't served the dog food, but get the real site.

Distinguishing search engines from regular users isn't terribly difficult, since the engines identify themselves and come from consistent IP addresses. In reality, "feeding the dogs" is just a modified form of browser detection. Search engines can do little to combat this approach, since they would have to consider eliminating dynamically built pages—which is impossible given their growing importance—or not informing sites that they are search engines while indexing. A few search engines have already begun to provide a link to a page that shows what was indexed, so users can determine if they are being shown something different than what a search engine indexed. Others revisit the page in multiple guises and see if things are dramatically different; if they are, cloaking is considered to be in play and the page is dropped. Of course, this may just be because the page is dynamically created; thus, many search robots will tend to exclude pages with complex URLs, like www.democompany.com/products.cfm?robots= army&cost=expensive. In order to address this, some site owners will rewrite page URLs to make them more search engine friendly. We'll address that in Chapter 17, on site delivery.

The problem with all the search engine promotion ideas is that they tempt the designer to stop building pages for users and start building them for search engines. This is just another form of designing more for your own needs than for your users.

> **Rule: Do not design pages solely to attract search engines, as, ultimately, pages are for people.**

One of the most interesting aspects about search engines is that many large organizations don't rely greatly on them for driving traffic. In fact, for many corporations, unless you type their name in directly, you'll be hard pressed to find them in a search engine. However, despite what appears to be a major oversight on their part, these sites continue to get huge amounts of traffic. According to studies such as the GVU Internet Survey, people type in URLs directly quite often.

How are they finding out about sites? Search engines aren't the only way to drive traffic. There are many ways to get users to visit your site. Banner ads, link exchanges, news group postings, mass e-mailings, and easily typed and remembered domain names all are well-known approaches to traffic generation. However, one increasingly popular way to attract visitors is to rely on things outside the Internet. Television, radio, print, billboard, direct mail, and a variety of other venues are being used to spread the address of the latest Web site.

Note   *This is by no means a complete discussion of search engine promotion, as the topic literally changes on a weekly basis. Readers looking for more up-to-date information are directed to the numerous site promotion sites that exist on the Web, especially Search Engine Watch (www.searchenginewatch.com).*

Summary

If browsing is about following predefined trails in a Web site, then searching is going off-path, blazing your own direction through content. While it would seem that search facilities appeal primarily to power users and frequent visitors, the fact is that novice users are familiar with public search engines and rely more and more on sites like Google for searching. Understanding how public search engines work and are used is the first step in designing a local site search facility. Designers should also understand how users move from public search sites to local sites and attempt to guide users to what they are looking for. Search facilities must be designed with the user in mind. The best way to do this is to consider what users would actually want to search for in a site. Do not fall into the trap of blindly imitating the free text search qualities of global Web search engines. When providing local search, make sure to provide both basic and advanced search forms. Format the search form carefully and provide instructions. This will help users form good queries, but in case things go wrong, make sure the negative result page provides extra help to get users back on track. Once users do get a positive result from a search engine, make sure that enough information is provided so they can narrow down the potential choices. Having too much data is nearly as bad as having none at all. However, always consider that searching isn't everything. Like all forms of navigation, searching is a means to an end, not the end itself. There are many ways to help users find what they are looking for. The next chapter will present a variety of other navigational aids, such as site maps, site indices, and help systems.

Chapter 10

Site Maps and Other Navigational Aids

Even when a site is well structured and search tools are provided, users may still have difficulty finding what they are looking for. Users may approach site navigation differently. Even when advanced search facilities are available, some users may prefer to browse or navigate by means of a site's structure, while others may prefer an alphabetized list. Still others might prefer a time-related aid, like a date-ordered list of changes to the site, or visual aids like graphical site maps.

Given the diversity of navigation possibilities, site designers should strive to provide as many navigational choices as possible—particularly site maps and site indexes. Even with these navigation systems in place, however, we must contend with the fact that some users may need additional assistance and turn to help systems or glossaries to further their understanding of the site.

Beyond Search

One of the biggest drawbacks to a search is that it doesn't provide a very accurate idea of scope, nor does it typically give the user an idea of content that is related or nearby the search in question. Consider how in a printed book like this one the sheer physical size of the work can give the reader some idea of the range of content contained within. The table of contents may also give an idea of the scope of the contents, as well as an indication of how the elements of the book are related. The index in the back of the book may indicate locations in the book where interesting content can be found. Even the indication of page numbers in the index provides hints to the reader as to the volume of information on a particular topic. Web sites should be able to provide all these features and more, since they are not constrained to one particular mode of presentation.

You may not need a search facility unless you have a very large site or very complex data. Even if you do need a search facility, it will not address every user's navigational questions. Users do not always know exactly what they are looking for. There is a huge range of possibilities—from a directed search for a known item to a casual browse around a site to see what is there. Sometimes a user will have a specific object in mind but will also be interested in seeing things that are somewhat similar. Looking through a list of related items easily addresses this desire. While search engines can provide alternative search queries as suggestions, sometimes the user just needs to browse to understand the items available. In this chapter, the common navigation aids used on Web sites beyond search, such as maps and indexes, are surveyed, with a discussion about current best practices and thoughts on improvements to them.

Site Maps

A map graphically represents the location of various elements within a set region or space. For example, a road map may represent the location of roads, cities, and landmarks in a bird's-eye style. A map provides both direction and distance information that a driver can use to find and reach a destination. Of course, maps aren't limited to driving directions, and some present information such as demographic data, political boundaries, animal migration patterns, weather, and just about anything else that intersects with the mapped geography.

Given that maps tend to present information related to geography, do they have any place on the Web, which does not exhibit such spatial characteristics? The answer appears to be "Yes," given the number of sites that do employ some form of navigational aid dubbed a "site map."

On the web, a *site map* is a structural overview of a site that shows pages generally related by structural proximity or, more appropriately, topic similarity. While often the physical and conceptual locations of pages are directly related, they do not have to be. In this sense, site maps for Web sites are more like the table of contents for a book, showing the organization of the book and providing a quick reference to major points of interest, such as chapter or section starts.

Just as the table of contents of a book is invariably in the same place—somewhere close to the front of the book—site maps should be easy to find. Typically, a site map should be accessible from every page within a site, but generally should not be a primary navigation choice. Often, a site map button or link is available within a global navigation bar, but its appearance or location is less prominent than main section navigation. Some site designs will cluster navigation aids like a site map and search facility together, as shown in Figure 10-1. The position of this navigational aid cluster is usually the upper-right corner or at the bottom, but the position of a site map, search facility, and index links aren't quite at the level of a Web convention. The most that can be said is that these secondary navigation items are generally not placed in a prominent location on the page.

The name of the Web site map link should be well considered. While simply "map" might seem appropriate, site designers must consider that if the site includes information about physical locations in the real world, the simple word "map" may be confusing. The term "site map" should be considered standard as the link name to access a structural diagram of a Web site. Do not confuse this with "site index," which will be discussed later in this chapter.

Rule: Name the link to a site map simply "site map."

In general, activating a site map link will load a page that provides a section-by-section overview of a site with links to many pages in the site. The user will scan the links in the map and then decide which page to access. The user could also use the site map to get a quick overview of the range of content within a site.

Textual Site Maps

The representation of a site map comes in many forms. The simplest map is a textual site map. A textual site map represents all links as basic HTML text with varying sizes,

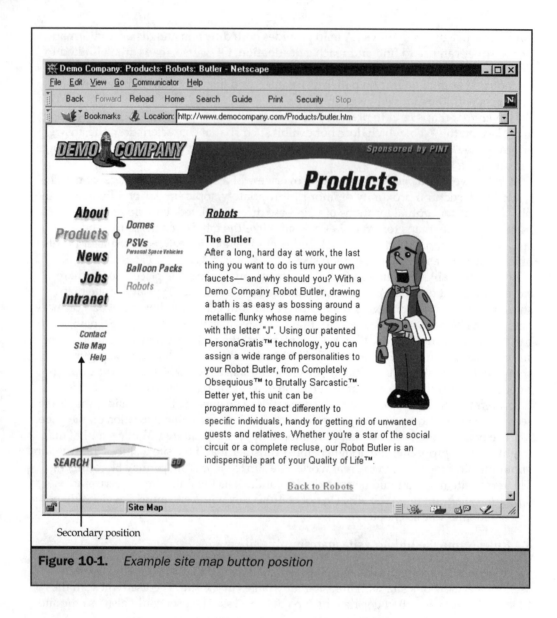

Figure 10-1. Example site map button position

colors, or indentation to show the importance of pages within a site. An example of such a map is shown in Figure 10-2.

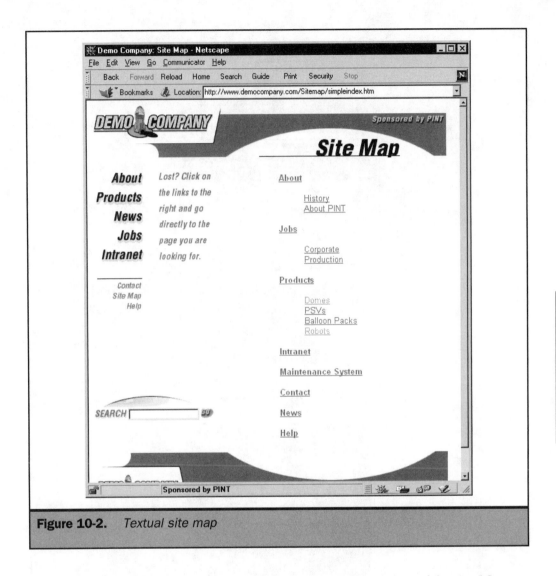

Figure 10-2.   *Textual site map*

The arrangement of the pages can aid in a user's understanding of the site. Many sites use colored boxes or columns to section various aspects of a site, as shown in Figure 10-3.

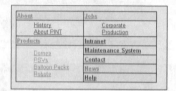

Intranet   Maintenance System   Contact   Help

About	Products	News	Jobs
History	Domes	Press Releases	Corporate
About PINT	Land	Newsletter	Production
	Underwater		
	Space		
	PSVs		
	Economy		
	Luxury		
	Cargo		
	Sport		
	Balloon Packs		
	Standard		
	Child		
	Two Person		
	Sport		
	Robots		
	Butler		
	Trainer		
	Security		
	Friends		

About	History	A brief but fascinating history of Demo Company
	About PINT	Info about this site's sponsor
Products	Domes	Our line of Habitat Domes: • Land • Underwater • Space
	PSVs	Personal Space Vehicles: • Economy • Luxury • Cargo • Sport
	Balloon Packs	Fun Balloon Packs: • Standard • Child • Two Person • Sport
	Robots	Our latest Robot models: • Butler • Trainer • Security • Friends
News	Press Releases	The latest Demo Company press releases
	Newsletter	Our staff newsletter
Jobs	Corporate	A list of all executive positions currently available
	Production	A list of all production positions currently

Figure 10-3.   Approaches to text map organization

In general, a column or downward-oriented approach to site mapping is better for larger sites, given screen width constraints and the lack of rightward scrolling.

Textual site maps are efficient to download, as well as easy to build and update. However, textual site maps may not be terribly memorable for the user. It may also be difficult to present complex organizational relationships in text form. Adding graphical icons to section heads may improve memorability and speed access by providing obvious site landmarks within a text map. It is also possible to use icons to indicate content types within the map or indicate password-restricted areas, page weights, external links, or other features. Figure 10-4 illustrates some of these ideas in practice. Yet even with added icons, some designers will find the aesthetic potential and presentation options of a textual site map to be limiting, and they will turn to a graphical site form.

Graphical Site Maps

While graphical site maps provide more possibility for visual design, they do have many drawbacks. As discussed in Chapter 4, most designers use a structural diagram or similar aid when organizing a site. It is not difficult to translate such a diagram into a visual and use it as a site map by making the various page icons clickable. A simple example of a graphical site map is shown in Figure 10-5.

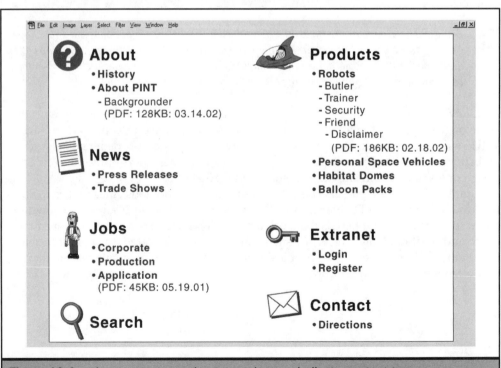

Figure 10-4. *Icons create good page markers or indicate content type*

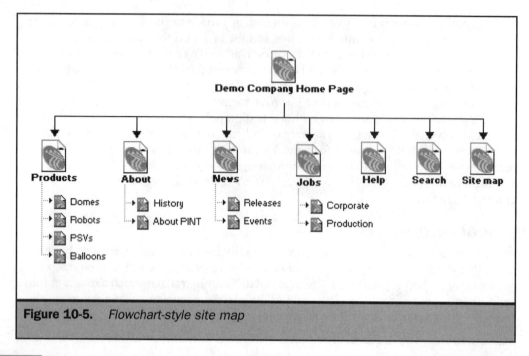

Figure 10-5.   *Flowchart-style site map*

Note	*Some site development products, like Macromedia Dreamweaver or Microsoft FrontPage, provide an easy way to save out site map images directly. Unfortunately, the maps often don't work as well as actual user site maps. Other flowcharting tools such as Visio may be useful in creating and exporting site maps to a Web-friendly format.*

Like flow diagrams, many site maps are hierarchical in structure, starting with the home page graphic at the top and proceeding down the page for deeper pages. Such a style will usually work well only with a relatively deep site. A broader site would probably not fit within a typical screen size. Thus, many designers opt for a circular design or less structured site map, as shown in Figure 10-6.

Graphical site maps can also be used to provide more obvious clues to depth. Some have found the use of 3-D–like maps (called an *isometric* style) appealing, as shown in Figure 10-7. The concept here is that such a map allows viewers to quickly determine depth and position. However, while such maps look sophisticated, they often provide little value for larger sites, as they typically can only represent a few pages. Further, they often are difficult to produce.

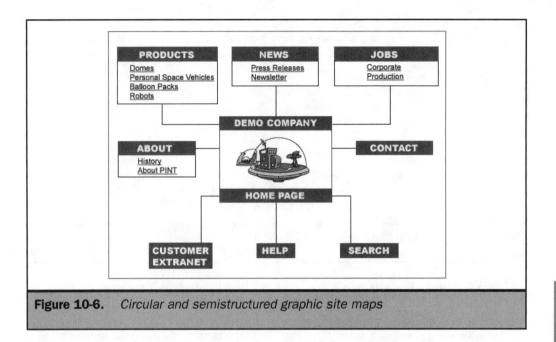

Figure 10-6. *Circular and semistructured graphic site maps*

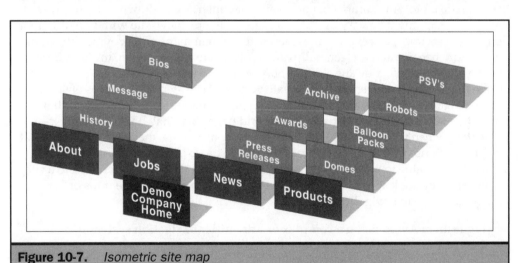

Figure 10-7. *Isometric site map*

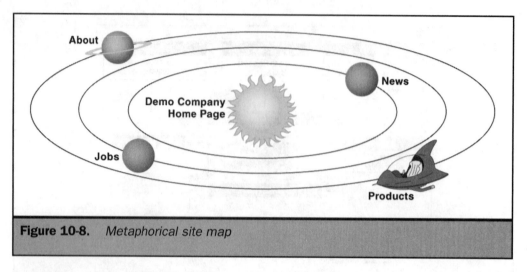

Figure 10-8.   *Metaphorical site map*

Despite potential production costs, one huge benefit of graphic site maps is that they can be extended to fit with the theme of the site, as shown by the example site map in Figure 10-8.

An interesting possibility with graphical site maps is using thumbnails representing the page linked to. An example of such a site map interface is shown in Figure 10-9. A thumbnail map might be very useful in a graphically intensive site with very different designs per section. However, in most cases, thumbnail maps will provide little in the way of extra benefits and are generally difficult to create and maintain. In short, despite looking sophisticated, they should probably be avoided.

Finally, some sites go so far as to create very sophisticated visual maps of sites, complete with animations and transitions, as shown in Figure 10-10. While such maps can show interrelationships between topics and pages that may be very complex—particularly when produced automatically from site meta data, they also can be difficult for users to figure out. So far, it appears that Web site visualization for navigation seems of little value to most users. Consider as well that users will often turn to a site map when they are lost or confused, so presenting them with an ingenious or unfamiliar site map navigation system may just drive them away.

> **Suggestion: Avoid using a complex or unfamiliar navigation system in a site map.**

While graphical site maps may provide more design possibilities, they do so at the expense of download time and updatability. Obviously, a visual site map will take more time to download than a text one. For users lost on a site, this may add insult to injury. Further, it will be difficult to keep the site map up-to-date, because any page changes will require a graphic change. Because of their update limitations, graphic site maps are reasonable only for relatively static sites, unless their detail is limited only to the highest-level pages.

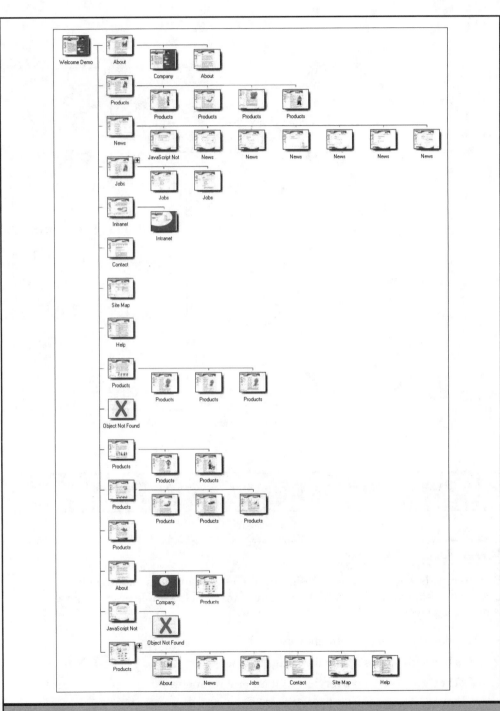

Figure 10-9.   *Thumbnail map*

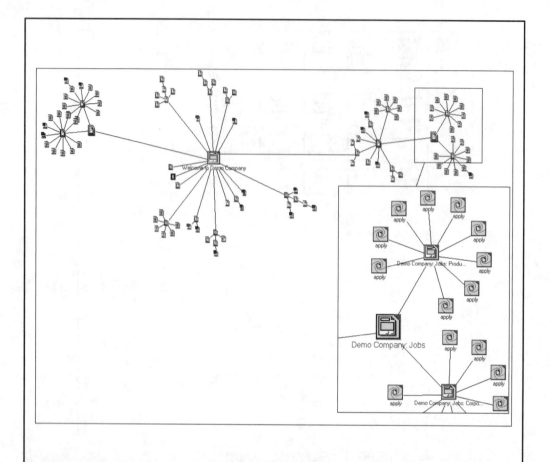

Figure 10-10. *Visualization-oriented site map*

Site Map Design

Before considering the issues of designing Web site maps, think about how maps are used in the real world. Standard geographical maps help people orient themselves in three basic ways:

- They show users where they are.
- They show users where they might go.
- They give users an overview of their environment.

Conceptually, a Web site map should serve the same purpose. In reality, they do not always meet these goals.

Showing Scope and Destination Choices

Clues to the size and scope of a site are usually found in most site maps, thus giving users a good overview of the site environment. A Web site map will provide links to various pages in the site, but not to all. A site map will also show the major sections and pages of a site, which should give the user an indication of the site's content. Of course, both of these map features are affected by the degree of detail provided in the map.

For all but the smallest sites, it may not be possible to show all the links in the site. Few site maps, even textual maps, show more than 100 to 200 direct links, because the map quickly becomes a tangle of links or icons. If you consider using a graphical structure, you may be limited to only a few dozen pages, at most, onscreen.

In short, the site map should be created to meet the following criteria:

- Provide the appropriate level of detail.
- Show important pages or site landmarks.

Determining the appropriate level of detail to represent will depend on the complexity of the site. For large sites, it is suggested to use pull-down menus within a site map structure or a similar dynamic structure, such as the expanding tree control shown here:

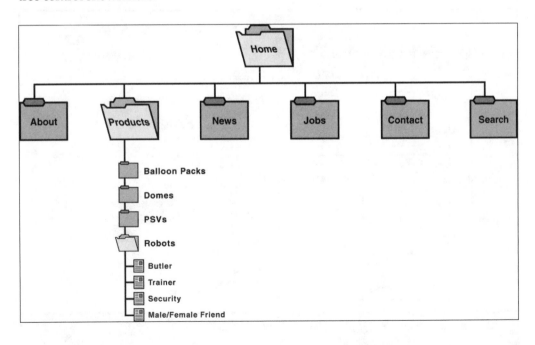

"You Are Here" Indication

Most site maps do not really show users where they are in the site. In some sense, this really doesn't matter, because most site maps load over the current page. However, it might be more appropriate to show the site map in a secondary window and provide a "you are here" marker within the page. This would be similar to location directories at malls, museums, and amusement parks that provide a "you are here" indicator to help the patrons find their way. The use of a similar construct on a Web site map would certainly give users more spatial orientation as they browse a site. An indication of the current document could be accomplished by distinguishing the page in the map by color, a graphic, or by size. Unfortunately, since the user could access the site map from any page on the site, adding this feature would require making the site map page dynamic. An example of this concept in action is shown in Figure 10-11.

Using a technology like JavaScript, it is not terribly difficult to augment a site map to provide such a feature. You can do this by looking at the referring page for a link and then having the site map highlight which page the user was on.

"Where You Were" Indicators

An even more sophisticated idea would be to show a user not only where they are, but where they have been during a site visit. You might augment a map automatically with information showing the user's trail through the site. While this can also be represented

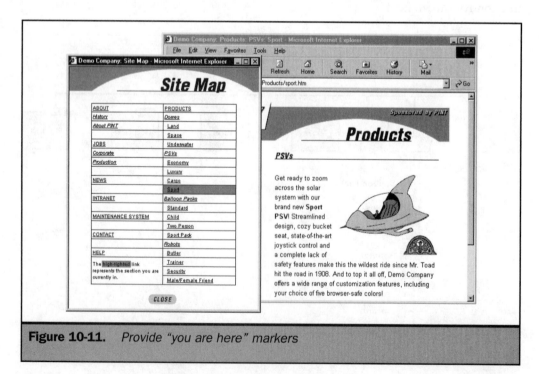

Figure 10-11.   *Provide "you are here" markers*

by the browser's history mechanism, a site map could be built to show page visit time or order. This may allow users to find pages they haven't visited recently. An example of one possibility of such a map is shown in Figure 10-12.

Producing Site Maps

For small sites, site maps are easy to produce manually, whether they take graphic or text form. For large sites, particularly those that have a great deal of dynamic content, developing a reasonably detailed map may be tedious. Automatic creation of a site navigation map is possible, but not always optimal. Tools do exist that can be used to produce textual or even graphical site maps. However, often these maps are geared more to a site maintainer looking for broken links on the site or performing similar structural maintenance.

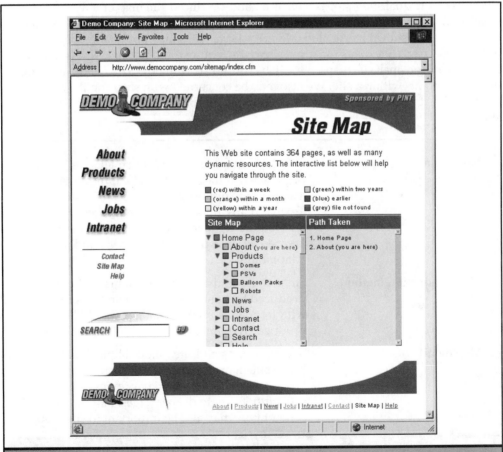

Figure 10-12.   *Site maps could show navigation history*

While automatic mapping would seem a good route, particularly for larger sites, showing the complete linking relationship of a site will often produce a tangled mess of page links. Given limited screen real estate, there is little real-world evidence to suggest that a graphical site map can show more than a few dozen pages without becoming unwieldy for the user. Textual maps are better. In either case, different levels of zooming could be useful—but potentially at the expense of showing content within the site.

Automatic mapping of a site may also fail to point out which pages are important in a site and should be identified as "site landmarks." It may be possible to use a heuristic, such as the number of links pointing to a page, hierarchy depth, or the amount of content in a page to determine which pages are important. However, these heuristics frequently fail, just as they do in search engines. The bottom line is that human guidance may be required for an automatic mapping tool to properly indicate the importance of pages.

Depending on the size of your site, you will have to choose between a graphical site map or a textual site map, as well as a hand-produced site map or a dynamically create map. No matter what the form, there will always be the question of how much detail should be shown in the map. Maps for larger sites may not be able to reasonably link to every page. Site maps for larger sites may require multiple zoom levels. However, in either large or small site maps, we will be concerned with how to show the importance of various points within a site. We also may be concerned with showing the amount of information at a particular location within a site. The basic site map design issues are summarized in Table 10-1.

Map form	Graphical maps are useful for small sites, particularly if they are static. Graphical maps also provide opportunity for visual design. Textual maps are useful for larger sites or those that require frequent changes. Textual maps are favored because of download speed and adaptability.
Map production method	Small maps and most graphical maps should be produced by hand. Large maps or maps for sites with frequent structure changes should be produced dynamically.
Map detail	Site maps for small sites should link to all pages. Large site maps should provide primary page links at a minimum and may provide zoom capability to get to deeper pages. Page size or content type may also be important to site maps.

Table 10-1.   *Site Map Design Considerations*

"Landmark" indication	Site maps should indicate important pages with graphic, text, color, size, or position cues.
Page characteristics	Site map entries should show important page characteristics, such as file size, access rights, or other pertinent information.
Location indication	Site maps should include a "you are here" feature when possible and spawn a separate window.

Table 10-1.   *Site Map Design Considerations* (continued)

While site maps can be useful, a survey of large sites shows that some have removed site maps in favor of search engines or site indexes. Some claim this trend is due to a lack of interest in site maps by users. Unfortunately, given common practices in site map design, it really is no surprise that their usage is limited. However, it is the author's opinion that a well-executed site map does have some value and should be included in every site.

Note *Site maps can provide more than navigation assistance. Web quality assurance tools may create maps to help developers find broken links or stale content. Further, a visual representation of site data can be used to discern data patterns in a site.*

Site Indexes

A site map may fail some users, particularly if they are scanning for a known item but are forced to guess the appropriate category. Even textual site maps that often resemble the table of contents of a book can be slow to scan if the user isn't familiar with the organization of the site. In the world of books, an index might be a more efficient way to find the page that a known item is referenced on.

An index for a book like this one provides an alphabetically organized reference of topics to page numbers. Thus, if a user wants to look up information on server logs they scan alphabetically to letter *S* and find a reference like this one,

```
Server logs, 381,743-746, 801
```

which indicates that six pages have references to server logs and the pages from 743 to 746 contain the most information on the subject. Given some sense of the scope of the book by its physical size, the discerning reader might think to look elsewhere for heavy

ELEMENTS OF
PAGE DESIGN

details on logging, given that the book devotes only a few pages to the subject. In view of the usefulness of an index in a book, many have tried to apply the idea to Web sites.

On the Web, a *site index* is an alphabetical listing of a site's contents. The label to reach a site index is typically called just that—a "site index"—but many sites unfortunately seem to mislabel this tool, calling it a "map" (or calling a map an "index"). While the simple label of just "index" might seem appropriate, site designers should consider that the word "index" on the Web has multiple meanings and is often considered to be a primary page of a section. Because of the inherent confusion with the label to this structure, some sites have more explicitly named links to the index, including "A–Z Index," "A–Z Topic Index," "Alphabetical Site Index," or some similar type of link name.

Suggestion: Label links to a site index as just "site index" or "A–Z index" if that is the only form of indexing provided.

A basic site index is shown in Figure 10-13. Notice how a lettering scheme with links is used to make it easy to navigate an index and that many pages may link to a particular topic.

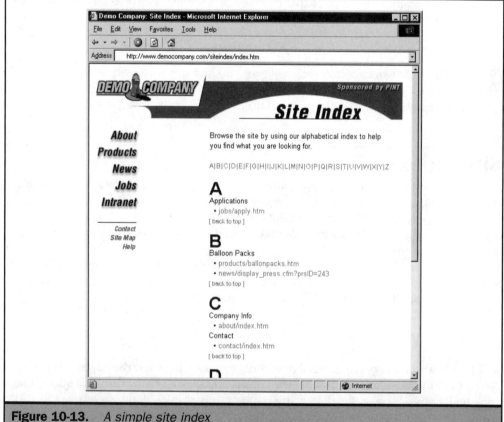

Figure 10-13.   *A simple site index*

As with a site map, access to a site index should be from every page within a site. Similarly, the site index should not be made a primary navigation choice. Like the site map, the site index link is often made available within a site-wide navigation bar, but its appearance or location is less prominent than main section navigation and is often clustered with other navigational aids.

Unlike site maps, the form of a site index is fairly regular and is nearly always text. It is possible to provide some graphical elements, such as icons, within a site index to indicate important index words or provide supplementary information such as content or page type. However, a graphical site index is not practical for all but the simplest sites; the only benefit would be stylizing the page to fit in aesthetically with the site. Other visual cues like color, font size, or font weight might be useful to distinguish more important concepts or pages within the index. A slightly more sophisticated-looking site index is shown in Figure 10-14.

Generation of an alphabetical site index can take some effort. For small sites, it may be possible to come up with topics and their associated pages quickly by hand; but as

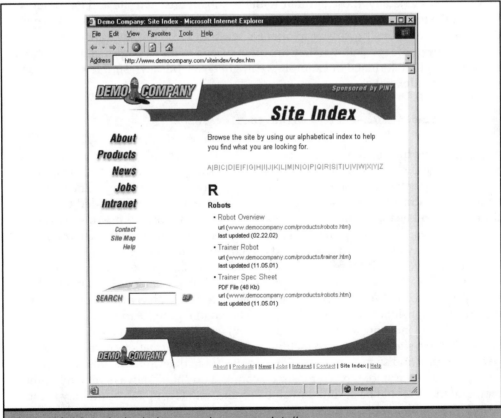

Figure 10-14.   *A site index may show page details*

ELEMENTS OF
PAGE DESIGN

the site grows, trouble may ensue both in volume and regularity of indexed terms. Two solutions present themselves: automation and controlled vocabularies.

Automation involves using an indexing tool like a search engine to analyze page content and determine word relevance on a per-page basis. Unfortunately, tool-created indexes will contain words of little or no relevance and will probably incorrectly associate some words and pages. The reason for this is obvious. Like search engine spiders, an index tool determines word/page relationships based upon word frequency and a variety of other criteria. This approach will not necessarily produce optimal results. Site designers should use tool-based results as a guide and produce the final index by hand.

A better solution would be to develop a *controlled vocabulary* and then to index pages to fit within the prescribed keywords in the defined vocabulary. Creation of the keywords in the controlled vocabulary can occur either in a top-down or bottom-up fashion. In top-down, you would come up with what are believed to be the keywords for the site without looking at the pages first and then try to fit pages into the keywords, making adjustments where required. A bottom-up approach would involve choosing keywords when looking at pages and then conforming similar keywords as they are encountered. Generally, those familiar with the subject area of a site and its contents will find the top-down with adjustments easier, but bottom-up may be useful to get started in the indexing process or to orient a new indexer to the site's content.

Once keywords are defined, they are often placed within a page using a **<meta>** tag or even in an RDF format. For example we might create our own simple **<meta>** tag value called **index-entry**,

```
<meta name="index-entry" value="Butler Robot" />
```

and then create the index by automatically collecting these values and associating them with the page URL. We may also store this information in a database and generate the index directly, rather than spidering **<meta>** tag information in a page. The value, of course, of the **<meta>** tag–based approach is that as static pages are added to the site, the content will be picked up in the index. However, as more sites are produced from an XML document, database, or content management system, the internal **<meta>** information may not need to be exposed directly in the document.

You may wonder if there are other ways to organize index content than alphabetically—the answer is a resounding "Yes!" (but alternatives have not yet been widely embraced in Web design). For example, in a site that has many updates, you may want to consider *time-based indexing*, as shown in Figure 10-15.

Time-based indexing (or temporal indexing) usually focuses on the time a page was added to a site and may also include modification information. Return visitors in particular may find such content sorting very useful to determine what exactly has changed in the site since their last visit. Of course, you should always remember that a temporal index would be of limited value in a site with few updates and may in fact reduce the credibility of the presented content by making it appear to be stale.

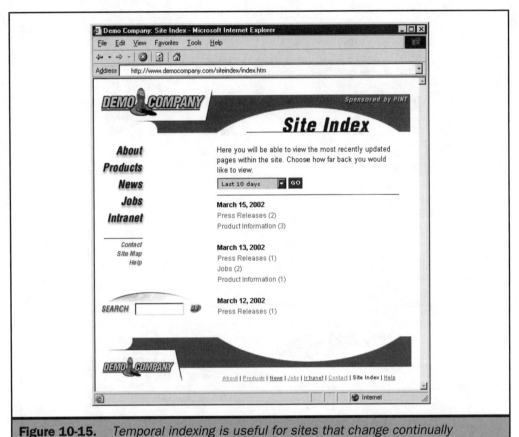

Figure 10-15.   *Temporal indexing is useful for sites that change continually*

Interestingly enough, temporal indexing of site content was actually popular on the Web in the early days in another form—the "What's New" page. You might consider keeping a "What's New" page along with a time-based index—the page could provide more details about additions or a summary of the more important additions to the Web site. More discussion of this structure can be found later in the chapter.

Another possible index organization might be a popularity-based index. You could show the pages ordered by how popular they are with visitors—how many unique page visitors viewed a page or how many times a page was requested. Such an index would help users determine which pages are deemed most important by the masses. Unfortunately, this may reveal information about site traffic you may not care to share, and it also may not help users find useful content that just isn't considered popular. It is also possible for such metrics to be manipulated by unscrupulous site visitors, and there is the possibility of creating a negative feedback loop as people go to falsely

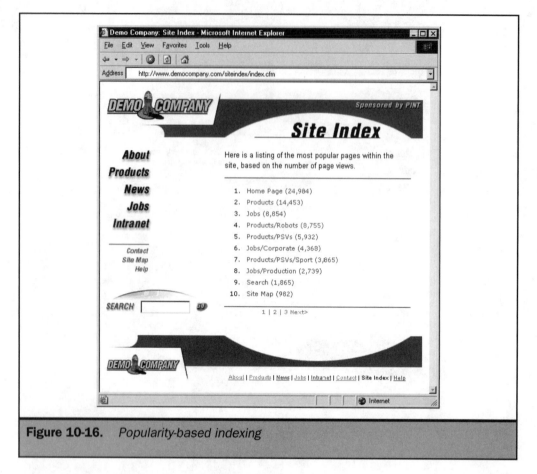

Figure 10-16.   *Popularity-based indexing*

popular sections just because it is top on the list. Figure 10-16 shows a popularity-based index slice.

Another possibility might be to show some satisfaction or quality ranking if users provide feedback on a page, as shown in Figure 10-17.

Another indexing possibility includes showing landmark pages by indicating which pages are heavily linked to and which pages have heavy outbound links. You might even consider indexing by file size or type. There are certainly other possibilities, but the value of adding more and more indexing schemes may diminish as users are overwhelmed by the site sorting possibilities.

While a site index today is not a common structure on the Web, it is in many ways preferable to a site map. A site index does not rely on a particular physical site organization, so maintenance is not difficult even for a dynamically generated site. A simple alphabetical site index is easy to use and is useful for known item searches, while a more complex site index allows users to slice site contents in whatever way

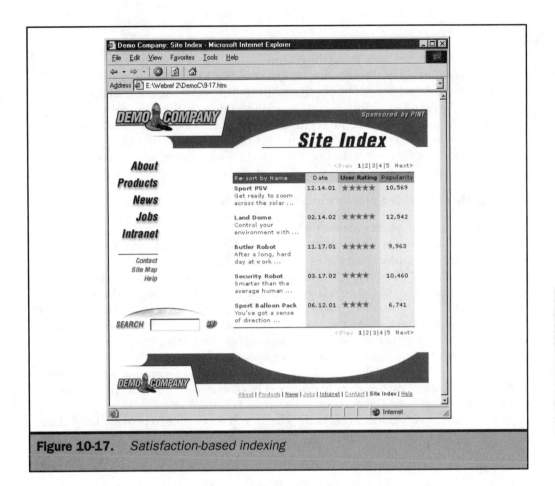

Figure 10-17.   *Satisfaction-based indexing*

suits them rather than with the predefined structure presented. A site index really encourages content-based navigation rather than structural navigation, which should fit user Web habits well.

Miscellaneous Site Navigation Aids

Beyond the site map and site index, numerous less popular navigation aids are being used in Web sites. Some of these are very useful in particular types of sites, but certainly many may become historical curiosities in the future. So, just because you can add them to your site, consider well their value first. If you do end up using them, study their usage in log files and solicit feedback from users about their usefulness to determine whether they make sense for your site in the long run.

Glossary

Many Web sites, particularly those filled with industry-specific jargon, would benefit from a little-used site aid—the *glossary*. A few sites that have complex jargon and appeal to people who may not be familiar with all the terms—online trading sites, for example—have employed glossaries successfully. However, there are relatively few glossaries used on the Web. Of the Fortune 100 companies, only seven had an easily identifiable glossary on their Web pages in the first half of 2002, up from two in the summer of 1999. Other sites, including those dealing with technical or financial material, also failed to show a heavy increase in glossary sections.

Suggestion: Provide a glossary in a site filled with complex jargon.

A glossary link may not necessarily be required on all pages, but should at least be readily accessible from a help page. Such links are often found within secondary navigation structures, like site indexes. Regardless of where it is found on a page, the link label should be "Glossary," "Site Glossary," or "Common Word Glossary."

A full-site glossary should be spawned as a separate smaller pop-up window. Otherwise, it will be difficult for users to utilize it properly, as they will have to consult word definitions without seeing the word in use. If the glossary is more than two-dozen entries long, a letter-style link list should be provided. Very long word lists should include a search feature. Like a site index, a glossary should be implemented in text and should be easily updatable. Site designers should consider creating a print-friendly version of a site glossary for users to print and have as a reference when they browse the site. An example of a site glossary is shown in Figure 10-18.

Rather than have a general link to the glossary, it is possible to provide links close to words that are often misunderstood.

DEMO COMPANY PRODUCTS

Robots
Habitat Domes
Balloon Packs
PSVs (glossary entry)

It is also possible to provide ToolTip information rather than a glossary link via the **title** attribute, which is a core attribute for nearly all HTML/XHTML elements. Acronyms and first-word occurrences of complex ideas make perfect candidates for this approach:

```
<span class="word-with-glossary-entry"
      title="Personal Space Vehicle-- a plutonium
      powered space car for personal use">
PSV</span>
```

If you use the ToolTip approach for word definition, make it obvious to the user that the item is selectable. The previous example related a style sheet rule by setting the **class** attribute to "word-with-glossary-entry." This **class** value should relate to a style entry to make the word look different from the common text.

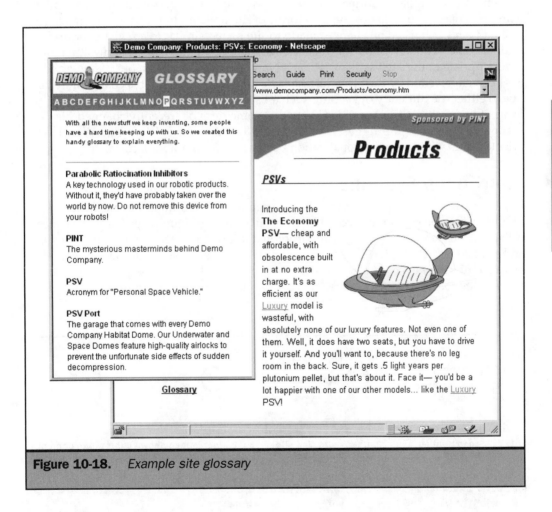

Figure 10-18.   *Example site glossary*

"What's New" Sections

Sites that are consistently updated should include some form of "What's New" section in the site to aid return visitors. The use of "last updated" text along with a date on a site's home page or at the bottom of a page is not appropriate because it does not indicate exactly what has changed on a site. Further, as many of these indications are script generated, simply opening and saving a page may change the date of update regardless of any actual changes made to the site.

Rather than forcing users to guess what has changed on a site, the site could employ a "What's New" section to alert return users to changes in site content. The section should contain only site-update information, but, unfortunately, many such sections are loaded with press releases and do not cover all forms of site updates. In the past, Web managers created pages that listed all changes made to site pages, similar to a revision or update list to the site. A survey of Fortune 500 sites at the time of this writing shows that the "every update in the site" style of "What's New" sections has fallen out of favor and has been superseded by the press release style of "What's New." This change may be due to either the difficulty of keeping such a list up to date or the heavy marketing focus of many sites. Over time, it is likely that some form of "recently changed files" section will become popular as WYSIWYW (What You See Is What You Want)–oriented sites with heavy personalization become more commonplace.

Keyword Jump Systems

One navigation system popular with larger organizations running various forms of offline and online promotions could be dubbed a "keyword jump system." The concept is that various keywords or codes are promoted in print advertisements, direct postal and e-mail interactions, television spots, and so on. A user visiting the site should be able to enter the keycode (often directly in a field off the home page) and then be transported to the advertised page. This concept is illustrated in Figure 10-19.

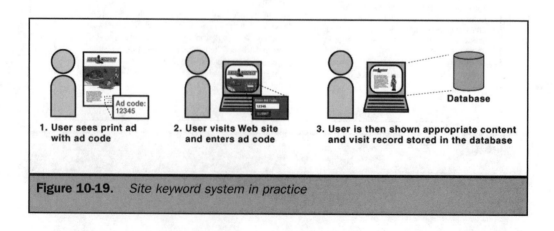

1. **User sees print ad with ad code**

2. **User visits Web site and enters ad code**

3. **User is then shown appropriate content and visit record stored in the database**

Database

Figure 10-19.   *Site keyword system in practice*

The value of keyword jump systems is that it allows organizations to avoid promoting long URLs in favor of easier ones to memorize keywords. These keywords can be used not only for navigation but for tracking, since many organizations may have the keywords indicate how the user found out about them. So far, such navigational systems are limited primarily to e-commerce sites; but given that the AOL Keyword system is widely known and browser vendors have been experimenting with keywords in the location bar, such systems may become much more popular in the future.

Site Tours

First-time visitors to complex sites as well as novice Web users may have a difficult time navigating, regardless of the site's structure or navigation aids (such as site maps). One way to help orient new users is the *tour*. A simple automatic or self-guiding linear path of pages can be implemented in a site, showing the site's most important pages along with explanations of how to navigate the site. A theoretical conception of a guided tour is shown in Figure 10-20.

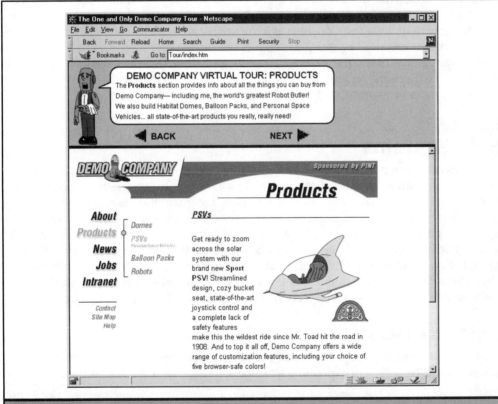

Figure 10-20.   *Guided tours are useful for first-time visitors*

As discussed in Chapter 6, a linear structure is very easy for new users to deal with. They may welcome the loss of control in exchange for introductory site use lessons. Theoretical support for tours as a navigation aid goes back to the earliest hypertext ideas presented by Vannevar Bush, who described "trails" through document sets that other users could follow. But despite anecdotal and theoretical support for the hypertext trail idea, the use of site tours and similar devices to help users navigate has so far been limited. They are primarily useful for novice or first-time users; advanced users will find them limiting or even annoying.

Following Traveled-Path Systems

Beyond preplanned guided tours of a particular site, there has been some growth in community-built tours or preplanned paths through the Web, the most prominent example being a Web ring (www.webring.com). Page popularity indexes and various voting systems that indicate site, page, or link popularity also show the possibility of directing users where to go. Even the popular "Similar items purchased by others" concept has been used successfully to guide people to likely purchases in e-commerce sites. Unfortunately, navigation related to following traveled paths of other users does have significant downsides. Consider that the unscrupulous site owner or even other site visitors may create a "beaten grass" effect by clicking on links or rigging the site to make it appear that users find a particular path appealing. Such manipulation certainly breaks trust with users, and site owners should be wary of popularity-based navigation systems that can be manipulated by unscrupulous visitors.

Help Systems

Regardless of the quality of implementation, some users will invariably be confused by a site's navigation or method of use. Unlike software, sites generally cannot rely on print documentation to answer questions. Online documentation is really the only approach to providing extra assistance for the user. Few sites actually have any help systems at all. A survey of the Fortune 100 sites during the summer of 1999 shows that only 11 had any form of help system. By 2002, the situation had vastly improved, with 23 having an obvious help system. However, considering that all had customer support phone lines, it seems there is still a long way to go in customer service online. On a more positive note, help systems were ubiquitous among the large e-commerce sites.

When to Use Help

While few sites employ fully developed online help systems, *all* sites should have at least a basic help system explaining site labels, navigation facilities, technology requirements, and contact information for technical support or bug reporting. Figure 10-21 shows an example of a very simple help page.

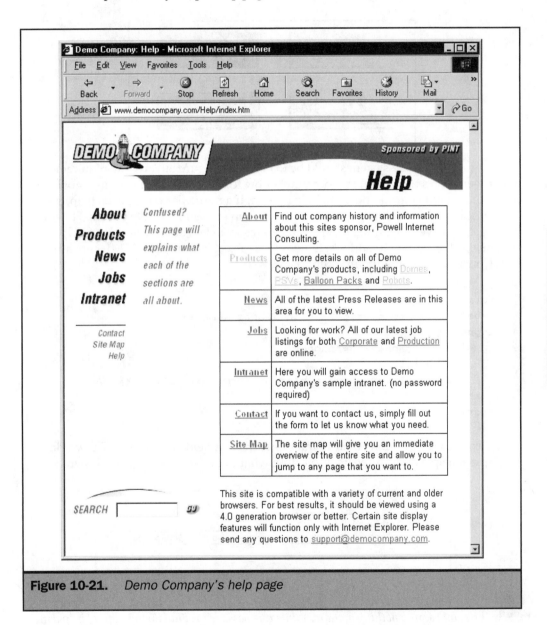

Figure 10-21. *Demo Company's help page*

Help pages would eliminate the need for a splash or home page covered with browser, plug-in, and technology requirement statements and buttons, as shown here:

The goal of the help system should be to help users figure out any site requirements, orient themselves to the site, and determine how to accomplish their desired goal. Be careful not to hide information in a help system. If a particular page needs help, put the help information within the page rather than burying it behind a Help button. However, if this gets too overwhelming, it is possible to resort to less obvious forms of help.

The most basic way to add a help item to an object is using the HTML core attribute **title**. Consider the following markup:

```
<form>
<label style="font-weight: bold">Phone Number:
<input type="text"
       name="phone" id="phone"
       size="15"
       title="Enter phone number of form (XXX) XXX-XXXX" />
</label>
</form>
```

When the user positions their pointer over the text field, a small ToolTip window similar to a help balloon appears, indicating what to do with the field, as shown here:

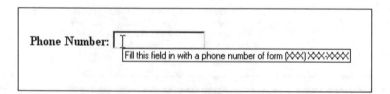

Note   *Older browsers may not support the use of the **title** attribute; however, degradation is graceful because nothing appears. While it is possible to simulate this type of help with JavaScript, it is not recommended.*

Rather than using a mouse-over, you could create a simple link, such as the word "Help" or a simple Question Mark icon, and have it create a small Help window explaining what to do with the field. The simple markup shown here,

```
<form>
<label style="font-weight: bold;">Phone Number:
<input type="text"
       name="phone" id="phone"
       size="15"
       title="Enter phone number of form (XXX) XXX-XXXX" />

<span style="font-size: xx-small">
<a href="javascript:alert('Enter phone number of form (XXX)
XXX-XXXX')">Need help?</a>;
</span>
</label>
</form>
```

can be used to create a simple JavaScript-style help system utilizing an alert box.

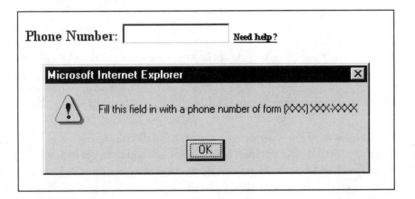

Complex Help Systems

Most Web sites should rely on help systems that are immediately apparent. Instructions should be in place, ToolTips should always be on, and a Help button should be prominent on every page. However, power users may find such a heavy degree of help annoying. Within intranets and some extranets, it may be desirable to follow more conventional Windows-style help forms. In most software environments, the help system is invoked by the F1 key, which brings up a Help window like the one shown next.

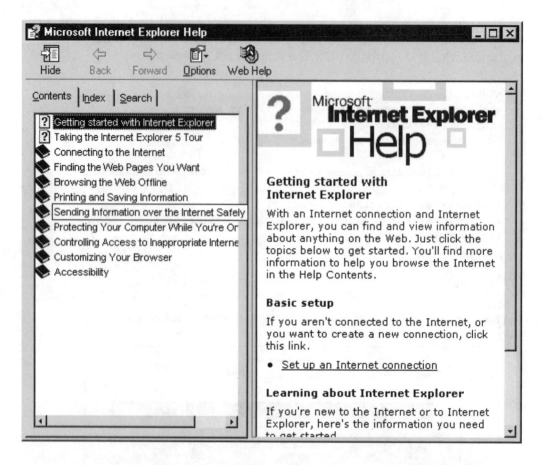

The typical Help window provides a Contents tab that shows a collapsible/ expandable outline form of the various help subjects available, an index that provides a quick lookup by a fixed vocabulary, and a free-text search query system. Setting up a similar help system for a Web site is possible. Microsoft's HTML Help (http:// msdn.microsoft.com/workshop/author/htmlhelp/default.asp) provides the ability to add sophisticated help systems to Web sites. Unfortunately, the strict Microsoft approach doesn't work in all browsers, because it relies on an ActiveX control only available to Internet Explorer 4.X and greater browsers. If you need cross-browser and cross-platform help, you will also have to provide Java- or JavaScript-based help. Some software vendors—notably, eHelp (www.ehelp.com)—offer systems to create cross-browser help. WebHelp from eHelp creates a help system that works under a variety of platforms and browsers. An example of this type of complex help system is shown in Figure 10-22.

While complex online help systems provide a great deal of power, they can be relatively time-consuming to create. However, if users (particularly intranet users) are

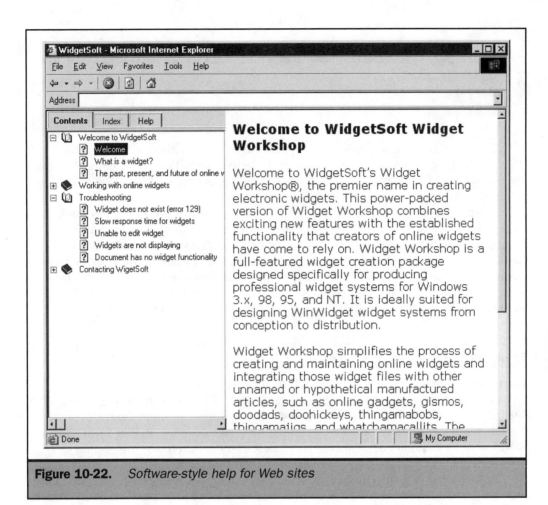

Figure 10-22.   *Software-style help for Web sites*

familiar with using standard help conventions, like the F1 key, it is important to accommodate them. Microsoft has defined a special JavaScript event, **onhelp**, that can be used with most HTML elements (particularly form fields) to associate actions with the press of the F1 key. This simple example shows how it might be used with a text field:

```
<form>
<label style="font-weight: bold;">Phone Number:
<input type="text"
   name="phone"
   id="phone"
```

```
   size="15"
   onhelp="alert('Enter phone number of form (XXX) XXX-XXXX');return
   false" / >
</label>
</form>
```

Notice that the code requires a false return value, since without this value the browser's help system will be invoked after the help information is presented. It turns out that we could instead invoke a Windows help file, but again this is somewhat Windows centric.

No matter how you do it, always remember that even if your help system is crafted properly, you still will not completely remove confusion from your site. Because users still might not understand everything, make sure to provide an e-mail form (or at least an address) for users to ask questions. Commonly, this is in the form: webmaster@domain.com. Unfortunately, beyond this simple e-mail, few Web sites seem to provide any major degree of technical support, but this will certainly change as sites become more complex and people become much more self-reliant.

Navigation Aid Trends

The future of navigation aids is unclear, but a few trends can be observed. First, site assistance is becoming more important. Examination of large e-commerce sites puts site maps, indexes, technical assistance, and other features clearly in the realm of customer service. Already, some e-commerce sites have adopted an idea from real world stores: a customer assistance section. Lost users are driven to this section to receive help to get back on track and complete their transactions.

Another trend is an increased role of browser navigation assistance. Already, some browser add-ons show page rankings, previous visitor paths, or even site overviews. In the future, a Web browser might be able to provide a visualization of a site, or even read an overview of a site's topics and provide its own views for users. Yet, even if the browser does the presentation, the content of such a map will still have to be developed and provided to the browser.

Last, the reliance on meta data to form sophisticated navigation systems will continue to increase. For example, in a *facet map* you could map all the site's content by its characteristics or facets. A common example might be to categorize types of beer by brand and type (such as pilsner or ale), color (such as red or brown), country of origin (such as Germany, New Zealand, or U.S.A.), and so on. You might then allow the user to slice the information by the facets presented. Some sites do this using "finding systems," while others use a style of search breakdown. Both are shown in Figure 10-23.

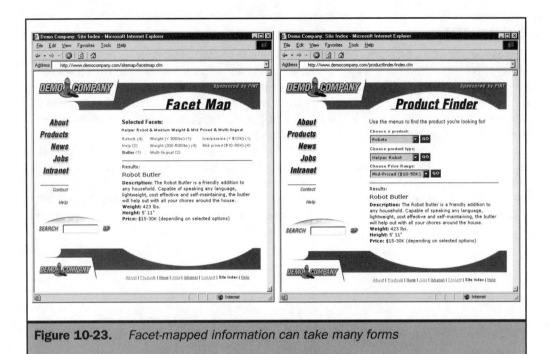

Figure 10-23.   *Facet-mapped information can take many forms*

Note that faceted classification favors regular data that is fully categorized, but it does enable a variety of interesting possibilities beyond the presented navigation scheme, such as generating "Related Links" to a particular page.

RELATED LINKS:
- **About Demo Company**
- **About Robots**
- **Artificial Intelligence**
- **Home Help Resources**

Even more complex are *topic maps* that show interrelationships among subjects through a variety of associations. For example, a subject like "Web Design" might have an association with this book. This book, in turn, has an association with this author and certain URLs online, while the author may have a variety of URLs related to the work in the book. A topic map helps organize these relationships in a structured manner. Once in such a form, topic maps may be exchanged or even combined when they are in an XML format. While they sound exciting, the complexity of producing and using topic maps has so far significantly hampered their use online.

Summary

Site maps provide a familiar construct for Web site visitors. Just as people use a map in the real world to find their way, a site map provides a guide for users to find their way to particular pieces of information on a site. Site maps may be graphical, textual, or a combination of both, and they are organized in a variety of ways. There are limits to the effectiveness of site maps. Users may not actually form mental models of site structures like designers do. A site index often provides greater benefit to users than a site map and can provide multiple ways to view data, including viewing data ranked by popularity or by some temporal criterion. Other aids such as glossaries or site tours may be useful in helping visitors figure sites out. A full-blown help system may even be required, particularly if complex forms need to be filled out. Finally, no single site aid meets all users' needs. The differences between users suggest that designers should strive to employ as many navigational aids as reasonable on a site.

The Complete Reference

Web Design

Part III

Elements of Page Design

The Complete Reference

Web Design

Chapter 11

Pages and Layout

The fundamental unit of a Web site is a page. Unlike with printed material, the characteristics of a Web page can vary dramatically between sites, as well as within a single site. Inspection of numerous pages shows that there are common page types—such as home pages, search pages, and content pages—that tend to have similar characteristics. However, the similarities between page types across sites can be slight. Even issues as basic as the width and height of pages can evoke contentious debate among designers. Despite this debate, Web design conventions suggest that some page layouts tend to work better than others. Designers should start exploring page layouts with these basic layouts in mind and then modify them to fit the content being presented. Extremely creative layout, while often visually inspiring, should be considered somewhat dangerous, as the purpose of page layout is always to assist the user in page use. Consistency in page layouts can go a long way towards improving page usability.

What Is a Page?

This concept of a page is at the very heart of a Web site. In the simplest sense, a page is what appears in a browser window. One page equals one URL. A user types in a URL and a document appears in the window. These days, things aren't so simple. A URL might load multiple documents in the browser window, and the so-called Web page might be broken up into many smaller windows or frames. Today a "screen" may be a better analogy, but "page" is the term we have and is unlikely to change.

In the print world, a page is a component of a document like a book or a press release. A page is a "chunk" of the larger structure. Of course the page itself is broken down into smaller chunks, such as paragraphs, sentences, headers, footers, illustrations, and the like. The Web world is no different. A Web site may contain a large amount of content on a particular subject, but it is divided up or "chunked" into different pages. Each of the chunks should be a self-contained "idea" that contributes to the whole. Ideas can span multiple pages in a coherent flow of steps, stages, or parts. The goal in setting up Web sites is to take a body of content and spread it across a series of interrelated pages for easy digestion by the user, as shown in Figure 11-1.

Chunking content is often more of an art than a science. A designer has to make some chunks bigger and some chunks smaller than others. Unlike in print, the dimensions of a Web page are not always fixed.

Page Sizes

The potential size of a Web page, in a theoretical sense, is both infinitely long and infinitely wide. However, given that overly long or wide pages would be difficult for a user to comprehend, use, or even print, there should be some consideration of appropriate page size. The most obvious question to ask yourself is what the appropriate size of a page should be. Even in paper, there are numerous sizes, but the Web certainly lacks an equivalent for the ubiquitous 8½ x 11-inch letter size. This is both good and bad.

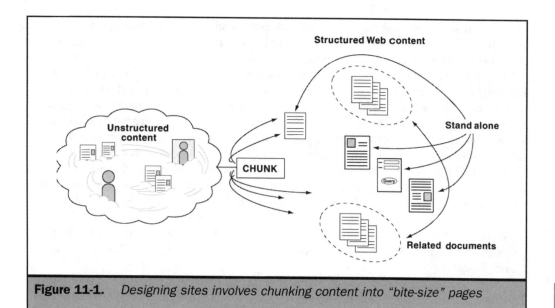

Figure 11-1.   *Designing sites involves chunking content into "bite-size" pages*

Is it really a problem that the Web lacks a standard page size? In the world of print, there are standard sizes rather than a single standard size. Printed materials might range from something as small as a fortune cookie message to something as large as a poster. Brochures, CD case liners, letters, business cards, paperback books, and so on all have different sizes. The Web is the same. Just as with print, the key to a successful Web page is whether the "size" is suited to the content. If the content is too little for the dimensions selected, you may find that the page has excessive white space, which may seem unusual to readers, particularly if they are accustomed to variable page sizes. Conversely, if there is too much content, it may not fit within the user's screen, forcing the content to be split across multiple screens.

Rule: Set the size of the page to fit the purpose and the content at hand.

Despite the variations in sizes resulting from differences in content, there are many reasons that standard sizes are a good idea. In the print world, if we didn't settle on a particular size of paper, such as standard letter size, it would be very difficult to buy paper, create laser printers, and so on. On the Web, some designers struggle with a lack of standardization. Numerous people have attempted to price Web site development services on a per page basis, but what exactly constitutes the size of a page? Aren't bigger pages, regardless of complexity, at least slightly more costly to do than smaller ones?

The fixed-page way of thinking may occasionally lead to lessened readability. If Web sites are priced on a "per page" basis, customers will try to cram as much data as possible into a single page. It doesn't really reduce production costs, and it may result in a long, dense, cluttered page that will lack both aesthetic appeal and onscreen readability. Also, fixed-size pages may result in page breaks at odd moments in the document, making it difficult to follow.

Fixed page sizes have definite advantages when trying to decide how to "chunk" information. Like a physical sheet of paper, there is a finite number of characters that will fit on the page. Further, a fixed size gives constructive boundaries for what may appear on a given page. Finally, fixed page sizes can also increase readability, as users know what to expect when viewing a page. They know it will be a certain size, with reliable elements, and will print or can be e-mailed in a predictable manner.

Given all the potential benefits of fixed page sizes, what size makes sense? First consider letter size paper. This is a standard 8½ x 11-inch paper size; on a system with a typical resolution of 72dpi, this works out to be 612 pixels by 792 pixels. Consider browser chrome in a browser like Internet Explorer and you'll see that this works out to be around three screens filled with content at 640 x 480, two screens or so at 800 x 600, a screen and a half at 1024 x 768. The entire page fits finally at 1280 x 1024, as shown in Figure 11-2.

What does this tell us? It lets us know that the user's screen is really the problem. The big question, then, is what is the user's screen size? Considering computer systems first, common screen sizes include 640 x 480, 800 x 600, 1024 x 768, 1280 x 1024, and 1600 x 1200. Numerous others sizes are important as well, such as MSNTV and Palm screen sizes. Table 11-1 details the common screen resolutions found.

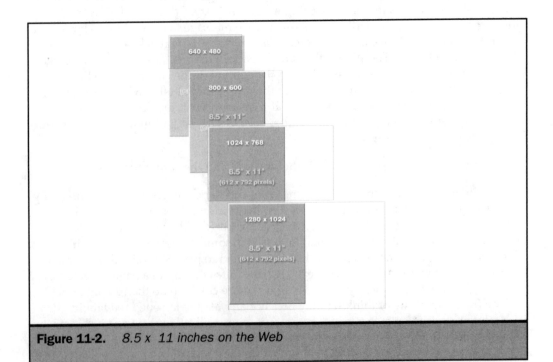

Figure 11-2.   *8.5 x 11 inches on the Web*

Resolution	Device	Comments
Varies dramatically from 3 lines by 12 characters to 320 x 240 pixels or more with cell-PDA hybrids	Cell phone	Resolution often measured in characters across and lines up and down rather than pixels.
320 x 240	Palm sized PDA	Scrolling difficult in this environment. Single screen-full approach common.
640 x 240	Windows CE "Breast pocket" form factor	Half-height VGA
544 x 372	MSNTV/WebTV	Rightward scrolling not possible. See http://developer.msntv.com for useful information.
640 x 480	Computer (low resolution)	Typical worst-case PC resolution.
800 x 600	Computer (standard resolution)	Probably a safe resolution assumption.
1024 x 768	Computer (high resolution)	About the limit of content expansion before significant usability problems might ensue.
1152 x 864	Computer (high resolution)	
1200 x 1024	Computer (high resolution)	
1600 x 1200	Computer (high resolution)	

Table 11-1. *Common Screen Resolutions*

Screen size really doesn't matter as much as designers might think. Even if users have a particular resolution, they may not size their browser to fit the entire screen, nor may they want to. The chrome of common browsers will take up screen space. Various operating system features, such as the Windows system tray, always will take up some room anyway. Even if you assume users have a 640 x 480 resolution, you may find as

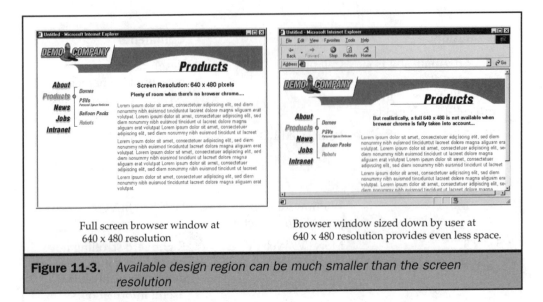

Full screen browser window at
640 x 480 resolution

Browser window sized down by user at
640 x 480 resolution provides even less space.

Figure 11-3. *Available design region can be much smaller than the screen resolution*

little as 570–580 usable pixels of screen width before scrolling, and 280–300 pixels of usable screen height, depending on the browser version. Figure 11-3 illustrates the screen region issues.

Designers often want a hard and fast screen height and width, but unfortunately the amount of room consumed by browser chrome varies dramatically. Consider an older browser like Netscape 3 under Windows with all options on. The browser chrome shown here takes up a whopping 150 pixels of vertical space.

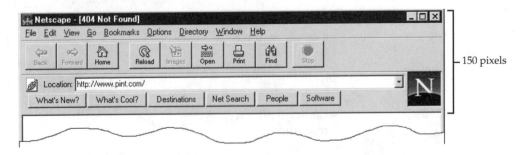

150 pixels

Newer browsers are generally more conservative in the amount of space they take up. Browser chrome will vary not just by browser, but by user preference. Compare standard Netscape and Internet Explorer browser chrome to their potentially minimized sizes, as shown in Figure 11-4.

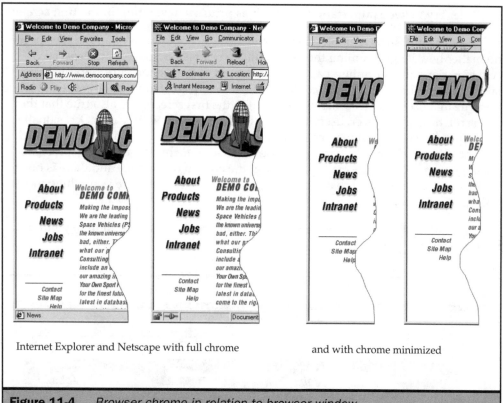

Internet Explorer and Netscape with full chrome   and with chrome minimized

Figure 11-4.   *Browser chrome in relation to browser window*

The reason that designers need to be concerned about screen size is that Web pages need to fit. It is well known that users will resist scrolling to the right, so pages need to fit the width of the screen if possible. Also consider that very wide pages rarely print well, especially if special printer style sheets are not employed.

Rule: Avoid wide pages, particularly those that cause rightward scrolling.

When it comes to page height, it is pretty obvious that users evaluate the first screen and then decide if they want to scroll or choose something on the first screen. Statistically, users will tend to pick items within the first screen over other items that they can't see yet. It is particularly important to make sure that important items like primary navigation elements appear on the first screen. The breaking point before something is off screen is termed the "fold," after the same concept in print design.

Rule: Try to keep important items such as primary navigation in the first screen.

Screen height isn't as troublesome as screen width. For example, pages can be printed no matter how long, assuming the user wants to print a long page. Some special considerations about printing pages are addressed in the section "Print-Specific Pages" later on in the chapter. Limiting content to fit screen height isn't a huge concern—while it is true that users will tend to favor content in the first screen, it is also true that they will scroll down. However, users will only scroll if they know they can. Occasionally the way a page is laid out may not indicate clearly that the page contains downward content, other than the scrollbar on the side of the screen. This is particularly problematic if a large amount of white space is exactly at the bottom of the page and there is no background tile or content that would suggest to the user that there is anything more. This idea is illustrated in Figure 11-5.

Suggestion: Be aware of the screen "fold" and try to hint at content beyond the first screen.

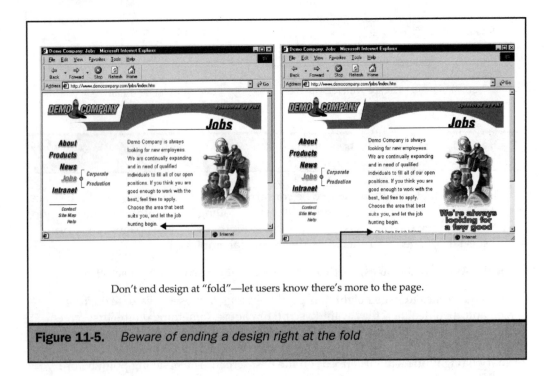

Don't end design at "fold"—let users know there's more to the page.

Figure 11-5. *Beware of ending a design right at the fold*

Dealing with Screen Size

Designers have a variety of ways of dealing with screen size. Some designers have taken a very anti-user stance by suggesting that users ought to have a certain size, such as 800 x 600; therefore, their sites will be designed to that resolution whether visitors like it or not. Sites practicing this philosophy often contain message like this:

> **This site best viewed under 800x600**

While it may be written in a nice tone, messages like this basically say "go away" to users who don't have such a resolution. It is very difficult to use sites like this with 640 x 480 or less. Some sites with frames are completely unusable at lower resolutions because the frames can't even be resized! Such exclusionary design based on resolution is a poor idea and really does not have a place in user-centered design.

Rule: Avoid resolution entry restrictions for sites if at all possible.

Resolution assumptions can really hurt non-PC based browsing. For example, MSNTV (previously known as WebTV) sets size exactly at 544 x 372. Particularly troublesome is that if a design goes beyond 544 pixels wide, it will not fit on a television screen. Rightward scrolling is not an option here. This is a pretty serious example of how a design approach restricting resolution to 800 x 600 would completely lock out users.

Rule: When designing for MSNTV/WebTV, consider a hard-and-fast page width of 544 pixels.

While television-based browsing is fairly limited, other devices with smaller screen sizes, like personal digital assistants, may also find the 800 x 600 fixed design style very troubling as well.

Assuming Page Size

WebTV's resolution restrictions play well to another crowd of designers, those who always assume the worst display will be the one used. Some go so far as to limit pages to be purely text-based and rely on percentage values to scale everything, while others aim to please almost everybody by trying to aim for some reasonable lowest common denominator, such as 640 x 480 resolution on a Windows system with a popular browser like Netscape or Internet Explorer. If you make assumptions about such minimum criteria, it may seem possible to figure out a typical screen size for the user. Consider this carefully, though. Given that the user has 640 x 480 resolution, what is the largest amount of screen area in the browser window? This is called the canvas space and is measured like this:

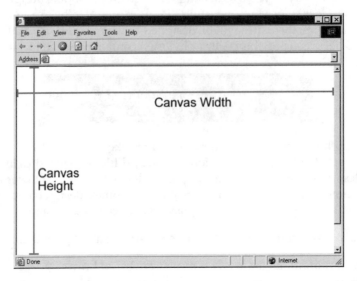

Obviously, canvas size varies. Did the user full-screen the browser, or are there other items taking up screen real estate? How much browser chrome do they have? If a user full-screens and leaves the settings alone in the browser, this could be your best-case possibility. On 640 x 480, this might equate to a width of 580 up to 620 pixels, depending on browser version, operating system, and variables such as whether the scrollbar is on or not. Vertical assumptions might range from as few as 290 pixels to up to 330 pixels or more. Similar variations, of course, are found for higher resolutions. Erring on the safe side is to assume 40 pixels off screen width and 190 off screen height. Given the common resolutions of 640 x 480, 800 x 600, and 1024 x 768, you would have the canvas size estimates in Table 11-2.

Alternatively, we could come up with a variety of measurements of the amount of chrome in a browser and how it tends to size on launch, size for whether scrollbars are on or off, and so on. This whole approach is very troublesome. What really is potential screen region? What happens if the user doesn't size their window up and just leaves it as it is or even sizes it smaller? The actual available size of a browser varies as well, and is often even less than what is presented in Table 11-2. Because of the uncertainty of

	640 x 480	800 x 600	1024 x 768
Probable canvas size	600 x 290	760 x 410	984 x 578

Table 11-2. *Potential Available Canvas Assumptions*

screen size, you might want to consider a "slop" factor in layouts. For example, if the available width is 600 pixels, you might want to provide 5% to 10% extra room for slop. It is obvious that assumptions, even when conservative and with a slop factor built-in, leave something to be desired.

Suggestion: If designing with assumed screen sizes, be conservative and give yourself a slop factor of as much as 10% of the available region.

Detecting Page Size

Rather than guess, it is possible to detect the available resolution using JavaScript. This simple script checks for screen size as well as available window size.

```
<!DOCTYPE HTML PUBLIC "-//W3C//DTD XHTML 1.0 Transitional//EN"
"http://www.w3.org/TR/xhtml1/DTD/xhtml1-transitional.dtd">
<html xmlns="http://www.w3.org/1999/xhtml">
<head>
<title>Resolution Checker</title>
</head>
<body>
<h2>Resize and reload</h2>
<hr />
<br /><br /><br /><br /><br />
<script type="text/javascript">
<!--
if (window.screen)
   {
    document.write("Screen: "+screen.width+"x"+screen.height+"<br />");
      winWidth = (window.innerWidth) ? window.innerWidth :
document.body.clientWidth;
    winHeight = (window.innerHeight) ? window.innerHeight :
document.body.clientHeight;

    if (winWidth && winHeight)
     document.write("Window: "+winWidth+"x"+winHeight+"<br />");
   }
  else
    document.write("<b>Requires 4.x generation browser or better</b>");
//-->
</script>
<noscript>
JavaScript must be on and you must use a 4.x generation or
better browser to detect resolution and canvas area.
</noscript>
</body>
</html>
```

While this script does generate a message on page resolution requirements, it would be better to sense for the available screen region and set content appropriately. For example, consider writing out style sheets that deal with all the various screen sizes. This next script example uses JavaScript available in the 4.*x* generation browsers to sense for screen resolution and outputs the appropriate link to a suitable style sheet. If an older browser views the page or the scripting support is off, the browser will resort to a worst-case scenario of using the lowest resolution settings.

```
<!DOCTYPE HTML PUBLIC "-//W3C//DTD XHTML 1.0 Transitional//EN"
"http://www.w3.org/TR/xhtml1/DTD/xhtml1-transitional.dtd">
<html xmlns="http://www.w3.org/1999/xhtml">
<head>
<title>Style Based On Resolution </title>
<script type="text/javascript">
<!--
if (window.screen)
   {
    if (screen.width < 641)
     document.write('<link rel="stylesheet" href="lowres.css" / >\n');
    else if (screen.width < 801)
     document.write('<link rel="stylesheet" href="mediumres.css" / >\n');
    else if (screen.width < 1025)
     document.write('<link rel="stylesheet" href="highres.css" / >\n');
    else
     document.write('<link rel="stylesheet" href="ultrahighres.css" / >\n');
   }
  else
    document.write('<link rel="stylesheet" href="lowres.css" / >\n');

//-->
</script>
<noscript>
<link rel="stylesheet" href="lowres.css" / >
</noscript>
</head>
<body>
Add your page content here
</body>
</html>
```

ELEMENTS OF
PAGE DESIGN

*The previous example will have a validation problem due to the **<noscript>** tag in the **<head>** of the document. This is an oversight in the XHTML specification; the mistake is intentional in that it makes the script perform adequately in all situations.*

Obviously, the previous example could be adjusted to output different images or background tiles or to set measurement sizes all based upon resolution or even window size. However, this brings up a familiar issue. Just because users have a 2000 x 2000 screen, do they necessarily want the content of a page to expand to fit the available screen? Consider that a 2000 x 2000 image will certainly take much longer to download! Relative sizing and scaling issues improve the situation and can restore a balance between users' wants and designers' need for control.

Relative Page Sizes

Another approach to dealing with page sizes relative to screen resolution is to not deal with it exactly. Why not use a relative size? For example, imagine a table layout like this:

```
<!DOCTYPE HTML PUBLIC "-//W3C//DTD XHTML 1.0 Transitional//EN"
"http://www.w3.org/TR/xhtml1/DTD/xhtml1-transitional.dtd">
<html xmlns="http://www.w3.org/1999/xhtml">
<head>
<title>Stretch Me</title>
</head>
<body>
<table width="100%" bgcolor="yellow">
<tr>
<td>
<p>This table is 100% of the width of the screen. Notice if you
stretch the content will expand to fit the available space.
Stretching may not always help with readability, as you can have
very long lines of text.</p>
</td>
</tr>
</table>
</body>
</html>
```

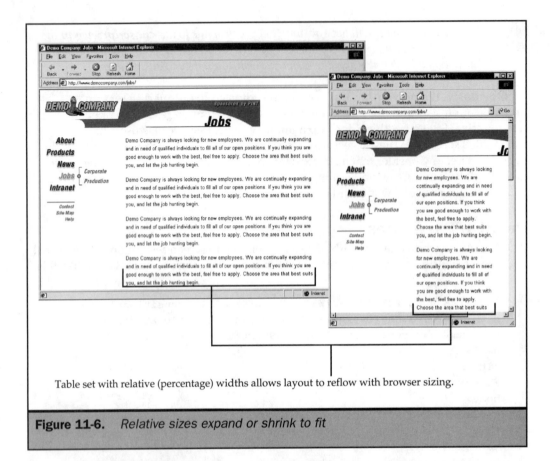

Table set with relative (percentage) widths allows layout to reflow with browser sizing.

Figure 11-6.   *Relative sizes expand or shrink to fit*

The page will stretch and shrink to the available window space, as shown in Figure 11-6. Notice that the content does not quite reach the top and left of the screen. A Web page will have default margins on. To adjust margins, see the section on page margins that follows this discussion.

Using CSS there are a variety of ways to implement the fluid or stretching design. Here is a simple example:

```
<!DOCTYPE html PUBLIC "-//W3C//DTD XHTML 1.0 Transitional//EN"
"http://www.w3.org/TR/xhtml1/DTD/xhtml1-transitional.dtd">
<html xmlns="http://www.w3.org/1999/xhtml">
<head>
<title>CSS Stretch</title>
<style type="text/css">
<!--
```

```
body {position: relative;
      margin: 15px;
      background: #ffffff;
      font-family: Verdana, sans-serif;}

#links {position: absolute;
        top: 26px; left: 0px;
        width: 100px;}

#content {position: absolute;
          top: 26px; left: 120px; right: 25px;
          padding: 10px;
          border: solid 5px #006699;
          color: #ffffdc; background: #0076A8;}

#content p { margin: 0 1em 1em;}
-->
</style>
</head>
<body>

<!-- start nav div-->
<div id="links">
<a href="#">Link 1</a><br />
<a href="#">Link 2</a><br />
<a href="#">Link 3</a><br />
<a href="#">Link 4</a><br />
<a href="#">Link 5</a><br />
</div>
<!--end nav links-->

<div id="content">

<p>Put some content here. It should stretch and act just like
the table design. Of course that assumes that Web
browsers have correct CSS implementations, which is simply not
true. Be careful, the older way may still be the safer way.</p>
</div>
<!-- end content div -->

</body>
</html>
```

The CSS example is deceptively easy—compatibility problems are numerous and all sorts of hacks are required to make a fluid design in CSS work in all CSS-aware browsers. For now, like it or not, using tables is still the safer way to go if you want to do this design.

It would seem that relative sizing would meet the needs of any resolution, but be careful, as relative sizing can distort a page layout greatly—and some things, like images, just aren't meant to scale. For example, if you set an image in HTML to have a percentage height or width, like this,

```
<img src="logo.gif" height="20%" width="40%" />
```

it will often look distorted, and users will see this as a mistake. Also consider that, even when you fix the size of some objects, layouts may become unreadable as the screen increases. Allowing a paragraph of text to expand to fit a 1600 x 1200 pixel resolution monitor will produce very long lines. Considering that optimal line length is around 12–15 words, allowing pages to stretch could actually result in significant usability problems. Of course, these problems would be the user's own doing rather than attributable to the designer. However, there is no guarantee that the user will see the problem from that perspective—the designer may still get blamed for creating a "bad" page. Figure 11-7 shows many of the downsides of relative layouts in action.

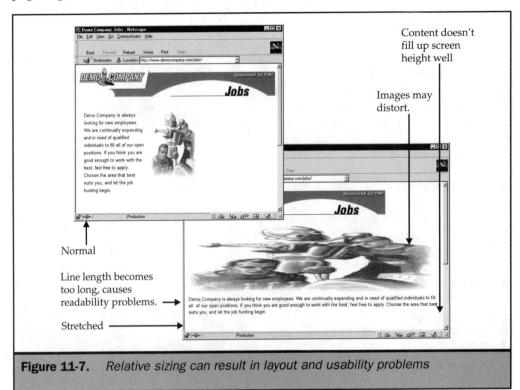

Figure 11-7.   *Relative sizing can result in layout and usability problems*

As one can see, the message of the page could be ruined by such distortion, and designers may therefore be unwilling to give up control of layout. A possible solution would be to scale content with window size.

Scaling Content

With very large windows, more content may be viewable—but is this always a good thing? Not necessarily, as page content may become too dense or too small to easily be read. It might be preferable to scale content with window size.

Scaling content need not be tricky if using cascading style sheets with relative measurement values, such as % or em, or using a JavaScript to adjust size on the fly. A basic example using JavaScript to adjust font size as the screen is resized is provided here; just add it to the previous examples or one of your own desire. Examples that are more drawn out can be found at the support site.

```
<script type="text/javascript">
<!--
var scaleFactor = window.screen.width - 300;

function changeSize()
{
  var windowWidth = (window.innerWidth) ? window.innerWidth :
document.body.clientWidth;

  document.body.style.fontSize = (windowWidth / scaleFactor) + "em";
}

window.onload = changeSize;
window.onresize = changeSize;
//-->
</script>
```

The problem with scaling content is that users may not necessarily want content to scale with window size, their view being that big monitors are made for showing more content. Meanwhile, those with less than perfect vision might want content to adjust in size. It seems that an option to toggle scaling on and off or at least to adjust font size for nonscaled content is required. The worst approach would be to have a stretchable design and use fixed point or pixel style sheets that cannot be easily overridden by the user.

Page Size Reality Check

Before racing off to make stretchable pages or ones that fit a user's resolution, carefully consider that the point of setting the page to a particular size is to make the content more presentable. Recall the discussion about paper sizes presented earlier. A fortune

ELEMENTS OF
PAGE DESIGN

cookie message doesn't belong on a letter size sheet of paper, no more than every page in your site has to stretch to fill some monster screen. Some pages ought to stretch and take advantage of every available pixel, particularly those overflowing with content. Notice that many portal sites or home pages for large e-commerce sites will stretch content to fit the screen resolution. However, do these sites necessarily allow all pages deeper in the site to stretch? Not often. The reality is that there is little benefit to letting a simple text document fill up a screen.

Ask a simple question: why *should* something fill the screen? One reason might be that a page doesn't look right if it doesn't fill up the screen. Some might complain that a site design looks "too small" on their big monitor, but does it need to be expanded to fit? Consider the pages shown in Figure 11-8. Both are a fixed size, but one is allowed to float to the center, while the other is fixed.

> **Suggestion: When using fixed page sizes, make sure to center your page to reduce the perception of empty space on larger displays.**

Another good trick to avoid the perception of empty space in fixed width designs is to utilize background tiles that set up boundaries for pages or fill up any extra space with a nice pattern, as shown in Figure 11-9.

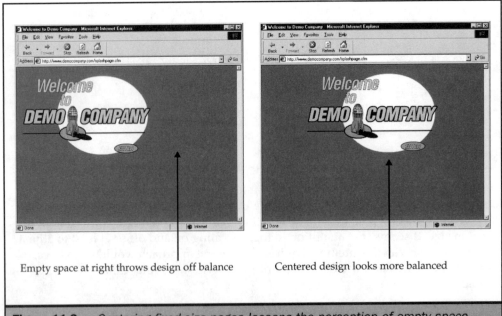

Figure 11-8.   *Centering fixed-size pages lessens the perception of empty space*

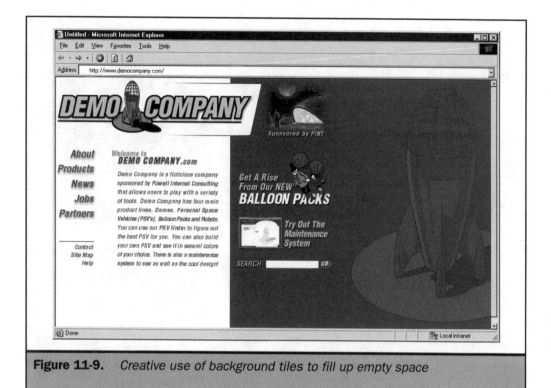

Figure 11-9. *Creative use of background tiles to fill up empty space*

Dealing with this last idea brings up an interesting question. Why do people full-screen sites? Considering that many, if not most, pages do not actually stretch, what's the point? One possible reason is that it allows the user to focus on the window. Beyond making the page look better, there are good reasons to allow layouts to grow. Sites that have a great deal of content can take advantage of the extra screen real estate. This will backfire if too little content is presented—particularly, if a single column is used. Notice in Figure 11-10 how strange a site with a minimal amount of content looks when set to full screen on a high-resolution monitor.

Suggestion: Avoid using stretchable designs on pages with little content.

Most of the discussion has focused on page width, but what about height? Recall that unless you want to limit the content so that it doesn't scroll up and down, this isn't as critical as width. While in some viewing environments, such as Palm Pilots, Kiosks, and WebTV, scrolling is frowned on, most Web sites do scroll up and down. The question, then, is how much scrolling should be allowed. Consider that if a page is too long it will be difficult to use, and probably will take a long time to load. If a page

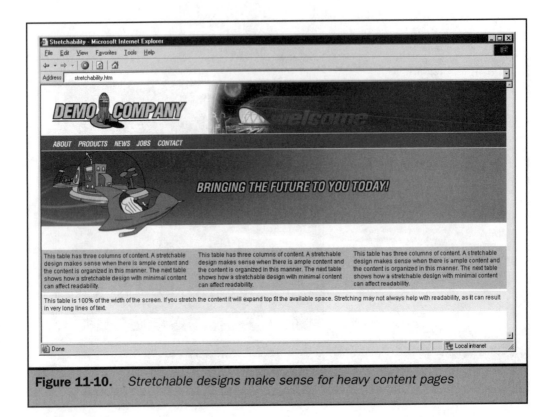

Figure 11-10.   *Stretchable designs make sense for heavy content pages*

must scroll up and down, a good limit is about three to five screenfulls. Of course what constitutes a full screen will vary greatly, so this is just a rule of thumb.

Suggestion: Try to fit content vertically within three to five screens if possible.

If pages are longer and the content can easily be split, then do so; otherwise, let it scroll. You do not want to break up a logical unit because of an arbitrary limit unless the page has become unwieldy. Another argument against splitting is that today users are getting used to scrolling; much effort, including improving mouse design, is being made to ease the scrolling burden on the user.

In the final analysis, no matter whether you fix content, whether your page size is 640 x 480 or 2000 x 2000, there will always be someone who finds the content too big or too small. Pages should be set not for monitors but for the needs of the content presented and the people viewing it. Making sure content fits the viewing environment is very important. An easy way to do this is to resize your browser window to simulate other resolutions. A variety of tools exist to do this (see http://www.webdesignref.com/), and most Web editors, including GoLive, HomeSite and Dreamweaver, also provide utilities for browser sizes.

Page Margins

Besides considering the overall size of a page, designers should be very aware of the margins. Browsers do have margins, and they vary from version to version. Background images do not respect the margins, but foreground images do. If a page is not designed to take into account margins or control them, it is very possible the layout may be ruined in some browsers, as shown in Figure 11-11.

Under older browsers, margins varied and could not be controlled using HTML. Today HTML and CSS provide facilities to turn off margins. If not controlled, margins will be set to anywhere from 5 pixels to 16 pixels from the left and top of the screen. Some UNIX variants of Netscape even have margin offsets to as much as 22 pixels! Providing a slop factor of upwards of 10 pixels left to right and 20 pixels up and down is about all that can be done if you aren't going to control things or have a very old browser audience to deal with—but now there are a variety of ways to remove margins.

Suggestion: Either control page margins or account for their variation with some layout slop factor.

Turning off the margins in HTML is not part of the specification, but both leading browser vendors have added propriety attributes to set page margins from the **<body>** tag. In Internet Explorer 4.*x* or later, set **leftmargin** and **topmargin** attributes for the **<body>** element to **0** or any desired pixel value. For Netscape 4.*x* or later, use **marginwidth** and **marginheight**. A statement like this,

```
<body topmargin="0" leftmargin="0" marginwidth="0" marginheight="0">
```

should turn off the margins in a page completely.

ELEMENTS OF
PAGE DESIGN

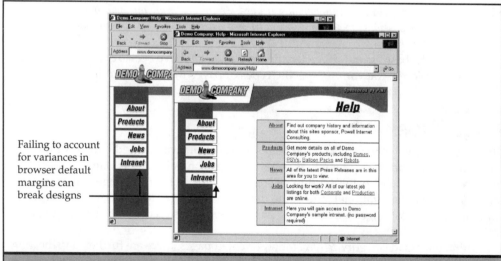

Failing to account for variances in browser default margins can break designs

Figure 11-11. *Margin problems can ruin layouts*

Unfortunately, some Netscape browsers may still render a 1-pixel margin at both top and bottom despite any manipulation.

For backward support, the HTML approach is the only reasonable approach. However, CSS is appropriate for layout control, so a rule like

```
body    {margin: 0;}
```

would do the same thing as the previous HTML. Here is an example of some content in a page set with and without margins to illustrate the effect:

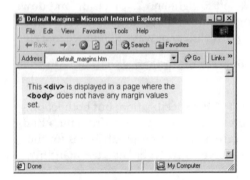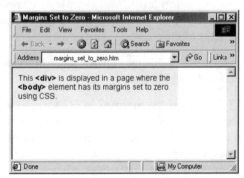

CSS provides greater control for page margins, which can be set individually for the left, top, right, and bottom.

 One interesting margin workaround still employed on some sites attempting to preserve layout on very old browsers is using frames. Frames have always had margin control, so it would be possible to use some sort of frames markup to kill margins on older browsers.

Now that the basic layout characteristics of Web pages have been discussed, we should turn our attention to the various specific types of pages that are found in Web sites.

Page Types

There are many ways to classify Web pages. One simple way is by the focus of the page. Is the page primarily a content page, a navigation page, a task page, or some mixture of types? Most pages tend to be some mixture, but certain pages, like site maps, are purely navigational, and some deep content pages in a site may be nearly all content based. Most pages—even home pages—will focus on content, navigation, and tasks to varying degrees.

Within the broad category of navigation-oriented pages, there are further classifications that can be made. As discussed in Chapter 7 on site navigation theory, users tend to view entrance and exit from a site as important steps. Because of the focus on entering and leaving a site, it is important to consider whether a page is an entrance page or an exit page. Entry pages should make it clear to the user which site they're on and what's available to them. A site's home page is often the primary entrance page, but, depending on how the site is used, many pages could serve as entry pages. Exit pages are less obvious than entrance pages, but an exit page should provide some closure to a user's site visit. A sense of completion is an important aspect in creating a positive take-away value for the user. Often, content pages serve as exit pages because users have found what they want. However, in task-oriented sites, like a shopping site, a special exit or order confirmation page may serve as a more explicit form of exit. In between would be pages that serve as steps during a user's visit. These intermediary pages range from providing content to acting as navigation points on the user's journey through the site. A successful journey will have a definite start (entry page), exposure to information, task and guidance (content and navigation pages), and, finally, a conclusion to the journey (exit page). A key to good Web design is making certain users do not lose their way between the start and the finish of the journey.

Content-oriented pages can be categorized by type. Content pages might include things like press releases, product specifications, biographies, stories, white papers, poems, frequently asked questions (FAQs), tutorials, release notes, and any other category of content imaginable. Some of the pages are particularly associated with the Web—FAQs, privacy pages, and so on, which will be discussed specifically in a moment—and have common features, but the particular form or meaning of content pages will vary with the organization running the sites. Navigation pages can also be categorized by type. Home pages tend to have distinct functions and "looks" that contrast with subsection navigation pages. Special navigation pages such as site maps, search pages, and site indices are also found in many sites. Each of these navigation pages has already been discussed in previous chapters.

There are a variety of other ways to categorize pages, such as how they are used, printed, or viewed online, and how often they are updated, and whether they are generated or are static—and *if* they are generated, whether they are unique for each viewer (in other words, "personalized"). However, the purpose of a taxonomy of page types is simply to allow designers to discuss things in a regular, organized way. Our simple taxonomy of entrance, navigation, content and exit pages will serve this purpose well enough.

Entrance Pages

Theoretically, any page in a site can serve as an entrance page if the user knows the page's URL. In Chapter 6, sites that did not limit entry to a particular set of pages were considered porous, while sites that limited entry could be dubbed semiporous or solid, depending on how limited entrance was. Regardless of any formal attempt to limit users, most sites tend to have only a few entry points. The home page is the main entry to a site, but certain important sectional pages or "sub-home" pages might also be entry points into a site, particularly if they have special URLs or unique domains. While most sites will focus traffic through a home page, some sites may have a special entry page called a splash page.

Splash Pages

A *splash page* is a page that is used to introduce a site, to "make a splash" and leave a strong impression. Often a splash page is used to set the tone of a site through the use of graphic layout, animation, or even sound. Figure 11-12 shows an example splash page. For some users, the often overly animated logos of a splash page serve as an unwanted download and may encourage them to leave. However, for some sites a splash page is very important to set the stage for the rest of the site experience. On such sites, not having a splash page could be similar to not having an opening title sequence for a movie, leaving the user confused or disoriented. Given that a splash page could be annoying to the user, there should be an easy way to skip the page. Usually a small text link labeled "skip intro" or simply "skip" is used towards the bottom of the page for bypassing the splash page.

Suggestion: Provide an obvious link to quickly skip a splash page.

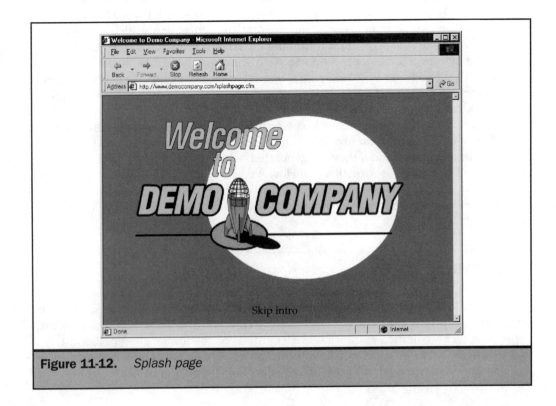

Figure 11-12. *Splash page*

When a splash page just orients users with spinning logos and other introductory material, frequent visitors to a site may become highly annoyed, even if they can skip the page. Skipping the intro itself becomes an annoyance. It need not be, as it is possible instead to issue a cookie to the user to enable showing a splash page only to a first-time visitor.

Tip: Consider showing splash pages only to initial visitors.

A splash page can be used for much more than just spinning a corporate logo. A splash page can be used to assist setup or installation for the site, such as determining if the user has the appropriate plug-ins installed. A splash page can also be used to engage the user while items used elsewhere in the site are downloaded. For many multimedia sites heavily using Flash, a splash page is used in the same manner as an installer for traditional software.

Tip: Use splash pages for installation or preloading of site content.

Be careful to ensure that, for a splash page that provides important information, installs software, or prefetches site information, the user actually enters through it. If not, the value is lost.

Because of the perceived lack of value provided and the download delays caused by splash pages in the eyes of some users, they should be used with caution. However, when well executed and used infrequently for the appropriate type of site, a splash page can be a useful way to grab the attention of users and orient them to a site.

Tip: Question the use of splash pages in a site.

Home Pages

A home page is generally the first page users see when they visit a site. The home page acts as the main entry point of a site and should be a prominent landmark in a site. As a landmark page, a home page's appearance should be distinct from all other pages in a site. Keep in mind that the home page is often the way people visually remember a site. If it is not different, users may feel lost in a site, needing an obvious starting point.

Rule: A home page should look significantly different than other pages in a site.

In order to be distinct, home pages often are more visual than deeper pages in a site and may more prominently display an organizational identity, such as a logo, than other pages. Consider the abstract page layouts shown in Figure 11-13. Can you identify the home pages?

A home page needs to set the tone for the site. The home page sets the basic design elements of a site, such as color, graphic style, font style, and so on, that are used in subpages. If a home page uses a particular font for buttons, users will probably expect the rest of the site to continue using the same font for buttons. Also, the type of navigation

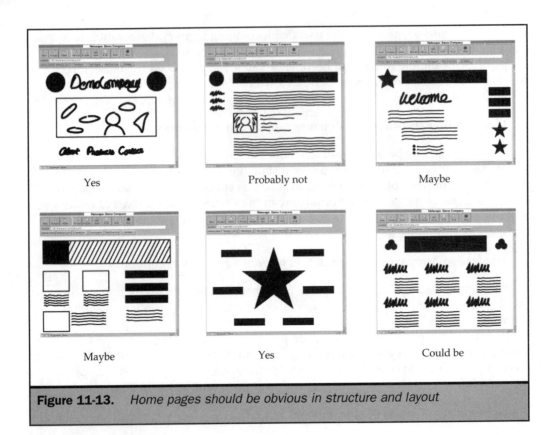

Figure 11-13. *Home pages should be obvious in structure and layout*

presented will be assumed to be consistent with that of the home page. If the home page uses blue graphical push buttons and pull-down menus for navigation, these should be used elsewhere in the site as well.

Rule: A home page should set the visual and navigational tone of a site.

Another aspect of a good home page is that it encourages people to look deeper in a site. Often, users will come to a site not knowing for sure what is provided. If the home page doesn't interest them, they may just leave. Inspection of a site's statistics logs will probably reveal that the home page is not only the primary entry page, but it is also one of the primary exit pages. Why is this? People may leave directly from the home page for a variety of reasons. Maybe they just landed at the page by accident. However, it is possible that the home page isn't doing its job. As the entry point for a site, the home page sets the user's first impression of the site. If the page loads slowly or doesn't look interesting, there may seem to be no reason for the user to look further.

Rule: A home page should load fast, but be informative and dramatic enough to encourage interest.

There are other reasons that a user might bail out from a home page. The home page might not indicate clearly what is at the site. Many home pages don't clearly present the site's purpose and the contents of the site. A home page is like a magazine cover. Magazine covers have to be flashy enough to attract attention on a crowded newsstand. They have to have a variety of cover blurbs indicating what's inside the magazine.

Rule: A home page should clearly indicate what's inside a site.

Like a magazine cover, the home page of a site must be "consistently different." What this means is that the page must be recognizable, but obviously changing and "fresh." Over time, the design of the site may have to change to keep the site fresh, but a complete redesign should not occur too often. Consider how often a major magazine changes its look. While it may not be a good idea to wait five years, it probably isn't a good idea to redesign your home page's look every six months. How often do the major Web sites like Yahoo! or Amazon significantly change their looks? The reality is that these sites are actually changing subtly all the time, but dramatic shifts are few and far between.

If return visitation is a key component of your site strategy, the home page is where to convince users to come back. You can try to encourage users to return in a variety of ways, but the most important is to provide informational value on the home page and show them things are changing. Don't expect users to come back day after day to a page that it is just a big graphic with a few buttons near by. Isn't this just a splash page with more buttons? Try to provide some value with your home page. Indicate the key changes made to the site directly on the home page. Remember—if the home page doesn't change over time, people may assume the site's content doesn't change either. The main elements could stay the same, while having secondary elements change and providing other clues to let people know the site has changed. A few ways to show change are:

- Putting the date somewhere on the page
- Rotating a primary image or Flash piece either randomly or at a set interval (daily, weekly, or monthly)
- Putting small amounts of important changing information (press releases, and so on) on the home page
- A direct statement of the last time the page was updated
- A link to a "What's New" area

Suggestion: A home page should provide informational value and an obvious indication of the site's change if change is occurring.

Some sites, however, will not change terribly often, so their home page will not look dynamic. Remember, if you aren't going to update the site, don't let people know that. Don't put press releases on the home page that are old or put dates on the home page that changes—if nothing changes in a site. Don't put ondated material on your homepage, or in turn, date material that won't be updated later on.

From this discussion, it is obvious that a home page has many roles to fill, as shown in Figure 11-14. It is the entry point, the update indicator, the tone setter, and the primary navigational landmark. Users will bookmark it or type in the URL directly; they might visit it frequently, but they probably won't do one thing common to other pages: print it. Usually a home page provides only basic or teaser information for a user about what's in a site, not detailed information that would be useful to print. Printing should therefore be considered a secondary requirement for home pages. This does give the designer more flexibility in color and background usage, multimedia, and screen width than with pages deeper in a site.

Tip: Consider printing a secondary design consideration for home pages.

Subpages: Navigation vs. Content

From the home page, the user will select a link to explore. At this point, users begin the middle of their visit. They have set off to do something. Because users tend to be more focused at this point, subpages don't have to be quite as visual or distinct as home pages. However, subpages generally must follow the lead of the home page, unless they are

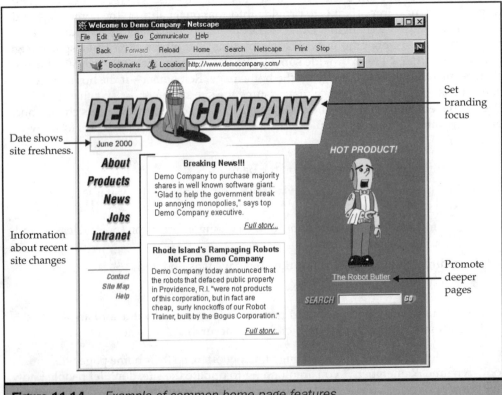

Figure 11-14.   *Example of common home page features*

attempting to act as a "sublandmark." For example, a subpage for a large section of a company such as Technical Support may be the entry page for many users. People who don't come through the "front door" of the site, so to speak, will need to orient themselves from this page. In this sense, the subpage is a landmark for a particular section. It is important that a subpage used this way be distinctly different from other pages in the site. However, avoid the temptation of making it look like a home page. If users did enter through the home page and then clicked to get to the technical support page, they would see something that looks like another home page. That would be quite confusing and could potentially ruin the landmark value of each page.

> **Suggestion: If a particular subpage is a landmark or common entry page, such as a "section home page," make it visually distinctive.**

Most subpages, however, will probably not be visually distinctive. In fact, most should take their design and navigation cues directly from the home page. While the purpose of the home page is to make the user keenly aware of being on a particular site, when a user journeys deeper into the site, the user's awareness needs to shift to the content. If subpages are presenting the user with new navigation, new logos, and new color schemes all along the way, the user's attention will be drawn away from the content.

Consider the home page and subpage shown in Figure 11-15 and notice how it is obvious they are related, but that the subpage is more content oriented.

> **Rule: Subpages should follow the style and navigation of the home page, at least in spirit.**

Subpages will often be more focused than home pages. A subpage is generally either focused on navigation or on content. A few pages, such as site maps, might be considered purely navigation. However, it is unlikely that a subpage is a pure content page because if it lacks navigation or links, it would be an "orphan" page (one that has no way for a user to exit from other than by the browser back button). Generally, there is a balance between content and navigation in a subpage.

Navigation-Specific Pages

A variety of special navigation-focused pages, beyond home pages or main sectional pages, can be found in many sites. These have been discussed in previous chapters so will only be briefly described here. Two of the most common special navigation pages are site maps and site indexes. A site map is used to provide a structural overview of a Web site, while a site index provides a list of a site's content organized alphabetically rather than structurally. (The design of these navigational pages was discussed in depth in Chapter 10.) A search page is the other common navigation-specific page. Search facilities generally include a query page, result pages (both positive and negative), and, ideally, a help page. These pages are very important for site navigation, particularly to power users. Special care should be paid to their design. Chapter 9 discusses search

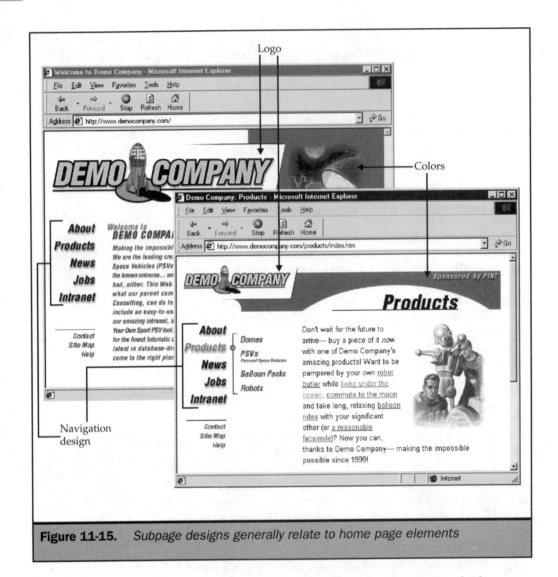

Figure 11-15. *Subpage designs generally relate to home page elements*

facilities in great depth. Given that the focus of site maps, search pages, and other navigation pages is almost purely navigational, there should conversely be some pages that are completely content focused.

Content Pages

Content pages are those subpages that are very focused on content presentation. In some sense, a content page is a destination page. Often they are the leaf pages in the site tree and represent the "bottom" of a site. Like other subpages in a site, a content page will probably have some navigational elements, lest it become an orphan page. The layout of a content-focused page will vary with the content presented, but it tends to take cues from ancestor pages, such as main section or home pages. Often, sites tend to get less visual the deeper in, but this is not necessarily a hard and fast rule. Common content pages found in commercial sites include things like press releases, product specifications, biographies, customer testimonials, technical support documentation, news articles, financial reports, legal information, and on and on. Personal Web sites might have stories, resumes, poems, and family trees, while educational sites might have syllabi, homework assignments, and presentations. Other forms of sites might have document types completely unique to themselves. The reality is that there are potentially as many types of content pages as there are people in the world. However, there are a few types of content pages that are common on Web sites or that are so specific to the Web as to warrant further discussion: FAQs, legal terms, and privacy pages.

FAQ Pages

Frequently Asked Question or FAQ pages are common types of documents on the Internet. The basic idea of a FAQ page is to provide concise answers to common questions in a single document, so that a user doesn't have to hunt all over a site for information. FAQs are often formatted as a single, long, scrolling document, with an index of questions at the top with links from each question that jump the user down the page to the appropriate answer. An example of a typical FAQ is shown in Figure 11-16.

There may be some question why FAQ files jump up and down a page rather than link to individual files. The main reason is that users will want to print the entire range of questions for future reference. However, if there are too many questions, the document can become unwieldy. If an FAQ is more than a dozen or so printed pages, it is probably wise to break it up into pieces that are linked together and to provide a separate printable version for users who want the whole document.

> **Suggestion: If FAQ pages are of a reasonable length, make them a single document for easy printing.**

When users reads an FAQ, they will often look for the question they are interested in, read the answer, and then want to return to the list of questions. To avoid users

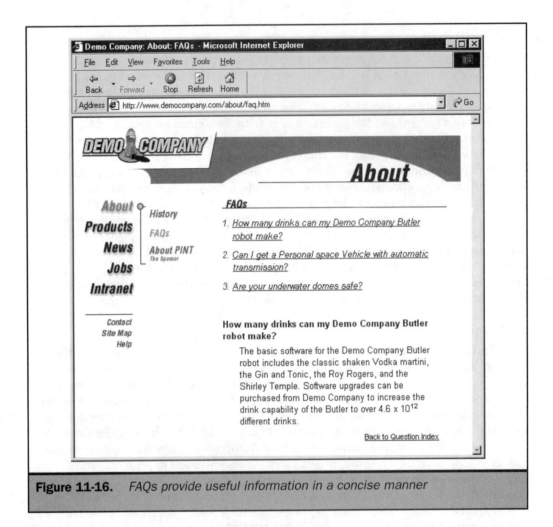

Figure 11-16. FAQs provide useful information in a concise manner

having to scroll around, make sure to provide a link at the end of each question to bring users back to the question index, which is usually at the top of the document.

Suggestion: Provide a link back to the top of the document or the list of the questions at the end of every answer.

FAQs are only useful if the answers provided actually answer the user's questions. It is a very good idea to provide a link or mechanism for users to indicate if their question was answered. Often links like are included with each question. Other questions, such as rating of usefulness, can be asked as well. Collected information can be used to indicate which questions users most commonly read and whether they are satisfied with the answers. This information could be useful to other users. Some sites actually provide a listing of the most popular questions accessed.

> **Tip: Provide a feedback mechanism for users to rate the value of the FAQ answers provided.**

Some sites have extended the idea of rating the usefulness of an FAQ to every page in the site. This does give great feedback to site designers about page use and user satisfaction. However, don't go overboard with user feedback and other popularity measurements because some very useful pages may be infrequently accessed or misunderstood by a few very vocal users but well understood by most others.

Legal Pages

Now that the Web is used for commerce, legal terms pages have become commonplace within many sites. Often, the bottom of a Web page on a public site includes a corporate statement of some kind. There may also be a short statement about site usage. Either of these short statements will generally include a link to another page describing the legal aspects of the site. The way legal information is linked to pages varies. Some examples are shown here:

Read our <u>Terms and Conditions of Use</u>.

<u>Copyright and Trademark Notice</u>

Please click here for Terms and Conditions of use regarding this site.

The actual legal page itself tends to lack much of the navigation or layout facilities of other site pages. However, it should still at least minimally include a way to return to the home page of the site, as well as a minimal amount of branding to associate it with the site. An example of a legal page is shown in Figure 11-17. You'll notice that the example does not provide much in the way of legal verbiage, other than some basic headings. Given that Web sites are software and, in the case of e-commerce or task-based sites, some harm could result from their usage, site designers should not try to use "boilerplate" legal pages modified from other sites. Designers should not attempt to practice armchair law. There is already enough room for mistakes in site building without adding in the potential for legal trouble.

> **Suggestion: Consult a legal professional for drafting pages with any legal terms.**

Copyright pages can be particularly troublesome. Designers are quick to add copyrights to pages. While the value of these statements is somewhat suspect and

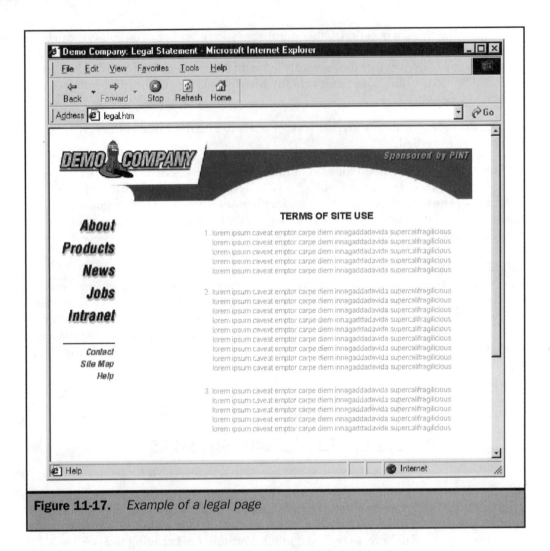

Figure 11-17. *Example of a legal page*

while some statements do not truly indicate any intention to apply for a copyright, they are important. Users often seem to look to copyright statements as an indication of content freshness. This then raises the question of whether a copyright statement should be changed every year to keep users thinking the site is up to date. In theory, if a change was made to a page, even a minor one, this is okay to do.

Tip: Be careful with copyright statements; users may judge site freshness by them.

However, utilizing the copyright statement as the only indication of a page's freshness isn't a great idea. Consider instead putting some sort of last-modified indicator on the page instead, like this:

Document last modified: August 23, 2002

Keeping freshness indicators up to date can be troublesome, but it is possible to automatically insert them with a program, or even to use a simple JavaScript, like the one shown here, at the bottom of every page:

```
<script type="text/javascript">
<!--
document.write('<font size="-1" class="lastmodified">');
document.write('<em>Last Modified: ');
document.write(document.lastModified);
document.write('</em></font>');
//-->
</script>
```

Suggestion: Add a last-modification indicator to pages.

Note *Be careful when adding automatic modification dates using JavaScript to dynamically generated pages. They will show an update every time the page is generated!*

Privacy Pages

A particular class of Web "legal" pages that has garnered much attention is the privacy statement page. Many sites collect sensitive or personal data from users, and what sites do with this data is of particular concern to many users. Because of this concern, which is often well founded, sites should provide a privacy statement that indicates what any collected data will be used for. Links to this statement should be available throughout the site and be prominently displayed on any data collection pages. The design of this page should be like other legal pages, with only basic navigation and graphics limited to those, like logos or colors, that identify the organization. The privacy page may also include icons associated with and links to various privacy organizations, particularly if the site is built to follow some industry standard. Figure 11-18 displays a privacy statement layout.

As with all legal documents, consulting a legal counsel is always suggested, but one agency, TRUSTe (http://www.truste.org), has stepped in to provide assistance to site designers looking to craft a privacy statement. Site designers are encouraged to use sites like TRUSTe to build privacy statements. However, be careful not to just add in a

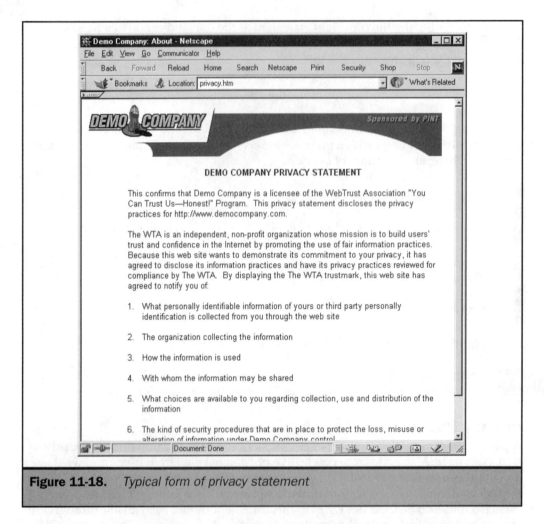

Figure 11-18. *Typical form of privacy statement*

large privacy statement without considering both whether it truly addresses a user's privacy concerns in an easy-to-understand manner and whether it can be enforced. The fallout of posting privacy statements only to break them is enormous. Some legal experts believe a site is better off with no privacy statement than with one that is faulty or is not enforced.

Rule: If sensitive or personal information is collected, provide an easily accessible and understandable privacy statement.

Task-Specific Pages

Task-specific pages are pages that allow a user to do something, particularly provide information through the interaction with various form elements. Some common task pages found in sites include shopping cart management pages, database query pages, search pages, download pages, registration forms, guestbook pages, discussion posting pages, and so on. As with content pages, there are too many possible task-specific pages to provide a reasonably complete list of them. However, contact pages and print pages are common enough that they should be discussed further.

Contact Pages

A contact page provides information for or even a form contacting the owners of a site. Usually a contact page will provide numerous methods to contact the site's owners, ranging from a simple e-mail address or phone number to a form or even an instant chat service. An example of a contact page is shown in Figure 11-19.

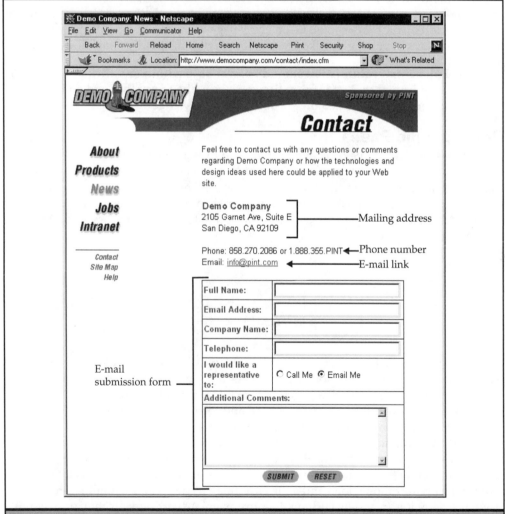

Figure 11-19. *Contact forms should provide multiple contact methods*

Links to site contact pages should be placed prominently on all pages within a site. Generally, the label for this link is simply "Contact." However, some sites prefer to use a more verbose link name, like "Contact Us" or "How to Contact Us." A compromise might be to provide the shortened label name, but then use a scope note or the **title** attribute to provide a tooltip with more information about the forms of contact available.

The downside of having a separate contact page reachable from content pages within a site is that it may not be associated closely enough with content, particularly if the user eventually prints the page out and consumes it offline. Because of this potential problem, some designers prefer to put full contact information on every page just in case a user prints a page and later wants to contact the organization by phone, fax, postal mail, or e-mail without revisiting the site. This might seem a little overboard, but some form of minimal contact information, such as organization name, site URL, main phone number, or e-mail address, probably should be on every page within a site. Companies with toll-free numbers increasingly make that number part of the page's visual design itself.

> **Rule: Full contact information should be available within one click of any page on a site; minimal contact information such as a phone number and e-mail address should be included on the bottom of every page.**

Print-Specific Pages

Some pages are likely to be consumed offline and thus are geared for printing. Occasionally, a site may be consumed both offline and online, and two forms of the same page will exist. Notice the rise of "print version" buttons on many Web sites. In fact, many sites are now including not only links to printable pages but special saving and e-mail facilities to make it easier for users to use content they find. An example of this is shown here.

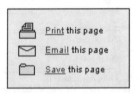

At this point, let's focus on printing pages. Many Web pages don't print well because the page is optimized for online consumption with larger text and narrow columns. A direct print of such a page tends to waste a great deal of paper. Printed pages should be generally set in smaller type and the layout modified to utilize standard letter size paper effectively. Colored text may not be important on a printed page, and backgrounds will burn more toner or ink than can be justified by any benefit in most cases. Further, users probably do not need to see site navigation, other than some indication of the site the page came from. This information may be as little as putting the organizational logo and an indication of a page's location in the site, such as what section it is in and its URL on the print page. Advertisements may or may not be a good idea to include in the print output.

There are a variety of ways to provide print versions of pages. One possibility is to create a special print version in HTML. This could be as simple as stripping most of the HTML out or might be as involved as creating a special new HTML layout optimized for print.

Another approach might be to utilize a secondary print-oriented layout using a style sheet. The CSS specification indicates that it is possible to provide multiple style sheets to apply to a page. To do this, two **<link>** elements would be included in the **<head>** of a Web page, like so

```
<link rel="stylesheet" href="normal.css" />
<link rel="stylesheet" href="print.css" media="print" />
```

The second style sheet could be used to change text size, reduce line-height, change color, remove navigation elements by setting their display property to none, and so on. Using CSS2, it is even possible to indicate where printer page breaks would occur. For example a CSS rule like,

```
.newpage    {page-break-after: always;}
```

sets all elements in the class "newpage" to cause a printer page break when the page is printed in a browser that supports this CSS2 property. Figure 11-20 shows an example

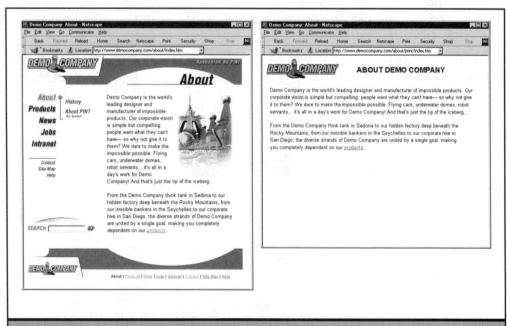

Figure 11-20.   *Printed versions can vary from online versions*

of how these ideas could be applied and shows a Web page onscreen as well as the resulting printed page.

Unfortunately, not all browsers support printer style sheets. A more degradable approach would be to simply link to a page that was formatted for the printer using either CSS or traditional HTML layout. Besides being downwardly compatible, this approach doesn't surprise the user. The user sees the page as it will print and is not surprised with something different than what is seen onscreen. Consider that just using a linked printer style could cause frustration for users. What happens if they want to see the page exactly as it looks onscreen? Maybe they actually want to print the advertisements.

Suggestion: Inform users that printed pages will be different from what is seen onscreen, or show the print version directly.

Another approach to the printing issue is to utilize Adobe's Acrobat technology (http://www.adobe.com/acrobat) and provide a PDF (portable document format) version of the page. Using PDF, it is possible to create a high-resolution, printer-oriented version of the information in a page, just as it might appear in a brochure. A common use of this format is for displaying highly complex information, such as technical specifications or mathematical formulas. An example of a PDF file associated with a Web page is shown in Figure 11-21.

Suggestion: Use Acrobat PDF files for highly complex information that needs to print perfectly, such as data sheets, technical drawings, and complex financial or mathematical information.

If a PDF is used, make sure to let users know what it is with an appropriately named link or PDF icon. Given the larger size of PDF files, it is also probably a good idea to indicate the file size of a linked PDF. The last time the document was modified may be useful to the user. Finally, make sure to provide information on where to obtain the Acrobat reader for users who may not have it. All these ideas are illustrated here:

Instruction Manuals		
📄	Robot Butler - User's Manual [437 Kb]	Revision RB-23 Revised 03/03/2002
📄	Sports PSV - User's Manual [789 Kb]	Revision S-PSV-03-B Revised 03/03/2002

Suggestion: Clearly indicate Acrobat files with text and an icon, and provide information on using these files.

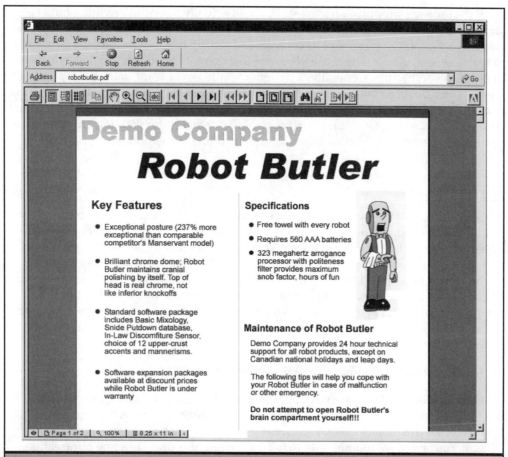

Figure 11-21.   *Acrobat files make useful supplements to HTML-based information*

Restricted Printing Pages

Some designers may actually conclude that some pages are not made for printing at
all. An interesting possibility is limiting printing of a page with a small CSS trick. It is
simple to create a linked printer style sheet named noprint.css:

```
<link rel="stylesheet" href="noprint.css" media="print" />
```

The linked file contains a single rule:

```
body    {display: none;}
```

If the browser supports a linked style, it will actually not print anything out at all. Of course, while this will limit most people, the page can still be printed. A user could easily screen-capture a page, save its contents and modify it, adjust the browser preferences to ignore style sheets, or simply use a browser that doesn't understand printer style sheets to avoid this restriction. Generally, a designer would never want to limit the printing of a page, since doing so takes a great deal of control away from the user. However, there may be some instances—for example information changes so quickly that it should not be saved, that the page is a sample of something purchased for viewing online only, or some bug with printing exists—when limiting printing is a good idea.

Exit Pages

While it's clear that the home page serves as the main entry point to a Web site, is there a similarly defined exit point? For content-oriented sites, there may not be one, and every page could be considered an obvious exit point. Ideally, in such cases the user will have found some interesting content and then left from a content page.

Not all sites can afford to lack a point of closure. Sites that have definable tasks, such as downloading software, buying a product, making a stock trade, and so on, should have an obvious exit page. The exit page provides a sense of completion or closure to a visit. Closure is very important to site usability, as it signifies to users that they have completed the task properly.

Rule: Provide an obvious conclusion page for a task.

Probably the most common exit page seen on the Web is what might be termed the "Thank You" page. A "Thank You" page comes after a user has filled in a form for further information or completed some transaction, such as buying a product. A "Thank You" page should not only thank a user, but also provide some information, such as confirmation of success, what to expect next, a tracking number, or other follow-up information, as in Figure 11-22. A very important aspect of an exit page is that it should provide a way back in to the site. E-commerce sites have found that just adding a link that states "Continue shopping," as well as providing a link back to the main home page, is a good way to get a few more sales.

Suggestion: Provide a way back to the site from an exit page.

Be careful with the idea of trying to get the user back into the site when they are about to leave. Some designers have abused this idea, using a form of "last chance" window to hit the user up one more time. With JavaScript it is fairly easy to perform a task on a page as it is unloaded. Consider this modification to the **<body>** element of an HTML page:

```
<body onunload="alert('Please visit again soon!');">
```

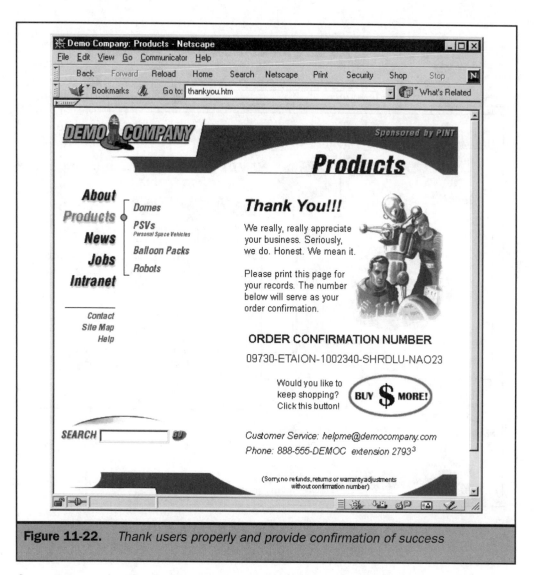

Figure 11-22.   *Thank users properly and provide confirmation of success*

Some sites use this idea to spawn a variety of advertisement windows, and a few even use it to trap users within the site, by endlessly redirecting them to related sites. Figure 11-23 shows a few examples of "last chance" pop-ups in action.

Hitting the user with numerous pop-up windows on exit is not a good way to leave a positive feeling in a user's mind. Each window has to be dismissed, so you have just created work for the user.

> **Rule: Let users leave in peace. Avoid "please don't go" or "last chance" pop-up windows.**

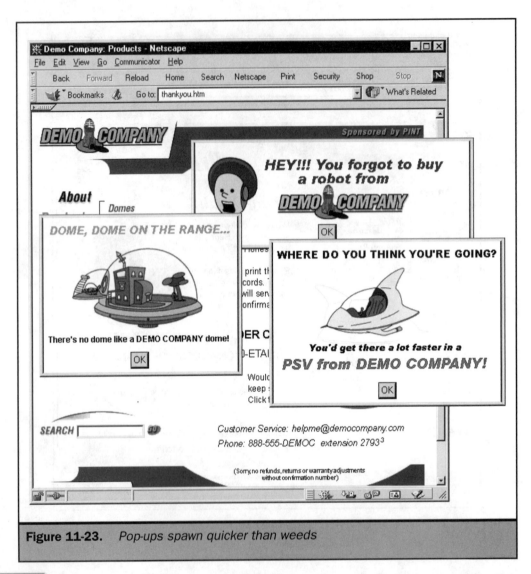

Figure 11-23. *Pop-ups spawn quicker than weeds*

Note *If, for some reason, such as extreme marketing pressures, you decide to not pay attention to the "last chance" rule, the least you could do is make the windows automatically dismiss themselves after a few seconds of viewing.*

The three major categories of pages—entrance, mid-visit, and exit pages—have all been covered, along with the difference between content pages and navigation pages. A few important page types like legal pages also have been discussed in depth. However, little has been said about how these pages look. To begin a discussion of this subject, let's explore the general ways people tend to design pages by considering the various Web design schools of thought.

Web Design Schools

As in other fields of design, there are different schools of thought about Web design. At this point in the history of Web design, these "schools" aren't well established or even clearly defined, but a few seem common on the Web.

Text

The simplest school of thought about Web pages suggests that text is the most important design element in a page. Designers who follow the text first approach favor the content over presentation and generally use minimal graphics, instead focusing on color or type choice. In the past, because of the limitations of HTML and poor support of CSS, people who took a text first approach to Web design tended to have somewhat dismal looking pages, such as the one shown in Figure 11-24.

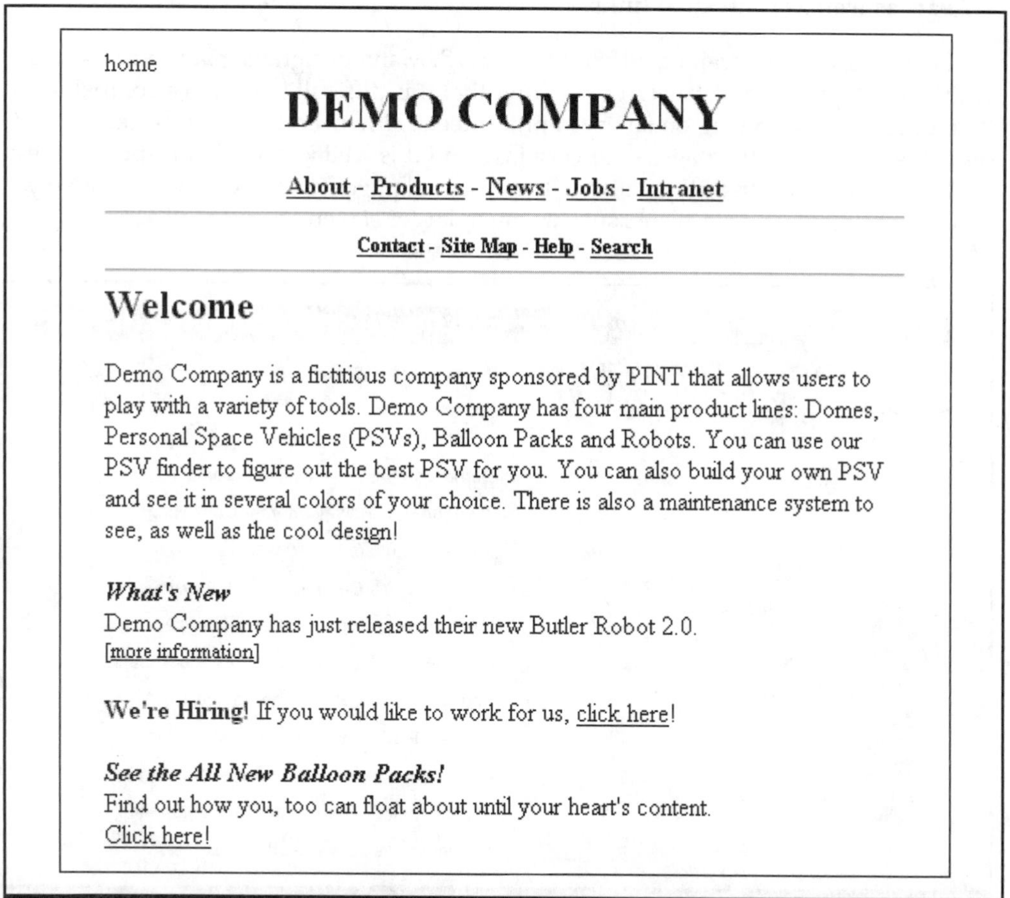

home

DEMO COMPANY

About - Products - News - Jobs - Intranet

Contact - Site Map - Help - Search

Welcome

Demo Company is a fictitious company sponsored by PINT that allows users to play with a variety of tools. Demo Company has four main product lines: Domes, Personal Space Vehicles (PSVs), Balloon Packs and Robots. You can use our PSV finder to figure out the best PSV for you. You can also build your own PSV and see it in several colors of your choice. There is also a maintenance system to see, as well as the cool design!

What's New
Demo Company has just released their new Butler Robot 2.0.
[more information]

We're Hiring! If you would like to work for us, click here!

See the All New Balloon Packs!
Find out how you, too can float about until your heart's content.
Click here!

Figure 11-24. *Initial Web technology limited, text-oriented design*

Many designers instead turned to putting text in a graphic form to achieve formatting, but did so at the expense of download time and scalability. Today, however, things are much better for text-oriented designers. Using CSS and downloadable fonts, it is possible to create nice pages with no imagery, as shown by the example in Figure 11-25.

One potential downside of advanced text design is that it relies on a technology that, so far, has been less than well supported by browsers. Second, text design—particularly when implemented in a traditional hypertext fashion—tends to favor somewhat unstructured or contextual links, interspersed within content, over regular navigation bars. As discussed in Chapter 8, this type of link is a very powerful way to create jumps to link-related ideas, but its lack of regularity can confuse novice users who expect to see consistent navigation in a site.

Suggestion: When using text-oriented design, consider providing navigation bars as well as contextual links.

Finally, text design can be difficult to do well. Many designers, particularly those with limited typographic backgrounds, find that it is difficult to design a compelling Web page without relying on fancy graphic effects. However, the major benefit of text design is significant: the pages load very fast, and it is well known that responsiveness is a key aspect of site usability. Further, text-oriented pages can be converted relatively easily to different environments, such as much larger screens, very small screens like PDAs or cell phones, and even speech-based browsers.

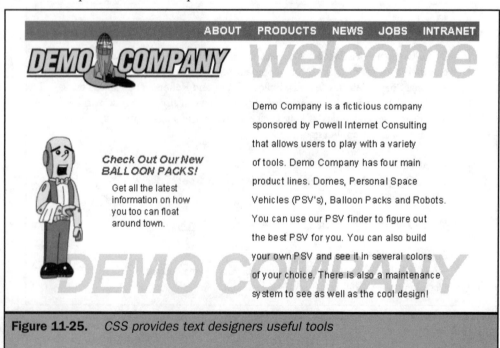

Figure 11-25.   *CSS provides text designers useful tools*

Suggestion: Consider using a text design philosophy on sites where download speed or display flexibility is of paramount importance.

Metaphor and Thematic

The metaphor and thematic design philosophy is interested in making Web pages look similar to what they are about in real life. If a site is about cars, then structuring the site's interface as a steering wheel is a good example of this design approach. Metaphor approaches tend to be highly visual, as shown by the example in Figure 11-26.

The metaphor design has two major benefits. First, given the heavy visuals and tie-in with the real world, the site is often highly memorable. Second, relying on metaphors based on real world objects may make the site seem familiar and easy to use. However, these benefits do come with some serious downsides. First, some users might not "get" the metaphor. For example, if you built your site interface to act like a Hewlett Packard reverse-Polish notation (RPN) calculator, some users might find it amusing and very intuitive, particularly if they are engineers. However, for others who blocked math class out of their brain long ago and have no clue how to use a RPN calculator, the metaphor-oriented interface may provide no benefit and even be a hindrance. Even users who understand the metaphor might not find it useful after a while. Expert users may find metaphor-oriented interfaces limiting, and frequent visitors to the site might find that the interface becomes tiresome.

Suggestion: Avoid using a metaphor design on sites geared toward expert users or heavy repeat use.

Figure 11-26.   *Metaphor-based Web design*

Finally, because metaphor design tends to be so visually heavy, such sites often are slower than other types of sites.

However, despite its downsides, on occasion metaphor design can be the best choice of all. Simulators are the best of example of this. For example, when you are trying to show how a car works, it is best to have a user click on the actual objects in the car, such as a steering wheel, the brakes, and so on. Figure 11-27 shows an example of this in the context of Demo Company. Here, clicking and rolling on objects will show products in motion, as well as text describing key features.

GUI Oriented

A very popular school of Web design could be termed "sites that act like traditional software applications." Granted, few sites following this design pattern will forsake

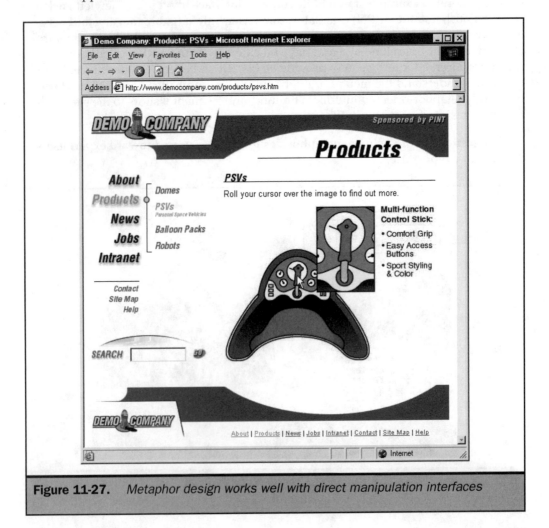

Figure 11-27.   *Metaphor design works well with direct manipulation interfaces*

color or graphics in favor of battleship gray menus and small icon-laden navigation bars, but the overarching sense of acting as software is at the heart of software- oriented/ GUI-oriented design. Sites that use a lot of text buttons organized in palettes across the top or left of the screen basically are imitating what software applications look like. The upside of GUI design is hard to ignore. Users know how to use software. They've come to understand what to expect from menus, text fields, buttons, and so on. This knowledge the designer gets for free. GUI-oriented Web design is consistent with what people already know, so in that sense GUI design is the safest design style to practice. Rarely will a GUI style site inspire, but at the same time it rarely upsets users. Figure 11-28 illustrates the GUI design style that is so frequently shown throughout this book.

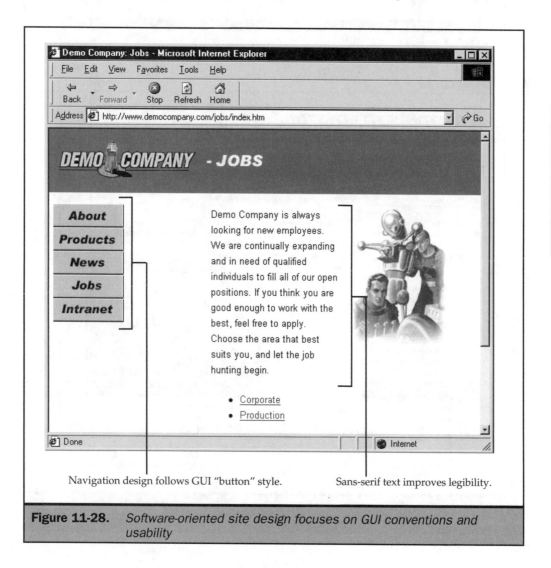

Navigation design follows GUI "button" style.   Sans-serif text improves legibility.

Figure 11-28.   *Software-oriented site design focuses on GUI conventions and usability*

Tip: GUI style site design is a safe bet, particularly when there is a range of user sophistication.

Be careful, though, and do not embrace GUI design so closely that you attempt to reinvent the user's desktop or traditional window environment within the browser window. This can confuse the user more than provide security through familiarity, as shown in Figure 11-29. Consider how difficult it would be to explain to novice users

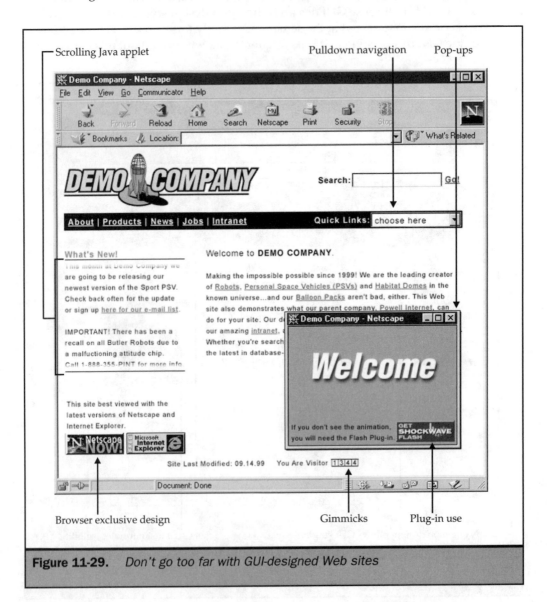

Figure 11-29.   *Don't go too far with GUI-designed Web sites*

that they use the Windows GUI to access a browser application to access a GUI within a browser window over the Internet. Someday it's surely going to be seamless, but for now don't take chances.

While the look of a GUI-oriented Web site might be more colorful than the typical software application, the general sense of consistency is there. This consistency could be the major downside of GUI design, as it doesn't always leave as much room for designers and limits their design possibilities to the choice of colors or the use of simple thematic buttons. Even font choice on navigation might be limited to common sans-serif fonts like Arial and Helvetica when GUI principles are subscribed to religiously. GUI design can be limiting to designers who want to stretch their creative wings.

Unconventional

The unconventional school of design favors creativity, unpredictability, and even randomness in design. Unconventional pages often damn the conventions and invent their own. The interface is an artistic opportunity for the designers to express their feelings. While these forms of designs can be the most powerful, they also can be the most dangerous to use. Unconventional interface design directly counters the usability idea of consistency. Why rely on what people already know? That's boring. Give them something new! Of course, a site following such practices forces the user to learn new interfaces, and this could send many users packing. On the other hand, when the experience is fun or provides a motivating payoff, users may stick around nonetheless. Remember, users can be quite curious, and, when their curiosity is piqued, what is considered usable may be not as important as what is considered new or unusual.

While the unconventional school of Web design is probably the most fun and certainly tends to attract great interest in the design community, it is practical for only a relatively small class of sites. Few corporations would be willing to risk their site to an unconventional design. Heavy-use sites or task sites may find the use of an unconventional design highly damaging. Imagine a user struggling with new bizarre interface concepts when trying to find information about a business or pay bills. Figure 11-30 suggests what a self-interested designer might have done with the Demo Company site.

> **Suggestion: Avoid unconventional or very artistically oriented interface designs on task-driven, heavy-content, or frequent-use sites.**

Of course, sites meant to entertain users may find unconventional design the best approach. Sites designed as art are an obvious place for unconventional design. Designer portfolios, personal homes, and any site whose primary purpose is to provide a creative outlet for the designer rather than serve the user will find unconventional design appropriate. In short, any site where the main goal is to interact with a user on an aesthetic or emotional level with no worry about leaving some people behind may find unconventional or art-first designs appropriate. Designers are highly encouraged to explore these boundaries of the Web and push the limits. It makes them better designers.

Figure 11-30. *An interesting design, but Demo Company management might not appreciate an unconventional design*

A pet project is a great way to safely do this and lets the designer not worry about what other people think or even if people understand the site. Of course, don't try this kind of design on a paying client unless they asked for it or you are willing to lose them!

> **Tip:** Sites designed purposefully to be unconventional are a great way to explore new ideas.

Layout Examples

This section provides some examples of the most common layouts used in Web sites. While there are countless variations of layouts, most tend to be somewhat related to the ones presented here. Of course, freestyle designs that seem to follow no pattern at all may seem to be the most common of all, and they are particularly popular among personal home page builders. The examples presented speak only about general layout and say nothing about the particular stylistic aspects of a particular layout. The use of color, text, and imagery is closely related to personal taste and current social and visuals trends. Some classical trends, such as the use of symmetry and white space, tend to weather short-lived fads, but there are few other such principles, so the focus of this discussion will be placed on general layout and leave the designers free to be as creative as they like within the defined regions.

"TLB"

TLB, top-left-bottom or top-left-backup, is one of the most common design styles used on the Web today. In this design, the top of the page is reserved for page labeling, branding information, and often primary navigation, and the left side of the page usually contains secondary navigation elements. If the site is small, the left side contains the site's primary navigation and the top contains solely labeling and branding information, but more often the left is reserved for secondary navigation information. As the user clicks through the main sections, the choices on the left change. This is really no different than a traditional GUI application. In a GUI, the user selects menus that drop down to present more specific choices. The only difference here is the position of the menu— fixed to the left of the screen. The last location in a TLB design is the bottom of the screen, which is generally reserved for text links to supplement or back up the other navigation and supplementary information, such as copyright information, legal terms, or contact info.

TLB designs are so common that users should already be very familiar with how to use sites with this layout. From a usability perspective, the major complaint about TLB designs is that the left-hand navigation often takes up a great deal of screen real estate that could be used for content, and the user in some sense has to "jump over" the navigation to reach the content. When using fixed page widths to account for small monitors, the column for content can be somewhat restrictive, so that some content, such as tables, has to be reformatted or the page will scroll a great deal. However, letting the content expand infinitely to the right is not always a good solution, as it may make the page difficult to read. In fact, often TLB designs are restricted eventually on the right by a third column of related information or a background color. This creates a familiar page approach to design. Figure 11-31 illustrates a TLB design in practice.

> **Tip: Consider limiting the right-hand margin in TLB designs to create a consistent page look.**

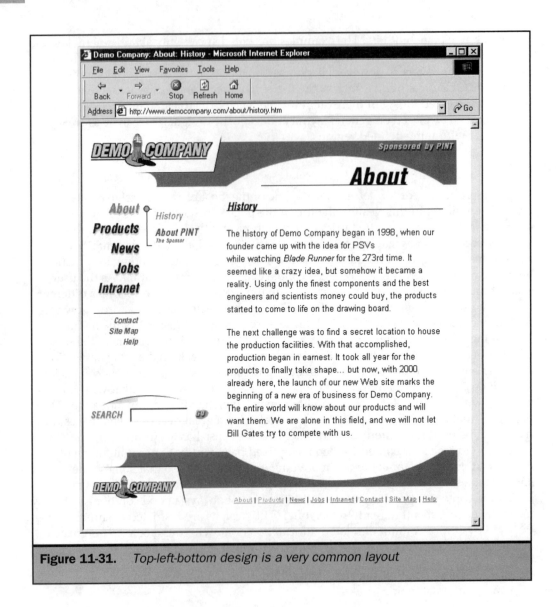

Figure 11-31. *Top-left-bottom design is a very common layout*

An example layout in this familiar style is presented here:

```
<!DOCTYPE HTML PUBLIC "-//W3C//DTD XHTML 1.0 Transitional//EN"
"http://www.w3.org/TR/xhtml1/DTD/xhtml1-transitional.dtd">
<html xmlns="http://www.w3.org/1999/xhtml">
<head>
```

```html
<title>TLB Template</title>
<style type="text/css">
<!--
body {margin: 0px;}
-->
</style>
</head>
<body bgcolor="#ffffff" leftmargin="0" rightmargin="0" topmargin="0"
marginheight="0" marginwidth="0">

<!--BEGIN: Label or primary nav table -->
<table width="100%" border="0" cellspacing="0" cellpadding="0">
<tr>
<td width="100%" bgcolor="yellow">
<h2 align="center">Site Heading and/or Navigation</h2>
</td>
</tr>
</table>

<!--END: Label of primary nav table-->

<!--BEGIN: Secondary nav and content -->
<table width="100%" border="0" cellspacing="0" cellpadding="0">
<tr>
<td width="10" bgcolor="red">   </td>
<td width="90" valign="top" bgcolor="red">

   <br />
<a href="#">Link</a><br />
<a href="#">Link</a><br />
<a href="#">Link</a><br />
<a href="#">Link</a><br />
<a href="#">Link</a><br />
<a href="#">Link</a><br />
</td>
<td width="10" bgcolor="white">   </td>
<td>
<br />
<h2>Page Heading</h2>
<hr />

<p>Lorem ipsum dolor sit amet, consectetuer adipiscing elit, sed
```

```
diam nonummy nibh euismod tincidunt ut laoreet dolore magna aliquam
erat volutpat. Ut wisi enim ad minim veniam, quis nostrud exerci
tation ullamcorper suscipit lobortis nisl ut aliquip ex ea commodo
consequat.</p>

<p>Lorem ipsum dolor sit amet, consectetuer adipiscing elit, sed
diam nonummy nibh euismod tincidunt ut laoreet dolore magna aliquam
erat volutpat. Ut wisi enim ad minim veniam, quis nostrud exerci
tation ullamcorper suscipit lobortis nisl ut aliquip ex ea commodo
consequat.</p>
</td>
<td width="10" bgcolor="white">   </td>
</tr>
</table>
<!-- END: tert nav and content -->

<!--BEGIN: footer navigation and legal-->
<div align="center">
<br />
<font size="-2">
<a href="#">Link</a> |
<a href="#">Link</a> |
<a href="#">Link</a> |
<a href="#">Link</a> |
<a href="#">Link</a> |
<a href="#">Link</a>
</font>
<br />
<em>&copy;2002 DemoCompany Inc.</em>
</font>
</div>
<!-- END: footer nav -->
</body>
</html>
```

The major downside of TLB layouts, besides their potentially limiting content region, is that they generally focus on navigation rather than content and may not provide as much design opportunity as some other forms of layout.

Header-Footer

A header-footer design provides navigation both on the top and bottom of the page, with the entire width of the page used for content. This type of design is good for content-oriented sites, though it does limit the amount of area used for navigation.

Generally, the top of the screen is used for branding, graphical navigation, and page headings, while the bottom of the screen is used to repeat text links and to provide supplementary text links, particularly if the top navigation can scroll off the page. Using frames, it is possible to fix the position of the top and bottom navigation regions so they don't scroll offscreen. CSS should eventually provide this functionality as well, but so far the required properties are not well enough supported to be relied upon. However, if it is not possible to fix navigation, a redundant set of navigation is not as necessary, and the bottom may be reserved instead solely for useful information like legal terms, copyrights, or contact information. Figure 11-32 shows an example of header-footer design.

Suggestion: Use header-footer design for content-focused sites, particularly when wide content is common.

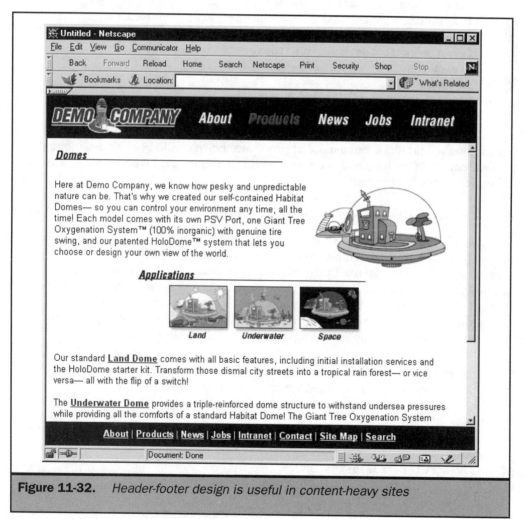

Figure 11-32. *Header-footer design is useful in content-heavy sites*

A basic header-footer template is presented here using frames. In this example, you would need to provide three more files to set the top navigation, contents, and bottom information.

```
<!DOCTYPE HTML PUBLIC "-//W3C//DTD XHTML 1.0 Frameset//EN">
<html xmlns="http://www.w3.org/1999/xhtml">
<head>
<title>Header Footer Frameset</title>

</head>
<frameset rows="125,*,50">
  <frame src="header.htm" id="header" name="header"
   frameborder="0" scrolling="no" />
  <frame src="content.htm" id="content" name="content"
   frameborder="0" scrolling="auto" />
  <frame src="footer.htm" id="footer" name="footer"
   frameborder="0" scrolling="no" />
</frameset>
</html>
```

It will also eventually be possible to create this design using CSS. Absolute CSS positioning would work, but a more appropriate choice would be fixed positioning. Unfortunately, at the time of this edition's writing, this method works only in Mozilla 1.0 browsers and is not predictable.

Centered and Floating Window Style

An increasingly popular page layout style could be termed the "floating card or window" style. The basic idea is to create a region in the middle of the screen for content. The region can be fixed in size from page to page, have a varying length, or be a scrolling window. Generally, the fixed-card style won't work unless a very limited amount of content is presented. A full, fleshed-out example of a centered-style page with a background or color is shown in Figure 11-33, while the following code provides a simple framework for implementing a centered-style design.

```
<!DOCTYPE HTML PUBLIC "-//W3C//DTD XHTML 1.0 Transitional//EN"
"http://www.w3.org/TR/xhtml11/DTD/xhtml11-transitional.dtd">
<html xmlns="http://www.w3.org/1999/xhtml">
<head>
<title>Simple Centered Page</title>
</head>
<body bgcolor="#3399ff">
```

```
<table width="600" align="center" bgcolor="white">
<tr>
<td>Content here</td>
</tr>
</table>
</body>
</html>
```

Utilizing frames, it is possible to create a variation on this design with a central region of content that scrolls. The benefit of this style of design is that it provides a fixed region to design for but doesn't look as unusual on varying screens, since it is usually positioned within a lush background and floats in the center of a screen. Of course, executing this design may require the use of frames, floating frames

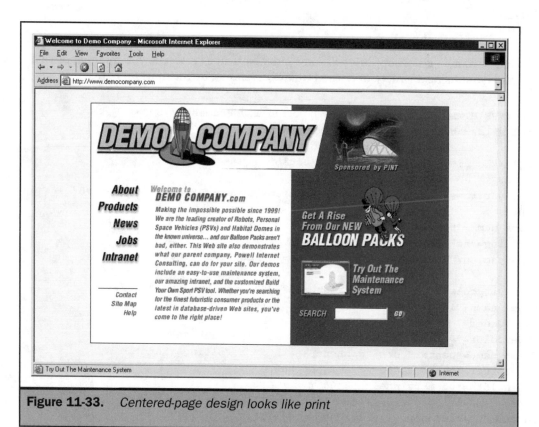

Figure 11-33.   *Centered-page design looks like print*

(defined by **<iframe>**), or style sheet-based positioning. The simplest way to execute a scrolled window style design might be to do something like this:

```
<!DOCTYPE HTML PUBLIC "-//W3C//DTD XHTML 1.0 Transitional//EN">
<html xmlns="http://www.w3.org/1999/xhtml">
<head>
<title>The Easy Way</title>
</head>
<body bgcolor="blue">
<div align="center">
<iframe src="http://www.democompany.com" height="90%" width="600"
border="0">
</iframe>
</div>
</body>
</html>
```

Since **<iframe>** is not supported in some older Netscape browsers, you might approach this layout using a variety of normal frames, as shown by the markup here:

```
<!DOCTYPE HTML PUBLIC "-//W3C//DTD XHTML 1.0 Frameset//EN">
<html xmlns="http://www.w3.org/1999/xhtml">
<head>
<title>Floating Window in Frames</title>
</head>
<frameset rows="71,*,34" border="0" frameborder="0" framespacing="0" >

<frame name="top" src="top.htm"
scrolling="no" frameborder="no"
framespacing="0" noresize marginwidth="0" marginheight="0" />

<frameset cols="170,423,*" frameborder="0" framespacing="0" />
<frame name="left" src="left.htm" scrolling="no"
frameborder="no" noresize framespacing="0"
bordercolor="#ffff00" marginwidth="0" marginheight="0" />
<frame name="center" src="contentpage.htm" scrolling="auto"
frameborder="no" noresize framespacing="0"
marginwidth="0" marginheight="0" />
<frame name="right" src="right.htm" scrolling="no"
frameborder="no" noresize framespacing="0"
marginwidth="0" marginheight="0" />
</frameset>
```

```
<frame name="bottom" src="bottom.htm" scrolling="no"
frameborder="no" framespacing="0" noresize
marginwidth="0" marginheight="0" />


<noframes>
<body>
This site heavily uses frames. If you do not have a
frames-compatible browser it is not possible to proceed
beyond this point. Please e-mail
<a href="mailto:gripes@democompany.com">gripes@democompany.com</a>
to register a complaint.
</body>
</noframes>
</frameset>
</html>
```

This markup sets up a set of frames that define the top, bottom, and sides of the window and leaves the middle for content. A final variation using CSS positioning in conjunction with a scroll option for the content is shown here:

```
<!DOCTYPE HTML PUBLIC "-//W3C//DTD XHTML 1.0 Transitional//EN"
"http://www.w3.org/TR/xhtml1/DTD/xhtml1-transitional.dtd">
<html xmlns="http://www.w3.org/1999/xhtml">
<head>
<title>Centered and Scrolling with CSS</title>
<style type="text/css">
<!--
body     {background-color: #33cccc;}
#content {width: 600px; height: 410px;
          overflow: scroll;
          padding: 10px;
          margin-top: 20px;
          margin-bottom: 20px;
          margin-right: auto;
          margin-left: auto;
          background: white;
          border: 5px solid #cccccc;}
-->
</style>
</head>
```

```
<body>

<div id="content">

<p>Lorem ipsum dolor sit amet, consectetuer adipiscing elit, sed
diam nonummy nibh euismod tincidunt ut laoreet dolore magna
aliquam erat volutpat. Ut wisi enim ad minim veniam, quis nostrud
exerci tation ullamcorper suscipit lobortis nisl ut aliquip ex ea
commodo consequat. Duis autem vel eum iriure dolor in hendrerit
in vulputate velit esse molestie consequat, vel illum dolore eu
feugiat nulla facilisis at vero eros et accumsan et iusto odio
dignissim qui blandit praesent luptatum zzril delenit Lorem
ipsum dolor sit amet, consectetuer adipiscing elit, sed diam
nonummy nibh euismod tincidunt ut laoreet dolore magna
aliquam erat volutpat.</p>

<p>Ut wisi enim ad minim veniam, quis nostrud exerci tation
ullamcorper suscipit lobortis nisl ut aliquip ex ea commodo
consequat. Duis autem vel eum iriure dolor in hendrerit in
vulputate velit esse molestie consequat, vel illum dolore eu
feugiat nulla facilisis at vero eros et accumsan et iusto
odio dignissim qui blandit.</p>

<p>Ut wisi enim ad minim veniam, quis nostrud exerci tation
ullamcorper suscipit lobortis nisl ut aliquip ex ea commodo
consequat. Duis autem vel eum iriure dolor in hendrerit in
vulputate velit esse molestie consequat, vel illum dolore
eu feugiat nulla facilisis at vero eros et accumsan et
iusto odio dignissim qui blandit.</p>

</div>
</body>
</html>
```

Note   *To avoid printing problems, if you use CSS to implement this approach, make sure
to have a special print style sheet. Also, be aware of CSS implementation problems.*

An example of a floating design in action is shown in Figure 11-34.

The challenge of using the fixed-window approach is dealing with the CSS and the
frame rendering problems in browsers. Testing is very important with this type of layout.

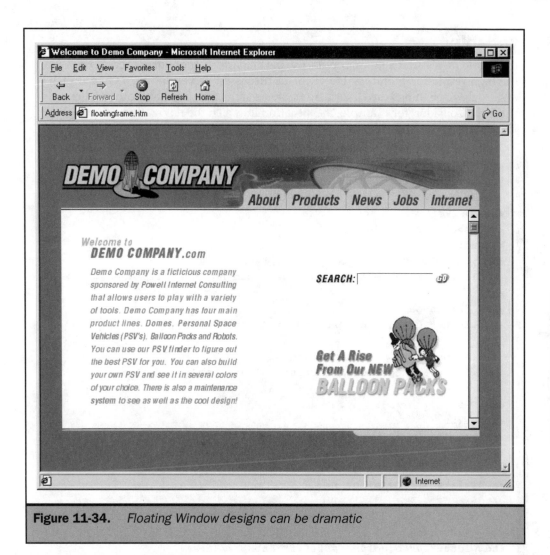

Figure 11-34. *Floating Window designs can be dramatic*

Tip: When building scrolling card style pages, be careful to make sure that frame line-up is precise under all browsers.

As mentioned earlier in the chapter when discussing page sizes, fixed pages may look rather small on large monitors. Unlike TLB layout, header-footer and scrolling windows can be centered to reduce the perception of empty space. Of course, the only way to truly deal with space issues is to create a stretchable page with relative sizing.

Stretchable

Stretchable pages are rising in popularity, particularly as more users access the Web with high-resolution monitors. However, as discussed earlier, letting a page stretch is dangerous, since things can distort. Some items should be fixed and others allowed to stretch. Consider, for example, the situation in which the navigation column and margins are fixed, while the center column is free to stretch however the user wants.

```
<!DOCTYPE HTML PUBLIC "-//W3C//DTD XHTML 1.0 Transitional//EN"
"http://www.w3.org/TR/xhtml1/DTD/xhtml1-transitional.dtd">
<html xmlns="http://www.w3.org/1999/xhtml">
<head>
<title>Stretch Me</title>
</head>
<body bgcolor="#006699">
<table border="0" width="100%" cellspacing="0" cellpadding="0">
<tr>
<!-- just a gap -->
<td width="20" bgcolor="#006699">   </td>

    <!-- navigation column fixed size -->
<td width="80" bgcolor="#ffcc00" valign="top">

<h3>Navigation</h3>
<br /><br />
<a href="#">Link</a><br />
<a href="#">Link</a><br />
<a href="#">Link</a><br />
<a href="#">Link</a><br />
</td>

<!-- just a gap -->
<td width="20" bgcolor="#ffffff"> </td>

<!-- content region variable size -->
<td width="100%" bgcolor="#ffffff" valign="top">
<h2 align="center">Stretch Demo</h2>
<hr />
<p>Content goes here. Content goes here. Content goes
   here. Content goes here. Content goes here. Content
   goes here. Content goes here. Content goes here.
   Content goes here.</p>
</td>
```

```
<!--right column-->
<td width="80" bgcolor="#ffcc00">Some other text here </td>

<!--right margin gap-->
<td width="20" bgcolor="#006699">   </td>
</tr>
</table>
</body>
</html>
```

While a stretchable or fluid design does fit to whatever screen the user wants, it can be rather limiting. Creating stretch points limits the design to simple colors or patterns, since the relative areas are elastic and would distort an image placed there.

Tip: Avoid stretchable pages when content is minimal, or they may distort when stretched.

The Road to Common Site "Looks"

Designers may feel that the previous discussion will stifle creativity. Yet consistency is common even in the world of print. Consistency can be *good*. Users know what to expect. They are faster and more efficient when they understand a site. The frame grabs of two popular e-commerce sites are shown in Figure 11-35. They really are the same design, and for good reason. Users will know how to shop right away.

Common layouts not only benefit the user, but the designer as well. Common layouts can be implemented as templates that allow for the cost effective construction of large sites. Even novices can easily apply common layouts with decent results. Remember, not everyone who is building sites will need or want to go to art school. Already, the W3 has issued core styles (http://www.w3.org/StyleSheets/Core/) that they are encouraging people to use. Hopefully, this will improve the look of many sites.

Consistency between sites does, however, limit creativity to some degree. Rather than be pessimistic about the design options open to you, it would be smarter to say that consistent site designs allow creativity to operate within certain parameters. Within a similar site, there may be many ways to do the same general design. Type choice, color, artistic devices such as the treatment of illustrations or photos, all can make sites with the same basic structure appear very different. This is not necessarily a limitation any more than are the accepted practices for designing books, which tend not to be triangular and usually have tables of contents. Truly great Web designers can stay within convention and still stand out.

Rule: Strive always in Web design to be the same, but different.

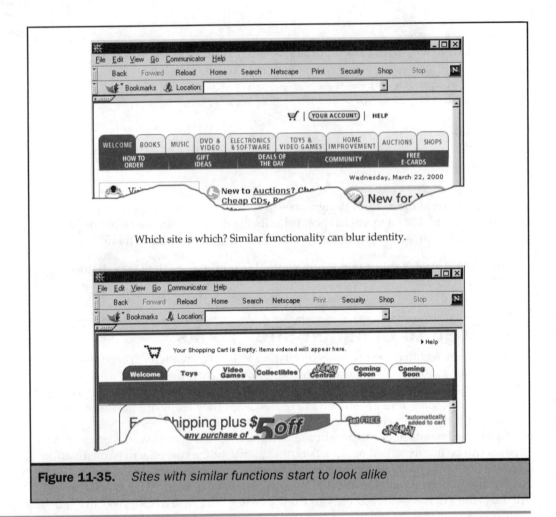

Which site is which? Similar functionality can blur identity.

Figure 11-35.   *Sites with similar functions start to look alike*

Summary

Web pages are not print pages. While certain characteristics like size and layout are often similar, the dynamic nature of the Web environment can create design difficulties that don't exist for books. Users can view pages under a variety of resolutions, and designs will literally break if designers aren't careful. Even something as simple as the user adjusting the font size can ruin a nice layout. The design of a page is influenced both by the type of the page and by its content. Always remember that the beauty of the Web is that pages can easily be changed to fit content. A few common schools of Web design exist, and there are common layouts as well. Designers should consider these designs, but also think about experimenting. So far, little has been said about the actual components of a page, such as text, color, images, and form elements. The next few chapters will investigate the proper use of these page elements.

Chapter 12

Text

The heart and soul of a Web page is text. Whatever anyone says about the future of multimedia online, most Web pages today are dominated by textual information. Assuming that your site relies heavily on text, the way that you use text may significantly influence the user's experience. The simple choice of a typeface could hurt site usability just as much as it could improve site "memorability" by building brand. Formatting text could also make the text easier or harder to deal with. The art or process of using type is traditionally termed *typography*. In short, typography is concerned with the aspects of text that make it readable—or if you prefer, simply usable—as well as expressive. The use of words themselves and the style of writing employed might affect the user's experience just as much as how the text is presented.

The Medium Matters

Like print or television, the Web is a medium that has its own particular limitations. While there is a great deal of knowledge concerning how type is used on paper, not all of it maps well to the Web. Technologies like HTML and CSS are not always powerful enough to do things that are feasible on paper, at least not easily. Even if we were provided with absolute control over page layout, we still would have trouble. As discussed in Chapter 11, the Web does not support any particular fixed page width or length. Even if there were such conventions and they were followed, page designers do not have as much control over the final presentation as they think. Users are always free to change their screen size, increase or decrease their font size, change the font used, or even change their browser's colors. Designers have to get used to the fact that the Web is not static—it's a fluid medium where presentation varies greatly from user to user and moment to moment. Nowhere is this lack of control more obvious than the use of text within Web pages. Text flow is very dynamic: users simply have to increase their font size, shrink their window, or expand their window to ruin a nicely formatted page, as shown in Figure 12-1.

Many designers cannot accept the fact that Web technologies like HTML don't allow them common typographic facilities like adjustable line spacing. They become very frustrated when they find that even simple things like relative text size are not predictable online. Notice the dramatic potential difference between font sizes on a Macintosh and PC screen shown in Figure 12-2.

Note *Most newer Mac browsers attempt to rectify the cross-browser sizing difference, but there is no guarantee such browsers are used or set correctly.*

Taking Control of Text

What's a designer to do? Some will invariably fight with the medium and attempt to wrestle control back. Typically, these designers put all their text into image format. Making their text graphic allows designers a degree of control over letter spacing, font choice, and a variety of other facilities they have come to expect from print.

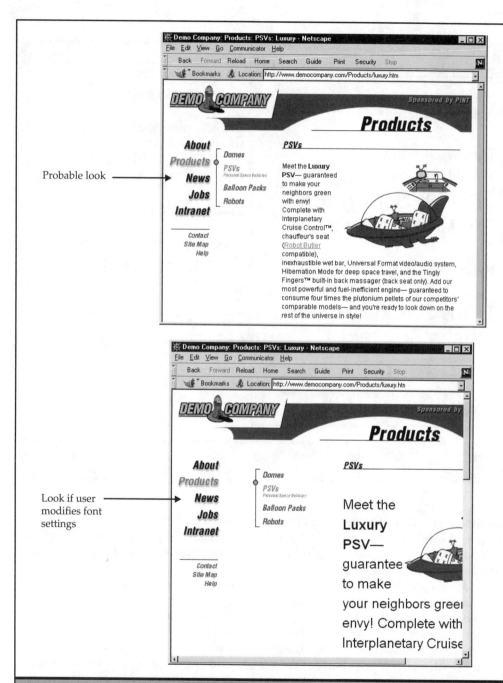

Probable look

Look if user modifies font settings

Figure 12-1. Text layout challenges on the Web

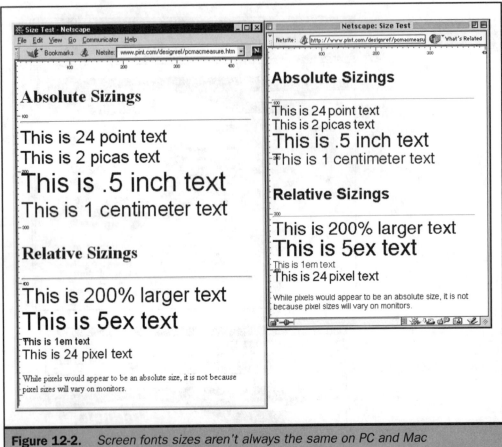

Figure 12-2.   *Screen fonts sizes aren't always the same on PC and Mac*

This approach is flawed to the core. Putting textual content into an image form makes a Web page load slower. No amount of graphic optimization is going to make the phrase "Web pages need to be fast" in a graphic form quicker than ASCII text saying the same thing, as shown in Figure 12-3.

Besides the problem of file size, graphic text must be formatted for a particular screen size. A graphic text label using a 24-point font size may look quite nice at 640 × 480 resolution. Consider what it looks like at 1,024 × 768. The pixels don't get any bigger, so either it is small or distorted, as shown in Figure 12-4.

Users have no way of fixing the sizing issue. If, however, text is presented as regular HTML text, it is possible for the browser to override any sizing. This enables the user to improve the page's readability. Other problems with using graphic text include the following:

- **Difficulty updating** You need to use an image manipulation tool to make a simple text change. If you use **alt** text, you actually have to update both the image and the text—doubling the work.

- **Accessibility limited** Users with nonvisual browsers will have problems with graphic text unless the **alt** attribute is used. As previously mentioned, accessibility may be limited regardless of **alt** attributes if the images do not size based on screen resolution.

- **Ignored by search engines** Search engines will not index graphical content, though they should be able to index **alt** text if it is provided.

Despite its problems, graphical text does have its place. Until downloadable font technology is straightened out, graphical headings and buttons that must be rendered with a particular effect will still have to be created as graphics. For most text, though, it is better to use text itself rather than images.

Note *Flash is another text control possibility—it should scale with screen size but has the other two drawbacks.*

Throwing Up Your Arms

On the other end of the spectrum are those who throw up their arms and don't even try to control text layout to any major degree. This is nearly as bad as the previous situation. The reason we want to control layout is to improve the readability of text. If our text is

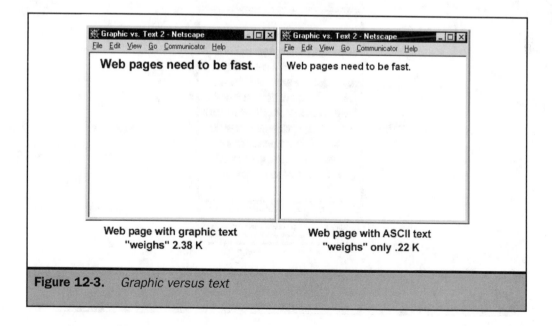

Web page with graphic text "weighs" 2.38 K

Web page with ASCII text "weighs" only .22 K

Figure 12-3. *Graphic versus text*

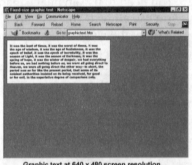

Graphic text at 640 x 480 screen resolution

Graphic text at 1024 x 768 screen resolution

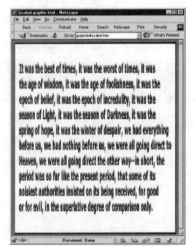

The <IMG> tag allows the use of percentage values
to define image height and width (100% for each
dimension in this example). This makes image
display completely dependent on how the user's
browser is sized, as shown here.

Figure 12-4.   *Absolute sizing of text backfires as graphic*

easier to read, it is more likely the user will actually bother to read it and act upon any message we are attempting to convey. The use of a particular typeface, size, and style and the overall layout of text all affect how well or how poorly text conveys information to the user. Traditional typographic conventions have striven to improve the legibility or readability of text (the "usability" of the text). Take a look at the Web pages shown in Figure 12-5. The page on the top is a typical page lacking any major typographic improvements. The one on the bottom has had some basic techniques applied to improve readability.

Modern-Day Baskerville

Should we strive to apply any and all typographic conventions from print to the Web directly? No, because some type conventions just don't make sense or need modification for use on the Web. For example, the practice of copy fitting is well known in print publishing. Copy fitting is the process of taking text and trying to fit it within a predefined space, such as a piece of paper. Copy fitting requires the designer to literally count the characters and determine how to fit them in the page by changing the type size, type family, line spacing, or layout or even by editing the text. On the Web, we could limit our pages to a particular size, as discussed in the previous chapter, but we could also let things scroll. We are not confined by the same limitations as paper, and this can be a blessing. We really can't worry about things like widows in Web text. Because text can reflow simply by the user resizing their screen or changing their font size, a paragraph may have a widow (a short line of text that appears by itself at the top of a page) no matter what we do. The concept of copy fitting just doesn't work for the Web.

Get used to the fact that many longstanding ideas of print type layout do not make sense for the Web. As a designer, you should strive to work with the medium, not against it. Consider the history of print design. John Baskerville was an English type designer in the mid-1700s who designed typefaces that took into account how the print process worked, starting from the properties of the metal used to manufacture type. Baskerville considered the whole process and the state of printing technology when he designed his typeface. We should always remember that the Web, and its support for text layout, is still very primitive. Be a modern-day Baskerville!

The rest of this chapter will provide a brief overview of typography and its terms. We'll follow with a discussion of many traditional tasks of type and how they may be accomplished using standard Web technologies like HTML or CSS. The chapter will conclude with a discussion of how to format text for usability.

Typography Terminology 101

Typography has a rich history, as well as many rules and terms. Web designers should be familiar with the vocabulary and some of the basic tenets of text usage that have been established in the print world. Don't fall asleep as you read on. Remember, the

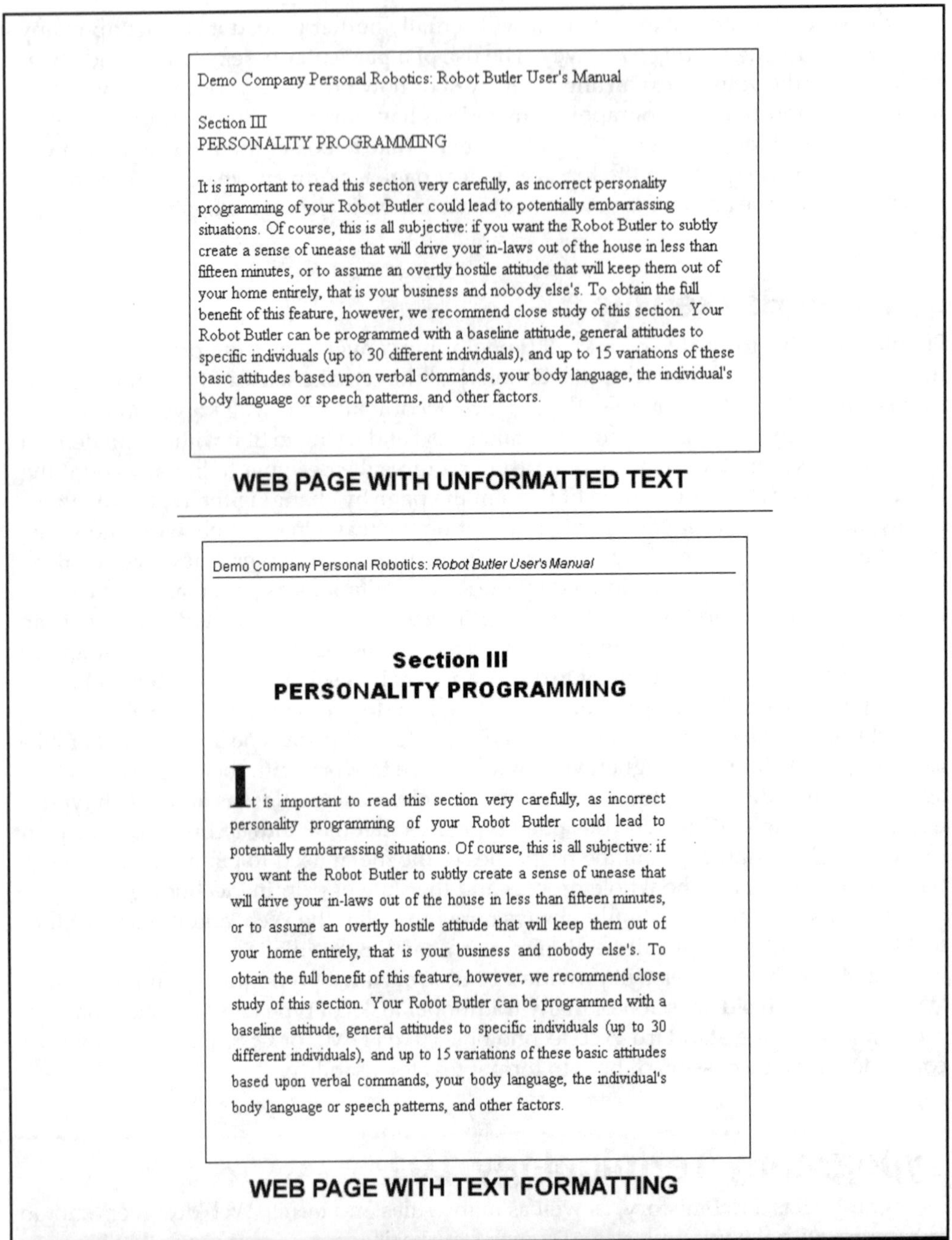

Demo Company Personal Robotics: Robot Butler User's Manual

Section III
PERSONALITY PROGRAMMING

It is important to read this section very carefully, as incorrect personality programming of your Robot Butler could lead to potentially embarrassing situations. Of course, this is all subjective: if you want the Robot Butler to subtly create a sense of unease that will drive your in-laws out of the house in less than fifteen minutes, or to assume an overtly hostile attitude that will keep them out of your home entirely, that is your business and nobody else's. To obtain the full benefit of this feature, however, we recommend close study of this section. Your Robot Butler can be programmed with a baseline attitude, general attitudes to specific individuals (up to 30 different individuals), and up to 15 variations of these basic attitudes based upon verbal commands, your body language, the individual's body language or speech patterns, and other factors.

WEB PAGE WITH UNFORMATTED TEXT

Demo Company Personal Robotics: *Robot Butler User's Manual*

Section III
PERSONALITY PROGRAMMING

It is important to read this section very carefully, as incorrect personality programming of your Robot Butler could lead to potentially embarrassing situations. Of course, this is all subjective: if you want the Robot Butler to subtly create a sense of unease that will drive your in-laws out of the house in less than fifteen minutes, or to assume an overtly hostile attitude that will keep them out of your home entirely, that is your business and nobody else's. To obtain the full benefit of this feature, however, we recommend close study of this section. Your Robot Butler can be programmed with a baseline attitude, general attitudes to specific individuals (up to 30 different individuals), and up to 15 variations of these basic attitudes based upon verbal commands, your body language, the individual's body language or speech patterns, and other factors.

WEB PAGE WITH TEXT FORMATTING

Figure 12-5. *"Do nothing" versus "do something"*

more we focus on the various aspects of letters and the use of type, the better we will be able to fix subtle problems that the reader may not be consciously aware of.

Text is made up of characters. Characters can be letters, numbers, punctuation, and a variety of special characters. With letters, we have both uppercase and lowercase letters. We can also describe various parts of the individual letters. For example, *ascenders* are the parts of lowercase letters that protrude upward away from the main part of the letter. *Descenders* are the parts of letters that protrude downward and hang below the baseline, which all characters sit on. The letters *b, d, f, h, k, l*, and *t* have ascenders, while the letters *g, j, p, q*, and *y* have descenders. Ascenders and descenders are important because they help readers to recognize words more easily by providing variation in letter forms when combined in a word. The *baseline* is a line, usually unseen, that text appears to sit on; descenders go below this line. The comparable line that marks the top of lowercase letters that lack ascenders is called the *meanline*. Between these two lines, characters may be measured by their *x-height*, which is the height of the body or main part of a lowercase letter not including any descender or ascender. Basically, it is the distance from the meanline to the baseline. It is simplest to think of x-height simply as the height of a lowercase *x* character. Figure 12-6 provides a graphical overview of all these type terms.

There are many more terms that help classify letter shapes. Some of these are shown in Figure 12-7. The purpose of knowing all these terms is simply to be able to understand the differences between different character styles.

Fonts

A "font" refers to the style of the type used on a computer. The term comes from the print publishing industry, where it referred to a particular size of a particular typeface. On the computer, this term is often interchangeable with the word "typeface." On the Web, typefaces are generally classified in only a few basic ways. First, by distinguishing if the typeface is *serif* or *sans serif*. A serif font is one that has short starting or finish strokes protruding from certain parts of letters, like *T* or *h*. In contrast, a sans-serif font

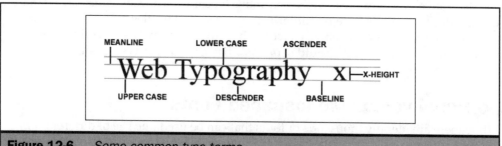

Figure 12-6.   *Some common type terms*

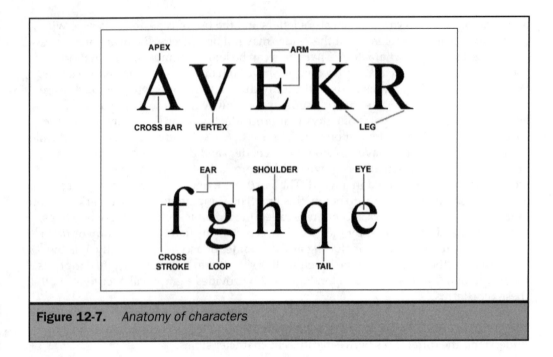

Figure 12-7. *Anatomy of characters*

lacks these extra strokes. Notice the difference between Arial, a common sans-serif font, and Times, the most common serif font on the Web.

Arial is a sans serif font

Times is a serif font

Beyond sans-serif and serif, some other common typefaces categories include script and decorative. Some may refer to the decorative typefaces as novelty or display typefaces. Other categories of type are possible, and many subcategories may also exist, but typographers continue to debate exactly what categories exist and which font is in which category. Table 12-1 should serve as a basic guide for Web designers to the common categories of typefaces that exist.

Proportional versus Monospaced Fonts

While there are literally thousands of fonts that can be used, the use of different font families within standard Web text is actually very limited. By default, Web browsers support only two basic font types: proportional and monospace fonts. A *proportional font* consists of characters that take up only as much space as they need within a

Kinds of Typefaces	Categories Within Each Typeface	Examples
Serif typefaces	**Old Style** This type appeared between the 15th to 17th centuries. Fonts have little contrast between thick and thin strokes, bracketed serifs, and small x-height.	Bembo Times Roman
	Transitional This is a group that combines elements from both the Old Style and Modern groups and appeared in the 17th and 18th centuries. The typical characteristics include a large x-height, more contrast between thick and thin strokes than is seen in Old Style faces, and thin, bracketed serifs.	Bodoni
	Modern This typeface originated in the 18th century and was used in the 19th century as well. Fonts in this category usually display a contrast between thick and thin strokes, small x-height like Old Style, and usually unbracketed serifs.	Clarendon
	Slab serif This typeface features heavy lines and curves of equal width, with rectangular serifs the same width as the strokes themselves. The x-height is generally large. Some slab serifs have an "Egyptian" feel to them.	
Sans-serif typefaces	**Geometric** The x-height of these tends to be small and the strokes of the characters tend to be the same width. Like their name, tend to be very mathematical in their proportions.	Century Gothic
	Grotesque These tend to have more stroke variation than other sans-serif fonts. Have a large x-height. Are not as "geometric" in feeling.	Gill Sans

Table 12-1.   *Common Typefaces*

ELEMENTS OF
PAGE DESIGN

Kinds of Typefaces	Categories Within Each Typeface	Examples
Sans-serif typefaces	**Humanist** Uses a small x-height, similar in proportion to Old Style.	
Script typefaces	**Brush script** This type looks as if it were lettered with a brush. **Calligraphic** In this kind of typeface, the designs appear to have been drawn with a broad-edged pen.	*Brush Script*
Decorative typefaces (also called Display or Novelty typefaces)	Many of these fonts are too intricate or irregular to be useful for text unless in very large size or for a few words.	RAnSOM NoTE

Table 12-1.   *Common Typefaces* (continued)

word or a line of type. By default, text in HTML is rendered in a proportional font when not specified—typically, Times. With *monospaced fonts* (also called fixed-width or nonproportional), each character occupies exactly the same amount of space regardless of its actual width. Web browsers also support a single monospaced font—typically, Courier. Setting Web text in a monospaced font is easy to do with HTML using the **<tt>** element, as shown here:

```
<tt>This is now monospaced</tt>
```

A specific monospaced typeface such as Courier can be specified using CSS or HTML's **<font>** tag. However, proportional fonts should be used for most text, as they have the following two advantages:

- You can include more characters in a given amount of space if they can vary in width.
- Text is easier to read because the words appear as a cohesive unit within a sentence.

Note the readability and the amount of room taken up by the sample text shown in Figure 12-8.

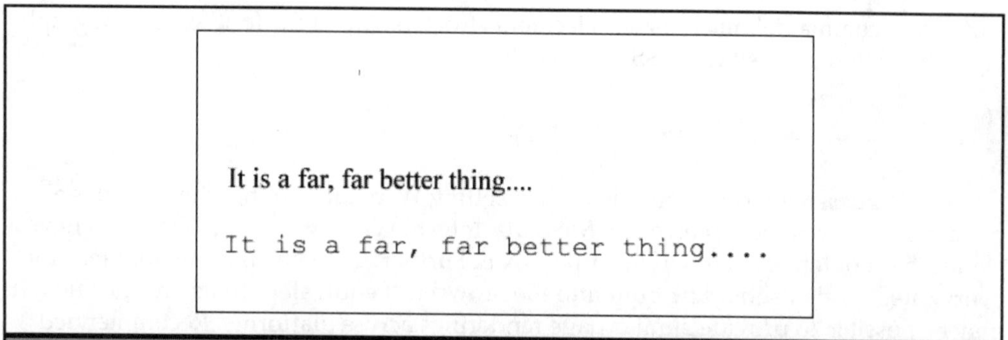

It is a far, far better thing....

It is a far, far better thing....

Figure 12-8. *Monospace versus proportional text*

In general, you should consider using monospaced type within Web pages for computer code, certain technical data, or to bring special emphasis to words or phrases.

Setting Fonts in Web Pages

While Web pages support two primary generic font types, proportional and monospaced, it is possible to set the font itself. Use the **face** attribute for the **<font>** tag to set the name of the font used to render text in a Web page:

```
<font face="Courier">This is now monospaced</font>
```

A Web browser will read this HTML fragment and render the text in the font named in the **face** attribute—but only for users who have the font installed on their systems. Multiple fonts can be listed using the **face** attribute:

```
<font face="Arial, Helvetica, Sans-serif">This should be in a
different font</font>
```

Here, the browser will read the comma-delimited list of fonts until it finds a font it supports. Given the fragment shown above, the browser would try first Arial, then Helvetica, and finally a sans-serif font before giving up and using whatever the current browser font is.

When using CSS, specify the **font-family** property to set the font, either by specifying a specific font such as Arial or a generic family such as sans-serif, which should be built into the browser. Quote any font names that contain white space, and be careful to note that font names may have to be capitalized. Like the **<font>** tag, CSS supports a comma-delimited list to select fonts from. So, to set the font for all paragraph tags, you would use a simple CSS rule like this:

```
p    {font-family: Arial, Helvetica, sans-serif;}
```

A little guesswork can be applied when setting Web fonts so that the page has a good chance of rendering correctly. Most Macintosh, Windows, and UNIX users have a standard set of fonts, as shown in Appendix E. Further, CSS specifies one font face for every category that should be built into the browser. If equivalent fonts are specified, it may be possible to provide similar page renderings across platforms. Recommended faces to use within Web pages are shown in Figure 12-9.

Because many of these fonts are specific to a particular operating system, you may have to specify fallback equivalents unless you decide to use downloadable fonts, which will be discussed in the next section. Traditionally, without relying on downloadable fonts, the combinations listed below have been considered useful to specify within Web sites because the fallback fonts are fairly similar and users generally have them installed:

```
Arial, Helvetica, sans-serif
Times New Roman, Times, serif
Courier New, Courier, Luxi mono, monospace
Georgia, Times New Roman, Times, serif
Verdana, Arial, Helvetica, sans-serif
```

Using Downloadable Fonts

With traditional HTML, and even basic CSS, font choice is very limited on the Web. Designers often resort to putting text into an image form in order to use a nonstandard font in a page. However, this solution is not optimal. Fortunately, the major browser

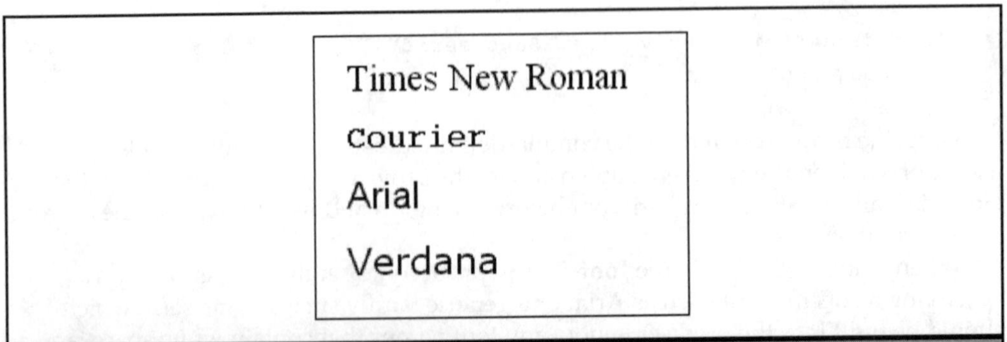

Figure 12-9.   *Common Web fonts*

vendors have begun to support downloadable fonts. Microsoft's solution is called OpenType (www.microsoft.com/typography) and has been built-into Internet Explore since version 4.0. Netscape's 4.x browsers used Bitstream TrueDoc technology (www.truedoc.com) natively. Unfortunately, Opera, Netscape 6/7, and Mozilla 1.0 browsers have not embraced downloadable fonts, so cross-platform font use can be challenging.

Microsoft's technology is the only reasonable way to embed fonts in a Web page. To include a font, you must first build the page using the **<font>** element or style sheet rules that set fonts that you own. When creating your page, don't worry about whether or not the end user has the font installed; it will be downloaded. Next, use Microsoft's Web Embedding Font Tool (WEFT), available from www.microsoft.com/typography, to analyze the font usage on the page. The program should create an .eot file that contains the embedded fonts. Then, add the font use information to the page in the form of cascading style sheets (CSS) style rules, which are basically those defined in CSS2, as shown here:

```
<!DOCTYPE HTML PUBLIC "-//W3C//DTD XHTML 1.0 Transitional//EN"
"http://www.w3.org/TR/xhtml1/DTD/xhtml1-transitional.dtd">
<html xmlns="http://www.w3.org/1999/xhtml">
<head>
<title>Microsoft Font Test</title>
<style type="text/css" media="all">
<!--

  @font-face {
    font-family: Ransom;
    font-style:  normal;
    font-weight: normal;
    src: url(fonts/ransom.eot);}

  .special {font-family: Ransom;
            color: green;
            font-size: 28pt;}
-->
</style>
</head>
<body>
<font face="Ransom" size="6">
Example Ransom Note Font
</font>
<br /><br />
<span class="special">
```

```
This is also in Ransom
</span>
</body>
</html>
```

Note in the example, how the **@font-face** selector allows you to bring any number of fonts into a page. It may be useful to define a fonts directory within your Web site to store font files, similar to storing image files for site use. Also, notice how it is possible to use both typical style sheet rules like a **class** binding, as well as the normal **<font>** tag. A possible rendering of font embedding is shown in Figure 12-10.

For more information on embedded fonts under Internet Explorer and links to font file creation tools like WEFT (Web Embedding Font Tool), see the Microsoft Typography site (www.microsoft.com/typography).

While downloadable font technology is improving, you must be careful with browser compatibility. Despite the fact that CSS2 defines the same syntax as Internet Explorer uses, not all IE versions across platforms support the technology, and even when done correctly, some minor screen flashing may occasionally occur, or the text may not work properly with background colors and images. Once perfected, downloadable font technology will drastically change type use on the Web, enabling users to create beautiful pages as well as ones overloaded with font families. Experienced designers should consider that a limited selection of fonts may be best for inexperienced page builders who might pick illegible fonts to use online.

Setting Font Styles

The most common font style is when the characters are upright. This is the *Roman* style (or simply *normal*, as is the case in CSS). By default, HTML uses Roman style, as does CSS, if you don't specify a particular style. To explicitly set font style to Roman, use a style rule like the following:

```
<span style="font-style: normal;">This text is Roman.</span>
```

Figure 12-10.   *Embedded fonts increase design choices*

The other font style is *italic*, where the letters slant to the right. In print typography, each font has its own particular italic style, but on the Web, italic style is generally just a simple slanting. Setting text in italic in HTML is simple using the **<i>** element:

```
<i>This is italic text</i>
```

It is also possible to use the **font-style** rule in CSS to set the style rule, as shown here:

```
<span style="font-style: italic;">This is italic</span>
```

Finally, you can specify to set text in a style called *oblique*. In print typography, oblique text is just a slanted font, while italic is a specially created slanted font. On the Web, oblique text appears identical to italic text, and so far Web browsers do not seem to differentiate between the two forms. Text style can be set to oblique only by using CSS:

```
<span style="font-style: oblique;">This is oblique</span>
```

Note   *Remember, an italicized font isn't necessarily one that is just tilted. If the font family supports an italic or oblique style, the actual characters may be different when the corresponding italic or oblique CSS rule is present. So far this is not commonplace, but it can happen.*

Setting Font Weight

The weight of a font refers to the thickness of its stroke. Changing the weight brings emphasis to text. Many designers prefer to bring emphasis to text using italics rather than bold, but the choice is up to you. However, note that text set bold tends to be less readable the smaller the text is.

Setting text bold in HTML is easy using the **<b>** tag. Given the trend towards logical markup and style sheets, developers are encouraged to use the **<strong>** tag instead.

```
<b>This is bold text</b>
<strong>This is logically bold text</strong>
```

HTML does not afford any great control over the weight of text. Under CSS, you can specify the weight using the **font-weight** property. Values for the property range from 100 to 900, in increments of 100, with 100 being very light and 900 being very bold. Normal text is set at 400 weight, and 700 corresponds to the use of the **<b>** tag. Keywords are also supported, including **bold**, **bolder**, and **lighter**, which are used to set relative weights. Some browsers may also provide keywords such as **extra-light**, **light**, **demi-light**, **medium**, **demi-bold**, **bold**, and **extra-bold**, which correspond to the 100 to 900 values.

Because font families also include bold values and the meaning within them varies, the numeric scheme is preferred. A few examples are shown here:

```
strong              {font-weight:    bolder;}
.special-emphasis   {font-weight:    900;}
h2                  {font-weight:    demi-bold;}
```

Unfortunately, many supposed CSS-compliant browsers do not support the various weights well and default to just bold or not bold text.

Specifying Font Variants

Yet another way that a font can add emphasis to text is the use of small capitals (or "small caps"). This style is often used in legal documents. In HTML, you will have to manually size text down and type in all-capital letters:

```
<small>THIS IS MANUAL SMALL CAPS</small>
```

CSS provides the **font-variant** property, which can be set to **small-caps** to display the current font as small uppercase letters:

```
em    {font-variant: small-caps;}
```

Reversing Text

Using white letters on a black or another color background can create a striking effect, but it may also be much harder to read. Reverse type appears smaller, and the color may overpower the text. On the Web, we don't have to worry about ink bleeding issues with reversed type, but because of readability issues, you will probably still have to up your font size 1 or 2 points when using reversed text. You should also avoid using very thin typefaces in a reversed fashion. Setting text in reversed style is fairly easy by creating a style sheet rule,

```
.reverse   {background-color: black;   color: white;}
```

and then accessing it whenever you want to reverse text—like so:

```
<span class="reverse">Reverse It!</span>
```

Using only HTML, it is much harder to reverse text. You will have to rely on tables and background colors to achieve the effect unless you want to resort to making an image. The markup below achieves the same effect as the style rule:

```
<table cellpadding="0" cellspacing="0">
<tr>
<td bgcolor="black">
<font color="white">Reverse It!</font>
</td>
</tr>
</table>
```

Not only is the HTML approach messy, it doesn't necessarily work well in all situations. Consider the following markup to reverse a single letter. It works, sort of, but it's awkward.

```
<table cellpadding="1" cellspacing="0" border="0">
<tr>
<td align="center" bgcolor="black"><font color="white">R</font></td>
<td>everse only the R</td>
</tr>
</table>
```

To effectively reverse a single character in a Web page without using style sheets, you will probably have to resort to an image.

Text Casing

One last way to change the general appearance of text is to case it differently. As you already know, text has both uppercase and lowercase. While uppercase letters set emphasis, you should be cautious about using uppercase in Web pages, as TYPING IN ALL UPPERCASE IS CONSIDERED THE EQUIVALENT OF SHOUTING ONLINE. Also consider that when you TYPE IN ALL UPPERCASE IT IS MUCH MORE DIFFICULT TO READ than when you type in mixed case because the letter forms are much less distinct.

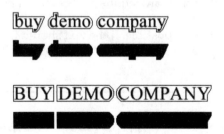

Last but not least, when type is set in all caps, it can be much longer than the same type set in lower or mixed case. This can be very important if you are making buttons or have a fixed region like a table or column to put text into. You may have to make the size of the text smaller to fit into the defined area. This could make the text illegible.

Setting the case of text is generally a manual process, though CSS does define the **text-transform** property that can be used to uppercase text automatically. The example here shows how a class called "upper" is changed to uppercase automatically:

```
.upper   {text-transform: uppercase;}
```

It is also possible to specify values of **lowercase**, **capitalize**, or **none** for the **text-transform** property. Uppercase text should be used sparingly, but it may be useful within navigation or within section labels or headings.

Sizing Font

Print text measurement tends to specify font size in points. A point is 1/72 of an inch. The point size of text is measured from the top of the ascender to the bottom of a descender. Even though text is set to a particular point size, two different fonts in the same point size may not look the same size on screen or paper. The size of the characters optically is determined greatly by their x-height measurement (see earlier in the chapter, "Typography Terminology 101"). Since most text will be composed of lowercase letters, a font with a small x-height will look smaller than one with a larger x-height, even though both may be set to the same point size. Figure 12-11 illustrates the point measurement system and shows the size variation between fonts.

Font Sizes in HTML

HTML does not provide a fine-grain measurement system for fonts. The **<font>** tag does provide a **size** attribute that sets the size of type. In a Web page, there are seven sizes for text, numbered from 1 to 7, where 1 is the smallest text in a document and 7 is the largest. To set some text into the largest size, use **<font size="7">This is big</font>**. By default, the typical size of text is 3; this can be overridden with the **<basefont>** tag. While sizing is not exact in HTML, if a user has not modified the browser settings, the size corresponds to the point sizes in Table 12-2. Designers are warned that these are only guidelines. If more exact sizes are required, CSS should be used or the text made into an image.

Relative sizing with HTML is possible. If the text should just be made one size bigger, use a relative sizing value such as **<font size="+1">** instead of specifying the

Figure 12-11.   *Font measurement in points and x-height*

<font size="*n*">	Typical Point Size
1	8
2	10
3	12
4	14
5	18
6	24
7	36

Table 12-2. Typical **<font>** size Attribute Values and Point Equivalents

size directly. Using the plus (+) and minus (–) signs makes it possible to move the font size up or down a specified number of settings. The values for this form of the **size** attribute should range from +1 to +6 and –1 to –6. It is not possible to specify **<font size="+10">** because there are only seven sizes. If the increase or decrease goes beyond acceptable sizes, the font generally defaults to the largest or smallest size, respectively. Finally, because under strict HTML and XHTML the **<font>** tag is deprecated, it is more appropriate to use the **<big>** and **<small>** tags, which correspond to **<font size="+1">** and **<font size="–1">**, respectively, or to focus only on CSS-based sizing.

Font Sizing Under CSS

CSS provides more control over font sizes than HTML. The **font-size** property sets the relative or physical size of the font. Values may be mapped to a physical point size or to a "relative" word describing the size. Physical point-size can be set in points (**pt**), picas (**pc**), centimeters (**cm**), millimeters (**mm**), inches (**in**), pixels (**px**), x-height values (**ex**) and em values (**em**). It is also possible to use keywords like **xx-small**, **x-small**, **small**, **medium**, **large**, **x-large**, and **xx-large** that map to browser defined sizes, which would probably be very similar to the HTML font sizes from 1 to 7. Relative sizing can be accomplished using the keywords **larger** or **smaller**, as well as positive percentage values like **50%** or **200%**. A few example rules are shown here:

```
p        {font-size: 18pt;}
strong   {font-size: larger;}
h1       {font-size: 200%;}
```

This is a clear case where CSS provides more control options than HTML. While point size may appear to provide the most control, unfortunately point size is not perfectly equivalent across PC and Macintosh displays. Without adjustment the PC tends to display text about 33 percent larger for the same point size as a Mac. Fortunately, most modern Macintosh Web browsers have settings to avoid this problem, but it is an issue in older Macintosh browsers.

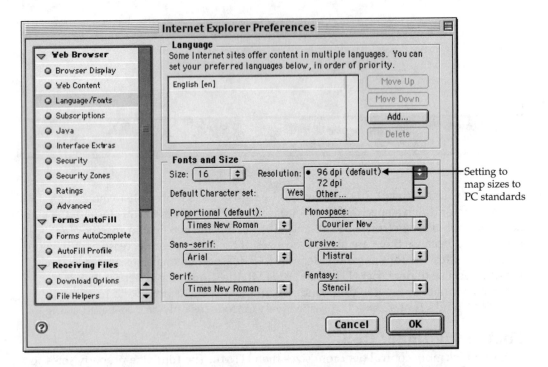

Setting to map sizes to PC standards

Designers looking for extremely precise control may have to resort to units of measure, such as pixels. Unfortunately, precise sizing raises the an issue of whether the user should be allowed to adjust font size upward or downward to improve reliability. Most browsers provide features to override set sizes, but relative sizes in percentages or em values provide more flexibility. We'll revisit the usability-related issues of text again at the conclusion of the chapter.

Text Layout

Once you have selected your font to use and begun to set basic features such as size and style, you may begin to experiment with formatting text in various ways. Traditionally, Web page designers have relied heavily on tables to lay out text on a page. We will provide only basic reminders of how this can be accomplished, as there is no doubt that over time this approach to text layout will be replaced with CSS. HTML tables are far too complex and bind layout very closely to content. Readers looking to find more information about table and CSS layout are encouraged to see the companion book *HTML: The Complete Reference* 3rd edition (Osborne McGraw-Hill, 2001).

Text Alignment

The first question about text layout usually has to do with aligning text. The default on the Web is to leave the text flush left with a ragged right side. In HTML you do not have to do anything to force this alignment, but you can explicitly set it with the **align** attribute on a common block tag like **\<p\>**.

```
<p align="left">This paragraph is aligned to the left</p>
```

This can also be done in CSS using the **text-align** property.

```
p   {text-align: left;}
```

Setting the alignment in the opposite style, flush right with a ragged left side, is possible simply by changing the value to **right** in the two examples. Making the text flush both left and right, or justified, is possible by setting the value to **justify**. To center text, you can use the **\<center\>** element, **\<div align="center"\>**, or an **align** attribute on some block elements like paragraph. This may not produce the desired effect unless you manually add line breaks at the appropriate points, because the text won't really seemed centered except as a block relative to the whole page. CSS also supports a center value for the **text-align** property. Finally, it is possible to format text in more of a random or asymmetrical style. The easiest way to accomplish this is using the **\<pre\>** element in HTML. Unfortunately, the **\<pre\>** element will also convert the text to a monospace font like Courier. The following example illustrates the use of all the formatting in both HTML and CSS. Notice that the CSS overrides the various **align** attributes and forces the **\<pre\>** tag to render in the default style. This example would work equally well in a CSS and a non-CSS supporting browser.

```
<!DOCTYPE html PUBLIC "-//W3C//DTD XHTML 1.0 Transitional//EN"
"http://www.w3.org/TR/xhtml1/DTD/xhtml1-transitional.dtd">
<html xmlns="http://www.w3.org/1999/xhtml">
<head>
<title>Text Alignment in HTML and CSS</title>
<style type="text/css" media="all">
<!--
.flushleft    {text-align: left;}
  .flushright  {text-align: right;}
```

```
  .centered    {text-align: center;}
  .justified   {text-align: justify;}
  .random      {font-family: Serif;
                font-size: 1em;}
-->
</style>
</head>
<body>
<p align="left" class="flushleft">
On the Web text is normally aligned to the left with a
ragged right side. This is the most common layout of
text and while it is highly readable with good variation
between lines, it can get somewhat boring.
Consider spicing up your layouts with other text layout
styles.</p>
<br /><br />
<p align="right" class="flushright">
Aligning your text to the right is not always considered
the best thing to do because it may make it difficult to
read.<br />
Readers may not be able to easily track the text because
of the uncommon layout style.<br />
However, for effect you may find that flush right text
can be bring attention to the content.</p>
<br /><br />
<p align="center" class="centered">
Centered text can be a real problem for large amounts of
copy. <br />
The reader's eye will bounce back and forth across lines
of varying length. <br />
In reality you are going to have to set all the lines of
centered text <br />one <br />by <br />one.<br />
If you just center whole paragraphs at a time you aren't
going to get the effect you are looking for.</p>
<br /><br />
<p align="justify" class="justified">
While justification seems like a good idea it really isn't.
Depending on how it is implemented in the browser and what
the text says, justification may result in rivers of
white space within your text. These rivers may break up
the layout of your text drawing undue attention to the
whitespace. Depending on your screen size the rivers may
```

```
grow or shrink. If you really want to justify your
text on the Web you are going to have to put up with
them.</p>
<br /><br />
<pre class="random">
  Asymmetrical or
    random
formatting
      seems like a lot of fun.
    It can be.
        However,
      this style of formatting
 isn't appropriate for everything and should be
      used sparingly for things like poetry.
Remember, it will be very
    difficult for a browser to reflow
 such random text and generally this
    will force
            RIGHT SCROLLING
for users
with smaller screens.
</pre>
</body>
</html>
```

The rendering for this example is shown in Figure 12-12. Notice that the flush right and centered text is difficult to read. The asymmetrical text is also very difficult to follow, but when used properly it can bring emphasis to text.

While justified text seems a good approach over the tried-and-true flush left, ragged right style, "rivers" of white space can be created in the document. Depending on the content and how the user resizes their browser, this may ruin the document's readability. Remember, justification works by inserting spaces between words to even the lines up. The more words in the line, the less noticeable will be the inserted spaces. If the text is in a small column or the browser window is resized dramatically, the gaps between words will become more noticeable, as shown in Figure 12-13.

Suggestion: Avoid using justified text in Web pages.

Line Length

When laying out our text, we should strive to make the length of a line of text somewhere between 50 and 70 characters, or roughly anywhere from 7 to 15 words.

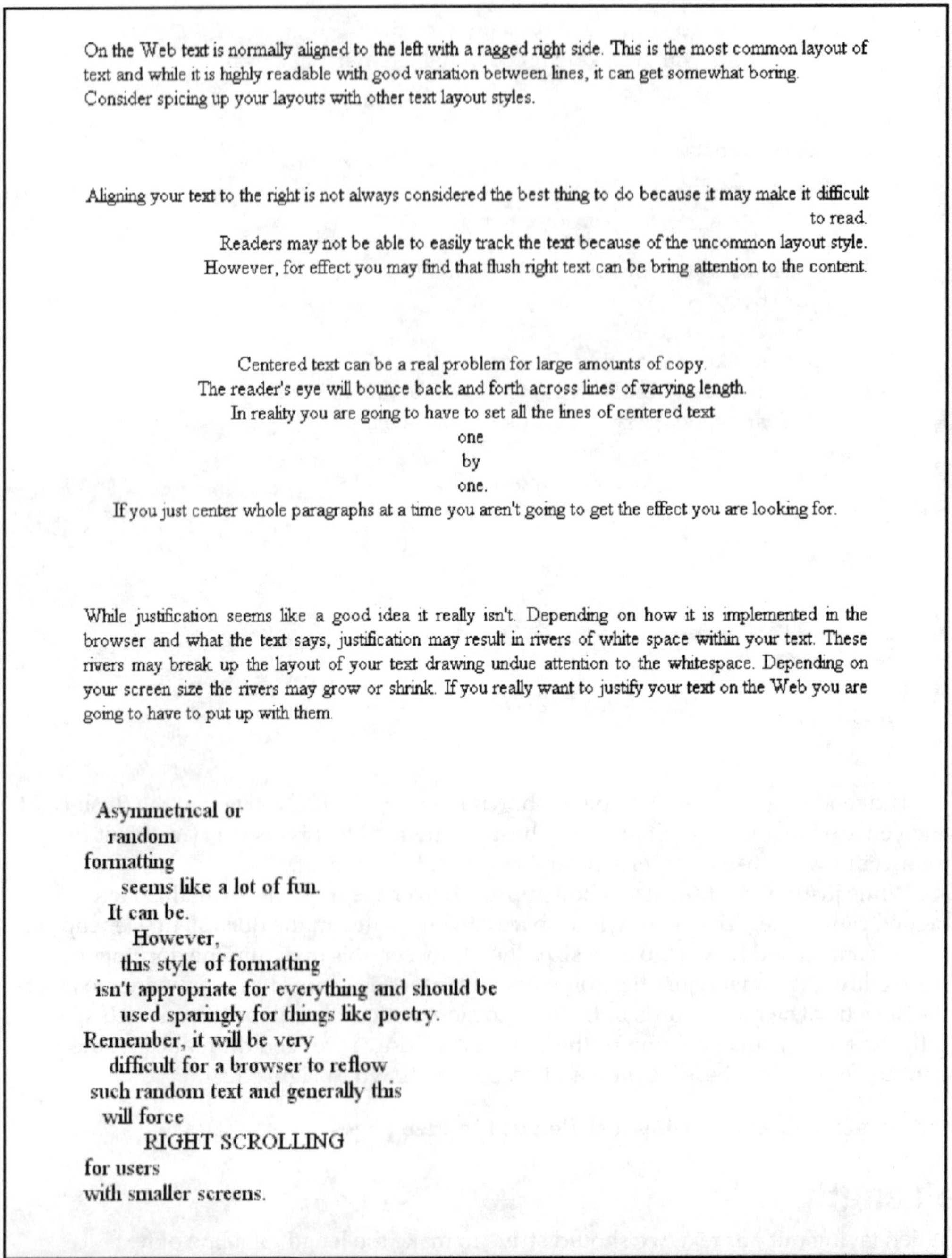

On the Web text is normally aligned to the left with a ragged right side. This is the most common layout of text and while it is highly readable with good variation between lines, it can get somewhat boring. Consider spicing up your layouts with other text layout styles.

Aligning your text to the right is not always considered the best thing to do because it may make it difficult
to read.
Readers may not be able to easily track the text because of the uncommon layout style.
However, for effect you may find that flush right text can be bring attention to the content.

Centered text can be a real problem for large amounts of copy.
The reader's eye will bounce back and forth across lines of varying length.
In reality you are going to have to set all the lines of centered text
one
by
one.
If you just center whole paragraphs at a time you aren't going to get the effect you are looking for.

While justification seems like a good idea it really isn't. Depending on how it is implemented in the browser and what the text says, justification may result in rivers of white space within your text. These rivers may break up the layout of your text drawing undue attention to the whitespace. Depending on your screen size the rivers may grow or shrink. If you really want to justify your text on the Web you are going to have to put up with them.

Asymmetrical or
random
formatting
seems like a lot of fun.
It can be.
However,
this style of formatting
isn't appropriate for everything and should be
used sparingly for things like poetry.
Remember, it will be very
difficult for a browser to reflow
such random text and generally this
will force
RIGHT SCROLLING
for users
with smaller screens.

Figure 12-12.   *Rendering of text formatting example*

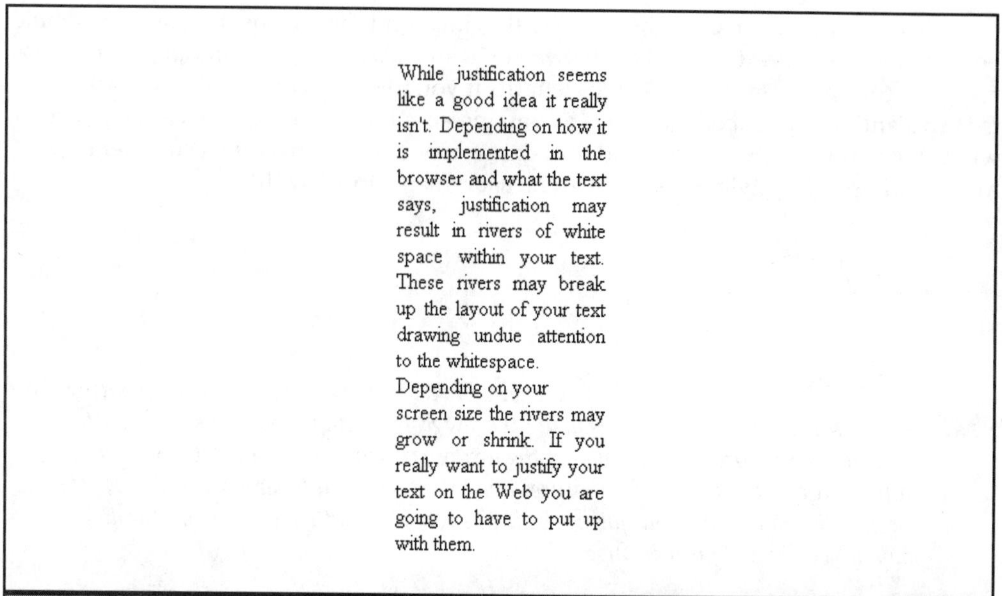

> While justification seems like a good idea it really isn't. Depending on how it is implemented in the browser and what the text says, justification may result in rivers of white space within your text. These rivers may break up the layout of your text drawing undue attention to the whitespace. Depending on your screen size the rivers may grow or shrink. If you really want to justify your text on the Web you are going to have to put up with them.

Figure 12-13. *Narrow columns of justified text can cause rivers*

While the common print rule of thumb is to aim for a line length of 66 characters, you usually don't want to break words, thus the size variation. When setting the length of lines in print, we often measure in picas. A pica is equal to 12 points and thus, given that a point is 1/72 of an inch, there are 6 picas per inch. Optimal line length is calculated by doubling the font's point size and taking the result as the number of picas per line. Thus, when using a 24pt font, we want to use line lengths of 48pc. If we set line lengths too short, the reader may have trouble reading the text, as phrases are often broken across lines. Lines that are very long will cause problems for the reader because it will be difficult for them to track text. You have probably experienced such problems.

The length-of-line suggestions are related to the cognitive science and usability concepts discussed in Chapter 2. Studies suggest that that the human eye can focus on an area about 4 inches wide without the observer having to turn his or her head. This space corresponds to around 24 picas for standard 12pt Times; thus we see the "double the point size in picas" rule of thumb in action.

To set line length, we may consider setting regions off by using **<div>** tags to create various line lengths, as shown here:

```
<div style="font-size: 12pt; width: 24pc;">
Insert your text here
</div>
```

However, if we are using tables in HTML with a 12pt Times font standard, we should be using columns of text somewhere between 350 and 400 pixels wide for optimum online reading. You can certainly use longer lengths if you like, but you should increase your font size and the space between lines as you increase line length. Otherwise, the text will become unreadable. Given that text sizing may not be in fixed measurements, you might end up using style rules with em measurements to set width.

```
p {width: 33em;
   text-align: left;
   font-family: Verdana, Arial, Helvetica, sans-serif;}
```

Note *The line length rules of thumb suggested will result in wasted paper when printing. To combat this problem, many sites using the suggested sizing provide a special button to get a "printer friendly" version of the text or even to link to an Adobe Acrobat equivalent of the text. As CSS matures and browsers begin to support media-based style sheets, this may change, but for now, always consider that sizing for monitor display may not be optimal for printing.*

Line Spacing

Line spacing or *leading* is the term for the space between lines of text. The purpose of line spacing is generally to provide space between the lines of type so that it is easy for a reader to track which line they are on. Normal HTML text will render generally in whatever style the browser decides, typically close to single spacing. If you want to increase line spacing, you will have to manually insert **
** tags at the end of every line. Not only is this approach tedious, but text will reflow when a user sizes the screen smaller than the longest line; this will ruin the layout unless the text is constrained by a fixed-width table cell. Even then, if the user overrides the default font size, all the spacing will be ruined.

CSS provides support for setting line spacing using the **line-height** property. The value of the line height can be specified in a variety of forms, but it would most often be written in points (**pt**), pixels (**px**), or relative values like percentage (**%**). We can set **line-height** for the entire body of a document or for selected areas of text, as shown here:

```
body      {line-height: 1.5em;}
p.double  {line-height: 200%;}
```

The print rule of thumb is to set line spacing to around one-third to one-half above the type size. So if you are using 12pt font, set **line-height** to 18pt or greater. If we don't know the current font size, it is easy to specify this as 2.5ex (1 ex corresponding to the x-height of the current font). Some typefaces, particularly sans-serif fonts like Arial or Helvetica, have very large x-heights, so they will need to have more line spacing to make it easier to read. Given how hard it is to read online text, you might consider using a **line-height** of 2em or 200%. If you plan on making very long lines, you should increase the **line-height** accordingly to improve readability.

Rule: Increase line height to improve online text readability.

Figure 12-14 shows the effect of **line-height** on various forms of text.

 The origin of the word "leading" has to do with the fact that in the days of mechanical type setting the operator would actually place small strips of lead between the lines to give them space.

Letter Spacing and Word Spacing

In addition to opening up the space between lines, we can modify the space between words or even characters. The technique of adjusting spacing between characters to improve readability is called *kerning*. Adjusting of letter spacing in HTML cannot be done accurately. While it is possible to insert a single full space between letters just by pressing the SPACEBAR between characters, HTML collapses multiple spaces, so any real formatting of this kind has to be done with the non-breaking space entity (** **).

No Spacing Set

Just because the Web may not afford as many facilities for type control as print does not mean that we should abandon all hope of control over our text. The reality is that type control is improving and with some effort we can improve the presentation of our text dramatically. Choosing the appropriate typeface, size, style, spacing, and line weight can go a long way to improving the readability of a Web page.

Just because the Web may not afford as many facilities for type control as print does not mean that we should abandon all hope of control over our text. The reality is that type control is improving and with some effort we can improve the presentation of our text dramatically. Choosing the appropriate typeface, size, style, spacing, and line weight can go a long way to improving the readability of a Web page.

1.5 em Spacing

Just because the Web may not afford as many facilities for type control as print does not mean that we should abandon all hope of control over our text. The reality is that type control is improving and with some effort we can improve the presentation of our text dramatically. Choosing the appropriate typeface, size, style, spacing, and line weight can go a long way to improving the readability of a Web page.

Just because the Web may not afford as many facilities for type control as print does not mean that we should abandon all hope of control over our text. The reality is that type control is improving and with some effort we can improve the presentation of our text dramatically. Choosing the appropriate typeface, size, style, spacing, and line weight can go a long way to improving the readability of a Web page.

Figure 12-14. *Line spacing should be adjusted to improve readability*

While formatting with spacing is not terribly accurate, this entity is littered throughout many Web pages.

CSS provides letter spacing control using the **letter-spacing** property. You can set the value of this property to a positive value like 3pt or a negative value like –4pt to enlarge or tighten up spacing between letters, respectively. Normally, we aren't terribly concerned with kerning HTML text unless the text is very large, such as in a headline. In fact, you should avoid adjusting letter spacing in lowercase body text. It is considered bad practice. However, in headlines we may notice large gaps between certain letter combinations like Yo, Ya, Wa, We, Te, To, and numerous others. Reducing the space between the characters is possible, but it can be tedious. However, in headlines, reducing the spacing between lines, words, and letters can make the text more pleasing to look at and easier to read.

CSS also provides control over intraword spacing using the **word-spacing** property. You can set this to a positive value like 2em to open spaces between words or a negative value like –5pt. In general, you should try to keep word spacing in your headlines and body text fairly close. The general rule of thumb from the print world for word spacing is to set the width of a lowercase *l* between words. Note that because the *l* character changes size with font choice and size, the word spacing would also change according to this rule. The following code illustrates adjusting a headline in various ways. The colored text is used solely to show which characters are being kerned.

```
<!DOCTYPE HTML PUBLIC "-//W3C//DTD XHTML 1.0 Transitional//EN"
         "http://www.w3.org/TR/xhtml1/DTD/xhtml1-transitional.dtd">
<html xmlns="http://www.w3.org/1999/xhtml">
<head>
<title>Kerning Is Here?</title>
<style type="text/css" media="all">
<!--

   .style1     {font-size: 36pt;
                color: red;
                line-height: .9em;
                letter-spacing: -2pt;
                word-spacing: .5em;}

   .style2     {font-size: 36pt;
                color: green;
                line-height: .9em;
                letter-spacing: -1pt;}

   .style3     {font-size: 36pt; color: green;}

   /* kerning classes */
```

```
     .tight      {letter-spacing: -5pt; color: yellow;}
     .tighter    {letter-spacing: -6pt; color: purple;}
     .tightest   {letter-spacing: -8pt; color: orange;}
-->
</style>

</head>
<body>
Full Kerning

<h1 class="style1">Demo Company Incorporated
<span class="tight">Wa</span>rmly
<span class="tight">We</span>lcomes
<span class="tightest">Yo</span><span class="tighter">u</span>
To Our Homepage</h1>

Simple Letter Spacing and Line-height Reduction

<h1 class="style2">Demo Company Incorporated Warmly
Welcomes You To Our Homepage</h1>

Regular Style

<h1 class="style3">Demo Company Incorporated
Warmly Welcomes You To Our Homepage</h1>
</body>
</html>
```

The improvement when adjusting spacing in a headline can be dramatic. You often find that you can fit much more type in the same area as well as create a more pleasing looking headline if you take the time to adjust the layout, as shown by the rendering in Figure 12-15. However, you will notice that certain characters, such as the lowercase *p* and the uppercase *Y* on the line below it tend to run a bit too close to each other for comfort.

While the support for character and word spacing is still pretty buggy in browsers, over time it will certainly improve. However, any graphic text that you produce—such as for buttons and labels, particularly if it is in larger text—should be kerned. If you are going to avoid using HTML and CSS text and incur all the downside of graphical text, you might as well enjoy the upside. Be aware that text manipulated in many programs may be autokerned in such a way as to look odd to some designers. If you want to examine your text, you should try to focus on the spaces between letters and look at the actual letters themselves. Techniques that designers often use are to squint while looking at

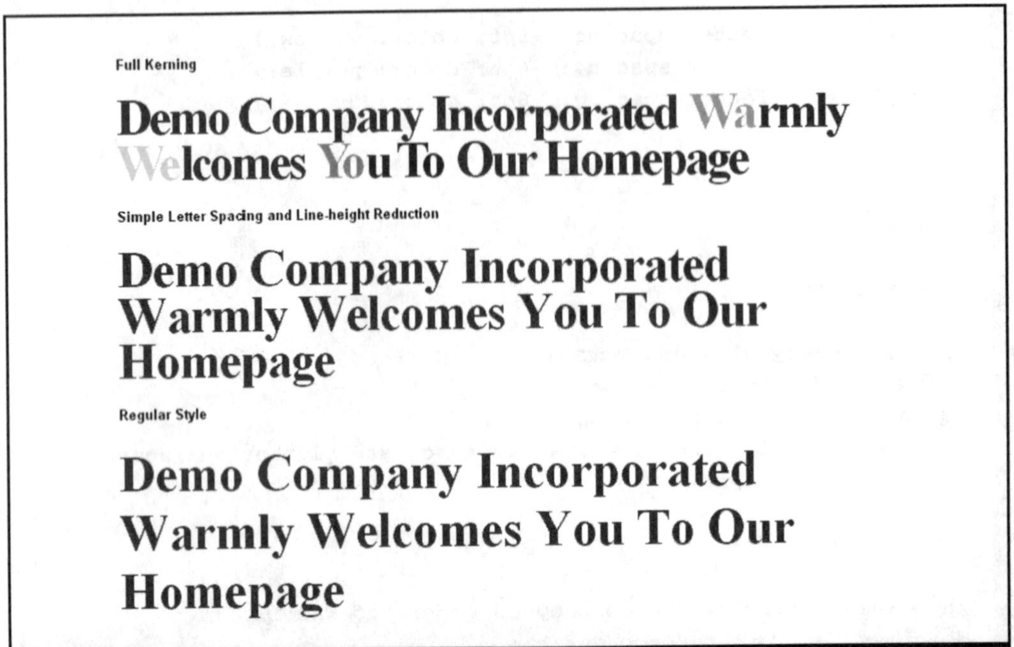

Full Kerning

Demo Company Incorporated Warmly Welcomes You To Our Homepage

Simple Letter Spacing and Line-height Reduction

Demo Company Incorporated Warmly Welcomes You To Our Homepage

Regular Style

Demo Company Incorporated Warmly Welcomes You To Our Homepage

Figure 12-15. *Headline text often needs adjustment*

text; to look at the text upside down, reversed, or backward; or to look at text in any other way that focuses not on the word, but the actual characters and the spaces between them.

Setting Type Hierarchy

Type hierarchy can be used to improve the organization of a page greatly and should be considered when creating Web pages. The concept here is to create a size and level of emphasis of text in a pattern that matches the importance of the page. Imagine setting your headlines in large font and your footer information in small font. This is the crudest type of example, but with simple sizing and style adjustments, we can give importance to the elements on the page that should help back up any page structure we may have come up with.

In order of importance, you should run your text objects from large to small, dark to light, dense to spread out, and so on. Each font and style you use should have a unique "voice," so your hierarchy is obvious. The concept of *type voice* is simple if you imagine the page being read aloud by a talking browser. You would probably want the device to read the important things loudly and the less important things softly. You might even consider that some things would be said with a different tone if they were a form of aside. HTML implicitly provides a very simple type hierarchy through headlines, body text, and links, but you could consider improving or extending this hierarchy.

> **Suggestion: Create a type hierarchy by varying text color, size, style, and position to improve page usability.**

Headings and Subheadings

Headings and subheadings can be used to draw a user into a page and also provide a structure for your page. The main heading is often used to indicate what the page is about, while the subheadings are used to indicate various sections of text. You should be careful not to have just a simple heading followed by huge amounts of body text broken into paragraphs and the occasional figure. Such text will look daunting for the reader and provide no easy entry points other than starting at the first line and reading.

In HTML, we generally indicate a heading with a heading tag like **<h1>**, **<h2>**, **<h3>**, **<h4>**, **<h5>**, or **<h6>**. The formatting provided by these tags is relatively simple. The more important the heading, the larger or more distinctively the heading is rendered. Headings in HTML are arranged from most important and largest (**<h1>**) to least important and smallest (**<h6>**). It has been noted that designers rarely use headings beyond **<h3>**. Mostly this has to do with the lack of visual distinction in standard HTML of the smaller headings. However, now that more logical markup is being employed, this should change.

Using style sheets, we can provide a greater distinction between our subheadings. The first thing to do to improve headings in Web pages is to remove the implicit returns from headings by setting their display property to **inline**. This improves headings by more closely relating subheadings to their content. In normal HTML, there is often quite a gap between headings and their related content. Next, we might consider making the headlines much more visually distinctive, using color, size, spacing, or even bars. The following markup illustrates a few possibilities:

```
<h2 style="display: inline; color: green;">Important Headline</h2><br />
<div id="section1" style="width: 24pc;">
Text here for section.</div><br /> <br />

<h2 style="display: inline; color: red;">
Important Headline</h2><br />

<div id="section1" style="margin-left: 1em; width: 24pc;">
Text here for section.</div><br /><br />
```

```
<h2 style="border-bottom-style: double; border-color: black;
color:orange; font-size: 24pt; width: 9em;
display: inline;">Important Headline</h2><br />
<div id="section1" style="width: 24pc;">Text here for section.</div>
```

The rendering of this example is shown in Figure 12-16.

The basic technique of bringing the headings out could also be applied to text such as frequently asked question (FAQ) pages. Consider making the questions visually distinct from the answers. This will improve the user's ability to quickly scan the page for the content being sought.

Formatting Paragraphs and Sections

When presenting large bodies of text, it is useful to break them up into smaller units such as paragraphs and sections (which may include multiple paragraphs). The most basic way to format paragraphs in HTML is with the **<p>** tag.

As a block level element, the **<p>** tag usually receives the equivalent of two line breaks after the element. In print, this style of paragraph is not indented. When paragraphs are indented, they generally do not receive two line breaks; rather, they receive only one. In plain HTML, a simple way to create this form of paragraph layout is to forego using **<p>** tags and to separate the logical paragraphs with the **
** tags and to use multiple non-breaking spaces (** **) or invisible images to indent the first

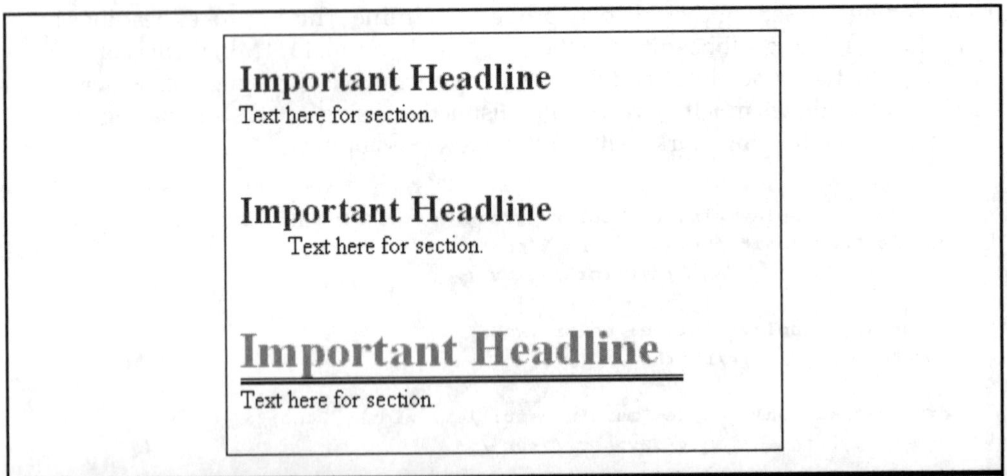

Important Headline
Text here for section.

Important Headline
    Text here for section.

Important Headline
Text here for section.

Figure 12-16.   *Vary headings to improve page hierarchy*

line of each paragraph. In CSS, you might instead set margins, text-indent, and line height properties to set this style, like this:

```
p  {text-align: left;
    width: 33em;
    line-height: 2em;
    margin-top: -1em;
    text-indent: 2em;}
```

While in print you might never want to both double space paragraphs and indent them, because of screen readability some designers seem perfectly happy to set text this way online. Figure 12-17 shows all three forms of paragraph renderings together.

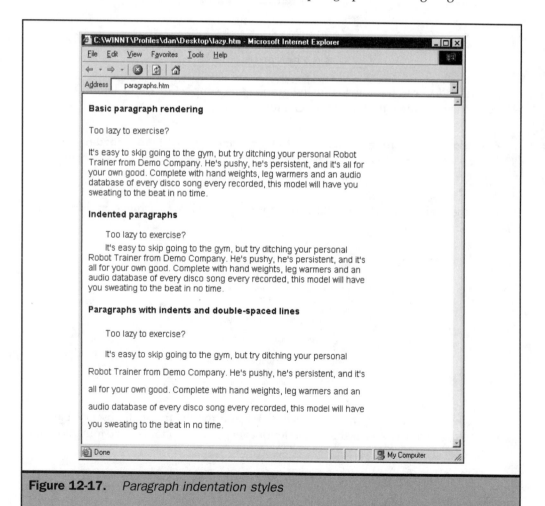

Figure 12-17. *Paragraph indentation styles*

Initial Caps

Another way to mark the beginning of a paragraph or section is to set off the first letter, or "initial cap." This is generally used more for sections than for paragraphs.

Raised Initials   One style of initial cap is the raised initial. In this case, the first letter of the section lies on the same baseline as the rest of the first line, but is much larger than the other text. This effect can be achieved using basic HTML, although, as shown below, it tends to create extra space between the first line and the rest of the text.

```
<font size="+5"><b>D</b></font>emo Company Robots are your best
investment in artificial intelligence...
```

A better effect can be achieved using graphics. A simple GIF of the letter *D* can be added to the first line with the **<img>** element.

```
<p><img src="bigD.gif" width="30" height="37" alt="D" border="0"
align="absbottom" />emo Company Robots are your best investment in
artificial intelligence...</p>
```

By using the non-standard **absbottom** attribute, it is possible to achieve an improved effect in most browsers.

Style sheets offer another means to set initial caps using the **first-letter** pseudo-element. For example, the rule here sets the first letter of every paragraph in a large font and bold.

```
p:first-letter {font-size: 48pt; font-weight: bold;}
```

However, while CSS provides the preferred standards-oriented solution, many browsers still render such rules with gaps in the text.

Drop Initials   Drop initials set the initial cap into the text, usually taking up the first part of several lines of text. Graphics provide the most efficient means to do this in Web pages, as shown here:

```
<p><img src="bigM.gif" width="35" height="35" alt="M" border="0"
align="left" />ixing drinks is just one of the many skills
available with our line of Robot Butlers....</p>
```

In this case, the image is aligned to the left of the text, which flows around it as shown here.

This is all very well and good using a letter like *M* with straight ascenders, but what if the first letter has a different shape like the letter *A*?

The slope of a character like *A* creates a significant gap between the uppercase *A* and other letters, which may make text difficult to read. Using CSS position rules, it is possible though messy to solve such problems, as shown in the following markup fragment:

```
<div id="layer1" style="position:absolute; width:80px;
height:130px; top: 15px; z-index:1; font-family: Arial;
font-size: 100px; font-weight: bold;">A</div><br />

<div id="layer2" style="position:absolute; width:350px;
height:115px; z-index:2; left:12px; top: 32px;
font-family: Arial; font-size: 13px;">
<img src="space.gif" width="50" height="1" border="0" />
```

```
11 Demo Company robots are<br />
<img src="space.gif" width="55" height="1" border="0" />
guaranteed against corrosion,<br />
<img src="space.gif" width="62" height="1" border="0" />
rust, and going berserk and<br />
<img src="space.gif" width="67" height="1" border="0" />
trying to take over the world.<br />
<img src="space.gif" width="72" height="1" border="0" />
Tampering with your robot's<br />
core programming may invalidate warranty.</div>
```

The outcome of the layout is shown here:

In this example, a layer is created for the letter *A*, which is set to a precise size of 100 pixels; using measurements that can vary between browsers and systems would make this a very unstable approach. Another overlapping layer is created for the rest of the text, which is set to a size of 13 pixels. Breaks were entered where needed with the **
** tag, and an invisible pixel was used to adjust the indentation of each line. The actual image is only 1 pixel by 1 pixel; its width is adjusted using the **width** attribute. Non-breaking spaces could be used instead, but this approach offers more control. It is also possible to achieve the effect using a positioned layer for each line of text.

Hung Initials   The third variety of initial cap, the hung initial, places the initial in the margin to the left of the text. In HTML, this can be simply done by using a graphic letter and a table, as shown here:

```
<table width="400" cellspacing="0" cellpadding="0" border="1">
<tr>
<td valign="top" width="39"><img src="bigM.gif" width="35"
height="35" border="0" hspace="2" vspace="2" alt="M" /></td>

<td valign="top" width="361">ixing drinks is just one of the many
skills available with our line of Robot Butlers...</td>
</tr>
</table>
```

The graphic letter goes into one table cell, while the text goes into another; Figure 12-18 shows a rendering of this with the table border turned on. This effect could also be achieved using style sheets, but for now many designers are sticking with tables when creating grids.

Pull Quotes

In print, it is sometimes useful to enhance a page of text with one or two pull quotes. In addition to varying the text flow, pull quotes are used to draw the reader's attention by highlighting a statement from the text. In Figure 12-19, most of the paragraphs are set to a default font size and face with no further embellishment beyond a left margin of 10 pixels. The pull quote, which is drawn from later in the text, is distinguished from the rest of the text by CSS rules:

```
<p style="background: #99ffff; width: 22pc; margin-left: 0;
padding: 12px; font-family: Arial; font-size: 12pt;
font-weight: bold; border-style: solid; border-width: thin;
border-color: #000000;">"I came up with the Robot Butler while
watching <i>Arthur</i> for the ninety-seventh time. That's when
it hit me: everyone wants a servant! Why not a robot?"...</p>
```

A similar effect achieved with HTML tables would work in many older browsers, but otherwise CSS is always preferred.

```
<table width="400" border="0" cellspacing="0" cellpadding="15">
<tr>
<td><font face="Times New Roman" size="-1">
<b>HOME &amp; ROBOT MONTHLY - January 2000</b><br /><br />

Insiders report that the latest models...</font></td>
</tr>

<tr>
<td bgcolor="#99ffff">
<font face="Arial, Helvetica, Sans-serif" size="+1"><b>"I came up
with the Robot Butler...</b></font></td>
</tr>

<tr>
<td><font face="Times New Roman" size="-1">Demo Company has done
well... </font></td>
</tr>
</table>
```

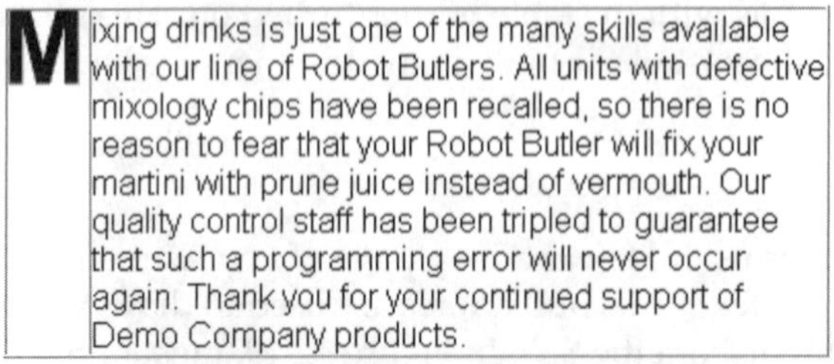

Figure 12-18. Hung initial created with graphic and table

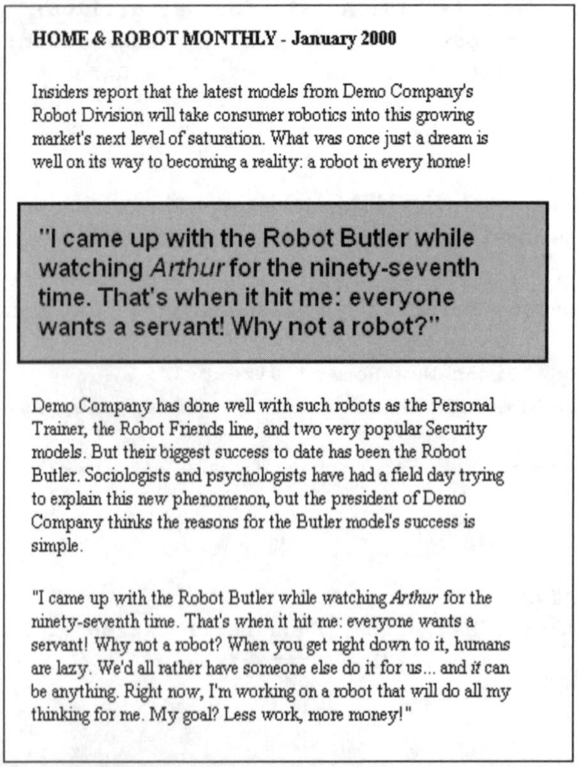

Figure 12-19. Pull quote created with CSS

Sidebars

Like pull quotes, sidebars stand apart from the rest of the text on a page. Instead of drawing attention to the main text, however, they serve to provide additional information related to the subject at hand. Tables are commonly used to create sidebars, as demonstrated here:

```
<table width="400" cellspacing="0" cellpadding="12" border="0">

<tr><td align="center" colspan="3"><b>HOME &amp; ROBOT MONTHLY -
January 2000</b></td></tr>

<tr>
<td width="200" valign="top">Insiders report...</td>

<td width="200" valign="top" bgcolor="#ccffff">
<font face="Arial, Helvetica, Sans-serif" SIZE="-1">
The history of Demo Company began in 1998...
</font></td>
</tr>
</table>
```

The result, shown in Figure 12-20, uses two side-by-side table cells, two different fonts, and a background color in the right cell to create two columns. The **cellpadding** attribute of the **<table>** element is used to create padding and prevent the two text areas from butting up against each other.

Formatting Tables

As demonstrated throughout this chapter, **<table>** and its associated tags can be used as a means to lay out text and graphics in a Web page. Tables were actually meant to be used as *tables*—as a means of presenting information in an organized fashion. Financial data, statistics, and concise summaries of information already covered in detail somewhere else are all prime candidates for this sort of presentation. Consider this simple table summarizing the selling points of a line of robots:

```
<table width="500" cellspacing="0" cellpadding="3" border="1">
<thead>
<tr>
<th width="170">Robot Model</th>
<th width="180">Standard Features</th>
<th width="150">Price</th>
</tr>
```

```
</thead>
<tbody>
<tr>
<td>Butler</td>
<td>Sarcasm, Drink Mixing</td>
<td>30,000 credits</td>
</tr>
<tr>
<td>Trainer</td>
<td>Enthusiasm, Gym Shorts</td>
<td>32,000 credits</td>
</tr>
<tr>
<td>Security (ToughGuy)</td>
<td>Limited vocabulary</td>
<td>40,000 credits</td>
</tr>
</tbody>
<tfoot></tfoot>
</table>
```

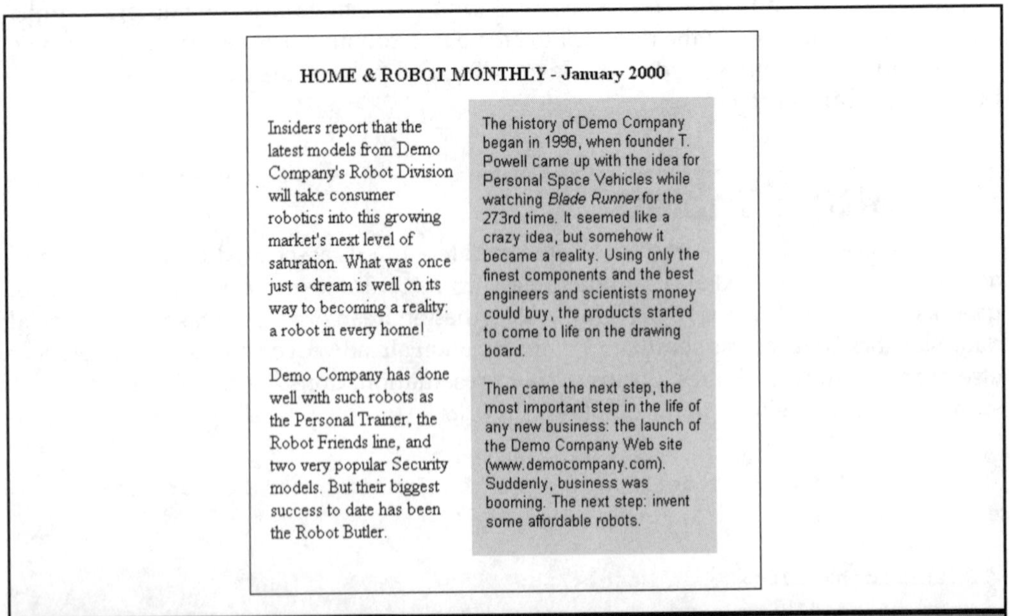
HOME & ROBOT MONTHLY - January 2000

Insiders report that the latest models from Demo Company's Robot Division will take consumer robotics into this growing market's next level of saturation. What was once just a dream is well on its way to becoming a reality: a robot in every home!

Demo Company has done well with such robots as the Personal Trainer, the Robot Friends line, and two very popular Security models. But their biggest success to date has been the Robot Butler.

The history of Demo Company began in 1998, when founder T. Powell came up with the idea for Personal Space Vehicles while watching *Blade Runner* for the 273rd time. It seemed like a crazy idea, but somehow it became a reality. Using only the finest components and the best engineers and scientists money could buy, the products started to come to life on the drawing board.

Then came the next step, the most important step in the life of any new business: the launch of the Demo Company Web site (www.democompany.com). Suddenly, business was booming. The next step: invent some affordable robots.

Figure 12-20. *Sidebar created with HTML table*

As shown in Figure 12-21, this isn't formatted very well. The table header element **<th>** has a default alignment of **center**, while the table data element **<td>** has a default alignment of **left**. (Note that the content of **<th>** is automatically rendered as bold text.)

It is possible to use style sheet rules to control layout of table constructs:

```
th   {font-family: Arial; font-size: 11pt; text-align: left;}
td   {font-family: Arial; font-size: 9pt;}
```

As Figure 12-22 shows, even with the border set to zero in the HTML, this stylized table is easier to follow. The larger text in the **<th>** cells clearly establishes the relationship of the columns, which is further enhanced by consistent alignment of the text in each column.

This table is clearly oriented along the horizontal axis; while a more vertical organization is possible, horizontal orientation is more suitable for Web pages. Even so, a larger table with more rows may tend to be harder to read. Figure 12-23 applies a background color to every other table row in order to improve readability and maintain the proper relationship between information.

In the code used to create Figure 12-23, the CSS information in the document head includes a class rule:

```
.shaded {background: #ccffff;}
```

In this case, the rule is applied to alternating table rows.

```
<tr class="shaded">
```

Robot Model	Standard Features	Price
Butler	Sarcasm, Drink Mixing	30,000 credits
Trainer	Enthusiasm, Gym Shorts	32,000 credits
Security (ToughGuy)	Limited vocabulary	40,000 credits

Figure 12-21.   *Table with no text formatting*

Figure 12-22. *Basic text formatting enhances tables*

This will work in CSS-compliant browsers. For backward compatibility, background color could be added to the table cells in alternating rows using the **bgcolor** attribute:

```
<tr bgcolor="#ccffff">
<td>Butler</td>
<td>Sarcasm, Drink Mixing</td>
<td>30,000 simoleons</td>
</tr>
```

Various design embellishments can also be added. Horizontal lines can be added to separate all the rows or to separate the header row from the other rows as well as to

Figure 12-23. *Alternating colors in table rows*

delineate the end of the table. In a three-column table like this one, the **colspan** attribute can be used to make a cell that spans three columns:

```
<tr>
<td colspan="3"><img src="line.gif" height="3" width="480" /></td>
</tr>
```

As shown in Figure 12-24, graphics lines are used in this example. The same image source was used for all the lines in this table; the thinner lines were created simply by setting the **height** attribute to **"1"** instead of **"3"**. (When working with solid colors, it is feasible to resize images in this fashion, but it is not advisable when working with more complicated images.)

There are many ways to lay out tables. In some cases, it is desirable to have the table borders turned on. The essential thing to remember is that the information in the table is more important than the look and feel of the table itself. Thick borders, excessive and inconsistent coloring of table cells, and extraneous graphics will not enhance a table's usefulness. When presenting information in table form, keeping it simple is your best bet.

Text Details

In Web page design, the devil is truly in the details. Users will often notice a bad copyright symbol or improper use of quotes before they notice that the navigation for the site is illogical. Formatting text is all about the details. Especially careful consideration should be paid to special characters and punctuation layout.

Adding special characters to Web pages is easy if you understand character entities. It is possible to insert special symbols, such as the copyright character, by specifying a character entity, like **©** or **©**. Unfortunately, we may not always be happy with the text layout of these characters because in many fonts they are oversized.

Robot Model	Standard Features	Price
Butler	Sarcasm, Drink Mixing	30,000 credits
Trainer	Enthusiasm, Gym Shorts	32,000 credits
Security (ToughGuy)	Limited vocabulary	40,000 credits

Figure 12-24.   *Table with horizontal lines for organization*

Consider reducing the point size on these characters either using the **<small>** element in HTML or using a style rule like **<span style="font-size: 0.8em;">** around the character entity. You need to be particularly careful to check if the font you are using supports the particular symbol you have selected. If necessary, you might even make your own small GIF images to replace troublesome special characters.

Dashes can be particularly troublesome for layout. First, make sure you are using the correct dash. A short dash (or en dash) is specified in HTML with **–**, while a long dash (or em dash) is specified with **—**. The purpose of the em dash is to shift to a new point in a sentence. A short dash is generally employed when specifying ranges, like 4–7. A particularly troublesome problem with dashes is that, when used with capital letters, they may not appear to line up vertically. The reason for this is that the dash is aligned to the middle of the lowercase *x*. The dash may look low next to some capital characters, particularly those in a font with a small x-height.

> LOOK AT THE DASH—DOES IT SEEM LOW?
> LOOK AT THE DASH NOW—BETTER?

You should shift the text up using the **vertical-align** attribute, as shown here:

```
<span style="font-size: 36pt;">
LOOK AT THE DASH&#151;DOES IT SEEM LOW?</span><br />
<span style="font-size: 36pt;">
LOOK AT THE DASH NOW<span style="vertical-align: 10%;">&#151;
</span>BETTER?</span>
```

As with the problem with dashes, you should consider reducing the size of any bullets that you use, even in lists. You may even consider setting their position relative to text differently.

Quotes can also be troublesome. Be aware of the difference between prime marks (" and ') and so-called smart or curly quotes ("" and "). The prime marks are used for measurements in feet and inches and for basic quotes within code. If we want to use smart quotes, we should resort to the entities **“** and **”** for opening and closing smart quotes. Unfortunately, this isn't always dealt with carefully—particularly when importing text from word processing programs. In this situation, the smart quotes may render on some systems as empty boxes or other strange characters.

It is also important to use an actual ellipsis (…) rather than three periods (. . .). HTML does support a special entity **…** that can be used to insert real ellipses. Some designers may not find this entity adequate, as it often looks as bad as three periods. If you want such fine control, consider adjusting letter spacing between the three periods to create your own style of ellipsis.

Finally, you may consider hanging your punctuation outside the current paragraph, particularly when using headlines or large type that is justified. If you do not, any punctuation characters starting or ending a line will cause small gaps in your nicely laid-out text. An example of hung punctuation is shown in Figure 12-25.

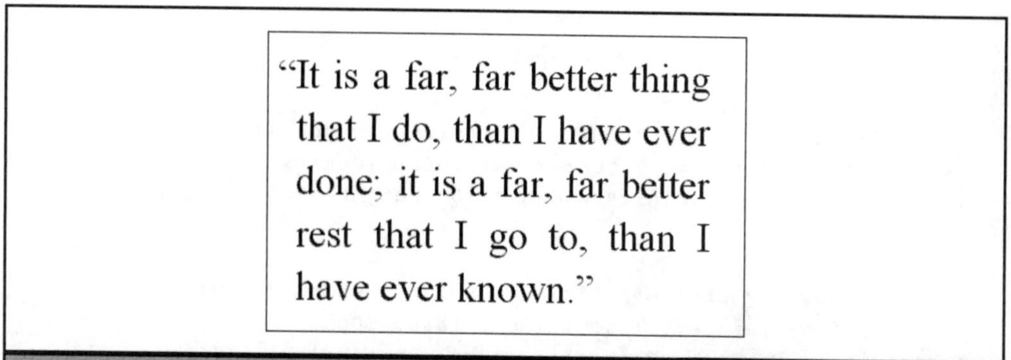

> "It is a far, far better thing that I do, than I have ever done; it is a far, far better rest that I go to, than I have ever known."

Figure 12-25. *Hanging punctuation in large justified text*

Note *Be careful with special characters and entities; if the wrong character set is in play, you will not end up with the result you are looking for and may instead see gibberish or box characters. In most cases, this problem can be avoided with a **<meta>** directive like **<meta http-equiv="Content-Type" content="text/html; charset=iso-8859-1" />** in the head of your document, which specifically defines the character set for the document .*

Fancy Text Layouts

Before finishing up the chapter with a Web text usability discussion, let's experiment a little with the layout power provided with CSS. For example consider the layout in Figure 12-26. This would have been nearly impossible in traditional HTML documents without resorting to graphics or Flash.

Unfortunately, laying a page out with such sophisticated runarounds can be a real chore. This is the code just to create the simple pyramid of text shown in the example:

```
<!DOCTYPE html PUBLIC "-//W3C//DTD XHTML 1.0 Transitional//EN"
"http://www.w3.org/TR/xhtml1/DTD/xhtml1-transitional.dtd">
<html xmlns="http://www.w3.org/1999/xhtml">
<head>
<title>Text Secrets of Ancient Egypt</title>
<style type="text/css" media="all">
<!--
body {background-color: #0035ff;
      margin: 10px;}
-->
</style>
```

```
</head>
<body>

<div id="layer1" style="position:absolute; width:440px;
height:345px; z-index:1; top: 20px; left: 20px;">
<img src="bluepyramid.gif" width="440" height="345" border="0" />
</div>

<div id="layer2" style="position:absolute; width:320px;
height:250px; z-index:2; top: 75px; left: 80px;
font-family: Verdana; font-size: 13px; line-height: 160%;
text-align: center;">

In<br />
ancient<br />
Egypt, all<br />
they wanted<br />
was to live forever.<br />
Their odds of success<br />
were much better than a<br />
Web designer's chances of creating<br />
a truly creative layout guaranteed to<br />
work correctly on all browsers, all the time.</div>
</body>
</html>
```

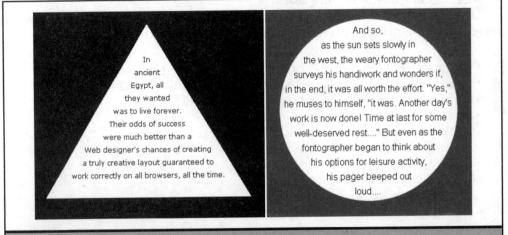

Figure 12-26.   *Sophisticated text layout is possible with CSS*

Given the lack of tools for creating style-sheet-based layouts, it is no wonder that we don't rush quickly back to image-based layouts. Not so fast—the hard work pays off. These designs scale, are searchable and printable, and much faster than image layouts on download.

Special Text Effects

The previous section suggested that it is possible to create sophisticated layouts using style sheets—what about buttons and fancy text effects? Actually, basic 3-D text, drop shadows, raised buttons, and just about anything you can come up with is possible in CSS.

Making drop-shadowed text, particularly if you can download a font, doesn't require you to go to PhotoShop. Making a button is just as easy. The button shown here (as rendered by Internet Explorer),

was produced with the following markup:

```
<div name="Layer1" style="position: absolute; z-index: 1; width: 125px;
height: 50px; top: 52px; left: 52px; background: #0000cc;"> </div>

<div name="Layer2" style="position: absolute; z-index: 2; width: 125px;
height: 50px; top: 50px; left: 50px; background: #99ffff;"> </div>

<div name="Layer3" style="position: absolute; z-index: 3; top: 66px; left:
57px; font-family: Arial; font-size: 18px; font-weight: bold; color:
#ffffff;">HOME PAGE</div>

<div name="Layer4" style="position: absolute; z-index: 4; top: 65px; left:
56px; font-family: Arial; font-size: 18px; font-weight: bold; color:
#0000cc;">HOME PAGE</div>
```

Note   *Complex CSS rules such as the ones used in these examples are not always consistently supported, even in browsers that claim compliance. This is yet another reason to fully test your Web pages.*

Creating dramatic text effects like this:

no longer requires any fancy filter or illustration work. Of course, you have to know CSS pretty well. The code that produces this effect is shown here, rendered in Internet Explorer 5.0:

```
<div name="Layer1" style="position: absolute; z-index: 1; width: 300px;
height: 215px; top: 10px; left: 10ox; background-color: red;"></div>

<div name="Layer2" style="position: absolute; z-index: 2; width: 295px;
height: 380px; top: 25px; left: 11px; font-family: Arial Black;
font-size: 18pt; text-align: center; line-height: 90%;">

THE TIME HAS COME<br />
FOR ALL BROWSERS<br />
TO GET REAL WITH</div>

<div name="Layer4" style="position: absolute; z-index: 4; top: 80px;
left: 10px; font-family: Arial; font-size: 50pt; color: white;
text-align: center; letter-spacing: -15px;">CSS</div>

<div name="Layer5" style="position: absolute; z-index: 5; top: 80px;
left: 30px; font-family: Verdana; font-size: 70pt; font-style:
italic; text-align: center; letter-spacing: -15px;
color: yellow;">CSS</div>

<div name="Layer6" style="position: absolute; z-index: 6; top: 80px;
left: 70px; font-family: Arial Black; font-size: 90pt;
text-align: center; letter-spacing: -15px;">CSS</div>
```

The code is used positioned layers to overlap text. The next example uses the Wingdings font to create a teardrop shape, then layers more text over it to create an initial cap effect:

```
<div name="Layer1" style="position: absolute; z-index:1;
width: 100; height: 100; left: 10px; top: 0px;
font-family: Wingdings; font-size: 202px;
color: black;">S</div>

<div name="Layer2" style="position: absolute; z-index:2;
width: 60; height: 100; left: 41px; top: 70px;
font-family: Verdana; font-size: 100px;
font-weight: bold; color: white;">S</div>

<div name="Layer3" style="position: absolute; z-index:3;
left: 116px; top: 148px; font-family: Verdana;
font-size: 20px; font-weight: bold; color:
black; letter-spacing: -2px;">omewhere on the Web...</div>
```

This last example uses Microsoft's proprietary filter extensions to CSS to create a glow around a section of text:

```
<html>
<head>
<title>Fuzzy Fonts Attack</title>
<style type="text/css">
<!--
.blur    {height: 10px; width: 400px;
          font-family: Arial Black;
          font-size: 35pt; font-style:
          bold; color: black;
          filter: Glow(Color = lightblue, Strength = 15); }
-->
</style>
</head>
<body bgcolor="#ffffff">

<div name="Layer1" class="blur">GLOW FILTER</div>

</body>
</html>
```

You might wonder why correct XHTML wasn't used in the last example. The reason is that such Microsoft extensions are not standard; when you introduce a **<!DOCTYPE>** statement that indicates Web standards usage, proprietary text filters and other non-standard features will generally not render. We end on this point purposefully as a reminder that fancy text effects often rely on nonstandard technologies that may not be cross-browser safe, so proceed with caution.

Text Design Issues for the Web

As has been continually stressed in this chapter, the Web page simply isn't like paper. The actual resolution of screens is usually very low: around 72 pixels per inch. Compared to even a typical laser printer, this is very low. Further, glare and refresh rate make reading online difficult. Eyestrain is frequent, and many usability experts—such as Jakob Nielsen (http://www.useit.com)—have suggested that people just don't read online, they scan, and when they do read carefully, it is much slower than with print. Designers should always strive to make their Web pages more readable. Standard rules like keeping your line lengths short and increasing your leading apply to the Web, as well as to paper. However, print rules of thumb about font sizing often have to be adjusted upward to deal with the lack of screen resolution. Some print practices don't work as expected, some are open to debate, and some just don't make sense at all. As an example of the latter, the precise text control with measurements in points or pixels that allows control of the space between characters and is not available on the Web.

Font Usage

Some design experts consider serif typefaces more readable than sans-serif typefaces because the serifs help define the characters, making them easier to recognize, and may even lead the eye to easily move from letter to letter. Traditional print design rules suggest that a legible serif font be used for body text, while a contrasting sans-serif font be used for large titles and headings. The Web, not breaking with tradition, generally uses Times as the default body copy for text; however, it does not change heading styles to a sans-serif font.

There is some debate to whether or not serif text should be used onscreen, particularly when small. Many Web designers opt for sans-serif fonts like Arial or Verdana, claiming better screen readability at smaller sizes. The choice can become particularly important if the text is graphic and anti-aliased. Aliased images are those that have jagged edges, while anti-aliased images are those that have their edges smoothed out. The problem with anti-aliased text is that when the text is small it tends to look fuzzy, not smooth—particularly when anti-aliasing is done on crisp sans-serif fonts like Arial.

Suggestion: Avoid anti-aliasing small text.

A demonstration of the readability problem with anti-aliasing is shown in Figure 12-27.

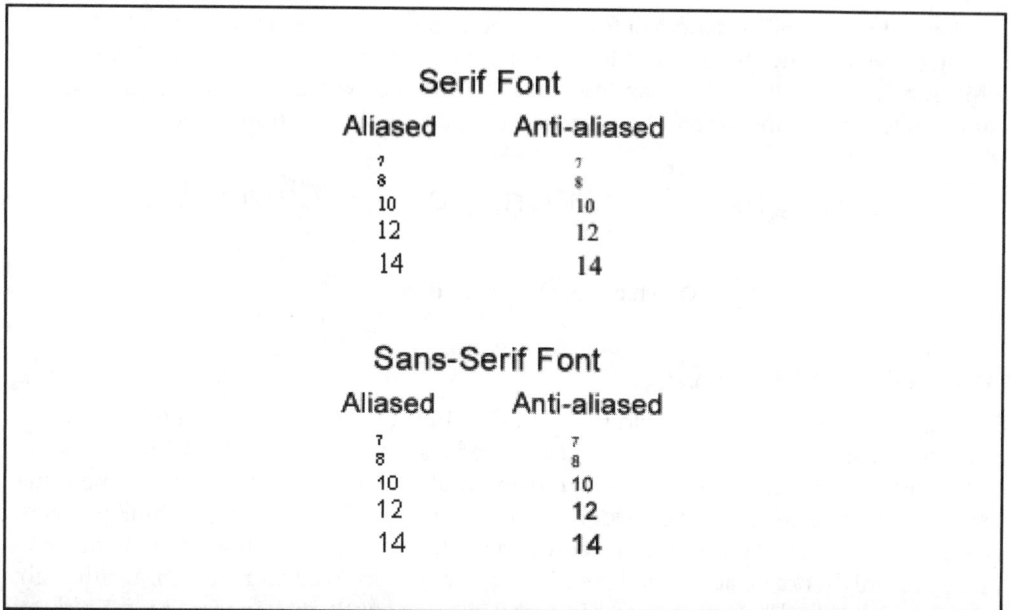

Serif Font

Aliased	Anti-aliased
7	7
8	8
10	10
12	12
14	14

Sans-Serif Font

Aliased	Anti-aliased
7	7
8	8
10	10
12	12
14	14

Figure 12-27.   *Comparison of aliased and anti-aliased text at varying point sizes*

Because of the desire to make extremely small text crisp and easy to read, many designers will employ special pixel fonts, drawn a single pixel at a time, for extreme readability. Many of these fonts can be found at http://www.minifonts.com. An example of a pixel font at 7pt is shown here, compared to common Web fonts at the same size.

Mini-7
ABCDE

Arial
ABCDE

Times New Roman
ABCDE

Be careful, though: pixel-precise fonts will distort when scaled up, so don't jump on the bandwagon too quickly and keep in mind those users who do want to size text upward. While small pixel fonts have some place in design, when sized up they also will distort—so be extremely careful when using them.

Beyond the usability aspect of font choices, you need to consider the implied feeling of the font. In the broadest terms, serif typefaces have a formal appearance, while sans-serif typefaces have an informal appearance. Not just usability, but also content should be considered when choosing a font, as demonstrated here:

Clown, Inc.   Clown, Inc.   Clown, Inc.

Q: Which font is most appropriate?

Number of Fonts to Use

Traditionally, designers have held that you should use only two types of fonts in a document, usually a sans-seriff or headlines and a serif for body text. Of course, the styles and size of these may change, but using multiple fonts—particularly of the same font type like sans serif—was considered to be poor style. Some designers think you can go higher, particularly if the contrast between the fonts is obvious enough. Remember that a user might not be able to tell the difference between Arial and Helvetica, although you can. If you establish your type hierarchy on such subtle differences, it is bound to fail. Worse, even if they do notice, they may consider such variations mistakes rather than intentional. Using radically different fonts next to each other brings attention to content and may aid greatly in setting up a type hierarchy.

However, while the "two fonts per document" rule works well in print, it might need to be modified for the Web. Instead, you may consider three fonts: one for your headlines, one for your body text, and one for your navigation.

> **Suggestion: Consider using three fonts per page: one for page labels and headlines, one for body text, and one for navigation.**

Columns on the Web

Traditional print design has relied extensively on columns when laying out text. Columns on the Web are very different. Unless you have very sophisticated sensing, it is not guaranteed that the user will be able to see your complete page at once. Columns that wrap up and down make little sense on the Web unless fixed page sizes are used. Remember, the text-read direction is not a top-left to bottom-right style, but more of a top-left down the page to its bottom. Imagine having the user scroll up and down the page just to follow text. When using columns, they should continue to run down the page until the content is finished, as shown in Figure 12-28.

> **Rule: Columns of text in Web pages should never wrap up and down unless they are all contained in a single screen.**

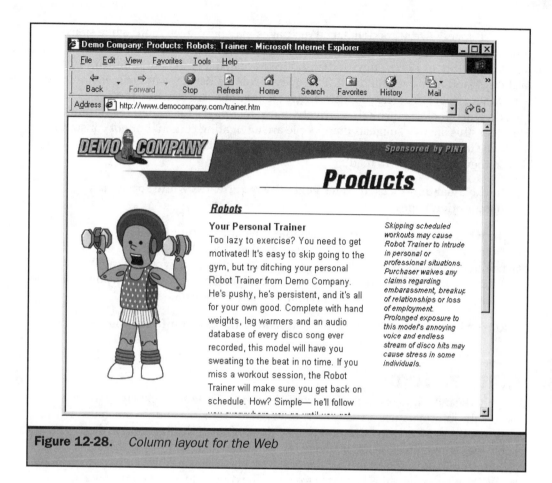

Figure 12-28. *Column layout for the Web*

The size of the columns should not be much more than around 300 pixels or so (around 24pc for 12pt font) if it is heavy on body text. You may find that a design with a main center column of around 300 to 400 pixels with a left navigation column and a right pull quote or supplementary column works well. Many heavily used sites have employed such a design successfully.

Is White Space Good or Bad?

Traditional type design suggests that judicious use of white space makes a page much more readable. The white space can give readers a place to rest their eyes, or it may direct a user's focus, emphasize certain bits of text, and just provide an open airy look to a page. Unfortunately, many Web designers tend to cram as much content into a screen as possible. Some experts suggest that this is very much a bad idea and that online is no different than print in this respect.

White space is very good. In fact, Web pages may need even more white space—as much as 40–60 percent white space on a page. However, some usability experts, notably Jared Spool (Spool 1999), suggest that white space actually may not improve page usability—and may even hinder it. This goes so far against conventional wisdom that it is very hard to believe. The probable answer is that the user can "cover more ground" quickly when looking through relatively dense text pages formatted for skimming. However, this answer suggests that people are navigating content but not consuming it. Maybe they are simply printing the content out for later use. Yet once they do, it is certain they want it easy to read!

Rule: Navigation-focused pages generally require less white space than consumption pages.

The white space issue is certainly troublesome; the concept that it may be bad makes sense if users are skimming. As discussed in navigation chapters, you need to balance clicking and scrolling. If you have a lot of white space, you may not be giving people the amount of content they need at an adequate pace. Always consider what the user is doing with data and where it will ultimately be consumed.

Rule: Always use white space to complement the use of information.

Print vs. Screen

Probably the most important thing to consider when discussing text layout on the Web is where the information is actually consumed. Many designers put so much text within pages that users invariably print the pages. Much of the time, these pages don't print terribly well. Other times, text is intended for online consumption. Often, this means much less text per page with lots of links. If there is some reason the user would want to print the content, it isn't easy with this approach to collect the content together for printing.

When users read online, they generally want less text, large size, narrow columns, and large line height. However, when printing, users may want a lot of content per page, possibly expanding to fit the paper or even using a smaller font size and line height. If printing becomes an issue, you may find it useful to provide a link to an Acrobat version of your content (http://www.adobe.com/acrobat) or provide a link to a page that is formatted for print output. Many sites now provide printable versions of text.

An article at an online magazine may be broken up into several pages for online reading, complete with graphics, advertisements, and site navigation. While these pages may be printable, the resulting printout may be too cluttered to be useful. And if the pages use advanced layouts such as the pyramid text shown earlier in this chapter, it may not be printable at all. This has led to the increased use of the already ubiquitous "Click here for a printer-friendly version" and similar links. However, using special style sheets for printing is a better approach. To define a different look for printing, use a linked style sheet and indicate the media to apply it to, like this:

```
<link rel ="stylesheet" href="styles/printer.css" media="print" />
```

Regardless of the approach, if users are to print, make sure the level of legibility of the print document is as high as that of the screen document.

Writing for the Web

As discussed in previous chapters, user involvement tends to be a mix of navigating content, consuming content, or performing a task such as filling out a form. Up to now we have focused a great deal on users navigating content—but what about when they are ready to actually read a page?

Reading vs. Scanning

If you're coming to the Web with a print-oriented mindset, you're in for a rude shock: studies have shown that reading on the Web generally takes a least 125 percent of the time it takes to read the same text on paper. If that wasn't bad enough, many users won't even read the page online. Web experts such as Jakob Nielsen have determined that users tend to scan quickly over the content of Web pages, looking for something that will catch their attention and lead them to click on a link, or back up and read the page more closely. If something doesn't grab them right away, they are highly likely to move on to another page or site. Page length can be daunting, too; a person skimming over a Web page hoping to be engaged probably won't feel like scrolling down to read more if the text in the initial screen hasn't already done its job. A few key concepts will help counter this trend:

- **Keep your text short and concise**   Experts suggest that you should write only half as much text as you would when writing for print. This makes the online reading process smoother by overcompensating for the slow reading rule mentioned above. Keep paragraphs short as well; nothing scares users away faster than long, unbroken columns of text that extend far below the bottom of their browser window.

- **Get to the point right away**   Don't preface your page with a long, rambling, and circuitous opening. If your English professor taught you to start with the general and work up to the specific, forget it. Cut to the chase and tell users your conclusion in the very first sentence. Use the journalistic technique known as the "inverted pyramid"—tell them what you're going to tell them immediately, *then* fill in the details, followed by whatever background material seems appropriate.

- **Use headings to provide meaning**   Headlines aren't much use if they're clever but don't tell the user what the main content is about. Headers should let users know why they should stop and read a Web page. Meaningful use of subheadings adds structure and additional meaning to a page.

■ **Highlight the ideas expressed in the page**   Pull quotes and highlighted text, if selected well, will emphasize what the page is about and help users decide if the page interests them. It's better to have someone leave a page because the topic leaves them cold than to have them leave simply because they can't figure out what the page is about. Don't emphasize text with underlining, as this may be confused with hyperlinks. If your hyperlinks are chosen well, the clickable text should provide additional hints to your page's meaning.

■ **Use lists to summarize information**   When dealing with important information, don't embed it in a paragraph if it can be broken out into bulleted or numbered lists instead. This places the information out in plain view of the skimming reader, instead of forcing the reader to dig for it in a large block of text.

The inverted pyramid structure is just one of the tools that can make online writing more user friendly. Applied to the Web, it can be used to get a basic point across and motivate users to scroll down to the more detailed information lower in the page. Hypertext adds even more variations to writing on the Web. On the simplest level, it can be used to break a piece of writing up into smaller pages that are connected by linear linking and read in sequence. This can keep page scrolling to a minimum and make page content easier for readers to process quickly. Ending each page in a fashion that will encourage readers to move on, and starting each page with writing that reinforces the reader's desire to continue can work wonders and keep users from defecting to another site.

Nonlinear Writing

Of course, the Web offers more choices than a simple linear progression. The options are many, but it is important not to go overboard. While it is possible to create an incredibly complex hypertext document that branches off in multiple directions, it would be wiser to provide short blocks of information to create a much larger whole. Optimally, the basic information you are trying to convey could be organized in a fairly linear fashion, while more detailed examinations of its implications could branch out in many directions.

If, for instance, you were an expert in canine health concerns, you might be tempted to create a huge Web page that imparts all your years of accumulated knowledge in one huge lump, but dog owners would be more likely to read a simple site about canine health. The main focus could be about nutrition and the basic care of dogs, with additional pages that go into more detail on those topics, with well-placed hyperlinks to pages discussing how to recognize the symptoms of canine diseases, and with even deeper pages that might be of more interest to veterinarians than to laypeople. Such a site could be a great resource for a wide variety of people, as long as it is written and structured to draw them in and guide them to the level of information they require.

Danger Words

It is important to remember that certain ordinary words have taken on extra meaning on the Web. The word "links" could easily refer to sausages or to golf, but on the Web those meanings may be secondary. Choice of vocabulary is an issue.

Suggestion: Be careful of using words that have alternative Web meanings.

For example, at a Web site about golf courses, it might be impossible to avoid using "links" as it relates to the game, so it would be imperative to use the word "hyperlinks" when referring to clickable text in the site in order to reduce any potential confusion. The following table lists a few words to use carefully because of their online significance.

Home	Page	Browse/browser
Explore/explorer	Navigate/navigator	Robot
Stop	Back	Forward
Source	Script	Spider
Map	Index	Site

Summary

While HTML may not afford the designer much possibility to lay out text on a page, CSS provides everything from leading to kerning. Perfect positioning is possible if you want to spend the time. While font control isn't perfect yet, downloadable fonts are on the way. Spending the time to lay out pages well by increasing line height, reducing line length, changing font size, and generally dealing with small details pays off in highly readable pages more likely to invite the user to stay and read awhile. However, now that we have better text control, we are armed and dangerous. If we're not careful, we can just as easily mess up our organized site and pages with poor type layout. More damage can result if we blindly utilize technologies that are not consistently supported in browsers and that can cause ruined layouts or pages that are difficult to read. With the power of CSS, we can take display control back away from the user. Just remember the lessons from previous chapters before you yank control from them—the user's experience should always be our number one concern.

Chapter 13

Color

Colors are used on the Web not only to make sites more interesting to look at, but also to inform, entertain, or even evoke subliminal feelings in the user. Yet, using color on the Web can be difficult because of the limitations of today's browser technology. Color reproduction is far from perfect, and the effect of Web colors on users may not always be what was intended. Apart from correct reproduction, there are other factors that affect the usability of color on the Web. For instance, a misunderstanding of the cultural significance of certain colors may cause a negative feeling in the user. In this chapter, color technology and usage on the Web will be covered, while the following chapter will focus on the use of images online.

Color Basics

Before discussing the technology of Web color, let's quickly review color terms and theory. In traditional color theory, there are three primary colors: blue, red, and yellow. By mixing the primary colors you get three secondary colors: green, orange, and purple. Finally, by mixing these colors we get the tertiary colors: yellow-orange, red-orange, red-purple, blue-purple, blue-green, and yellow-green. We now have a total of twelve colors, which are generally arranged as a color wheel, as shown in Figure 13-1. It is more colorfully presented at http://www.webdesignref.com/examples/colorwheel.htm.

We add to our basic color palette the neutrals: black, white, and gray. Recall that black is the absence of color while white is the combination of all colors.

From the twelve basic colors and the neutrals all the rest of the colors are born. Given a particular color, or more appropriately hue, we might modify the *value* or *brightness* of

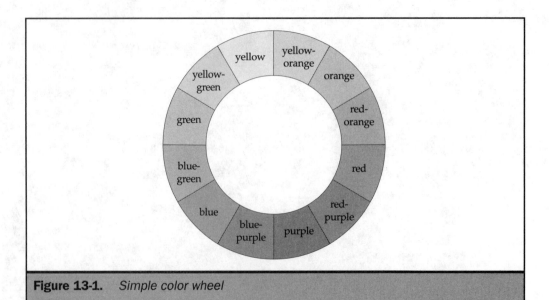

Figure 13-1. *Simple color wheel*

Hue	The color attribute identified by color names, such as "red" or "yellow."
Value	The degree of lightness or darkness of a color.
Saturation	The relative purity of a color; also referred to as "intensity." The "brighter" the intensity of a color, the more saturated it is. New jeans are saturated with blue; faded ones are a less-saturated blue.
Chromatic hues	All colors other than black, white, and gray.
Neutral colors	Black, white, or gray—otherwise known as "non-chromatic hues."
Monochromatic	A color combination based on variations of value and saturation of a single hue.

Table 13-1. *Basic Color Terminology*

the color to create variations. For example, we might take the color blue and vary it from light blue to dark blue. It is also possible to modify the *intensity*. Intensity controls how bright or dull a particular color appears. You might think of intensity as purity; the higher the intensity, the more pure the color. Intensity is also described using the term *saturation*. These basic terms and a few others are defined in Table 13-1.

Computer Color

Computer monitors display colors using varying amounts of red, green, and blue, called RGB color. This is considered an additive form of color, because red, green, and blue light in equal amounts "add" up to white light. All other colors are formed on screen by varying the amounts of each color. For example, red and green are combined to form yellow, blue and green to form cyan, and red and blue to form magenta. This is demonstrated at www.webdesignref.com/examples/rgbcolor.htm.

Note *RGB color is completely different from the way colors are set in print. In print, CMYK (cyan, magenta, yellow, black) is the more common color scheme. The colors you see on a printed piece are the parts of the spectrum reflected back to your eyes as white light hits the ink. CMYK is considered subtractive color since, in theory, if you were to mix pure cyan, magenta, and yellow, they should absorb all color to produce black (because of impurities in all printing inks, however, these three don't actually produce black, which is why black (K) ink must be added).*

Bits	Number of Possible Colors
32	16,777,216 (24 bits) plus 8 bits used for control information
24	16,777,216
16	65,536
8	256
7	128
6	64
5	32
4	16
3	8
2	4
1	2

Table 13-2.   *Bit Depth and Possible Colors*

Each of the various dots or pixels (picture elements) on a computer monitor is set to a particular color to create imagery on screen. *Bit-depth*, sometimes referred to as *color depth*, is the term given to the number of bits used to describe color in an image or on a monitor. The basic idea is simple: the more bits used to specify a color, the more possible colors are available—more bits equals more colors. One bit can be used to specify two colors, typically black and white, two bits can describe four colors, three bits can describe eight colors, and so on. Notice that the number of colors specified by the bit-depth is simply 2 raised to the nth power, where n is the number of bits, as shown in Table 13-2.

A firm understanding of bit depth is important for a Web designer, as the bit depth of a visitor's monitor affects color reproduction, and the manipulation of bit-depth in images can be used to significantly decrease file size. Put simply, the higher the bit depth, the greater the number of colors; the greater the number of colors, the larger the file size. Reducing the number of colors will aid in lowering the file size of images and improve the download time of Web pages. Further consideration of this idea is given in Chapter 14.

Web Color Basics

Anyone familiar with Photoshop or similar programs will probably know the basics of RGB color. In such a graphics program, each of the three color elements, red, green, and blue, can have values from 0 to 255, generally expressed as three numbers separated by commas. So, in the RGB triplet 102,153,204, the number 102 is the red value, 153 is the green value, and 204 is the blue value. All this is very well and good when you're working in a graphics program, but Web technologies do not always measure color with decimal values, but often rely on hexadecimal (base-16) values.

In HTML, color is specified by a hexadecimal RGB triplet preceded by the pound sign (#). The color is six digits long, two hex digits for each byte. So, in the RGB triplet #FF12AC,

■ The first two digits (FF) represent the intensity of the red component of the pixel, which is at full strength because a byte cannot be greater than FF.

■ The next two digits (12) represent the intensity of the green component of the pixel, which here is fairly low.

■ The last two digits (AC) represent the intensity of the blue part of the pixel, and here it's fairly high.

The end result is a bright pink color that might be used in markup like this:

```
<font color="#ff12ac">Hot Pink!</font>
```

In HTML and CSS, we measure color in a hexadecimal range of 00–FF, which is equivalent to 0–255 in decimal. It's relatively easy to translate RGB values to hexadecimal values by referring to a translation chart, such as the one found in Appendix F. Given such a chart, a mid-range blue like rgb (102,153,204) would be represented in hex as #6699CC.

It also is possible to reference the color by name in the code (for example, "black"). The 16 basic names originally defined by Microsoft are now part of the HTML specification; these appear alongside their hexadecimal values in Table 13-3.

Color Name	Hex value
Black	#000000
White	#ffffff
Gray	#808080
Silver	#c0c0c0
Green	#008000
Lime	#00ff00
Olive	#808000
Yellow	#ffff00

Table 13-3. *HTML Specification Colors*

ELEMENTS OF
PAGE DESIGN

Color Name	Hex value
Aqua	#00ffff
Teal	#008080
Blue	#0000ff
Navy	#000080
Fuchsia	#ff00ff
Purple	#800080
Red	#ff0000
Maroon	#800000

Table 13-3. *HTML Specification Colors* (continued)

These are just a few of the colors available. By using RGB triplets translated to a hex value, it is possible to use 256 shades of red, green, and blue to create colors—somewhere around 16.4 million colors! There are over one hundred more color names originally introduced by Netscape and based upon the X11 windowing system colors. These colors are largely supported by most Web browsers. Believe it or not, they include such varied color names as "tomato," "thistle," and "lightcoral."

Online: The full list of color names and their hexadecimal and RGB equivalents can be seen online at http://www.htmlref.com/Reference/AppF/colorchart.htm

One could, of course, use any word, such as pineapplesherbet (not a real value), as a color value; browsers will attempt to render them, but if they are not recognized color names, the rendering will have no relation to the meaning of the word. Our imaginary value pineapplesherbet renders as a shade of blue in Internet Explorer, but as a completely different, much darker blue in Netscape. Either way, it doesn't look like pineapple sherbet. Therefore, it is important to specify the exact color you wish to reproduce with its correct hexadecimal value in order to avoid different browser interpretations. For example, the defined color name aquamarine is equivalent to an RGB value of 127,255,212, which translates to a hexadecimal value of #7FFFD4. Unfortunately, as with many of the other named colors, this is not a browser-safe color. In general, it is preferable to use a hexadecimal code to indicate color. Doing so greatly reduces the chance that the color will be rendered incorrectly.

Rule: To ensure that the appropriate color is produced, always use a hexadecimal value over a named color, except in the case of basic VGA colors like white, black, red, and so on.

HTML Color Use

There are numerous ways to set colors in HTML. The elements (tags) that allow setting the color as an option include the background color of the document body, the default color of text in the document, the colors of links, the color of fonts used in the document, and background colors in tables.

Two basic document-wide color settings can be defined using the **body** element:

```
<body bgcolor="#ffffff" text="#000000">
```

This will provide the document with a white background, and the default color for text in the document will be black. In addition, the **<body>** tag has three attributes that define the colors for three different text link states:

```
<body link="blue" alink="red" vlink="purple">
```

The **link** attribute defines the color of unvisited links in a document. For example, if you've set your background color to black, it might be more useful to have a light link color instead of the standard blue. The **alink** attribute defines the color of the link as it is being clicked. This often happens too quickly to be noticed, but it can create a flash effect, if desired. For a more subdued Web experience, it might be better to set the **alink** attribute to match either the **link** attribute or the next one, **vlink**. The **vlink** attribute defines the color of a link after it has been visited, which under many browsers is purple. Many authors wish to set the value of the **vlink** attribute to red, which makes sense given standard color interpretation. So, using the code above, creating a white page with green text, red links, and fuchsia-colored visited links could be accomplished using the code presented here.

```
<body bgcolor="#ffffff" text="#008000" link="#ff0000"
      vlink="#ff00ff" alink="#ff0000">
```

Try not to choose link colors that might confuse your viewers. For example, reversing link colors so that visited links are blue and nonvisited links are red could confuse a user. While it is unlikely that a page designer would do such a thing, it has been seen more than once—particularly in situations where the look and feel is the driving force of the site. Other common problems with link color changes include setting all link values to blue in the belief that users will revisit sections, thinking they haven't been there before! While this may make sense from a marketing standpoint, the frustration factor due to the lost navigation cues may override any potential benefit from extra visits. As the last example showed, setting the link colors all to red could have the similar effect of encouraging users to think they have seen the site already.

It is also important to make sure that you do not set your links to the same color as the regular text on the page. Relying on underlining to be the definition of the link is extremely dangerous, since most browsers have the option to turn off underlining. Make sure that your link color is going to contrast enough with the paragraph containing it in order to avoid forcing your user to spend time figuring out if there are any links on the page.

Font colors, as well as all other font values, are controlled under traditional HTML through the **<font>** tag. Focusing on colors exclusively, using **<font>** is pretty simple. The following,

```
<font color="red">Red text!</font>
```

will produce red text, as will

```
<font color="#ff0000">Red text!</font>
```

Tables also can be assigned background colors in several ways. The **bgcolor** attribute is valid for **<table>**, **<tr>**, **<th>** and **<td>**.

```
<table border="1" cellspacing="0" cellpadding="8" bgcolor="green">
<tr>
<th bgcolor="lightblue">Lightblue</th>
<th bgcolor="lightblue">Lightblue</th>
<th bgcolor="lightblue">Lightblue</th>
</tr>

<tr bgcolor="orange">
<td>Orange</td>
<td>Orange</td>
<td>Orange</td>
</tr>

<tr>
<td bgcolor="red">Red</td>
<td bgcolor="white">White</td>
<td bgcolor="blue">Blue</td>
</tr>

<tr>
<td>Green</td>
<td>Green</td>
<td>Green</td>
</tr>
</table>
```

In this code, the header cells (**th**) in the first row will have a light blue background; all three cells (**td**) in the second row will have an orange background, as defined for the entire row (**tr**); the three cells in the third row will have different background colors, as defined by the **bgcolor** attribute for each **<td>** tag; and the cells in the last row, which have no background color defined for themselves or their row, will default to the green background color defined in the **<table>** tag, as shown here:

Lightblue	Lightblue	Lightblue
Orange	Orange	Orange
Red	White	Blue
Green	Green	Green

Note that the **cellspacing** attribute for **<table>** is set to zero; if it is set to a higher value, the background color will display in the areas between cells in Internet Explorer:

Lightblue	Lightblue	Lightblue
Orange	Orange	Orange
Red	White	Blue
Green	Green	Green

Don't forget that if the **cellspacing** attribute is not included, most browsers will render the table with several pixels of cell spacing by default. Be sure to set it to"0" to prevent inadvertent spacing.

Some grouping elements associated with tables, like **<thead>** and **<tfoot>**, as defined in the HTML 4.0 spec, also accept **bgcolor**, but make sure to test for browser computability.

Additional proprietary attributes have also been defined for table elements. Internet Explorer supports a **bordercolor** attribute for **table**. Under IE 4 and higher, the following code,

```
<table bordercolor="#ff0000" border="1">
<tr>
<td>. . . content . . .</td>
</tr>
</table>
```

will render a table with a red border around all the entire table and its cells. Netscape may render a red outline only around the four sides of the table and the effect is completely different from the IE rendering. Under IE, **bordercolor** can also be applied to rows (**tr**), headers (**th**), and cells (**td**).

Internet Explorer also provides two more border color attributes: **bordercolordark** and **bordercolorlight**.

```
<table bordercolordark="#ff0000" bordercolorlight="#0000ff"
border="4">
<tr>
<td>...content...</td>
</tr>
</table>
```

Under Internet Explorer, this will render a two-tone outer border for the table in which the top and left outer borders are blue, while the lower and right outer borders are red. It will have no effect in Netscape. Proprietary attributes are not recommended but are commonly employed, given the heavy Internet Explorer penetration.

Finally, on certain browsers some other HTML elements may support color. A common one is the horizontal rule (**<hr>**) tag. This is a proprietary use of the **color** attribute defined by Microsoft, so while

```
<hr noshade="noshade" size="1" color="red" />
```

will render a solid red rule under Internet Explorer 3 and higher, other browsers will ignore the **color** attribute and render the rule in default gray. Color setting for anything other than page background, table, link, and text should be left to style sheets.

CSS1 Color Use

So far we have discussed applying color values to various HTML elements using named values like **red** or hexadecimal values like **#ff0000**. The number of HTML elements that support such attributes as **color** and **bgcolor** is rather limited. Using CSS1 (Cascading Style Sheets, Level 1) opens up a whole new world of color possibilities, both in terms of expressing color values and of the number of HTML elements to which you can apply color.

First, CSS allows color to be applied both to the foreground and background of almost any HTML element. For example, to make all text in a document red, use the simple style rule:

```
body {color: red;}
```

You can also specify background color using the background-color property; so the following rule would specify a black background for the page with red text:

```
body {background-color: black; color: red;}
```

The specification of colors can happen on single tags or groups of tags so that instead of using **<table>** tags with background colors, you might resort to simple rules like,

```
em {background-color: orange; color: black;}
strong {background-color: yellow; color: purple;}
```

to accomplish the same look with far less markup. Consider what it would take to implement the look here:

CSS make setting *colors and background* easy!

Without CSS, it would certainly take some careful table code—or you might just give up and make it an image.

Color in CSS, as in HTML, can be specified using traditional hexadecimal color values, for example:

```
body {background-color: #000000; color: #FF0000;}
```

However, you could also use this approach in this case for a red font:

```
body {background-color: #000; color: #F00;}
```

CSS1 andCSS2 support a sort of condensed hexadecimal code, where black would be #000, blue would be #00F, and so on. Browser support is variable, so be careful when applying these color values.

PhotoShop users will appreciate another CSS color value approach: RGB values. No need to convert RGB values to hex with this technique.

```
span {color: rgb(0,0,255);}
```

Most CSS browsers support this approach, in which the color value is defined by the letters rgb (lowercase) followed by three-comma-separated RGB values in parentheses. It is also possible to use percentage values instead of decimal values, as for example:

```
span {color: rgb(100%,0%,0%);}
```

CSS2 Color Use

The main change in CSS2 in regard to color is the ability to set color values that are related to the user's current graphical environment. The idea here is that we can now specify colors in a relative manner so that the Web page integrates itself into the user's graphical environment. Imagine a user with a customized red desktop. We might want our various page and GUI elements to match this desktop. Apart from aesthetics, system settings may be adjusted to suit a user's accessibility needs. If we adjust page colors to suit, it may improve the accessibility of the page. The color values defined in Table 13-4 can be applied to any color property, like **color** or **background-color**. They should be cased as presented below for readability.

CSS2 Color Value	Description of Color Relation
ActiveBorder	Active window border
ActiveCaption	Active window caption
AppWorkspace	Background color of multiple document interface
Background	Desktop background
ButtonFace	Face color for 3-D display elements
ButtonHighlight	Dark shadow for 3-D display elements
ButtonShadow	Shadow color for 3-D display elements
ButtonText	Text on push buttons
CaptionText	Text in caption
GrayText	Grayed (disabled) text
Highlight	Item(s) selected in a control
HighlightText	Text of item(s) selected in a control
InactiveBorder	Inactive window border
InactiveCaption	Inactive window caption
InactiveCaptionText	Color of text in an inactive caption
InfoBackground	Background color for tooltip controls
InfoText	Text color for tooltip controls
Menu	Menu background

Table 13-4. *CSS2 System Color Values*

CSS2 Color Value	Description of Color Relation
MenuText	Text in menus
Scrollbar	Scroll bar gray area
ThreeDDarkShadow	Dark shadow for 3-D display elements
ThreeDFace	Face color for 3-D display elements
ThreeDHighlight	Highlight color for 3-D display elements
ThreeDLightShadow	Light color for 3-D display elements
ThreeDShadow	Dark shadow for 3-D display elements
Window	Window background
WindowFrame	Window frame
WindowText	Text in windows

Table 13-4.   *CSS2 System Color Values* (continued)

You use these values just as you would use any other color; for example, a simple rule that sets the background of the page to match the desktop background would be

```
body {background-color: Background;}
```

The 6.*x* generation browsers have provided some support for these values. However, page authors are encouraged to use them carefully, as the distinction between desktop and Web application for now should be kept clear.

Possible CSS3 Color Use

While it is still early to state safely what browsers will support in the upcoming CSS3 specification, some aspects of color support deserve at least a brief mention so as to point at future possibilities.

First, the CSS3 specification allows for opacity to be set for elements. This can also be set via a modified color specification indicated by rgba, which adds alpha as a fourth value. The alpha value ranges from 0.0 (fully transparent) to 1.0 (fully opaque). Under CSS3, we might use rules like this:

```
em {color: rgba(255,0,0,1);} /* red fully opaque */
strong {color: rgba(0,0,255,0.5);}  /* partially transparent green */
```

Another improvement introduced in CSS3 is the ability to set color in Hue Saturation Lightness (HSL) format. HSL colors are specified as a triple (hue, saturation, lightness). Hue is represented as an angle of the color circle, where red is 0 or 360, green is 120, blue is 240, and the other colors spread in between. Saturation is represented in a percentage, so 0% is no saturation or a shade of gray, while 100% is full saturation of the hue. Lightness is also represented as a percentage value, with 100% lightness being white and 0% lightness being black. A lightness value of 50%, specifying a "normal" value, would be commonly used. Given these specifications, the following CSS rules make sense:

```
.red {color: hsl(0, 100%, 50%); }
.green {color: hsl(120,100%,50%);}
.darkgreen {color: hsl(120,100%,75%);}
.lightgreen {color: hsl(120,100%,25%);}
.blue {color: hsl(240,100%,50%);}
.white {color: hsl(0,0%,100%);}
.black {color: hsl(0,0%,0%);}
```

While this may seem to be just another way to specify color, the HSL color specification is more intuitive to adjust, and it is generally easier to create variations of colors by keeping the hue the same and adjusting saturation and tint.

Like the RGB color specification, HSL colors under CSS3 should also support alpha values and are measured by HSLA (hue, saturation, lightness, alpha). For example,

```
.translightgreen {color: hsla(120,100%, 25%, 0.5);}
```

would specify a semitransparent light-green color.

Finally, CSS3 should introduce properties like color-profile, which will allow the specification of an ICC (International Color Consortium) color profile (http://www.color.org). For example, to correct colors for images in the page under CSS3, a rule like

```
img {color-profile: url("http://example.com/profiles/eg.icm"); }
```

might be employed. The ability to improve color reproduction in browsers has been a long time in coming. The real challenge we see with color on the Web is that, with such a wide variety of viewing environments, the difference between what colors we specify and what actually shows up can be quite large if we are not careful.

Practical Web Color

The reality is that color often does not reproduce correctly in Web pages. The most common reason is related to bit-depth, as a color may be beyond the range of the viewing display environment. Alternative colors may be employed, or color shifting may occur. Of course, even when a visitor's system is capable of displaying a color, technical features ranging from hardware age to Gamma control may cause that lovely shade of brown to turn into onscreen mud. The improper reproduction of color isn't just an issue of aesthetic integrity, as such problems may result in such poor contrast as to render pages all but unusable. Given today's technology, color manipulation in the Web environment can be challenging.

Browser-Safe Color

What are the browser safe colors, and why is it important to use them? The first step in answering this question is to ask another question: What controls the colors that can be displayed on a computer? These colors are controlled by the computer's video card and limited by the capacities of the monitor being used. The range of colors can vary anywhere from 256 colors and below on the low end all the way up to millions (and "true color") on the high end. Some older systems may even support only 16 colors. In order to be completely safe for all systems, Web design must concentrate on the lowest common denominator, but how can we predict what that is going to be? We can't, really. Many of the newer systems available today are more than likely to have all the colors needed to display all of your images, but we must play it safe and assure that those who have only 256-color capability will not have a terrible experience.

So how do we figure what those 256 colors are? The 256 colors supported by a PC are not the same as those supported by a Macintosh; most of them are the same, but 40 are actually different. That leaves 216 colors that will be guaranteed to be "safe" and display correctly, regardless of the platform or video card. What happens if you use a color that is not one of the 216 Web-safe colors? Quite often, nothing; if a user's computer can display more colors, then it will not have any problems rendering the color you chose, as long as the color is in that computer's palette, but what happens if they do have only 256? In these cases, their computer will try to re-create the color by using a technique called *dithering*.

Dithering is a process through which the computer attempts to re-create the desired color by using those it has available. It will do this by using two or more colors in a dithered (speckled or dotted) pattern to try to match the color it doesn't have, as shown in Figure 13-2. You can see a better example of this in our dithering demo at http://www.webdesignref.com/examples/dither.htm. Dithered images can look terrible and reflect poorly on the designer. By paying attention to the Web safe palette, it is possible to avoid most instances of dithering.

So how do we use the browser-safe colors? Well, it is pretty easy to make simple hex colors. Given the normal hex color triplet, you have RRGGBB, where RR, GG, and BB represent the hex values for red, green, and blue. Safe colors are those where RR, GG, and BB are only the values 00, 33, 66, 99, CC, or FF. Thus #FF00CC is a safe color, while #FFF5EE is not. You might wonder why these values? They represent exact 20% increments in saturation that give us a wide range of colors. So converting from hex, we see decimal values of 0, 51, 102, 153, 204, and 255 as the allowed values for **rgb** (R,G,B) measurements. The percentages for the safe values are 0%, 20%, 40%, 60%, 80%, and 100%

Not safe—true color

Not safe—256 color

Figure 13-2.   *Dithering example*

respectively. Table 13-5 summarizes these basics rules, which you should commit to memory if you plan on producing Web graphics frequently.

A complete palette in full color with both hex and RGB values is present in most graphics programs and can also be found at http://www.htmlref.com/reference / AppE/index.htm.

RGB Value	Percentage Value	Hexadecimal Value
255	100%	FF
204	80%	CC
153	60%	99
102	40%	66
51	20%	33
0	0%	00

Table 13-5.   *RGB/Hexadecimal Equivalents*

If you use colors outside the safety range in an 8-bit viewing environment, you should see dithering or color shift. To ensure that colors reproduce correctly, particularly in GIF images, you will want to use a graphics program like Adobe PhotoShop or Macromedia Fireworks and make sure the palette used is "Web-safe" or that you "snap" to the safety palette once you save out.

Given how quickly computer technology is advancing and how few people probably use 8-bit displays, does any of this matter? As we discussed earlier, the majority of newer systems today will have a much greater color capacity than 256. So what do you design for? Or, to put it differently, why should you limit your designs to the lowest common denominator? It's very hard to say. If you have a specific target audience and you know what they have, such as an internal company intranet, then you can definitely design for that audience's capability. Since the majority of the time you don't know what your users are going to have, you are either going to have to assume some minimum platform or detect for user capabilities. However, if you end up assuming a base platform, remember that some users might not see colors properly—since it is possible to do exciting, high-quality design within the boundaries of Web-safe color palettes, why take the risk at all? We will examine next a few approaches for breaking the browser safety barrier. However, be sure to read the section entitled "Color Shifting and the Reality of the Web Palette" to gain a proper perspective on this issue.

<table>
<tr><td>**Note**</td><td>*Another interesting trend that seems to encourage the use of the browser-safe palette regardless of monitor support is download time. With GIF images, color reduction is the easiest way to reduce file size, so even though most Web users can see more than 256 colors, many sites continue to design around very restrictive color palettes.*</td></tr>
</table>

Hybrid Colors

In their quest to beat the 216-color limitations of the Web-safe palette, designers have come up with a simple workaround generally referred to as *hybrid colors*. Taking advantage of the smallness of pixels and the human mind's tendency to fill in the blanks in visual information, hybrid colors simply take two or more Web-safe colors and combine them in some pattern—usually a checkerboard, but sometimes stripes—to trick the eye into seeing a different color. In a sense, this is a form of controlled dithering that, if done properly, the end user will not notice.

> **Suggestion: To safely break the 216-color barrier, use pre-dithered patterns (so-called "hybrid colors").**

In the next illustration, the area on the left that appears to be gray is actually a checkerboard made up of single-pixel black and white squares, as shown on the right.

Normal view
of hybrid color

Close-up
of hybrid color

**Online: Demos of hybrid colors can be viewed at
http://www.webdesignref.com/examples/hybridcolor.htm.**

Various tools, such as BoxTop's ColorSafe plug-in for PhotoShop (http://
www.boxtopsoft.com), can aid designers in creating hybrid colors quite easily.
In the end, however, the real decision is whether you can design within the
constraints of the Web-safe palette. By remaining within that range as much as
possible, you maximize the usability of your Web site.

Color Detection

Another approach to dealing with the color variability issue is to detect for user
capabilities using JavaScript. In 4.*x* generation browsers and better, the JavaScript
Screen object can be used to determine the bit-depth of the user's monitor by accessing
the **colorDepth** property. For example, this short script displays the current color
depth in an alert dialog:

```
<script type="text/javascript">
<!--
if (window.screen)
alert(window.screen.colorDepth+"bit");
//-->
</script>
```

The dialog box is shown here:

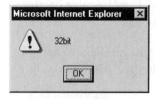

In view of the color detection capability, you might consider setting screen colors based upon user screen conditions. A style sheet reference based upon the color support could be written:

```
<script type="text/javascript">
<!--
var bitDepth;

if (window.screen)
  bitDepth = window.screen.colorDepth;
else
  bitDepth = 8;

if (bitDepth > 8)
 document.write('<link rel="stylesheet" href="hicolor.css" media="screen" />');
else
 document.write('<link rel="stylesheet" href="locolor.css" media="screen" />');
//-->
</script>
<noscript>
<link rel="stylesheet" href="locolor.css" media="screen" />
</noscript>
```

It might be a lot of work, but detection is a slight improvement over mere guesswork in achieving accurate color reproduction. Unfortunately, so far, without color reproduction profiles in Web browsers, there are many things that can derail our efforts.

Troublesome Color Reproduction Issues

There are many other issues that can affect the display of colors on the Web. This section will discuss several of them, including color shifting, gamma correction, and types of monitors. Remember, while you may develop your designs on a 21-inch top-of-the-line monitor, your users will probably be viewing your creation on something much different.

Color Shifting and the Reality of the Web Palette

Here's the bad news: even the Web-safe palette isn't Web-safe under many conditions. The monitor does not really determine the number of colors that can be displayed. The number of available colors is actually defined by the computer's video card. In our lowest common denominator scenario of 256 colors, 8 bits are employed to display colors. (Remember: 2 to the 8th power is 256.) For more colors, the computer must allocate more memory to process colors. High color (16-bit) produces over 65,000 colors, while 24-bit provides literally millions of colors. This may really be overkill, as studies have shown that the average person cannot tell 16-bit and 24-bit color apart. On the other hand, 8-bit and 16-bit are fairly easy to distinguish.

For reasons of simple mathematics, 16-bit displays have some problems with the accurate display of the 216 Web-safe or browser-safe colors discussed earlier in this chapter. High color monitors were originally intended for print designers, who work with CMYK—a four-value system—rather than RGB—a three-value system. If you're working in CMYK, 16 divided by 4 yields a handy 4 bits per color channel. But if you're working in RGB, you run up against a troublesome issue. You can't split a bit, so in 16-bit RGB you wind up with 5 bits per color channel; the 16th bit either vanishes into some electronic limbo or is assigned arbitrarily to one of the three channels, depending on the system. A color channel with 5 bits can produce 32 different colors; raise that to the power of 3, and you get 32,768 colors—not quite the 65,000+ you'd get in CMYK. Ever get the feeling you're being cheated?

The Web-safe palette, on the other hand, divides each color channel into six values. Because 32 can't be divided exactly by 6, the colors defined by the Web-safe palette won't necessarily match the colors defined by a 16-bit color setting. Thus, on some systems, some of the Web-safe colors may shift their values slightly. It turns out that only about 22 of the supposed Web-safe colors don't shift at all. The Web-safe color palette appears to be unsafe! To many Web designers, this is the equivalent of saying the earth is flat, but it is true. See http://www.morecrayons.com for links to articles that go into great detail on this issue.

Given this potentially earth-shattering information, should a designer even care about the Web-safe colors anymore? The answer: probably not as much. An alternative palette that is more 16-bit friendly contains 4096 colors and can also be found at http://www.morecrayons.com. This certainly helps increase what we can design with and addresses the majority of Web users—but you might wonder if color shifts occur on a 24-bit display and how 8-bit folks will view your site? You might just want to stick to primary colors, as many designers do. Other designers just completely ignore the problem and design with the full 16-bit palette. Finally, you could use JavaScript to detect for bit-depth and go from there, but that could get complex.

To add even more complexity to the color shifting issue, different components of a Web page may be affected differently. Remember, a Web browser is a program; the part of that program that processes GIF images may process a certain color one way, while the part of that program that processes HTML may shift the same value somewhat differently when rendering a background color. This can result in an image not matching a background, even though you've taken great pains to keep that shade of red to the correct value. More information on this issue can be found at http://www.macromedia.com/go/13901/. The unpredictable nature of interactions between video cards and monitors is further compounded by the rendering inconsistencies of the browsers themselves.

Gamma Correction

Gamma correction changes the overall brightness and color saturation of an image as it is displayed on a monitor. If a display is gamma-corrected, the nonlinear relationship between pixel value (the number assigned to a particular color tone) and displayed intensity (the way it actually looks) has been adjusted for. To get an idea of what this means visually, take a look at http://www.webdesignref.com/examples/gamma.htm.

To understand gamma, we need to delve a little deeper into the inner workings of monitors. The purpose of gamma correction is to adjust a monitor so that it boosts the voltage in a manner consistent with other monitors. Computers send a certain voltage to monitors, which control the electron emissions that tell the pixels on the screen which colors they should display. The monitor, in turn, boosts the signal by increasing that voltage a certain amount, which may be as high as 2.5 times the original voltage. But since the original voltage, which varies for different colors, is usually less than 1 volt, this may not account for much. Variations in the amount a monitor boosts this voltage will cause different monitors to display the same color differently. Brightness and contrast are both affected. Browsers with incorrect gamma correction will look darker and have less contrast. This is not just a matter of brightness, as gamma settings also affect the ratios between the levels of red, blue, and green.

Macintosh computers are generally regarded as better in this department, and with good reason: they were meant to be used in the creation of graphics (originally for print), while this has only become a recent concern for PCs. As it stands, Macs are set to a gamma setting of 1.8, and PCs are set to 2.5. Macs default to "corrected" gamma, which means the video signal is absolutely true to the source data—which is what a print designer needs. Most Windows PCs display "uncorrected" gamma, just like television, which skews midtones to be 10–15% darker and more saturated. For this reason, many experts suggest that once Web designers get their gamma set up correctly, they should work with an average gamma of 2.2 in mind. Gamma-correction software can be implemented by technicians, or you can do it yourself. PhotoShop allows designers to preview an image's appearance under various gamma settings. Recent Web-specialized graphics programs like Fireworks and ImageReady have the ability to gamma-preview images, as well as to batch-process images to use a selected gamma value. If you are working on low-contrast designs, understanding the lack of gamma correction on the average PC monitor will help you avoid creating muddy, indistinct imagery.

In theory, gamma issues should not affect CSS and HTML colors, but the reality is that there are at times differences between colors in PC and Mac environments. Until color profile information is included, it might be best to stick with common colors or put up with imperfect color reproduction, as even the latest display technology seems to make things more complicated.

Monitor Types: CRT vs. LCD

Most desktop computer monitors are CRT (Cathode Ray Tube) display devices, just like a television monitor. The inside of a CRT monitor screen is covered with thousands of phosphor dots. Three of these dots—one red, one green, one blue—make up a pixel. The phosphor dots glow in response to charges emitted by an electron gun at the back of the monitor. As noted above, however, color processing begins in a computer's video card, not in the monitor. Using a Digital to Analog Converter (DAC), a computer monitor translates the digital information from the video card into an analog signal that controls the monitor's electron gun. Sudden and erratic variations in a monitor's color display may be caused by problems with the DAC circuit. When encountering serious color distortion, always test the monitor on a different computer before blaming the wrong piece of hardware for the problem.

Other issues with CRT monitors include flicker; this occurs when the phosphor dots inside the screen, which have been stimulated by electron streams, begin to lose their charge before it is refreshed. Setting your monitor to a refresh rate above 70 Hz should take care of this; although the Video Electronics Standards Association (VESA) defines 85 Hz as the standard, this may be more than is required. Setting the refresh rate too high can cause damage to a monitor. There are several types of CRT monitors, such as aperture-grille and shadow-mask, but this area is beyond the scope of this discussion.

LCD (Liquid Crystal Display) monitors, long used for laptop computers, are becoming more commonly used as desktop monitors, as the technology has improved sufficiently to make larger screens feasible and affordable. Since LCD monitors don't need room for an electron gun, they are "flat" and take up, on average, only a third of the space needed for bulkier CRT monitors. Other factors in their favor include a complete lack of cathode ray emissions, making them easier on the eyes, and significantly lower power requirements. The upswing in LCD monitor use has several ramifications in terms of color use.

First, many LCD screens, particularly smaller ones, may handle only thousands, or even hundreds, of colors and also tend to support a narrower range of screen resolutions. Larger and/or more expensive ones are more likely to handle millions of colors, or true color. Brightness may also be a concern, as LCD monitors are backlit, and their brightness levels may vary more than those of CRTs. The most important color issue for LCD monitors has to do with the angle of view. They need to be viewed head-on for best results, but even then, light variations caused by the orientation of the screen surface may cause the same color to look somewhat darker at the top of the screen and lighter at the bottom, or vice versa. Given this, LCD screens are probably a poor choice for doing graphics design for Web sites (or any other medium), unless your lighting conditions are very well controlled. From a designer's viewpoint, this reinforces the importance of choosing well-contrasted and coordinated colors for Web pages.

Using Color

Even when color is reproduced properly, it isn't difficult to abuse it. A few too many drastically different colors in use at once might be so garish as to drive users away. Color harmony attempts to find pleasing combinations of colors. Yet even when harmonious, colors may not provide enough contrast and thereby affect usability. Finally, colors have implied meanings that should be considered.

Color Harmony

When using color, designers generally attempt to put things in balance. Too much color can be over stimulating and chaotic, while too little color can be boring. When using color, we strive for harmony—in other words, we use color in a pleasing way. Of course, while this may seem to be more a matter of taste, color theory has long shown how certain color combinations work well together, while others do not.

The most basic tips for good color use are

- Use only a few different colors on a page.
- Do not use an excessive amount of colors.
- Use hot and cool colors together.

We can come up with some common schemes for finding pleasing color combinations using the color wheel presented earlier in the chapter. The simplest way to do this is to select colors near each other on the color wheel. The scheme is described as *analogous*. Colors directly opposite on the color wheel also work well together and are considered *complementary*. For variation, you can try nearly complementary colors or three colors that form an equilateral triangle in the color wheel. Such a color scheme is called a *triadic* color scheme. Color harmony diagrams illustrating the previous ideas are shown in Figure 13-3, with examples found at www.webdesignref.com/examples/colorharmony.htm.

Finally, plain black and white plus a color is the easiest harmony. While a little boring, it is safe and looks pleasing, particularly if the color used is vibrant so as to show contrast with the neutral black and white.

Color and Usability

Page authors must also be extremely careful when setting text and background colors. Readability must be preserved. Page designers are often tempted to use light colors on light backgrounds or dark colors on dark backgrounds. For example, a gray text on a black background might look great on your monitor, but if the gamma value of another person's monitor is much different than your monitor, it will be unreadable. An online demonstration of contrast problems can be found at http://www.webdesignref.com/examples/contrastandusability.htm.

The simple solution to the color usability problem is to make sure to never have elements that require a precise rendering in order for the difference to be apparent. A non-main element, one whose disappearance wouldn't affect the overall look of the page, might qualify as an exception to this rule, but if your design requires that everything appear precisely rendered in order for the whole to not fall apart, then you will need to modify your design.

To avoid color contrast problems, white and black always make a good pairing, and red is certainly useful. The best color combination in terms of contrast is yellow and black, but imagine the headache from reading a page that looks like a road sign!

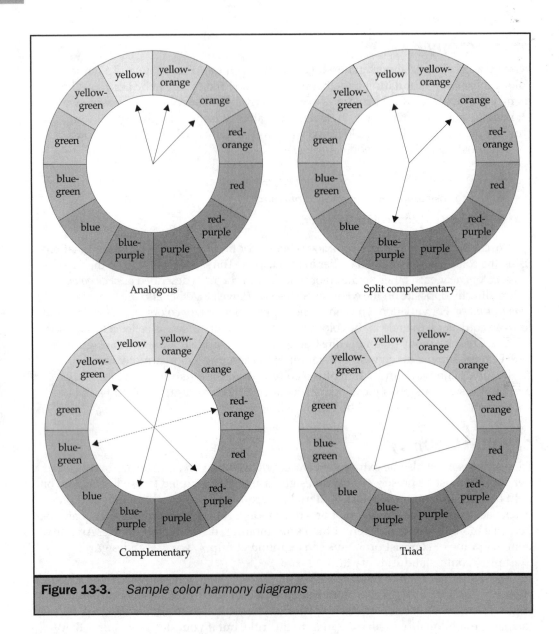

Figure 13-3. *Sample color harmony diagrams*

Despite the high contrast, designers should be careful of white text on a black background when font sizes are very small, particularly on poor-resolution monitors. Yet be careful also of exaggeratedly high contrast. Bright neon colors on a black background offer a great deal of contrast, but is it an effective or usable design? As mentioned in the previous section on color harmony, using color and contrast to call attention to particular parts of a site is a balancing act. Making the navigation colorfully obvious without making it obtrusive and at the same time highlighting a special site feature can be challenging, because just as fast as you grab attention, you may generate a negative response.

Another aspect of color and usability to consider is the variation of visual capabilities in Web users. Human color perception simply does not adhere to some exact standard (considering that the health and structure of each person's eyes varies greatly, this is somewhat to be expected). For example, it is estimated that approximately eight percent of all men and one percent of women have color vision deficiency to some degree or another. Users with vision that is somewhat color-deficient are often unable to differentiate between colors of similar hue when those colors are of the same lightness and saturation. Someone with the most common color deficiency, red-green color blindness, would have trouble distinguishing between red and green when the red and green are close in saturation and lightness. Such color vision issues can be troublesome when you consider the difficultly in distinguishing between red and green traffic lights. Does the color-deficient driver really know when to stop or go? Probably yes, since position also provides meaning in a traffic signal. However, on the Web, if links are similar in hue, lightness, and saturation, it might be difficult for someone to determine which links have been visited and which have not. If color is being used to draw something out, try to have something that also indicates importance, just in case the user can't perceive color properly.

Color perception problems may get worse with the proliferation of PDAs, cell phones, and Palm devices. What do you do when you are not working with lots of color? Can you design a site that works well in all conditions? Two-tone devices, usually displaying with a greenish-gray background and grayish-black text, challenge design ingenuity in a number of ways. The safest approach is probably to design a separate site for each browsing platform so that you can design completely within a particular visual environment. Browser-sensing then directs incoming users to the version of the site appropriate to their display device.

The last point about color and usability on the Web is once again related to links. Like it or not, on the Web blue equals go and purple equals stop or go away. Making something blue will encourage a person to click on it, making it purple will probably not. If you use lots of purple on the page, you might just be subliminally telling people that this site is one they should pay less attention to. Color isn't just for decoration; it can have meaning.

The Hidden Meaning of Colors

On the Web, particularly when dealing with international visitors, it's easy to get messed up by a potentially tricky issue: the meaning of color. Artists, philosophers, scientists, religious thinkers, and others from all walks of life have pondered this issue for centuries, but no consensus has been reached. The nineteenth century German writer and thinker Goethe spent a large portion of his life developing a theory of colors—most of which has been consigned to the dustbin of philosophy by modern thinkers. Even setting aside highly codified color/concept schemas—such as those used in Tibetan religious art or the changing colors of the liturgical seasons in Western churches—it is difficult to apply specific meanings to specific colors. In the West, black is largely associated with death and somber thoughts—while in Japan, the color associated with death is white, a complete reversal of the Western viewpoint. Considering that the Web is an international medium of communication, it may not be practical to take culturally accepted color meanings for granted. Bearing in mind the Western cultural background of this book's production, Table 13-6 lists some common meanings people may associate with certain colors.

red	hot	aggression
	error	fire
	stop	lushness
	warning	daring
pink	female	
	cute	
	cotton-candy	
orange	warm	
	autumnal	
	Halloween	
yellow	happy	cheerful
	caution	slow down
	sunny	
brown	warm	
	fall	
	dirty	
green	envy	inexperience
	pastoral	fertility
	jealousy	newness
blue	peaceful	
	sadness	
	water	
	male	
purple	royalty	
	luxury	

Table 13-6. *Common Concepts Associated with Colors (Subject to Cultural Bias)*

black	evil	ghostly	cool
	death	night	
	mourning	fear	
gray	overcast		
	gloom		
	old age		
white	virginal	winter	
	clean	cold	
	innocent		

Table 13-6. *Common Concepts Associated with Colors (Subject to Cultural Bias)* (continued)

Even without the complications of cultural associations, Web conventions also use color to convey meanings. The significance of hyperlink colors is brought up throughout this book—people are used to clicking on blue text to go somewhere else, and they know that purple text means they've already been there. Changing the color of hyperlinks is always a questionable proposition, especially if the audience for the site are not experienced users—they may see light blue text and never think to click, because they know that regular links are blue. However the messages may be subtler and more difficult to pin down. Reflect on what you think when you see a Web page with red text on a black background. How often does this make you think "Amateur!" in terms of the site's designer? How do you respond to sites that do not have a white background on text-heavy pages? Every Web user brings a host of unacknowledged expectations about what colors, or combinations of colors, mean in the browser window.

Summary

Color is important to Web designers, as it makes pages both pleasing and meaningful to visitors. Unfortunately, color use on the Web can be difficult. With the wide variability of viewing environments, designers need to continue to rely on the 216-color browser-safe palette. Hybrid colors and color depth detection can help us break the 216-color limit safely, but even then things may not work. Without color correction technology that can deal with differences in the user's viewing environment, color reproduction on the Web is far from an exact science. This is a rather unfortunate situation. Color preciseness is important if we want to make sure that the blue shirt users buy online is exactly the shade of blue they thought it was. Just think of the cost of returns due to a serious color shift! With the eventual introduction of color profiles in CSS (and PNG images, discussed in the next chapter), things should improve. Yet even when color is displayed properly, it is easy to misuse color by not using harmonious colors, providing too little contrast, or not considering the meaning of color.

ELEMENTS OF
PAGE DESIGN

The
Complete
Reference

Web
Design

Chapter 14

Images

Today, for most people, the Web is a visual medium. While the disabled or those accessing the Web from a non-graphical environment can still interact with Web pages, they often miss a great deal of information that only images can provide. Graphics may not only enhance a user's comprehension of material; when aesthetically pleasing, they may even improve the user's experience. At the same time, overuse of graphics can have a negative effect and result in a slow and unusable site. Correct image use on the Web is not just a matter of taste. It requires complete understanding of the various file formats, such as GIF, JPEG, and PNG. A major goal of designers is to balance image quality with download size. This chapter will present the technical issues surrounding the use of images on the Web, with a focus on usability and cross-browser compatibility. It will be up to you to determine what is pleasing and appropriate to present to your users.

Image Formats

A computer monitor is composed of numerous small dots, or pixels (picture elements). Images are formed onscreen by setting the colors of particular pixels. An image format describes the color and position information necessary to create an onscreen image. There are two basic image format varieties: *vector images* and *bitmapped images*.

In its raw form, a *bitmap* or *raster* image is simply a collection of pixels of different color values. Because of the large number of pixels and color information in an image, raw bitmaps can be very large. An uncompressed bitmap image at 800×600 pixels with 24 bits of color information would take up over 1MB ($800 \times 600 \times 24 = 11,520,000$ bits / 8 bits per byte = 1,440,000 bytes). Given their potential size, bitmapped image formats almost always employ some form of compression. In general, there are two forms of image compression: *lossless* and *lossy*. Lossless image compression means that the compressed image is identical to the uncompressed image. Because all the data in the image must be preserved, the degree of compression, and the corresponding savings, is relatively minor. Lossy compression, on the other hand, does not preserve the image exactly, but can provide much higher degrees of compression. With lossy compression, the loss in image quality achieves a smaller byte count. Because the human eye may barely notice the loss, the trade-off may be acceptable.

A *vector* image stores image information in a much different manner, describing the image as a collection of mathematical curves, points, and colors. Given the compact manner in which vector images are described, the format has the advantage of being very small in file size. Because the image is created or rendered mathematically, it can easily be scaled, in comparison to bitmap formats, which tend to become distorted during size changes. With all their advantages, vector images do have tradeoffs. First, a vector image must go through an extra step, called *rendering*, where the image is calculated and drawn onscreen. This process does take some time compared to bitmap images, which simply decompress and display. The difference between the two basic image formats is shown next.

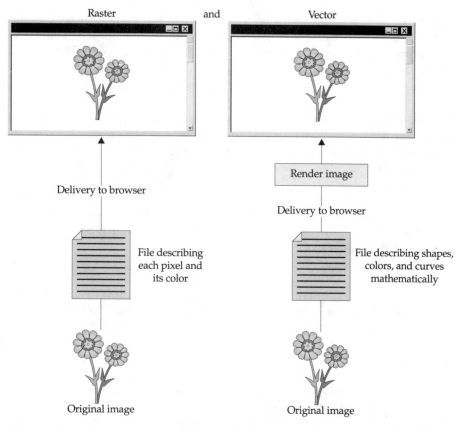

In most cases—those in which the image is rather simple—the render time for a vector image is negligible. As the image becomes more complex, the rendering process can take an increasingly significant amount of time. Remember that, at the end of the day, everything must become a bitmap in order to be displayed onscreen. Vector formats do a good job on illustrative-style graphics, text, and logos, while bitmaps handle photographs well. Interestingly enough, many vector formats will import bitmap images for textures, and vectors are often rasterized for inclusion in bitmap images. Both types of formats have their merits and work well together.

While the HTML standard says nothing about what image formats can be used on the Web, browsers tend to support the same image types. On the Web, the primary bitmap image formats are GIF (Graphics Interchange Format) and JPEG (Joint Photographic Experts Group). The PNG (Portable Network Graphics) format is now finally gaining some ground, but it is so far not that prevalent online. Where vector graphics are concerned, the Flash format is dominant on the Web, but the W3C-endorsed SVG (Scalable Vector Graphics) format is gaining some ground. Other image formats, such as the various UNIX-related formats like XBM (X Bitmaps) and XPM (X Pixelmaps) and the Windows format (.BMP), are often supported natively by browsers, but are primarily of historical interest and are not to be used. Esoteric formats, such as wavelet-based formats, will eventually emerge into the mainstream; but at least for now, stick with the tried-and-true GIF and JPEG. We discuss the main image formats and some of the important features directly.

GIF

GIF images are the most widely supported image format on the Web. Originally introduced by CompuServe (and occasionally referred to as "CompuServe GIFs"), the GIF format actually comes in two types: GIF 87 and GIF 89a. Both forms of GIF support 8-bit color (256 colors), use the LZW (Lempel-Ziv-Welch) lossless compression scheme, and generally have the .gif file extension. GIF 89a also supports transparency and animation, both of which will be discussed later in this section. Today, when speaking of GIF images, we always assume the GIF89a format is in use and make no distinction between the formats, regardless of whether or not animation or transparency is actually used in the image.

GIF images use a basic form of compression called *run-length encoding*. This lossless compression works well with large areas of continuous color. Figure 14-1 shows the GIF compression scheme in practice. (To see an extended online version of this, go to http://www.webdesignref.com/examples/gifcompression.htm.) Notice how the test images with large horizontal continuous areas of color compress a great deal, while those with variation do not. As shown in the demo, simply taking a box filled with lines and rotating it 90 degrees shows how dramatic the compression effect can be. Given GIF's difficulty in dealing with variability in images, it is obvious why the format is good for illustrations and other images that contain large amounts of continuous color.

As mentioned earlier, GIF images only support 8-bit color for a maximum of 256 colors within the image. Consequently, some degree of loss is inevitable when representing true-color images, such as photographs. Typically, when an image is remapped from a large number of colors to a smaller color palette, dithering occurs. As discussed in Chapter 13, the process of dithering attempts to create a color that is outside of the palette. It does this by taking two or more colors from the palette and placing them in some sort of checkered or speckled pattern as a way of visually creating the illusion of the original color.

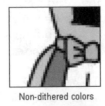

Non-dithered colors

Dithered colors

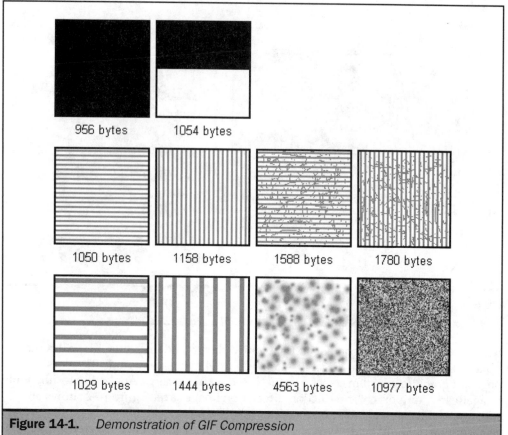

956 bytes   1054 bytes

1050 bytes   1158 bytes   1588 bytes   1780 bytes

1029 bytes   1444 bytes   4563 bytes   10977 bytes

Figure 14-1.   *Demonstration of GIF Compression*

Note   *There is a fairly esoteric use of GIF images that allows them to exceed the 256-color barrier by using multiple image blocks, each with its own color palette within the same GIF file. The so-called true-color GIF could provide support for thousands of colors, but with a much larger file size. Those looking to exceed the 256-color limitation of GIF should look to JPEG or PNG files.*

Ensuring that the appropriate file format is used for the right types of images and that flat or illustrative type images use Web safe colors will help reduce the amount of dithering that takes place.

While having only an 8-bit color depth seems problematic, sometimes designers will further downward adjust the bit-depth of GIF files to reduce file size. Recall that the higher the bit-depth in an image, the more colors and the greater amount of information required. It would make sense then that, by limiting the number of colors as much as possible without reducing the quality of the image, you could create some extremely small files. The key to doing this is using just enough colors in the image to

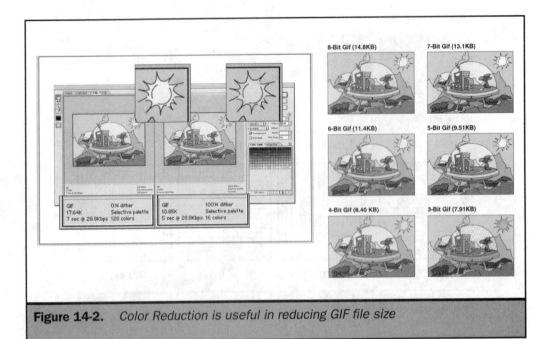

Figure 14-2.   *Color Reduction is useful in reducing GIF file size*

support what is there or what is reasonable to dither. Standard 8-bit GIFs will contain up to 256 colors, 7-bit up to 128 colors, 6-bit up to 64 colors, 5-bit up to 32 colors, and so on. Most graphics programs, such as Macromedia Fireworks or Adobe Photoshop with ImageReady, support color reduction directly on image save. Figure 14-2 shows an example of the file reduction possibilities using GIF color reduction. A complete demo can be found online at http://www.webdesignref.com/example/gifcolorreduction.htm.

GIF images also support a concept called *transparency*. One bit of transparency is allowed, which means that one color can be set to be transparent. Transparency allows the background that an image is placed upon to show through, making a variety of complex effects possible.

without
transparency

with
transparency

Online: For transparency examples, got to http://www.webdesignref.com/ examples/giftransparency.htm.

GIF transparency is far from ideal. Given that only a single color can be made transparent, it can be difficult to avoid a halo effect when placing transparent GIF images on backgrounds, as shown here:

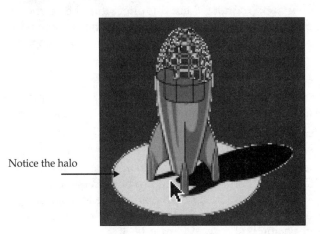

Notice the halo

The main problem with 1-bit transparency is that *anti-aliasing* uses variable colors to blur the jagged edges of an image and smooth things out. A variety of issues related to transparency are displayed at the online demo. Remember: everything that is displayed onscreen is made up of pixels. Pixels are square. It should therefore be obvious that creating an image that has rounded edges may pose some problems. Anti-aliasing allows us to create the illusion of rounded or smooth edges by partially filling the edge pixels in an attempt to blend the image into the background, as shown here:

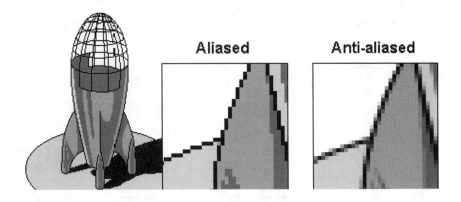

Aliased   Anti-aliased

There are a variety of solutions to the anti-aliasing-transparency halo problem. First, you could simply not anti-alias the image. This can produce unwanted "jagginess" in the image. A second possibility might be to avoid setting the transparency image on a complex background and instead prefill the image with the appropriate background. This approach is seamless and completely avoids any trace of halo, but it limits what we can put images over. For this reason, designers often will avoid transparency in conjunction with complex backgrounds where this effect might be difficult to accomplish. The final approach is to try to solve the transparency problem by creating a mask. All of these approaches are illustrated online at http://www.webdesignref .com/examples/giftransparency.htm.

When using small text in a graphic, it is often a good idea to leave the text aliased. Anti-aliasing introduces an element of fuzziness, which may make smaller font sizes very difficult to read.

GIF images also support a feature called *interlacing*. Interlacing allows an image to load in a venetian-blind fashion rather than from top to bottom one line at a time. The interlacing effect allows a user to get an idea of what an image looks like before the entire image has downloaded, thus keeping users from being frustrated as images download. The idea of interlacing is shown in Figure 14-3.

The previsualization benefit of interlacing is very useful on the Web, where download speed is often an issue. While interlacing a GIF image is generally a good idea, occasionally it comes with a downside: interlaced images may be larger than non-interlaced images. It would also be a bad idea to use interlacing for images that

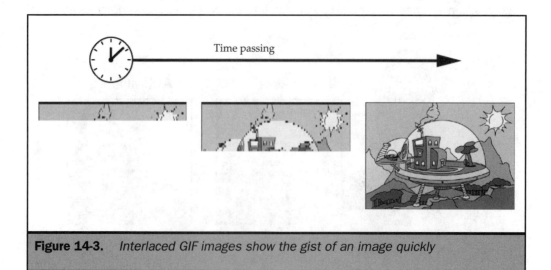

Figure 14-3.   *Interlaced GIF images show the gist of an image quickly*

have text on them, since it would be impossible for the text to be read easily until the download was complete.

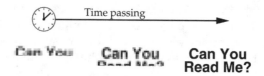

Online : For more on GIF interlacing visit http://www.webdesignref.com/examples/interlacedgif.htm.

Finally, the GIF format also supports animation. This works by stacking GIF after GIF to create the animation, in a manner similar to a flip book. The animation extension also allows timing and looping information to be added to the image. Most popular graphics programs, such as Fireworks, support animated GIFs. An example of the interface to control GIF animation in Fireworks is shown in Figure 14-4.

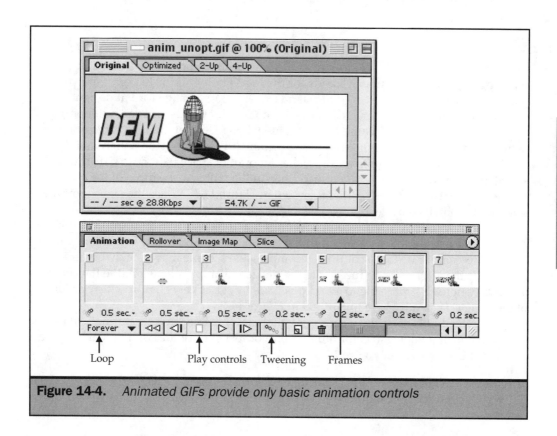

Figure 14-4.   *Animated GIFs provide only basic animation controls*

Animated GIFs are one of the most popular ways to add simple animation to a Web page because nearly every browser supports them. Browsers that do not support the animated GIF format generally display the first frame of the animation in its place. Even though plug-ins or other browser facilities are not required, authors should not rush out to use animation on their pages. Excessive animation can be distracting for the user and makes for inefficient downloads. Since the animation is basically image after image, the file size is the total of all the images within the animation combined; this can result in a much larger image than the user is willing to wait for. Thus, it is very important to make sure that every frame of the animation is compressed as much as possible. One approach to combat file bloat is to optimize the image by replacing only the moving parts of an individual animation frame. This is often called *changing rectangles* optimization. By replacing only the portion of the frame that is changing, you can use smaller images in some frames to help cut the file size down. Many of the GIF animating applications have a feature built in that will go through and optimize the images for you. Doing this may result in a dramatic saving of file size, as shown in Figure 14-5.

Online: http://www.webdesignref.com/examples/animatedgif.htm

JPEG

The other common Web image format is JPEG, which is indicated by a filename ending with .jpg or .jpeg. JPEG—which stands for the Joint Photographic Experts Group, the name of the committee that wrote the standard—is a lossy image format designed for compressing photographic images that may contain thousands, or even millions of colors or shades of gray. Because JPEG is a lossy image format, there is some trade-off between image quality and file size. However, the JPEG format stores high-quality 24-bit color images in a significantly smaller amount of space than does GIF, thus saving precious disk space or download time on the Web. An example of the quality versus file size tradeoff with JPEGs is shown in Figure 14-6. Notice the significant file size savings obtained by sacrificing just a little quality.

The trick with JPEG's lossy compression is that it focuses on slight smudging in areas of heavy detail that a viewer is unlikely to notice. However, in a situation where continuous color or text is used, JPEG's compression scheme may quickly become evident, as the artifacts introduced into the image will appear heavy in the flat color and text regions. It is possible to avoid this issue by selectively compressing portions of the image. These ideas are illustrated in Figure 14-7.

While the JPEG format may compress photographic images well, it is not well suited to line drawings, flat color illustrations, or text. Notice the comparison between GIF and JPEG file sizes in Figure 14-8.

Online: For comparison of GIF and JPEG formats, go to http://www .webdesignref.com/examples/gifvsjpeg.htm

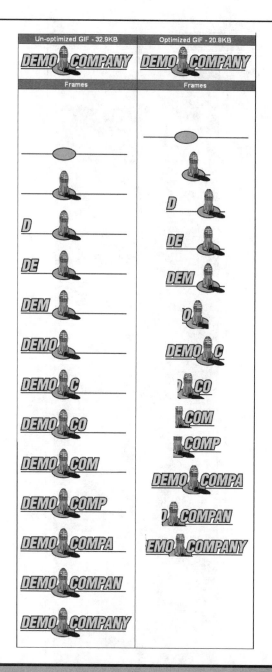

Figure 14-5. *Example of animated GIF frames and optimization*

TECHNOLOGY AND
WEB DESIGN

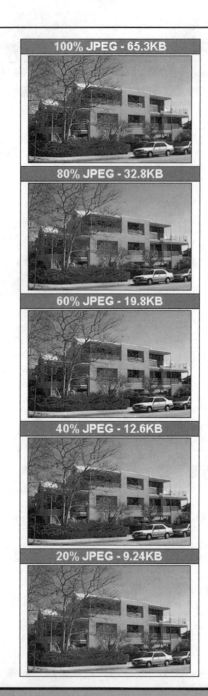

Figure 14-6.   *JPEG file size and quality comparison*

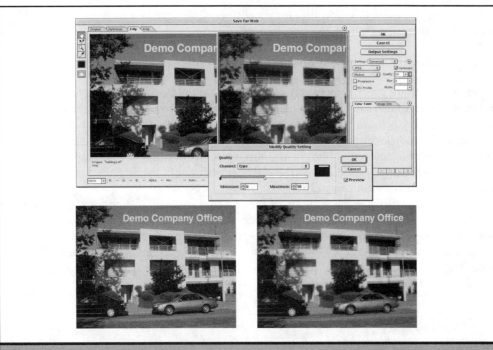

Figure 14-7. *Distortions around flat color areas and text can be reduced with selective compression*

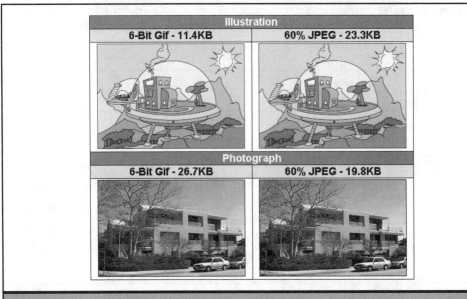

Figure 14-8. *Comparison of GIF and JPEG file sizes*

Choosing between GIF and JPEG is usually very straightforward: do photos with JPEG and illustrations with GIF.

Rule: Use GIFs for illustrations and JPEGs for photos.

However, there are instances where developers may be willing to distort a photo to put it in GIF to use the format's features, since JPEG images do not support animation or any form of transparency. However, JPEG images do support a feature similar to GIF interlacing in a format called *progressive JPEG*. Progressive JPEGs fade in from a low resolution to a high resolution, going from fuzzy to clear, as shown in Figure 14-9. Like interlaced GIFs, progressive JPEG images are slightly larger than their non-progressive counterparts.

Finally, some designers are aware of the fact that since JPEG images are heavily compressed, decompression time can occasionally be a factor. With today's more powerful computers and higher-speed lines, the decompress time of a JPEG will not be an issue much of the time. However, if you make an extremely large dimension JPEG and compress it highly, you will notice a delay. Of course, if you used a GIF, you'd have a worse-looking image that might be just as large.

PNG

The Portable Network Graphics (PNG) format is an emerging format that has all of the features of GIF in addition to several other features. First, the compression algorithm for PNG is not proprietary, unlike that of GIF's, which is LZW (owned by Unisys). Some designers have worried about the potential problems stemming from Unisys patent claims on LZW compression, but so far this has been a nonissue. PNG's

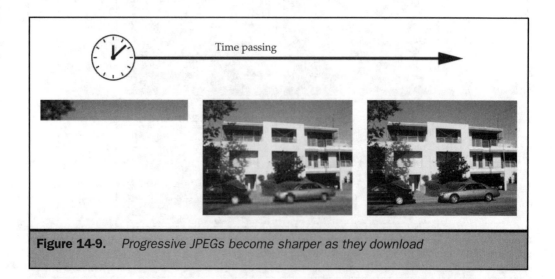

Figure 14-9.   *Progressive JPEGs become sharper as they download*

compression algorithm is also slightly better than GIF's, as shown in Figure 14-10; but this alone is probably not much of a reason to give up GIF images, given the browser compatibility problems that still plague the format. PNG also supports slightly improved interlacing.

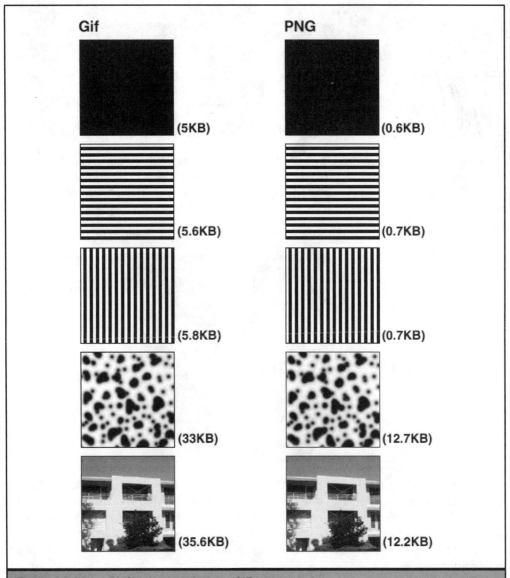

Figure 14-10.   *PNG compression vs. GIF compression*

PNG images break the 8-bit color barrier normally found in GIF images; but with the degree of compression available in PNGs today, it would not make sense to favor PNG files over JPEGs, in all cases, though this examples shows that PNG is the best format:

A significant plus for PNG images is the improved transparency possibilities. Rather than being limited to a single color for transparency masks, PNG files can use up to 256 colors in a mask, thereby lending themselves to smooth transparent edges and shadow effects.

Another problem addressed by PNG is the apparent color shifting in images that are developed on a system with one Gamma or brightness value and then shown on a system with a different Gamma value. Notice in Figure 14-11 how the images do not quite look the same at different Gamma values. PNG avoids this problem.

Finally, PNG supports animation through MNG that is similar to what is provided in GIF animations.

With all these great features, one wonders why PNG is not more common online. The main reason is that the browser vendors still don't consistently support PNG images. Even when the image format is supported, many features like transparency are not fully implemented. In fact, no browser other than Mozilla 1.0 supports PNG well enough to

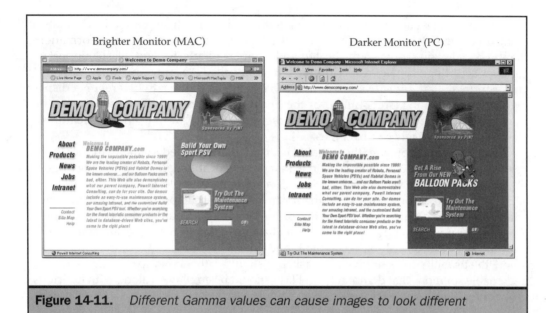

Figure 14-11. *Different Gamma values can cause images to look different*

rely on the format, so Web designers are warned to avoid using PNGs unless browser sensing is utilized.

> **Suggestion: Limit bitmap graphics formats in Web pages to JPEG and GIF until other formats become more widely supported.**

Flash

One vector-based image format is becoming relatively common on the Web: Macromedia's Flash, which is indicated by the .swf file extension. The format is primarily known for animations, but it can also be used to create static, scalable, still images (see http://www.webdesignref.com/examples/staticflash.htm). The advantage is that the image can scale easily to the screen size available, or it can show more detail, as shown in Figure 14-12. In many cases, the images are as small as GIF images.

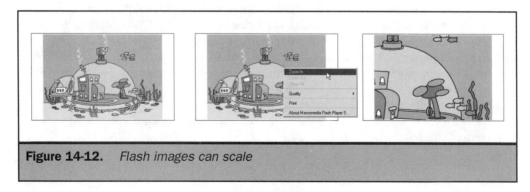

Figure 14-12. *Flash images can scale*

TECHNOLOGY AND
WEB DESIGN

Animation is what most people equate with Flash. A Flash animation is far superior to an animated GIF in several ways. First, it can contain a great deal more information than a GIF, allowing more sophisticated and complex effects. Second, Flash supports complex scripting using a JavaScript-like language called ActionScript. Third, as a vector format, Flash files are scalable and can expand or contract to fit a relative display region, thus becoming larger on top-of-the-line monitors, yet are able to scale down to fit reasonably comfortably within low-end displays. Finally, despite all these features, Flash files are relatively compact files.

It might seem surprising, then, that Flash isn't well regarded by many in the usability community. The main reason is that designers abuse Flash by making huge files which don't take users into consideration. Plain and simple: if you make Flash support mandatory, you are just asking for trouble. A certain portion of your audience will not have the plug-in at all, another portion will have an outdated version and be unwilling or unable to upgrade, others may have installation conflicts, and some users may not want to see Flash-based content. The pragmatic designer wouldn't either ignore the usability folks or give up Flash, but should rather embrace the fact that degradable solutions that do not rely on Flash should be employed, along with judicious browser and Flash detection.

Other Image Formats

There are numerous other image formats out there that can be used in browsers but are generally not appropriate for public Web site development. First is the BMP format. While Internet Explorer supports this format, it lacks any major degree of compression, and it is not supported in many other browsers. Second, there are numerous historical image formats like XBM and XPM that were popular in the UNIX environment, but today are simply historic holdouts from Web days past. Last, some sites do support a variety of other image formats that might be considered exotic: ActiveX controls, Java applets, or plug-ins. These formats, which generally provide some special feature like zooming or support for extremely large file sizes, use extreme compression.

One potentially important format that deserves at least a brief mention is JPEG 2000. Though still in the works as far as browsers are concerned (despite its "2000" sticker), this format promises developers a JPEG standard that will vastly improve the display of photographic images on the Web. Regular JPEGs use a compression system, known as DCT, that compresses visual information into blocks of 8 pixels by 8 pixels; the blocks load in sequence as the image is rendered. The JPEG 2000 standard, in turn, uses *wavelet compression* that converts images into a series of wavelets, rather than square blocks of pixels, and that does not need to discard as much information as the current JPEG approach. In addition to getting improved compression, designers will be able to choose from a range of resolution levels for each JPEG 2000 image—and users will be able to select how much of that resolution they want to display. JPEG 2000 will also allow for possible CMYK display on the Web and correct color display for a variety of systems and platforms.

Now that we have covered all the image formats and their basic features, it is time to discuss how they are used within Web pages and to describe some of the nuances of their usage that designers should be aware of. We will not, however, focus on step-by-step image preparation, as we assume readers are either schooled in the basics of graphic programs or will want to consult detailed tutorials on Photoshop or Fireworks usage.

HTML and Images

To insert an image into a Web page, simply use the **<img>** tag and set the **src** attribute of the element equal to the URL of the image. The form of the URL may be either an absolute URL or a relative URL. The best approach is to use a relative URL to an image found in a centralized images directory, often just "/images" off the main Web site root directory. So, to insert a GIF image called logo.gif residing in that directory, use

```
<img src="images/logo.gif" />
```

An absolute URL could also be used to reference an image on another server:

```
<img src="http://www.democompany.com/images/logo.gif" />
```

Although using absolute URLs for linking in your images works, it is going to limit the mobility of your Web site. Imagine trying to make a copy on a CD-ROM or switching your site to a new domain name. Therefore, using relative links will be a better long-term solution. Using an external URL is not advised, since images may move and cause the page to load at an uneven pace.

Besides **src**, there are numerous other attributes of the **<img>** element. Some commonly used attributes that have some important features are discussed briefly next; a full list can be found in Appendix C, which covers HTML/XHTML. A detailed examination of **<img>** tag syntax can be found in Chapter 5 of the companion volume *HTML: The Complete Reference*.

Alternative Text

The **alt** attribute provides alternative text for user agents that do not display images or for graphical browsers where the user has turned off image rendering.

```
<img src="images/logo.gif" alt="Demo Company Logo" />
```

The **alt** attribute's value may display in place of the image or be used as a tool tip or placeholder information in image-based browsers. Any HTML markup found in the **alt** element will be rendered as plain text. If the option to display images is turned off, the browser will display the alternative text, as shown here:

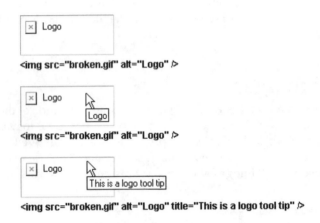

A browser may also show the **alt** text as images load, giving the user something to read as the page renders.

Many modern graphical browsers will also display the **alt** text as the tool tip for the image once the pointer is positioned over the image for a period of time. However, the core attribute **title** should override this and be displayed instead of the **alt** text in a conforming browser.

While theoretically there is no limit to the alternative text that may be used, anything more than a few hundred characters may become unwieldy. Some browsers do not handle long tool tips and **alt** text properly, or they might not wrap the descriptive text. Be warned that if you insert entities like  to format the **alt** or **title** text, you may wreak havoc in voice browsers that read screen content, though the visual presentation might be improved.

The **alt** attribute's importance becomes clear when you consider how many people might access the Web from a text-only environment. Unfortunately, much of the alternative text set does not always provide a substantial benefit. Do the examples above really help by backing up the Demo Company's logo graphic with the actual words "Demo Company logo"? Would simply "Demo Company logo" be sufficient? or insufficient? Try to make **alt** text reflect the meaning of an image; if an image is merely decorative, like a graphic bullet for a list item, setting it to no value (**alt=""**) is perfectly acceptable.

> **Suggestion:** *alt* **text should reinforce the meaning of significant images; if an image does not convey essential meaning, leaving the** *alt* **value blank may be better than adding noise information to screen readers or cluttering the page with unnecessary** *alt* **text or tool tips.**

Sizing Images in HTML

One all-too-common sight on the Web is text that loads quickly, only to suddenly reflow all over the place when the images pop in a few seconds later. This is caused by designers neglecting to use the **height** and **width** attributes of the <img> tag:

```
<img src="images/sequoia.jpg" height="150" width="40" />
```

Using these attributes resolves the problem because, when visual browsers read these attribute values, they reserve the space defined by those dimensions.

Rule: Always use the height and width attributes with the <img> tag.

When these attributes are used in an HTML document, text will flow around where the images are supposed to go, even if the images finish loading long after the text. For more complicated layouts, where cut-up images may be assembled jigsaw-puzzle style in a table, it is very important to use these attributes accurately and in a way that matches the dimensions of the table cells holding the images. Using these attributes has the additional benefit of improving the perceived download time, since users can begin reading the page before the all of the images have finished loading.

Some designers misuse the **height** and **width** attributes to resize images with HTML. It is usually easy to spot this mistake: whether they are shrunken or expanded by decreasing or increasing the attribute values, images resized in HTML tend to look distorted. For flat images or simple patterns, stretching may work; but in most cases, it should be avoided.

Rule: Avoid using the *height* and *width* attributes to resize images with HTML because distortion may occur.

Image Borders

Browsers tend to render images with an undefined **border** attribute as having no border, with one notable exception. While the image

```
<img src="images/robotfag.gif" height="150" width="40">
```

will render without a border, making it a link

```
<a href="robotfaq.htm"><img src="images/robotfaq.gif"
    height="150" width="40" alt="Robot FAQ" /></a>
```

will render with a colored border, usually blue. This is the Web's graphic equivalent of underlining text links. In the early days, this was a good way to let users know that an image was a link. Nowadays, with graphic navigation conventions fairly well established, this is more of a nuisance than a boon. Setting all images to have a border of zero is a good idea most of the time.

Rule: Always set an image's *border* attribute to zero unless you have a specific design reason to do otherwise—and remember that linked images with no *border* attribute will render with colored borders by default.

Image Toolbar

A special browser-specific feature for images that deserves some special comment is Internet Explorer 6's image toolbar. If you have ever held your mouse over a large image in a Web page using IE6, you might have noticed a strange pop-up toolbar:

The toolbar supports quick saving-out of images to a special "My Images" folder. The browser uses image size for determining which images to show this toolbar for, and it does a pretty good job of not showing this feature of navigation buttons and banner ads—for everything else, it depends on its size threshold. To turn off the image toolbar on an individual image, just add the **galleryimg** attribute and set its value to No, like so:

```
<img src="democompanylogo.gif" alt="Demo Company" galleryimg="no"
    height="50" width="100" />
```

If you just want to be rid of the whole feature altogether in a page, either have your server issue an HTTP response header of **Imagetoolbar: no** or, more easily, use a **<meta>** tag in the **<head>** of each page.

```
<meta http-equiv="imagetoolbar" content="no" />
```

Of course, there are numerous other **<img>** tag attributes to consider, but they should already be familiar to readers and may be found in Appendix C.

Background Images in HTML

To set a background image for a Web page, simply use the **background** attribute with the **<body>** tag and set the value just as you would with **<img src>**:

```
<body background="images/background.gif">
```

The image should be a GIF or a JPEG file. Internet Explorer also supports bitmap files (.bmp), but this is not really a viable option unless users will be limited to a Microsoft-exclusive environment. Images accessed in this fashion repeat, or *tile*, in the background of a Web page. This can make or break a Web page design. Imagine someone who used the **background** attribute to place a 200 × 300 pixel JPEG of a favorite dog on his or her home page. The dog's image would repeat, both vertically and horizontally, in the background of the page. This would make the dog's owner very happy—and make the page very difficult to read. Figure 14-13 shows an example of a bothersome repeating background.

In most situations, complex background images tend to be a poor design decision. Taking a subtle approach can backfire as well. Some designers attempt to create a light background, such as a texture or watermark, thinking that, as on paper, it will have a sophisticated effect. The problem is that, under many monitors, the image may be

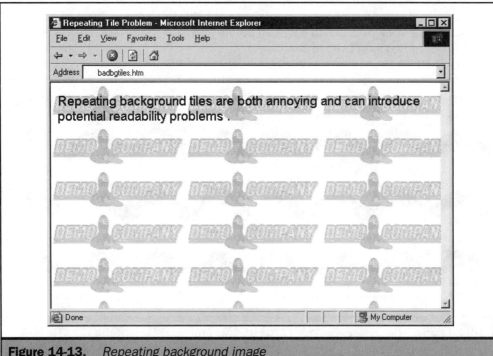

Figure 14-13. *Repeating background image*

difficult to make out at all, or the texture may even blur the text on top of it slightly. Just as with setting background colors, the most important consideration is the degree of contrast. Always attempt to keep the foreground and background at a high level of contrast so that users can read the information. Unless you are absolutely certain the background image will not interfere with text readability, don't use it.

If a background is desired, image manipulation programs such as PhotoShop can be used to create seamless background tiles that are more pleasing to the eye and show no seam. Figure 14-14 demonstrates the idea of a repeating background tile execution.

The best use of the background tile, however, is to enhance page layout by framing certain zones on the page rather than filling the entire display area. Often the backgrounds are kept outside of content areas or are limited to navigation or labeling zones. A common design is to create backgrounds to show navigation areas and leave the rest of the page for content. For example, a single GIF image 5 pixels high by 1,600 pixels wide could be used to create a useful page layout. The first 200 horizontal pixels of the GIF could be black, while the rest could be white. Assuming 1,600 pixels as the maximum width of a browser, this tile would only repeat vertically, thus creating the illusion of a two-tone background. This has become a very common use of a background image on the Web. Many sites use the left-hand color for navigation buttons, while the remaining area is used for text, as shown in Figure 14-15. To guarantee that content appears on top of the appropriate section of the background image, you may be forced to use tables so the tile won't repeat, as shown in Figure 14-16.

The repeat issue is a problem if you aren't aware of the width of the user's screen. Given today's monitor technologies, it might be possible to assume a 1,600-pixel or 2,000-pixel-wide background will cover all but the most unusual cases. However, by using CSS, even that won't be required.

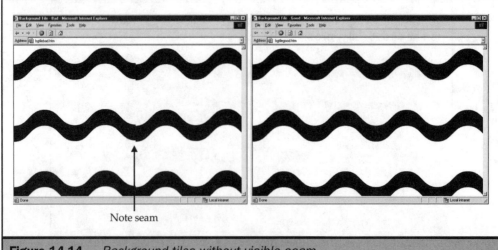

Note seam

Figure 14-14.   *Background tiles without visible seam*

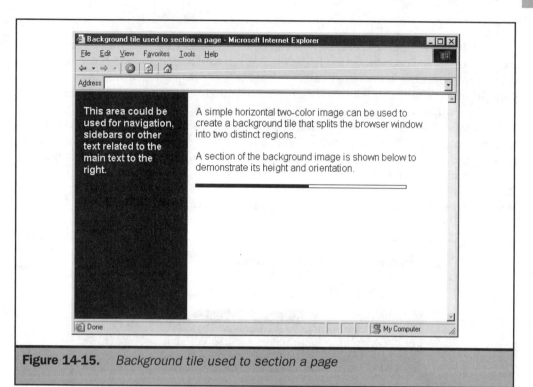

Figure 14-15.   *Background tile used to section a page*

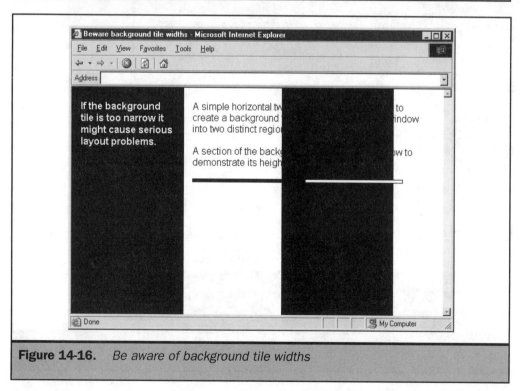

Figure 14-16.   *Be aware of background tile widths*

In plain HTML, background control can be a real issue. Consider that a vertical section such as the one shown in Figure 14-17 is not safe to develop in HTML without using frames or CSS. Unless pages are a fixed size, long pages, text sizing, or simple page reflow due to width adjustment may cause content to flow over backgrounds.

A final variation of page backgrounds was introduced by Microsoft: the *fixed background*. A fixed background is attached and doesn't scroll with content; instead, content scrolls over it. Some would call this a watermark style. It is easy to set such a background: just set the **bgproperties** attribute of the **<body>** tag to a value of **"fixed"** when specifying a background.

```
<body background="democompanylogo.gif" bgproperties="fixed">
```

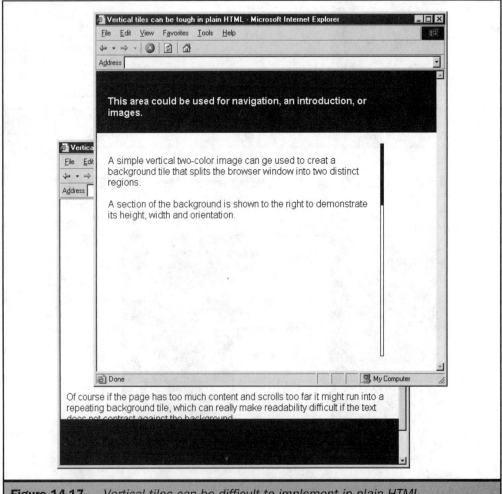

Figure 14-17. *Vertical tiles can be difficult to implement in plain HTML*

Background Images in Tables

Using simple HTML, it is possible to apply background images to tables as well. Defining a table with the code

```
<table width="220" border="1" cellpadding="0" cellspacing="0"
        background="smalltabletile.gif">
.... other table elements...
</table>
```

would place a repeating background tile behind the table, as shown here:

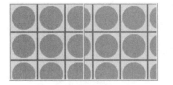

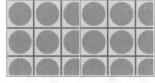

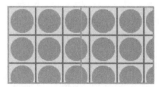

Internet Explorer   Netscape 4.7   Mozilla

The tables on the left and right, displayed in Internet Explorer and Netscape 6/ Mozilla, respectively, render the tile in a repeating background behind the entire table. The table in the center, displayed in Netscape 4.7, applies the background to each separate table cell. This is a radical cross-browser split that can really screw things up.

The same attribute can be applied to table rows (**<tr>**), but this will not display in Internet Explorer; and in Netscape 4, as in the preceding illustration, the tile applies to each cell in the row, not to the row as a whole. It will work in a standards-focused browser such as Mozilla 1.0/Netscape 6 and better. Interestingly, if you look at the HTML specifications, you'll discover that image backgrounds aren't supposed to be supported in tables at all, or so says the W3C.

Last, table cells as defined by the **<td>** tags often have their backgrounds set as demonstrated here:

```
<table width="220" border="1" cellpadding="0" cellspacing="0">
<tr>
<td width="110" background="bigtabletile.gif"> </td>
<td width="110" background="smalltabletile.gif"> </td>
</tr>
</table>
```

Be careful with using table backgrounds. Content sizing and reflow may result in interesting variations, just as they would as a document-wide background, as this example shows:

Once again, these problems can be better controlled through the use of CSS, which is the standards approach and is more future oriented.

Images and CSS

CSS itself is not used to insert foreground images into Web pages. This task is still handled by the **<img>** tag. However, it is used to control foreground images and to insert and control background images. Consider the markup here to insert an image:

```
<img src="demo.gif" alt="demo" id="demoimg" />
```

You could use CSS to size, position, and stroke the image. For example,

```
#demoimg {height: 100px; width: 100px;}
```

could be used instead of HTML **height** and **width** values. Of course, browsers will probably continue to rely on the HTML attributes, so don't dump them quite yet.

You could also avoid basic alignment settings in HTML and rely on CSS instead.

```
#demoimg {float: left;}
```

You could use margins or other features, but, for greater precision, you can position the image on the page with more specific use of CSS:

```
#demoimg {position: absolute; left: 100px; top: 50px; z-index: 3;}
```

As you saw in the last rule, you can even set z-index values and stack images on top of other page objects.

Last, some style effects like borders might make sense to set for some images:

```
#demoimg {border-style: double; border-width: 2px; color: orange;}
```

Most of these features can be accomplished with HTML, though less cleanly; it is with background images that CSS really shines.

CSS and Backgrounds

CSS can be used to apply background images to any display tag in HTML. For example, to set a background image for a page, just apply a rule to the **<body>** tag.

```
body {background: url(tile.gif);}
```

CSS isn't limited to page backgrounds; you could set them on anything, even paragraphs or **<span>** tags surrounding a few words.

```
<p style="padding: 5px; background: url(spottedtile.gif);">
Talking over<br />a busy tile<br />
can sure be<br />hard to read!
I wonder if <span style="background: url(bricks.gif); ">
this text is any more readable</span>
than the last section.
</p>
```

This markup would produce the following:

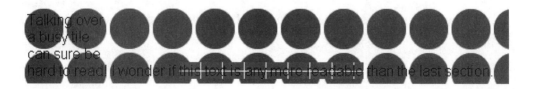

This still could be accomplished with tables, though in a very messy fashion.

CSS does have a very useful feature in that the repeat pattern of the background can be controlled. Recall that misbehaving background tiles can ruin an otherwise excellent design. For example, suppose you wished to use one large image in the background of a page. Using only regular HTML, you would have to create an estimated maximum size image and hope that no one would view it on a larger monitor or with a larger browser window than you had estimated. There is no way to guarantee that no one would use a larger monitor, and you would risk ruining the viewing experience of users with smaller monitors. Luckily, CSS provides a way to limit background tiling in Web pages:

```
<body bgcolor="#99ccff" style="background-image: url(sunnybeach.gif);
background-repeat: no-repeat;">
```

The background will only appear once:

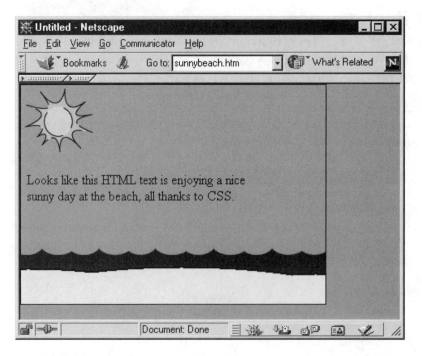

Other values you can use instead of **no-repeat** are **repeat-x** and **repeat-y**, which limit tiling to one axis only.

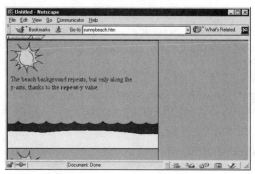   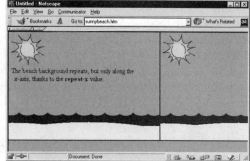

repeat-y   repeat-x

Needless to say, this will only work in CSS-compliant browsers. If you want the background image to display in older browsers, even though it will repeat, be sure to include it using the **background** attribute:

```
<body bgcolor="#99ccff" background="images/sunnybeach.gif"
  style="background: url(images/sunnybeach.gif) no-repeat;">
```

CSS1 also supports positioning of background images so that we don't have to rely on table cell backgrounds and background attachments to create the same effect as the **bgproperties="fixed"** value does in Internet Explorer. Appendix D contains a summary of the various CSS properties. Now we turn to a short discussion of image usage issues.

Image Usage

There are a number of issues associated with the use of images on the Web. Usability issues top the list, but correct sizing is very important—not just for usability, but also for simple economical reasons. Remember: images use bandwidth, and bandwidth costs money. Now you know why the really high traffic sites are dumping complex designs. We'll also discuss issues of image management and a few "gotchas" with image delivery, and end with a brief discussion of image usage concerns that designers should be aware of.

Usability and Images

Images definitely improve the Web, but there are downsides to their use. First, there are issues with color that was touched on in Chapter 13. When building a site that relies heavily on color, it is important to consider those who, for physical reasons, will perceive color in a dramatically different way than the average user. Many people suffer from some form of color-vision deficiency, commonly known as color blindness.

The most common color-vision problem is red-green color blindness. A person suffering from this form of color blindness lacks red cones in their eyes and thus confuses red and green. Given the prevalent use of red as a danger color and green as a safe color, this is a rather troublesome predicament.

Other forms of color blindness, such as blue-yellow color blindness—or even true color blindness, where the person can see only in shades of gray—are less common than red-green color-vision deficiency. Dealing with color-vision problems on the Web boils down to the following when it comes to images:

Suggestion: Don't rely solely on color, not only in links but also in informational graphics.

When using color as a key in an informational graphic such as a pie chart, consider using labels or patterns in case color cannot be seen, as shown in Figure 14-18.

Consider using colors in informational images with different lightness values. While color perception is a problem for some, intensity is usually not. Even if some users won't be able to distinguish color, they will be able to distinguish intensity.

Then there is always the option to simply not use images. This is obviously not the most visually pleasing solution. Using only text is going to be far less interesting, and

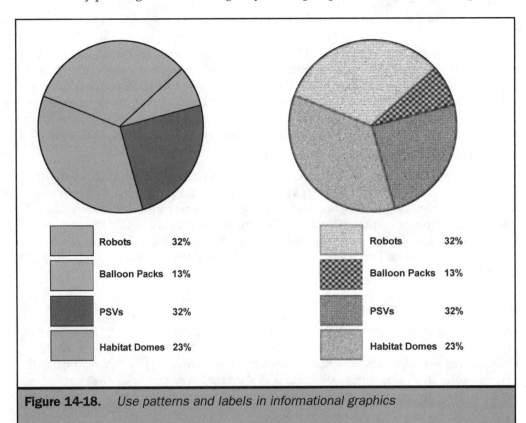

Figure 14-18.   *Use patterns and labels in informational graphics*

there may be information that requires the use of images to make sense. It is possible to have two versions of a site, one that is text-only and one with text and images. This is a possible solution, but data maintenance efforts could create an enormous amount of work to serve the needs of a small audience (if, for example, a database was not used to populate content). How about alternative text? Writing really good **alt** text could be extremely useful. If the user can't see the images, then the **alt** text will take their place. Speech-based browsers, once developed, might "speak" the **alt** text for the visually impaired. Overall, judicious use of carefully selected and optimized imagery in conjunction with thoughtful use of color will allow you to create powerful Web pages that are usable for the large majority of users.

Download/File Size Issues

Another concern is the matter of images slowing page download speeds. In fighting this problem, choosing the correct file format can make a huge difference. By choosing the correct format, you will be able to greater compress the images, thereby reducing the file size and allowing the page to download faster. It is important to be careful not to over-optimize by cutting the image into smaller pieces. While this does work to a certain extent, every image is a request to the server. Too many server requests can also start to slow the page down. The key is to find a good balance between the number of files and the overall page size.

Also remember that size really doesn't matter. You really only need to make users *think* they downloaded a large amount of data—by reusing the same images over and over—as long as they don't become bored. In short, you literally try to fool the user. An obvious way to speed up pages is to reuse imagery across pages. If you use the same navigational area across the top of all of your subpages, calling the same images on multiple pages takes advantage of the browser's cache. This means that the user downloads an image once and then reuses it, speeding up the experience of the site. Cutting things up appropriately so that images appearing on multiple pages can be cached will save the browser from having to re-download the images on every page.

While not exactly an "image" issue, the importance of good underlying code cannot be emphasized enough. The number of visually exciting sites brought to grief by poorly executed code is a shame, especially when good code is more a matter of attention to detail and good testing than anything else. The bottom line is that your images will perform better when your HTML and CSS are at their best.

Compression Issues

Another way of improving the usability of images with respect to download is to reduce the byte count in an image through compression. As discussed previously, image compression is handled by the image file format, so choosing the correct format for a particular image is integral to reducing byte count. A basic rule of thumb is to use GIF images for illustrations and JPEGs for photographs. Also, by setting the degree of compression when using a JPEG image, you can reduce file size with small sacrifice of image quality. Because the human eye can't often perceive the difference between an image of high quality and one of medium quality, tuning the image can often result in significant file size savings without a visual penalty.

While image size is certainly important to improving the loading time of Web pages, designers shouldn't get carried away with optimizing images without consideration for the rest of the Web process. There are many more factors that affect Web page performance, including the type and configuration of the Web server, the distance "traveled" on the Internet between the server and the end user, the traffic levels on the Internet at the time of site access, the software being used on the server to deliver the site and on the user's system to view the site, and even the processing speed of the user's computer. All of these factors affect the user's experience. Chapter 17 discusses this subject in depth.

Background Image Sizing Problems

Don't get too aggressive with your bandwidth reduction techniques; they can often backfire on you. For example, you might be tempted to minimize the file size of your background tile in order to reduce download time. Sometimes you will encounter a situation where you can see a screen "paint" the background image. This happens because a designer made the background image a single pixel tall, causing the background to tile as many times as the screen is high in pixels. With a slow video card, this may produce an annoying sweeping effect as the image fills in, pixel by pixel, down the screen. To avoid the background painting problem, balance physical file size and download size. If colors are kept to a minimum, there is no harm in making the image 20 or 30 pixels high. It will still be only a few kilobytes in size and will not incur any significant download penalty.

> **Suggestion: Do not make a background tile a very small height or width (for example, 1 or 2 pixels), since an annoying monitor flashing effect may result as the screen paints.**

Preloading Images

Preloading images is a possible method for improving Web page performance. You could selectively place an image or two for a successive page at the bottom of a previous page, scaled to a 1×1 pixel size in the code, which renders it invisible on the page where it preloads. Once it has been placed in the user's browser cache, it will render very quickly when the user requests the page where it is normally sized and is supposed to display. There are limited uses for this trick. It works best when you have a series of pages where the user will spend some time reviewing the visual materials before moving in a linear fashion to the next page in the series. This way, each image has been prepared for a guaranteed viewing session. This works well to a certain extent, but don't forget that it still has to download on whatever page you hide it on. The first page of the series will always have a significantly longer download time than the other pages, and this may cause users to exit before they get into the progression of images. Make sure that you don't try to preload too many images in this manner, and make sure that it isn't going to hurt the preloading page too much. You can also use JavaScript to try to be more judicious in your preloading. Some site acceleration services have begun to offer client-side preloading as a way to improve site usability.

Delivery Image Distortion

Occasionally, your images can be ruined by the sheer act of Web delivery. For example, America Online and some larger ISP users often encounter blurry images when viewing Web pages, particularly pages off their network. The reason for this is that many large networks, particularly AOL, use special proxy caches and acceleration systems that may recompress graphics for further bandwidth savings. In the case of AOL, the browser built into the client employs its own compression format, created by the Johnson-Grace company (now owned by AOL), which converts GIF, JPEG, and even BMP files into their own .ART format. On the consumer end, AOL users can deselect "User Compressed Graphics" from their Web preferences menu. On the designers end, there aren't many things you can do to *try* to minimize display issues under AOL. Thumbnail information in images has been known to mess up AOL compression, so don't save with previews or thumbnails when creating a Web image. However, there is really not much else that is known, at least publicly, about what the AOL compression does, though it can severely distort JPEG images at times.

Image distortion is not limited to AOL, since many Web caching and acceleration products will recompress graphics to save bandwidth; generally, they re-JPEG images, so it is quite easy for your graphics to be ruined in transit. So far, there is really no way to tell such recompressing systems to leave certain images alone, and you frankly don't know what your pages go through before hitting their end users. As you will see in Chapter 17, delivery really is important, since all your hard visual design work can be ruined by speed, network issues, and a variety of other things!

Image Management

When preparing images for use on your Web site, there are several things to keep in mind beyond file size, compression, and delivery. First, where do you store the images? It is a good idea to keep your images in their own directory. For most sites, you are going to end up with a lot of images, and it is much better, for organizational reasons, if you have them separated from everything else. Create a directory named "images" and keep all of the site images in it. It will dramatically improve maintenance operations on the site if all images are in one location.

> **Rule: Always store your images in a separate directory (usually /images).**

It is extremely important to name your images in a manner that makes sense. When viewing the directory, they will be in alphabetical order, so you want to make related images show up next to one another. For example, you could name your navigational images HNabout.gif, HNproducts.gif, and HNcontact.gif (HN standing for Home Navigation). That way, alphabetically, all the HNs will show up together in the directory. If the images were to have rollovers, you could name those HNOabout.gif, HNOproducts.gif, and HNOcontact.gif (HNO standing for Home Navigation On). Again, they will always show up next to one another in the images directory. You could continue this throughout the entire site by using names such as SN for Sub Navigation or PI for Product Images. Create your own standards, but keep the names as short and to the point as you can, while still making sure that you can figure out what they are.

Rule: Name your images in a logical fashion that groups them by purpose or usage.

Some Web design tools will cut up images and name them by the rows and columns in layout tables. While this seems logical, in practice, it often leads to confusion, so avoid naming by location and instead focus on use.

Protecting Images

A frequent question is how to protect images on the Web from being stolen. A common suggestion is to deny the user's ability to right-click the image to use the Save Image As feature of a browser. This is easily accomplished using JavaScript and the **oncontextmenu** event. For example, to disable right-click in an entire page, use the following code:

```
<body oncontextmenu="return false;">
```

You could even add a message telling the user the situation:

```
<body oncontextmenu="alert('Images (c) 2002 Demo Company, Inc'); return false; ">
```

Of course, you have just denied users the use of their context menu on anything. This can really annoy experienced users who like to right-click to navigate pages. Instead, you could put the **oncontextmenu** handler on each individual image,

```
<img src="robot.gif" alt="robot" oncontextmenu=" alert('Images (c)
2002 Demo Company, Inc'); return false;" />
```

so that only if the user were trying to copy it would they see the message shown.

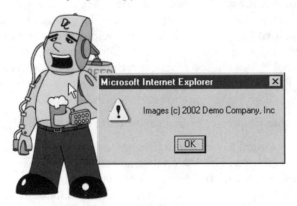

Of course, these approaches really only stop nonsavvy users. Everything will almost always be in the user's browser cache unless you've added special cache directives to avoid local saving, and even then, many browsers ignore such directives. Using a program to explore their cache or manually rummaging through their temporary files will uncover what they are looking for, regardless of right-click disabling. The user can also disable scripting and save images at will, or use an older browser that doesn't understand context-menu JavaScript directives. It's also quite simple to enter an image's URL directly into the browser. At this point, the solution might seem to be to put images in Flash or Java, but users can screen-grab the image if they really want it. The main thing to do is try to protect images and then make sure to watermark them in a graphics program for enforcement purposes later on. Some users think that image appropriation, as they call it, is their right. Unfortunately, some designers do as well.

Image Legalities

So you see all the really cool sites out there, but where do you get the cool images? There are a variety of ways in which to obtain great images. The first way would be to buy them. You can go about this a couple of ways. You could commission a photographer to take some pictures for you—in other words, pay for the photo shoot. You could also buy images from a vendor. There are many vendors that do nothing but sell images. As you might expect, good images cost significant amounts. There are also usability rights that must get cleared. You may get charged depending on how you plan to use the images—don't assume that paying one price will always get you limitless usage rights. The right to use an image might apply only on one page of your site, or only on the Web, or not on related print materials, and so on. These issues will vary from vendor to vendor. Obtaining images is actually relatively easy, but obtaining good images on a relatively tight budget with unlimited usage rights can be challenging. Finally, there are few images that can be used "as is," even if they are of good quality.

The expense of licensing images and the ease with which images can be copied have convinced many people that they can simply appropriate whatever images they need. Unfortunately, this is stealing the work of others. While there are stiff penalties for copyright infringement, it can be difficult to enforce these laws. Also, some page designers tend to bend the rules, thanks to the legal concept called *fair use*, which allows the use of someone else's copyrighted work under certain circumstances.

There are four basic questions used to define the fair-use doctrine.

First, is the work in question being appropriated for a nonprofit or profit use? The fair use defense is less likely to stand up if the "borrowed" work has been used to make money for someone other than its copyright holder.

Second, is the work creative (for example, a speculative essay on the impact of a recent congressional debate) or factual (a straightforward description of the debate without commentary)? Fair use would tend to apply more to the use of the factual work than to the use of the creative one.

Third, how much of the copyrighted work has been used? It is possible to use someone else's image if it is changed substantially from the original. The problem is determining what constitutes enough change in the image to make it a new work. Simply using a photo-editing tool to flip an image or change its colors is not enough. There is a fine line between using portions of another person's work and outright stealing. Even if you don't plan on using uncleared images, be careful of using images from free Internet clip art libraries. These so-called free images may have been submitted with the belief that they are free, but some of them may have been appropriated from a commercial clip art library somewhere down the line. Be particularly careful with high-quality images of famous individuals and commercial products. While such groups may often appreciate people using their images, the usage is generally limited to noncommercial purposes.

The third fair use question leads to the fourth. What impact does the image have on the economic value of the work? This whole discussion begs many legal questions that are far beyond the scope of this book. Suffice it to say that, in the long run, it's always safer to create original work, license images, or use material in the public domain. Just because many Web designers skirt the law doesn't mean that you should.

If you are artistically gifted, you can try creating the images yourself. You can use programs such as Adobe PhotoShop to create entirely new and unique images. If you are not an artist, you can hire a graphic designer or a design firm to create original images for you. This can be an expensive proposition and usually means that you will still have to purchase some stock imagery to use as the building blocks for your new designs. At best, unless you wish to limit your visual expression to unaltered clip art, you will need to invest part of your Web site budget into development of images.

Now that you are an image creator, you have to worry about controlling your visual property. How do you prevent someone from stealing your images from your Web site? You could try to use some advanced scripting or programming to prevent it, you could create images that are multipart and difficult to collect, you could embed a watermark within PhotoShop using Digimarc technology (http://www.digimarc.com), and so on. The issue, however, comes down to determining how you will know if someone takes images from your site and knowing what your legal options are if they do. You could have a legal team to constantly check for illegal use and then decide if you want to prosecute image thieves to stop them from using your images. Or, you could limit the images you use on your site to those you are willing to lose control over. You will always want to protect your logo and your brand name and images of your products, for instance. However, after applying the tips of the preceding section about watermarks and right-click limitations, you've done all you can without getting into digital rights issues, which are not well supported in today's browsers.

Summary

To recap, this chapter has examined various issues surrounding the use of images on the Web. Without images, Web sites can become quite boring. However, images should be properly optimized lest download time becomes a key concern. Choosing the correct file type, either GIF or JPEG, and tuning color and quality are the best ways to reduce image file size. New image formats such as PNG promise improved download support and image use for the Web; but so far, their use is not advised. Flash files make a lot of sense and will continue to be used, particularly when animation is required. Always be aware of the numerous usage details—for example, the improper use of transparency and anti-aliasing can ruin an image, and background tiles can be easily ruined when seams are seen in the tile or when tiles are too small or too wide. Designers certainly have their hands full with the images on the Web, even before considering how to make something look pleasing. The next chapter will look at the relationship between Web page design and graphical interface design and what Web designers can and should learn from it.

Chapter 15

GUI Widgets and Forms

A Web site is really a modified form of a traditional graphical user interface (GUI) program. While not all conventions survived the translation to the environment of the Web, such as double clicking, many conventions have. It is important for Web designers to understand the traditions of GUI design so as not to utilize GUI widgets like menus, fill-in fields, and so on, in ways that may confuse a user already familiar with how software applications tend to use these items. However, never assume that the Web is exactly the same as a GUI-driven software application. Differences do occur; some Web technologies like HTML forms do not yet provide all the interactive elements commonly found in software applications. This chapter presents the commonly used forms and GUI widgets found in Web sites, with an emphasis on usage that can improve site usability.

Web Sites vs. GUI Applications

It is tempting to simply apply the rules of interface design used to build typical GUI software applications to the Web. Considering that a Web site really is a form of software, this makes a great deal of sense. However, Web design is not quite GUI design. It borrows heavily from GUI design principles, but it has its own conventions as well.

What makes Web sites different from GUI applications? First, consider the delivery of Web sites and the medium of the Web. Web sites generally are delivered incrementally, often a page at a time. Software applications tend to be installed, either after downloading a complete package from the Internet or by using a CD-ROM or diskette. The simple fact that the software application is completely installed in most cases makes it much more responsive than a Web-delivered one. However, the benefit of the Web's incremental delivery approach is that users do not have to actually install anything more than they need. Web sites lack what could be called the "install-uninstall barrier" of a traditional application. With most software, users have to have the initiative to find, download, or purchase a piece of software and then install it—just to try it out. If the program isn't quite what they are looking for, they may even have to reverse the procedure with an uninstaller. Because of the hassle of installation and removal, users may be hesitant to try something new and slow to remove a less-than-ideal package. However, Web sites do not have such an install-uninstall barrier. A simple click, and users are off to another site.

The install-uninstall barrier has interesting ramifications for Web design. Because Web sites do not have this barrier, they often have to perform very well because the user can easily move on to a competing site. Because of this, many sites strive to become "sticky." Sticky sites keep users coming back often by providing a valuable service that is difficult to transfer to another site. Consider why sites offer free e-mail accounts, a calendar, and massive customization. It makes users less likely to want to move on, even if the site isn't quite perfect.

> **Suggestion: Provide a useful service that is difficult to transfer between sites to improve site "stickiness."**

Another interesting aspect of software design versus Web design is the heavy reliance on documentation by software. Web site designers building public sites generally cannot expect users to read a manual in order to use their site, whether the manual is provided online in the form of a help section or offline in the form of a printed manual. The function and use of sites must be obvious. Unfortunately, creating such a site can be difficult; there are bound to be aspects or operations of the site that users will not understand, no matter how well the site is designed. Documentation should still be provided. Public sites may provide help in the form of online help pages. Internal Web projects such as intranet or extranet sites may provide hard copy documentation or even training classes. However, as with software applications, expecting users to access help documents or read the manual is unrealistic. Given that users have come to expect Web sites to be easy to use, it is problematic to rely on documentation to make up for site flaws.

> **Suggestion: Provide online documentation (or in some cases printed documentation) for sites, but don't rely on the user accessing it.**

The degree of marketing influence on interface design is much greater with Web sites than for most commercial software applications. Given two word processing programs, it would be somewhat difficult to correctly identify the programs after only a brief inspection. Most software applications only subtly brand with their interface. Rarely do you see software programs with hot pink and oddly shaped buttons; most tend to lay out the screen in about the same way and utilize similar icons. On the Web, however, marketing is often directly integrated into the user interface. In some sense, you could say that, with a Web site, the box and the application are one and the same. In the case of software, often the branding is done mostly through the box, documentation and other collateral material, the installation screen, a splash dialog shown on startup, and subtle interface details in the program. Web sites are often more heavy handed in their integration, with marketing demands a priority because they lack many of the outlets for branding beyond the interface.

However, one of the biggest differences between GUI design and Web design is that, with GUI design, there is a lack of recognized groups, such as operating system vendors, to set a standard. While the World Wide Web Consortium (http://www.w3.org) and browser vendors certainly try to influence how people approach Web design, they do not wield the power of interface standards that Apple and Microsoft have with application developers. The Web lacks recognized standards of interface design. Instead, conventions of design have arisen online, influenced by the innovations of browser vendors and individual site creators, as well as by previous GUI design ideas. Understanding GUI design conventions is important for Web designers because many of them can be quickly applied to Web sites.

GUI Design Implications

Graphical interface design has nearly 20 years of commercial experience. Many of the ideas of Web design follow directly from early findings from Xerox and Apple and, later, Microsoft. Apple, in particular, has been very influential in the field of interface design. In fact, the Macintosh operating system was developed with ten interface principles in mind, most of which relate directly to the usability ideas of Chapter 2. Given the great importance of these principles in shaping modern interface design, it would be interesting to see how they apply to the Web. As it turns out, most hold up quite well, and Web designers should try to apply these principles to their sites. However, some of the rules should be modified with the Web in mind, and a couple of new rules ought to be added, given the different medium of the Web. Remember that network and content aspects of the Web are different from those of traditional software. Table 15-1 presents the original Apple interface design principles, along with commentary and possible modification for use on the Web.

While the preceding discussion shows just how much GUI conventions influence Web conventions, new conventions are still emerging, and many designers seem

GUI Principle	Commentary	Web Principle	Commentary
1. Metaphors from the real world	Concrete metaphors from the real world should be applied so that users have expectations to apply to the computer environment.	1. Metaphors from the real world, including GUI metaphors.	Given the familiarity people have with GUI systems, the Web variation could be "Metaphors from the real world including existing software metaphors." The window, icon, mouse, and pointer approach is a metaphor of its own for many users. Break with these common metahors too much within a Web page and you'll go against a user's expectations of how the site should act.
2. Direct manipulation	Users want to feel that they are in control of the computer's activities.	2. Direct manipulation	This is as true for a Web site as for a software application. The only downside is that direct manipulation may be difficult to sustain in a network delivery environment with relatively slow response times.
3. See-and-point (instead of remember-and-type)	User interfaces should rely on recognition rather than recall. In practice, make sure to present choices plainly onscreen so a user can simply choose from them.	3. See-and-point (instead of remember-and-click)	No major difference here, except that we do not have to deal with the downsides of keyboard command interfaces on the Web. Given the amount of sites a user may see, this becomes more important within a sequence of Web sites, as users will probably not be able to memorize many specific details from all the sites they visit.

Table 15-1. *General Principles of GUI Design Modified for the Web*

ELEMENTS OF PAGE DESIGN

GUI Principle	Commentary	Web Principle	Commentary
4. Consistency	Effective applications are both consistent within themselves and with one another.	4. Consistency	This applies directly to the Web. Web sites should be consistent internally *and* follow conventions set by other Web sites. The only nuance in this idea on the Web is that a centralized body such as an operating system vendor is lacking to enforce conformance to conventions.
5. WYSIWYG (what you see is what you get)	The users get exactly what they see—no more, no less. Secrets are not kept from the user. A particularly important aspect of this idea early on was to make sure that what is seen onscreen is what shows up on paper when printed.	5. WYSIWYW (what you see is what you want)	For the Web, WYSIWYG should be modified to WYSIWYW (what you see is what you want). Users may like to modify sites to display information they are interested in rather than what is set out for them. In a diverse environment like the Web—with many ways to access information (including cell phone, PDA, and computing systems of all shapes and sizes)—the idea of WYSIWYG doesn't work well. The printing aspect may still be somewhat important, but for many users, exact printing may be less important than appropriate printing. Notice all the print versions versus Web version pages that exist in content-rich sites.
6. User control	The user, not the computer, initiates and controls all actions.	6. Balance of control	Control should be given to the user (Chapter 2), but the appearance of control is more the issue. Users should be guided in many situations, depending on the purpose of the site.
7. Feedback and dialog	Keep the user engaged and provide plenty of feedback, such as messages and status indicators, to let a user know what is going on.	7. Feedback and dialog	On the Web, this is more important than ever, especially considering the responsiveness problem of the Web. Sites should provide more feedback to the user.

Table 15-1.   *General Principles of GUI Design Modified for the Web* (continued)

GUI Principle	Commentary	Web Principle	Commentary
8. Forgiveness	Users will make mistakes, so we have to forgive them and allow them to undo things or keep them from doing things that could be very damaging.	8. Forgiveness	This rule certainly applies to Web sites. Not every site provides adequate confirmation of important actions, such as order placement, that are difficult to undo. As sites become more software-like, this rule will become more and more important.
9. Perceived stability	Users will find comfort in a computer environment that remains familiar rather than changing randomly.	9. Perceived stability	This rule is well applied in GUI applications. Notice that menus don't jump around the screen or change their ordering. Unfortunately, Web sites often do not give an appearance of perceived stability and may change button style or position or even choices, seemingly arbitrarily. Sites could be improved dramatically just by strict conformance to this principle.
10. Aesthetic integrity	An interface should be clear and pleasing. Design should be consistent, but objects that are different should be distinctly different.	10. Aesthetic integrity	For the Web, this is very important. Users will judge sites severely if they have poor appearances.
		11. Quality content	Web sites are heavily geared toward content. Web sites should provide high-quality content that is well written, provides the appropriate level of detail, is clear and easy to comprehend, and is—above all—accurate.
		12. Time sensitive	Web sites need to be sensitive to time. Time of delivery is the most important aspect of many sites. Users will not stand for inefficient delivery. Timeliness of content and interface may also be important. Sites tend not to be as static as traditional software.

Table 15-1.   *General Principles of GUI Design Modified for the Web* (continued)

completely oblivious to useful GUI design ideas. The rest of the chapter will present the various interface widgets used in interactive design and will explain how they are used on the Web. Careful attention will be paid to widgets that are used slightly differently than those in traditional software applications.

Windows

The first interface component to consider is the window. All Web pages are displayed in a window—the browser window. The browser window serves as the frame for a page. Without this framing device, site design may often look strange, as shown in Figure 15-1.

The exact look of the browser window varies from browser to browser. In some situations, the browser window may not be terribly evident. Television browsers, like WebTV/MSNTV, and many embedded browsers, such as cellular phone browsers, provide few framing features. A textual browser like Lynx running from a UNIX prompt also does not provide much framing. Figure 15-2 shows a range of framing effects for a browser.

It is even possible now to customize the look of browsers. Various Internet Explorer browser extensions, such as HotBar (http://www.hotbar.com) and the core Mozilla

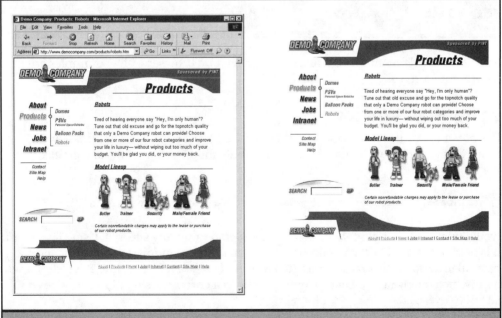

Figure 15-1.   *The browser window frames a Web page*

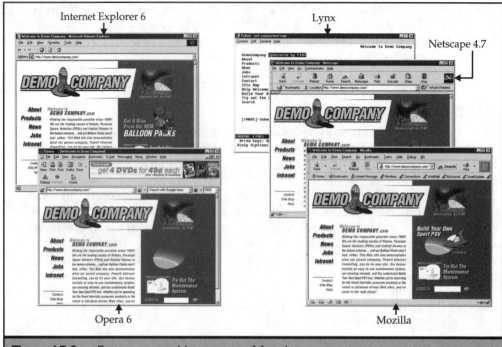

Figure 15-2. *Browsers provide a range of framing*

browser, provide methods to offer custom skins for a browser. A few examples are shown in Figure 15-3.

Creating New Windows

It is possible to customize windows in HTML and JavaScript. The simplest way to create a new window is to use the target attribute modification of the anchor element. For example,

```
<a href="http://www.democompany.com" target="_blank">Open window</a>
```

would open a new browser window with the Demo Company site in it. Using JavaScript, it is possible to modify the window that is opened. The window can be sized, and the particular buttons shown can be limited as well. For example, consider the code shown here, which opens up the Demo Company site in a chromeless window and sizes it to 600×500 pixels:

```
<a href="http://www.democompany.com"
onclick="newwindow=window.open('http://www.democompany.com','democompany',
'width=600,height=500'); return false;>
Open window</a>
```

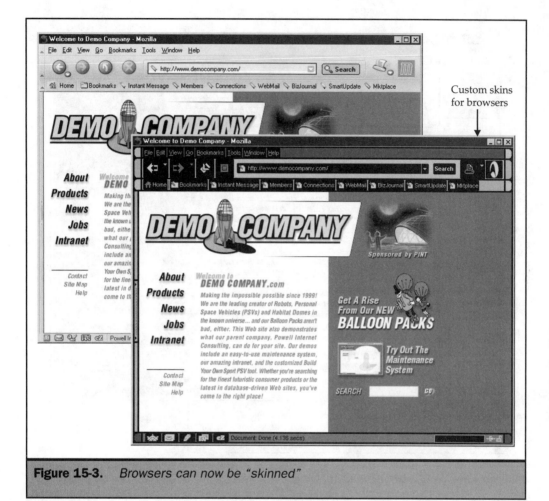

Figure 15-3.   *Browsers can now be "skinned"*

Note *It is possible using JavaScript to turn on some buttons, status bars, and so on. It isn't an all-or-nothing situation when creating new windows. See JavaScript documentation on the **window.open( )** method for specific syntax on allowing buttons.*

Figure 15-4 shows the rendering of the chromeless window. Notice in the figure that much of the control has been taken away from the user. They aren't sure where they are, since the URL is hidden, browser buttons they may have come to rely on have been hidden, and even scrolling the page seems difficult. It should be evident that browsing a site within this type of window might be frustrating for some users, particularly novices. Unfortunately, some designers use this technique to create a fixed page size, so they don't have to worry about their design stretching to fit a browser window. While the framing effect of the perfectly sized chromeless window might improve the look, the usability

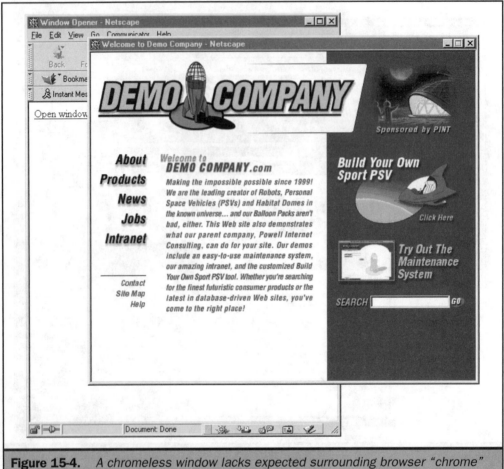

Figure 15-4. *A chromeless window lacks expected surrounding browser "chrome" and buttons*

tradeoffs are significant. Designers are warned not to use this technique unless absolutely necessary. Secondary windows that present a short message such as an alert can be significantly modified, but the primary window the user will use to navigate your site should not be modified in most situations.

Suggestion: Avoid modification of the appearance of the user's primary browser window.

When opening new windows, you have to be sure that the window is visible to the user. Occasionally, it may move out of the way, or it may be positioned behind other windows if it is automatically lowered. In order to combat these problems, you may wish to position and raise created windows. To set the position in Netscape 4, set the *screenX* and *screenY* parameters when creating the window. For Internet Explorer 4 and beyond, set the top and left parameters. Mozilla 1.0 appears to support both forms of syntax. Simply focusing the created window using its **focus( )** method should bring it back to the top. The following code shows how this would be accomplished, using a link to trigger the new window:

```
<a href="http://www.democompany.com"
onclick="newwindow=window.open('http://www.democompany.com',
'democompany','width=600,height=500,screenX=100,screenY=100,
top=100,left=100'); newwindow.focus(); return false";>
Open window</a>
```

Full-Screen Windows

Creating a window that fills up the screen and even removes browser chrome is possible in many browsers. It is possible under 4.*x* generation browsers and beyond to figure out the current screen size and then create a new window that fits most or all the available area. In the case of Netscape, you may have difficulty covering the entire window because of the way the height and width of the screen are calculated. However, the script presented here should work to fill up the screen in both browsers.

```
<script type="text/javascript">
<!--
newwindow=window.open('http://www.democompany.com','main','height='+screen.height+
',width='+screen.width+',screenX=0,screenY=0,left=0,top=0,resizable=no');
//-->
</script>
```

The preceding "poor man's" script does keep the browser chrome and may not quite fill up the window. It is possible under many browsers to go into a full-screen mode that completely fills the screen. Using Internet Explorer, it is quite easy using a JavaScript statement like this:

```
newwindow=window.open('http://www.democompany.com', 'main',
'fullscreen=yes');
```

However, Netscape needs a much more complicated script and will even prompt the user if a security privilege should be granted to go full-screen. A script that works in both browsers is shown here:

```
<script type="text/javascript">
<!--
```

```
if (window.navigator.appName == "Netscape")
{
netscape.security.PrivilegeManager.enablePrivilege('UniversalBrowserWrite');
 window.open('http://www.democompany.com','newwin','titlebar=no,width=' +
window.screen.availWidth+',height='+window.screen.availWidth+',screenX=0,screenY=0')
}
else if (window.navigator.appName == "Microsoft Internet Explorer")
    {
      window.open('http://www.democompany.com', 'newwin', 'fullscreen=yes');
    }
   else
   { /* do the best we can to go fullscreen */
  newwindow=window.open('http://www.democompany.com','main','height='+screen.height+
',width='+screen.width+',screenX=0,screenY=0,left=0,top=0,resizable=no');
   }

//-->
</script>
```

It is important to note that many users will not know how to get out of full-screen mode. The key combination ALT-F4 should do the trick on a Windows system. However, users may not know this, so you should provide a Close button or instructions on how to get out of full-screen mode.

Rule: When using a full-screen window, inform the user how to exit or provide a Close button.

While it seems annoying that Netscape prompts the user, it is probably a good idea not to force a full screen on people. Users may want to keep another window open while they browse your site or copy content from your site into another document. Forcing full-screen mode takes their options away.

Suggestion: Do not go full screen without asking the user first.

Sub-Windows

Sub-windows are secondary windows that are presented to users to allow them to perform a task on, or inform them about what's going on in, the primary browser window. In GUI parlance, these windows are generally called "dialog boxes," since they are used to carry on a dialog with a user. A common use of a dialog box on the Web is to alert users about errors made during form fill-out, to warn them about irreversible actions such as deleting content or making a payment, and to collect small bits of information from them such as login or password information. Dialog boxes can contain just about any amount of information and may be customized to look a particular way. However, in the case of most Web sites, dialogs are created using simple JavaScript and tend to have a standard look and feel, unless the designer has gone specifically out of their way to customize their presentation.

Alerts

In a GUI application, an *alert* is a small dialog box used to present an important message to the user. Often, alerts are used to inform users of errors made—particularly during form fill-out. Alerts can be created directly in JavaScript using the **alert( )** method of the Window object. For example, consider this markup:

```
<form>
 <input type="button" value="Press Me"
 onclick="window.alert('Red Alert!')" /;>
</form>
```

Pressing the form button creates a browser modal dialog with a short message saying "Red Alert!" in a JavaScript-capable browser. The alert usually contains a special icon, a message indicating that it is the browser issuing the alert and not some other application on the user's system, and an OK button used to dismiss the dialog. However, the specific rendering of the alert box varies fairly significantly from browser to browser. Figure 15-5 shows a variety of renderings for the alert.

It is important to consider the modal nature of an alert message. An application *modal window* is one that blocks action within the application. In the case of the alert, users must dismiss the dialog in the window before continuing on in the current browser window, though in many modern operating systems they can switch to another application before closing the alert. A *system modal* dialog would be one that blocks all action on the user's system until dismissed. While it may be possible to create a system modal dialog in Internet Explorer, doing so would be in extremely poor taste. Even though alerts are commonly just browser modal dialogs, they should be used sparingly. Avoid welcoming people to your site or providing noncritical information to the user by using an alert.

> **Suggestion: Use alerts to inform the user of important issues, not general information.**

The look and feel of JavaScript-generated alert boxes may leave something to be desired. The size and style of the dialogs are not easily modified using the basic **window.alert( )** JavaScript method. However, it is possible to create custom alert dialogs—complete with their look and feel and buttons. For example, consider the custom alert shown here:

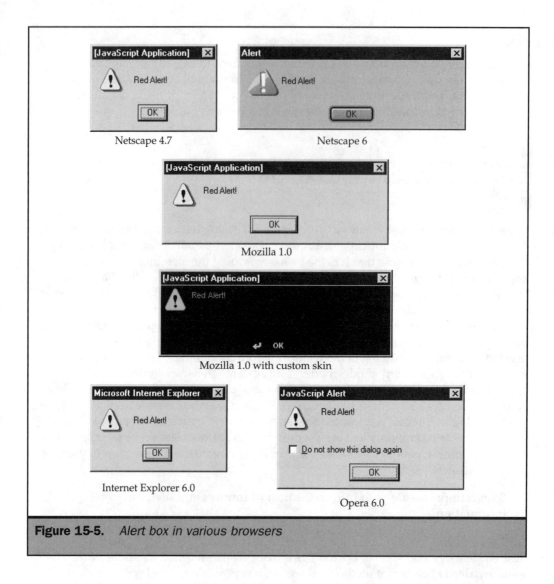

Figure 15-5. *Alert box in various browsers*

To create an alert of this style requires coding a custom piece of JavaScript that creates a special modal window that acts like an alert, complete with an OK button to dismiss the dialog. However, consider when custom alerts should really be used. While it may be nice to create alerts that fit with the marketing aspects of a site, it may be more important to do more than just make improvements to the meaning of the alerts. In traditional GUI design, there are three forms of common alerts: informational alerts, which provide important information; warning alerts, which warn the user about actions taken or reversible mistakes made; and error alerts, which present very important information, such as the occurrence of a serious error or failure. The typical icons for each of these dialogs are shown in Figure 15-6.

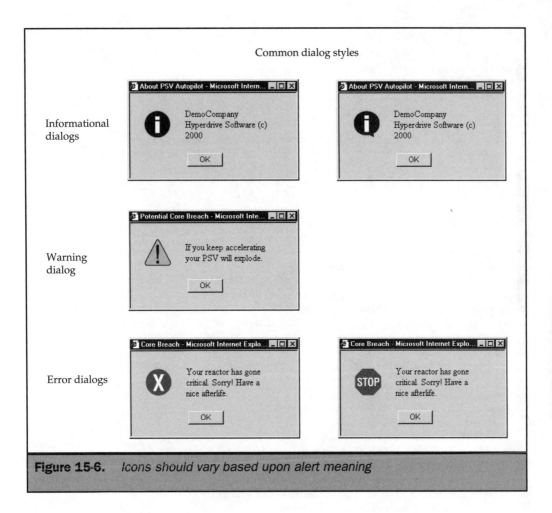

Figure 15-6. *Icons should vary based upon alert meaning*

A custom alert script to present informational, warning, and error alerts is presented here:

```
<!DOCTYPE HTML PUBLIC "-//W3C//DTD XHTML 1.0 Transitional//EN"
"http://www.w3.org/TR/xhtml1/DTD/transitional.dtd">
<html xmlns="http://www.w3.org/1999/xhtml">
<head>
<title>Custom Alerts</title>
<script type="text/javascript">
<!--
function customAlert(alerttype, title, msg)
{
var icon;
```

```
if (alerttype == "error")
 icon = "icons/stop.gif";
else if (alerttype == "info")
 icon = "icons/info.gif";
 else
 icon = "icons/exclaim.gif";

if (window.navigator.appName == "Microsoft Internet Explorer")
  newalert = window.open("", "alertwindow", "width=300,height=150,modal=yes");
else
  newalert = window.open("", "alertwindow", "width=300,height=150");


newalert.document.writeln('<!DOCTYPE HTML PUBLIC "-//W3C//DTD XHTML 1.0
Strict//EN" "http://www.w3.org/TR/xhtml1/DTD/xhtml1-strict.dtd">');
newalert.document.writeln('<html xmlns="http://www.w3.org/1999/xhtml">');
newalert.document.writeln('<head>');
newalert.document.writeln('<title>'+title+'</title>');
newalert.document.writeln('</head>');
newalert.document.writeln('<body bgcolor="#CCCCCC" onblur="self.focus()">');
newalert.document.writeln('<table cellpadding="10">');
newalert.document.writeln('<tr>');
newalert.document.writeln('<td width="50">');
newalert.document.writeln('<img src='+icon+' width="50" height="50" border="0"
alt="['+alerttype+']" align="left" />');
newalert.document.writeln('</td>');
newalert.document.writeln('<td width="150">');
newalert.document.writeln(msg);
newalert.document.writeln('</td></tr>');
newalert.document.writeln('<tr><td align="center" colspan="2"><form>');
newalert.document.writeln('<input type="button" value="   OK
  " onclick="window.close()" />');
newalert.document.writeln('</form></td></tr></table>');
newalert.document.writeln('</body></html>');

newalert.focus();

}
// -->
</script>
</head>
<body bgcolor="#cccccc">

<form>

<input type="button" value="Info Dialog" onclick="customAlert('info','Core
Breach', 'Demo Company Hyperdrive Software (c) 2000';)" />

<input type="button" value="Warning Dialog" onclick="customAlert('warn','Potential
```

```
Core Breach', 'If you keep accelarating your PSV will explode.');" />

<input type="button" value="Error Dialog" onclick="customAlert('error','Core
Breach', 'Your reactor has gone critical. Sorry! Have a nice afterlife.');" />

</form>
</body>
</html>
```

Online: http://www.webdesignref.com/examples/customalerts.htm

Note that the scripts presented here assume the user has the images locally for each type of dialog. These icons can easily be saved from the working example online.

Confirms

In a GUI application, a confirm dialog box is presented when a confirmation is required before performing some task. The confirm is often used as an "Are you sure?" question for the user, and it is usually presented before the user performs a task that may not be easily reversible, such as deleting a file or placing an order. Confirmation dialogs can be created directly in JavaScript using the **confirm( )** method of the Window object:

```
<form>
 <input type="button" value="Press Me"
 onclick="window.confirm('Do you really want to blow up the ship?');" />
</form>
```

The JavaScript **confirm( )** method creates a browser modal dialog with a short message asking the user a simple question and providing an OK and a CANCEL button for making the response. As with the alert dialog, the specific rendering of a confirmation dialog varies from browser to browser. Figure 15-7 shows a variety of renderings of confirm dialogs generated from JavaScript.

The use of confirms should be limited to those situations where you want to warn users of an action they are about to take or to have them answer a simple question. Typical uses of the confirm dialog would be to ask the user if the contents of a form should be cleared or submitted for processing, or if an irreversible task such as deleting an online account should be allowed to take place.

Suggestion: Use a confirmation dialog to verify the execution of an irreversible or important task, such as form submission.

When asking confirmation questions, consider the formation of the question carefully, since the standard JavaScript confirmation dialog buttons are labeled OK and CANCEL. Asking a "Yes or No" question like "Do You Want to Delete the File?" may

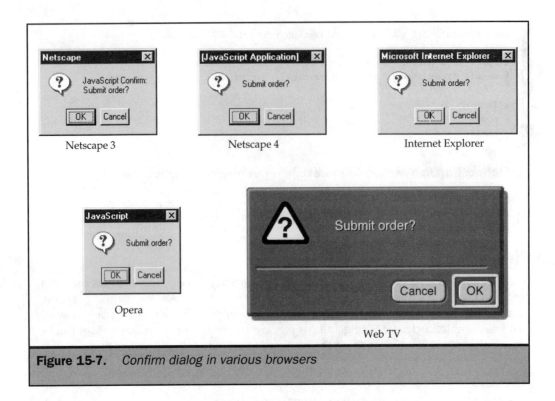

Figure 15-7. *Confirm dialog in various browsers*

be confusing to a novice user faced with the JavaScript confirmation dialog buttons. Instead, write a message like "Delete the file?"

The look and feel of JavaScript-generated confirmation dialogs, like that of alert dialogs, may leave something to be desired. The size, style, and buttons cannot be modified using the basic **window.confirm()** JavaScript method. As with alerts, it is, of course, possible to create custom confirm dialogs that fit with the look and feel of the site, as shown here:

However, besides controlling the look and feel of the window, designers should provide different icons and button text for confirm dialogs, depending on the type of confirmation. A custom confirmation dialog script could be created similar to the one presented for alerts, but for full emulation we will have to require our routine to return True or False depending upon the user's choice.

Prompts

A prompt dialog box is presented when a small amount of information is needed from the user to perform some task. Usually, a prompt dialog is used to collect a single line of information in answer to some question. For example, the user may be prompted to enter a special offer code. Prompt dialogs can be created directly in JavaScript using the **prompt( )** method of the Window object:

```
<form name="testform" id="testform">
Answer: <input type="text" value="" name="favcolor" id="favcolor" size="20" />
<input type="button" value="Ask Me"
onclick="document.testform.favcolor.value=window.prompt('What is your favorite
color?',' ');" />
</form>
```

The **prompt( )** JavaScript method creates a browser modal dialog with a short message asking the user a simple question. A default answer can also be provided. When prompted, the user can press the OK button when done or CANCEL to not respond. As with the alert and confirmation dialogs, the specific rendering of a confirmation dialog varies from browser to browser. Figure 15-8 shows a variety of renderings of prompt dialogs generated from JavaScript.

The use of prompts should be limited to those situations where you want to collect a single line of text—usually a short answer to a simple question. Typically, the prompt dialog is used to ask users for their name or for a value to put in a form field that wasn't filled in.

> **Suggestion: Use prompt dialogs only to ask a user to provide a short word or numeric answer to a simple question. Do not ask questions that would result in a multiple-line answer.**

Make sure that you clearly indicate what type of information you are looking to collect, such as number or text string.

The look and feel of JavaScript-generated prompt dialogs, like the previously described dialogs, may leave something to be desired. The size, style, and buttons cannot be modified using the basic **window.prompt( )** JavaScript method. As with

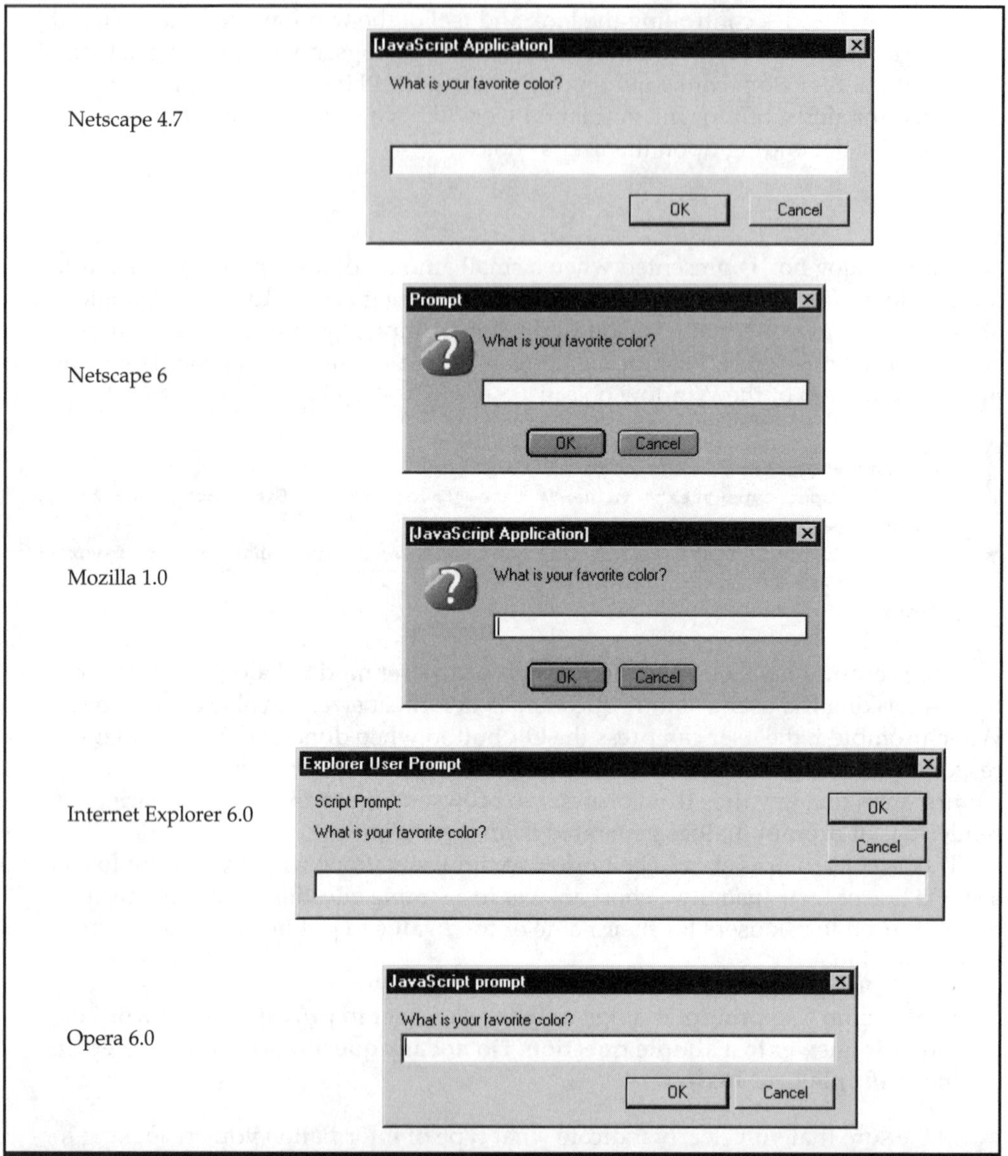

Netscape 4.7

Netscape 6

Mozilla 1.0

Internet Explorer 6.0

Opera 6.0

Figure 15-8.   *Prompt dialog in various browsers*

alerts and confirms, it is obviously possible to create custom prompt dialogs that fit with the look and feel of the site, as shown next.

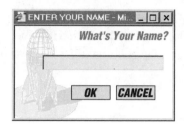

Forms

The primary way that a user interacts with a Web site besides selecting links is through the various form elements, such as text fields, radio buttons, pull-down menus, and so forth. GUI design theory has a great deal to say about how to use these elements properly; but, unfortunately, given the limited capabilities of HTML form widgets, sometimes it is difficult to implement a modern GUI from within a Web page. The next few sections discuss each of the form elements and provide an overview of their proper use.

Labels

Form elements should be clearly labeled. A label should provide a description that indicates what a form element does or what kind of data should be entered in the element. Labels may include both text and graphics. Here are a few examples of labels:

Email: ▯

email ▯

✉ *email* ▯

The position of labels should be close to the field they are describing. Often, the label is either to the left or above the field. Sometimes, a table may be used to associate the label and the field together. All three ideas are shown here:

Name: ▯

Name:
▯

Name: ▯

HTML 4.0 and XHTML define the **<label>** to be used to signify the label for a particular field, but few developers seem to use it. However, the **<label>** tag can be used in interesting ways. For example, consider having CSS rules like the ones shown here:

```
label {color: black; font-weight: bold;}
label.required {color: red;}
```

In the form, it would be easy enough to wrap the individual fields with **<label>** tags and even indicate required fields, like so:

```
<label>Name:
 <input type="text" name="name" id="name" />
</label>

<label class="required">E-mail:
 <input type="text" name="email" id="email" />
</label>
```

Labels and Field Selection

In some browsers, the **<label>** contents can be clicked to select the field. The idea is that when the label receives focus from the user, either by clicking it or using an accelerator key, the focus should switch to the associated field. The reality is that, in many browsers, this doesn't work. This is a big reason not to use an **accesskey** attribute on a label, but rather on the field, as discussed later in the chapter. However, the click-select action of the label can easily be simulated using a little bit of JavaScript:

```
<form name="myform" id="myform">
<label onclick="document.myform.firstname.focus();">
 First Name:
<input type="text" name="firstname" id="firstname" />
</label>
</form>
```

In this example, a modern browser will bring the cursor to the associated field when the user clicks the label by using the **focus()** method on the field. Fortunately, older browsers will just ignore the **<label>** tag, as well as the JavaScript on the associated intrinsic event handler attribute.

Text Fields

HTML provides for single-line text fields using markup like this:

```
<input type="text" />
```

For eventual processing by server-side programs or validation by client-side scripts, the fields should always be named with the **name** as well as **id** attribute.

```
<input type="text" name="age" id="age" />
```

In the future, the **id** attribute will be the only naming required, but the **name** attribute should be used for backward compatibility and is still actually favored by some newer browsers, notably Internet Explorer 6.0.

Setting the size of the text field will depend on the data being entered, but it is far better to use HTML to limit the field size to a particular range than to permit the user to enter more data than is allowed. For example, if you are asking for the user's age, two or perhaps three digits should be the maximum allowed. Two digits would allow a range of 0–99. Setting the size of the text field is easy in HTML—it requires specifying the size of the field in number of characters to show using the **size** attribute, like so:

```
<input type="text" name="age" id="age" size="2" />
```

Suggestion: Set the length of text fields to reasonably fit data being provided.

Age: `58` *not* Age: `58`

One troublesome aspect of the text input field in HTML is that the size of the field doesn't seem to always match the amount of data that can be input in the field visually. Consider the fields and data shown in Figure 15-9. Without applying style sheet rules, there isn't necessarily any guarantee the data will not extend past the region provided or not fill up the region itself. This is an annoying quirk that varies among browsers and versions.

The visual size of a field doesn't necessarily limit the amount of data that can be put in the field under HTML. To limit the field, you would have to use the **maxlength** attribute like so:

```
<input type="text" name="age" id="age" size="2" maxlength="2" />
```

Once the user hits the limit, the browser should not allow more data to be entered and will probably sound the system beep or perform some other indication the limit has been reached if the user continues to type.

If you do not set the **maxlength** attribute, the data will not be limited and the field will scroll to the right as a user types in data. You should really always try to set **maxlength**. A user maliciously pasting, say, 10,000 characters into a field may cause problems for server-side processing. Hackers often utilize unconstrained fields that are run on servers to try to run commands from the form. Of course, **maxlength** doesn't really provide much help, since it is easy enough to falsify the form and remove the

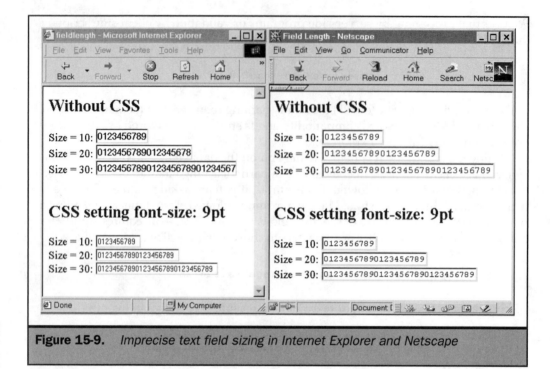

Figure 15-9. *Imprecise text field sizing in Internet Explorer and Netscape*

maxlength restriction. Improved security comes by checking the passed form data no matter what, but don't use that as an excuse not to set **maxlength** because not doing so is just plain careless.

> **Rule: Always set a maxlength value for a text field.**

Always attempt to make a text field large enough to hold the data without scrolling. Users should be able to see all the text they have input in case they forget what they entered. The only time the **maxlength** value should be larger than the actual size of the text field is when the field is too big to fit the available screen real estate.

> **Rule: Allow a text field to scroll rightward only when there is a premium on screen real estate and the data to be entered is larger than the available screen region.**

Password Fields

A password field is a modified single-line text field that does not echo the characters typed to the screen, instead showing an asterisk or similar character. The main purpose of the password field is to provide limited security by making "shoulder surfing"—

where a person looks over your shoulder to see your password—more difficult. The syntax for the password text field form is similar to a single-line text field:

```
<input type="password" name="secret" id="secret" size="10" maxlength="10" />
```

The rendering of the password field is fairly similar in browsers and should look something like this:

Password: `**********`

Given that users will not be able to see what they are typing, it is very unwise to let the field scroll. A user typing a very long password may suddenly forget what letter was just typed as the field scrolls. The user will not be able to easily determine the number of characters typed, so will probably be forced to reenter the entire password. To combat this potential problem, set the **maxlength** and **size** the same to avoid scrolling.

Rule: Never allow password fields to scroll.

Another consideration with passwords is that they tend to have a maximum length. Make sure to limit the password field to match the length.

Rule: Limit the length of password fields to match password sizes.

An obvious rule that should not have to be stated is not to use default values with password fields. All the user has to do is view the source in order to see what the password is!

Rule: Do not use default values with password fields.

Multi-Line Text Entry

A multi-line text area defined in HTML using the **<textarea>** tag is used to collect larger amounts of data, such as comments. The text area size can be established by setting the **cols** attribute to the number of characters across and the **rows** attribute to the number of lines to show in the box before scrolling. For example, the HTML markup,

```
<textarea name="comments" id="comments" rows="8" cols="40">

</textarea>
```

creates a multi-line text entry region 40 characters across with 8 lines showing at a time.

One interesting aspect to the **<textarea>** tag is that there is no obvious way to set the maximum amount of content that can be entered in the field. For browsers that support all the core events such as **onkeypress**, we could easily limit the field, for example,

```
<form name="myform" id="myform">
Comments:<br />

<textarea name="comments" id="comments" rows="4" cols="40"
 onkeypress='return (document.myform.comments.value.length < 100)'>

Will be limited to 100 characters in a compliant browser.

</textarea>
</form>
```

Of course, in many browsers, such as Netscape 4.*x* generation and Opera 6.0 or before, the preceding script will not work, despite the fact that this is a standard event. The only workaround to deal with the unlimited field length would be to sense the field length when its contents change or at submit time and reduce it to the proper number of characters. The following example illustrates one approach to this problem.

```
<!DOCTYPE HTML PUBLIC "-//W3C//DTD XHTML 1.0 Transitional//EN"
"http://www.w3.org/TR/xhtml1/DTD/transitional.dtd">
<html xmlns="http://www.w3.org/1999/xhtml">
<head>
<title>Limited Text Area</title>
<script type="text/javascript">
<!--
function checkLimit(field, limit)
{
 if (field.value.length > limit)
 {
 alert("Field limited to "+limit+" characters");
 // Change it to the limit

  var revertfield = field.value.slice(0,limit-1);
  field.value = revertfield;
  field.focus();
 }
```

```
}
//-->
</script>
</head>
<body>
<form name="myform" id="myform">

Comments:<br />

<textarea name="comments" id="comments" rows="8" cols="40"
 onchange='checkLimit(this, 100);>

Try entering 10 more characters to pass 100 characters
in this field. Then click outside.

</textarea>
</form>
</body>
</html>
```

Tip: Be careful with <textarea> fields, as they have no limit to the amount of entered text without scripting.

A default value can be set for the element by including text information within the tag. Be careful, though, because this area takes plain text, and all returns, tabs, spaces, and even HTML markup will be shown onscreen, though character entities should be interpreted.

```
<textarea name="comments" id="comments" rows="8" cols="40">
S P A C E S work here
so do
      TABS and

RETURNS.
Watch out for <b>HTML</b> in here.
What about character entities like &copy;
</textarea>
```

Probably the most troublesome aspect of the **<textarea>** tag is that the wrapping of text is not supported in a standard way between browsers. In fact, by default, older versions of Netscape, such as Netscape 4, will not wrap text, while Internet Explorer will, as shown here:

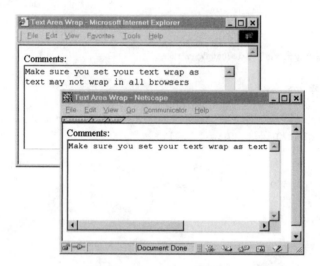

The solution to this is simply to define the **wrap** attribute to a value of "soft," so that both browsers will exhibit the same behavior:

```
<textarea name="comments" id="comments" rows="8" cols="40" wrap="SOFT">
Everything is fine with this field now that the wrapping
has been set.
</textarea>
```

Suggestion: Set text wrapping in multi-line text regions for backward compatibility.

Check Boxes

Check boxes should be used to indicate optional values. The basic idea with a group of check boxes is that the user may select as many or as few as they like of the set values. Setting check boxes in HTML is easily done using **<input type="checkbox">**, as shown here.

```
<form name="myform" id="myform">

<strong>PSV Options</strong>
<br /><br />
<label>
```

```
Asteroid Bumpers:
<input type="checkbox" name="bumpers" id="bumpers" />
</label>
<br />
<label>
Blackhole Detector:
<input type="checkbox" name="detector" id="detector" />
</label>
<br />
<label>
Autopilot:
<input type="checkbox" name="autopilot" id="autopilot" />
</label>
<br />
</form>
```

The rendering of the check box does vary under some browsers, but the major browsers render the markup nearly identically, as shown in Figure 15-10.

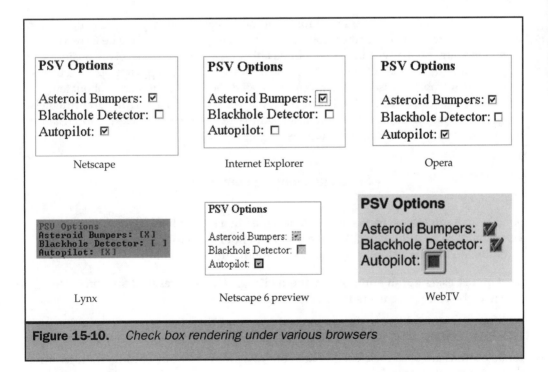

Figure 15-10.   *Check box rendering under various browsers*

It is possible to modify the look and feel of a check box using a set of images to represent the on and off stages. Radio buttons can be handled in much the same way, and a script to customize the look of both will be presented in the section on radio buttons, later on in this chapter.

When using check boxes, designers should think carefully about the amount of mouse travel between choices. Notice, for example, how the check boxes here when laid out horizontally incur more mouse travel:

PSV Options

Asteroid Bumpers: ☑
Blackhole Detector: ☐
Autopilot: ☑

PSV Options

Asteroid Bumpers: ☑   Blackhole Detector: ☐   Autopilot: ☑

Traditionally GUI design has tended to cluster items together; but Web pages do scroll, so a vertical element might make more sense.

Suggestion: Consider vertical aligning of related check boxes to decrease mouse travel.

Be careful when creating large groupings of check boxes, sine they may take up a great deal of screen real estate. Further, consider that while check boxes may be easy to use, when there are too many, a user may not be able to scan them effectively. Consider the 7 (+/–2) limit (discussed in Chapter 2) for the number of choices appropriate for a user's memory; it is probably wise to keep groups of related check boxes limited to about ten.

Setting a check box to be selected by default is very easy using HTML. Unfortunately, very often, forms are designed with values that must be deselected by a user—for instance, to opt out of receiving e-mail solicitations.

Send me annoying email!   ☑

Some e-mail solicitation forms are even designed in a somewhat sneaky fashion, with very small text near the label. Because users will not necessarily read check box labels carefully, do not use default check boxes for follow-up information.

Tip: Let users opt in and not out of e-mailings. Do not preselect any such check box—require users to select it themselves.

Radio Buttons

Radio buttons are used to select one item out of a group. Groups of radio buttons are defined similarly to check boxes. The main difference syntax-wise, besides setting the

type attribute for the **<input>** tag to **radio,** is that all the fields must have the same value for the **name** and **id** attributes to preserve the radio functionality between the fields. Consider the markup here that demonstrates the problem as well as the correct approach:

```
<form>
<h2>Incorrect radio usage</h2>
<input type="radio" name="notequal" id="notequal" value="firstchoice" /> choice 1
<input type="radio" name="names" id="names" value="secondchoice" /> choice 2
<input type="radio" name="donotwork" id="donotwork" value="thirdchoice"
checked="checked" /> choice 3

<h2>Correct radio usage</h2>
<input type="radio" name="samename" id="samename" value="firstchoice" /> choice 1
<input type="radio" name="samename" id="samename" value="secondchoice" /> choice 2
<input type="radio" name="samename" id="samename" value="thirdchoice"
checked="checked" /> choice 3
</form>
```

Notice in the rendering shown here that it is possible to select all the choices in the first example, while the second one preserves the one-of-many radio selection method:

Incorrect radio usage

⊙ choice 1 ⊙ choice 2 ⊙ choice 3

Correct radio usage

○ choice 1 ○ choice 2 ⊙ choice 3

Another small implementation problem with radio buttons under HTML is that a value is not selected by default. This creates a mysterious state that users are unable to return to, as shown here:

Mysterious initial state with nothing set

○ choice 1 ○ choice 2 ○ choice 3

Once clicked unable to return to first state

● choice 1 ○ choice 2 ○ choice 3

Setting the first field selected by inclusion of the **checked** attribute solves this troublesome interface quirk.

Rule: Always select an initial radio button by default.

Another more potentially troublesome aspect of radios is determining when they should be used. Some designers feel that radios should be used for "Yes or No" questions rather than pull-downs. This makes sense when you consider that they show both choices at once. The screen real estate saved by the pull-down is minimal. However, some designers further suggest that maybe a check box with a different label makes more sense, since it is only one control to manipulate rather than two. It makes some sense until you consider that the wording of the label may get somewhat confusing. Consider the example shown here, asking whether a user wants to receive e-mail solicitations. Radio buttons provide the best way to present this information, since the normal pull-down hides possible choices; the pull-down with all choices shown looks nonstandard, and the check box is confusing.

Send me annoying email! ☑

Do you want to receive our annoying e-mail? Yes ⊙ No ○

Do you want to receive our annoying e-mail? | yes ▾ |

Do you want to receive our annoying e-mail? | yes / no |

Rule: Use radio buttons for "Yes or No" questions rather than pull-down menus or check boxes.

The main advantage of radio buttons is that they are all exposed, allowing the user to easily choose from them. However, since all choices must be looked at in a radio group, the number of selections has to be limited enough for the user to consider all at once to avoid making a mistake. This means the short-term memory rule of 7 (+/–2) items should be strictly enforced.

Suggestion: Avoid more than ten items in a radio group.

Beyond memory considerations, when more than ten items are presented, screen real estate may become an issue.

Suggestion: Use pull-downs if more than ten items are in a selection of "one-choice-of-many" to save screen real estate.

If radios are to be used, the grouping of radio buttons isn't quite as critical (unlike with check boxes), since the user will make only one choice, but it is wise to consider vertical alignment with radios as well—particularly when there are many choices.

Tip: Vertical alignment is useful for larger groups of radio buttons.

Like check boxes, the rendering of radio buttons is similar among the major browsers, but there are differences in some viewing environments, as shown in Figure 15-11.

Netscape

> **On a scale of (1-5) how satisfied are you with your DemoCompany Butler robot?**
>
> ○ 1 *(Be careful I know where you live!)*
> ○ 2 *(Well at least it didn't explode when I was home.)*
> ◉ 3 *(He grumbles when he does the dishes, but I would too.)*
> ○ 4 *(I named my child DemoCompany in honor of your wonderful company.)*
> ○ 5 *(Can I give you all my money? Please.)*

Internet
Explorer

> **On a scale of (1-5) how satisfied are you with your DemoCompany Butler robot?**
>
> ○ 1 *(Be careful I know where you live!)*
> ○ 2 *(Well at least it didn't explode when I was home.)*
> ◉ 3 *(He grumbles when he does the dishes, but I would too.)*
> ○ 4 *(I named my child DemoCompany in honor of your wonderful company.)*
> ○ 5 *(Can I give you all my money? Please.)*

Opera

> **On a scale of (1-5) how satisfied are you with your DemoCompany Butler robot?**
>
> ○ 1 *(Be careful I know where you live!)*
> ○ 2 *(Well at least it didn't explode when I was home.)*
> ◉ 3 *(He grumbles when he does the dishes, but I would too.)*
> ○ 4 *(I named my child DemoCompany in honor of your wonderful company.)*
> ○ 5 *(Can I give you all my money? Please.)*

Lynx

```
On a scale of (1-5) how satisfied are you with your DemoCompany Butler
robot?
( )  1   (Be careful I know where you live!)
     ( )  2   (Well at least it didn't explode when I was home.)
     (*)  3   (He grumbles when he does the dishes, but I would too.)
     ( )  4   (I named my child DemoCompany in honor of your wonderful
company.)
     ( )  5   (Can I give you all my money? Please.)
```

WebTV

> **On a scale of (1-5) how satisfied are you with your
> DemoCompany Butler robot?**
>
> ◉ 1 *(Be careful I know where you live!)*
> ● 2 *(Well at least it didn't explode when I was home.)*
> ● 3 *(He grumbles when he does the dishes, but I
> would too.)*
> ● 4 *(I named my child DemoCompany in honor of
> your wonderful company.)*
> ● 5 *(Can I give you all my money? Please.)*

Figure 15-11.   *Radio buttons are relatively consistent in appearance*

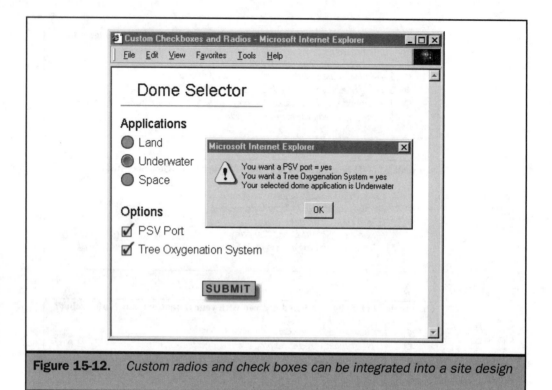

Figure 15-12. *Custom radios and check boxes can be integrated into a site design*

As mentioned in the section on check boxes, it is possible to modify the appearance of both GUI elements using JavaScript. The markup and script code presented here show this in action. A rendering is shown in Figure 15-12.

```
<!DOCTYPE HTML PUBLIC "-//W3C//DTD XHTML 1.0 Transitional//EN"
"http://www.w3.org/TR/xhtml1/DTD/transitional.dtd">
<html xmlns="http://www.w3.org/1999/xhtml">
<head>
<title>Custom Checkboxes and Radios</title>
<script type="text/javascript">
<!--
  /* needed for Netscape 4 hack */
  ns4 = (document.layers)? true:false;

  /* preload the images */
  loadImage('button0','images/button0.gif');
  loadImage('button1','images/button1.gif');
  loadImage('radiobutton0','images/radiobutton0.gif');
  loadImage('radiobutton1','images/radiobutton1.gif');
  loadImage('checkbox0','images/checkbox0.gif');
  loadImage('checkbox1','images/checkbox1.gif');
```

```
function initialize()
{
 psv = new checkBox('DomeSelector','psvImg','yes','no');
 tree = new checkBox('DomeSelector','treeImg','yes','no');
 dome = new radio('DomeSelector','domeImg',3,'Land');
}

function loadImage(imgObj,imgSrc)
{
 eval(imgObj+' = new Image()');
 eval(imgObj+'.src = "'+imgSrc+'"');
}

function submitForm()
{
   str = "You want a PSV port = " + psv.value + "\n";
   str += "You want a Tree Oxygenation System = " + tree.value + "\n";
   str += "You selected dome application is " + dome.value + "\n";

   alert(str);
}

function changeImage(layer,imgName,imgObj)
{
   if (ns4 && layer!=null)
eval('document.'+layer+'.document.images["'+imgName+'"].src = '+imgObj+'.src');
   else document.images[imgName].src = eval(imgObj+".src");
}

function radio(layer,imgNames,length,defaultValue)
{
   this.layer = layer;
   this.imgNames = imgNames;
   this.length = length;
   this.change = radioChange;
   this.value = (defaultValue)? defaultValue : "undefined";
}

function radioChange(index,value)
{
   this.value = value;
   for (var i=0; i<this.length; i++)
     changeImage(this.layer,this.imgNames+i,'radiobutton0');
   changeImage(this.layer,this.imgNames+index,'radiobutton1');
}

function checkBox(layer,imgName,trueValue,falseValue,defaultToTrue)
{
```

```
          this.layer = layer;
          this.imgName = imgName;
          this.trueValue = trueValue;
          this.falseValue = falseValue;
          this.state = (defaultToTrue) ? 1 : 0;

          this.value = (this.state) ? this.trueValue : this.falseValue;
          this.change = checkBoxChange;
        }


      function checkBoxChange()
      {
        this.state = (this.state) ? 0 : 1;
        this.value = (this.state) ? this.trueValue : this.falseValue;

        changeImage(this.layer,this.imgName,'checkbox'+this.state);
      }
//-->
</script>
<style type="text/css">
<!--
  #DomeSelector  {position: relative;}
  body {font-family: Arial, Helvetica, sans-serif; color: black;
background-color: white;}
-->
</style>
</head>
<body onload="initialize()">

<div id="DomeSelector">
<table border="0" cellspacing="0" cellpadding="3">
<tr><td colspan="2" align="center">
<h2>Dome Selector</h2>
<hr />
</td></tr>

<tr><td colspan="2">
<h3>Applications</h3>
</td></tr>

<tr><td>
<a href="javascript:dome.change(0,'Land');"><img name="domeImg0"
src="images/radiobutton1.gif" width="20" height="20" border="0" alt="" /></a>
</td>

<td>Land</td></tr>
```

```
<tr><td>

<a href="javascript:dome.change(1,'Underwater');"><img name="domeImg1"
src="images/radiobutton0.gif" width="20" height="20" border="0" alt="" /></a>
</td>

<td>Underwater</td></tr>

<tr><td>
<a href="javascript:dome.change(2,'Space');"><img name="domeImg2"
src="images/radiobutton0.gif" width="20" height="20" border="0" alt="" /></a>
</td>

<td>Space</td></tr>

<tr>
<td colspan="2">
<br /><h3>Options</h3>
</td></tr>

<tr><td>
<a href="javascript:psv.change();"><img name="psvImg" src="images/checkbox0.gif"
width="20" height="20" border="0" alt="" /></a>
</td>

<td>PSV Port</td></tr>

<tr><td><a href="javascript:tree.change();"><img name="treeImg"
src="images/checkbox0.gif" width="20" height="20" border="0" alt=""></a></td>

<td>Tree Oxygenation System</td>
</tr>

<tr><td colspan="2" align="right">
<br />
<a href="javascript:submitForm()"
onmousedown="changeImage('DomeSelector','submitImg','button1');"
onmouseup="changeImage('DomeSelector','submitImg','button0');"
onmouseout="changeImage('DomeSelector','submitImg','button0');"><img
name="submitImg" src="images/button0.gif" width="85" height="30" alt="Submit"
vspace="10" border="0"></a>
</td></tr>
</table>
</div>
</body>
</html>
```

Online: http://www.webdesignref.com/examples/customradios.htm

ELEMENTS OF
PAGE DESIGN

One disturbing use of radio buttons that bears mentioning before moving to the next GUI element is the use of radio buttons to navigate a site. This is a completely nonstandard use of this widget and is highly confusing. While pull-downs have been used successfully for navigation on the Web and offer the same "one-choice-of-many" that radios do, users have tended to understand from software applications that a menu selection will trigger an action while a radio button will not.

Rule: Do not use radio buttons for navigation.

Pull-Down Menus

Pull-down menus, as defined in HTML using the **<select>** tag, provide a simple "one-of-many" selection capability similar to radio buttons. The main advantage of pull-downs is that they save screen real estate. However, pull-downs do hide values from the user, forcing them to expose the values—which takes effort as well as potentially requiring memorization of the values shown (in case of second thoughts later on). Certainly, pull-downs do not rely on recognition, but rather on recall, the downsides of which have been discussed previously. However, the screen real estate issue alone makes pull-downs worthy of consideration. Setting up a simple pull-down can be done with the following code:

```
<form>
<select name="robotchooser" id="robotchooser">
    <option value="Butler">Butler</option>
    <option value="Security">Security</option>
    <option value="Trainer">Trainer</option>
    <option value="Friend">Friend</option>
</select>
</form>
```

Indicating a default choice isn't as great of a problem as it is with radio buttons. A pull-down menu will always start on the first choice presented. It might be a good idea to utilize the **selected** attribute to preselect a choice, similar to setting the first radio button rather than relying on the default action of the browser.

Tip: Do not rely on the browser's default action with pull-down menus; always set an initial state explicitly.

Designers occasionally create nonchoice items, which may in some sense ruin the logic of the widget—which is "now choose one of the items but not the first one," as shown here:

```
<form>
<select name="robotchooser" id="robotchooser">
```

```
    <option>Choose your robot</option>
    <option>Butler</option>
    <option>Security</option>
    <option>Trainer</option>
    <option>Friend</option>
</select>
</form>
```

The assumption would be that we would validate the form in the preceding situation and alert users that they have to choose something. Another potential downside of **<select>**-based menus is that they lack any form of separator or grouping facility. Occasionally, designers will use an entry filled with dashes or a blank entry to simulate a separator, like this:

```
<form>
<select name="robotchooser" id="robotchooser">
    <option>Choose your robot</option>
    <option>--------------------</option>
    <option>Butler</option>
    <option>Security</option>
    <option>Trainer</option>
    <option>Friend</option>
    <option>    Male</option>
    <option>    Female</option>
</select>
</form>
```

Tip: Be wary of using special characters in pull-downs—particularly non-breaking spaces—as they often do not render properly.

HTML 4 introduced the **<optgroup>** tag, which should be used to segment choices into groups, or even to create sub-menus. Consider the markup shown here:

```
<form>
<select name="robotchooser" id="robotchooser">
    <option>Choose your robot</option>
    <option>--------------------</option>
    <option>Security</option>
    <optgroup label="Security Models">
      <option>Man</option>
      <option>K-9</option>
    </optgroup>
    <optgroup label="Friend Models">
```

```
      <option>Female</option>
      <option>Male</option>
   </optgroup>
   <option>Trainer</option>
</select>
</form>
```

In Netscape 6/7 or Mozilla browsers, this renders with a section name that cannot be selected, as shown here:

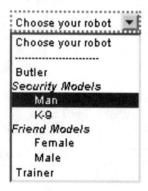

However, browser support for <**optgroup**> is still spotty, so until the tag is more commonly supported in browsers (it is currently supported by Internet Explorer 6), it should be avoided and the workarounds with dashes or spaces considered.

The renderings of traditional pull-downs are fairly similar in the major browsers, but there are, of course, differences in the appliance or text-only environments, as shown in Figure 15-13. These environments may find radios a much better choice.

Tip: Consider radio buttons over pull-downs if you are dealing with alternative access users.

One interesting aspect of the use of a pull-down menu is that when the **size** attribute is added, it generally results in a window that acts like a pull-down, allowing only one choice out of many, but looks like a scrolled list. Many users won't understand that the widgets shown here do the same thing.

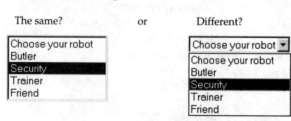

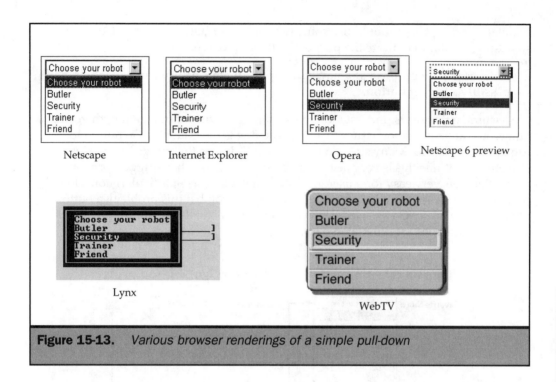

Figure 15-13.   *Various browser renderings of a simple pull-down*

> **Suggestion: Avoid changing the display of single-choice pull-down menus with the size attribute.**

It is possible, of course, through the use of style sheets, to significantly change the look and feel of pull-downs and, in fact, to create your own. Many designers have experimented with a variety of cascading menu scripts to create navigation systems for sites. An example of this is presented in the section later in this chapter entitled "Advanced Web GUI Widgets." For now, let's take a look at the use of pull-downs for navigation in Web pages.

Using Pull-Downs for Navigation

A common use of pull-down menus in Web sites is for navigation. The basic idea is that a selection of sites or pages is shown in a pull-down, and, when one is selected, the user is instantly whisked to the page. The pull-down, like a typical application menu, tends to be on the top of pages and uses a great deal less screen real estate than do conventional navigation bars—of course, it does so by hiding the links. While this use for the pull-down seems perfectly acceptable, it means there are two types of pull-downs: one for navigation, the other for form elements. Some users may be confused with the dual meaning if the context of use is not kept clear. A pull-down used for navigation should not be used within a form. It should be clearly labeled—"quick links" is popular—and probably should use some type of trigger button labeled "Go" or something similar to indicate the purpose of the pull-down.

Rule: Make the purpose of a navigation pull-down clear by context, labels, and possibly a trigger button.

Assuming that users understand the use of pull-downs for navigation, there are numerous implementation issues to avoid. The first is the issue of a Go button to trigger the page load. Many sites prefer to use pull-downs that trigger a page load immediately. While this is very fast, it can be somewhat of a hair-trigger form of navigation. It is very easy for a user to slip up on the mouse—particularly on a long pull-down—and accidentally trigger a page load. To combat this problem, a button often with a label of "Go" is used next to the menu to actually trigger the page load. The two approaches are illustrated here:

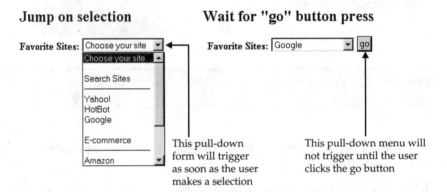

A big problem of sites that don't take the Go button approach is what to do when the user has turned their JavaScript off. In many sites, without JavaScript, the navigation completely breaks and the user is left pulling menus that don't do anything. The use of the Go can trigger a back-up call to a server-side program to redirect the page.

Rule: Make sure pull-down navigation degrades gracefully when JavaScript is off.

It is possible to have the Go button show up only when script is off, or it can be left on the screen all the time. However, leaving it onscreen does result in a troublesome usability problem, since the user is never able to click the button before a new page loads, which could annoy the user greatly.

Rule: If a Go button is shown onscreen with pull-down navigation, make sure the user can actually click it to trigger page load.

Having the Go button trigger the page load is probably a better way to go rather than automatic selection, since it does give a sense of closure to the user's action and avoids the hair-trigger effect this form of navigation often exhibits.

The last problem with pull-downs for navigation concerns the state the menu is left in. For example, the user may pull the menu down and select a separator. Shouldn't the menu reset to the top like a traditional menu in an application? Most, for some reason, do not. Or, for another example, a user does select a legitimate choice and is sent to a new page. Once at that page, the user backs up, only to find the pull-down selecting the choice they just made. Suddenly deciding that the page they had selected was correct, they have to either reload the page to reset the pull-down or make some false choice and try again. The basic problem is that, most of the time, the menu is not reset when the user reloads the page or selects a nonactive item like a separator.

Rule: Reset a pull-down when users back out of a page or select separator items.

The best way to really understand these problems is by accessing the examples located at http://www.webdesignref.com/examples/pulldownproblems.htm. A complete script is presented here that deals with all the problems and provides cosmetic improvements to the pull-down navigation style.

```html
<!DOCTYPE HTML PUBLIC "-//W3C//DTD XHTML 1.0 Transitional//EN"
"http://www.w3.org/TR/xhtml1/DTD/transitional.dtd">
<html xmlns="http://www.w3.org/1999/xhtml">
<head>
<title>Select Navigation</title>
<style type="text/css">
<!--
.nochoice {color: black;}
.choice {color: blue; }
-->
</style>
<script type="text/javascript">
<!--
function redirect(pulldown)
{
 newlocation = pulldown[pulldown.selectedIndex].value;
 if (newlocation != "")
   self.location = newlocation;
}

function resetIfBlank(pulldown)
{
 possiblenewlocation = pulldown[pulldown.selectedIndex].value;
 if (possiblenewlocation == "")
   pulldown.selectedIndex = 0; // reset to start since no movement
}

//-->
</script>
</head>
```

```html
<body>
<form name="navForm" id="navForm" action="redirector.cgi" onsubmit="return false">
<label>Favorite Sites:
<select name="menu" id="menu" onchange="resetIfBlank(this)">
<option value="" class="nochoice" selected>Choose your site</option>
<option value="" class="nochoice"></option>
<option value="" class="nochoice">Search Sites</option>
<option value="" class="nochoice">--------------------------</option>
<option value="http://www.yahoo.com" class="choice">Yahoo! </option>
<option value="http://www.hotbot.com" class="choice">HotBot</option>
<option value="http://www.google.com" class="choice">Google</option>
<option value="" class="nochoice"></option>
<option value="" class="nochoice">E-commerce</option>
<option value="" class="nochoice">--------------------------</option>
<option value="http://www.amazon.com" class="choice">Amazon</option>
<option value="http://www.buy.com" class="choice">Buy.com</option>
<option value="" class="nochoice" class="choice"></option>
<option value="" class="nochoice">Demos</option>
<option value="" class="nochoice">--------------------------</option>
<option value="http://www.democompany.com" class="choice">Demo Company</option>
</select>
</label>
<input type="submit" value="go" onclick="redirect(document.navForm.menu); return
false;" />
</form>
<script type="text/javascript">
<!--
document.navForm.menu.selectedIndex = 0;
//-->
</script>
</body>
</html>
```

Note   *The preceding example relies on the use of a CGI program called redirect.cgi in the event that JavaScript is off, which is not presented here. The execution of that script is simply to take a passed URL and redirect the user's browser to that page.*

Online: http://www.webdesignref.com/examples/pulldownnavigation.htm.

Certainly, using pull-downs as a navigation device is a break from traditional GUI conventions. Another interesting difference is that GUI conventions suggest that, when there are over 15 items, designers should forego use of a pull-down in favor of a scrolled list of some sort. Yet scrolled lists, which are discussed next, are relatively rare in Web sites.

Scrolled Lists

A *scrolled list* is one where the user can select multiple items from the choices presented. Functionally they are equivalent to the check box, though they take up less screen real estate. To create a scrolled list, simply change a **<select>** tag by adding the attribute **multiple** and setting a **size** attribute equal to the number of choices that show at a given moment. An example is shown here:

```
<form>
<label>Security Robot Extras:<br />
<select name="extras" id="extras" size="3" multiple="multiple">
    <option>Austrian accent</option>
    <option>Flame thrower</option>
    <option>One-liner catch phrase software upgrade</option>
    <option>Permanent facial sneer</option>
    <option>Rocket fists</option>
</select>
</label>
</form>
```

Browser rendering examples of a scrolled list are shown in Figure 15-14.

Note that in the alternative browsers, like TV browsers, phone browsers, or text-only environments, scrolled lists are significantly modified or even changed into check boxes.

Suggestion: Avoid scrolled lists if you expect alternative browsing environments; use check boxes instead.

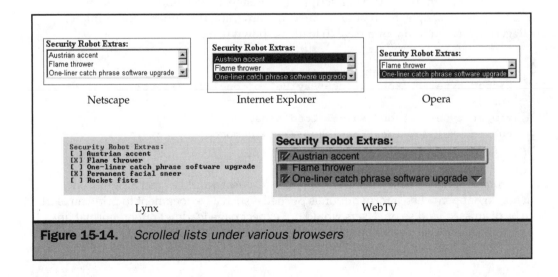

Figure 15-14.   *Scrolled lists under various browsers*

What's interesting is that scrolled lists are actually relatively unused in large public Web sites. Probably the main reason is that, for some users, they are confusing compared to check boxes. Consider, how do you select multiple noncontiguous items in the list? Which key is held down? CTRL? SHIFT? Now consider different operating systems and browsers—is this method of selection performed in the same way? What you'll find if you actually watch novice users is that they often approach these form elements in a trial-and-error fashion. Therefore, if scrolled lists must be employed, always provide a statement about what keys should be held for multiple selections.

Rule: When using scrolled lists, make sure to provide some form of instructions for novice users on how to select multiple items.

Push Buttons

HTML forms support simple push buttons using this syntax:

```
<form>
<input type="button" value="Push Me" />
</form>
```

The rendering of such buttons is very plain and tends to look something like this.

It is also possible to use the **<button>** tag to create a simple push button, but given its limited support in older browsers, it is best to stick with the presented syntax.

However, without the use of a scripting language, a push button will do nothing. With the use of scripts, push buttons can cause anything to happen—for example, triggering an alert to fire or a page to load, as shown here:

```
<form>
<input type="button" value="Say Hello" onclick="alert('Hello');" />
<br />
<input type="button" value="Load a page"
onclick="window.location='http://www.democompany.com';" />
</form>
```

From experience with software applications, a user would expect a significant action to happen when a form button is pushed—such as a document to print, an alert to be dismissed, and so on. Users would not expect page loading; rather, normal links or graphical buttons tend to be used for that action.

> Suggestion: Do not use default form-style push buttons for navigation; instead, reserve them to cause actions to take place.

Reset Buttons

A reset button may be useful to include on complex forms to reset values back to their default state. The syntax for the reset button is one of the simpler forms of the **<input>** element:

```
<input type="reset" value="Clear Fields" />
```

Web conventions seem to suggest that the reset button be placed near the form submission and be labeled simply something like "Reset," "Reset Fields," or "Reset Form." If there are no default values used in the form, a more appropriate label might be "Clear Form" or "Clear Fields."

The main problem with the reset button is that it is often so close to the submit button that the user might literally slip and press it accidentally, thus possibly losing a great deal of entered information. To avoid a hair-trigger reset button, attach a JavaScript to get confirmation from the user, as shown here:

```
<form onreset="return confirm('Clear form fields?');">
...other fields in the form...
<input type="reset" value="Clear Fields" />
</form>
```

> Rule: Provide a confirmation on a form reset button to avoid accidents.

One might wonder why the reset button is so close to a form submission button. While this is somewhat of a mystery, convention seems to place it there. You might consider putting it at least a few pixels away from the submit button.

> Suggestion: Consider moving your reset button away from the submit button.

Submit Buttons

A submit button is a special class of push button that triggers the contents of a form to be sent to a server-side program, as specified by the value of the **action** attribute in the **<form>** tag. For example,

```
<form action="saveit.pl" method="POST" name="testform" id="testform">
...form elements here...
<input type="submit" value="Submit" />
</form>
```

would trigger the execution of the program "saveit.pl," which would receive the contents of the form. Because a submit button may cause an action that could be irreversible, it is always a good idea to warn a user before they submit something by using a confirmation dialog, as discussed previously in the chapter and as shown here:

```
<form action="saveit.pl" method="POST" name="testform" id="testform"
onsubmit="return confirm('Are you sure?');">
...form elements here...
<input type="submit" value="Submit" />
</form>
```

Rule: Provide a final chance to change a decision before submitting important information or starting a difficult-to-reverse action.

The location of a submit button is generally at the bottom of a form. However, unlike many form applications on the Web, it is not necessarily at the far right or the center of the screen. On the contrary, it generally appears on the left or the center of the bottom of the screen—generally near the reset button.

Suggestion: Keep the submit button at the bottom of the form, either center or left side.

The look and feel of the submit button is usually the same as any normal push button, though designers may wish to change the style of the button using an image, as discussed in the next section.

Image Buttons

With script, it is possible to utilize an image instead of a typical HTML form field as a push button. Unlike using plain HTML form controls, multiple states (including animated states) are possible. One example of an image button is shown here:

Using the **<input type="image">** element to make image buttons more visually appealing is relatively straightforward. An example of this is presented here:

```
<form onsubmit="alert('The form would be submitted.'); return false;">
<input type="text"><br />
```

```
<input type="image" src="button.gif" width="85" height="30" border="0" />
</form>
```

Before designers quickly run out to change all form buttons, consider first the download expense as well as the degradability of these buttons. Designers should consider whether the visual improvement of the button is that important to the user experience and whether the buttons will even be viewable under all browsing conditions. A simpler idea might be just to apply some basic style sheet rules to color buttons to match a site design.

Suggestion: Provide a degradable state for image buttons with scripting or images off.

*HTML 4 and XHTML 1 support the **<button>** tag, which is a much more flexible approach to adding image buttons. However, this element is not well supported in newer browsers and not at all in very old browsers, and should be avoided for the moment.*

File Upload Controls

A special type of form control supported in HTML is the file upload control. This control can be used to browse the user's local system and attach a file for uploading. The syntax of the field is relatively simple, as shown here:

```
<input type="file" name="upfile" id="upfile" />
```

File upload does not work on every browser; but on the ones that are supported, it looks fairly similar, as shown in Figure 15-15. Notice that, as expected, this form element does not work in alternative or restricted browsing environments.

Rule: Make sure to consider the environment of use before using a file upload facility. This facility may not make sense for users that do not have file storage.

The file upload facility as implemented under HTML provides little room for customization. The only possibility is that the size of the path field may be set. However, designers should not modify or limit the size of the file field, given that they will have no idea of the length of the directory path that may be required to attach a file on a user's system. Also, there is really no option to change the layout of the field or the associated browse button.

It is possible to implement a file upload system using Java or JavaScript and produce an interface similar to the one shown in Figure 15-16.

Now that we have covered all the various types of form widgets, it is time to discuss how they can be used properly.

ELEMENTS OF
PAGE DESIGN

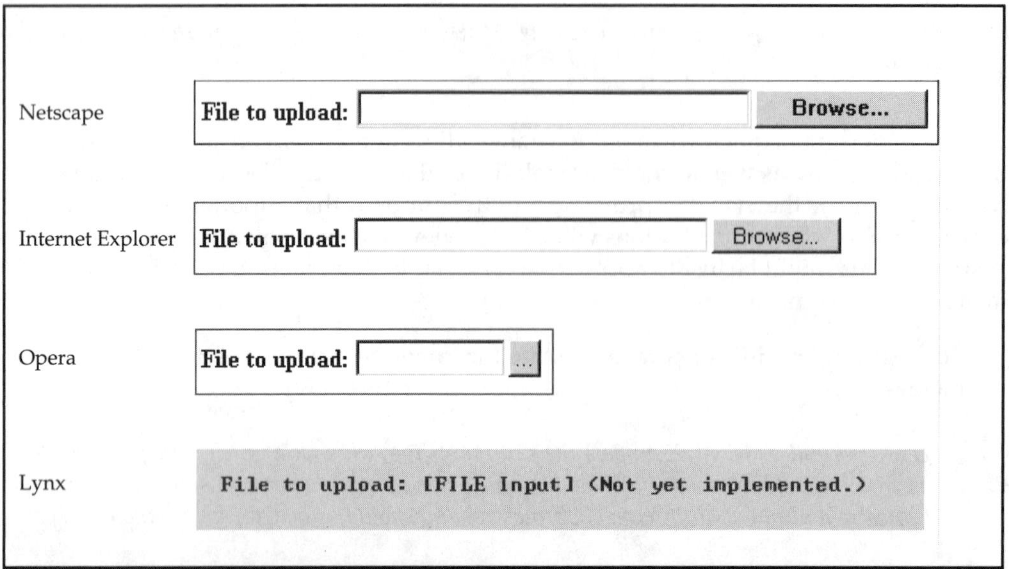

Netscape	**File to upload:** [_____] **Browse...**
Internet Explorer	**File to upload:** [_____] Browse...
Opera	**File to upload:** [_____] [...]
Lynx	`File to upload: [FILE Input] (Not yet implemented.)`

Figure 15-15. *Rendering of the file upload control*

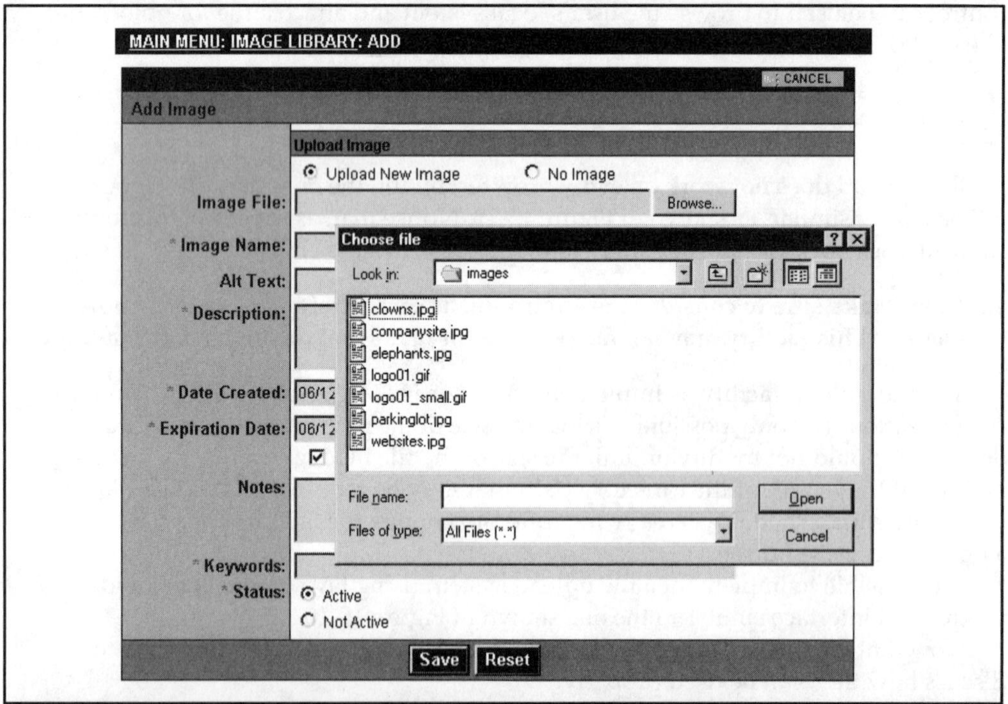

Figure 15-16. *Advanced technologies allow improved file upload interfaces*

Usable Forms

Creating a usable form need not be hard. The most common failing is that forms are simply not well laid out. Consider the forms shown in Figure 15-17. The form with well-aligned fields at least appears easier to fill out.

Forms will be laid out in an up-and-down fashion on a Web page, rather than a left-to-right fashion, to fill up a fixed-sized dialog. However, the exact layout of the form will depend greatly on the data presented. For example, consider the two possible layouts for collecting a user's name shown here:

First: Thomas   Initial: A Last: Powell

versus

First: Thomas
Initial: A
Last: Powell

ELEMENTS OF
PAGE DESIGN

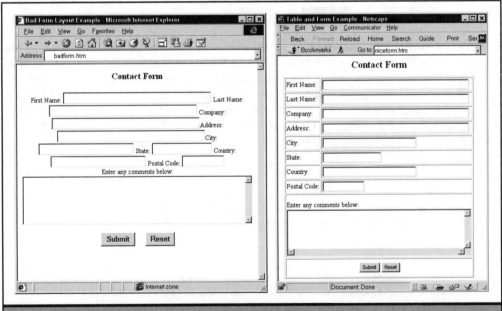

Figure 15-17.   *Clean form layout improves usability*

Which field layout is easier to understand? Which is the more efficient use of screen real estate? On the Web, fields tend to be filled out generally up to down, though it might make sense to arrange fields left to right because of context.

Suggestion: Lay out form elements generally up to down, but consider left to right based upon the context of the information being asked for.

Regardless of how forms are laid out, in most cases, HTML tables will be used. CSS can be used to improve form layout, but things don't often work properly when mixing the two technologies. For the near term, consider using tables and CSS rather than just plain CSS for form pages.

Suggestion: Consider keeping table borders on when formatting table elements, since they help associate labels and fields.

To format text fields, you might try to use HTML markup like **\<font>**, **\<tt>**, and **\<b>** around form elements. However, browsers will typically only interpret the markup for the label and not for the field itself. Consider the example here:

```
<form>
<font color="red"><i>
Username: <input type="text" name="username" id="username" size="20" />
</i></font>
</form>
```

The label of the field will be rendered in red and italic in every browser; however, what happens to the content in the text field varies. A few browsers, will actually render the typed text in italic, but not red. However, in most browsers the text field is unaffected.

CSS provides much greater control over the look and feel of various form fields. It is possible to set colors, background, width, borders, and a variety of other visual characteristics of form fields in a CSS1-compliant browser. The following examples illustrate some possible uses of CSS:

```
<form>

Username: <input type="text" name="username" id="username" size="20"
style="background-color: #ffcc66; border-width: 1px; border-color: black;" />

<br /><br />

Code Number: <input type="text" name="code" id="code" size="20"
style="background-color: #333300; border-width: 1px; color: #00cc66; border-color:
black; font-variant: small-caps;" />

<br /><br />
```

```
Offer Code: <input type="text" name="offercode" id="offercode" size="8"
style="width: 8em; background-color: #ffffcc; border-width: 1px; color: #006699;
font-family: Verdana; border-color: black; border-style: dashed;" />

</form>
```

Style can be applied to a field to indicate what state it is in. For example, as the user tabs through a set of fields, consider having the background color of each field change slightly. Under CSS2, it is possible to do this easily using the focus pseudo-class. For example, the rule

```
input.textfields:focus   {background-color: yellow;}
```

would set all **<input>** tags in class textfields to a background color of yellow when selected. Using JavaScript, it is possible to color fields both as they are focused and when they are in error.

As we can see, online forms provide interesting new possibilities. In fact, probably one of the biggest mistakes designers make when working with forms online is directly copying the look and feel of an existing paper form. When users are very familiar with a particular type of form that they fill in everyday, such copying may be useful in improving the users' comfort level with the form and not requiring that people be retrained to use the online version. However, in most cases, written forms have differences from online ones that affect usability. It is important to gear the form to how the user is going to be filling it out—using a keyboard and a mouse, probably. To improve usability, make the form simpler to read and use online.

> **Suggestion: Imitate real world forms directly if users are very familiar with them; otherwise, focus on reducing the amount of data entry.**

Users will have to use the keyboard to enter in text data, and there may be a great deal of keyboard-to-mouse and back movement in a form. Try to minimize this by making the form keyboard friendly: encourage tabbing, use accelerator keys, and provide default data values. How to implement each of these ideas is discussed later in the chapter.

> **Rule: Make forms keyboard friendly.**

Also, make sure to limit mouse travel between form elements. If users are going to be moving from field to field with their mouse, try to limit the distance between fields.

> **Rule: Limit mouse travel between form elements.**

In order to limit mouse travel, you often end up grouping associated items together.

ELEMENTS OF PAGE DESIGN

Fields that are associated with each other should be grouped together. The easiest way to do this is to put the fields within a table. The table may have a background color to make the grouping more obvious. It is also possible using the HTML elements **<fieldset>** and **<legend>** to quickly create form grouping. The two approaches are illustrated here:

It is important, of course, to group items that make sense together, not just to limit mouse travel or to create colored sections. Next, we discuss one of the most important steps to take in improving forms: ensuring that fields that are required are clearly noted to the user.

Required Fields

When a user is trying to fill in a form, it is very important to indicate which fields in the form are required. Nothing can annoy a user more than trying to guess what fields are required and being forced to keep resubmitting until all the mandatory fields are filled in. The most common way that required fields are indicated on the Web is using an asterisk next to the field. Despite the common use of the asterisk for required fields, it is a good idea to explicitly indicate somewhere on the form that the asterisk indicates a required field. Color is also used on the asterisk itself. However, avoid just coloring a field name to indicate a required field, since a user may be unable to see the color. Last but not least, it might just be best to indicate the required field by explicitly putting the word "required" next to it. All these techniques for showing required fields are illustrated here:

Rule: Label all required fields carefully using an asterisk or the word "required."

Occasionally, there is the opposite situation—all fields are required except one or two. In such cases, use the marker "optional" on either the right or left of the field. Do not attempt to reuse the asterisk and change its meaning with some label.

Tabbing Forms

One good way to improve form fill-out is to improve the movement between fields by using the TAB key. Normally, a browser will tend to tab through fields left to right, top to bottom. However, the basic tab movement is more an artifact of the order in which fields are defined. If you want to explicitly set a tabbing order, HTML 4.0 introduced the **tabindex** attribute for many elements.

Set the **tabindex** to a value between 0 and 32767. Hopefully, you don't have 32,000 fields in your form, but the specification says you can set tab values that high! Tabbing will proceed from the lowest positive value to the highest value. Fields with a **tabindex** set to 0 will be tabbed in order of definition after all other fields have been navigated. Fields with negative **tabindex** values are skipped in some browsers like Internet Explorer, but in others they are treated normally. Disabled fields will not be tabbed at all. The following example demonstrates the use of the tabbing index with form elements:

```
<form>
<input type="text" name="field1" id="field1" value="tabbed after set fields" />

<br />
<input tabindex="1" type="text" name="field2" id="field2" value="first field" />
<br />

Check me: <input type="checkbox" name="field3" id="field3" tabindex="4" />
<br />

<input disabled="disabled" type="text" name="field4" id="field4"
       value="skip this field" />

<br />
<select tabindex="10" name="field5" id="field5">
   <option>Choice 1</option>
   <option>Choice 2</option>
</select>

<br /><br />

<input type="text" name="field6" id="field6" tabindex="-5"
       value="skip this field? maybe" />
```

ELEMENTS OF PAGE DESIGN

```
<br /><br />
<input tabindex="3" type="submit" value="Submit" />
</form>
```

The **tabindex** attribute is supported in most browsers, and those that don't support it just default to their normal form of navigation, so it is fairly safe to use this attribute.

Suggestion: Add tabindex attributes to improve form navigation.

First Field Focus

For efficient form use, the user should be able to quickly use the keyboard to enter data in the form. While the TAB key can be used to quickly move between fields, you should notice that most browsers will not focus the first field by default, and the user may be forced to click the field before starting keyboard entry. Using JavaScript, it is fairly easy to focus the first field in a form. This should improve form fill-out in a subtle but noticeable way.

Suggestion: Focus the first field of a form page immediately.

The example presented here shows a short JavaScript associated with the **onload** event handler attribute for the **<body>** that focuses a form field. Just change the form name and field name in the script and it should work without modification in nearly any page.

```
<!DOCTYPE HTML PUBLIC "-//W3C//DTD XHTML 1.0 Transitional//EN"
"http://www.w3.org/TR/xhtml1/DTD/transitional.dtd">
<html xmlns="http://www.w3.org/1999/xhtml">
<head>
<title>Focus First Field</title>
</head>
<body onload="window.document.testform.firstname.focus();">

<form name="testform" id="testform">
<label>First Name:
<input type="text" name="firstname" id="firstname" size="30" maxlength="30" />
</label>
<br />
<label>Last Name:
<input type="text" name="lastname" id="lastname" size="30" maxlength="30" />
</label>
<br />
</form>

</body>
</html>
```

Keyboard Shortcuts

HTML 4.0 introduces the use of the **accesskey** attribute for many elements, including form elements. The access key can be used to set an accelerator for a field so that the user can access the field using a key combination—usually ALT and the defined access key. Note that the actual key combined with the defined accelerator may vary based on the underlying system. For example, Macintosh users may use CMD instead of ALT to activate accelerators. Regardless of the key combination, the syntax of the accelerator is the same. For example,

```
<input type="text" size="40" accesskey="n" name="username" id="username" />
```

sets the letter *n* as the accelerator for the field. In a browser such as Internet Explorer that recognizes this attribute, the key combination ALT-N will move the cursor to the field immediately. All other browsers will just ignore the key combination.

> **Note** *Avoid using the **accesskey** attribute on the **<label>** element. In many browsers, it will not focus the associated field.*

One potential problem with access keys is users not knowing exactly what key combinations are used to access fields. In traditional GUI interfaces, a particular letter choice is underlined to indicate an accelerator key. For example in File the F key is used to access the menu. While this approach could be used on the Web, the user might consider the underlined letter a link. Given the context of the underline and the lack of color, the user will not jump to this conclusion. However, because of this potential concern, it may be okay to indicate accelerators in another fashion, such as reversing them out.

The best approach to indicating accelerators is to use a style sheet. For example, you might define a class accesskey in a style sheet using a rule like this:

```
.accesskey    {text-decoration: underline;}
```

and then reference it later on in the form using a **<span>** tag around the particular letter being used as the accelerator:

```
<span class="accesskey">N</span>ame:
```

Using style sheets will allow you to experiment easily with different styles and will also allow easy removal of the key indications when a browser doesn't support the **accesskey** attribute. It is very important to turn off the key indication, since it would frustrate a user greatly to see an indication of a keyboard shortcut and not have it work. Many older browsers such as Netscape 4 do not support the **accesskey** attribute. Using a little JavaScript to add the style sheet rule based upon the browser would fix the problem, but doing so is actually a little involved, as shown here. There really is no way to account for browser spoofing, so it isn't foolproof.

```
<!- - Use this in the HEAD section of the document only -->
<script type="text/javascript">
<!--

var agent=navigator.userAgent.toLowerCase();
var version = parseInt(navigator.appVersion);

var is_gecko = (agent.indexOf('gecko') != -1);
var is_ie    = ((agent.indexOf("msie") != -1) && (agent.indexOf("opera") == -1));
var is_ie4up = (is_ie && (version >= 4));

if (is_gecko || is_ie4up)
{
    document.writeln('<style type="text/css">');
    document.writeln('.accesskey    {text-decoration: underline; font-weight: bold;}');
    document.writeln('</style>');
}
//- ->
</script>
```

Another potential problem with accelerator keys besides browser support is accidentally masking or even overriding browser accelerator keys. Normally, a browser like Internet Explorer uses key shortcuts to access its primary menus. What would happen if you were to assign one of these preassigned letters to a form field? Well, either it wouldn't work and the menu would pop down from the browser instead, or you would kill the default action of the accelerator key in favor of your form. The user may be used to pressing F to access the file menu on the browser and become highly annoyed.

Rule: Do not override or mask browser accelerator keys.

Table 15-2 shows the current mappings for Internet Explorer and Netscape. Make sure to look carefully in your browser to see if mappings have changed before using a particular letter as an accelerator.

Given the potential problems with accelerators, one might wonder if there is really any point to using them. The reality is that for a single-time visit form, the benefit of accelerators is somewhat limited. A user will probably not be familiar enough with the form to use the shortcuts. However, for forms that a user must fill in frequently—for example, within an intranet or Web application—accelerators could really improve the

Key	Description
F	File menu
E	Edit menu
V	View menu
N	Navigation menu (Opera 6)
G	Go menu (Netscape/Mozilla) Messaging menu (Opera 6)
B	Bookmarks menu (Netscape/Mozilla only)
A	Favorites menu (Internet Explorer only)
T	Tools or Tasks menu
M	E-mail menu (Opera 6)
S	Search menu (Netscape 6), News menu (Opera 6)
W	Window menu (Netscape 7/Mozilla)
H	Help

Table 15-2. *Common Browser Reserved Accelerator Keys*

user's ability to fill things out. Moving the hand from the keyboard to the mouse does take time. For fast form fill-out, accelerators are very useful.

Suggestion: Use accelerator keys for forms that will be used repeatedly.

Tool Tips and Form Fields

A tool tip can be set to provide a small amount of information about the meaning of a particular form field or even instructions on its use. Tool tips can be set most easily using the **title** attribute for the various HTML form elements. For example, the HTML markup

```
<form>
Phone Number:
<input type="text" size="10" name="phone" id="phone"
      title="Enter your phone number without dashes" />
</form>
```

would render something like the image shown here when the user put the mouse over the field.

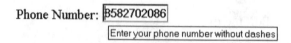

Phone Number: 8582702086

Enter your phone number without dashes

Providing extra information about a field using a tool tip is an easy way to improve form use. Be careful, however, not to put critical information in the tool tip, in case the user has a browser that will not display them.

Suggestion: Use tool tips to provide extra information about field use and format.

It is possible to use some JavaScript to simulate a tool tip in other browsers or to provide information in the browser's status bar instead.

Status Messages

Besides using tool tips, it may be helpful to utilize the status bar to provide information to the user on the meaning and use of various form fields. While the status bar may not be in the primary area of focus for the user, unlike the tool tip, it is not transitory and can be set to display as long as the field is in focus. For example, notice the status bar message in the example here and how it relates to the field currently focused.

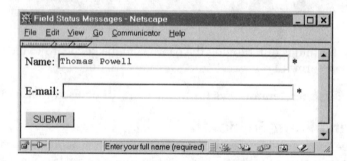

A sample script to use in any form is provided here; just alter the values passed to the *setStatus* function in each form field and include the script in the **<head>** section of your page.

```
<!DOCTYPE HTML PUBLIC "-//W3C//DTD XHTML 1.0 Transitional//EN"
"http://www.w3.org/TR/xhtml1/DTD/transitional.dtd">
<html xmlns="http://www.w3.org/1999/xhtml">
<head>
<title>Field Status Messages</title>
```

```
<script type="text/javascript">
<!--
function setStatus(msg) { window.status = msg;}
//-->
</script>
<style type="text/css">
<!--
 label {font-weight: bold;}
 label.required {color: red;}
-->
</style>
</head>
<body>
<form>
   <label class="required">
    Name:
   <input type="text" size="40" name="name" id="name"
          title="Enter your full name (Required field)"
          onfocus="setStatus('Enter your full name (required)');"
          onblur="setStatus('');" /> *
   </label>
   <br /><br />

   <label>
   Age:
   <input type="text" size="2" name="age" id="age"
          title="Enter your age in years"
          onfocus="setStatus('Enter your age')"
          onblur="setStatus('')" />
   </label>
   <br /><br />

   <label class="required">
E-mail:
<input type="text" size="40" name="email" id="email"
          title="Enter a complete well formed email address
(required)"
          onfocus="setStatus('Enter a complete well formed email
address (required)');"
          onblur="setStatus('');" /> *
    </label>

    <br /><br />
```

```
     <input type="submit" value="submit" />
</form>
</body>
</html>
```

Suggestion: Use the status bar to provide messages about field use.

Form Field Help

Given all the problems with form fill-in, it is obviously just a plain good idea to provide help wherever possible. While some browsers, notably Internet Explorer, do provide online help integration associated with the **onhelp** attribute that can be triggered with the F1 key, most users are unaware of this possibility. Besides tool tips and status messages discussed previously, the easiest way to provide help is simply to write the help information near the field in question or provide a link or icon indicating help is available, as shown here:

Robot Serial Number: [   ] ⑦

Robot Serial Number: [   ] Help

Suggestion: Provide a help button near complex form fields for context-sensitive help.

Form Validation

A key aspect of usable forms is helping people not to make mistakes. One of the easiest ways to do this is to check the contents of the forms before the user submits them. This is called form validation and can be performed both using a client-side technology like JavaScript or a server-side technology. While a server-side technology may not rely on any particular browser capability, designers should add client-side validation to pages, since they will appear more responsive to a user and avoid the round trip time to the server and back.

Rule: Validate forms client side when possible.

However, a user may not have JavaScript or similar technology useful for client-side validation. In such cases, you must rely on server-side checks. In order to get the best of both worlds, consider adding a hidden form field to a form that indicates the state of validation. For example,

```
<input type="hidden" name="validated" value="false" />
```

would be used to indicate the state of the form. If the form could be validated using JavaScript, the last task to do before submission would be to change the value of the hidden field to True. On the server-side, the program that deals with the form data would then look at the field value to determine if validation were required or not. When using this technique, we keep from doing double the work and always check whether a page is really validated. However, the security implications of this approach are troubling. If you do not perform a check on the server side, a potential hacker might figure this out and set the hidden variable to show data to be okay even though it isn't. For both security and usability reasons, you should always perform server-side validation.

Rule: Always provide backup validation on the server side.

If you end up using server-side validation, make sure that you preserve form data when the page is returned. Giving users a simple error page and then allowing them to back up may clear the form out, but it will force users to fill out the entire form again. This is very annoying and should be avoided.

Tip: Preserve filled-in form data when using server-side validation to allow for easy correction.

A big question with form validation is when to actually validate the fields. Many people wait until the very end, when the user has pressed the Submit button to check for mistakes. An error is presented, the user corrects it and moves to press the Submit button. The process repeats until all the errors are removed from the form. It would actually be better to try to correct the errors either all at once or as the user moves from field to field in the form, since it would reduce the amount of trial and error for the user.

Suggestion: Try to validate as people type using masking or as they move from field to field.

The only downside to validating as users go along is that users doing a quick heads-down fill-in of a form may prefer not to be interrupted until they have finished. You may want to consider this when dealing with validation on frequently used forms. Regardless of when errors are caught in a form, it is very important to provide a clear indication of what the errors are and how to correct them.

Rule: During form validation, provide a clear indication of what fields are in error and how to correct the error.

A subtle nuance that can greatly improve the validation experience for the user is to bring focus to a field in error. This allows the user to quickly correct the error instead of having to remember which field was in error and scroll back through the form looking for it.

Rule: Bring immediate focus to fields in error.

Finally, make sure you always consider extreme cases in validation. Don't just go for the obvious mistakes; assume edge cases, like extremely small and extremely large values, and pretend the user is trying to break your form on purpose. Given the range of data that could be entered, it might be wisest to try to limit what the user can enter rather than deal with it once they have.

Field Masks

Using JavaScript, it is possible to limit the type of data that is entered into a field as it is typed. This goes along with the idea of catching errors as they happen rather than waiting for validation later on. For example, the following script could be used in Internet Explorer or Netscape 4.x or higher to limit a field to only numeric characters.

```
<!DOCTYPE HTML PUBLIC "-//W3C//DTD XHTML 1.0 Transitional//EN"
"http://www.w3.org/TR/xhtml1/DTD/transitional.dtd">
<html xmlns="http://www.w3.org/1999/xhtml">
<head>
<title>Numerics Only Demo</title>
<script type="text/javascript">
<!--
function numbersOnly(field, event)
{
var key,keychar;

 if (window.event)
   key = window.event.keyCode;
 else if (event)
   key = event.which;
 else
   return true;

keychar = String.fromCharCode(key);

if ((key==null) || (key==0) || (key==8) ||
   (key==9) || (key==13) || (key==27) )
   {
   window.status = "";
   return true;
   }
else if ((("0123456789").indexOf(keychar) > -1))
   {
   window.status = "";
```

```
      return true;
      }
 else
    {
    window.status = "field accepts numbers only";
    return false;
      }
}
//-->
</script>
</head>
<body>
<form name="testform" id="testform">
Robot Serial Number:
<input type="text" name="serialnumber" id="serialnumber"
       size="10" maxlength="10"
       onkeypress="return numbersOnly(this, event);" />
</form>
</body>
</html>
```

The benefit of masking a field is, obviously, that it avoids having to do heavy validation later on by preventing errors from happening.

Suggestion: Mask text fields to limit the type of characters entered.

This idea can be extended to account for formatting of data as well. For example, you might let a user enter a credit card number or phone number without dashes and format it to include them automatically using JavaScript. You should always aim to fix things for users rather than to require them to enter things in a special way.

Another way to avoid errors is to modify form controls to not let users make errors. For example, why let a user type in their state of residence when a simple pull-down might work? While this may improve validation, it may actually slow down the filling out of the form for keyboard users.

It is important to note that automatically masking or formatting form data may cause confusion to international users. For example, a centered site may format dates in a way that an international user might not be accustomed to. Make sure you consider nuances like this before you start formatting data automatically.

Finally, another possible way to prevent users from making mistakes is not to let them edit a field at all if it shouldn't be modified. Through HTML or scripting, it is possible to disable a field or set its value to read-only.

Disabling Fields

A disabled form field should not accept input from the user; it is not part of the tabbing order of a page and is not submitted with the rest of the form contents. The presence of the **disabled** attribute, as shown here,

```
<input type="text" value="Can't Touch This" disabled="disabled" />
```

would be all that's necessary to disable a field under an HTML 4.0-compliant browser. A browser rendering of a disabled field is usually a "gray out" of the field. It is always a good idea to disable labels as well, either manually with a style sheet or with the **disabled** attribute.

A scripting language would have to be used to turn disabled fields on and off depending on context. The following markup, which shows how this might be used, works in most modern browsers.

```
<form name="myform" id="myform">

Color your robot?  
Yes <input type="radio" name="colorrobot" id="colorrobot"
value="yes" checked="checked"
onclick="document.myform.robotcolor.disabled=false;robotcolorlabel.
style.color='black';" />
No <input type="radio" name="colorrobot" id="colorrobot" value="no"
onclick="document.myform.robotcolor.disabled=true;robotcolorlabel.
style.color='gray';" />


<br /><br />

<label id="robotcolorlabel">
Color:
<select name="robotcolor" id="robotcolor">
    <option>Silver</option>
    <option>Green</option>
    <option>Red</option>
    <option>Blue</option>
    <option>Orange</option>
</select>
</label>
</form>
```

Unfortunately, the preceding example does not work in Netscape 4 or other browsers that lack full HTML 4 support and that vary in their scripting capabilities. The use of this field does not degrade well, as shown in Figure 15-18.

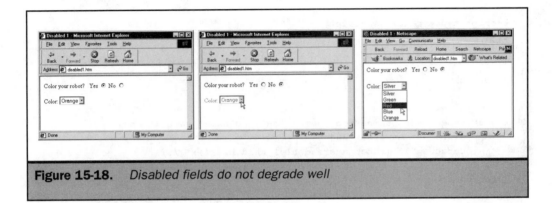

Figure 15-18. *Disabled fields do not degrade well*

If possible, it is better to redesign a form so it does not rely on a disable function, but if required, disabling can be accomplished by use of the HTML 4 **disabled** attributes and JavaScript that either hides a field or clears its value if it is disabled.

Suggestion: Disable or hide fields that are not necessary in a particular context.

Read-Only Fields

Text fields can also be set not only to a disabled state but also to read-only. A read-only text field can be clicked but not changed. Unlike disabled fields, the values of a read-only field are submitted to the server when a form is submitted. Under HTML 4, it is easy to set a text field to this state by simply including the **readonly** attribute, like so:

```
<input type="text" value="Can't touch this!?" readonly="readonly" />
```

Like the disabled feature of HTML 4, read-only does not degrade well, as older browsers will simply ignore the **readonly** attribute they don't understand, leaving the field modifiable. Using JavaScript, it is pretty easy to simulate the function of read-only simply by blurring a read-only field as soon as a user tries to select it. The example shown here demonstrates this in action.

```
<form name="myform" id="myform">

Change standard name of robot?  
Yes <input type="radio" name="colorrobot" id="colorrobot" value="yes"
checked= "checked" onclick="robotnamereadonly=false;" />
No <input type="radio" name="colorrobot" id="colorrobot" value="no"
onclick="robotnamereadonly=true;document.myform.robotname.value='Robby';" />

<br /><br />
```

```
<script type="text/javascript">
<!--
robotnamereadonly=false;
//-->
</script>

Name:
<input type="text" name="robotname" id="robotname" value="Robby"
     size="20" maxsize="20"
     onfocus="if (robotnamereadonly) this.blur();" />

</form>
```

If you plan to add your own form of read-only to deal with down-level browsers, make sure to let the user know what is read-only with an alert or a visual change. Fortunately, the need for this type of workaround will soon no longer be required, as more browsers support the **readonly** attribute.

Default Data

Even after applying every usability improvement in this chapter, filling out a form can still be an arduous process for a Web user. Before adding more questions, think of how many forms and fields you are asked to fill out during a few hours of browsing. One simple thing that can be done is to provide users with default data—data that are likely to be used. For example, if most users order only a single item, why not fill out the quantity field this way automatically? This is easily done using the **value** attribute for a field.

```
Quantity: <input type="text" name="quantity" id="quantity"
           size="2" maxlength="2" value="1" />
```

Suggestion: Provide defaults and always set values to the most likely entry.

Of course, users will not always enter the same data, so defaults are not going to help all the time. If data is stored about a user, it might be possible to populate fields with data the user has entered before. Many e-commerce sites already remember common data about a user, including address, shipping preferences, and credit card number, and may fill out the form in advance for a user. Of course, the data storage and complexity required for such personalization may be beyond some sites. Fortunately, newer browsers, such as Internet Explorer 5 and beyond, provide auto-completion facilities for form fields, which should speed up data entry significantly.

Internet Explorer AutoComplete

An important form-use improvement introduced in Internet Explorer 5 is called AutoComplete. The concept of AutoComplete is to help users fill out forms by providing a pick list of previously used values for similar form names or even by relating the information in their personal data profile or vCard to form fields.

For users to fully enjoy AutoComplete features for forms, they must enable them. In IE, select Internet Options on the Tools menu, select the Content tab, and then click the AutoComplete button. Users might also want to fill out their personal information by selecting the My Profile button in the same dialog. Once AutoComplete is enabled, the browser should provide a pick list for text fields either when the user presses the DOWN ARROW key or the characters they are typing match a previously entered value for a similar field, as shown here:

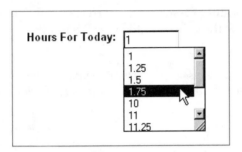

From an HTML perspective, there are a few things that are important to know about AutoComplete. First, on some fields, you may want to disable AutoComplete for privacy reasons. You can set an attribute called **autocomplete** to off in either the **<form>** or the **<input>** tag:

```
<form autocomplete="off"> ... </form>
```

or

```
<input type="password" autocomplete="off"
       name="supersecret" id="supersecret" />
```

Turning the attribute on will provide no benefit, as the user must enable AutoComplete in the first place. The key to using AutoComplete is to make sure to use similar field names as other sites out there on the Internet. The browser first presents information from previously completed form fields, and it also looks at a common name list drawn from popular Web sites. In short, if you use the same field names, the user will be prompted to reuse data. Therefore, make sure that you name fields with simple common names, like firstname, lastname, address, city, state, zip, and so on.

Suggestion: Name your field names with simple common names to take advantage of browser AutoComplete features.

Besides using common values, AutoComplete may pull information automatically from a user's vCard schema as set in the Profile Assistant. Many users have begun to use profiles such as those provided by a vCard to provide the equivalent of an electronic business card. To focus on accessing the user's profile information, use the **vcard_name** attribute in the form fields. For example, to allow someone to automatically fill in form data from their vCard profile, you might have an **<input>** tag like this:

```
<input type="text" size="40" name="company" id="company"
       vcard_name="vCard.Company" />
```

Of course, it is important to associate the correct vCard field with each field in your form. Table 15-3 provides the values for the **vcard_name** attribute categorized by the type of information.

Note   *The Mozilla 1.0 browser also supports form completion, but it requires manual intervention by the user and does not have a clearly defined interface for site designers.*

General Info	Home Info	Business Info
vCard.FirstName	vCard.Home.StreetAddress	vCard.Company
vCard.MiddleName	vCard.Home.City	vCard.Department
vCard.LastName	vCard.Home.State	vCard.Office
vCard.DisplayName	vCard.Home.Country	vCard.JobTitle
vCard.Gender	vCard.Home.Zipcode	vCard.Business.StreetAddress
vCard.Email	vCard.Home.Phone	vCard.Business.City
vCard.Homepage	vCard.Home.Fax	vCard.Business.State
vCard.Notes		vCard.Business.Zipcode
		vCard.Business.Country
		vCard.Business.Phone
		vCard.Cellular
		vCard.Pager
		vCard.Business.Fax
		vCard.Business.URL

Table 15-3.   *vcard_name* Values by Category

Before concluding this chapter, let's take a brief look at some of the very advanced GUI ideas that are starting to be applied on Web sites.

Advanced Web GUI Widgets

With careful use of JavaScript, it is possible to create a variety of advanced GUI widgets, many of which are used for navigation purposes. For example, a cascading menu that triggers page loads could be used to create a site-wide navigation bar, as shown in Figure 15-19.

The use of such a navigation bar flattens the site by reducing the number of clicks made by users to a particular page. However, it also makes a site look more and more like a typical GUI application. Adding a navigation bar to a site isn't difficult, but the

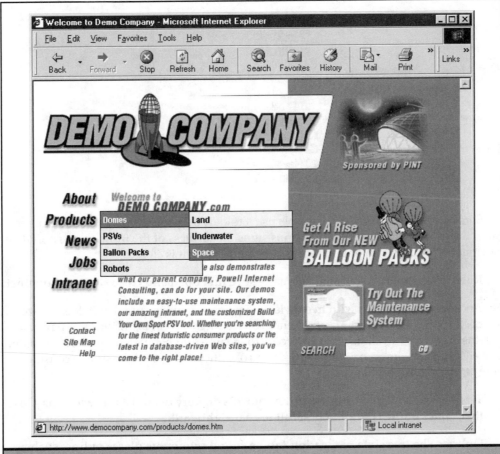

Figure 15-19.   *DHTML menus are popular for navigation*

code is far to complex too present here. Interested readers are directed to the numerous online tutorials at http://www.hiermenuscentral.com/ to learn about adding menus to their site. The code used in Figure 15-19 that shows the context of how this menu might be used in the Demo Company site can be found at http://www.webdesignref.com/examples/hiermenu.htm.

Tree Navigation

Another GUI navigation facility is the use of tree controls or expandable/collapsible outlines for navigating a site, as shown here:

Sometimes, tree navigation controls use a folder/document icon pair, while other times they use arrows or plus and minus signs. Regardless of the form, there should be a distinction between an option that is open and one that is closed.

Rule: When using a tree control, make sure that open and close states are distinct.

Another consideration with tree-style navigation is making sure that it does not get too deep. While this widget may tremendously reduce the number of clicks to navigate a site, the amount of scrolling that may occur for a large number of items both left to right, as well as up and down, could make the control difficult to use. Make sure to consider how far the control could expand.

Tip: Beware of using tree or outline controls on very deep lists, as users may lose their place or the control may scroll too far rightward.

Online: The tree style navigation can be found numerous places online, such as http://www.webdesignref.com/examples/outline.htm.

Tabbed Dialogs

With DHTML it is possible to create a tabbed dialog, as shown in Figure 15-20.

In GUI applications, a tabbed dialog is commonly used in very complex dialog boxes, and thus its use isn't always favored. However, on the Web, there may be some use for this style of interface because, in some implementations, all the contents of each tab are loaded before display, which makes the interface appear very responsive.

> **Online: The tabbed dialog example can be found at http://www.webdesignref.com/ examples/tabbeddialog.htm.**

Sliders

A slider is a relatively rare GUI interface element found mostly in color adjustment dialogs. It is possible, using JavaScript, to build a slider, as shown in the example in Figure 15-21.

> **Online: The slider demo can be found at http://www.webdesignref.com/ examples/slider.htm**

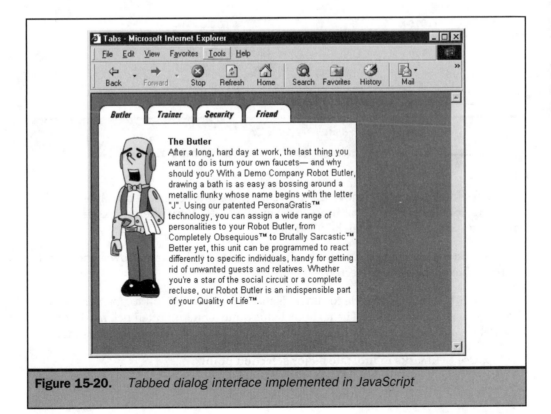

Figure 15-20.   *Tabbed dialog interface implemented in JavaScript*

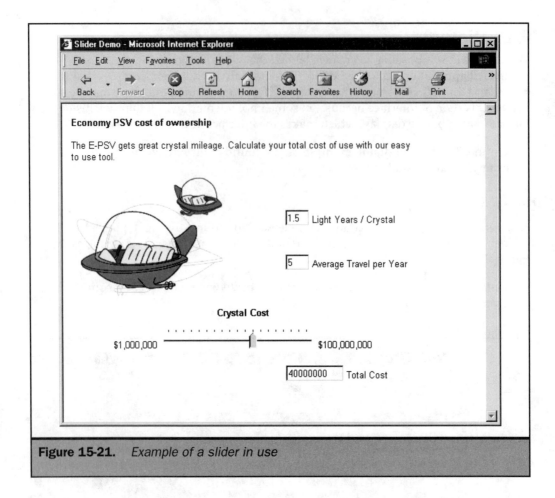

Figure 15-21.   *Example of a slider in use*

Often sliders are used to move through a large continuous range of values. Therefore, it may be difficult for users to set exact values. Very often, a text field is associated with a slider that can be filled in directly.

Tip: Add a text box near a slider to show a selected value and allow a user to set the value of the slider directly.

Another potential downside to sliders is that it is often difficult to position them directly to a particular value. The text box helps quite a bit, but often tick marks or other labels are used to indicate increments or useful stopping points for the slider.

Tip: Use tickmarks to indicate major selection points.

Context Menus

The last advanced GUI facility is the use of the context menu. Since the introduction of Internet Explorer 5, the single mouse button barrier has been broken. Now, with scripting, it is possible to sense the use of the right mouse button and perform some actions, such as creating a context menu or even suppressing the use of the menu. Some designers, hoping to make it difficult for people to steal their images, have resorted to putting a line like this in their **<body>** tag:

```
<body oncontextmenu="return false;">
```

However, turning off JavaScript or using an older browser easily thwarts this approach. An example of how a custom context menu could be created is shown in Figure 15-22.

Online: The context menu example can be found at http://www.webdesignref.com/ examples/contextmenu.htm.

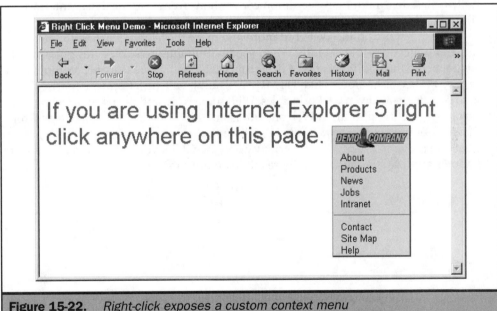

Figure 15-22. *Right-click exposes a custom context menu*

When Web Applications Are Just Applications

The preceding section indicates that the gap between what is possible in a Web site using standard technology like JavaScript, CSS, and HTML and a desktop application is narrowing all the time. In fact, using Java, ActiveX, or even Flash, it is pretty much possible to simulate any GUI widget known. When compatibility problems become less prominent, the difference between what is considered a Web application interface and what is just a plain application will somewhat blur. Already, many Windows applications are capable of accessing Internet facilities, and Web applications are acting like desktop applications. Once the gap is closed, the need for designers to be more aware of standard GUI interface conventions may become crucial. However, until the time that the two meet, it is important to try to integrate conventions. When using object technologies like JavaScript or Flash, avoid building an application interface within a Web page, or you may end up with a confusing mess. For now, keep the distinction between Web and desktop clear.

Summary

Web sites often do exhibit many common conventions from graphical user interface (GUI) design theory. Some ideas, such as double-clicking or drag-and-drop, have yet to really see much use on the Web, but more and more the Web is starting to look like a GUI application—particularly when used within intranets. Web designers must understand both the traditions of GUI design as well as what is reasonable to implement using core HTML technologies like HTML, CSS, and JavaScript. Forms, in particular, stand to benefit greatly from GUI principles. With some work and the use of a technology like Java, designers could turn a Web site into something that looks just like a desktop application—but should they? Web sites do have their own design aesthetics, as discussed in previous chapters, and strictly applying GUI layout and conventions from a Windows application might actually result in an unusable site.

The Complete Reference

Part IV

Technology and Web Design

Chapter 16

Web Technology
Best Practices

621

Correct use of technology is not necessarily a given in today's Web sites. Shifting standards and browser problems are partially to blame, but there are many other problems that are due simply to developers' lack of knowledge of best practices. In this chapter, many of the best practices that should be employed in Web building are presented. The focus is mostly on core technologies, such as URLs, HTML, CSS, JavaScript, and images, but suggestions are made for other technologies that are relevant to site design and user interaction. This is by no means a complete discussion, as each of these technologies warrants a large book of its own. Needless to say, what is presented represents the most important issues, which should not be overlooked during site construction.

Pragmatic Web Development

Before addressing specific site building best practices, we must acknowledge a few golden rules of Web development that any pragmatic Web designer should follow. First, users won't always place blame correctly. While that little display problem or error message might really be due to a non-standards–compliant browser, will users blame the browser vendor or the site owners and designers? It is unlikely users will blame the browser, unless they are savvy in Web development practices.

Rule: Users often don't blame browsers for site errors—they blame sites.

Regardless of who made the mistake, users do not want to be impacted by problems. They are at your site to accomplish a goal, not to fight with error dialogs or address Web technology problems like JavaScript, HTML, CSS, and Flash incompatibilities. This leads us to our second golden rule of Web best practices.

Rule: Users don't care how sites are built, just if they work.

You might call this the "no exposed wiring" rule. Users don't want or need to see the behind-the-scenes operation. While some visitors schooled in Web design might be impressed or curious to see your site's plumbing, for everyone else, exposing such things may cause users to be confused or to proceed with great trepidation. They are leaving the correct construction and setup of the site to us; if we appear to break this trust, they are unlikely to like the site.

However, don't assume that just because users think a site works properly, that it is necessarily a good one. Far too often Web designers are bending rules, creating work-arounds, or just plain ignoring various Web specifications. Base cases are tested, but extreme cases may be ignored or skipped. Something that looks right isn't necessarily right—you have to verify and test things. Know your site's tolerances. If it is impossible to build the site to fit all situations, define what situations it will fail under and make sure everyone involved understands the limits Don't wait to try to explain to a client or boss why your site broke under some browser; address it up front. Finally, remember that quite often people don't necessarily notice a poorly constructed building until it topples to the ground in an earthquake, and it is the same with Web sites.

Rule: Site construction must be truly solid—follow standards and conventions, verify correct execution, and openly indicate limitations.

When mistakes in site construction do happen—and inevitably they will in such an emerging field—acknowledge the problem and figure out how to address it. Do not try to shift blame to tools or the medium. Skilled painters don't blame their brushes, nor should you blame your WYSIWYG editor because it generated faulty code. Either stop using the editor, learn how to use it correctly, or fix any mistakes it makes. Also avoid blaming the medium. The Web, with all its delivery problems, is what we have. Again, the painter does not blame his canvas or his paint. Last and most important of all, do not blame the users. While the painter screaming at people who don't understand him might be put up with as a temperamental artist, an engineer who berated his customers for not knowing how to use his product would probably just end up out of a job. Web sites aren't art projects; they marry engineering and design, so tread carefully before you start blaming users for not having the appropriate browser, connection, or the sophistication to use your site properly. Address the problem and fix it to their liking. We work for our users, not the other way around. The customer (or, more appropriately, visitor) is always right—or at least must always feel right!

Rule: Acknowledge site problems and avoid placing blame on tools, the Web medium, or users.

Browser Best Practices

The first aspect of Web technology to consider is the browser. As it is the interpreter of our site, it is very important to understand a user's Web browser and what capabilities it has. The two most common browsers at the time of this book's publication are Microsoft's Internet Explorer and Netscape's Communicator/Navigator product. Other browsers, such as Opera, are used, but not to the degree of the two most popular browsers, so browser compatibility doesn't seem a big deal to some designers. However, there are numerous versions of each of the common browsers as well as betas—not to mention just plain vocal users who might use something outside the mainstream and then complain about compatibility. To address the problem of browser compatibility, designers tend to take one of the following approaches:

- Ignore the problem and assume everybody has the most common browser.
- Warn the user that the site requires a new browser, but leave it at that.
- Allow the user to self-profile and choose a version of the site that suits his or her browser or situation.
- Automatically detect and update pages to suit the browser and technology being used.
- Degrade seamlessly to the user's capabilities.

To ignore the problem is not reasonable, unless you are running in a closed environment like an intranet, or possibly an extranet, where you can define what browsers the end users must have in order to use the site. On a public site using this approach, visitors outside the browser range may have a poor experience, so often users are warned through a message indicating technical or browser requirements:

Warning users of browser requirements is not necessarily the best approach, but if you take it, clearly indicate the requirements and help users to find out how to visit the site properly. If the visit will be catastrophic using their browser, you really should lock them out of the site.

Tip: If relying on browser compatibility warnings, make the warnings clear and informative.

A slightly better version of the browser warning approach is to offer choices to the user, rather than simply warning them. This might be called self-profiling, because you ask users to make a choice based upon their particular browser version or technology, as illustrated in Figure 16-1. However, be careful with self-profiling, since you are asking the user to make a choice, and a wrong choice may result in a poor viewing experience. Further, understand that self-profiling may require that parallel sites for different browsers be created and maintained.

It is obviously better to sense or address user capabilities directly and to custom-tailor error messages or pages to the user, but carefully consider the implications of doing this. Browser sensing isn't always easy, and it may require a great amount of conditional logic or multiple versions of the same content. With browser sensing taken to extremes, one could imagine a dozen different versions of a site, running in parallel.

Browser Detection Basics

If you decide to go down the browser detection route, you need to decide first what you want to detect, what you plan on doing once you detect something, and finally how you are going to perform the detection.

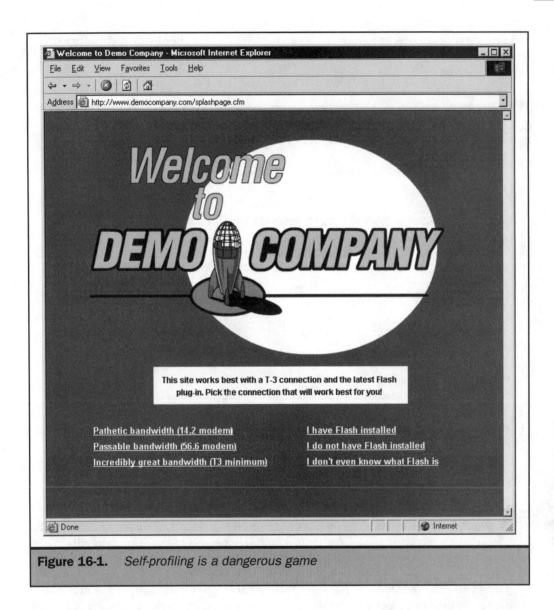

Figure 16-1.   *Self-profiling is a dangerous game*

The most basic detection indicates the particular browser and version being used. Generally, this information is retrieved by looking at the user-agent string associated with the browser. This information is transmitted by the **HTTP User-Agent** header for reading server-side programming, or it can be accessed via client-side technologies such as JavaScript. The following script demonstrates accessing browser information with JavaScript.

```
<!DOCTYPE HTML PUBLIC "-//W3C//DTD XHTML 1.0 Transitional//EN"
"http://www.w3.org/TR/xhtml1/DTD/xhtml1-transitional.dtd">
<html xmlns="http://www.w3.org/1999/xhtml">
<head>
<title>Browser Detect Example</title>
</head>
<body>
<script language="JavaScript" type="text/javascript">
<!--
var browserName = navigator.appName;
var browserVersion = parseFloat(navigator.appVersion);
var userAgentString = navigator.userAgent;
document.write("Your browser is "+ browserName + " "+
browserVersion+ ".");
document.write("<br>The user agent string is "+userAgentString);
//-->
</script>
<noscript>
 Sorry, I can't detect your browser without JavaScript on.
</noscript>
</body>
</html>
```

The example rendered under some common browsers is shown in Figure 16-2.

Note *Be careful with relying on the User Agent data, as it is easily forged directly in some browsers and in others using an add-on. Users change the string, for fun or occasionally because of privacy concerns, but it often limits their access to some sites or results in a different version of the site being delivered.*

Once you have detected the browser, then what to do? One possibility would be to deny users who don't meet a particular base requirement and redirect them to a special error page. Alternatively, you might send them to a different page built for their browser, or you might conditionally include different markup, style sheets, or other technology to suit their particular environment. For example, the page here detects to see if the user has a Microsoft or Netscape browser of at least 4.0 and redirects them to

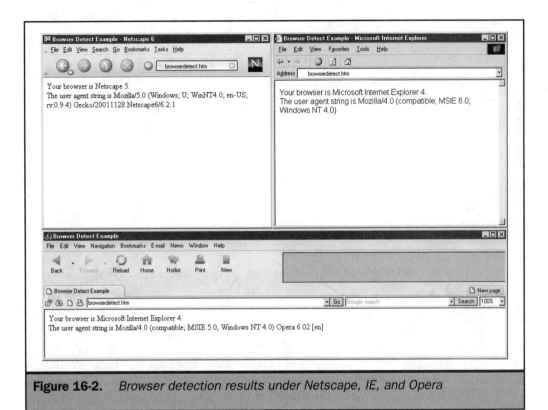

Figure 16-2.   *Browser detection results under Netscape, IE, and Opera*

the appropriate site version; otherwise it prints an error message of some sort. You could, of course, substitute an alternative page version instead.

```
<!DOCTYPE HTML PUBLIC "-//W3C//DTD XHTML 1.0 Transitional//EN"
"http://www.w3.org/TR/xhtml1/DTD/xhtml1-transitional.dtd">
<html xmlns="http://www.w3.org/1999/xhtml">
<head>
<title>Browser Detect Example 2</title>
</head>
<body>
<script language="JavaScript" type="text/javascript">
<!--
```

```
var browserName = navigator.appName;

if ((browserName == "Microsoft Internet Explorer") ||
 (browserName == "Netscape"))
 majorBrowser = true;
else
 majorBrowser = false;
var version = parseFloat(navigator.appVersion);

if (majorBrowser && (version >= 4))
  location = 'index.htm';
// -->
</script>
<h1>Browser Error</h1>
<hr />
<p>This site <strong>requires a 4.0 or better</strong> version of a
Microsoft or Netscape compatible browser.</p>
</body>
</html>
```

Instead of page redirection, you might have conditional page logic and output different page contents or style sheets based upon the accessing browser.

Browser detection as presented here is commonly performed—but sometimes incorrectly. The reason is that the check is performed only at the home page of the site. However, since most sites are porous, the user may enter the site at any publicly accessible URL. Browser detections should really occur at any possible point of entry.

Tip: Perform browser detection upon any point of entry, not just on the home page.

Browser Capabilities Detection

Detecting for browsers allows you to sort users into groups, such as standards-supporting browsers, CSS-supporting browsers, and so on. However, most developers want finer grain control than that. You can roughly divide the useful detectable information into four categories:

- Technical Issues (JavaScript support and Java, plug-ins)
- Visual Issues (color depth and screen size)
- Delivery Issues (connection speed or type)
- User Issues (language spoken or previous visitor)

Out of these four categories, you will most often end up using JavaScript to obtain at least some of the required information. Microsoft has done its part to promote improved browser detection in JavaScript using its client capabilities facility introduced in Internet Explorer 5. Using client capabilities detection, it is easy to check various user capabilities, including connection speed, as demonstrated here:

```html
<!DOCTYPE HTML PUBLIC "-//W3C//DTD HTML 4.01 Transitional//EN"
"http://www.w3.org/TR/html4/loose.dtd">
<html xmlns:ie>
<head>
<title>IE Specific Browser Detect</title>
<style type="text/css">
<!--
@media all { IE\:clientCaps {behavior:url(#default#clientCaps)}}
-->
</style>
</head>
<body>
<ie:clientcaps id="oClientCaps" />
<script language="JSCRIPT" type="text/javascript">
<!--
document.write("<h2>Screen Capabilities</h2>");
document.write("Screen Height: " + oClientCaps.height + "< /br>");
document.write("Screen Width: " + oClientCaps.width + "< /br>");
document.write("Available Height: " + oClientCaps.availHeight + "< /br>");
document.write("Available Width: " + oClientCaps.availWidth + "< /br>");
document.write("Color Depth: " + oClientCaps.colorDepth + "bit< /br>");
document.write("<h2>Browser Capabilities</h2>");
document.write("Cookies On? " + oClientCaps.cookieEnabled + "< /br>");
document.write("Java Enabled? " + oClientCaps.javaEnabled + "< /br>");
document.write("<h2>System and Connection Characteristics</h2>");
document.write("Connection Type: " + oClientCaps.connectionType + "< /br>");
document.write("CPU: " + oClientCaps.cpuClass + "< /br>");
document.write("Platform: " + oClientCaps.platform + "< /br>");
document.write("<h2>Language Issues</h2>");
document.write("System Language: " + oClientCaps.systemLanguage + "< /br>");
document.write("User Language: " + oClientCaps.userLanguage + "< /br>");
//-->
</script>
</body>
</html>
```

TECHNOLOGY AND WEB DESIGN

A rendering of this example in Internet Explorer, which appears in Figure 16-3, shows that nearly every bit of information necessary to customize a site for a user is easily found.

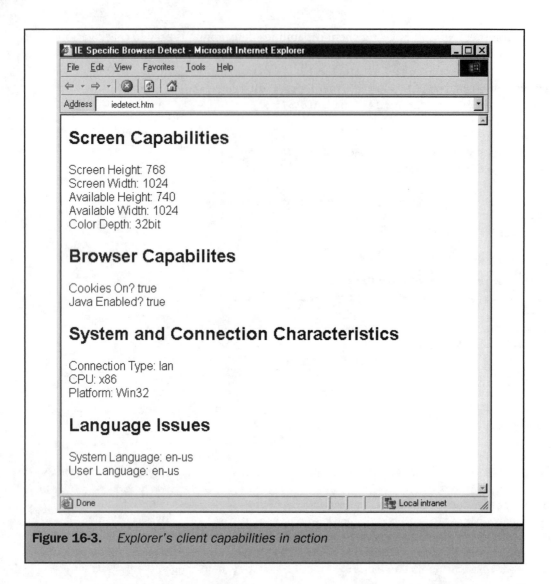

Figure 16-3. *Explorer's client capabilities in action*

Browser Detection in Practice

There are a few problems using browser detection in the way described. First, you have to make sure JavaScript can even be executed. Therefore, you may want to do some basic browser detection using server-side technologies, first looking at the user-agent string sent and then probing more deeply using JavaScript, if it is on. The next problem has to do with saving all the hard detection work performed. You should save this information to a cookie and then detect only those features that have changed. You will also have to make sure that your detection is fail proof by considering all the things that could go wrong, like script being off, a new browser version coming out, and so on. Finally, you'll have to be a browser capabilities expert. Given the number of browsers out there, this can be rather difficult. Just counting the major versions of the browsers, you'll find literally dozens. When you consider older browsers or the emerging device-based browsers, like phones and PDAs, the information will quickly become a lot to deal with. Fortunately, if you need to deal with all sorts of browser conditions, help is out there. Consider looking into browser detection and control software such as BrowserHawk (http://www.browserhawk.com).

HTML Best Practices

After the browser itself, developers are often very concerned with the various technical aspects supported, the most fundamental technology being HTML. Despite being the base technology on which Web pages are built, HTML is actually poorly understood by a good number of its practitioners. Many commercial editors produce malformed markup, and tutorials and books on the subject contain numerous and significant falsehoods. The reason is that the rules of HTML are not enforced, which leads to complacency on the part of developers. Web browsers are the root of the problem. Traditionally, browsers have been permissive in what they allowed to render. In fact, just about anything renders. Go ahead and invent a new element, like **<bogus>**:

```
<bogus>What happens?</bogus>
```

The browser isn't going to complain when it sees this. Browsers typically aren't going to complain if you don't follow the rules. Forgot to quote your attributes? No problem. Close tags not used? No big deal. Syntax is not enforced, and when browsers read pages that have errors, they will make assumptions on how to fix flawed markup or just plain ignore things they don't understand. This environment has led developers to take a loose, browser-focused approach to building Web pages. Unfortunately, HTML does have rules, and when they aren't followed, bad things can and do happen. HTML serves as the foundation of a Web page—if you build on top of shaky foundation, things are bound to fall down sooner or later. This isn't idle chatter—once you move to XHTML, these rules really may be enforced by the browser!

Rule: Write pages using standard HTML 4 or XHTML 1.0 or as much as the browser can support.

The various rules of HTML are described in Appendix C, as well as in the companion text *HTML: The Complete Reference*.

Doctypes

Regardless of how the browsers have interpreted things in the past, the syntax of HTML and XHTML is now very well defined by a document type definition, or DTD. In fact, all Web pages should begin with a **<!DOCTYPE>** declaration, which is used to indicate the particular version of markup being employed in a page. Table 16-1 shows the most common HTML DTD indicators. You might recall having noticed them at the top of the source of many Web pages.

Note *On occasion you may see other HTML doctype indicators, notably one for the 3.0 standard that was never really adopted in the Web community.*

Version	**<!DOCTYPE> Declaration**	Comments
2.0	**<!DOCTYPE HTML PUBLIC "-//IETF//DTD HTML//EN">**	This version of HTML is equivalent to what is supported by early versions of Netscape. Few sites use strictly HTML 2.0, given its limited capabilities.
3.2	**<!DOCTYPE HTML PUBLIC "-//W3C//DTD HTML 3.2 Final//EN">**	This version of HTML is similar to what is supported by 3.x generation browsers. Many of the acceptable browser-introduced proprietary tags were adopted for this version of HTML.
4.0 Transitional	**<!DOCTYPE HTML PUBLIC "-//W3C//DTD HTML 4.0 Transitional//EN" "http://www.w3.org/TR/REC-html40/loose.dtd">**	The transitional version of HTML 4.0 is roughly equivalent to what 4.x generation browsers support. However, few browsers at the time of this book's writing are fully HTML 4.0-compliant, despite the specification having been out for more than three years. The transitional form of HTML 4 preserves most of the presentational markup aspects commonly employed by Web designers.

Table 16-1. *Common HTML DOCTYPE Declarations*

Version	<!DOCTYPE> Declaration	Comments
4.0 Frameset	**<!DOCTYPE HTML PUBLIC "-//W3C//DTD HTML 4.01 Frameset//EN"**	The frameset DTD is an auxiliary definition to deal with the use of frames in a document. It defines only the frame syntax and otherwise relies on the transitional DTD.
4.0 Strict	**<!DOCTYPE HTML PUBLIC "-//W3C//DTD HTML 4.0//EN">**	The strict version of HTML 4 removes nearly all the presentation-oriented markup elements in favor of using CSS for page formatting. This greatly simplifies the language, but it forces the developer to rely on CSS, which is not properly supported in 4.x or even 5.x generation browsers.
4.01 Transitional	**<!DOCTYPE HTML PUBLIC "-//W3C//DTD HTML 4.01 Transitional//EN">**	A minor update release of the 4.0 specification that addresses errors and oversights in the original release.
4.01 Frameset	**<!DOCTYPE HTML PUBLIC "-//W3C//DTD HTML 4.01 Frameset//EN">**	The update release of the frameset auxiliary DTD.
4.01 Strict	**<!DOCTYPE HTML PUBLIC "-//W3C//DTD HTML 4.01//EN">**	A minor update release of the 4.0 strict specification that addresses errors and oversights in the original 4.0 specification.
XHTML 1.0 Transitional	**<!DOCTYPE HTML PUBLIC "-//W3C//DTD XHTML 1.0 Transitional//EN" "DTD/ xhtml1-transitional.dtd">**	The XHTML 1.0 version of the HTML 4 transitional specification.
XHTML 1.0 Strict	**<!DOCTYPE HTML PUBLIC "-//W3C//DTD XHTML 1.0 Strict//EN" "DTD/xhtml1-strict.dtd">**	The XHTML 1.0 version of the HTML 4 strict specification.
XHTML 1.0 Frameset	**<!DOCTYPE HTML PUBLIC "-//W3C//DTD XHTML 1.0 Frameset//EN" "DTD/xhtml1-frameset.dtd">**	The XHTML 1.0 version of the HTML 4 frameset specification.

Table 16-1.   *Common HTML DOCTYPE Declarations* (continued)

TECHNOLOGY AND
WEB DESIGN

The doctype defines HTML syntax very carefully. Making sure that a document complies with the indicated doctype—basically that it follows the rules—is called *validation*. Producing valid markup is not a given, and more than a few Web tools produce invalid markup. Fortunately, many popular Web editors also offer built-in validation. Online validation is also possible using a site like http://validator.w3.org, and stand alone validators such as the CSE Validator (http://www.htmlvalidator.com) are also available. To understand the benefits of validation, consider the HTML shown here. This example has numerous errors, including proprietary attribute usage, missing quotes, bad nesting, tags used in inappropriate ways, and tags that aren't closed.

```
<!DOCTYPE HTML PUBLIC "-//W3C//DTD HTML 4.0 Transitional//EN">
<HTML>
<HEAD>
<TITLE>Messed <B>Up!</B></TITLE>
</HEAD>
<BODY BGPROPERTIES="fixed">

<H1 ALIGN="center">Broken HTML
<HR>
<UL>
<P>Is this <B><I>correct</B></I>?<BR>
<A HREF=HTTP://WWW.DEMOCOMPANY.COM>
Visit DemoCompany</A>
<PRE>
    Should we do <B>this?</B>
    How about entities &copy; ?
</PRE>
</UL>
</BODY>
<HTML>
```

Running the page through a validator catches the errors, as shown in Figure 16-4.

The benefit of validation can't be overstated. Remember that HTML will serve as the foundation of a Web page. Other technologies like JavaScript and CSS rely on HTML to be well formed, so it is best to have it as error free as possible.

Rule: Validate all HTML pages.

The Doctype Switch

One new wrinkle to the use of the doctype declaration is known as the *doctype switch*. The change from syntactically loose browsers to standards-focused browsers requires the ability to provide both backward and forward compatibility for Web pages. This is

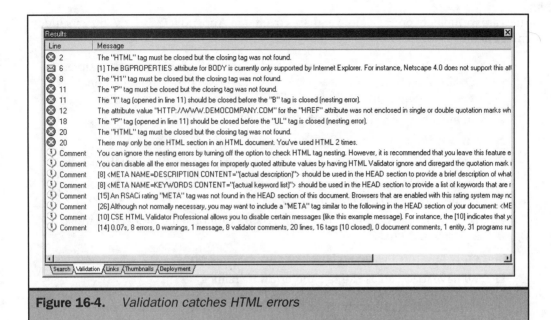

Figure 16-4.   *Validation catches HTML errors*

accomplished through the doctype. The 6.0 versions of the two main browsers now support both a standards mode and what is known as a *quirk mode*. The quirk mode allows for all the various HTML tricks and looseness commonly employed in Web pages. The browser determines the mode for reading pages by the doctype. Generally, if the doctype is missing, the browser will enter into quirk mode. Also, if the doctype indicates an older version of HTML, such as 3.2, is in use, it enters into quirk mode. However, if a more modern version of HTML is indicated, such as XHTML, the browser will switch into standards mode. This switch between modes has caused more than a few headaches for designers who didn't pay extremely close attention to their markup. In some instances, the entire box model of the page is disrupted, and visual distortions can occur—so suddenly the rules really do matter!

Rule: If you use a doctype, specify it correctly and adhere to it.

Move to XHTML

The new version of HTML, called XHTML, became a W3C Recommendation in January 2000. XHTML is a reformulation of HTML using XML, and it attempts to change the direction and use of HTML to the way it ought to be. So what does that mean? In short, rules now matter. In the past you could feed your browser just about anything and it would render. XHTML ends all that. Now, if you make a mistake, it matters significantly: the page may have problems or possibly not render at all. The rules are fortunately pretty simple and are covered in Appendix C. Briefly, they include things like

- You must have a doctype indicator and conform to its rules. For example: <!DOCTYPE HTML PUBLIC "-//W3C//DTD XHTML 1.0 Transitional//EN" "http://www.w3.org/TR/xhtml1/DTD/xhtml1-transitional.dtd">.

- You must have **<html>**, **<head>**, and **<body>**.

- **<title>** must come first in the **<head>** element.

- You have to quote *all* your attributes, even simple ones like **<p align=left>**.

- You must nest your tags properly, so ****text**** is ok, but ****text**** is not.

- You cannot omit optional close tags, so **<p>** cannot stand alone; you must have **<p>** and **</p>**.

- Empty tags must close, so tags like **<hr>** become **<hr />**.

- You have to lowercase all tag and attribute names.

There's more, but these are most of them. See the XHTML specification (http://www.w3.org/TR/xhtml1/) for all the rules. Except for a few changes in syntax, like the empty tag changes and the forced lowercase, just do your HTML correctly as you should have done before.

While XHTML doesn't appear to be a big deal, it is. Enforcing rules is going to cause problems, and most pages will have to be restructured somewhat. So the big question is will this really come to pass? If it does, XHTML will probably not sweep the Web in a short period of time. In some sense, the technology should be a big deal, since the payoff of well-formed HTML, actually XHTML, is huge—easier document conversion, improved editors that can generate clean markup, a continued movement towards the separation of Web page presentation from structure, and even automated extraction of content, since pages can be precisely parsed. Yet what will happen when the first XHTML-enforcing browser is released and it doesn't render 99 percent of the pages on the Net? Browsers already include a compatibility mode for some old markup handled through the doctype switch, as discussed previously. Designers aren't getting away from old HTML anytime soon. You might call HTML the DOS of the Web, always lurking around some place. However, moving to XHTML is not difficult, and the benefit is great. With careful formatting, normal Web pages can be written to conform to XHTML. Tools like HTML Tidy (http://tidy.sourceforge.net/) and editors should make the job of creating new documents and migrating old ones easier.

Suggestion: Conform to XHTML today to "future-proof" Web pages.

Avoid HTML/XHTML for Presentation

Another concern for designers is that with the focus on standards-oriented HTML, particularly XHTML, and the introduction of CSS, there really is a different way of building pages. In the past, HTML has been used for laying out pages visually. This was primarily accomplished using HTML tables. Unfortunately, HTML is not really designed with layout in mind, and designers have struggled to force layouts. A variety of techniques have been used to try to overcome HTML's layout limitations, including

- HTML tricks and misuse of invisible pixels and ** **
- Using proprietary browser-specific elements
- Tables
- Putting most layout and content in images
- Using binary formats like Flash to avoid HTML entirely

All these approaches have significant problems. Using browser-specific elements only works when the user has the appropriate browser. Putting layout and text entirely within images is not download friendly, accessible for those who can't see images, easy to update, or scalable to different resolutions properly. While file formats like Flash solve the scaling problem, they too are not accessible and are still unfriendly download-wise. Further, updating a site with content in image format is not easy. The use of trick HTML is very popular, but it requires extreme care on the designer's part, since not all browsers support the various work-arounds in the same manner. Layout using HTML tables is probably the only reasonable solution, but it produces excessive markup that can be difficult to update.

At its heart, HTML is supposed to be a logically oriented language to structure documents. When using an element like **<h1>**, we aren't saying make an object big; we are saying make it a headline. How the browser decides to present things is determined separately. Even a tag as simple as **<p>** that defines a paragraph says nothing about whether blank lines should be used after paragraph, how many blank lines should be used, or if the paragraph should be indented. Consider something as simple as formatting a paragraph to be indented 100 pixels. Using traditional HTML for presentation, you might have something like:

```
<!DOCTYPE HTML PUBLIC "-//W3C//DTD HTML 4.0 Transitional//EN">
<html>
<head>
<title>HTML for presentation</title>
```

```
</head>
<body>
<table border="0" cellpadding="0" cellspacing="0">
<tr>
<td width="100"> </td>
<td><p><font face="Arial, Helvetica, Sans-serif" size="+1">I am a paragraph
and I am indented around 100 pixels.</font></p></td>
</tr>
</table>
</body>
</html>
```

while using CSS in conjunction with XHTML you would have

```
<!DOCTYPE HTML PUBLIC "-//W3C//DTD XHTML 1.0 Transitional//EN"
"http://www.w3.org/TR/xhtml11/DTD/xhtml11-transitional.dtd">
<html xmlns="http://www.w3.org/1999/xhtml">
<head>
<title>CSS for layout</title>
<style type="text/css">
<!--
 #para1    {position: absolute;
            left: 100px;
            font-size: 150%;
            font-family: Arial, Helvetica, Sans-serif;}
-->
</style>
</head>
<body>
<p id="para1">I am a paragraph and I am indented around 100 pixels.</p>
</body>
</html>
```

Notice that the HTML in the second example is much simpler. The presentation and the structure of the document have not been mixed together. This will provide significant benefits when changing presentation later.

However, it should also be said that quickly embracing an all-CSS layout does have some problems. First, the browsers are very quirky in their handling of complex layouts. Second, users may turn off or override your CSS and ruin the layout. Of course, this may be what they want. Last, there are still users who won't have CSS-capable browsers. Because of this, some designers still rely on at least basic HTML formatting or continue to use layout for basic page structure and improve upon it using CSS. If your audience allows it, you should move to CSS.

> **Suggestion: Try to separate visual layout from HTML structure using CSS if possible.**

Moving away from using HTML for presentation generally requires a shift to a more logical tagging style for HTML documents. Instead of relying on headings like **<h1>** to size things, think about making headings and styling them later. Use tags like **<strong>** or **<em>** instead of **<b>** or **<i>** to provide emphasis to text. Use **<div>** and **<p>** tags liberally and try to set **id** and **class** attributes to associate meaning with the markup. Finally, stay away from visual presentation attributes and tags such as **<font>** unless you are trying to provide backward compatibility.

> **Suggestion: Use logical markup elements (for example, <strong> vs. <bold>).**

Miscellaneous HTML Best Practices

There are a variety of other best practices for markup beyond the themes presented earlier in this section. We present a few of the more common ones here, with a brief discussion of each, but be aware that the ultimate best practice for markup languages like HTML or XHTML is to simply treat their syntax as seriously as you would a programming language.

Even When Writing Traditional HTML, Lean Toward XHTML

In some cases, because of browser compatibility problems, you may need to avoid creating documents with XHTML. For example, some sites avoid pure XHTML because using the **<?xml?>** directive within an XHTML document will cause problems with many 3.0 generation browsers. Most will write pages that do not use this directive. If you are a conservative site builder not going to move to XHTML soon, consider at least following its basic tenets, such as using lowercase, quoting, tag closing, and a **<!DOCTYPE>** indicator. This should improve the situation with compatibility and minimize the work necessary to convert markup in the future.

Watch Out for HTML Space Handling Quirks

Browsers will collapse white space between characters down to a single space. Consider this markup:

```
<strong>T e s t o f s p a c e s</strong><br />
<strong>T   e   s   t   of   spaces </strong><br />
<strong>T
```

```
e s
t o f s p                           a c e s</strong><br />
```

As shown below, all the spaces, tabs, and returns are collapsed to a single element:

T e s t o f s p a c e s
T e s t o f s p a c e s
T e s t o f s p a c e s

In some situations, HTML doesn't collapse white space characters. For example, in the case of the **<pre>** tag, white space is not collapsed. Also, white space is preserved within the **<textarea>** tag when setting default text for a multi-line text entry field.

Subtle errors tend to creep into HTML files where white space is concerned; be especially careful with spacing around **<img>** and **<a>** elements. For example, consider the markup here:

```
<a href="http://www.democompany.com">
<img src="democompany.gif" width="221" height="64"
border="0" alt="Demo Company" />
</a>
```

Notice the return character after the **<img>** tag just before the closing **</a>** tag. Under some browsers, this will result in a small little "tail" to the image, often referred to as a *tick*, as shown here:

Note tickmark

Some browsers will fix the tick problem, and others won't. What is interesting is that the browsers with the tick are actually interpreting the HTML specification properly. If you have a link like

```
<a href="http://www.democompany.com">Visit Demo Company</a>
```

you would expect the space between words to be underlined—so why wouldn't other white space characters be underlined as well? Many of the recent versions of browsers eliminate ticks by making assumptions, but at what cost?

Avoid Using   for Spacing

One troubling aspect of HTML spacing is the use of the nonbreaking space entity, or ** **. Some might consider this the duct tape of the Web—useful in a bind when a little bit of formatting is needed or an element has to be kept open. While the ** ** entity can be used in many useful ways, such as keeping empty table cells from collapsing, designers should avoid relying on it for significant formatting. While it is true that markup like

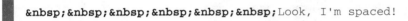

```
      Look, I'm spaced!
```

w:// create space in some text, the question is, exactly how much? In print media, using spaces to format is dangerous and things rarely line up. It is no different on the Web.

Comment and Format for Readability

Given that HTML is not space sensitive, many developers will format their code for easy readability and update and comment complex structures, such as tables. For example,

```
<!-- Sample Table -->
<table>
<!-- Row 1 -->
<tr>
     <td>Lorem</td>
     <td>ipsum</td>
</tr>

<!-- Row 2 -->
<tr>
     <td>Lorem</td>
     <td>ipsum</td>
</tr>
</table>
```

is obviously far more readable than

```
<table>
<tr><td>Lorem</td><td>ipsum</td>
</tr>
<tr>
<td>Lorem</td>
    <td>ipsum</td></tr></table>
```

even though both are equivalent. However, be careful not to reveal information that may be considered sensitive if you are not removing your comments before delivery.

Crunch for Delivery

The inverse of the comment-and-format approach is to remove white space and other nonessential items like comments to reduce file size. This is often referred to as *HTML crunching*. HTML crunching, as illustrated in Figure 16-5, can improve file size significantly for complex files. However, when using tools to automatically crunch

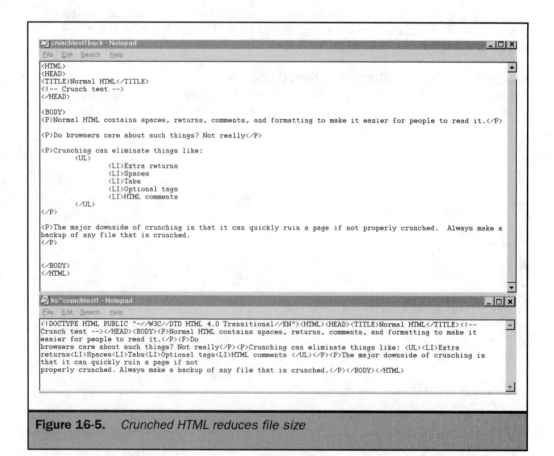

Figure 16-5.   *Crunched HTML reduces file size*

markup, always test carefully, as crunched files do not always render as intended. Further, make sure to keep original readable source around for future editing.

Specify Character Set Usage Explicitly and Be Cautious of Character Entities

Make sure that characters, particularly higher number character entities, render properly in browsers by setting the language explicitly with a **<meta>** tag, as shown here:

```
<meta http-equiv="content-type" content="text/html;
charset=iso-8859-1" />
```

Failing to do this may result in some characters not being rendered properly, often appearing as boxes. Further, be aware that many browsers, particularly older ones, do not necessarily implement higher value character entities such as mathematical operators, arrows, and various dingbats, despite their definition in the HTML 4 specification.

Use <meta> Tags Liberally

Use numerous **<meta>** tags to specify search information and related meta information, like this,

```
<meta name="Keywords" content="Demo Company, Robots, Fake Example" />
<meta name="Description" content="Demo Company is a fake company that
is used to demo various Web design and technology ideas in books.">
<meta name="Author" content="Thomas A. Powell" />
```

and also to specify HTTP header information for cache control, page refresh, content rating, and so on:

```
<meta http-equiv="expires" content="Wed, 5 June 2002 08:21:57 GMT" />
```

See Chapter 17 for more information on these delivery-related issues.

Use Consistent Naming Conventions

One aspect of HTML document construction that can be contentious for some designers is whether to use an .htm or an .html file extension. There is some benefit to using .htm, since it is slightly more transportable, but the reality is that it really doesn't matter. The only important thing is to be consistent. It is sad but somewhat amusing to watch developers struggle with files called index.htm and index.html in the same directory and not understand why changes are hot showing up. Save yourself the aggravation and be consistent in whatever you choose. Note that naming conventions go beyond simple file extensions; you should also consider the following:

- Use common directories like /images, /styles, and /scripts; this helps to keep sites organized and improves the possibility of caching site content.

- Use lowercase filenames without special characters, including dashes or underscores.

    Some servers are case sensitive, so lowercasing everything makes sites a little more portable. Many special characters will be encoded in an URL, and while some characters, like dashes, may seem harmless, they make URLs slightly harder to type. In the case of underscores, they are often mistaken for spaces. The simple solution is just to run long URLs together without special characters, but again, filenames should probably be short and easy to type and spell.

- Come up with a naming scheme for HTML tags using **name**, **id**, and **class** attributes.

The last naming suggestion could be taken further to state that naming schemes for markup objects should be not only page-unique but also site-unique to make it easy to move content from one document to another.

Use HTML Templates

Rather than make up markup for pages individually, consider using set templates. This will both ease production and lead to a more maintainable and potentially usable Web site. Why make ten different press releases, when a single press release template can be created and modified? Unfortunately, many tools and design books alike tend to take a page-at-a-time approach. Avoid doing this and instead create generic templates. Using a template will speed up development and make resulting pages more consistent in style and structure.

Consider putting in a particular doctype, style sheet links, comments, common meta tags, and other sitewide items in your template, as illustrated in the following example:

```
<!DOCTYPE HTML PUBLIC "-//W3C//DTD XHTML 1.0 Transitional//EN"
"http://www.w3.org/TR/xhtml1/DTD/xhtml1-transitional.dtd">
<html xmlns="http://www.w3.org/1999/xhtml">
<head>
<title>DemoCompany Template</title>
<meta http-equiv="content-type" content="text/html; charset=iso-8859-1" />
```

```
<meta name="Keywords" content="" />
<meta name="Description" content="">
<meta name="Author" content="" />
<meta name="Create Date" content="5/15/99" />
<meta name="Last Modification" content="1/5/02" />

<!--
   Specific Page Comments: Used SuperDuperEdit 7.0 to build the page.
-->
<link rel="stylesheet" href="styles/global.css" media="screen" />
<link rel="stylesheet" href="styles/printer.css" media="print" />
</head>
<body>
...
</body>
</html>
```

Use the Correct Authoring Tool for the Job

What's interesting about HTML is that, quite often, Web designers are more concerned with how they create HTML documents than with how well they do it or how appropriate their method of creation is. There are pros and cons for every method of page creation, from hand editing of markup to using the latest WYSIWYG editor. Each of the basic methods with some pros and cons are presented in Table 16-2.

The reality is that there are probably occasions to use each of these approaches for creating HTML documents. For example, making a quick change of a single tag is often fastest in a pure text editor. Saving out large existing print documents might make sense using a translator. Precision coding of an HTML template might best be performed within a tagging editor. Building a modest site in a visual manner is easily done using a WYSIYWG editor. Always consider the applicability of the tool to the job before applying it.

The tools change all the time, but at the time this book was written the HTML tools mentioned in Table 16-3 are popular. Certainly, many tools exist, all with their own features and benefits, but given their use at large-scale Web firms, the combination of Dreamweaver and a text editor is suggested for professional developers. An updated short list of some of the popular tools is maintained online at http://www.webdesignref.com/resources.

In the end, regardless of the tool used, always remember the following tip:

Tip: Don't blame the tool; fix the markup.

Method	Example	Pros	Cons
By hand	Coding pages with Notepad	+Great deal of control over the HTML +Can address bugs and new HTML elements or CSS properties immediately	−Slow −Error prone −Requires intimate knowledge of HTML elements and CSS properties −No direct visual representation
Translation	Saving from another tool, such as Microsoft Word	+Quick +Simplifies conversion of existing documents	−Produced HTML is often problematic −Still requires editing to add links and clean up problems
Tagging Editor	Using HomeSite	+Great deal of control +Faster than hand editing +Provides help addressing errors and writing structured HTML or correct CSS	−Can be slow −Requires intimate knowledge of HTML and CSS
WYSIWYG Editor	Using FrontPage	+Works on visual representation of page +Requires no significant knowledge of HTML or CSS +May be faster to develop page layouts	-Often generates incorrect HTML or CSS -Precise control of layout often requires direct markup editing

Table 16-2.   *Methods of HTML and CSS Creation*

CSS Best Practices

Cascading style sheets (CSS) offer an alternative to HTML-based presentation and are now being embraced by the Web design community. However, adoption of CSS does require some changes from Web developers. Unlike traditional HTML, CSS is much more syntax sensitive, and small mistakes can result in complete rule failure. Thus, designers must be aware of CSS specifications and check their rules.

   Rule: Follow CSS1 standards and validate rules.

Product	Platform(s)	URL	Comments
Dreamweaver	Windows Macintosh	http://www .macromedia.com/	A good visual design tool that balances WYSIWYG design capabilities with code editing. Strong CSS and DHTML support. Now includes the basic code editing features of the old Allaire/ Macromedia HomeSite product.
GoLive	Macintosh Windows	http://www.adobe.com /products/golive/	Very popular with the Macintosh set, this tool has a visual designer-oriented interface. Some generated markup problems have limited its popularity with strict standards developers.
FrontPage	Windows	http://www.microsoft. com/frontpage	Popular with the small developer and internal corporate development crowds. It has improved greatly, but still has a reputation for generating bad or too Microsoft-specific pages.

Table 16-3. *A Selection of Popular HTML Development Tools*

TECHNOLOGY AND WEB DESIGN

Note   *An online validator for CSS can be found at http://jigsaw.w3.org/css-validator/.*

Unfortunately, even when following the rules, significant bugs exist in modern browser implementations, and rendering quirks abound. Note the vast rendering differences under various browsers displayed in Figure 16-6. Sites like http:// style.webreview.com attempt to track the moving target of browser CSS support.

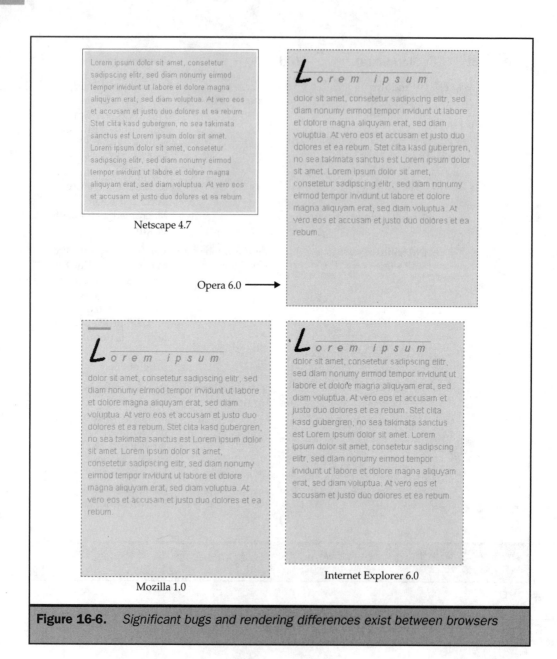

Netscape 4.7

Opera 6.0 ⟶

Mozilla 1.0

Internet Explorer 6.0

Figure 16-6. *Significant bugs and rendering differences exist between browsers*

In the future, browsers should support CSS properly, but for now developers should be aware of CSS implementation problems and test and track browser support for CSS religiously.

Rule: Test CSS rules very carefully.

There is a great deal to know about CSS, and new features are being added all the time. CSS1, the first style sheet specification, defines more than 50 properties, and CSS2 defines over 50 more. Very important, CSS2 incorporates the positioning facilities known as CSS-P (supported in the 4.*x* generation of browsers and beyond). A new version called CSS3 plans on further developing the presentation capabilities, as well as integrating better with other technologies, including scripts and vector-based graphics. Table 16-4 provides a quick summary of the various CSS specifications that can be found at http://www.w3.org/style.

Consider HTML Usage

It is important to keep in mind that HTML is the underlying foundation of a Web page. Style sheets, in fact, rely directly on the proper use of HTML/XHTML, or even XML elements. CSS does not replace HTML; it is a separate technology that binds directly to HTML tags. However, style sheets will not necessarily work predictably if bound to malformed markup.

Rule: Bind style only to correct markup.

Version	Overview of Features
CSS1	* Text handling, including fonts, sizing, style, and spacing * Background and colors * Margins, borders, and padding control of objects * List styles
CSS2	* Printing specific features * Aural renderings * Downloadable fonts * Positioned elements (CSSP) * Table support * Support for CSS with XML * Some interface control, such as cursor display * Limited behaviors, such as hover effects on links
CSS3	* Support for vertical running text * Multicolumn layout facilities * Increased support for associating behaviors and styles * Integration with graphics, color, and font technologies

Table 16-4. *CSS Versions Overview*

While it is obvious that we want to attach meaning to logical tags, be aware that this does not give you license to use CSS to obfuscate HTML markup. Rules that change the limited presentation of some tags should not be used. For example, here we make **<b>** tags act unusually and remove all forms of link decoration:

```
b  {font-style: italic; font-weight: normal;}
a  {text-decoration: none; color: black;}
```

If there is some overriding reason to use such rules, make sure they are commented.

Suggestion: Be careful when overriding default HTML tag renderings.

Because of the problem with default tag meanings in HTML, you may find the **<div>** and **<span>** tags particularly useful. Recall that the **<div>** tag is a block tag that has no default rendering, so it is useful in styling large sections of a document:

```
<div style="background: lightblue; font-weight: bold; color: black;">
<p>This paragraph is highlighted in blue.</p>
<p>So is this one.</p>
<p>Not to mention this final paragraph...</p>
</div>
```

Similarly, the **<span>** tag has no predetermined meaning or rendering, but as an inline tag includes no carriage return, so it is useful when attaching style information to just a few words or letters, like this:

```
<p>Calling out <span style="background-color: yellow; font-weight: bold;
color: black;">special sections of text</span> isn't hard with SPAN</p>
```

Include CSS Carefully

There are a variety of ways to include CSS in an HTML document, and all have pros and cons that should be carefully weighed before an approach is taken.

First, you can link to an outside style sheet by specifying a linking relationship to an external style sheet in the head section of an HTML document:

```
<link rel="stylesheet" href="styles/global.css" media="screen" />
```

External style sheets can be linked from any location. When using local style sheets, designers should set up a central directory to store style definitions.

Tip: Keep all your style sheet documents in a central styles directory.

A remote style sheet could also be referenced using an URL, such as http://www.democompany.com/styles/corpstyle.css. Designers should be careful not to rely on remotely hosted style sheets that may move or incur a download delay. Web designers should always try to use external style sheets, particularly if styles are going to be similar from page to page. An external style sheet facilitates update and is more bandwidth friendly than document-wide style (to be discussed next), since a browser can cache an external CSS file.

Rule: Use external style sheets whenever possible.

The second way to include an external style sheet is to embed it. When you embed a style sheet, you write the style rules directly within the HTML document. Document-wide style is a very easy way to begin using style sheets. It involves using the **<style>** tag placed within the head of an HTML document. Because multiple forms of style sheets may be included (beyond the standard CSS format), you should still include the **type** attribute to indicate which format of style sheet you are using, regardless of the browser's default support for style sheet technologies. You can have multiple occurrences of the **<style>** element within the head of the document, and you may even import some styles, link to some style rules, and specify some styles directly.

One concern with embedded style sheets is that not all browsers understand style information. To avoid problems, comment out the style information by using an HTML comment, such as **<!-- -->**, so that the comments aren't displayed onscreen or misinterpreted by older browsers.

Rule: Always comment out document-wide style blocks to avoid interpretation by older browsers.

A simple example of a document-wide style is shown here:

```
<style type="text/css">
<!--
   body {background-color: white; font-size: 16pt;}
   h1 {color: red;}
  /* other style rules here */
-->
</style>
```

Note that document-wide styles have a noticeable disadvantage in comparison to linked styles in that they have to be copied into each page that uses them. This makes updating sites that use document-wide styles a little harder and does not effectively use the browser's local cache. However, many designers continue to use document-wide styles because they encounter bugs with linked style rules in some browsers.

The final way to use CSS is to apply inline style to specific elements using the common style attribute:

```
<p style="color: red; font-size: 14pt;">This is red text at 14pt.</p>
```

This sort of style information doesn't need to be hidden from a browser that isn't stylesheet–aware, because browsers ignore any attributes that they don't understand. However, it does not achieve many of the major benefits of using CSS, because the style rules are closely bound to the tag. In fact, one would argue that this approach is not much better than using new tags to describe page appearance. However, some designers use CSS in this manner to provide a bridge from old HTML markup habits to CSS. For example, using inline style, you might overload HTML presentation elements like the **<font>** tag. For example, try to set text size to around 22 points. You can come close with HTML browsers—and get it just right in CSS browsers—like this:

```
<font size="5" style="font-size: 22pt;">HTML comes close; CSS hits it right
on!</font>
```

A variety of CSS properties like font sizing can be used for CSS-oriented browsers, and HTML can be used for older ones.

Suggestion: If backward compatibility is a concern, use CSS to overload HTML presentation tags like <font>**.**

Address CSS Browser Issues

Some designers use CSS just for minor page improvements, while others style their whole page with it. However, if CSS is used aggressively and older browsers access the site or users turn off style sheet support, the results can be catastrophic, as shown here:

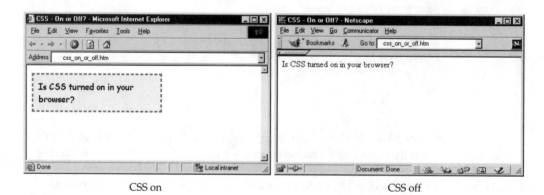

CSS on   CSS off

As you can see, when positioning and other advanced CSS rules aren't supported, the difference can be dramatic. Under older browsers, the layout completely fails; even under some modern browsers, the layout is significantly altered. Because of the problems with CSS support, designers should use script to detect the browser in use, or they can rely on older technology like tables, unless only CSS compatible browsers hitting the site can be guaranteed.

Suggestion: Avoid relying solely on style sheets for layout unless non-CSS–compliant browsers can be limited or detected and dealt with.

Another way to include CSS in a page is to depend on it less. Consider setting double spacing in a page using a CSS property. If the browser picks it up, great; if not, users won't know what they are missing. However, if you must rely on CSS for page layout, then use either browser detection or clearly labeled error messages to account for non-CSS–aware browsers and users who disable CSS. For example, consider using the following HTML markup with an inline style rule:

```
<div style="display: none;">
<table width="100%" bgcolor="red" align="center">
<tr><td align="center">
  <b>CSS Required for proper site display</b>
</td></tr>
</table>
</div>
```

This table will only show up when the user's browser ignores the style directive. We could clean this up with a class rule and provide links to more information about CSS support, but as it is, the demonstration shows that it is possible to inform users about CSS requirements easily. The example below shows our hack in place:

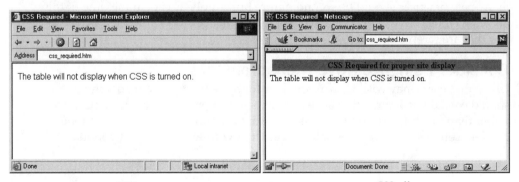

CSS on   CSS off

Rule: Account for CSS being off in browsers.

Finally, make sure that you address browser-CSS compatibility issues. Probably the best way to do this is to insert style rules programmatically, either on the server side or using JavaScript on the client side. For example,

```
<script type="text/javascript">
<!--
 if (document.layers)
  document.writeln('<link rel="stylesheet" href="nav4.css" />');
 else
  document.writeln('<link rel="stylesheet" href="standard.css"
/>');

//-->
</script>
<noscript>
  <link rel="stylesheet" href="standard.css" />
</noscript>
```

will insert a different set of style rules for Netscape 4 users than for other site visitors. In the case of being unable to run scripts, we would insert the standards-based sheet and hope for the best.

Rule: Use technologies like JavaScript to account for CSS implementation differences or provide different style sheets based upon browser.

Miscellaneous CSS Best Practices

Despite its age, CSS is still an emerging technology for many Web developers, and many best practices should be second nature but simply are not at the time of this book's writing. We will quickly cover some obvious best CSS practices, as well as a few that are rarely employed.

Consider Using Relative Measurements

Given that users may wish to increase their font size to improve readability, you should consider using relative measurements in percent (%) or em measurements rather than pixels (px) or points. This way, font may scale as users adjusts their browser settings. It is even possible to scale font with window size if you like.

Consider Using Alternative Style Sheets

Some browsers, such as Mozilla 1.0, allow users to easily select among many available styles for a page. Specifying an alternative stylesheet is easy with the **<link>** tag. Just set the **rel** attribute's value to "alternate stylesheet" and make sure to set a title so the user knows what the style is.

```
<link rel="alternate stylesheet" type="text/css" media="screen"
      title="big fonts" href="/styles/bigfonts.css" />
<link rel="alternate stylesheet" type="text/css" media="screen"
      title="fancy fonts" href="/styles/fancyfonts.css" />
```

The alternative style sheets will then be selectable under Mozilla 1.0's View menu, provided that the .css files are located where the code indicates.

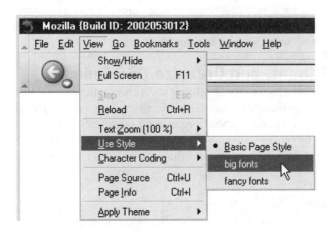

Alternate style sheets might be used to provide different themes for a page or improve usability for those users who may be visually impaired.

Provide Printer Style Sheets

CSS2-aware browsers can support printer style sheets, which allow designers to change the look of the printed page as compared to what is shown on screen. Printer styles might be referenced like this:

```
<link rel="stylesheet" type="text/css" media="print"
      href="/styles/print.css" />
```

When using printer style sheets, since some browsers do not support them, you might want to provide a link to a special print page. However, you should try to make sure that what prints in a CSS2-aware browser is the same as what is on the special printing page.

Match CSS Selector Cases

CSS is not specific, necessarily, to HTML and can be used with any arbitrary markup language. The selectors used in a style sheet should match tags exactly. So if you are using XHTML and case all tags lowercase, you should use lowercase selectors, even if the browser will work using uppercase.

Use id and class Rules Properly

The value of a particular **id** attribute is supposed to be unique to the tag, while a **class** value may be used on many tags. While this may seem obvious, many CSS developers continually use **id** values multiple times or use **class** on a single unique tag because browsers will render appropriately. This is just poor style and will cause problems once scripting is used to access the tag object.

Comment, Format, and Organize CSS Rules

As with HTML, if you plan on hand-editing style sheets, they should be neatly formatted and commented using the /* */ syntax. Matching the braces for rules can also help improve readability. Be careful about organizing your CSS rules. Some document authors may wish to group various selectors together or even alphabetize rules by selector—be careful, as the cascade relationships of rules can spoil your organization scheme.

Compress Style Sheets

CSS is also like HTML in not being terribly dependant on white space; thus, rule files can be crunched by removing white space characters. CSS rules can be further reduced by shorthand rules. For example, many rules for fonts, backgrounds, borders, and so on have a master rule that can set many properties at once. So, instead of

```
p {font-weight: normal;
   font-size: 16pt;
   font-family: Arial, Helvetica, Sans-serif;
   line-height: 150%;}
```

you might write

```
p {font: normal 16pt/150%  Arial, Helvetica, Sans-Serif;}
```

The only downside to using shorthand rules is that it can be difficult to find syntax errors in complex compound rules.

XML Best Practices

As we already know, traditional HTML isn't perfect, but it works pretty well, particularly if you consider the millions of documents created by people all over the world with varying markup knowledge levels. Yet, HTML does have two major weaknesses—it does not enforce rules, and it is not extensible.

As mentioned earlier, browsers do not strictly enforce HTML rules. While this makes it easy for mere mortals to create documents, it makes it difficult for programs to read our inconsistent results. This could have serious ramifications if structure were important. Imagine if you created an electronic invoice in HTML to send to a customer. The customer might write a program to read the invoice and automatically submit the appropriate information to their accounts payable system. However, their program would have to assume a particular structure for the document. What happens if you or your editor changes the structure of the HTML invoice? Obviously the client's program breaks. Even without changing structure, just the loose, imprecise nature of HTML could make pulling apart the document a difficult chore.

The second problem with HTML, that it's not extensible, means that we can't define our own elements. Consider again the idea of the electronic invoice. If a tag were defined called **<TOTAL>**, it would be pretty easy to parse the document and find the amount owed. A whole range of tags could be defined for the invoice language, including **<ADDRESS>**, **<RATE>**, **<DESCRIPTION>**, **<HOURS>**, **<TAX>**, and so on. We might get so excited about our language that we name it IML, for Invoice Markup Language. We could even create a simple document in our language, like so:

```
<?xml version="1.0"?>
<INVOICE>
<TITLE>Invoice</TITLE>
  <CUSTOMERINFO>
   <NAME>Demo Company</NAME>
   <ADDRESS>
    <STREET>2105 Garnet Ave., Suite E</STREET>
    <CITY>San Diego</CITY>
    <STATE>CA</STATE>
    <ZIP>92109</ZIP>
   </ADDRESS>
  </CUSTOMERINFO>

  <SERVICES TYPE="CONSULTING">
   <DESCRIPTION>Jabbering about things</DESCRIPTION>
   <RATE>250.00</RATE>
```

```
    <HOURS>3</HOURS>
    <TOTAL>750.00</TOTAL>
    </SERVICES>
</INVOICE>
```

and name it invoice1.xml. This document would actually render as something in an XML-aware browser like Internet Explorer 6, as shown in Figure 16-7. Of course, if mistakes are made, a conforming XML browser will display errors, as shown in Figure 16-8.

A few questions probably arise after considering this last example. First, how exactly do you define an XML language? Next, how do you provide a rendering for it? Finally, what is the point of doing all this? Let's begin with the technical issues and address usage issues as we go.

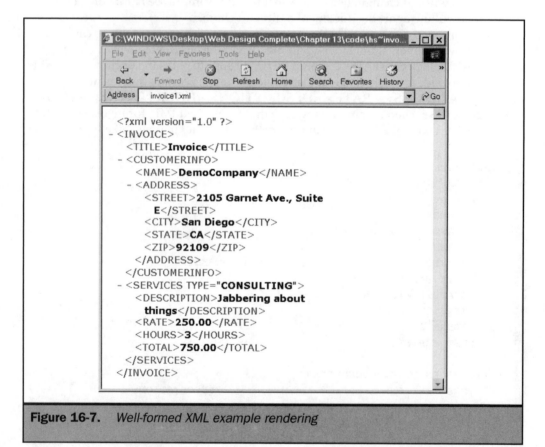

Figure 16-7.   *Well-formed XML example rendering*

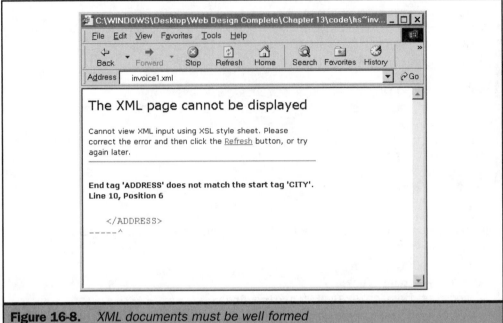

Figure 16-8. *XML documents must be well formed*

Defining an XML language is rather easy: just make up some tags and follow the basic syntax rules like nesting, quoting attributes, casing things the same, and so on. Documents that follow such basic XML syntax are called *well formed*. Of course, carefully following syntax is fine and good, but these tags don't really have any meaning. To make this a valid document, we have to define the rules of our particular language by writing a document type definition (DTD). A DTD defines how a language can be used, by indicating what elements can contain what other elements, the values of attributes, and so on. A simple DTD to define a grading language for the invoice example is defined here. Readers looking for basics on XML might find the W3C (http://www.xmlfile.com/) site useful, and the various sections of the W3C site—such as http://www.w3.org/XML/, as mentioned in Chapter 3—are also valuable, though a little more technically dense.

```
<!-- INVOICE DTD -->
<!ELEMENT   INVOICE   (TITLE,CUSTOMERINFO,SERVICES)>
<!ELEMENT   TITLE (#PCDATA)>

<!ELEMENT   CUSTOMERINFO   (NAME,ADDRESS)>
<!ELEMENT   NAME (#PCDATA)>
<!ELEMENT   ADDRESS   (STREET, CITY, STATE, ZIP)>
```

```
<!ELEMENT  STREET (#PCDATA)>
<!ELEMENT  CITY (#PCDATA)>
<!ELEMENT  STATE (#PCDATA)>
<!ELEMENT  ZIP (#PCDATA)>

<!ELEMENT  SERVICES  (DESCRIPTION,RATE,HOURS,TOTAL)>
<!ATTLIST  SERVICES  TYPE  (CONSULTING | PLUMBING | HOUSEWORK)
#REQUIRED>
<!ELEMENT  DESCRIPTION (#PCDATA)>
<!ELEMENT  RATE (#PCDATA)>
<!ELEMENT  HOURS (#PCDATA)>
<!ELEMENT  TOTAL (#PCDATA)>
```

This DTD file, named invoice.dtd, would be referenced by the example XML file, such as the one shown here:

```
<?xml version="1.0"?>
<!DOCTYPE INVOICE SYSTEM "invoice.dtd">
<!-- the document instance -->
<INVOICE>
<TITLE>Invoice</TITLE>
  <CUSTOMERINFO>
   <NAME>Fake Company</NAME>
   <ADDRESS>
    <STREET>123 Fake Street</STREET>
    <CITY>San Diego</CITY>
    <STATE>CA</STATE>
    <ZIP>92117</ZIP>
   </ADDRESS>
  </CUSTOMERINFO>

  <SERVICES TYPE="HOUSEWORK">
   <DESCRIPTION>Fixing the hole in the ceiling</DESCRIPTION>
   <RATE>25.00</RATE>
   <HOURS>2</HOURS>
   <TOTAL>50.00</TOTAL>
  </SERVICES>
</INVOICE>
```

The example would not only be syntactically checked, but we could also validate the document against the DTD. If this last example leaves you wondering why you would ever want to define your own language, it should. There are certainly many reasons to define a language, but there also many reasons not to. In fact, with everyone going around defining languages, we could easily turn the Web into a modern day equivalent of the Tower of Babel, with HTML cast aside in favor of languages that many organizations don't know or agree upon. There is no reason for everyone to be writing DTDs. Most developers should be more concerned with using a language rather than defining their own. Many useful languages—such as SMIL (Synchronized Multimedia Interchange Language) used to create presentations (http://www.w3.org/TR/REC-smil/); WML (Wireless Markup Language) the primary cellular language (http://www.wapforum.org); and, of course, XHTML—are already in fairly widespread use.

Suggestion: Rely on standard XML languages rather than in-house–developed languages.

The fact of the matter is that XML from a designer's point of view is like concrete in the mind of an architect. You use it to build things, but you don't play around in it or wonder about its chemical composition.

What should be considered next is what can be done with XML. It doesn't seem to look like much in a browser. While that's true, we could convert it into HTML or even attach a style sheet to it. Consider the style sheet here, called invoice.css.

```
INVOICE         {font-family: Arial; font-size: medium;}
TITLE           {text-align: center; text-decoration: underline;
                {display: block; font-size: x-large;}
CUSTOMERINFO    {text-align: right;    display: block;}
NAME            {font-size: smaller; font-weight: bold;
                 display: block;}
ADDRESS, CITY   {display: block;}
STATE, ZIP      {display: inline;}
SERVICES        {text-align: left; position: relative; top: 50px;
                 background-color: #EEE88A; display: block;
                 border: solid;}
DESCRIPTION {position: absolute; left: 20%; font-style: italic;}
RATE        {position: absolute; left: 50%; font-family: Courier;}
TOTAL       {position: absolute; left: 80%; color: green;
                font-weight:bold}
```

This could be associated to the XML file invoice.xml with a simple statement like this:

```
<?xml-stylesheet href="invoice.css" type="text/css" ?>
```

In a browser supporting both CSS and XML, the page would begin to take shape as shown in Figure 16-9.

> *This style sheet will have rendering issues. There are shortcomings in the approach taken and the use of CSS in this fashion, but it does show that something could be rendered without changing it into HTML.*

This last example explicitly shows the idea of separation of logic and presentation. However, what's going to happen in older browsers? The answer is absolutely nothing. For now, client-side XML doesn't make sense, so you will need to convert XML tags into HTML or XHTML with CSS to render safely in browsers.

Suggestion: Transform XML on the server side into something that can be viewed on the client side.

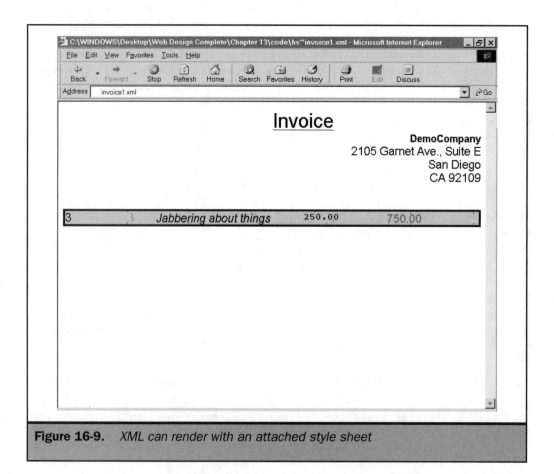

Figure 16-9. *XML can render with an attached style sheet*

What XML will eventually bring is the power to make data more regular and more specific to particular applications or industries. Migrating Web data to and from databases, exchanging documents with other parties, and navigating large collections of documents could get significantly easier because documents will follow a rigid structure. XML's rule enforcement should allow data interchange between many organizations, making our example of an automated invoice exchange system a reality, and it will signal a move away from just publishing documents, but writing programs to handle them.

Suggestion: Use XML as a neutral storage format and for exchange.

Web Programming Best Practices

Sometimes a big challenge in Web-based programming is making sure to choose the right technology for the job. More often than not, designers are quick to pick a favorite technology, whether it is JavaScript, ASP, ColdFusion, or Java, and use it in all situations. The reality is that each technology has its pros and cons. In general, client-side and server-side programming technologies have characteristics that make them complementary rather than adversarial.

Consider, for example, the situation of adding a form to a Web site to collect data to save in a database. It is obvious that checking the form to make sure that the user entered the correct information would make more sense to perform on the client side, since it would not force a network round-trip to the server just to check the input data. Client-side programming would make the form validation more responsive and frustrate the user less. On the other hand, putting the data in the database would be best handled by a server-side technology, given that the database would be located on the server side of the equation. The reality is that each general type of programming has its place, and a mixture is often the best solution.

Rule: Consider using both client-side and server-side technologies in a site, rather than just one or the other.

Server-Side Programming Best Practices

Server-side programming comes in many flavors, including CGI scripts, server-API programs like Apache Modules and ISAPI programs, Java servlets, and server-side scripting environments such as Microsoft's Active Server Pages (ASP/ASP.NET) and Macromedia's ColdFusion. Each technology has its pros and cons, but all forms of server-side programming share one common quality: *control.*

The server is really the only part of the client-server equation that the developer has real control over, and we can carefully dictate how a server-side program will run. Server-side programs don't rely to any major degree on client-side variations, so in theory, a site using interactivity running on the server can deliver pages to any type of browser. Despite a great deal of hype about client-side technologies, most web large sites rely to a great degree solely on server-side technology to develop interactive elements. Of course, the major downside of server-side programming is the negative effect on speed. Because all the interactivity takes place on the server, the user may perceive delays due to server response time limitations or network round-trip time. The best practices presented here focus on performance, security, and maintainability, which are core to any Web site server-side program, regardless of what it is written in.

Create a Capacity Plan When Using Server-Side Technologies

Capacity plans are not trivial, and they do reveal that it often takes a great deal of hardware and bandwidth to service users. Numerous examples of sites faltering under enormous user loads show how difficult it is to capacity plan sites. However, it is possible to do. If you know that a typical page takes two seconds to build and is 50KB in size, you can actually calculate things like the number of simultaneous users that can be handled with 1 Mbps of bandwidth.

Carefully Monitor Responsiveness of Server-Side Technologies

Even with a capacity plan in place, you should constantly monitor your server-side programs to make sure they are responding quickly enough to user requests. Slow pages will simply drive visitors away.

Use Compiled Languages or Server Modules to Improve Server-Side Performance

Many server-side programs are written in interpreted scripting languages. Regardless of your take on which scripting language is better, all will not fare well performance-wise under heavy load. Consider using a compiled language like C for server-side programming tasks when performance is key. If you want very high performance, you may have to rewrite your application to utilize a Web-server API, such as Apache Modules for Apache-based Web sites or ISAPI modules or filters for Microsoft IIS-based systems. You also may find that, even if performance is not an issue, you still want to separate out complex business logic into compiled binaries and leave server-side scripting technologies for page generation.

Pregenerate or at Least Cache Server-Scripted Pages if Possible

Many sites using server-side scripting needlessly regenerate page content over and over again for visitors. If the press release is the same for every visitor, why query a database and build it fresh each time? It might be better instead to build pages into static HTML ahead of time, if they do not change from visitor to visitor. This can be performed manually or by using some form of server-side cache that holds generated page results.

Try to Separate HTML Markup from Script Logic

Many scripting environments and CGI programs intermix markup and script code freely. While this may seem appealing, like mixing in CSS into HTML, it will make maintenance difficult. Consider pulling HTML fragments or templates into scripts rather than to hard-code markup information into scripts.

Use a Centralized Directory for Server-Scripts, Particularly cgi-bin Programs

If you use server scripts, it is often a good idea to keep them in one directory. Commonly, this is a cgi-bin directory if you are writing CGI programs. The value of following this convention is that it not only organizes your site, but it also allows security restrictions to be more easily placed on scripts. You do not necessarily have to name such a directory cgi-bin, and you may want to name it something less revealing, like /scripts or /programs.

Avoid Showing File Extensions of Server-Side Programs

Just because you use Perl to write CGI programs or use other server-side technologies, your users shouldn't care. Don't expose such information inadvertently via file extensions like .pl. Instead, try to use more generic extensions like .cgi or, in some cases, no extension at all. While worrying about extensions might seem trivial, hackers trying to compromise a server take note of such little bits of information.

Avoid Complex URLs if Possible

Along the same lines as the previous best practice suggestion, it is not a good idea to use complex URLs, particularly if they are easily decipherable. The example here shows a query string that might be manipulated.

```
http://www.democompany.com/scripts/prod.php?product_id=57&status=view
```

Guess what happens if you set the **product_id** value yourself or start playing with the status value? Hackers will certainly try to play around with query strings to crack into a system or get it to dump information via an error page. In many cases, this rule will require you to use the POST method rather than the GET method, which may be preferable from a usability point of view, as it keeps URLs very simple.

Avoid Exposing Back-End Information in Diagnostics and Errors

Often when a server-side program yields errors, it will dump out valuable diagnostic information, such as the name of the server, the directory path used, the software being used, and so on. This information is highly coveted by persons trying to crack a Web server, so they will purposefully try to cause errors to reveal such information. Make sure that you provide sanitized error messages to avoid such information leakage.

Carefully Check Incoming Data

When running server-side programs, you need to be very careful to screen incoming data. Very often potential hackers will attempt to send too much data via forms or GET strings in hopes of causing some form of buffer overflow to reveal useful information. In other cases, they may try to directly manipulate sent data to crack a site or cheat an e-commerce system. Such "front door" attacks are increasingly common, and server-side programs should carefully check data before doing anything with it.

Avoid Running Command Line Programs via a Script

An especially dangerous form of server-side program will run command-line programs using submitted data. Generally, such server-side programs should be avoided, if possible; if you must write such a script, you should be very careful to check incoming data.

 As we have seen in this discussion, many of the best practices for server-side programming are related to delivery—a more in-depth discussion of the various delivery requirements can be found in Chapter 17.

Client-Side Programming

The major drawback of server-side programming is, of course, a lack of speed due to the round-trip time over the network. Programs executed client side, however, appear to be quite fast to a user in most cases. This makes sense, if you consider that no network travel is required to show the result of some action. Of course, client-side programming does come with one serious drawback—a lack of control. For example, when designing public Web sites it is hard to say exactly what kind of users are going to hit a site. What browser is being used, what features are turned on, what kind of processor the user has are all questions that are not always easy to answer.

Even with browser sensing, client-side programming does leave things more up to chance. There is always that one user who doesn't want to play by the rules, who wants to use a beta browser release, turn off their scripting support mid-visit, or modify their browser in some unpredictable way, such as removing or modifying their user-agent header. Client-side programming often won't be able to recover from such changes, because it relies on the browser for more than mere display of data. Therefore, client-side programming doesn't always work. The best approach is to assume that it will work, but to account for it not working by providing some fallback state. Consider the approach to form validation again: go ahead and check the form client side, but if it needs to be checked once it reaches the server, perform the check again.

Rule: Provide a fallback state for all client-side programming technologies.

The idea of always accounting for potential problems is a recurring theme of this chapter. Now, let's take a look at some best practices with client-side programming, first with a special focus on using JavaScript, followed by a discussion of object technologies, such as Netscape plug-ins, Microsoft ActiveX controls, and Java applets.

JavaScript Best Practices

JavaScript is certainly the premier client-side scripting language in use today on the Web and is used for a variety of tasks such as form validation, implementing navigation systems, and adding special page effects. Originally developed by Netscape and then supported by Microsoft browsers in the form of JScript (a clone language used in Internet Explorer), the language is now standardized as ECMAScript, a cross-platform Internet standard for scripting. Browser vendors generally comply with the specification, but vendors and developers alike will still use the commonly recognized JavaScript name.

While standards have improved the situation with JavaScript, compatibility problems still abound, and very often it is used very sloppily. Little consideration is given to browsers that have scripting off or do not support particular objects, and errors are most often left unhandled. The majority of the best practices for JavaScript address various contingency cases for that language, but a few also address other issues, such as programming style or performance.

Consider Carefully How JavaScript Is Included in Pages

There are four standard ways to include script in an HTML document:

- Within the **<script>** tag
- As a linked file via the **src** attribute of the **<script>** tag
- Within an HTML event handler attribute such as **onclick**
- Via the pseudo-URL **javascript:** syntax referenced by a link

The following simple example shows each form of inclusion in action, including a linked script that adds some support functions, a link triggered script, a **<script>** tag in the head of the document, and finally an event handler on a button that triggers the script in the head.

```
<!DOCTYPE HTML PUBLIC "-//W3C//DTD XHTML 1.0 Transitional//EN"
"http://www.w3.org/TR/xhtml11/DTD/xhtml11-transitional.dtd">
<html xmlns="http://www.w3.org/1999/xhtml">
<head>
<script language="JavaScript" type="text/javascript"
```

```
        src="scripts/global.js"></script>
<script language="JavaScript" type="text/javascript">
<!--
function alertTest( )
{
  alert("Danger! Danger!");
}
//-->
</script>
</head>
<body>
<div align="center">
<form id="form1" name="form1">
<input type="button" value="Don't push me!"
        id="button1" name="button1"
        onclick="alertTest()" />
<br /><br />
<a href="javascript: alert('ouch');">Push me</a>
</form>
</div>
</body>
</html>
```

Use Linked Scripts

A very important way to include a script in an HTML document is by linking it via
the **src** attribute of the **<script>** tag. The example here shows how we might put the
function from the previous example in a linked JavaScript file:

```
<!DOCTYPE HTML PUBLIC "-//W3C//DTD XHTML 1.0 Transitional//EN"
"http://www.w3.org/TR/xhtml1/DTD/xhtml1-transitional.dtd">
<html xmlns="http://www.w3.org/1999/xhtml">
<head>
<script language="JavaScript" type="text/javascript"
        src="danger.js"></script>
</head>
<body>
<div align="center">
```

```
<form id="form1" name="form1;">
<input type="button" value="Don't push me!"
       id="button1" name="button1"
       onclick="alertTest()" />
</form>
</div>
</body>
</html>
```

Notice that the **src** attribute is set to the value "danger.js." This value is a URL path to the external script. The linked file will contain only the JavaScript code to run, no HTML or other Web technologies. So, in this example, the file danger.js should contain the following script:

```
function alertTest( )
{
  alert("Danger! Danger!");
}
```

The benefit of script files that are external is that they separate the logic, structure, and presentation of a page. With an external script, it is possible to easily reference the script from many pages in a site and update only one file to affect many others. Further, a browser can cache external scripts, so their use effectively speeds up Web site access by avoiding extra download time spent refetching the same script.

While there are many benefits to using external scripts, they are often not used because of some of their potential downsides. First, not all JavaScript-aware browsers support linked scripts. Fortunately, this problem is mostly related to older browsers, specifically Netscape 2 and some Internet Explorer 3 releases. Another challenge with external scripts has to do with browser loading. If an external script contains certain functions referenced later on, particularly those invoked by user activities, programmers must be careful not to allow them to be invoked until they have been downloaded, or else error dialogs may be displayed.

Tip: Be aware of script load order when using linked scripts.

Finally, there are just plain and simple bugs when using external scripts. Fortunately, most of the problems with external scripts can be alleviated with good defensive programming styles, as demonstrated throughout the book. However, if stubborn errors won't seem to go away and external scripts are in use, a good practice is to include the code directly within the HTML file.

Focus on Using Common Event Handlers

Under the HTML 4.0 specification, nearly every tag should have one of the core events, such as **onclick, ondblclick, onkeydown, onkeypress, onkeyup, onmousedown, onmousemove, onmouseout, onmouseover,** and **onmouseout,** associated with it. For example, even though it might not make much sense, you should be able to specify that a paragraph can be clicked using markup and script like this:

```
<p onclick="alert('Under HTML 4 you can!')">Can you click me</p>
```

Many older browsers, even from the 4.*x* generation, won't recognize event handlers for many HTML elements, such as paragraph. Most browsers, however, should understand events such as the page loading and unloading, link presses, form fill-in, and mouse movement. Unfortunately, the degree to which each browser supports events and the ways in which they are handled vary significantly, and numerous extended events have been introduced by Microsoft.

Avoid HTML Event Handlers if Possible

HTML event handlers should remind readers of the inline style attribute. Like inline styles, scripts using HTML event handlers such as **onclick** are closely integrated with markup. This can make pages messy and maintenance difficult. It is possible in many scripts to register events in a different way to clear up this situation. Consider this rewrite of the running example that removes the **onclick** handler.

```
<!DOCTYPE HTML PUBLIC "-//W3C//DTD XHTML 1.0 Transitional//EN"
"http://www.w3.org/TR/xhtml1/DTD/xhtml1-transitional.dtd">
<html xmlns="http://www.w3.org/1999/xhtml">
<head>
<script language="JavaScript" type="text/javascript"
        src="danger.js"></script>
</head>
<body>
<div align="center">
<form id="form1" name="form1">
<input type="button" value="Don't push me!"
        id="button1" name="button1" />
</form>
```

```
</div>
<script language="JavaScript" type="text/javascript" >
<!--
document.form1.button1.onclick=alertTest;
//-->
</script>

</body>
</html>
```

We could continue to clean the markup by using a linked script to register the various event handlers. We see that separating logic in JavaScript from page markup can be just as important as separating CSS from markup!

Avoid the javascript: pseudo-URL

The JavaScript pseudo-URL is often used in links, but it is not very degradable. In the following, what will happen if script support is off or unsupported by the browser?

```
<a href="javascript:alert('Javascript running');">Click me</a>
```

Most likely, a page load error would occur. If a link trigger is required, a better approach is to use an **onclick** event handler for JavaScript and provide a link to an alternative rendering or error page in case script is off, as demonstrated here:

```
<a href="javascriptoff.htm" onclick="alert('JavaScript
running');return false;">Click me</a>
```

Note that the returned **False** value is used to kill the default action of a link, so the backup page is not loaded.

Use HTML Comments to Hide JavaScript Code in the `<script>` Tag

As with CSS, it is important to hide script code enclosed in the **<script>** tag from nonsupporting browsers. This is accomplished either using a linked script or commenting out the code. Notice that the comment structure is slightly different: the HTML close comment --> is actually similar to JavaScript syntax.

```
<script type="text/javascript">
<!--
/* Insert JavaScript below */

// -->
</script>
```

Handle the JavaScript Off Situation with <noscript>

When a browser does not support JavaScript or JavaScript is turned off, you should provide an alternative version or at least a warning message telling the user what happened. The **<noscript>** element can be used to accomplish this very easily. All JavaScript-aware browsers should ignore the contents of **<noscript>** unless scripting is off. The following example illustrates a simple example of this versatile element's use.

```
<!DOCTYPE HTML PUBLIC "-//W3C//DTD XHTML 1.0 Transitional//EN"
"http://www.w3.org/TR/xhtml1/DTD/xhtml1-transitional.dtd">
<html xmlns="http://www.w3.org/1999/xhtml">
<head>
<title>noscript Demo</title>
</head>
<body>
<script type="text/javascript">
<!--
    alert("Your JavaScript is on!");
//-->
</script>
<noscript>
    <em>Either your browser does not support JavaScript or it
        is currently disabled.</em>
</noscript>
</body>
</html>
```

Figure 16-10 shows a rendering in three situations: first a browser that does not support JavaScript, then a browser that does support it but has JavaScript disabled, and finally a modern browser with JavaScript turned on.

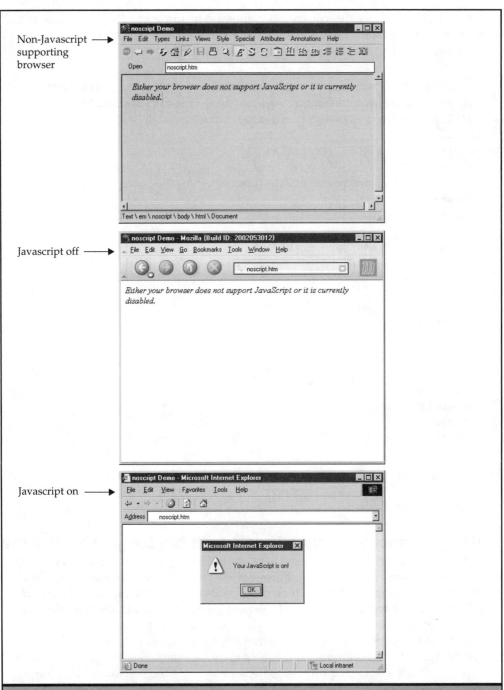

Figure 16-10.   *Use <noscript> to handle browsers with no JavaScript*

One interesting use of the **<noscript>** element is to automatically redirect users to a special error page if they do not have scripting enabled in the browser or are using a very old browser. The next example shows how this might be done:

```
<!DOCTYPE HTML PUBLIC "-//W3C//DTD XHTML 1.0 Transitional//EN"
"http://www.w3.org/TR/xhtml1/DTD/xhtml1-transitional.dtd">
<html xmlns="http://www.w3.org/1999/xhtml">
<head>
<title>Needs JavaScript</title>
<noscript>
    <meta http-equiv="Refresh" content="0;URL=noscript.htm" />
</noscript>
</head>
<body>
<script type="text/javascript">
<!--
 document.write("Congratulations! If you see this you have
JavaScript.");
//-->
</script>
<noscript>
  <strong>JavaScript required</strong><br />
  <p>Read how to <a href="noscript.htm">rectify this problem</a>
</p>
</noscript>
</body>
</html>
```

Note *Interestingly enough, the **<noscript>** tag is not defined in the XHTML specification as being allowed in the **<head>** of a page, though **<script>** is. This specification oversight will cause a validation error.*

Address JavaScript Version Issues with the Language Attribute

Even if scripting is available, problems may occur. During its short lifetime, JavaScript has undergone many changes. Not all browsers support it to the same degree, if at all. JavaScript has a few major dialects, including JavaScript 1 (=Netscape 2.*x*), JavaScript 1.1 (=Netscape 3.*x*), and JavaScript 1.2 (=Netscape 4.*x*). JScript in Internet Explorer 3 is approximately equivalent to JavaScript 1; it doesn't support JavaScript 1.1 features, such as dynamic image replacement. Internet Explorer 4 appears to support JavaScript 1.1, but with a richer object model and is able to modify page elements at will. Finally, there is the ECMAScript standard. Table 16-5 summarizes the versions of JavaScript.

Browser Version	JavaScript Support
Netscape 2.*x*	1.0
Netscape 3.*x*	1.1
Netscape 4.0–4.05	1.2
Netscape 4.06–4.08, 4.5*x*, 4.6*x*, 4.7*x*	1.3
Netscape 6.*x*/7.*x*	1.5
Internet Explorer 3.0	JScript 1.0
Internet Explorer 4.0	JScript 3.0
Internet Explorer 5.0	JScript 5.0
Internet Explorer 5.5	JScript 5.5
Internet Explorer 6	JScript 5.6

Table 16-5.   *Browser Versions and JavaScript Support*

The reason designers need to be aware of all these versions is that each varies in what it can do. For example, if you code for Netscape 4, it probably won't work in older browsers, or maybe even Internet Explorer 4!

One way to deal with different versions of JavaScript is to utilize the **language** attribute of the **<script>** tag. Script-aware browsers will ignore the contents of **<script>** tags using language attributes they do not understand. Because browsers act this way, it is possible to create multiple versions of a script for varying versions of the language, as you would imagine here:

```
<script language="JavaScript">
Netscape 2.0 version here
</script>

<script language="JavaScript1.1">
Netscape 3.0 version here
</script>

<script language="JavaScript1.2">
Netscape 4.0 version here
</script>
```

It is probably a better idea to try to selectively insert the script required using a server-side technology to cut down on potential problems and download size (just as it's better not to use multiple CSS rules at one time), but this technique is still often employed.

 *The **language** attribute is not considered standard, but all JavaScript-aware browsers use it, and it is more commonly found than the **type** attribute.*

Practice JavaScript Defensive Coding, such as Object Detection

Fall-through code isn't the best way to do things. In some cases, it is just better to check to see whether it is possible to do something. For example, you might be interested in whether it is possible to do rollover buttons. Netscape 3 browsers and beyond, as well as Internet Explorer 4 and beyond, can all do rollovers, so you might be tempted to do a browser sensing to help determine whether rollovers should be activated. Unfortunately, what happens if a new browser comes out, say, SuperBrowser 1.0, that supports rollover capability but doesn't match up in name or version with the other rollover capable browsers? Well, your code simply won't work.

Tip: Object detection is generally better than browser detection in scripting.

Rather than knowing everything about which browsers support what versions of JavaScript, it is probably just better to detect for capabilities by checking if the appropriate object is available. For example, a script here would check to see if your browser could support rollover images by simply looking to see if the image object is defined.

```
<script type="text/javascript">
if (document.images)
 alert("Rollovers possible")
else
  alert("Sorry no rollovers");
</script>
```

Using conditional logic in this manner can be applied to the existence not only of objects, but of methods as well. The goal is to never assume that something is available but to test for it and then fail gracefully if necessary.

Handle or Suppress Script Errors

Even if we deal with different script versions and browsers that don't support script, there are bound to be errors that happen in a page. Users are probably all too familiar with messages like the ones shown here popping up every second:

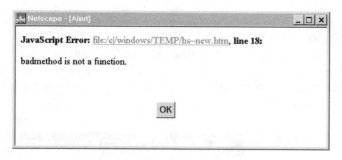

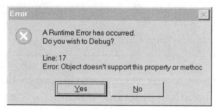

Script errors are so significant that by default some browsers suppress them to a console. The only clue that something has gone wrong is a small message in the status bar, like this one:

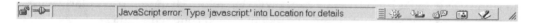

Of course, if you do actually access the JavaScript console, you'll eventually see the same errors.

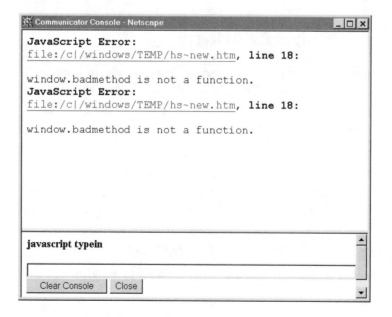

The fact of the matter is that errors will occur. It is probably better to handle them gracefully, rather than let the browser do so. You can even just suppress the error messages if you like, but it is better to show the problem and then fix it.

Note that the browsers do things very differently in the case of error handling, so it would be beyond this discussion to present their approaches here, but it is possible to provide custom error messages like this,

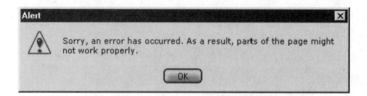

or even collect information from users, as shown in Figure 16-11, with a custom handler. More information on error handling practices in JavaScript can be found in the companion volume *JavaScript: The Complete Reference*.

Comment and Format Scripts for Maintainability

JavaScript should be formatted for readability using tabs and white space. White space can be used liberally, since like HTML and CSS, JavaScript is not extremely sensitive to white space, though it does have issues with the return character, particularly with semicolons. Nested structures should be indented, and comments indicated by // or /* */. Meaningful variable names like username should be used to improve readability. In short, common coding techniques from languages like C should be employed. However, such coding style can introduce significant bulk, which leads to the next best practice.

Crunch Large Scripts for Delivery

The addition of JavaScript to HTML documents can result in very long documents. Like HTML, it is possible to crunch JavaScript. For example, returns can be eliminated from statements if semicolons are used. Consider that in JavaScript,

```
document.write("Hello ")
document.write("world!");
```

and

```
document.write("Hello);document.write("world");
```

are equivalent. Of course, if you don't use semicolons, crunching can ruin a script.

Tip: Beware of semicolon problems if crunching JavaScript.

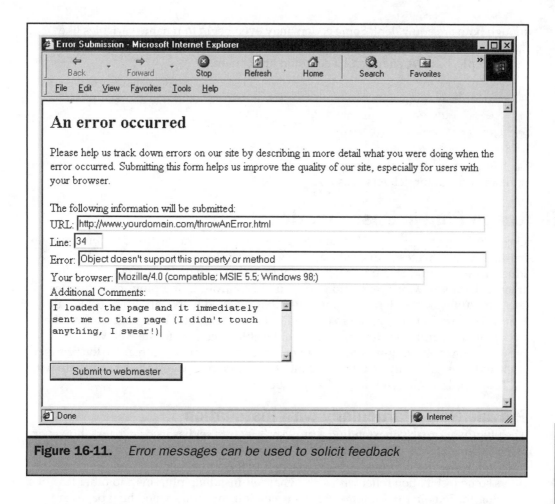

Figure 16-11.   *Error messages can be used to solicit feedback*

TECHNOLOGY AND
WEB DESIGN

It is also possible to utilize shorthand notations to further crunch files. For example, some JavaScript authors prefer this,

```
(quantity > 10) ? alert("You get a discount!") : alert("Sorry, no discount.");
```

to this,

```
if (quantity > 10)
  alert("You get a discount!");
else
  alert("Sorry, no discount.");
```

though both are equivalent. Some coders may even begin to rename variables like *quantity* to simple single letters like *q*, or even map common object names into variables. For example, here we shorthand a common object name:

```
var d=document;
d.write("Much shorter huh? ");
d.write("Yes it is! ");
```

Such techniques do create unreadable code, so consider keeping original source around and only crunch for delivery reasons.

Netscape Plug-in Best Practices

Object technologies such as Netscape plug-ins are used primarily to add more complex features to Web pages than can be added via a scripting language like JavaScript. Plug-ins were introduced by Netscape in Navigator 2 and have limited support in Internet Explorer, which relies more on ActiveX controls. Using plug-ins addresses the communication and integration issues that plagued helper applications. Recall that helper applications are not integrated into the design of a Web page; rather, they appear in a separate window and may not be able to communicate well with the browser. However, plug-ins are components that run within the context of the browser itself and thus can easily be integrated into the design of a page and communicate with the browser through technologies like JavaScript.

Provide Help, Particularly with Installation

The plug-in approach of extending a browser's feature set has its drawbacks, however. Users lacking a particular plug-in must locate and download plug-ins, install them, and even restart their browsers. Many users find this rather complicated. Netscape 4 offers some installation relief with somewhat self-installing plug-ins and other features, but plug-ins remain troublesome. Scripting can improve things, and help pages are certainly in order, but the problem should be avoided if possible.

Focus on Popular Plug-ins

Because of problems with installation and availability, many of the most commonly requested plug-ins, such as Macromedia's Flash, are being included as a standard feature with Netscape browsers. The standard plug-ins are primarily geared toward media handling and include Macromedia Flash and Shockwave, Adobe Acrobat, RealVideo, RealAudio, and simple download and play multimedia technologies supporting AVI movies or WAV sound files. If plug-ins are considered, focus on providing the popular ones first to make it most likely that users will be spared installation hassles.

Detect for Plug-in Availability

It is possible using JavaScript to see if a plug-in is installed and enabled. A simple detection scheme would be to check for a plug-in's existence using the **plugins[ ]** array found in JavaScript's **Navigator** object. This array contains information about the specific vendor and version of installed plug-ins. As an example, to look for a Flash plug-in you might write:

```
<script type="text/javascript">
<!--
if (navigator.plugins["Shockwave Flash"])
  alert("You have Flash!");
else
    alert("Sorry no Flash");
//-->
</script>
```

You need to be careful to use the exact name of the particular plug-in that interests you in order to access it. Also, be conscious of the fact that Internet Explorer defines a faux **plugins[ ]** array as a property of Navigator. It does so in order to prevent poorly written Netscape-specific scripts from throwing errors while they probe for plug-ins. We would need to deal with this cross-browser nuance by first checking to make sure we are not using Internet Explorer when doing the **plugins[ ]** array probe, and then writing out the appropriate **<embed>** syntax if it's found or giving an error or alternative rendering if it's not found, as shown here:

```
if (navigator.appName.indexOf('Microsoft')==-1 &&
   (navigator.plugins && navigator.plugins.length))
 {
   if (navigator.plugins["Shockwave Flash"])
     {
       document.write('<embed src="Movie1.swf" quality=high bgcolor="#FFFFFF"
 ');
       document.write(' swLiveConnect="false" width="550" height="400"');
       document.write(' type="application/x-shockwave-flash"
pluginspage="http://www.macromedia.com/shockwave/download/index.cgi?P1_Prod_
Version=ShockwaveFlash" />');
     }
   else
     window.location ="noflash.htm";
 }
```

Fortunately, if Internet Explorer is in use, we can rely on the **<object>** tag to install the appropriate object if the user allows it.

Use <noembed> to Support Browsers That Are Not Plug-in–Aware

What should be done with browsers that do not support plug-ins at all? Use the **<noembed>** tag as demonstrated here:

```
<embed src="welcome.avi" height="100" width="100" />
<noembed>
<img src="welcome.gif" alt="The history and philosophy of
        Demo Company is both humorous and mysterious." />
</noembed>
```

When encountering this code, a browser not aware of the **<embed>** syntax will skip the first element and utilize the **<img>** tag. If the browser did not support images, it would then display the **alt** attribute. With careful coding, it is possible to fall back to an acceptable state in nearly every situation. We'll see that this can be worked into ActiveX deployment as well.

ActiveX Best Practices

ActiveX is the Internet portion of the Component Object Model (COM) and is Microsoft's component technology for creating small components, or controls, within a Web page. ActiveX is intended to distribute these controls via the Internet as a way of adding new functionality to Internet Explorer. Microsoft maintains that ActiveX controls are more similar to generalized components than to plug-ins, because ActiveX controls can reside beyond the browser even within container programs such as Microsoft Office. ActiveX controls are similar to Netscape plug-ins in that they are persistent and machine-specific. Although this makes resource use a problem, installation is not an issue: the components download and install automatically. However, security is a big concern for ActiveX controls. Because these small pieces of code can potentially have full access to a user's system, they can cause serious damage.

Consider Installation Time of ActiveX Objects

Adding an ActiveX control to a Web page requires the use of the **<object>** tag. For example, this markup is used to add a Flash file to a page:

```
<object classid="clsid:D27CDB6E-AE6D-11cf-96B8-444553540000"
  codebase="http://download.macromedia.com/pub/shockwave/cabs/flash/
```

```
swflash.cab#version=5,0,30,0"
id="Movie1" width="550" height="400" />
<param name="movie" value="Movie1.swf" />
<param name="quality" value="high" />
<param name="bgcolor" value="#FFFFFF" />
Sorry, you don't have ActiveX.
</object>
```

If the browser does not have this particular ActiveX component it will be downloaded from the URL indicated in the **codebase** attribute. Installation can be troublesome for users and may cause significant wait time, so as with plug-ins, try to focus on using commonly found controls, if possible.

Address Browsers Lacking ActiveX

What appears in a browser without ActiveX? In the previous example the message "Sorry you don't have ActiveX" would be output. A better approach would be to include alternative technologies in the page for other browsers to fall back to, such as Netscape plug-ins or even images. The following example demonstrates how that could be done for Flash. Notice how all issues are dealt with ActiveX: no plug-ins, no scripting, and even no images on.

```
<!DOCTYPE HTML PUBLIC "-//W3C//DTD XHTML 1.0 Transitional//EN"
"http://www.w3.org/TR/xhtml1/DTD/xhtml1-transitional.dtd">
<html xmlns="http://www.w3.org/1999/xhtml">
<head>
<title>Flash Demo</title>
</head>
<body>
<object classid="clsid:D27CDB6E-AE6D-11cf-96B8-444553540000"
codebase=""http://download.macromedia.com/pub/shockwave/cabs/flash/swflash.c
ab#version=5,0,30,0"
id="Movie1" width="550" height="400">
<param name="movie" value="Movie1.swf" />
<param name="quality" value="high" />
<param name=bgcolor value="#FFFFFF" >
<!-- here is the detection for plug-in for Netscape -->
<script type="text/javascript">
<!--
var plugin = (navigator.mimeTypes && navigator.mimeTypes["application/x
shockwave-flash"]) ? navigator.mimeTypes["application/x-shockwave
```

```
flash"].enabledPlugin : 0;
if ( plugin &&
parseInt(plugin.description.substring(plugin.description.indexOf(".")-1)) >=
4 ) {
   // Check for Flash version 4 or greater in Netscape
   document.write('<embed src="Movie1.swf" quality="high" bgcolor="#FFFFFF"
');
   document.write(' swLiveConnect="false" width="550" height="400"');
   document.write(' type="application/x-shockwave-flash"
pluginspage="http://www.macromedia.com/shockwave/download/index.cgi?P1_Prod_
Version=ShockwaveFlash" />');
} else if (!(navigator.appName && navigator.appName.indexOf("Netscape")>=0
&& navigator.appVersion.indexOf("2.")>=0)){
   // Netscape 2 will display the IMG tag below so don't write an extra one
   document.write('<img src="Movie1.gif" width="550" height="400" border="0"
/>');
}
//-->
</script>
<noscript>
  <img src="Movie1.gif" width="550" height="400" alt="Flash Rules!" />
</noscript>

<noembed>
  <img src="Movie1.gif" width="550" height="400" alt="Flash Rules!" />
</noembed>

</object>
</body>
</html>
```

While this script may look complicated, it can be generated automatically using editors like Dreamweaver; once a single detection script is written, it can be reused in many situations.

Accept ActiveX's Security Problems

Many users will be paranoid about the potential security hazards involved in using ActiveX. Make sure that you provide information on changing security levels and what exactly what your ActiveX control is doing. In short, be clear and honest with users about security issues related to object technologies.

Java Applets Best Practices

The main downside of component technologies like Netscape plug-ins and ActiveX controls is that they are platform-specific. Unfortunately or fortunately (depending on how you look at it), not every user runs on Windows or even Macintosh. How do we deal with cross-platform issues? One way is to make a new platform that is common to all systems. This is one of the core ideas of Java.

Java promises a platform-neutral development language, somewhat similar in syntax to C++, that allows programs to be written once and deployed on any machine, browser, or operating system that supports the Java virtual machine (JVM). Web pages use small Java programs, called applets, that are downloaded and run directly within a browser to provide new functionality. Applets are written in the Java language and compiled to a machine-independent byte-code in the form of a .class file, which is downloaded automatically to the Java-capable browser and run within the browser environment.

Be Mindful of Java Performance Issues

Even with a fast processor, a user's system may appear to run Java byte-code slowly compared to a natively compiled application, because the byte code must be interpreted by the JVM. This leads to the common perception that Java is slow. The reality is that Java isn't necessarily slow, but its interpretation can be. Even with recent Just-In-Time (JIT) compilers in newer browsers, Java often doesn't deliver performance equal to natively compiled applications.

Address non-Java Supporting Browsers

Adding a Java applet to a Web page is relatively easy and can be done using the **<applet>** or **<object>** element, though **<applet>** is preferred for backward compatibility. If, for example, we had a .class file called helloworld, we might reference it with the following markup:

```
<applet code="helloworld.class"
        height="50"
        width="175">
<h1>Hello World for you non-Java-aware browsers</h1>
</applet>
```

In the preceding code example, anything except for **<param>** tags found with the **<applet>** element is considered an alternative rendering for browsers that don't support Java or the **<applet>** element or that have Java support disabled.

Java Detection

It is possible to detect for Java availability fairly easy using the method **javaEnabled( )** found in JavaScript's **Navigator** object. This method returns **True** if Java is available and turned on and **False** otherwise.

```
if (navigator.javaEnabled())
   // do Java stuff or write out <applet> tag
else
  alert("Sorry no Java");
```

You can find out more about Java once it is available by accessing a Java applet; then you can even determine what type of virtual machine is supported. In order to do this, you will have to access the public methods and properties of a Java applet.

Be Realistic About Java Support

Unfortunately, the reality of Java applets for a Web designer is that they really aren't useful on public sites. The truth is that there are so many different Java Virtual Machines (VM) in browsers that the idea of "write once, run everywhere" has been turned into "write once, debug everywhere." The major benefit of Java applets just isn't there. Further, Microsoft's latest Internet Explorer browsers do not even ship with a Java VM, but that may change some time in the future, or maybe not. Because of this uncertainty, Java isn't a great choice for public sites. However, within intranets, on the server side in the form of Java servlets, or with very careful coding, Java applets can be used.

Cookie Best Practices

An interesting programming topic that is often discussed is the use of cookies. Make sure you understand the basics of cookies, even if you plan on avoiding programming at all costs, since invariably you'll have to explain more than a few times what cookies are to concerned colleagues or clients.

A *cookie* is a small amount of information sent by a Web server that is stored on a user's system for later retrieval. The main purpose of a cookie is to save information for later. The major use of cookies is to store user identification and passwords so they don't have to always retype them. Another common use of cookies is to store any preferences you may set when you access a site. From a programming point of view, cookies are used to solve the state management problem. Basically, the state problem relates to the idea that servers don't remember a user from one visit to a next, so cookies are needed to create features such as shopping baskets that last across multiple visits. Other state preservation forms, such as hidden data within forms or complex URLs, can be used within visits, but between visits cookies are really the only possible solution.

Many users are absolutely paranoid about cookies. The reality is that they really aren't anything more than a small string of information. If you look for cookies on your hard drive you will probably come across a file called cookies.txt in your browser folder or even a whole directory of cookie text files, generally in C:\Windows\Cookies. Taking a look at a cookie, you might see something like

```
.google.com   TRUE  /  FALSE   2147368374   ID   112005d255531c2c
```

This particular cookie is associated with the Google search engine. What it is used for, one can't be quite sure. It is likely being used to know how often users search, when they search, what language they use and so on. However, in general the purpose of a cookie is simply to act somewhat like a Web laundry ticket. It allows the user to pick up the items in their shopping cart, keep their preferences set, and so on. In and of itself, the cookie doesn't say much about a user. Like a laundry ticket, it is just a code number. However, when associated with user-provided information, it is possible to build a profile about a user.

The fear of tracking through cookies has led to some pretty serious worries on the part of users. In reality, cookies are relatively harmless if they can't be associated with personal information. Despite any claims to the contrary, a cookie cannot be used to retrieve data from a user's hard drive other than the value of the cookie itself. The cookie can't steal sensitive information such as user's e-mail address or browser preferences. However, a cookie can be used to track users. Often, this tracking capability can be used in connection with the display of banner ads or other advertising directed to users based upon their past browsing habits. Some users who do not like the fact they are so carefully tracked will disable their cookies.

Inform Users of Cookie Usage

To avoid cookie problems and instill some trust in users of their sites, designers are encouraged to be honest with users about cookie use within those sites. Make sure that users can find out what cookies are used for in an easily accessed privacy policy or usage statement.

Avoid Using Too Many Cookies

Because users may have their preferences set to warn about cookies being issued you do not want to bug them too much. Consider trying to use a single cookie on your site to track the user and provide state preservation features. Issuing multiple cookies can be a nuisance for the user who has to accept each and every one.

Provide Alternatives for Cookie-Denying Visitors

Of course, some people are just going to reject cookies outright. If at all possible, provide another way for users to access your site without cookies and, if you have to use cookies, rely on session or memory cookies rather than disk or permanent cookies. If this is not possible, at least gracefully fail and indicate to the user that they will not be able to use your site if they are going to be so paranoid.

Multimedia Best Practices

Finally, we consider the best use of multimedia technology on Web pages, which is becoming increasingly important as the Web moves away from a print design style. Many sites use animation, and audio and video usage is becoming popular as well. However, while multimedia may improve the presentation of a site, it often comes with significant bandwidth and technology restrictions. Designers should first consider if the addition of multimedia elements would actually improve the user's ability to understand information or will make the experience of visiting the site more pleasing. If it will not, it really shouldn't be included. Designers should then determine how the multimedia elements should be added, which is a very important consideration. Designers should stick to common technologies, lest they create a barrier to entry to a site. A few simple best practices for animation, audio, and video follow.

When Trying to Draw Attention, Avoid Competing Animations

Consider, for example, two very animated banner advertisements on the same page. How will the user be able to focus on one banner ad if another one continues to signal them? While the user's ability to tune sensory input (as discussed in Chapter 2) is great, competing animations will likely distract users and cause their eyeballs to bounce like ping-pong balls.

Avoid Continuously Running Animation Loops

While it may be possible to get a user to notice animations by running loops, after awhile they will probably tune them out or get annoyed. Therefore, continuously looped animation should be avoided.

Inform Users of Formats and Download Sizes

Given that multimedia files tend to be large and that compatibility problems with various audio and video plug-ins are common, we need to let users know what they should expect with a link "price" indicating the size and nature of the download. Consider, for example, this simple link to an audio file in WAV format:

```
<a href="democompanyjingle.wav">Demo Company's Corporate Jingle
(7 second WAV - 180K)</a>
```

We have indicated not only the format, but also the length of the clip and the file size. Always try to let users know such information before the access a multimedia element.

Don't Assume or Require Audio Support

Accessing sound in a Web site shouldn't be an infuriating experience for Web users. The first thing to do is not put something very important only in audio form. Remember: not all users will have speakers on their computers or be in an environment where sound can or should be heard. Always provide alternative forms of access for important audio-based content, such as a text transcript. Even when a user can hear audio, do they necessarily want to? Consider the business user hitting a site, only to have some theme music play in the background letting everyone know what he or she is doing.

Allow Sound to Be Turned Off

When sound is used, make sure you provide an easy way for the user to turn it off—particularly if it is continuous. A common sound toggle button should be used and would look something like this:

Make Sure Multimedia Adds to the Message

Once again, the most important best practice for multimedia is just to question its value. Even with heavy compression and increased user bandwidth, multimedia is going to require more user wait time. Thus audio, video, and animation should really only be used in situations where it adds to the presentation of content. One such situation would be teaching someone to dance via a Web page. While dance moves could be described in text, they would certainly work better as a picture, animation, or even movie. Unfortunately, far too often it seems that multimedia content is not significantly better than text content, just fancier in appearance. The user will notice this sooner than later.

Summary

Any designer who has tried to build a Web site has occasionally been doused by a bucket of cold water known as Web technology problems. Even ten years after its inception, Web technologies are immature and ever changing. Designers are encouraged to fully investigate the strengths and weaknesses of any technology before using it online and to follow the best practices presented in this chapter.

TECHNOLOGY AND
WEB DESIGN

While the tips presented here go a long way to improving Web site construction, at the end of the day the most important point is once again to understand that the use of technology is to support the users and address their needs. However, do not take some of the cautionary points presented as an excuse to avoid pushing the limits of Web technology. If we are too conservative, we might create a site that takes no chances with technologies, a site that is limited to simple HTML and server-side programming—one that users may not find to be motivating. If a new technology can be implemented properly, and provides an exciting enough new technology, users will probably deal with the downsides. However, only use emerging technologies when there is a very good reason to.

Pragmatic designers know that execution challenges will always exist, even with the emergence of standards-based browsers, and will continue to strive to address such issues rather than bury their head in the sand and pretend that such problems don't exist. Unfortunately, errors on the Web happen more often than we'd like, and it is our job to try to correct this. The next chapter addresses one of the most challenging and underappreciated aspects of Web design: consistent and reliable delivery.

The Complete Reference

Web Design

Chapter 17

Site Delivery
and Management

Delivering a site to a user is just as important as building the site. A site's usability is heavily influenced by its responsiveness, which has a direct impact on the end user's overall feeling about the site. Most designers are painfully aware of the need for speed. Although designers often focus on image file size or end-user connection rate, to explain why a site is slow, the actual cause may not be so obvious. Speed may be dictated by a multitude of things, including network effects like traffic, protocol issues, server issues, and site content. Designers will have to address all aspects of delivery, because the end user is not going to evaluate the individual components of transmission, but will consider the site as a single system.

Even when a Web site is delivered properly, running it can be challenging and time consuming. There is always something for the Webmaster to do: content must be maintained, broken links repaired, and the site monitored for availability. One interesting aspect of site maintenance is usage analysis. On the Web, it is possible to understand what users do when they visit our sites by analyzing log files. We can use this information to better design our sites, but collecting such usage data brings up concerns of privacy. This chapter will provide an overview of the delivery and maintenance of Web sites, with a focus on how these issues influence site design.

The Importance of Delivery

Unfortunately, delivery issues are often contemplated only after a Web site has been designed and built. In many cases, the budget for the site doesn't adequately consider delivery costs, and so corners are cut. This is like spending significant money to design and print a corporate brochure, only to have it delivered via third-class postal mail because no funds were left after design and printing. The effect of the brochure would be severely diminished by its slow arrival. Delivery of Web sites is even more critical, particularly given the rise of task-oriented Web sites or e-commerce sites, where any delay may be the difference between a successful sale and a lost one. It is well known that shopping cart abandonment increases with download time as users become frustrated with site browsing or checkout delays.

While designers may admit that users don't like slow sites, they tend to focus only on a few aspects of what makes a site slow. Consider that users will not be able to distinguish which aspect of site delivery is causing a page to load slowly. They are going to view it as a slow site, whether or not the graphics were optimized properly. Web site designers often place too much emphasis on optimizing file size and not enough on servers, network choice, and even the characteristics of the medium itself. Consider all the possible reasons a site may be slow, as illustrated in Figure 17-1.

While there are numerous potential problems to consider when delivering a site, the one inescapable fact is that, eventually, data will have to be transferred. Whether you download now or download later, you eventually have to do it. From the user's perspective, how much data is downloaded doesn't really matter; it only matters how

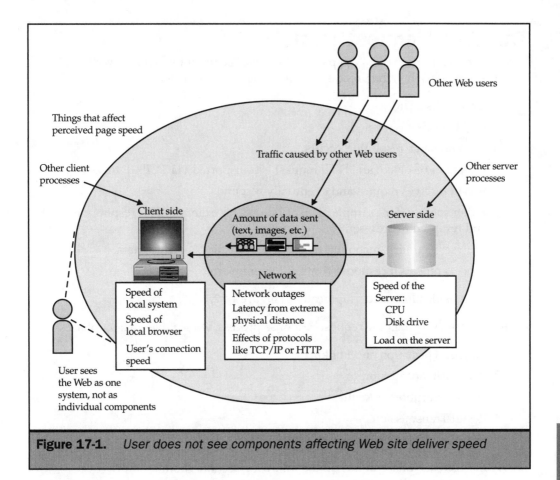

Figure 17-1.   *User does not see components affecting Web site deliver speed*

responsive the site is. The user typically only notices the seconds going by, not the number of bytes delivered. Simply put, how much data comes down doesn't matter to the end user.

> **Rule: The amount of bytes delivered to create a page is not as important as how fast the user perceives the page to be delivered.**

If you are using huge graphics by downloading them during the idle moments, the user certainly won't care. Time is everything, and the bottom line is simply keeping the user happy. If your design requires a great deal of bandwidth, has many individual requests, or requires real-time delivery, you may have to shelve it. Once again, always respect the medium of the Web. Just as a print designer understands that ink may bleed on paper, the Web designer should understand the nature of the network and servers used to deliver their creations. We start first with a brief overview of an individual Web process and isolate each step for its effect on site performance.

The Web Request Cycle

Looking at each portion of a Web page request we see room for error, as well as improvement. Roughly, the process of requesting a page is as follows:

1. User types a URL.

2. HTTP request is formed.

3. Domain name resolution occurs.

4. If name is resolved, an HTTP request is transported via TCP/IP to server.

5. Server receives request and eventually responds.

6. Either success (for example, 200) or failure (for example, 404) response is built and returned to browser.

7. Browser examines incoming response and displays or saves data.

8. Process repeats if response contains other objects.

This process is illustrated graphically in Figure 17-2.

If we were to abstract the request-response process, we see five distinct phases:

1. Request Formation and Lookup

2. Request Transmission

3. Server Execution of Request

4. Result Transmission

5. Browser Processing of Result

We discuss each phase in turn in the following sections, both to improve understanding of the Web medium and to illustrate areas for improved execution.

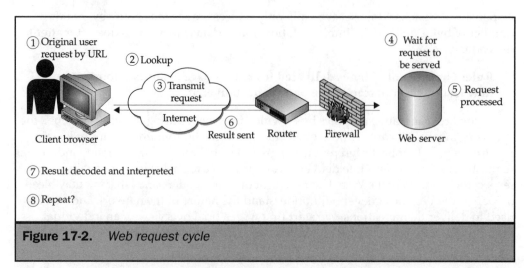

Figure 17-2. *Web request cycle*

Request Formation and DNS Lookup

When looking to improve the Web site request process, the first step is to make addresses easy to type and remember. Never underestimate the power of a good domain name. Many sites have an easy to remember (and type) domain name to at least partially thank for their success. Some sites have even found that having a domain name like "cheaptickets" or some generic expression is a good way to attract customers. However, beyond the marketing aspects, domain names should be well thought out, as some Web users can become confused on how to actually address a site.

Contingency Domains

Given a domain name such as democompany.com, domain name servers should be configured to map all the following fully qualified domains to the same place:

```
democompany.com
ww.democompany.com
www.democompany.com
wwww.democompany.com
```

Here we have mapped typos with two and four *w* characters (instead of three) as well as the omission of the www machine name altogether. Extra machine names are easily added to DNS, and you may also consider adding others, such as *w* and "web," as they really only act as backups for mistakes. If at all possible, consider registering slight typo domain names, particularly if the domain is long, difficult to spell, or hard to type.

Suggestion: Provide numerous domain name forms for a site.

In the future, domain names may change. We may see a rise in popularity of both new domain name forms and unique addresses, often generically referred to as Uniform Resource Names, or even keyword-based navigation directly from within a browser. Whatever the form of address, it is important that it get the user to find and continue to use a site.

URL Fixes

Similar to domain name fixes is the setting of special entry points for your Web site. For example, for easy access to the employment section of your site, you may opt for domains with synonymous terms—like jobs.democompany.com, careers.democompany.com, employment.democompany.com, and hr.democompany.com—that all map to the same place. The same could be said of directory paths, so www.democompany.com/hr, www.democompany.com/jobs, www.democompany.com/careers, and so on would also map to the employment page for the site.

Suggestion: Add multiple guessable URLs for common site sections.

Beyond static mappings, you should consider the robustness of the directory and filenames in the URLs themselves. Be cautious with using cased filenames because UNIX systems will treat these files differently than Windows systems, which are not case-sensitive. If your site is hosted on a UNIX system, make sure to enable both lowercase and uppercase URLs. Also consider adding a spell-checking feature for URLs, so that if a page is requested with a typo, the server will fix the request. The Apache Web server supports the extension mod_speling, which can correct simple URL mistakes. Similar systems can be found for popular Web servers like IIS.

Suggestion: Try to fix simple user URL typos and casing problems at the server level.

Web Address Trickery

Some sites utilize Internet Protocol (IP) addresses or encoded URLs rather than domain names, often to mask their identity. For example, notice that URLs are often displayed in a special form called "URL encoded," where special or problematic characters such as spaces and even slashes are translated into special codes. This translation is often seen in the URL of a CGI program using the GET method or a search engine. For example, try running a query for "Robert O'Reilly's Robot Repair Shop." Many search engines will show a query string in the URL like this:

```
http://www.fakesearchengine.com/run-search.cgi?query=
Robert+O%27Reilly%27s+Robot+Repair+Shop
```

Notice that, in the encoding, spaces were converted to plus signs, and special characters were translated to a value (the apostrophes became %27). This format, which may appear cryptic, is the highly regular format of URL encoded. The basic idea is to encode characters that would be unsafe as part of a URL in another format, such as hex values or plus signs. Because browsers should have no problem decoding URL-encoded addresses, some less scrupulous Web users—particularly people who send a great deal of junk mail—attempt to mask their identity with an encoded URL. For example, www.democompany.com would appear as

```
http://%77%77%77.%64%65%6D%6F%63%6F%6D%70%61%6E%79.%63%6F%6D
```

Some sites instead might just utilize a simple IP address like

```
http://206.252.142.209
```

Note *Some newer browsers will not allow this type of trickery in the URL, which is a welcome change.*

While valid, neither of these address forms is as good as a real domain name, particularly since the mysterious encoding may suggest to the end user that some sort of funny business is going on. So don't use things like this in links or play other encoding games—and be very wary of those people who do.

Running DNS

The Web's reliance on the domain name service cannot be overstated. When a user types in a URL like http://www.democompany.com, the address www.democompany.com must first be translated into the underlying IP address before a request can be made. The first time a user accesses a particular site, there can be a substantial delay (on the order of a few seconds) to perform the name translation. Users notice this delay by the messages shown in the browser status bar, like the one shown here:

Connect: Looking up host: www.democompany.com...

For slow connections or infrequently accessed hosts, the initial lookup may time-out and force the user to look up the host again. If the domain name server that does the translation is down, the site will be effectively down unless the user somehow knows the underlying IP address of the site. Because of the heavy reliance on domain name service, a site should have multiple domain name servers that are geographically and network dispersed to improve the likelihood that at least one server is available and responsive. Although domain name translation requests are small in terms of data, the servers should also be designed for responsiveness.

Suggestion: Make sure that domain name service for a Web site is fast and robust.

While the Web server may be a critical component in the delivery of a Web site, don't forget: if users can't get to the server, they won't care how fast it is.

Request Transmission

Once a URL is selected either by manually entering it or following a link, a request is formed and sent to a Web server. The request is made in Hypertext Transfer Protocol (HTTP), the basic application-level network protocol used to coordinate the exchange of data to and from a Web server and a browser. However, the request itself is transported using the lower level network protocols of TCP/IP. The basics of how HTTP works is presented next as a groundwork for discussing its limitations and impact on design.

TECHNOLOGY AND WEB DESIGN

HTTP

The HTTP protocol is a very simple request/response protocol designed primarily to deliver static content. The basic idea of the protocol is that a browser will request a page from a server, using a request such as

```
GET /products/index.htm HTTP/1.1
```

and then provide any parameters, if required. A complete request from a browser tells all sorts of interesting information, such as the type of browser being used, the language being used, the character sets supported, and so on. An example of a complete request is shown here:

```
GET /products/index.htm HTTP/1.1
Connection: Keep-Alive
User-Agent: Mozilla/4.0 (compatible; MSIE 5.01; Windows 98)
Accept: application/x-comet, image/gif, image/x-xbitmap,
image/jpeg, image/pjpeg, */*
Accept-Language: en-us
```

Note that header information can be used to determine a user's environment and dynamically configure a page to match the user's native language or browser. This concept is usually termed *browser sniffing* or *browser detection*.

   Most of the header data passed by a browser is completely harmless, but some users may actually go through the trouble of hiding their request headers, particularly the user agent value. This does nothing but limit their ability to receive customized pages.

Once a complete request has been made to the server, it will then answer with its own code. 404 Not Found is a common server response seen when a requested page does not exist. If things are going well, a response like

```
HTTP/1.1 200 OK
```

with a bunch of other header information following is returned, as shown here:

```
HTTP/1.1 200 OK
Date: Tue, 18  June 2002 02:37:58 GMT
Server: Apache/1.3.4 (Unix)
Last-Modified: Tue, 12 Oct 2001 21:04:18 GMT
Content-Length: 7947
Connection: close
Content-Type: text/html

<html>

... HTML document follows...

</html>
```

One particular header to pay attention to is the Content-Type header. This header indicates the MIME type of the data to be passed back. A MIME type is comprised of two parts: a data type and subtype separated by a slash, as shown here:

```
Content-Type: type/subtype
```

The type is set to a general data type such as image, audio, text, video, application, multipart, message, or extension-token. The subtype gives more specific detail about the type of data, such as whether it is a GIF image or an HTML file. A few sample MIME types are listed here:

text/html	image/gif
text/xml	audio/x-wav
video/quicktime	application/x-shockwave-flash
video/x-msvideo	application/x-zip-compressed

Once a browser receives the reply, it will look at the Content-Type header to determine how to handle the request. For example, the lookup table for Netscape Communicator 4.*x*–generation browsers is shown here.

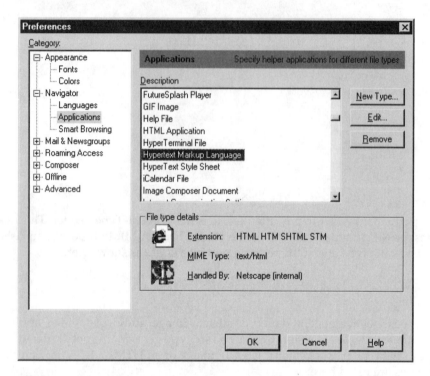

Notice that, in the example, the type is text/html and the actual HTML document is passed back after all the headers are finished. The dialog indicates that the browser itself will handle the file internally. Also notice that the browser indicates that it recognizes the file extensions .html, .htm, .stm, and .shtml as HTML files. However, other file extensions seem to appear as normal HTML when they are viewed online. The MIME type returned by the browser in the Content-Type header is the key to why a file with an extension like .cfm, .asp, .jsp, and so on is treated as HTML by a Web browser when delivered over a network, but may not be read if opened from a local disk drive. The reason is that these extensions often are associated with dynamically generated pages that are stamped with the HTML MIME type by the server; when reading off the local drive, the browser relies instead on the file extension like .htm to determine the contents of a file. If a browser attempts to read a file that it is unsure about, either because of file extension or MIME type, it should respond with a dialog like the one shown here, as Netscape does:

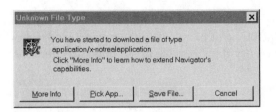

What's very interesting is how Internet Explorer prompts the user to immediately save data if the MIME type is not understood, as shown by this dialog:

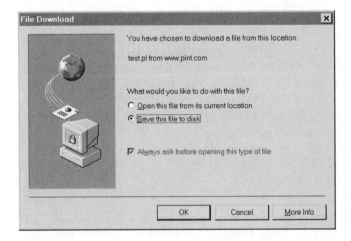

Normally, Web pages are delivered properly, so these dialogs are not seen. The browser would first read the HTML being delivered and then retrieve any other objects—GIF images, sound files, Flash files, Java applets, and so on— that are associated with the page. Each object would result in another request to the server. If the browser encountered something like

```
<img src="images/logo.gif" height="100" width="200"
alt="Demo Company" />
```

it would then form a request like

```
GET /images/logo.gif HTTP/1.1
Connection: Keep-Alive
User-Agent: Mozilla/4.0 (compatible; MSIE 5.01; Windows 98)
Accept: application/x-comet, image/gif, image/x-xbitmap,
  image/jpeg, image/pjpeg, */*
Accept-Language: en-us
```

The server would then respond with a similar answer as before, but this time indicating that a MIME type of image/gif is being returned, followed by the appropriate form of binary data to make up an image, as demonstrated here:

```
HTTP/1.1 200 OK
Date: Tue, 18 Jan 2000 04:41:15 GMT
Server: Apache/1.3.4 (Unix)
Last-Modified: Wed, 13 Oct 1999 23:37:38 GMT
Content-Length: 28531
Connection: close
Content-Type: image/gif

GIF87a— æ÷ÿïÿÿÆì÷÷òÒÖ÷ìîõñî½Öìììèñ½ìèóÆçã¿Æçõ½çç÷áß´µçÞì-çÝç½
Þñ¥çß÷´Þì-ÞÞÖä¥Ü÷œÞÖì°Õç"ÞÏ®ŒÞÕî™×÷"ÖÇµŒÖÆ-„ÖÆ-{ÖÅÓsÖ½-½½¥À½œsÎ½
¥¿¹ZkÎÌµ¬-zyµÏ©¨<¥¥¥ ¡-œ>Œ¥Ã{""‡'<<Unicode: 90>>
X
< ^ŒŒ{„Œ{j<<Unicode: 90>>¢„„s,<<Unicode: 81>><<Unicode:
84>>'}l<<Unicode: 81>><<Unicode:
81>>{„{s,fT{{s zjq|~¦eUmogKvŠ<<Unicode: 90>>]QljZckZoe
PfegccZccRZcRX
… binary file continues …
```

With the MIME type set properly, it is possible to serve literally any object. Designers often avoid serving custom forms of data beyond HTML or common media types like GIF, JPEG, or WAV because of unfamiliarity with the MIME-type configuration possibilities on client and server.

Tip   *Consider adding a MIME type to handle a proprietary information format rather than convert it to HTML, particularly on an intranet.*

That's really all there is to HTTP. First, the browser makes an HTTP request, and the server responds in the appropriate fashion with a MIME type attached. This cycle repeats as each of the individual elements that make up a page is requested. A full discussion of HTTP headers and methods can be found in Appendix G. Even with all the extra details added in, the HTTP protocol is really quite simple, and that's what causes many of its problems. Fortunately, during the request phase the size and number of requests made are generally not significant, so there are few possibilities for improvement, except reducing the latency between browser and server. It is once we hit the server that we run into potential bottlenecks.

Web Servers

To many, Web servers seem mystical. In reality, a Web server is just a computer running a piece of software that fulfills HTTP requests made by browsers. In the simplest sense, a Web server is just a file server—and a slow one at times. However, a Web server isn't just a file server, because it can also run programs and deliver results. In this sense, Web servers could also be considered application servers—if, occasionally, simple or slow ones.

Recall from earlier in the chapter that the user will not be able to single out the individual components of Web delivery. If a site is slow, users often don't know why. It could be the network, it could be the server, or it might even be their own machine. Designers should always try to improve the user's perception of a site and thus should strive to control what *can* be controlled—namely, the server and its connection out to the Internet. Let's consider each in turn.

Web Server Components

A Web server is composed of both hardware and software. The primary operation of a Web server is to copy the many (generally small) files making up a Web page from disk to network as fast as possible for numerous simultaneous users. A secondary mission is to run programs for numerous individuals and deliver the results as fast as possible. Given these requirements, consider the hardware requirements of a Web server shown in Table 17-1.

> **Suggestion: Don't skimp on Web server hardware—focus on systems with high-speed hard drives, a great deal of memory, and good network interfaces.**

Beyond getting the best hardware you can afford, it is important to consider that the operating system running on the hardware and the available server and development software options are going to have a great effect on the speed of the Web server. In general, given that Web servers have to deal with multiple requests simultaneously and need a rich set of development options, most developers tend to use either Windows NT or some variant of UNIX, including Linux, for their operating system. Table 17-2 presents the major operating system choices, as well as some of the issues in using them for Web serving.

While Table 17-2 presents a good overview of some of the issues faced when choosing one operating system over another for a Web server, the decision may often be based on familiarity or personal taste. While one person may argue about the merits of UNIX, introducing a UNIX server into an environment with heavy Windows investment would be foolish. The bottom line is to always remember suitability and total cost over time. A relatively low-traffic site for a school might do well on a Macintosh. A Windows system might make a great departmental server in a corporation that favors Windows systems. A Linux system might appeal to a technical-minded individual looking to avoid spending money on hardware and software, and a high-end Sun server running Solaris might be appropriate for a large e-commerce venture. Some sites may find that a server-appliance that does not obviously expose operating system issues may also be appropriate if maintenance is a significant concern. The point is always to choose an operating system for a server based on the practicality of performance, development, and long-term maintenance characteristics of the OS.

Hardware Component	Considerations
Processor	While a fast processor seems key to a fast Web server, the reality is that computational requirements of a Web server are limited. Multiple processors may be more useful than a single fast processor when dealing with numerous requests made on a server.
Memory	A Web server may need a large amount of RAM to hold numerous individual processes running CGI programs for users or fulfilling file requests.
Bus	Web data will constantly move from disk to memory to network. Don't limit the data path with a slow bus.
Disk drive	Since a Web server's primary task is delivering files to a user, a high-speed disk drive that is kept optimized is a primary goal. Spend extra on drives with high-speed adapters such as SCSI-3.
Network interface	Once files are retrieved from disk, they are delivered back to the user via the network. Don't limit a server by its network interface card. Consider Fast Ethernet or better. For high-volume servers, multiple network interfaces may be mandatory.
Other	Most other aspects of a Web server have little bearing on the delivery of a site. However, some peripherals such as tape drives or other backup storage facilities are mandatory for site maintenance.

Table 17-1.   *Web Server Hardware Issues*

Suggestion: Don't choose an operating system for a Web server solely based on popularity; consider total cost of ownership and suitability for development and long-term maintenance.

Web Server Software

Once the hardware and operating system are selected, it is time to consider which Web server package to use. Only a few years ago, there were only two major Web servers available: NCSA's httpd server for UNIX and CERN's httpd server for UNIX, both free servers that required a fairly substantial knowledge of UNIX and programming to use and for development. Today, there are dozens of different Web servers—both commercial and freeware—available on a variety of machines. Rather than considering all Web

Operating System	Pros	Cons
UNIX	+Tends to run on fast hardware such as UltraSparc and Alpha systems. +Very flexible development environment. +High-end applications and servers are available.	–Can be complicated to use and difficult to set up and maintain. –Labor costs may be high. –Buy-in costs for hardware and software are relatively high.
Windows NT/ 2000/XP	+Runs on both high- and low-end hardware. +Many servers and development tools available. +Basic administration is simple.	–May require multiple servers for high-volume sites. –Advanced administration may rival UNIX in difficulty. –Guaranteeing server stability can be troublesome.
Linux	+Available on low-end equipment. +Cost is low. +Many servers and development tools available.	–Can be complicated to use and difficult to maintain. –Lacks some commercial software support found with mainstream UNIX systems like Solaris.
Windows 98/ME	+Easy to run. +Low equipment costs. +Inexpensive software.	–Not a multiuser environment. –Not as robust as NT or UNIX for server applications. –Selection of Web software is limited, compared to Windows NT or UNIX variants. –Security concerns can be significant.
Macintosh	+Easy to run and administer. +Low equipment costs. +Inexpensive software.	–Traditional Macintosh OS is not suitable for Web serving, though the UNIX based OSX is. –Selection of Web software is limited compared to Windows or straight UNIX. –Often not as robust as NT or UNIX for serving.

Table 17-2.   *Operating Systems and Web Serving Considerations*

servers in your decision, it might be wise to look at the most common Web servers used. On the basis of surveys and analysis of reachable servers on the Internet (http://www.netcraft.com), the following are considered to be some of the most common Web servers used, though their exact market percentage is a topic of hot debate.

Apache	Zeus
Microsoft's IIS	WebStar
IPlanet servers (formerly Netscape)	Domino

Each of the popular Web servers is discussed next. This should by no means be considered as approval of these products, but rather just a synopsis of each product highlighting some of its known characteristics.

Serverwatch (http://www.serverwatch.com) provides links and reviews of most of the popular Web servers available.

Apache (http://www.apache.org/)

A descendant of NCSA's httpd server, Apache is probably the most popular Web server on the Internet, at least as far as public Web sites are concerned. Apache's popularity stems from the fact that it is free and fast. It is also very powerful, supporting features like HTTP 1.1, extended server-side includes (SSIs), a module architecture similar to NSAPI/ISAPI, and numerous free modules that perform functions such as content negotiation, text compression, spell checking, and much more. However, Apache is not for everyone. The main issue with Apache is that it isn't a commercial package. Some firms are hesitant to run their mission-critical systems on a user-supported product. However, as with operating systems like Linux, various third parties offer commercial implementations of Apache or sell support for the free version. Another potential limiting factor for Apache is that the system currently is mainly for UNIX. Although there is a port of Apache to Windows 32-bit systems, as well as one for the Macintosh OS X environment, the server was initially built for popular UNIX and Linux variants. The lack of heavy NT support may limit the use of Apache within many Windows-centric enterprises, but the Apache 2.0 release aims to change that. However, given the development integration Microsoft IIS provides, it may be a hard sell to the Windows crowd. Probably the most troublesome aspect of Apache for some developers is that it might require modification of configuration files or even compilation in order to install properly. If you like to tinker or desire speed, have a UNIX system, or don't have a lot of money, then Apache might just be for you. You'll be in good company; some of the largest Web sites on the Internet swear by this product.

For Web trivia buffs, the name "Apache" is derived from the description of the software as a patched version of NCSA. Think "a patchy NCSA server."

Microsoft Internet Information Services (http://www.microsoft.com/iis/)

IIS is Microsoft's server for Windows NT/2000/XP. Other Windows variants also support a similar but much less powerful version of IIS called the Personal Web Server (PWS). While PWS is certainly popular, of the two, most organizations favor IIS. One very important aspect of IIS is that it is very tightly integrated with the Windows environment. In fact, today it is hard to distinguish IIS as a stands–alone service within Windows 2000. Unfortunately, being so Windows specific is also one of the problems with IIS. Because of hardware and clustering issues, IIS initially isn't quite as scalable as some UNIX-based servers. With new Microsoft clustering technologies and integration with a transaction processor, this scalability problem is likely to change. For an intranet environment—particularly one with heavy Microsoft investment—it is difficult to beat the features offered by IIS, particularly its Active Server Pages development platform and its integration with other Microsoft technologies and products. The price for IIS is currently a major positive point for the software—it's freely bundled with the operating system.

Sun (Servers formerly known as iPlanet or Netscape) (http://www.sun.com/software/)

Sun servers born from the iPlanet joint venture between Sun and Netscape after the merger between Netscape and AOL, constitute a large number of Web servers. These servers continue a long history started by Netscape of supporting high-end Web and application servers running on most major variants of UNIX (Solaris, SunOS, AIX, HP-UX, Digital UNIX, and IRIX), as well as Windows 2000. The servers are well developed, as they represent more than four generations of software releases. The servers are also very developer friendly and powerful, with support for databases and directory services, content management, HTTP 1.1, and a variety of other features. Given Sun's involvement, a focus on Java is core to the server offering. If you are in a cross-platform or UNIX environment and you are looking for commercial-quality Web serving solutions, then consider using these servers.

4D WebStar (http://www.starnine.com/)

Initially a popular Web server for the Macintosh originally based on MacHTTPD, WebStar integrates well with the traditional Macintosh interface. The server has solid security features and supports native Macintosh technologies, as well as UNIX-style CGI programs, PHP, a Java virtual machine for server-side Java, and extended SSI. The performance of most Macintosh Web servers has often left much to be desired, though it is improving and is probably more than adequate for intranets or small Web sites. Apache on OSX tends to be a better choice for larger Macintosh-powered sites.

Lotus Domino (http://www.lotus.com/domino)

Domino is an example of the collision between traditional Web serving and messaging and groupware. Domino runs on Windows servers, variants of UNIX, and even large IBM systems such as AS/400s. It is often used in corporate intranet and extranet environments where workflow and integration with messaging and backend systems may be more important than raw Web serving performance.

Zeus (http://www.zeus.com)

Finally, we have Zeus as a contender for the fastest Web server. This server is becoming popular with extremely high volume Web sites. The Zeus server does not lack development capabilities, as it provides not only Java compatibility but supports both IIS's ISAPI interface and the NSAPI interface introduced on Netscape Enterprise servers.

Making the Choice

There are numerous Web server software choices. Remember that different packages will have different performance characteristics. Using the same hardware, one Web server software package may far outperform another. When planning to build a Web server, start either from the hardware and build up or from the particular software and build down, picking the best possible hardware. If you make good software and hardware choices, the performance of the site can be significantly improved. Always try to base your choices on usage requirements, such as a target number of simultaneous users or requests per minute or second. However, don't forget that you will have to maintain the site. If you are unfamiliar with UNIX systems and your company uses only Windows servers, your decision is probably already made for you. Once all the requirements of the site have been carefully determined, it is possible to best choose how to serve a site.

Server Capacity Issues

The first thing to determine when building a Web server is exactly what kind of load the machine will come under. Exactly how many users does the site need to serve, worst case? For public Web sites, this is hard to predict, but educated guesses can be made, and over time your serving requirements will become clearer by looking at usage logs. The simultaneous user requirement suggests not only how much hardware may be needed but how much bandwidth. Consider 100 users simultaneously looking at pages that are 50KB in size and it is easy to calculate the amount of bandwidth needed. It also shows why it is so important to consider the size of pages not only from a usability point of view, but a cost point of view. The incremental costs of serving heavy Flash-laden pages are significantly higher than using a lightweight XHTML with CSS page. Now you understand why so many e-commerce sites skimp on any visual design beyond pictures of products—it just doesn't pay!

Server load calculations for capacity are not always very simple. Normal Web sites will have bursty load, and we may find that peak load may be much higher than simply dividing the number of users a day by the amount of time in the day.

When considering server capacity, you will begin to see that one machine just isn't going to be able to handle infinite load. To address this, you may create a *server farm*—a collection of Web servers all serving the same information. A server-farm is diagrammed in Figure 17-3. Incoming users will be distributed across all the servers in the farm, hopefully improving both uptime and performance. The distribution of users can be performed simply by using a modified form of DNS, called *DNS round-robin*, that allocates users one-by-one in a round-robin fashion to different IP addresses or in a more complicated fashion using a *load balancer*. A load balancer may have more sophisticated distribution schemes, such as least busy or closest geographically, which leads us to our next issue. Even if you have capacity, the actual location of the server plays a big role in responsiveness.

Server Location

Server location influences both site response time and maintenance costs. The basic choice boils down to whether to have a server at your own location or at another location(s) offsite, such as at an Internet service provider or hosting vendor. Choosing whether to run your own server or outsource the server and maintenance to a third party can be a complex question, but you should always try to put the server close to users. The reason for this is that by minimizing the network path between a server and a user, you minimize the possibility of problems caused by the network.

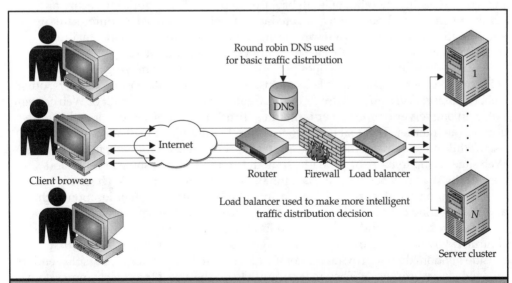

Figure 17-3.   *Server farms are built to scale Web sites*

Rule: Always strive to minimize network distance between a site and its users.

For an intranet, it is pretty obvious that the server should be on your local network. But what about for an external site? Many people prefer to host their own site, which requires a full-time connection to the Internet. However, is the server as close as it could be to the end users? Further, will a locally hosted site provide enough bandwidth for users? Having enough bandwidth available can be important for mission-critical Web sites. Regardless of server bottlenecks, a mere fractional-T1 or full-T1 leased line might not provide enough bandwidth to deal with the bursty nature of Web access. However, installing multiple T3 leased lines just to deal with the occasional flash crowd that may swamp a site seems wasteful, given the significant investment required. Rather than bringing bandwidth to the server, why not move the server to the bandwidth? Even if bandwidth is not an issue, there may be other reasons for network closeness. It is unlikely that you'll be able to install leased lines to multiple connectivity providers. Even if you can, your site will still be more hops away from central exchange points than the providers you may purchase bandwidth from.

Another motivation for not placing an external Web server locally is the security implications. Many companies are still very afraid of the security problems associated with the Internet. Firewalls and security policies can help, but if a public Web server is located on the firm's LAN, allowing Web viewers to access it is similar to asking potential robbers to come knock on your door. Putting public use information on outsourced Web servers keeps casual intruders away from a firm's network access point and allows stronger security policies to be put into place at the corporate firewall.

The actual facility housing the server is often an overlooked aspect of locating a Web server. Does your own location provide a safe environment for a server? Are power systems highly reliable, with backups in place? Is the building secure and staffed twenty-four hours a day, seven days a week? Is there a computer-safe fire suppression system? The cost of providing the physical and personnel facilities necessary for a high-end Web site should not be underestimated.

Finally, outsourced hosting does provide the possibility of moving away from a single point of serving to multiple locations. In fact, large-scale hosting vendors, often dubbed *content distribution networks* or *CDNs,* attempt to serve the bulk of Web content not from one server or one server farm but a distributed set of servers or caches at the edge of the Internet. The goal here is once again to minimize the distance to the end user. While edge delivery makes a great deal of sense, it does fundamentally change Web site serving to more of a broadcast model and introduces some expense and complexity that may be inappropriate for all but the highest traffic Web sites.

Don't automatically assume that placing a Web server at another location such as a Web hosting vendor is the only way to go. Certainly, the network and services provided by hosting vendors can exceed local hosting, but you give up security and control. If you need to provide access to highly sensitive data, you may find that outside vendors do not provide the comfort level you desire. Further, outside vendors are by their nature *outside.* They may promise to do their best to protect your system from harm and provide high-quality support, but some people want the control of doing things themselves. Finally, if the requirements for a site are minimal and the infrastructure is in place, it just may not be cost effective to outsource site delivery.

> **Suggestion: Choose to host your own Web site when security or control is a primary concern.**

Outsourcing Web Hosting

As Web sites become more critical to the information infrastructure of companies, there is a growing need to provide high-quality, high-availability solutions. For example, a business selling something only online can't afford to have its site go down at all. The serving of a site to an e-business is as critical as power and telephone services would be to a traditional business. This trend might be termed the "utilization" of the Web, as some may consider the health and delivery of their Web site as important as other utilities like water and power. However, given that the site must be run in a very efficient and reliable manner, firms quickly discover that it is in fact quite expensive for companies to develop in-house the talents and facilities to run a mission-critical Web site. Therefore, many firms have decided to outsource their Web facilities. Web server outsourcing comes in many flavors, but many of the differences revolve around two factors. The first differentiating factor is whether your site is sharing a machine with other sites. The second is whether or not the machine being used is owned and managed by you or the outsource vendor. Each type of service will be discussed in turn, with special focus on their pros and cons.

Shared Hosting

The most basic form of hosting, shared hosting, ranges from free Web space added to other services or in exchange for advertisement placement to high-end *application service providers* (ASPs). At the low end, many Internet service providers will provide a directory on one of their Web servers with a few megabytes of disk space and possibly access to a few shared tools that can be used on your Web site, such as simple form-handling scripts, counters, or message boards. Usually, the URL for a site like this is of the form http://www.isp.net/~enduser or http://www.isp.net/enduser. The hosting service lacks any customization like your domain name (yourname.com), and it may impose limits on traffic delivered or programming tools that can be used. The upside to these types of services is that they are often free or may be included in the cost of your Internet connection. There are also many vendors who will provide free Web serving in exchange for personal information for marketing purposes, or if you agree to show banner advertisements, they book on your Web site. While these services are appealing to home users or those looking to put up a site for fun, most will prefer other forms of shared hosting.

Shared hosting services that provide a domain name (www.yourname.com), often called a *virtual server*, generally are not free. These services also provide improved development facilities, like your own cgi-bin directory, statistical reports on site traffic, shopping cart facilities, and other useful features. The costs for virtual server accounts on a shared system usually start around $20 or more per month. However, costs vary greatly and the more bandwidth your site consumes or the more special requests you have, the higher it may cost—even if the machine is not dedicated to you. In fact, with complex shared hosting services, where you may have access to content management systems or e-commerce facilities, the cost can literally skyrocket to hundreds or even thousands of dollars per month.

The major downside of shared Web hosting is that it involves using the shared server facilities of a hosting vendor. This means that the site will share Web server resources and bandwidth with other hosted sites. Server responsiveness may be significantly affected because of other hosted Web sites, particularly if those sites become popular. Further, many customers are wary of sharing a server with others, because security often cannot be guaranteed on these shared systems. Despite its drawbacks, shared hosting is very popular—mainly due to price.

Dedicated Hosting

Because of the downside of sharing a server with others—most notably security and control—many people opt to use a dedicated server. Dedicated servers are advantageous because you can customize your server with whatever tools or programs you like, and you are not affected by other sites as much. However, the trade-off is cost. Dedicated servers tend to be more expensive.

There are two forms of dedicated server hosting. The first is where the outsource vendor owns and maintains the equipment. This may be called *fully managed* or *dedicated hosting*. The other is where you own and may even be responsible for maintaining your server. This is usually called *co-location*. With co-location, the vendor provides space at their facility, electrical power, a network connection, a certain amount of bandwidth, and very limited system management for your server (like rebooting it if it crashes or maybe doing tape backups). Co-location is generally cheaper than fully managed services, but for those who don't want to be bothered with the details of Web site delivery, co-location is not as great of a deal as it might seem.

Dedicated hosting solutions are very attractive to those who want control, security, and power, but don't want to deal with many of the day-to-day issues of running a Web server. The major downside of these solutions is price. Services provided by top-tier vendors might run many thousands of dollars per month—the amount dependent on the equipment and bandwidth required, as well as any services added, such as security monitoring or sophisticated hosting requirements like mirroring a site at multiple locations. However, if a business really relies on robust fast Web site delivery, many of these vendors are a bargain, even at what appears to be a high price. Think of the actual cost of maintaining a telephone company-grade equipment room filled with servers connected to numerous Internet providers being monitored twenty-four hours a day, seven days a week by capable system and network administrators— you'll see that the cost may be well worth it. When you consider that some of the largest sites for content, search engines, and e-commerce don't run their own servers, it will seem more plausible that an outside hosting vendor is a good idea.

Companies looking to save money on Web delivery may find outsourcing very attractive, but some flexibility and security may have to be sacrificed. With less-experienced hosting companies, this lack of control can be disastrous, resulting in hidden costs or problems with reliability. Those who want more control over their Web services should consider co-location or running their own servers locally.

Tip	*Links to commercial hosting vendors can be found at http://www.webhostlist.com.*

Delivering the Payload

Once a page is built it is time to consider finally delivering it and its associated components, like images and other multimedia files, back to the user. Obviously the size of the payload in proportion to the user's bandwidth will increase user wait time. However, don't go overboard with size reduction for speed improvements; things aren't always what they seem when you consider network interactions. Remember time matters more than bytes!

Networking, Protocols, and Web Design

While HTTP isn't really the most sophisticated or fastest network protocol, it is well understood by all browsers in use. The simplicity of this request/response application causes some potential problems, particularly when mixed with other protocols such as Transmission Control Protocol (TCP). The first thing to consider is that the HTTP protocol requests each object within a Web page separately. Consider an HTML page with eight images. There is one request first, for the HTML, followed by eight more requests for the images. There may even be an extra request at the beginning if the URL is partially formed, like http://www.democompany.com/products, and a trailing slash would have to be added and be directed to an index file.

With nine or ten separate requests, there is bound to be some extra overhead added, as opposed to a single request for all the objects at once. Consider this carefully when building a page. Say that one page has a single large image nearly 75KB in size, while another has ten images totaling 70KB. While the total bytes to be delivered would suggest that the second page should be faster, the first page may actually download more quickly as far as the user is concerned.

Suggestion: Try to keep the number of unique individual objects in a page small to reduce the number of HTTP requests.

Note	*The HTTP 1.1 protocol does attempt to address performance problems with HTTP and multiple requests, but generally the rule of "fewer connections is better" holds.*

While there will always be overhead associated with individual requests, HTTP protocol is notorious for its inefficiency at times—particularly when paired with the congestion avoidance features of the lower-level TCP used to control the transmission of data from browser to Web server. TCP uses a variety of techniques, such as slow start and backoff once traffic is encountered, to keep networks from clogging up. Users certainly notice the slow-start facility of TCP when downloading large files, since the download speeds keep increasing until reaching a plateau.

The problem with congestion avoidance is significant when considering the size of typical Web objects, which are often less than 20KB. Given the small size of Web objects, most connections never reach the full potential of the connection given the slow-start facility. This is one of the reasons that a single image at 100KB may beat a few images totaling 80KB, particularly on a fast connection. Browsers may try to address this issue by requesting numerous objects at once, but this only serves to create bursts on servers that may already be overwhelmed servicing many requests.

The effect of network protocols on Web page delivery is obvious even to the casual Web user. Notice when using a high-speed connection, such as a cable modem or leased line, that the improved bandwidth doesn't make as much of a difference on typical sites as it does when downloading large files or accessing sites that use large binary formats, like Macromedia Flash. The reason is partly the network protocols being used and partly the way that sites are designed. Typically, users accessing sites with slow connections find splitting up files into multiple pieces better than delivering large files. It goes back to usability: keep the users happy with a little bit at a time. However, a high-speed user may find sites with a few large images to be more responsive. Designing for high-speed connections and low-speed ones is not just about the size of the objects that can be delivered, so always design with the type of connection in mind—not just the amount of data to transfer.

Suggestion: Match data types, number of items, and size of data items to be delivered to the speed of the user's connection.

Exploiting Expiration and Caches

In an effort to improve Web usability, it is best not to re-request unchanging contents. Users are generally familiar with the concept of the browser cache. The browser cache stores images, HTML files, style sheets, and other items so that they do not have to be downloaded over and over. Other forms of network caches also are used at both the corporate LAN and the Internet provider level to avoid retransmission of the same data. While caches may be commonplace, the number of site designers taking advantage of them is relatively uncommon.

Simply re-referencing the same image files over and over from a common directory may appear to improve site access speeds, but it does not go as far as it could. In fact, even if the image is the same, a browser will issue a request to a server to see if the item has been modified recently. If unchanged, the server will respond with a 304 code indicating the cached resource can be used, as the requested item is unchanged. Unfortunately, all these 304 requests do add up. It would be smarter to indicate which items in a Web site do not need to be looked at and which do, as well as how frequently. You can accomplish this using expiration and cache directives. For HTML files, you can use a **<meta>** tag like **<meta name="Expires" content="Tue, 01 Jun 1999 19:58:02 GMT" />** to indicate expiration date. Needless to say, images change far less often and should be cached locally more often. To set expiration times on such objects, you typically need to access the Web server and selectively set expiration headers per item. A good way to accomplish this is to put unchanging graphics like navigation items and section labels in a special directory, say /images/cache, and then set a long expiration time for all these items.

> **Suggestion: Consider setting expiration dates for unchanging items such as site graphics.**

One downside of using expirations is that you can't clear remotely cached items easily and you generally will be required to change filenames to force a re-request of information.

Dealing with State

HTTP is considered a stateless protocol because it doesn't maintain a constant connection between the browser and server. As discussed in previous chapters, the stateless nature of HTTP also presents significant challenges—particularly to interactive Web sites—since it can be difficult to preserve information from page load to page load. Cookies, extended path information, and hidden form fields are all used to deal with this limitation. By its nature, HTTP does not make this easy; designers should make sure to implement complex interactive sites carefully and in such a way that they are not overly optimistic about the presence of a particular technology such as cookies. However, don't consider the stateless nature to be a serious flaw with HTTP; it is exactly these characteristics that allow Web servers to service numerous users simultaneously, because the overhead of a connection does not have to be maintained.

Real-Time Data and the Web

An interesting aspect of the TCP protocol that is not well considered by many Web designers is the protocol's inability to efficiently deal with real-time data. If you've used the Internet for any period of time, you've encountered occasional delays. The network is "bursty" by nature. The TCP/IP protocols used on the Internet were designed this way for robustness and scalability. The Internet is a packet-switched network that breaks data up into little chunks and sends them separately, to be reassembled at the other end, because these packets may be lost along their journey or arrive out of order. However, the Transmission Control Protocol, or TCP, solves this problem with retransmission and proper assembly of data packets that guarantees the integrity of the data. This way, many users can share a fixed circuit, which allows for economies of scale.

Packet-switched networks have distinct advantages over circuit-switched networks like the telephone system. If your connection is cut off during a phone call, you have to redial. If there are already too many calls going across a circuit, you get a busy signal.

When a packet-switched network like the Internet faces increased traffic and failing connections, it just slows down and reroutes (although servers and overloaded Internet providers can create the equivalent of a busy signal). However, most packet-switched networks like the Internet have one serious problem—they cannot guarantee delivery time without special modifications. This makes streamed audio, video, and other "real-time" applications difficult on packet-switched networks.

Packet-switched networks can be augmented with protocols like RTP (Real Time Transport Protocol), RTSP (Real Time Streaming Protocol), and RSVP (Resource Reservation Protocol), which help format or even control the delivery of time-sensitive data over the Internet. However, some of these ideas—particularly the idea of being able to reserve bandwidth—are not well supported yet and, additionally, introduce economic considerations. For example, how would you charge or limit bandwidth reservations? Wouldn't a user always want maximum bandwidth? True real-time delivery protocols are still in development, so another approach to real-time data on the Internet is necessary.

The current approach to real-time data on the Internet is really just an assumption— you hope the end user has the end-to-end bandwidth to receive the file in real time. For example, consider a user with a 14.4 Kbps modem. On average, we predict the user can receive about 1KB per second. If we can compress one second of audio down to 1KB, we could deliver it to the end user and have the sound play in real time. Whatever the bandwidth, from 14.4 Kbps to T1, an assumption like this is made. When the assumption holds, the sound can be streamed effectively. However, when the assumption doesn't hold, there are glitches and the sound may drop out. If you get too much dropout, the user turns off the audio stream. One way to avoid dropout is to buffer data. This process gives you a head start by preloading a certain amount of data in a buffer so that rough spots can be overcome. An initial buffering delay of 10 or 15 seconds is acceptable for long audio clips; buffering short sounds is counterproductive. Many Internet audio solutions use a combination of major compression, buffering, and the bandwidth assumption to achieve streaming.

The bottom line is that there is really no way to guarantee that bandwidth will be available. Traffic conditions on the Internet are unpredictable. Even worse, the base Internet protocols like TCP were never designed to provide the guarantee of delivery time in the first place. About the only thing to do is to make conservative estimates of available bandwidth, minimize the path between server and client so latency is reduced and there are fewer points of failure, and hope for the best. Today's Web content distribution networks do this, and various new protocols are being adopted to try to "fast track" real-time data. However, assuming that radio- or television-quality delivery of audio or video over today's Internet is possible, is a naïve assumption that does not consider the medium. Will reliable, high-quality real-time data transmission be possible in the future? Probably, particularly with new protocols and improved network infrastructure, but for now designers should consider the limitations of real-time data before relying too greatly on it.

Rule: Predictable and error-free delivery of real-time data on the Internet cannot be reliably guaranteed with today's protocols and usage.

Browser Rendering

Once site content finally reaches the browser, it is time to decode the data. As mentioned earlier, browsers should look at the Content-Type HTTP header and examine it before rendering the content; passing it to a plug-in, control, or helper application; or simply prompting the user to save or delete the information. Note that some browsers like Internet Explorer seem to even look beyond the MIME type or even file extension and will aggressively assume HTML is the data type once tags are seen. After content is rendered, it may be examined for further requests. In the case of an HTML file, it would be parsed and then any images, applets, movies, sounds, style sheets, scripts, and so on would be requested individually, unless they were already in local browser cache—thus repeating the browser the cycle mentioned at the beginning of the chapter. That's all there is to Web delivery.

Managing Web Servers

Once a Web server is installed and successfully delivering content to users, there are a great number of maintenance tasks that should take place. Servers must be continually monitored for availability, performance, and security. Checking availability might be simply a matter of utilizing a tool to "ping" the server every few minutes by sending it a small data packet to see if it is alive. However, such simple checking doesn't ensure that the server is working—just that it is reachable on the network. More sophisticated server monitoring actually requests a page on a site and may even look for some key phrase or element to make sure that the page is completely formed. Make sure your hosting vendor provides such monitoring facilities for your site. If not, consider purchasing a tool that includes site monitors and alarms.

A monitoring tool shows availability of your server only from a particular location. You may want to test the reliability and availability of your network connection to other locations on the Internet. The best way to do this is to employ a site-monitoring service that can test your site from multiple locations online.

> **Suggestion: Utilize a monitoring tool or service to ensure that your site is constantly available to users.**

The responsiveness of the server should also be carefully monitored. While a server may not necessarily crash, it can become so overloaded that it is effectively unusable. Make sure that the load on a server is carefully monitored as well.

Web Server Security

With the rise of e-commerce on the Web, monitoring site security has become of paramount importance. A lax attitude towards security leads to intrusion by hackers or crackers—or whatever term, probably derogatory, that you wish to use to describe an unsavory character who compromises your site. Why people decide to intrude into other people's sites ranges from simple curiosity to a malicious or criminal purpose. People *do* attempt to enter into a site to steal credit cards or other valuable information, as well as to try to ruin the reputation of a firm by posting profane or incorrect information to the site. A great number of people point to the fact that many intrusions do not result in significant damage as some indication not to worry too much about it. However, that is a naïve viewpoint that will be less tolerated as more and more businesses begin to do business on the net and damaging intrusions continue to happen. In the "real world," casual intrusion into a store in the middle of the night by an individual who claims they are doing this just to see if they can is just plain illegal. It is unlikely that a defense like "the locks should have been stronger" or even "they should have locked the door" will satisfy any sane jury. Regardless of your take on the hacking/cracking issue, site owners should still take precautions and attempt to fortify their site against unauthorized access. In order to do so, you must first consider the methods of intrusion employed. A few of the common intrusion techniques are briefly summarized in Table 17-3.

To combat some of these attacks consider employing all the methods described in Table 17-4.

What's interesting about these rules is that they must all be considered together in order to create a complete security policy. The strongest firewall in the world isn't going to keep someone out of your network if they can look through your garbage to find configuration information or simply call up and pretend to be an important executive. In some ways, security is somewhat an all-or-nothing venture if you are serious about it. Many people plug the obvious holes and then don't worry about security, but when money is exchanging hands, as in the case of an e-commerce site, that is a dangerous approach.

> **Rule: Create, implement, and test a full-site security policy that goes beyond a simple firewall.**

Keeping up with security matters can be a full-time task. Numerous sites like http://www.cert.org issue warnings literally weekly, and other sites post any and all exploits for all to see. So, consider that any person interested in cracking a system will have little problem finding sites that detail how to exploit common system holes. Thus, it should be no surprise that many of the most common intrusions and worm attacks that plague sites are due to "cookbook hacking" of the common holes and can be easily prevented just by patching systems. Because of the constant vigilance required to maintain secure systems, you may consider hiring an outside firm that specializes solely in security to audit your site and plug any exploitable holes.

Other Web Server Management Duties

Beyond ensuring the performance, availability, and security of a server, a Webmaster must often perform tasks such as upgrading hardware and software as well as backing up the server software and site on a regular basis. Backups may be performed both to

Method	Discussion
Password guessing	A common way sites are exploited is through easily guessable system passwords. Cracking tools can be employed that try common passwords or even try every word in the English dictionary.
Operating system exploitation	The underlying operating system may be open to exploitation because of bugs or known flaws. Once the operating system is compromised, the intruder will have the run of the site.
Spoofing	Not necessarily used for intrusion, spoofing is a technique where an intruder appears to be someone else. This may be used for intrusion when the intruder spoofs a trusted site. Spoofing can also allow an intruder to pretend to be the site when a user is conducting a transaction.
Network sniffing	Monitor network traffic to grab passwords and other data useful to gain entry to servers. In some cases there may be no need to actually enter a server, as valuable data may be transmitted around the network and scooped up directly.
Denial of service	A denial of service attack is not necessarily performed to gain access to a site. Denial of service is generally employed to cause damage or ruin reputation. Typical denial of service includes crashing the system, using up all server resources and thus locking out legitimate users, or flooding a network with bogus requests.
Social engineering	Social engineering is when an intruder attempts to trick unsuspecting site owners or associated staff members into divulging important information, such as system passwords. Typically, the intruder will attempt to impersonate a trusted or important individual over the phone or via e-mail, since physical deception can be difficult.
Physical compromise	Probably the least common attack form, but still important to consider, is physical intrusion of a site location, including actually stealing a system.

Table 17-3.   *Typical Site Attack Methods*

TECHNOLOGY AND
WEB DESIGN

Method	Discussion
Use and rotate strong passwords	Use longer, difficult to guess passwords. Make sure there is a limit to the life of passwords. Consider using hardware-generated passwords.
Maintain your OS	Keep operating system software up-to-date by applying all patches and upgrades.
Limit access points	Remove services that are not in common use. Limit Web servers to only providing Web services and consider removing any form of network protocol access to a server except HTTP.
Set up a firewall	Configure a firewall so as to limit network traffic. Consider using both packet filtering and application protocol limitations.
Use strong encryption	When transmitting sensitive data, either via e-mail or HTTP, encrypt the information using the strongest possible ciphers allowed.
Use digital certificates	Install digital certificates from organizations like VeriSign (http://www.verisign.com) so that identity can be verified.
Reduce information leakage	Don't freely expose information that a hacker could utilize to find a hole to exploit on your system. Don't allow a remote login, even with a prompt. If you do allow remote login, at least modify any prompts returned to not indicate the variant of the software or operating system in use. Modify your HTTP server headers to not reveal the type of Web server in use. Don't reveal the type of technology used in programmed Web pages, like Perl. Consider using generic file extensions like .cgi instead of language specific ones like .pl. Avoid exposing information about your network through domain name services. Avoid naming systems in such a way as to reveal their operating system (like solaris1.democompany.com). Modify your WHOIS record to not include personnel information that can be used in social engineering attacks.
Employ physical security	Limit physical access to important servers. Destroy sensitive documents, including documents that detail network or server configurations.

Table 17-4.   *Common Site Protection Methods*

offline storage like a DAT tape and to hot spare servers when any downtime could be detrimental. What's interesting is that, given the focus on availability, on security, and on routine system tasks, a Webmaster may spend much of his or her time acting as a traditional system or network administrator—only with a focus on Web services. Of course, other organizations may consider the Webmaster the individual responsible less for the maintenance of the Web server itself than for the content of the site. Content management is a key aspect to Web site management, but it does intersect with traditional system administration duties once usage analysis is considered. Certainly the lines between system, network, and content management blur on occasion.

Content Management

Maintaining content is just as important as maintaining the server itself. Large sites or those with numerous contributors will quickly degrade if special care is not taken. First, make sure there is a set policy for naming files. For example, consider avoiding special characters such as underscores (_) in filenames, because it will be difficult for users to notice them in the address line of a browser. Instead of robot_butler.htm, consider robot-butler.htm or just robotbutler.htm.

> **Suggestion: Avoid using underscores in filenames. Consider using dashes or no space between words.**

However, be careful with using filenames like RobotButler.htm or even capitalizing directory names. The domain aspect of a URL is not case-sensitive, and the user may not be consistent in the use of case. Although some servers such as UNIX systems have case-sensitive filenames, Windows systems don't, so moving sites between the systems could be troublesome. You can use a server configuration to address this, but it is easiest just to always use lowercase to avoid such problems.

> **Suggestion: Do not use mixed or uppercase letters in file or directory names.**

Set a file extension policy and stick to it. Shorter extensions are generally better if you consider the extra characters to type as well as the fact that some older systems prefer three-character extensions. However, regardless of your take on .htm vs. .html, pick one and be consistent.

> **Rule: Pick either .htm or .html as a file extension and stick with it.**

Consider limiting filename length, or even using consistent naming schemes. For example, some files may include dates in them, such as press releases. Filenames of pr021299.htm and pr010500.htm could reference press releases on 2/12/1999 and 01/05/2000, respectively.

Make sure to use the same care with directories as you do with files. Pick short, easy to type and spell directories in all lowercase letters that lack special characters.

Also, consider using common directory names to hold site assets. Table 17-5 details a few common directory names and their usual contents.

What probably causes the most difficulty in dealing with site content are all the changes that are made. When many people are working on a site, it is easy for conventions to be overlooked and for simple errors to be introduced. To reduce the possibility that content degrades, first carefully limit who can make changes to a site. Second, resist the desire to fix site problems or add content on a moment's notice. It is far better to make regular updates, such as once a day or once a week. This allows backups to be made and provides a stable base to roll back to in case problems are introduced.

Suggestion: Try not to update on demand; instead create a regular update schedule.

If a site is heavily updated, consider employing a content management tool. A simple source code control system can be used that will provide an audit trail and rollback facilities and will force site contributors to check out pages to make changes to

Directory Name	Contents
/cgi-bin	The traditional location for executable programs on a Web server, particularly CGI programs.
/scripts	Contains scripts for the site, including JavaScripts, CGI scripts, and server-parsed languages like Cold Fusion or Active Server pages. Occasionally, the directory may be named after the type of script stored—for example, /js or /javascripts for linked JavaScript files.
/styles or /css	Contains any linked style sheets used on a site.
/images	Contains all site images, including GIFs, JPEGs, and PNG files.
/video	Contains video assets—primarily nonstreamed video clips.
/audio	Contains audio assets—primarily nonstreamed audio files.
/pdfs	Contains PDF files such as a library of datasheets.
/download or /binaries	A central location for any programs or software distributions that are to be downloaded from the site.

Table 17-5.   *Common Site Directory Names*

them. More powerful content management systems with easy-to-use browser-based front ends, including form-based page editing, can be built or purchased. The DemoCompany site (www.democompany.com) itself uses such a tool, as shown in Figure 17-4.

Interested readers who have not experienced content management systems are encouraged to try this system. More advanced systems provide even more advanced capabilities and are used to run complex Web sites, particularly heavily updated sites like news sites. The point here is simply to illustrate the concept of content management.

Regardless of the methodology used to control the update of a site, one rule cannot be stressed enough: *Never work directly on a live site*. Be aware that users may see your changes as they happen and even see pages in half-finished form. Further, any serious blunder may be difficult to recover from if the live site is being edited directly.

Rule: Do not work directly on a live site!

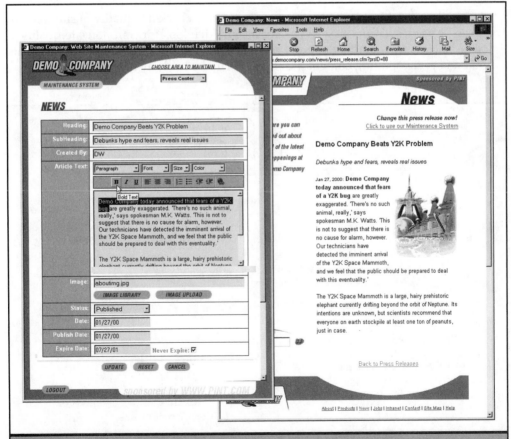

Figure 17-4. *DemoCompany's homegrown content management system*

Rather than working on a live site, consider using a three-site architecture, as illustrated in Figure 17-5. First, set aside a development server where a copy of the site is kept and major changes and programming features can be added and tested. Second, create a staging server with an exact duplicate of the published site. The staging server is where changes are made and tested. Last, a production server should be utilized to actually hold the site being delivered. Changes should be made only on the development or staging site, which is later synchronized with the production server.

Even with careful planning, errors are bound to creep in. In fact, some things may even be beyond your control, such as the availability of external servers you link to. Because of the potential for broken links, a link-checking tool should be utilized often. However, beware of just running link checking on a huge site and then trying to correct all the errors at once. It may be wiser to check sections of the site on a rotating basis. For example, every day a different part of the site tree might be examined and any broken links repaired.

Rule: Check site links constantly.

Besides link checking, it is important to continually check the quality of site content. Tools can be used, such as Coast (www.coast.com), that look for common site-quality problems such as slow-loading pages, spelling errors, or poor HTML, but nothing beats the human eye for spotting content problems. Focus particularly on page details such

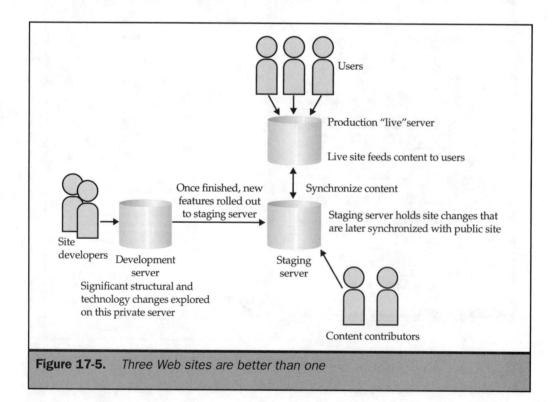

Figure 17-5. *Three Web sites are better than one*

as copyright information, page titles, and text sizing. Subtle variations can mean the difference between a positive user visit and a negative one. One good way of finding problems is to actually print pages and look them over carefully.

> **Suggestion: Check regularly for page details including spelling, legal terms, and font usage. Perform a print test if necessary.**

While careful checking will ferret out many problems, errors will still occur in most sites. Make sure that users have a form or e-mail address to use to send in any found errors. Sites should always consider the address webmaster@*yourdomainname*.com as a default address published for users to send problems to.

> **Suggestion: Provide the address webmaster@*yourdomainname*.com for users to contact you with suggestions and error reports.**

Even if users don't tell you where your errors are, looking at the way users browse a site by examining access logs may provide valuable clues to sections that should be examined further.

Usage Analysis

A very important task in managing a Web site is analyzing site traffic. Many sites use very simple measurements, such as page counters showing the number of visitors, to monitor usage. The true benefit of these counters is unknown. One possibility is that a visitor to the site may make a determination to stay or go based on the counter. If the counter shows only a few visitors have ever been to the site, they may assume there is nothing there and just leave. The counter, of course, is under complete control of the designer, and the number of visitors showing can be adjusted. If you decide to roll your counter to a much higher number, you may still have problems, as the user may believe the counter to be misleading—which could cast suspicion on the accuracy of the site's content. The bottom line is the user doesn't need to know how many people are visiting your site. Further, visitor counters are not found on most high-quality sites, and many users may feel that a site with one is amateurish.

> **Suggestion: Do not put a visible page counter on your site.**

Rather than counters to indicate site usage, you should rely on server log files, as they show what users actually look at in a site and can be used to glean important information about site usage and success. For example, by analyzing a log file, you can see which files users read and which they do not. From this information, you might decide to promote heavily used pages closer to the top of the site or prune lesser-used pages from the site. Managing log files is not difficult, but it does require some planning to deal with them properly, and they must be analyzed carefully so as not to jump to false conclusions about a site. If you decide you'd rather not keep statistics, there are numerous services that will monitor your site traffic for you—for example, HitBox (www.hitbox.com).

Regardless of who does the collection or what kind of server is used, log files are fairly similar. Web servers generally provide two basic logs: the access log and the error log. There may also be a referrer log, which records users following links from other sites to your site, and an agent log, which records information about the user agents (usually browsers) that are accessing the site. Often, the referrer information and user-agent information is recorded in the access log as well. The most common format of access log is called, appropriately, the *common log format*. The format of the common log format is

```
Host identd authenticated-user [Time of request]
"request made" result-code bytes-transferred
```

Each field in a typical common log is explained in Table 17-6. A few examples entries from an access log are shown here:

```
206.251.142.45 - - [22/Jan/2000:19:29:09 -0800]
"GET /badfile.htm HTTP/1.0" 404 222
sj.ix.netcom.com - - [22/Jan/2000:19:29:12 -0800]
 "GET / HTTP/1.1" 200 7947
sj.ix.netcom.com - - [22/Jan/2000:19:29:13 -0800]
 "GET /images/about.gif HTTP/1.1" 200 506
sj.ix.netcom.com - - [22/Jan/2000:19:29:14 -0800]
 "GET /images/staff.gif HTTP/1.1" 200 580
sj.ix.netcom.com - - [22/Jan/2000:19:29:14 -0800]
 "GET /images/products.gif HTTP/1.1" 200 620
phoenix.goodnet.com - lsw [22/Jan/2000:19:40:50 -0800]
 "GET /images/whatsnewtop.gif HTTP/1.1" 200 874
```

The example entries show bad requests, a series of requests that constitute a full page, and an entry that was authenticated. Given that every single individual object requested on a site is recorded, log files become enormous relatively quickly. Log file information should be cut into manageable chunks for analysis.

 Split logs on a regular basis such as daily, weekly, or monthly to avoid log files getting unwieldy and rotate or back up older logs to avoid filling up your drive with mountains of usage data.

Once a log file is generated, it should be periodically analyzed. Many software packages exists that can be used to batch analyze Web server logs. Many of these packages can be automated to fetch log files and run reports at a specified time. For example, WebTrends (www.webtrends.com) Log Analyzer, as shown in Figure 17-6, is a particularly popular log analysis package.

Field	Description	Examples
Host	The address of the client making the request. Often, this is just an IP address, since domains may not be resolved until later on.	192.102.249.5 pc1.fakedomain.com
Identd	The information returned by identd. If this is not used, a dash is recorded instead.	-
Authenticated user	This field indicates any username sent for authentication. A dash is found if no user challenge was issued.	- bigboss
Time of request	This field indicates the time the request was made. It should be in the form *DD/Mon/YYYY:hh:mm:ss –GMT* where *DD* is the day, *Mon* the month, *YYYY* the year, *hh* the hour on a 24-hour clock, *mm* minutes, *ss* seconds, and *–GMT* the offset from Greenwich mean time.	[22/Jan/2000:13:52:54 -0800]
Request made	This is the actual HTTP request made by the client.	"GET /products/robotbutler.htm HTTP/1.0"
Result code	This is the HTTP numeric status code returned by the server indicating the success or failure of the request made.	200 404
Bytes transferred	This field records the number of bytes sent back to the requesting client.	2358

Table 17-6.   *Access Log Fields*

TECHNOLOGY AND WEB DESIGN

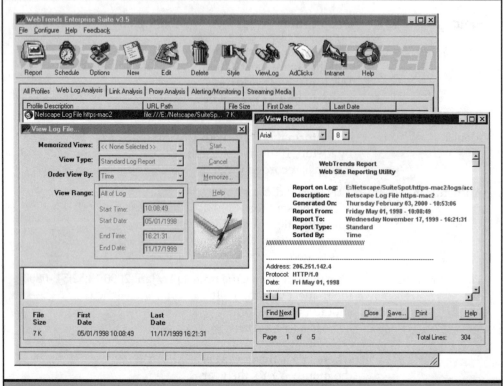

Figure 17-6.   *WebTrends presents an easy-to-use log file analyzer*

One important consideration when choosing a log file program is whether or not the usage data is stored in a database. Some lower-end analysis programs will simply read a log file and create a report. If you desire to see a different report, the entire log file must be reread. For quick and dirty analysis, such batch log file analysis is probably adequate, but many designers will want to investigate results dynamically and may want to run comparisons over long time periods. Sites with more than a few thousand visitors per month should consider using a database-enabled log analyzer and save statistical data over time in a data warehouse. However, the amount of usage data a site collects grows quickly, so think carefully about how much data is really necessary to save. Also, if your site gets a reasonable amount of traffic, you should consider dedicating a machine solely to process and analyze log files. Sites with large volumes of traffic find that keeping up with usage is very difficult, and they are forced to try to process log data in real time because of the time that will be mandatory to offload the server—particularly if usage analysis is going to be performed in real time.

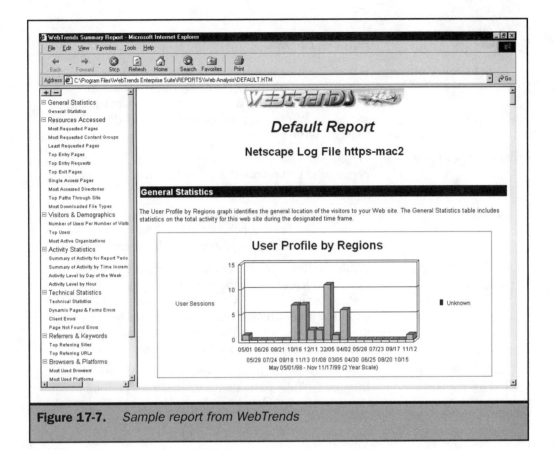

Figure 17-7.   *Sample report from WebTrends*

Analyzing Site Usage

The ultimate purpose of saving log files is to process them and create reports to reveal site usage. Statistical analysis programs can generate fancy reports showing various aspects of site use. An example report is shown in Figure 17-7.

While log analysis reports often contain pretty graphs and charts that look useful, a significant problem is that there is often only little meaning that can be distilled from the reports. In fact, far too often Web site managers focus too much on gross usage statistics, such as total page views, or concentrate on general trends rather than on what is actually happening on the site. Often, without close inspection, such metrics can be misleading. For example, are all the visits to a site a single visitor or multiple visitors? Are pages being reloaded? Are the page views coming from your own organization being filtered out? There is much more to measuring the use of a site than looking at the number of pages viewed. Consider performing the tasks listed in Table 17-7 when looking at log analysis reports.

Task	Purpose of Task
Look for entry points	Determine where users enter a site. If users are not entering through the home page, then how are they entering the site? The users may have bookmarked the site or are entering through search engines deep-linking to pages within the site.
Look for exit points	Which pages are users commonly viewing last? Are these pages valid exit points at the conclusion of a typical task, or are users bailing out of a site visit midstream?
Find common paths	What paths did users take through a site? Did these paths lead to valid conclusion pages? Are these paths efficient, or could the number of clicks be reduced?
Look at average visit length	While the time of the visit may be difficult to determine exactly, at least look at the numbers of pages viewed and the time estimate. Make sure to consider if the length of time is reasonable. Don't assume the longer the visit, the better. A visitor may just want to get a particular piece of information and leave.
Look for domain and user spikes	Look to see which domains and users visit the site frequently. Take particular note of surges of domains or users. It may be related to a particular event. Be careful to filter out local users, as an organization tends to be its own heaviest visitor.
Look for single visit or multivisit trends	Determine if site users are inclined to visit the site frequently or not by looking for return visits. If the site is geared towards heavy return visitation, attempt to track individual users with cookies.
Watch for day and time patterns	When do users visit the site? Is the site a night or day site? Is it heavily used during the week or on the weekend? Business sites often find their logs closely match business hours, while entertainment sites may show heavier use at night. Look for the heaviest traffic periods and try to understand the reason. It may be just that it is the time of day or week that the most users are likely to use the site, or it may be related to events that happened on the site, such as a new software release or the posting of an earnings report.

Table 17-7.   *Common Tasks to Perform During Log Report Inspection*

Task	Purpose of Task
Look for language and geography patterns	Look to see if users from foreign countries are using the site. Consider language changes or localization if heavy usage is found.
Look at browser usage	Look at the types of browsers using the site. Optimize the site for use by the most common browsers, but account for limitations of uncommon browsers seen in the log file.
Look for referring sites	Determine how users reach the site. If referring links are followed, backtrack and see what sites are pointing to yours. Keep a database of referring sites, particularly if links are paid for, to judge cost per visit.
Look at search engine keywords	If users are utilizing search engines to reach the site, make sure to monitor which keywords they are using to find the site.
Look for errors	Make sure to look at the error log and look for "404" page requests, server response problems, and any other errors that might have occurred.

Table 17-7.   *Common Tasks to Perform During Log Report Inspection* (continued)

Remember, one of the major reasons to look at a log file is to study how users actually use a site—these are real users with real goals, so try to determine what they are trying to accomplish at the site. Measuring the success or failure of visits is particularly important. It may be better to first focus on the number of software demos downloaded, forms submitted, products purchased, and so on, rather than to focus on the number of pages viewed.

Rule: Analyze your log files carefully and use them to improve a site or measure its effectiveness.

Log analysis can also be used to show the economic effectiveness of a site. For example, an e-commerce site might measure the number of visitors per sale, the number of page views per sale, the number of bytes delivered per sale, and so on. In fact, for e-commerce sites it is wise to consider visitation costs as related to sales. Remember, delivery of sites is not free, so it is important to try to understand the cost of each visit.

When used carefully, site promotion techniques can also be evaluated to determine their effectiveness. For example, consider the placement of a magazine advertisement for a new product. Rather than promoting the standard URL for an organization, like

www.democompany.com, use a special URL—for example, www.democompany.com/
robot/magad or something less obvious, like www.democompany.com/robot4.html—
so that each advertisement has a URL with a different number at the end. Some
organizations even create special URLs like robot.democompany.com, or even full
sites like www.robotbutler.com (often termed *microsites*) that can be associated with
a particular site promotion. Whether using just a special URL or creating a whole
new site, a unique entry point can be monitored in the log files to determine the
effectiveness of the advertisement. Further, the entry page can be created to be more
contextually appropriate to the advertisement, as shown in Figure 17-8.

  *When providing site addresses to the public, set up special entry URLs to track usage
and provide more focused information to users.*

While log files can be used very effectively to understand site use, don't fall into
the trap of thinking the logs tell the whole story. A log file isn't going to say if a user
enjoyed a visit to a site or found it confusing. For example, a user may get to a
particular page in the shortest number of clicks, but may have guessed or been forced
to very carefully read information in order to do so. Analyzing log files does not
remove the need to communicate with users. You should still solicit comments from
users and even hold surveys to determine user satisfaction.

**Rule: Do not rely solely on log files to understand a site's effectiveness. You still
have to talk to the site's users.**

Figure 17-8.   *It is often better to push users to specific URLs or sites*

Also, because of assumptions made by log analysis software, as well as the people analyzing the files, it is very easy to jump to incorrect conclusions. This is further compounded by network and protocol effects, which may taint log data.

Accuracy of Logs

Be careful when looking at log files not to infer too much. For example, the domain name or IP address of a user requesting a page is recorded in the log files. Some people are tempted to relate the domain name to the physical location of the organization that holds the domain name. This could then be used to determine what geographical regions people are coming from. However, the Internet isn't as geographically sensitive as many people might think. For example, if a user is coming from aol.com, that says nothing about where they are physically located. In fact, relating domain names to geographical locations will make you believe that California and Virginia account for the majority of a public site's traffic. The problem here is that many large Internet connectivity vendors are based in these regions and their domain names show this. Further, don't assume that just because a user comes from a .com domain that they are in the United States. Many foreign firms use the shorter domain names as well.

Another problem with log accuracy is related to network and protocol issues. Remember that HTTP is a stateless protocol. Because of this, it is very difficult to tell how long a user visit lasts. For example, a user may request the home page at a particular moment in time and, a minute later, click on a link to visit a subpage, and then leave by shutting down the system or entering a URL of another site directly in the browser. Question: how long was the visit? You can't really tell. The user may have lingered on the subpage for 10 seconds, 10 minutes, or even 10 hours. You can't see them leave. You just know they didn't view any more pages in your site. Most statistics analysis packages make an assumption to end a particular visit after so many minutes of inactivity. Tune the package to use a longer amount of time and your reports will suddenly show longer visitation times.

It is important to consider how aspects of the network, such as dynamic IP addresses and proxy servers, will affect log accuracy. Many users access the Internet from a machine that is given a new IP address dynamically each time it connects to the Internet. If you measure visitors by their IP address, you may easily over-report the number of unique visitors if dynamic IP addresses are issued. Further, when a proxy cache is used, you may see only a single visitor rather than numerous ones, because all users appear to come from a single IP address. It is possible to get around some of these issues by handing out a cookie to the user. The cookie can be used to identify the user, and will identify users uniquely regardless of what IP address they are coming from. Unfortunately, users may not accept cookies and may become suspicious of the amount of tracking going on. While it is important to track users to understand their likes and dislikes, it is also important not to appear to be monitoring them too closely. Privacy is a growing concern for users and is discussed in the next section. First, however, we'll consider the implication of site usage accuracy.

Some readers may be familiar with the expression, "There are lies, damn lies, and then there are statistics." It is true that it is easy to be misled by site usage statistics, particularly when making assumptions such as one IP address equals one user. As long as the assumptions are kept the same, useful patterns can be determined. The only real danger with site usage analysis is when the unscrupulous designer learns that it is easy to modify or even create results. Far too often, it seems sites strive to show heavy usage, and in some cases may misrepresent the usage level. Some sites play word games, talking about "hits" rather than "page views." A *hit* is simply a request for an object in a page. If a page has nine images in it, it produces ten hits or more—one for the page itself and nine for the images. If you want to look like you have a lot of traffic, put many small objects in every page and talk about your hits.

Some sites have even gone so far as to create results by either writing a program to browse the site or by paying people to click on the site. In fact, creating realistic-looking usage data complete with unique IP addresses is far easier than you think. It is no wonder that advertisers are hesitant to pay for mere banner views and prefer paying for clicks or results. Usage data trickery does nothing but hurt the industry. Legitimate sites already have begun relying on third-party auditing to verify usage for advertisers and other concerned parties. The "fake it until you make it" strategy is a dangerous game that no site should play.

Privacy

What is done with data collected from a user visit can be just as important as the delivery of the site itself. As more and more users rely on the Web for day-to-day business and personal tasks, the issue of privacy grows in importance. Many users, particularly novice users, are worried about being tracked by sites and may not want to transmit a credit card number over the Web for fear of interception. While some of these fears are certainly not warranted, Web designers should never quickly dismiss user concerns, as this would go against the very nature of user-centered design.

First, consider the user's fear of privacy as it relates to tracking their online movements. Indeed, sites do track users both openly and legitimately through log files, and occasionally they do so surreptitiously using cookies or even HTML tricks. While cookies may be useful to rectify various environment problems, such as the stateless nature of HTTP or dynamically assigned IP addresses, they are indeed used to track the user to some degree. Now, how you decide to utilize the information collected will vary, but it is important to inform the user of what is collected and what it is used for. A privacy policy should be written that explains the policy for collecting and using sensitive information. Organizations like TRUSTe (http://www.truste.org) will help sites create a privacy policy. However, enforcement of policy is problematic, and users are still wary of sites—even those that may have been audited by organizations such as TRUSTe.

Rule: If you are collecting sensitive data online, post a privacy policy or statement in an obvious place on the site and abide by it.

The crux of online privacy really gets back to control. Should users be in control of their online personal information and know what is being collected about them and what is stored in various databases? Or should Web sites be able to freely collect and trade information about users? Unfortunately, at least in the United States, the power to regulate personal information is not truly in the hands of users. Even when it comes to credit reports, think how difficult it can be to obtain and correct your own credit report. Now consider how damaging incorrect entries can be on your report when trying to apply for a home loan. The Web brings this to a whole new level.

Sites can and do develop profiles on users and use these profiles to market more selectively to them. In some situations, sites may even sell or trade user profile information with others. In fact, the degree of personal information that can be obtained online is quite scary. One recent news story detailed how a boy with a high school crush gone wrong used the Web to obtain and post information about the whereabouts of his obsession. He eventually found and murdered the girl. However, don't leap to conclusions about the evils of the Internet. The medium itself does nothing. There are few stories run about how people used the telephone to plan a crime, which is certainly done frequently. The key to improving the Web is to make sure to apply common sense to its usage and consider or even monitor carefully what is consumed.

Because privacy policies are typically hard to find and filled with legalese, it is not surprising that most users rarely (if ever) take the time to read and understand them in their entirety. To address this problem, the W3C has developed the Platform for Privacy Preferences (P3P), which provides an automated way for Web sites to publish and users to retrieve privacy information for a given site. The Webmaster runs a program that asks a series of questions in order to determine how to characterize the nature of the site's usage of user data. Once this short interview has been completed, the program places a special file that contains a summary of this information at a predetermined place on the Web server. Then, when a user wishes to retrieve privacy information on the site the browser fetches the summary and presents it to the user, as shown in Figure 17-9.

The truth of the matter is that P3P has not yet been widely adopted and has some critics in the privacy community. However, it probably cannot hurt to employ this technology or at least keep abreast of the developments in this area—especially in light of the fact that Microsoft is heavily behind the initiative. You can learn more about P3P and find programs such as the one just mentioned at www.w3.org/P3P/.

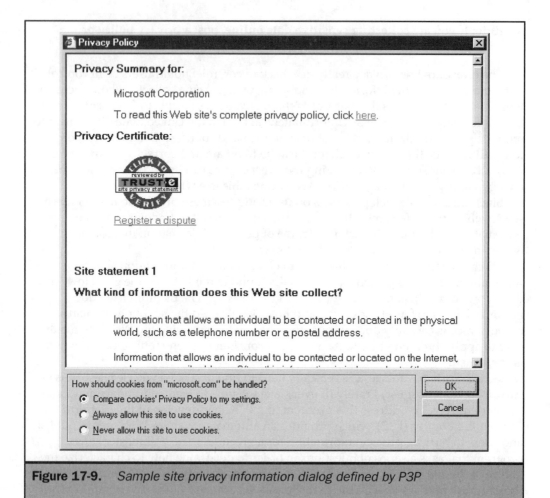

Figure 17-9.   *Sample site privacy information dialog defined by P3P*

Content Concerns

Like privacy, the delivery of data and interaction with a user are not just technical matters. These aspects of the online experience raise feelings and beliefs about the acceptability of content. Many parents, and now even employers, are concerned with the content that is easily available online. It seems that far too often children are able to easily find less than desirable material online, such as hateful sites or hardcore pornographic material, without their parent's knowledge. Of course, much of the blame can be placed on parents who do not carefully monitor what their children are doing and interact with them in a positive way to warn them about such sites.

While what constitutes "unacceptable" will certainly vary from individual to individual, few will argue that there are not at least a few sites that should be kept away from children, if possible. Of course, deciding what is acceptable and what is not should not be strictly determined and enforced by a third party—particularly the government—since this would inhibit freedom of speech and introduce censorship. However, parents, teachers, and even employers should have the tools to help monitor and control content usage where acceptable. Site filtering is probably the most common technique employed. The basic method of site filtering involves the use of special filtering software that looks first for a content rating before allowing a page to be loaded. If the content is deemed acceptable, it is presented to the user; if not, it is rejected. From a site delivery perspective, the key concern about content acceptability is the accuracy in labeling content as acceptable or unacceptable.

The W3C has proposed the Platform for Internet Content Selection, or PICS (http://www.w3.org/pub/WWW/PICS/), as a way to address the problem of content filtering on the Web. The idea behind PICS is relatively simple. A rated page or site will include a **<meta>** tag within the head of an HTML document. This **<meta>** tag indicates the rating of the particular item. A rating service, which can be any group, organization, or company that provides content ratings, assigns the rating. Rating services include independent, nonprofit groups such as the Internet Content Rating Association (ICRA) (http://www.icra.org/). The rating label used by a particular rating service must be based on a well-defined set of rules that describes the criteria for rating, the scale of values for each aspect of the rating, and a description of the criteria used in setting a value.

To add rating information to a site or document, a PICS label in the form of a **<meta>** tag must be added to the head of an HTML file. This **<meta>** tag must include the URL of the rating service that produced the rating, some information about the rating itself (such as its version, submitter, or date of creation), and the rating itself. Many rating services allow free self-rating. Filling out a form and answering a few questions about a site's content is all that is required to generate a PICS label. After you complete and submit the questionnaire, you receive a page or e-mail containing the appropriate meta information, which can then be placed in the head of your HTML documents. An example of a PICS label in the form of a **<meta>** tag using the RSACi rating is shown here:

```
<meta http-equiv="pics-label" content='(pics-1.1
"http://www.icra.org/ratingsv02.html" l gen true for
"http://www.democompany.com" r (cz 1 lz 1 nz 1 oz 1 vz 1)
"http://www.rsac.org/ratingsv01.html" l gen true for
"http://www.democompany.com" r (n 0 s 0 v 0 l 0))' />
```

Under the ICRA rating system, information is rated based on nudity, sex, violence, and language on a scale of 0 to 4, with 0 being harmless and 4 being the most extreme form of each criterion. In the previous case, nothing was offensive, so the site received 0 on all counts. Remember that, when filtering, software reads a file that contains a rating, and then it determines whether the information should be allowed or denied.

Very strict filtering environments may deny all sites that have no rating, so sites with a broad audience are encouraged to use ratings to avoid restricting readership.

Filtering technology that supports PICS is beginning to achieve widespread acceptance and use. For example, Internet Explorer already includes PICS-based rating filtering, as shown in Figure 17-10.

Of course, the technology itself can't cure the problem. Lack of trust in a particular ratings system is a major stumbling block in adoption of the filtering idea. Even when trust is gained, if the rating system seems confusing or arbitrary, its value is lowered. In the real world, Hollywood's MPAA movie rating system assigns a single value of G, PG, PG-13, R, or NC-17 for each movie. The assignment of a particular movie rating is based on many factors that often seem arbitrary to casual observers. When considering movies, parents may wonder how scenes of a dinosaur ripping a person to shreds merits a PG or PG-13 rating, while the use of certain four-letter words indicates an R rating. Certainly, similar situations occur on the Internet. Because of the imprecise nature of ratings, the topic is a loaded one, both off and on the Internet. Be careful not to inadvertently cause problems for your site by not rating it, particularly if some users could construe the content as unacceptable.

Rule: If your content is in any way questionable, have it rated.

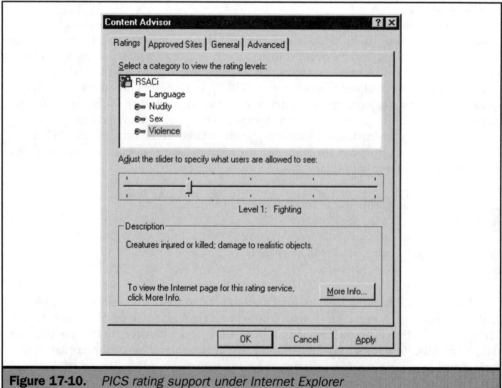

Figure 17-10. *PICS rating support under Internet Explorer*

Summary

Speedy site delivery is very important because the user's feeling about a site is heavily influenced by its responsiveness. When optimizing sites for speed, make sure to consider all aspects of delivery, including the protocols, the servers, and network location. When building a Web server, make sure to first consider the site's delivery requirements and then choose the hardware, operating system, and server software to match. Hosting choices should also be carefully evaluated, and outsourcing should be considered a viable option for many sites. Once the site is being delivered, make sure to monitor it carefully. Site maintenance will have to be performed not only on server hardware and software, but on the content itself. Analyzing log files and checking for broken links is an important aspect of proper site maintenance. However, always consider that delivering sites to users is akin to having a conversation with them, and the issue of security, privacy, and acceptability of the content will certainly come up.

Part V

Appendixes

Appendix A

Core Web Site
Design Principles

Throughout *Web Design: The Complete Reference*, key concepts have been summarized as Rules, Suggestions, and Premises. Useful Definitions have also been provided when necessary. This appendix collects all of these in one place, grouped by chapter, to give the reader the chance to quickly review the basic ideas of this book.

What Is Web Design?

These rules from Chapter 1 summarize some essential concepts for effective Web design.

> **Rule: YOU are NOT the USER.**
>
> **Rule: USERS are NOT DESIGNERS.**
>
> **Rule: Design for the common user, but account for differences.**
>
> **Rule: Make sure the visual form of a site relates to its function.**
>
> **Rule: A site's execution must be close to flawless.**
>
> **Rule: Know and respect the Web and Internet medium constraints.**
>
> **Rule: Appropriately respect GUI and Web interface conventions.**
>
> **Rule: There is no form of "correct" Web design that fits every site.**

User-Centered Design

These rules, suggestions, and definitions from Chapter 2 emphasize the importance of considering your target audience—the actual users of the site—when designing for the Web.

> **Definition: Usability is the extent to which a site can be used by a specified group of users to achieve specified goals with effectiveness, efficiency, and satisfaction in a specified context of use.**
>
> **Rule: There is no absolute description of what constitutes a usable site.**
>
> **Rule: Usability depends on the medium of consumption.**
>
> **Rule: Usability depends on the type of site, as well as the user's familiarity with it.**
>
> **Rule: Usability and user satisfaction are directly related.**

Rule: Browsers don't use sites, people do.

Suggestion: There are no generic people. Always try to envision a real person visiting your site.

Suggestion: Avoid using text, graphics, and backgrounds of similar hue.

Suggestion: Avoid combining text, graphics, and backgrounds of similar saturation.

Rule: Keep contrast high. Avoid using text, graphics, and backgrounds of similar lightness.

Suggestion: Avoid using busy background tiles.

Rule: Make sure colors that are meant to distinguish items like links are significantly different in two ways, such as hue and lightness.

Rule: Users try to maximize gain and minimize work.

Rule: Recognition is easier than recall.

Rule: Do not make visited links the same style or color as unvisited ones.

Suggestion: Make pages that will be remembered visually different from the rest.

Suggestion: Limit groups of similar choices, such as links, to between five to nine items.

Suggestion: Aim for memorization of only three items or pages sequentially.

Rule: The amount of time a user will wait is proportional to the payoff.

Rule: When response times such as page loads take more than 30 seconds, try to provide your own feedback to the user, such as a load-time progress bar.

Suggestion: Make page elements obviously different if they are different.

Suggestion: Limit page noise, and segment page objects so that they don't compete so much visually that users are unable to focus on what they are interested in.

Rule: Sensory adaptation does occur on the Web. If you want a user's full attention, you'll have to vary things significantly and often.

Rule: Try to optimize keyboard access for all pages in a site, not just form pages.

Rule: Minimize mouse travel distance between successive choices.

Rule: Minimize mouse travel between primary page hover locations and the browser's Back button.

Rule: Make clickable regions large enough for users to move to them quickly and press them accurately.

Suggestion: Always remember that you need to bring a site into the user's world, not the other way around.

Rule: Account for the characteristics of the probable environment in which the user will access a site.

Suggestion: Aim to create an adaptive Web site that meets the requirements of novices, intermediates, and advanced users.

Suggestion: Design for the intermediate user if an adaptive Web interface is not possible.

Rule: Users bring past experiences with the world, software, and the Web to your site. Make sure your site meets their expectations.

Rule: Do not stray from the common interface conventions established by heavily used sites.

Suggestion: Perform user testing early and often.

Suggestion: When performing even an informal usability test, avoid talking too much or guiding the user.

Suggestion: Do not use usability concerns as a way to avoid or eliminate visual, technological, or economic aspects of a site.

Suggestion: Practice "Las Vegas" Web design. Provide the user with a pleasant experience complete with perks and the illusion of unlimited choices, but control the situation strictly at all times.

The Web Medium

These rules and suggestions from Chapter 3 emphasize correct approaches to the capabilities and limitations of the Web medium.

Rule: Beware of relying on published browser usage figures; track actual browser usage on *your* site.

Rule: Users often don't blame browsers for simple errors—they blame sites.

Rule: Consider using both client-side and server-side technologies in a site, rather than one or the other.

Suggestion: Rely on helper applications when translation to a native Web format is impractical.

Suggestion: Focus on using only the more popular plug-in technologies unless automatic installation can be performed.

Suggestion: If ActiveX controls are used on a public site, make sure to provide alternatives for Netscape or other browsers.

Rule: Consider end-user system performance carefully when using Java applets.

The Web Design Process

These rules and suggestions from Chapter 4 focus on the importance of developing and sticking to a process when approaching Web design.

Suggestion: Always collect content as soon as possible.

Rule: Visual design should proceed in a top-down fashion, from home page to subsection pages and finally to content pages.

Suggestion: Always consider the bordering effect of the browser window when developing visual composites.

Rule: Don't marry your design prototypes. Listen to your users and refine your designs.

Rule: Sites always have bugs, so test your site well.

Rule: Testing should address all aspects of a site, including content, visuals, function, and purpose.

Rule: User testing is the most important form of testing and should always be performed last.

Rule: Site development is an ongoing process—plan, design, develop, release, repeat.

Evaluating Web Sites

These rules and suggestions from Chapter 5 concern approaches to evaluating existing Web sites.

Rule: Pay attention more to what users do than to what they say.

Suggestion: Consider having a person not involved in the site design process conduct a user test.

Site Types and Architectures

These rules, suggestions, definitions, and premises from Chapter 6 are concerned with defining and understanding the many types of Web sites and site structures.

Definition: A public Web site, an Internet Web site, an external Web site, or simply a Web site is one that is not explicitly restricted to a particular class of users.

Definition: An intranet Web site is a site that is private to a particular organization, generally run within a private network, rather than on the Internet at large.

Definition: An extranet site is a Web site that is available to a limited class of users, but is available via the public Internet.

Definition: A static site is one where content is relatively fixed, and users are unable to affect the look or scope of the data they view. In short, the visitor has minimal ability to interact with the site's content other than choosing the order in which to view content.

Definition: An interactive site is one where the users of the site are able to interact directly with the content on the site or with other users of the site.

Definition: A personalized site is one where content is directly geared towards a particular user, and the user generally can explicitly determine the content, look, or technology contained within a page.

Definition: A dynamically generated page is created at request or view time for the user.

Premise: The overriding purpose of any commercial site is to serve the user in a way that will benefit the company either directly or indirectly.

Premise: Entertainment sites may find novelty or surprise in design more useful than structure or consistency.

Definition: A portal is a site that is generally a primary starting point for a user's online journey and serves to help people find information. Portals often attempt to provide as much information and serve as many tasks for the user as possible in order to encourage them to stay or to at least continually revisit the site.

Definition: A community site is any site that allows easy interaction between site visitors and serves as a meeting area for site visitors, rather than simply a viewing area for visitors to view canned content.

Premise: The design of artistic sites may purposefully defy common Web conventions.

Premise: A Web site's logical structure is more important to a user than its physical structure.

Rule: Do not expose physical site file structure, if possible.

Rule: A site's logical document structure does not have to directly match physical structure.

Suggestion: Aim for a site click depth of three.

Suggestion: Aim for positive feedback indicating progress toward a destination for every click, with a maximum of three clicks without feedback.

Suggestion: Even for wide site structures, consider a range of 25–81 links per page when page links are ideally clustered.

Premise: The more important the page, the more redundant links should be provided to it.

Suggestion: Redundant links in a site should be no more than 10 to 20 percent of a page's total exit links.

Premise: Novice users prefer sites with predictable structure and may put up with extra clicks or a lack of control to achieve a comfortable balance.

Premise: Power users or frequent site users want control and will favor structures that provide more navigation choices.

Navigation Theory

These rules, suggestions, and definitions from Chapter 7 approach the important issue of Web site navigation both from a theoretical and a practical standpoint.

Rule: Use simple and memorable URLs to improve navigation.

Rule: Do not hide or obscure URLs unless you are trying to keep people from direct linking.

Rule: Use consistent and explicit page labels for all pages in a site.

Rule: Site-wide labeling of icons or words, such as the organization name or logo, should always return a user to the home page of the site when clicked.

Suggestion: Button states should be considered a secondary form of page labeling, and the selected state should always be subdued, not prominent.

Suggestion: When using color-coding to imply section location, make sure the colors used are significantly different from each other.

Suggestion: Do not go so overboard with theme-based location hints that you fall into a designer-defined metaphor.

Suggestion: Do not attempt to mimic the browser history mechanism with links.

Rule: Avoid links named simply "Back." Always explicitly indicate where a back link will go.

Rule: Do not hijack a user's back button unless the site's functionality requires it.

Definition: A cookie is a small bit of textual information handed out by a site that is stored on the user's system.

Rule: Users remember their start page as a permanent landmark and the home page of a visited Web site as a semipermanent landmark. Because of this, these pages should be stable in their presentation but look noticeably different than other pages visited.

Suggestion: Don't hide a destination choice from a user unless the link is less important or clutter forces sacrifices.

Suggestion: Avoid placing primary navigation on the far right of the screen.

Suggestion: Home pages or other landmark pages should consider using center-oriented navigation to distinguish themselves from other pages in a site.

Rule: Placement of navigation should be consistent within a page layout.

Rule: Navigation should be consistent and elements should exhibit stability in position, order, and contents.

Suggestion: When separating navigation choices by position onscreen, understand that four locations is a hard barrier.

Suggestion: Navigation-oriented pages should fit vertically within the screen whenever possible, as should primary navigation in all other types of pages.

Suggestion: Minimize the distance between primary site navigation buttons and the Back button.

Suggestion: Always attempt to limit mouse movement between subsequent navigation items.

Suggestion: Do not make a remote the mandatory form of navigation.

Rule: Limit scrolling and mouse travel in navigation as much as possible.

Rule: Consider a maximum of three page loads before a result.

Basic Navigation Practices

These rules, suggestions, and definitions from Chapter 8 examine the many ways to create links in a Web site.

Suggestion: Occasionally provide some unstructured links within document text to promote exploration and thought.

Definition: A static link is one where the destination file is hard-coded into the anchor by the document author.

Definition: A dynamic link does not have a fixed destination. Instead, the destination document is computed at page view time according to the environment and needs of the viewer.

Suggestion: Always provide textual links at the bottom of pages when using long pages or pages with graphical buttons.

Suggestion: When using image maps, always provide a secondary navigation form such as text links.

Rule: Never completely remove visited link indication.

Rule: Avoid changing link colors.

Rule: Avoid underlining non-linked text in Web documents—use italics or bold instead.

Suggestion: Avoid automatically turning off link underlining. If you do, add another link indicator form.

Suggestion: Avoid using ellipses in links, as they are generally redundant.

Suggestion: Graphical buttons should have at a minimum an unselected and a selected state. Mouseover states and active press states should be considered optional.

Suggestion: Provide good labels indicating the form of the content. Consider using icons to show content types.

Suggestion: Make sure to indicate if the link will jump them within a page, within a site, or to an external site. Don't hide the URL, in case the user can deduce the answer from it.

Suggestion: Indicate an external link by exposing the URL or using an icon. Indicate file size if triggering a download.

Suggestion: Use an icon or symbols, or issue an Alert dialog before the link.

Suggestion: Avoid changing visited link colors. Add the last modification date, where necessary. Use a "New" icon.

Suggestion: Use an Alert dialog, or warn with an obvious label.

Suggestion: When using status bar messages, consider providing URL information with the text when linking externally.

Rule: Broken links should be considered catastrophic failure.

Suggestion: Avoid automatic redirects for 404 errors.

Suggestion: Avoid using frames for layout. Use them for navigation.

Suggestion: When using frames, make smaller frames control larger adjacent frames.

Suggestion: Do not turn off frame resizing and scrolling unless resolution is very well accounted for.

Suggestion: Do not allow further navigation in spawned windows if at all possible.

Search

These rules and suggestions from Chapter 9 examine the concept of designing a site in a way that optimizes search functions.

Rule: Utilize past user experience with public search engines by using similar layout and labeling in local search facility design, but avoid imitating aspects of public search engines that deal with the uncontrollable nature of public Web sites.

Suggestion: When search is available in a site, include a search button or field on all pages.

Rule: Search forms and result pages must match the look and feel of a site.

Rule: A search form should match the content being searched.

Suggestion: Primary search text boxes should be about twice as big as secondary search text boxes.

Suggestion: It is generally better to limit a scoped search to a topic, category, or idea rather than a section of a site.

Rule: Advanced search facilities must provide instructions and examples.

Rule: Result pages should provide as much information as possible so users can decide what items to peruse further.

Rule: The format of search results should fit the data that is being returned.

Rule: Negative search result pages must include information on why a query failed and potentially how to fix the query.

Suggestion: Disallow blank queries unless they return a complete page set.

Definition: A Web directory is a human-edited and organized collection of site links and associated information such as descriptions and reviews.

Rule: Do not design pages solely to attract search engines, as, ultimately, pages are for people.

Site Maps and Other Navigational Aids

These rules and suggestions from Chapter 10 concern best practices for Web site navigation aids.

Rule: Name your link to a site map simply "site map."

Suggestion: Avoid using a complex or unfamiliar navigation system in a site map.

Suggestion: Label links to a site index as just "site index" or "A-Z index" if that is the only form of indexing provided.

Suggestion: Provide a glossary in a site filled with complex jargon.

Pages and Layout

These rules and suggestions from Chapter 11 concern aspects of pages and page layouts, from screen size to function-specific pages.

Rule: Set the size of the page to fit the purpose and the content at hand.

Rule: Avoid wide pages, particularly those that cause rightward scrolling.

Rule: Try to keep important items such as primary navigation in the first screen.

Suggestion: Be aware of the screen "fold" and try to hint at content beyond the first screen.

Rule: Avoid resolution entry restrictions for sites if at all possible.

Rule: When designing for MSNTV/WebTV, consider a hard and fast page width of 544 pixels.

Suggestion: If designing with assumed screen sizes, be conservative and give yourself a slop factor of as much as 10 percent of the available region.

Suggestion: When using fixed page sizes, make sure to center your page to reduce perception of empty space on larger displays.

Suggestion: Avoid using stretchable designs on pages with little content.

Suggestion: Try to fit content vertically within 3–5 screens if possible.

Suggestion: Either control page margins or account for their variation with some layout slop factor.

Suggestion: Provide an obvious link to quickly skip a splash page.

Rule: A home page should look significantly different than other pages in a site.

Rule: A home page should set the visual and navigational tone of a site.

Rule: A home page should load quickly, but be informative and dramatic enough to encourage interest.

Rule: A home page should clearly indicate what's inside a site.

Suggestion: A home page should provide informational value and an obvious indication of site change if change is occurring.

Suggestion: If a particular subpage is a landmark or common entry page, such as a "section home page," make it visually distinctive.

Rule: Subpages should follow the style and navigation of the home page, at least in spirit.

Suggestion: If FAQ pages are a reasonable length, make them a single document for easy printing.

Suggestion: Provide a link back to the top of the document or a list of the questions at the end of every answer.

Suggestion: Consult a legal professional for drafting or inspection of any legal terms page used to cover Web site usage.

Rule: If sensitive or personal information is collected, provide an easily accessible and understandable privacy statement.

Rule: Full contact information should be available within one click of any page on a site; minimal contact information such as a phone number and e-mail address should be included on the bottom of every page.

Suggestion: Inform users that printed pages will be different than what is seen on screen, or show the print version directly.

Suggestion: Use Acrobat PDF files for highly complex information that needs to print perfectly such as data sheets, technical drawings, and complex financial or mathematical information.

Suggestion: Clearly indicate Acrobat files with text and an icon, and provide information on using these files.

Rule: Provide an obvious conclusion page for a task.

Suggestion: Provide a way back to the site from an exit page.

Rule: Let users leave in peace. Avoid "please don't go" or "last chance" pop-up windows.

Suggestion: When using text-oriented design, consider providing navigation bars as well as contextual links.

Suggestion: Consider using a text design philosophy on sites where download speed or display flexibility is paramount.

Suggestion: Avoid using metaphor design on sites geared towards expert users or heavy repeat use.

Suggestion: Avoid unconventional or very artistically oriented interface designs on task-driven, heavy-content, or frequent-use sites.

Suggestion: Use header-footer design for content focused sites, particularly when wide content is common.

Rule: Strive always in Web design to be the same, but different.

Text

These rules and suggestions from Chapter 12 offer ideas to guide your usage of text, typography, and writing on the Web.

> **Suggestion: Avoid using justified text in Web pages.**

> **Rule: Increase line height to improve online text readability.**

> **Suggestion: Create a type hierarchy by varying text color, size, style, and position to improve page usability.**

> **Suggestion: Avoid anti-aliasing small text.**

> **Suggestion: Consider three fonts per page: one for page labels and headlines, one for body text, and one for navigation.**

> **Rule: Columns of text in Web pages should never wrap up and down unless all contained in a single screen.**

> **Rule: Navigation-focused pages generally require less text white space than consumption pages.**

> **Rule: Always use white space to complement the use of information.**

> **Suggestion: Be careful of using words that have alternative Web meanings.**

Color

These rules and suggestions from Chapter 13 focus on the use of color on the Web, from basic font coloring to advanced uses of CSS with colors.

> **Rule: To ensure the appropriate color is produced, always use a hexadecimal value over a named color except in the case of basic VGA colors like white, black, red, and so on.**

> **Suggestion: To safely break the 216-color barrier, use pre-dithered patterns or so-called hybrid colors.**

Images

These rules and suggestions from Chapter 14 focus on the use of images on the Web.

> **Rule: Use GIFs for illustrations and JPEGs for photos.**

Suggestion: Limit bitmap graphics formats in Web pages to JPEG and GIF until other formats become more widely supported.

Suggestion: *Alt* text should reinforce the meaning of significant images; if an image does not convey essential meaning, leaving the *alt* value blank may be better than adding noise information to screen readers or cluttering the page with unnecessary *alt* text or tool tips.

Rule: Always use the *height* and *width* attributes with the *<img>* tag.

Rule: Avoid using the *height* and *width* attributes to resize images with HTML, as distortion may occur.

Rule: Always set an image's border attribute to zero unless you have a specific design reason to do otherwise—and remember that linked images with no border attribute will render with colored borders by default.

Suggestion: Don't rely solely on color not only in links but informational graphics.

Suggestion: Do not make a background tile have a very small height or width (e.g. 1-2 pixels), as an annoying monitor flashing effect may result on screen paint.

Rule: Always store your images in a separate directory (usually /images).

Rule: Name your images in a logical fashion that groups them by purpose or usage.

Forms and GUI

These rules and suggestions from Chapter 15 consider Web design and form creation in the light of GUI (Graphical User Interface) principles that have been long established in the field of software design.

Suggestion: Provide online documentation (or in some cases printed documentation) for sites, but don't rely on the user accessing it.

Suggestion: Avoid modification of the appearance of the user's primary browser window.

Rule: When using a full-screen window, inform the user how to exit or provide a close button.

Suggestion: Do not go full-screen without asking the user first.

Suggestion: Use alerts to inform the user of important issues, not general information.

Suggestion: Use prompt dialogs only to ask a user to provide a short word or numeric answer to a simple question. Do not ask questions that would result in a multiple line answer.

Suggestion: Set length of text fields to reasonably fit data being provided.

Rule: Always set the *maxlength* for a text field.

Rule: Only allow a text field to scroll rightward when there is a premium on screen real estate and the data to be entered is larger than the available screen region.

Rule: Never allow password fields to scroll.

Rule: Limit the length of password fields to match password sizes.

Rule: Do not use default values with password fields.

Suggestion: Set text wrapping in multiline text regions for backward compatibility.

Suggestion: Consider vertically aligning related checkboxes to decrease mouse travel.

Rule: Always check an initial radio button by default.

Rule: Use radio buttons for yes/no questions rather than pull-down menus or check-boxes.

Suggestion: Avoid more than ten items in a radio group.

Suggestion: Use pull-downs if more than ten items are in a selection of one-choice-of-many to save screen real estate.

Rule: Do not use radio buttons for navigation.

Suggestion: Avoid changing the display of single choice pull-down menus with the size attribute.

Rule: Make the result of pull-down navigation clear by context, labels, and possibly a trigger button.

Rule: Make sure pull-down navigation degrades gracefully when JavaScript is off.

Rule: If a "Go" button is shown on screen with pull-down navigation, make sure the user can actually click it to trigger page load.

Rule: Reset a pull-down when users back out of a page, as well as select separator items.

Suggestion: Avoid scrolled lists if you expect alternative browsing environments; use check boxes instead.

Rule: When using scrolled lists, make sure to provide some form of instructions on how to select multiple items for novice users.

Suggestion: Do not use default form-style push buttons for navigation; instead, reserve them to cause actions.

Rule: Provide a confirmation on a form reset to avoid accidents.

Suggestion: Consider moving your reset button away from the submit button.

Rule: Provide a final chance before submitting important information or starting a difficult-to-reverse action.

Suggestion: Keep the submit button at the bottom of the form, either center or left side.

Suggestion: Provide a degradable state for image buttons with scripting or images off.

Rule: Make sure to consider the environment of use before using a file upload facility. This may not make sense for users who do not have file storage.

Suggestion: Lay out form elements generally up to down, but consider left to right based upon the context of the information being asked for.

Suggestion: Consider keeping table borders on when formatting table elements, as they help associate labels and fields.

Suggestion: Imitate real-world forms directly if users are very used to filling them out; otherwise, focus on reducing the amount of data entry.

Rule: Make forms keyboard friendly.

Rule: Limit mouse travel between form elements.

Rule: Label all required fields carefully using an asterisk or the word required.

Suggestion: Add *tabindex* attributes to improve form navigation.

Suggestion: Focus the first field of a form page immediately.

Rule: Do not override or mask browser accelerator keys.

Suggestion: Use accelerator keys for forms that will be used repeatedly.

Suggestion: Use tool tips to provide extra information about field use and format.

Suggestion: Use the status bar to provide messages about field use.

Rule: Validate forms client-side when possible.

Rule: Always provide backup validation on the server-side.

Suggestion: Try to validate as people type using masking or as they move from field to field.

Rule: During form validation provide a clear indication of what fields are in error and how to correct the error.

Rule: Bring immediate focus to fields in error.

Suggestion: Mask text fields to limit the type of characters entered.

Suggestion: Disable or hide fields that are not necessary in a particular context.

Suggestion: Provide defaults and always set values to the most likely entry.

Suggestion: Name your fields with simple common names to take advantage of browser AutoComplete features.

Rule: When using a tree control, make sure that open and close states are distinct.

Web Technology Best Practices

These rules and suggestions from Chapter 16 take a closer look at the underlying technologies of the Web and how they impact design considerations.

Rule: Users often don't blame browsers for site errors—they blame sites.

Rule: Users don't care how sites are built, just if they work.

Rule: Site construction must be truly solid—follow standards and conventions, verify correct execution, and openly indicate limitations.

Rule: Acknowledge site problems and avoid placing blame on tools, the Web medium, or users.

Rule: Write pages using standard HTML 4 or XHTML 1.0, or as much as the browser can support.

Rule: Validate all HTML pages.

Rule: If you use a doctype, specify it correctly and adhere to it.

Suggestion: Conform to XHTML today to future-proof Web pages.

Suggestion: Try to separate visual layout from HTML structure using CSS if possible.

Suggestion: Use logical markup elements (e.g. *<strong>* vs. *<bold>*).

Suggestion: Even when creating traditional HTML, lean toward XHTML.

Suggestion: Watch out for HTML space-handling quirks.

Suggestion: Comment and format for readability.

Suggestion: Crunch for delivery.

Suggestion: Specify character set usage explicitly and be cautious of character entities.

Suggestion: Use *<meta>* tags liberally.

Rule: Use consistent naming conventions.

Rule: Use HTML templates.

Suggestion: Use the correct authoring tool for the job.

Rule: Follow CSS1 standards and validate rules.

Rule: Test CSS rules very carefully.

Rule: Bind style only to correct markup.

Suggestion: Be careful when overriding default HTML tag renderings.

Rule: Use external style sheets whenever possible.

Rule: Always comment out document-wide style blocks to avoid interpretation by older browsers.

Suggestion: If backward compatibility is a concern, use CSS to overload HTML presentation tags like *<font>*.

Suggestion: Avoid relying solely on style sheets for layout unless non-CSS compliant browsers can be limited or detected and dealt with.

Rule: Account for CSS being off in browsers.

Rule: Use technologies like JavaScript to account for CSS implementation differences or provide different style sheets based upon browser.

Suggestion: Consider using relative measurements.

Suggestion: Consider using alternative style sheets.

Suggestion: Provide printer style sheets.

Rule: Match CSS selector cases.

Rule: Use id and class rules properly.

Suggestion: Comment, format, and organize CSS rules.

Suggestion: Compress style sheets.

Suggestion: Rely on standard XML languages, rather than in-house developed languages.

Suggestion: Transform XML on the server side into something that can be viewed on the client side.

Suggestion: Use XML as a neutral storage format and for exchange.

Rule: Consider using both client and server-side technologies in a site rather than one or the other.

Rule: Create a capacity plan when using server-side technologies.

Suggestion: Carefully monitor responsiveness of server-side technologies.

Suggestion: Use compiled languages or server modules to improve server-side performance.

Suggestion: Pre generate or at least cache server-scripted pages if possible.

Suggestion: Try to separate out HTML markup from script logic.

Suggestion: Use a centralized directory for server-scripts, particularly cgi-bin programs.

Suggestion: Avoid showing file extensions of server-side programs.

Suggestion: Avoid complex URLs if possible.

Suggestion: Avoid exposing back-end information in diagnostics and errors.

Suggestion: Carefully check incoming data.

Suggestion: Avoid running command-line programs via a script.

Rule: Provide a fallback state for all client-side programming technologies.

Rule: Consider carefully how JavaScript is included in pages.

Suggestion: Use linked scripts.

Suggestion: Focus on using common event handlers.

Suggestion: Consider avoiding HTML event handlers if possible.

Suggestion: Avoid the javascript: pseudo-URL.

Suggestion: Use HTML comments to hide JavaScript code in the *<script>* tag.

Suggestion: Handle the JavaScript off situation with *<noscript>*.

Suggestion: Address JavaScript version issues with the *language* attribute.

Suggestion: Practice JavaScript defensive coding such as object detection.

Rule: Handle or suppress script errors.

Suggestion: Comment and format scripts for maintainability.

Suggestion: Crunch large scripts for delivery.

Suggestion: Provide help for plug-ins, particularly with installation.

Suggestion: Focus on popular plug-ins.

Rule: Detect for plug-in availability.

Suggestion: Use *<noembed>* to support non-plug-in aware browsers.

Suggestion: Consider installation time of ActiveX objects.

Rule: Address browsers lacking ActiveX.

Suggestion: Accept ActiveX's security problems.

Suggestion: Be mindful of Java applet performance issues.

Rule: Address non-Java supporting browsers.

Suggestion: Be realistic about Java support.

Suggestion: Inform users of cookie usage.

Suggestion: Avoid using too many cookies.

Suggestion: Provide alternatives for cookie-denying visitors.

Rule: When trying to draw attention, avoid competing animations.

Rule: Avoid continuously running animation loops.

Suggestion: Inform users of formats and download sizes.

Suggestion: Don't assume or require audio support.

Rule: Allow sound to be turned off.

Suggestion: Make sure multimedia adds to the message.

Site Delivery

These rules and suggestions from Chapter 17 provide an overview of site delivery issues as they impact Web design and the importance of designing sites with future site management concerns in mind.

Rule: The amount of bytes delivered to create a page is not as important as how fast the user perceives the page to be delivered.

Suggestion: Provide numerous domain name forms for a site.

Suggestion: Add multiple guessable URLs for common site sections.

Suggestion: Try to fix simple user URL typos and casing problems at the server level.

Suggestion: Make sure that domain name service for a Web site is fast and robust.

Suggestion: Don't skimp on Web server hardware—focus on systems with high-speed hard drives, a great deal of memory, and good network interfaces.

Suggestion: Don't choose an operating system for a Web server solely based on popularity; consider total cost of ownership and suitability for development and long-term maintenance.

Rule: Always strive to minimize network distance between a site and its users.

Suggestion: Choose to host your own Web site when security or control is a primary concern.

Suggestion: Try to keep the number of unique individual objects in a page small to reduce the number of HTTP requests.

Suggestion: Match data types, number of items, and size of data items to be delivered to the speed of the user's connection.

Suggestion: Consider setting expiration dates for unchanging items such as site graphics.

Rule: Predictable and error-free delivery of real-time data on the Internet cannot be reliably guaranteed with today's protocols and usage.

Suggestion: Utilize a monitoring tool or service to ensure that your site is constantly available to users.

Rule: Create, implement, and test a full-site security policy that goes beyond a simple firewall.

Suggestion: Avoid using underscores in filenames. Consider using dashes or no spaces between words.

Suggestion: Do not use mixed or uppercase letters in file or directory names.

Rule: Pick either .htm or .html as a file extension and stick with it.

Suggestion: Try not to update on demand; instead create a regular update schedule.

Rule: Do not work directly on a live site!

Rule: Check site links constantly.

Suggestion: Check regularly for page details including spelling, legal terms, and font usage. Perform a print test if necessary.

Suggestion: Provide the address webmaster@*yourdomainname*.com for users to contact you with suggestions and error reports.

Suggestion: Do not put a visible page counter on your site.

Rule: Analyze your log files carefully and use them to improve a site or measure its effectiveness.

Rule: Do not rely solely on log files to understand a site's effectiveness. You still have to talk to the site's users.

Rule: If you are collecting sensitive data online, post a privacy policy or statement in an obvious place on the site and abide by it.

Rule: If your content is in any way questionable, have it rated.

Appendix B

Site Evaluation Form

This appendix presents a sample site evaluation worksheet based upon the procedure outlined in Chapter 5. The purpose of this type of site evaluation is to determine the basic characteristics of a Web site to identify obvious usability and execution problems. Tools will be useful to uncover site execution flaws beyond what can be spotted by a competent evaluator. Site delivery and capacity will also require rigorous testing using a tool or server. Finally, further evaluations using actual site users may be required in order to fully understand the real usability of the site.

Electronic copies of the worksheet are available in Adobe Acrobat, Microsoft Word, and RTF format on the book support site at http://www.webdesignref.com/evaluation. Readers are encouraged to adapt the evaluation form to their own needs. Any useful modifications should be forwarded to the author at tpowell@pint.com for potential future inclusion.

■ **Site Evaluation Worksheet: Preliminary Information**

Site name: _____

URL: _____

Purpose of evaluation: _____

Evaluated by: _____

Date: _____

Time: _____

First Impression:—[1 (poor) – 5 (excellent)] _____

General Comments: _____

After the first impression, you should perform a few pretests.

■ **Navigation Pretest   Print the page or do not touch anything. Identify clickable areas on the screen by inspection:**

Number of believed clickable areas: _____

Actual number of clickable areas: _____

Accuracy: _____

Comments: _____

■ **Identity Pretest   Based solely on information presented, identify site owner and describe general type of site.**

_____

_____

■ **Purpose Pretest**   Based upon quick inspection, identify the basic points of the site. What basic functions would it likely provide?

_____

_____

■ **Audience Pretest**   Based upon quick inspection, consider who the audience for the site would be.

_____

_____

GENERAL SITE CHARACTERISTICS

Site Structure

Is a site diagram provided?
Are there any broken links in the site? (use a tool)

❒ Yes

❒ No

If yes, are they broken links to external sites or internal pages?

❒ External

❒ Internal

❒ Both

What is the maximum page depth in the site (clicks from the home page)?

_____

Are there orphaned files in the site?

❒ Yes

❒ No

Are there clear entrance and exit pages to the site?

❒ Yes

❒ No

❒ Describe: _____

Does the site use pop-ups?

❒ Yes

❒ No

If yes, in what situations?

_____

Visuals and Layout

Describe the visuals used in the site:

_____

Do you like the visuals?

❑ Yes

❑ No

Why or why not?

_____

Are the visuals purely decorative, or do they add to the site's function or information?

❑ Only decoration

❑ Improve function

Print out the home page, as well as a subpage and content page. Mark up the printouts to illustrate previous answers and attach to report.

How is the screen contrast [(poor) 1–5 (excellent)]?

_____

If poor, describe why:

_____

Describe text size:

❑ Too small

❑ Just right

❑ Too large

Make browser text size larger or smaller using the browser. Does the text change size?

❑ Yes

❑ No

Does the layout still work with text modifications?

❑ Yes

❑ No

Resize the browser very large or very small. Does the layout still work?

❑ Yes

❑ No

Do the text or images scale with the window size?

❏ Yes

❏ No

Is the layout width static (stays the same size), or does it grow with the screen size?

❏ Static

❏ Stretchable

If the site has a static width, does the page fit, or is there rightward scrolling at:
640 × 480?

❏ Fits

❏ Scrolls right

800 × 600?

❏ Fits

❏ Scrolls right

1024 × 768 and greater?

❏ Fits

❏ Scrolls right

With respect to vertical screen size, does the primary navigation fit on screen at:
640 × 480?

❏ Fits

❏ Scrolls off

800 × 600?

❏ Fits

❏ Scrolls off

1024 × 768 and greater?

❏ Fits

❏ Scrolls off

Note   *You may want to perform this test at resolutions other than those mentioned, depending on your target platform.*

Do pages print correctly as is, or is a special print feature provided?

❏ Prints correctly without special print page

❏ Prints correctly with special print page

❏ Doesn't print correctly

If a special print feature is provided, describe:

- ❐ Special printer page
- ❐ Printer style sheet
- ❐ Adobe Acrobat file
- ❐ Other: _____

What kind of images are used in the site?

- ❐ GIF
- ❐ JPEG
- ❐ PNG
- ❐ Other: _____

Are the images generally used correctly (e.g., GIF for illustrations, JPEG for photos)?

- ❐ Yes
- ❐ No

Are the images optimized properly (e.g., small file size, safe colors)?

- ❐ Yes
- ❐ No

Are there image execution problems (e.g., color matching, seams showing in background tiles, etc.)?

- ❐ Yes
- ❐ No
- ❐ Describe: _____

Is ALT text used for images?

- ❐ Yes
- ❐ No
- ❐ Partially

Is the site usable without images on?

- ❐ Yes
- ❐ No
- ❐ Partially

General Content Statistics

Approximate number of content pages in the site:

_____

Percentage of content pages in site (content pages/total pages):
Content Quality:

Is there enough detail to answer simple user questions?

❒ Yes
❒ No

Is there enough content detail to answer complex user questions?

❒ Yes
❒ No

Does content appear accurate and truthful?

❒ Yes
❒ No

If no, describe what suggests this belief:

_____

Are there obvious misspellings in the site?

❒ Yes
❒ No

Are there egregious spelling errors such as misspellings in buttons or headlines?

❒ Yes
❒ No

Are there obvious grammar or usage errors in the site?

❒ Yes
❒ No

If yes, describe these errors: (e.g., fragments, run-ons, heavy use of acronyms without explanation)

_____

Describe the tone of content in the site (e.g., playful, business like, serious, humorous):

_____

Does the tone of content fit what is presented?

- ❏ Yes
- ❏ No

If no, describe why not:

_____

Is content updated on the site?

- ❏ Yes
- ❏ No

Is update necessary?

- ❏ Yes
- ❏ No

Answer the following questions only if content is being actively updated:
If content requires update, is it fresh?

- ❏ Yes
- ❏ No
- ❏ Partially

On average how often does it appear the content is updated?

- ❏ Daily
- ❏ Weekly
- ❏ Monthly
- ❏ Yearly
- ❏ Other

How was freshness determined? (copyright, label of last update, etc.)

_____

TECHNOLOGY USAGE

HTML
Version(s) used:

- ❏ HTML 2.0
- ❏ HTML 3.2
- ❏ HTML 4.0 Transitional
- ❏ HTML 4.0 Strict

❏ XHTML Transitional
❏ XHTML Strict
❏ No consistent compliance

Proprietary tag use:

❏ Yes
❏ No

Home page validation:

❏ Pass
❏ Fail
❏ Comments
❏ _____

Subpage validation:

❏ Pass
❏ Fail
❏ Comments
❏ _____

Style of HTML: (e.g., tag case, formatting, comments, etc. [(poor) 1–5 (excellent)]

_____

HTML style consistency [(poor – many styles) 1–5 (excellent – strict guidelines)] :

_____

Method of creation:

❏ By hand
❏ Editor/editor(s) used: _____
❏ Translator (e.g., Save as…) From what: _____
❏ Dynamically created/Method: _____

CSS
Version(s) used:

❏ CSS1
❏ CSSP (Positioning features)
❏ CSS2
❏ CSS3

Proprietary properties:

❏ Yes

❏ No

If yes, provide examples:

_____

_____

Do all CSS rules work correctly?

❏ Yes

❏ No

CSS rules inclusion method(s):

❏ Linked style sheet

❏ Document-wide style sheet

❏ Inline style

Quality of rules (e.g., simplicity, style, naming) [1 (poor)–5 (excellent)]:

_____

CSS use consistency [1 (poor, many styles)–5 (excellent, strict guidelines)]:

_____

Method of creation:

❏ By hand

❏ Editor/editor(s) used:_____

❏ Translator (e.g., Save as…) From what:_____

❏ Dynamically created/Method:_____

Compatibility: (CSS compatibility with browsers)

❏ Site works only in the latest CSS browsers

❏ Site uses CSS conservatively

❏ Site uses browser-specific CSS based upon viewer

Degradability: (works without CSS)

❏ Perfect degradation

❏ Degradation with cosmetic or subtle differences

❏ Degradation with serious differences in appearance

❏ Significant layout problems without CSS

XML
Is XML Used?

❐ Yes

❐ No

If yes, where is it used (client side or server side)?

_____

If present, what is it used for?

❐ Data storage

❐ Document structure

❐ Data exchange

❐ For presentation using CSS or XSL

Is the name of XML language used? If not indicate "unknown" or "proprietary".

_____

Is DTD available?

❐ Yes

❐ No

DTD clarity [1 (complex and confusing)–5 (simple and commented)]:

_____

Is the site usable with non-XML aware browsers?

❐ Yes

❐ No

If no, describe how dealt with:

_____

PROGRAMMING

Server-side Technology
Are server-side programming facilities used?

❐ Yes

❐ No

If yes, which ones?

- ❐ CGI (using Perl, C, etc.)
- ❐ Cold Fusion (.cfm)
- ❐ Traditional Active Server Pages (.asp)
- ❐ ASP.NET (.aspx)
- ❐ PHP (.php)
- ❐ Java Server Pages (.jsp)
- ❐ Server-APIs (ISAPI, NSAPI)
- ❐ Other

Describe usage of server-side technologies: (e.g., form processing, dynamic page generation, etc.)

_____

Describe the performance of the server application:

_____

Describe any errors encountered:

_____

Is a database used in the site?

- ❐ Yes
- ❐ No

If yes, describe how the database is used:

_____

Client-side Scripting: JavaScript

Is JavaScript used?

- ❐ Yes
- ❐ No

If yes, describe uses:

_____

How are scripts included?

- ❐ Directly in document
- ❐ Linked to external .js file

Do the scripts function properly?

❏ Yes
❏ No

JavaScript version(s):

❏ 1.0
❏ 1.1
❏ 1.2
❏ 1.3
❏ Other

JavaScript style [(convoluted and not commented) 1–5 (clear and well commented)]:

_____

Is the JavaScript degradable (works on older browsers or without scripting)?

❏ Yes
❏ No

Client-side Component Technology

Java

Are Java applets used?

❏ Yes
❏ No

If yes, describe how they are used and applet(s) name:

_____

Is the Java degradable (warning messages or alternate for no Java)?

❏ Yes
❏ No

Are there functionality problems (e.g., errors)?

❏ Yes
❏ No

If yes, describe how they are used:

_____

Are there performance problems?

❏ Yes

❏ No

If yes, describe:

_____

Are there security problems?

❏ Yes

❏ No

If yes, describe:

_____

ActiveX

Are ActiveX controls used? (e.g., Flash)

❏ Yes

❏ No

If yes, describe:

_____

Does the site work properly without ActiveX controls?

❏ Yes

❏ No

Are there functionality problems? (e.g., errors)

❏ Yes

❏ No

If yes, describe:

_____

Are there performance problems?

❏ Yes

❏ No

If yes, describe:

_____

Are there security problems?

❐ Yes

❐ No

If yes, describe:

_____

Netscape Plug-ins

Are Netscape plug-ins used? (e.g., Flash)

❐ Yes

❐ No

If yes, describe how they are used and the plug-in(s) name:

_____

If a plug-in is not present, is assistance provided to obtain it?

❐ Yes

❐ No

Does the site work properly without plug-ins?

❐ Yes

❐ No

Are there functionality problems? (e.g., errors)

❐ Yes

❐ No

If yes, describe:

_____

Are there performance problems?

❐ Yes

❐ No

If yes, describe:

_____

Are there security problems?

❐ Yes

❐ No

If yes, describe:

_____

Cookies

Are cookies used on the site?

❏ Yes
❏ No

If yes, describe:

_____

If cookies are used, does the site work with cookie support off?

❏ Yes
❏ No

If yes, describe:

_____

Is a privacy policy used on the site explaining cookie use?

❏ Yes
❏ No

BROWSER SUPPORT

Does the site work in Netscape or Mozilla? What versions?

_____

Does the site work in Internet Explorer? What versions?

_____

Does the site works in Opera? What versions?

_____

Are there other browsers supported?

_____

Does the site identify a browser that it does not work in?

❏ Yes
❏ No

If compatibility problems exist, are they explained in the site?

❐ Yes

❐ No

NAVIGATION

Placement of navigation elements:

Primary Navigation (select one or more):

❐ Top

❐ Bottom

❐ Left

❐ Right

Secondary Navigation (select one or more):

❐ Top

❐ Bottom

❐ Left

❐ Right

Tertiary Navigation (select one or more):

❐ Top

❐ Bottom

❐ Left

❐ Right

Does the site use assistance links (breadcrumbs)?

❐ Yes

❐ No

Consistency of navigation placement [1 (random)–5 (very stable)]:

_____

Comments on navigation placement:

_____

Is a navigation hierarchy used? Describe:

_____

Average number of navigation items per page:

_____

What is the average number of navigation items per navigation cluster?

_____

Are alternative forms of navigation provided? Describe:

_____

Does navigation in the site rely on the Back button?

❏ Yes

❏ No

Is a "Back-to-top" button used on longer pages, which requires the user to scroll?

❏ Yes

❏ No

Navigation label clarity: [1 (unclear)–5 (very clear)]

_____

Are scope notes used for labels?

❏ Yes

❏ No

Are tool tips used?

❏ Yes

❏ No

What is the organization of navigation labels?

❏ Alphabetical importance

❏ Random

❏ Other

What forms of navigation feedback are employed?

❏ Font type

❏ Font size

❏ Color

❏ Position

❏ Looks pressable

❏ Underlined

❏ Rollovers*

❏ Sound

❏ Other

Is the navigation feedback useful?

❐ Yes

❐ No

Discuss:

_____

If a link results in a download (e.g., PDF), is the size of the download clearly indicated?

_____

Are link colors modified from the blue, red, and purple defaults?

❐ Yes

❐ No

If yes, is the color combination logical?

_____

Are link colors used consistently throughout the site?

❐ Yes

❐ No

How is location indicated?

❐ URL

❐ Page label

❐ Deselected labels

❐ Depth gauge/breadcrumbs

❐ Color

❐ Design style

Are frames used?

❐ Yes

❐ No

If yes, are they for navigation or layout?

_____

Can pages be bookmarked?

❐ Yes

❐ No

Search

Does site have an internal search system?

❐ Yes

❐ No

If No should one be included?

❑ Yes

❑ No

Why?

_____

How is search accessed?

❑ Within page

❑ Separate page

❑ Both

Search integrated with design?

Type of search:

❑ Free text

❑ Parametric

❑ Both

If parametric is used, describe search parameters:

❑ Search forms

❑ Simple

❑ Advanced

❑ Both

Clarity of search form—[(poor) 1–5 (excellent)]

_____

Are instructions for search form included?

❑ Yes

❑ No

Do negative queries provide reasonable result and help?

❑ Yes

❑ No

Do positive queries provide reasonable results?

❑ Yes

❑ No

Is refinement of queries easily performed?

❑ Yes

❑ No

Known item searching accuracy [(poor – not found) 1–5 (excellent - #1 position)]:

Is meta information provided (for internal and external search engines) on all pages?

❏ Yes

❏ No

If yes, what meta tags are used?

❏ Title

❏ Description

❏ Keywords

❏ Others

Navigation Aids

Site map
Is the site map included?

❏ Yes

❏ No

If no, should a site map be included?

❏ Yes

❏ No

Reason:

What is the method to access the site map?

❏ Link on all pages

❏ Link on one or few pages

❏ Help system or search engine

What is the scope of the site map?

❏ Whole site

❏ Most pages

❏ Main sections

❏ Unknown scope

What is the format of the site map?

❐ Graphical
❐ Text

Is the site map static or dynamic?

❐ Static
❐ Dynamic

If static, is it up to date?

❐ Yes
❐ No

Comments on site map:

_____

Site Index

Is a site index used?

❐ Yes
❐ No

If no, should a site index be included?

❐ Yes
❐ No

Reason:

_____

What is method to access the site index?

❐ Link on all pages
❐ Link on one or few pages
❐ Help system or search engine

What is the scope of the index?

❐ All topics
❐ Main topics
❐ Unknown selection of topics

Is the index static or dynamic?

❐ Static
❐ Dynamic

If static, is the index up to date?

❐ Yes

❐ No

Comments on site index:

_____

Glossary

Is the glossary included?

❐ Yes

❐ No

If no, should a site term glossary be included?

❐ Yes

❐ No

Reason:

_____

What is the method to access the glossary?

❐ Link on all pages

❐ Link on one or few pages

❐ From the help page

Number of terms in glossary:

_____

Comments on glossary:

_____

Form Usage

Are required fields clearly indicated in the form?

❐ Yes

❐ No

Are clear messages and indicators used to show form errors?

❐ Yes

❐ No

Is the first field focused on the form?

❏ Yes
❏ No

Does the form use accelerator/access keys?

❏ Yes
❏ No

Does the form support tabbing well?

❏ Yes
❏ No

Does the form support browser auto-fill in?

❏ Yes
❏ No

Is an adequate confirmation page provided upon form submit?

❏ Yes
❏ No

Help and General Site Error Handling

Does the site deal with common DNS typos? (e.g., ww.xyz.com, wwww.xyz.com)

❏ Yes
❏ No

Is there helpful information with broken links (404 errors)?

❏ Yes
❏ No

If yes, describe:

_____

Is there helpful information when a page has been moved?

❏ Yes
❏ No

If yes, describe:

_____

Does the site deal with browsers, technology, or screen characteristics outside its optimal range?

❑ Yes

❑ No

If yes, how? (clear error message, alternate site, adapted pages, reasonable degradation of pages)

_____

Does the site provide an online help page?

❑ Yes

❑ No

If yes, describe:

_____

Does the site provide basic contact information?

❑ Yes

❑ No

Does the site provide contact for Web-specific problems?

❑ Yes

❑ No

Does the site provide an Online help system?

❑ Yes

❑ No

If yes, describe:

_____

Delivery

What operating system is used on the Web server?

_____

What Web server software with version number is being used?

_____

Where is the site being hosted?

❏ Internal

❏ Externally

Who is the closest "upstream" Internet Service Provider from the server?

_____

What is the amount of bandwidth available for the server if known or determinable?

_____

Rate the responsiveness of the server [1 (very slow)–5 (very fast)]:

_____

What is the largest page in the site, byte wise?

_____

What is the average page size in the site?

_____

What are the theoretical download times for the average and largest pages at:
Modem speeds (56 Kbps) _____
ISDN (128 Kbps) _____
Cable (600 Kbps +) _____
DSL/T1/Ethernet (1 Mbps +) _____

Are real download times similar?

❏ Yes

❏ No

If no, provide times for tested speeds:

_____

THE FINAL SCORE

Final Score [(Dislike) 1–5 (Like a lot)]:

_____

Key reasons for final score:

_____

The Complete Reference

Web Design

Appendix C

XHTML Chart

This appendix provides a quick guide to XHTML rules.

Basic Rules

When using XHTML, one should always follow these basic rules:

- Always include the correct DOCtype declaration at the beginning of the file.
- Add the attribute **xmlns="http://www.w3.org/1999/xhtml"** to the **<html>** tag.
- Tags must be all lowercase.
- Tags must nest properly.
- End tags are required (for example, omitting **</p>** is not valid anymore).
- Empty tags must have an end tag, or the start tag must end with **/>** (for example, **<hr>** becomes **<hr />**).
- Attribute values must be quoted (for example, **<p align="right">**).
- Attribute values cannot be minimized (for example, **<ul compact="compact">**).
- **id** attribute replaces the **name** attribute.
- Script and style characters such as "**<**" and "**&**" are treated as markup characters, so use **&** instead of **&** and **<** instead of **<**.
- Use all mandatory elements: **html, doctype, head, title, body.**

Document Type	Namespace	Description
Transitional	<!DOCTYPE html PUBLIC "-//W3C//DTD XHTML 1.0 Transitional//EN">	The more forgiving, more backwards-compatible version of XHTML
Strict	<!DOCTYPE html PUBLIC "-//W3C//DTD XHTML 1.0 Strict//EN">	The more rigorous, more XML-style version of XHTML
Frameset	<!DOCTYPE html PUBLIC "-//W3C//DTD XHTML 1.0 Frameset//EN">	DTD for frames

XHTML Tags and Attributes

These conventions apply in the following table:

- The attribute entries **Core, International,** and **Event** refer to attribute groups listed in more detail under "Core Attributes," "International Attributes" and "Events Attributes."

■ An asterisk following an attribute indicates a deprecated tag.

Name	Attributes	Description
a	accesskey = character charset = charset coords = Coords href = url lang = language code name = cdata onblur = script onfocus = script rel = link type rev = link type shape = Shape tabindex = number target = frame target type = content type Core International Event	anchor

Note: Cannot contain other a elements.

Name	Attributes	Description
abbr	Core International Event	abbreviation (e.g. WDVL)
acronym	Core International Event	acronym (e.g. WWW)
address	Core International Event	information on author
applet	height = length* width = length* align = Ialign* alt = text* archive = cdata* code = cdata* hspace = pixels* name = cdata* vspace = pixels* Core	Java applet

Name	Attributes	Description
area	alt = text accesskey = character coords = Coords href = url nohref onblur = script onfocus = script shape = Shape tabindex = number *target = frame target* Core International Event	client-side image map area
b	Core International Event	bold text style
base	href = url *target = frame target*	document base URI
basefont	size = cdata* color = color* face = cdata* id = id	base font size
bdo	dir = ltr | rtl id = id style = Style Sheet title = text International	I18N BiDi over-ride
big	Core International Event	large text style
blockquote	cite = url Core International Event	long quotation

Name	Attributes	Description
body	alink = color* background = url* bgcolor = color* link = color* onload = script onunload = script text = color* vlink = color* Core International Event	document body
br	clear = left | all | right | none* Core	forced line break
button	accesskey = character disabled name = cdata onblur = script onfocus = script tabindex = number type = button | submit | reset value = cdata Core International Event *Note: Cannot contain input, select, textarea, label, button, form, fieldset, iframe, isindex*	push button
caption	align = calign* Core International Event	table caption
center	Core International Event	shorthand for div align = center
cite	Core International Event	citation

Name	Attributes	Description
code	Core International Event	computer code fragment
col	align = left | center | right | justify | char char = character charoff = length span= number valign = top | middle | bottom | baseline width = multi length Core International Event	table column
colgroup	align = left | center | right | justify | char char = character charoff = length span= number valign = top | middle | bottom | baseline width = multi length Core International Event	table column group
dd	Core International Event	definition description
del	cite = url datetime = datetime Core International Event	deleted text
dfn	Core International Event	instance definition
dir	compact* Core International Event	directory list

Name	Attributes	Description
div	align = left | center | right | justify* Core International Event	generic language/ style container
dl	compact* Core International Event	definition list
dt	Core International Event	definition term
em	Core International Event	emphasis
fieldset	Core International Event	form control group
font	color = color* face = cdata* size = cdata* Core International	local change to font
form	action= url accept=charset = charset enctype = content type method = get | post onreset = script onsubmit = script target = frame target Core International Event	interactive form

Note: Cannot contain other form elements.

Name	Attributes	Description
frame	frameborder = 1 l 0 longdesc = url marginheight = pixels marginwidth = pixels noresize scrolling = yes l no l auto src = url Core	subwindow
frameset	cols = multilengths onload = script onunload = script rows = multilengths Core	window subdivision
h1, h2, h3, h4, h5, h6	align = left l center l right l justify* Core International Event	heading
head	profile= url International	document head, contains BASE, link, meta, SCRIPT, style, title.
hr	align = left l right l center noshade* size = pixels* width = length* Core Event	horizontal rule
html	version = cdata* International	document root element
i	Core international Event	italic text style

Name	Attributes	Description
iframe	align = ialign* frameborder = 1 | 0 height= length longdesc = url marginheight = pixels marginwidth = pixels name = cdata scrolling = yes | no | auto src = url width = length Core	inline subwindow
img	alt = text src = url align = ialign* border = length* height = length hspace = pixels* ismap longdesc = url usemap = url vspace = pixels* width = length Core International Event	Embedded image

Name	Attributes	Description
input	accept = ContentText accesskey = character align = ialign* alt = cdata checked disabled maxlength= number name = cdata onblur = script onchange = script onfocus = script onselect = script readonly size = cdata src = url tabindex = number type = input type usemap = url value = cdata Core International Event	form control
ins	cite = url datetime = date time Core International Event	inserted text
isindex	prompt = txt* Core International	single line prompt
kdb	Core International Event	text to be entered by the user

Name	Attributes	Description
label	accesskey = character for = idref onblur = script onfocus = script Core International Event	form field label text
	Note: Cannot contain other label elements.	
legend	accesskey = character align = lalign* Core International Event	fieldset legend
li	type = li style* value = number* Core International Event	list item
link	charset = charset href = url hreflang = language code media = media desc rel = link type rev = link type *target = frame target* type = content type Core International Event	a media-independent link
map	name = cdata Core International Event	client-side image map area
menu	compact* Core International Event	menu list

Name	Attributes	Description
meta	content = cdata generic meta information* name = name scheme = cdata International	HTTP-EQUIV = name
noframes	Core International Event	alternate content container for non-frame–based rendering
noscript	Core International Event	alternate content container for when a script is not executed
object	align = ialign* archive = url border = length* classid= url codebase = url codetype = content type data = url declare height= length hspace = pixels* name = cdata standby= text tabindex = number type = content type usemap = url vspace = pixels* width = length Core International Event	generic embedded object
ol	compact* start = number* type = ol type* Core International Event	ordered list

Name	Attributes	Description
optgroup	label = text disabled Core International Event	option group
option	disabled label = text selected value = cdata Core International Event	selectable choice
p	align = left | center | right | justify* Core International Event	paragraph
param	name = cdata id = id type = content type value = cdata valuetype = dat | ref | object	named property value
pre	width = number* Core International Event *Note: Cannot contain img, object, big, small, sub, sup*	preformatted text
q	cite = url Core International Event	short inline quotation
s	Core International Event	strike-through text style
samp	Core International Event	sample program output, scripts, etc.

Name	Attributes	Description
script	type = content type charset = charset defer language = cdata* src = url title = text	script statements
select	disabled multiple name = cdata onblur = script onchange = script onfocus = script size = number tabindex = number Core International Event	option selector
small	Core International Event	small text style
span	Core International Event	generic language/style container
strike	Core International Event	strike-through text
strong	Core International Event	strong emphasis
style	type = content type media = MediaDesc title = text International	style info
sub	Core International Event	subscript

Name	Attributes	Description
sup	Core International Event	superscript
table	align = talign* bgcolor = color* border = pixels cellpadding = length cellspacing = length frame = tframe summary = text width = length Core International Event	table
tbody	align = left | center | right | justify | char char = charset charoff = length valign = top | middle | bottom | baseline Core International Event	table body
td	abbr = text align = left | center | right | justify | char axis = cdata bgcolor = color* char = character charoff = length colspan= number headers = idrefs height = pixels* nowrap* rowspan= number scope = scope valign = top | middle | bottom | baseline width = pixels* Core International Event	table data cell

Name	Attributes	Description
textarea	cols = number rows = number accesskey = character disabled name = cdata onblur = script onchange = script onfocus = script onselect = script readonly tabindex = number Core International Event	multi-line text field
tfoot	align = left	center	right	justify	char char = character charoff = length valign = top	middle	bottom	baseline Core International Event	table footer
th	abbr = text align = left	center	right	justify	char axis = cdata bgcolor = color* char = character charoff = length colspan= number headers = idref height = pixels* nowrap* rowspan= number scope = scope valign = top	middle	bottom	baseline width = pixels* Core International Event	table header cell

Name	Attributes	Description
thead	align = left | center | right | justify | char char = character charoff = length valign = top | middle | bottom | baseline Core International Event	table header
title	International	document title
tr	align = left | center | right | justify | char bgcolor = color* char = character charoff = length valign = top | middle | bottom | baseline Core International Event	table row
tt	Core International Event	teletype or monospaced text style
u		underlined text style
ul	compact* type = ul style* Core International Event	unordered list
var	Core International Event	instance of a variable or program argument

Attribute Reference

The following three tables list the attributes referenced by the **Core**, **International**, and **Event** notations in the table above.

Core Attributes

The following table lists the "core" XHTML attributes.

Attribute	Data Type	Description
class	cdata	Space-separated list of classes
id	id	Document-wide unique id
style	style sheet	Associated style information
title	text	Advisory title/amplification

International Attributes

The following table lists the International XHTML attributes.

Attribute	Data Type	Description
dir	ltr | rtl	Direction of weak/neutral text
lang	language code	Language used on the page

Event Attributes

The following table lists the "Event" XHTML attributes.

Attribute	Data Type	Description
onclick	Script	A pointer button was clicked
ondblclick	Script	A pointer button was double-clicked
onkeydown	Script	A key was pressed down
onkeypress	Script	A key was pressed and released
onkeyup	Script	A key was released
onmousedown	Script	A pointer button was pressed down
onmousemove	Script	A pointer was moved within
onmouseout	Script	A pointer was moved away
onmouseover	Script	A pointer was moved onto
onmouseup	Script	A pointer button was released

The Complete Reference

Web Design

Appendix D

CSS Quick Reference

This appendix provides quick reference charts for CSS properties, grouped by category.

Text or Font Properties   Table D-1 lists CSS properties associated with text display.

Background, Border, Margin, and Padding Properties   Table D-2 lists CSS properties associated with backgrounds, borders, margins, and padding. Properties with the prefix "-moz-" are not part of the official CSS specification, but are adaptations for recent Netscape and Mozilla browsers of styles that may eventually be part of the CSS3 spec.

Page Layout Properties   Table D-3 lists CSS properties associated with page layout.

Element Type (Classification) Properties   Table D-4 lists CSS properties used to define and classify elements.

User Interface Properties   Table D-5 lists CSS properties associated with user interface display.

Generated Content   Table D-6 lists CSS properties associated with generated content.

Printing   Table D-7 lists CSS properties associated with printing content.

New in CSS2	Property	Description	Value	Example
	color	Used to describe the text (foreground) color of an element.	Name: aqua, black, blue, fuchsia, gray, green, lime, maroon, navy, olive, purple, red, silver, teal, white, yellow RGB: color: #0000FF; color: #00F; color: rgb(0,0,255); color: rgb(0%, 0%, 100%)	h1 {color: #66633;}
	font-weight	Specifies the weight, or boldness, of the type.	Descriptive: normal, bold, bolder, lighter Numeric: 100, 200. . .900	strong {font-weight: 700;}
	font-family	Font families may be assigned by a specific font name or a generic font family. Any font name containing white space must be quoted, with either single or double quotes.	Family name (the font needs to be present on the user's machine in order to display). Generic family name (serif, sans-serif, monospaced, cursive, fantasy)	p {font-family: "Trebuchet MS", Verdana, sans-serif;}
	font-size	Specifies the size of the text element. There are four methods for specifying font size.	Absolute: xx-small, x-small, small, medium, large, x-large, xx-large Relative: larger, smaller Length: number + em, ex, px, pt, pc, mm, cm, in Percentage: n%	h1 {font-size: large;} h1 {font-size: larger;} h1 {font-size: 24pt;} h1 {font-size: 125%;}
X	font-size-adjust	Allows authors to specify the "aspect value" that they wish to maintain. It becomes helpful when a specified font is unavailable and the system needs hints to determine the most suitable substitute.	inherit, none, number	h5.med {font-size-adjust: 0.58;}

Table D-1.   *CSS Properties Associated with Text Display*

New in CSS2	Property	Description	Value	Example
	font-variant	Determines if the font is to display in **normal** font or SMALL-CAPS.	normal, small-caps	p {font-variant: small-caps;}
	font-style	Specifies that the font be displayed in one of three ways: **normal**, *italic*, or *oblique* (slanted).	normal, italic, oblique	h1 {font-style: italic;}
X	font-stretch	This is the CSS indication of the condensed or expanded nature of the face relative to others in the same font family.	condensed, normal, expanded	h2 { font-stretch: expanded; }
	text-decoration	Allows text to be decorated through one of five properties.	none (default), underline, overline, line-through, blink	a: link {text-decoration: underline;}
	text-transform	Affects the capitalization of the element.	none, capitalize, lowercase, uppercase	h1.title {text-transform: capitalize;}
X	text-shadow	Specifies one or more comma-separated shadow effects to be applied to the text content of the current element.	inherit, none, [shadow effects]	blockquote {text-shadow: black 3px 3px, yellow -3px -3px;}
	letter-spacing	Specifies an amount of space to be added between characters.	normal, *length*	h5.close {letter-spacing: 0.1cm;}
	word-spacing	Specifies an additional amount of space to be placed between words of the text element.	normal, *length*	h3 {word-spacing: .5em;}

Table D-1.   *CSS Properties Associated with Text Display (continued)*

New in CSS2	Property	Description	Value	Example
	line-height	Will accept a value to control the spacing between baselines of text.	normal, number, *length*, *percentage*	p {line-height: 200%} p {line-height: 1.2em;}
	vertical-align	Affects the vertical alignment of an element.	baseline (default), bottom, middle, sub, super, text-bottom, text-top, top, *percentage*	p.opener {vertical-align: text-top;}
	text-indent	Specifies an amount of indentation (from the left margin) to appear in the first line of text in an element.	*length*, *percentage*	p.first {text-indent: 3em;}
	text-align	Affects the horizontal alignment of the contained text elements.	center, justify, left, right	div.center {text-align: center;}
X	direction	Specifies the direction of text.	ltr, rtl, inherit	div {unicode-bidi: embed; direction: rtl;}
X	unicode-bidi	Defines levels of embedding with regard to Unicode bidirectional algorithm.	inherit, normal, embed, bidi-override	div {unicode-bidi: embed; direction: rtl}

Table D-1.   *CSS Properties Associated with Text Display* (continued)

New in CSS2	Property	Description	Value	Example
	background-color	Sets the background color of an element.	color name or transparent	p.warning {background-color: red;}
	background-image	Sets a background image for the element.	URL, none	body {background-image: url(stripes.gif);}
	background-attachment	Determines whether the background image scrolls along with the document or remains in a fixed position.	scroll (default), fixed	body {background-image: url(stripes.gif); background-attachment: scroll;}
	background-repeat	When a background image is specified, this property specifies whether and how the image is repeated.	repeat, repeat-x, repeat-y, no-repeat	body {background-image: url(stripes.gif); background-repeat: no-repeat;}
	background-position	When a background image has been specified, this property specifies its initial position relative to the box that surrounds the content of the element (not including its padding, border, or margin).	*percentage, length,* top/center/bottom, left/center/right	body {background-image: url(stripes.gif); background-position: bottom left;}
	background	Shorthand property for specifying all the individual background properties in a single declaration.	background-color, background-image, background-repeat, background-attachment, background-position	body {background: aqua url(stars.gif) no-repeat fixed;}

Table D-2.   *CSS Properties Associated with Backgrounds, Borders, Margins, and Padding*

New in CSS2	Property	Description	Value	Example
	border-width	Shorthand property for specifying the width of the border for all four sides of the element box.	thin, medium, thick, *length*	p.header {border-width: thin}
	border-top-width, border-left-width, border-bottom-width, border-right-width	Specifies the border widths of the respective sides of an element's box.	thin, medium, thick, *length*	p.sidebar {border-right-width: medium; border-bottom-width: thick}
	border-color	Sets the border color for each of the four sides of an element box.	*color name*, *RGB value*	blockquote {border-color: red blue green yellow}
X	border-top-color, border-right-color, border-bottom-color, border-left-color	Specifies the border colors of the respective sides of an element's box.	inherit, transparent, *color*, -moz-use-text-color	div {border-top-color: green}
	border-style	Sets the style of border for an element's box.	inherit, none, dotted, dashed, solid, double, groove, ridge, inset, outset, -moz-bg-inset, -moz-bg-outset,	p.example {border-style: solid dashed}

Table D-2. *CSS Properties Associated with Backgrounds, Borders, Margins, and Padding (continued)*

New in CSS2	Property	Description	Value	Example
X	border-top-style, border-right-style, border-bottom-style, border-left-style	Specifies the border style of the respective sides of an element's box.	inherit, none, dotted, dashed, hidden, solid, groove, ridge, inset, outset, double, -moz-bg-inset, -moz-bg-outset,	strong {border-top-style: groove}
	border-top, border-left, border-bottom, border-right	Each of these is a shorthand property for setting the width, style, and color of a specific side of a box.	*border-top-width, border-style, border-color*	h1 {border-left: .5em solidblue}
	border	Shorthand property for setting the border width, style, and color for all four sides of an element box.	*border-width, border-style, border-color*	p.example {border: 2 px dotted #663333}
	margin	Shorthand property for specifying all the margins of an element.	*length, percentage, auto*	img {margin: 0px 12px 0px 12px}
	margin-top, margin-left, margin-bottom, margin-right	These properties specify the amount of margin on specific sides of the element.	*length, percentage, auto*	img {margin-top: 0px}
	padding	Shorthand property for specifying the padding for all sides of an element.	*length, percentage*	p.sidebar {padding: 1em}
	padding-top, padding-left, padding-bottom, padding-right	These properties specify an amount of padding to be added around the respective sides of an element's contents.	*length, percentage*	p.sidebar {padding-top: 1em}

Table D-2. *CSS Properties Associated with Backgrounds, Borders, Margins, and Padding* (continued)

New in CSS2	Property	Description	Value	Example
X	position	Determines whether normal, relative, or absolute positioning methods are used to render the current element box.	inherit, static, relative, absolute, fixed	h2 {position: absolute; top: 20px; right: 50px; bottom: 20px; left: 50px;}
X	direction	Specifies the base direction (reading order) for text content in an element. It is also meant to control the directionality of table columns, text overflow, and positioning of justified text.	inherit, ltr, rtl	div {direction: ltr;}
X	top	Describes the vertical offset for the top edge of the absolutely positioned element box from the top edge of the element's containing block.	inherit, auto, *length*, *percentage*	h2 {top:20px; right: 50px; bottom: 20px; left: 50px;}
X	left	Describes the horizontal offset for the left edge of the absolutely positioned element box from the left edge of the element's containing block.	inherit, auto, *length*, *percentage*	h2 {top:20px; right: 50px; bottom: 20px; left: 50px;}
X	bottom	Describes the vertical offset for the bottom edge of the absolutely positioned element box from the bottom edge of the element's containing block.	inherit, auto, *length*, *percentage*	h2 {top:20px; right: 50px; bottom: 20px; left: 50px;}
X	right	Describes the horizontal offset for the right edge of the absolutely positioned element box from the right edge of the element's containing block.	inherit, auto, *length*, *percentage*	h2 {top:20px; right: 50px; bottom: 20px; left: 50px;}
	width	Sets the width of the element. It can be applied to text elements or as a way to resize images.	*length*, *percentage*, auto	img.photo {width: 75%;}

Table D-3. *CSS Properties Associated with Page Layout*

New in CSS2	Property	Description	Value	Example
X	min-width	Allows a minimum width to be set for an element box.	inherit, *length*, *percentage*	h5 {min-width: 100px;}
X	max-width	Allows a maximum width to be set for an element box.	inherit, none, *length*, *percentage*	h5 {max-width: 150px;}
	height	Sets the height of the element.	*length*, *percentage*, auto	img.photo {height: 75%;}
X	min-height	Allows a minimum height to be set for an element box.	inherit, *length*, *percentage*	h5 {min-height: 100px;}
X	max-height	Allows a maximum height to be set for an element box.	inherit, none, *length*, *percentage*	h5 {max-height: 150px;}
X	z-index	Controls the placement of elements along the z-axis.	inherit, auto, *integer*	h2 {position: absolute; top: 20px; right: 50px; bottom: 20px; left: 50px; z-index: 3;}
X	visibility	Controls whether the content of an element box is rendered (including the borders and backgrounds).	inherit, visible, hidden, collapse, hide, show	p {visibility: hidden;}

Table D-3. *CSS Properties Associated with Page Layout* (continued)

New in CSS2	Property	Description	Value	Example
X	overflow	In cases where content in an element falls outside the element's rendering box (due to negative margins, absolute positioning, content exceeding the width/height set for an element, etc.), the overflow property describes what to do.	inherit, visible, hidden, scroll, auto, -moz-scrollbars-none, -moz-scrollbars-horizontal, -moz-scrollbars-vertical	blockquote {width: 50px; height: 50px; overflow: scroll;}
	float	Positions an element against the left or right border and allows text to flow around it.	left, right, none	p.sidebar {float: right}
	clear	Specifies whether to allow floating elements on an image's sides.	none, left, right, both	h1, h2, h3 {clear: left;}
X	clip	A clipping area describes the portions of an element's rendering box that are visible (when an element's "overflow" property is not set to "visible").	inherit, auto, *shape*	p {overflow: scroll; position: absolute; width: 50px; height: 50px; clip: rect(5px 40px 40px 5px);}

Table D-3.   *CSS Properties Associated with Page Layout (continued)*

New in CSS2	Property	Description	Value	Example
	display	Defines how and specifies if an element is displayed.	block, inline, list-item, none	p {display: block;}
	white-space	Defines how white space in the source for the element is handled.	normal, pre, nowrap	p.haiku {white-space: pre;}
	list-style-type	Specifies the appearance of the automatic numbering or bulleting of lists.	disc, circle, square, decimal, lower-roman, upper-roman, lower-alpha, upper-alpha, none	ol {list-style-type: upper-roman;} (A., B., C., D., etc)
	list-style-image	Specifies a graphic to be used as a list-item marker (bullet).	*url*, none	ul {list-style-image: url(3dball.gif);}
	list-style-position	Specifies whether list items should be set with a hanging indent.	inside, outside	ol {list-style-position: outside;}
	list-style	Shorthand property for setting the list-style type, image, and position (inside, outside) in one declaration.	list-style-type, list-style-image, list-style-position	ul {list-style: list-item url(3dball.gif) disc inside;}
X	table-layout	Controls the layout algorithm used to render table structures.	inherit, auto, fixed	table {table-layout: fixed;}
X	border-collapse	The rendering of table borders is divided into two categories in CSS2—collapsed and separated. This property specifies which border rendering mode to use.	inherit, collapse, separate	table {border-collapse: separate;}
X	border-spacing	Specifies the distance between the borders of adjacent table cells in the "separated borders" model.	inherit, *length*	table {border-spacing: 10pt 5pt;}

Table D-4. *CSS Properties Used to Define and Classify Elements*

New in CSS2	Property	Description	Value	Example
X	cursor	Controls the type of cursor that is used when a pointing device is over an element	inherit, default, auto, *url*, n-resize, ne-resize, e-resize, se-resize, s-resize, sw-resize, w-resize, nw-resize, crosshair, pointer, move, text, wait, help, hand, all-scroll, col-resize, row-resize, no-drop, not-allowed, progress, vertical-text, alias, cell, copy, count-down, count-up, count-up-down, grab, grabbing, spinning	blockquote {cursor: help;}
X	outline	Shorthand method for specifying the outline-color, outline-style, and outline-width properties using a single property notation	inherit, outline-color, outline-style, outline-width	button {outline: red solid thick;}
X	outline-width	Specifies the width for the outline of an element	inherit, thin, medium, thick, *length*	input {outline-width: thin;}
X	outline-color	Specifies a color for the outline for an element	inherit, invert, *color*	img {outline-color: black;}
X	outline-style	Specifies an outline line style for the current element	inherit, none, dotted, dashed, solid, groove, ridge, inset, outset, double	button {outline-style: groove;}

Table D-5.   *CSS Properties Associated with user Interface Display*

New in CSS2	Property	Description	Value	Example
X	content	Automatically generates content to attach before/after a CSS selector (using the :before and :after pseudo-elements.)	inherit, *string*, *url*, *counter()*, open-quote, close-quote, no-open-quote, no-close-quote, *attr(x)*	em:before {content: url("head.gif");}
X	quotes	This property determines the type of quotation marks that will be used in a document.	inherit, none, ([*string*] [*string*])	blockquote: before {content: open-quote} blockquote:after {content: close-quote}
X	counter-reset	The counter-reset property acts like a variable assignment in a programming language—it sets a new value for the specified counter whenever the current CSS selector is encountered.	inherit, none, [*identifier integer*]	h1:before {counter-increment: main-heading; counter-reset: sub-heading;}
X	counter-increment	The counter-increment property acts like an incremented variable in a programming language—it specifies the amount to increment the specified counter by when the current CSS selector is encountered.	inherit, none, [*identifier integer*]	h1:before {counter-increment: main-heading; counter-reset: sub-heading}

Table D-6.   *CSS Properties Associated with Generated Content*

New in CSS2	Property	Description	Value	Example
	@page	Sets page rules.		@page doublepage {size: 8.5in 11in; page-break-after: left;}
X	page	Used to specify a specific page type to use when displaying an element box.	auto, *identifier*	body {page: doublepage; page-break-after: right;}
X	size	Describes the orientation or dimensions of the page box.	inherit, auto, portrait, landscape, *length*	body {size 8.5in 11in;}
X	marks	Printed documents in the printing industry often carry marks on the page outside the content area. These marks are used to align and trim groups of papers. This property specifies what sort of marks should be rendered just outside the rendered page box.	inherit, none, crop, cross	body {marks: crop cross;}
	margin	Shorthand property which allows an author to specify margin-top, margin-right, margin-bottom, and margin-left, properties using a single property and value notation.	inherit, auto, *length*, *percentage*	body {margin: 5px 0px 2px 25px;}
	margin-top, margin-left, margin-bottom, margin-right	Specifies the margin properties of the respective sides of an element's box.	inherit, auto, *length*, *percentage*	address {margin-top: 33%;}
X	page-break-before	Specifies the page-breaking behavior that should occur before an element box and on what side of the page the content that follows should resume on.	inherit, auto, avoid, left, right, always, *empty string*	p {page-break-before: always;}

Table D-7. CSS Properties Associated with Printing Content

New in CSS2	Property	Description	Value	Example
X	page-break-after	Specifies the page-breaking behavior that should occur after an element box and on what side of the page the content that follows should resume on.	inherit, auto, avoid, left, right, always, *empty string*	p {page-break-after: always;}
X	page-break-inside	Specifies the page-breaking behavior that should occur inside an element's rendering box.	inherit, auto, avoid	p {page-break-inside: avoid;}
X	orphans	Specifies the minimum number of lines of content for the current element that must be left at the bottom of a page in a paged display environment.	inherit, *integer*	p {orphans: 4;}
X	widows	Specifies the minimum number of lines of content for the current element that must be left at the top of a page in a paged display environment.	inherit, *integer*	p {widows: 1;}

Table D-7. *CSS Properties Associated with Printing Content* (continued)

The Complete Reference

Appendix E

Fonts

T his appendix contains a quick reference for the commonly available fonts and a brief discussion of downloadable fonts.

Specifying Fonts

Under HTML 4.01 and transitional XHTML 1.0, the **<font>** tag can be used to set a font in a page by setting the **face** attribute:

```
<font face="Britannic Bold">This is important</font>
```

The Web browser will read this HTML fragment and render the text in the font named in the **face** attribute—but only for users who have the font installed on their systems. Multiple fonts can be listed using the **face** attribute:

```
<font face="Arial, Helvetica, sans-serif">
This should be in a different font</font>
```

Here, the browser will read the comma-delimited list of fonts until it finds a font it supports. Given the preceding fragment, the browser would try first Arial and then Helvetica and, finally, a sans-serif font, before giving up and using whatever the current browser font is.

CSS supports the same approach to setting fonts using **font-family** and **font** properties. For example, to set the font to Arial for all text in paragraph tags, we would use a rule like

```
p {font-family: Arial;}
```

Of course, the same restriction of fonts available on the local system applies, so a comma-delimited list of fonts should be specified like so:

```
p {font-family: Verdana, Arial, Helvetica, sans-serif;}
```

Regardless of the approach, a little guesswork can be applied to use fonts properly if you consider that most Macintosh, Windows, and UNIX users have a standard set of fonts. If equivalent fonts are specified, it may be possible to provide similar page renderings across platforms.

Fonts for Microsoft Platforms and Browsers

The following fonts are available for Microsoft browsers and systems; they are displayed in Figure E-1.

Font	Systems
Andale Mono	Internet Explorer 4.5 & 5
Arial	Windows XP, Windows 2000, Windows ME, Windows 98, Windows 95, Windows 3.1x, Windows NT 3.x, Windows NT 4.x, Internet Explorer 4.5 & 5
Arial Bold	Windows XP, Windows 2000, Windows ME, Windows 98, Windows 95, Windows 3.1x, Windows NT 3.x, Windows NT 4.x
Arial Italic	Windows XP, Windows 2000, Windows ME, Windows 98, Windows 95, Windows 3.1x, Windows NT 3.x, Windows NT 4.x
Arial Bold Italic	Windows XP, Windows 2000, Windows ME, Windows 98, Windows 95, Windows 3.1x, Windows NT 3.x, Windows NT 4.x
Arial Black	Windows XP, Windows 2000, Windows ME, Windows 98, Internet Explorer 3, 4, & 5
Comic Sans MS	Windows XP, Windows 2000, Windows ME, Internet Explorer 3, 4, & 5
Comic Sans MS Bold	Windows XP, Windows 2000, Windows ME, Internet Explorer 3, 4, & 5
Courier New	Windows XP, Windows 2000, Windows ME, Windows 98, Windows 95, Windows 3.1x, Windows NT 3.x, Windows NT 4.x
Courier New Bold	Windows XP, Windows 2000, Windows ME, Windows 98, Windows 95, Windows 3.1x, Windows NT 3.x, Windows NT 4.x
Courier New Italic	Windows XP, Windows 2000, Windows ME, Windows 98, Windows 95, Windows 3.1x, Windows NT 3.x, Windows NT 4.x
Courier New Bold Italic	Windows XP, Windows 2000, Windows ME, Windows 98, Windows 95, Windows 3.1x, Windows NT 3.x, Windows NT 4.x

Font	Systems
Georgia	Windows XP, Windows 2000, IE 4 & IE5 (add-on)
Georgia Bold	Windows XP, Windows 2000, IE 4 & IE5 (add-on)
Georgia Italic	Windows XP, Windows 2000, IE 4 & IE5 (add-on)
Georgia Bold Italic	Windows XP, Windows 2000, IE 4 & IE5 (add-on)
Impact	Windows XP, Windows 2000, Windows ME, Windows 98, Internet Explorer 3, 4, & 5
Lucida Console	Windows XP, Windows 2000, Windows ME, Windows 98, Windows NT 3.*x* (except NT 3.0), Windows NT 4.*x*
Lucida Sans Unicode	Windows XP, Windows 2000, Windows 98, Windows NT 3.*x* (except NT 3.0), Windows NT 4.*x*
Marlett	Windows XP, Windows 2000, Windows ME, Windows 98, Windows 95, Windows NT 4.*x*
Minion Web (Adobe)	Microsoft lists this as one of their "core fonts," but it seems to be available (for sale) only from Adobe (http://www.adobe.com).
Monotype.com	Old version of Andale Mono, still available for Windows 3.1 and 3.11 (add-on)
Symbol	Windows XP, Windows 2000, Windows ME, Windows 98, Windows 95, Windows 3.1*x*, Windows NT 3.*x*, Windows NT 4.*x*
Times New Roman	Windows XP, Windows 2000, Windows ME, Windows 98, Windows 95, Windows 3.1*x*, Windows NT 3.*x*, Windows NT 4.*x*
Times New Roman Bold	Windows XP, Windows 2000, Windows ME, Windows 98, Windows 95, Windows 3.1*x*, Windows NT 3.*x*, Windows NT 4.*x*
Times New Roman Italic	Windows XP, Windows 2000, Windows ME, Windows 98, Windows 95, Windows 3.1*x*, Windows NT 3.*x*, Windows NT 4.*x*
Times New Roman Bold Italic	Windows XP, Windows 2000, Windows ME, Windows 98, Windows 95, Windows 3.1*x*, Windows NT 3.*x*, Windows NT 4.*x*

Font	Systems
Tahoma	Windows XP, Windows 2000, Windows ME, Windows 98
Trebuchet MS	Windows XP, Windows 2000, IE 4 & IE5 (add-on)
Trebuchet MS Bold	Windows XP, Windows 2000, Windows 2000, IE 4 & IE5 (add-on)
Trebuchet MS Italic	Windows XP, Windows 2000, IE 4 & IE5 (add-on)
Trebuchet MS Bold Italic	Windows XP, Windows 2000, IE 4 & IE5 (add-on)
Verdana	Windows XP, Windows 2000, Windows ME, Windows 98, Internet Explorer 3, 4, & 5
Verdana Bold	Windows XP, Windows 2000, Windows ME, Windows 98, Internet Explorer 3, 4, & 5
Verdana Italic	Windows XP, Windows 2000, Windows ME, Windows 98, Internet Explorer 3, 4, & 5
Verdana Bold Italic	Windows XP, Windows 2000, Windows ME, Windows 98, Internet Explorer 3, 4, & 5
Webdings	Windows XP, Windows 2000, Windows ME, Windows 98, Internet Explorer 4 & 5
Wingdings	Windows XP, Windows 2000, Windows ME, Windows 98, Windows 95, Windows 3.1x, Windows NT 3.x, Windows NT 4.x

More information about these fonts can be found at http://www.microsoft.com/typography/fontpack/.

Fonts for Apple Macintosh System 7

The following fonts are available for Macintosh System 7; they are displayed in Figure E-2.

Chicago	Courier Regular	Geneva
Helvetica	Monaco	New York
Palatino	Symbol	Times

Andale Mono
Arial
Arial Bold
Arial Italic
Arial Bold Italic
Arial Black
Comic Sans MS
Comic Sans MS Bold
Courier New
Courier New Bold
Courier New Bold Italic
Courier New Italic
Georgia
Georgia Bold
Georgia Italic
Georgia Bold Italic
Impact
Lucida Console
Lucida Sans Unicode
M ⌄ ✕ ⌐ ⌐ ▲ ▲ (Marlett)
Minion Web
Σψμβολ (Symbol)
Times New Roman
Times New Roman Bold
Times New Roman Bold Italic
Times New Roman Italic
Tahoma
Trebuchet MS
Trebuchet MS Bold
Trebuchet MS Italic
Trebuchet MS Bold Italic
Verdana
Verdana Bold
Verdana Bold Italic
Verdana Italic
▶🏛 ⊛ ♥ ①●▧ ? (Webdings)
✛✕◼ ϒ⋄⚖✕◼ ϒ⋄✦ (Wingdings)

Figure E-1.   *Font families available for Microsoft browsers and systems*

Chicago
Courier Regular
Geneva
Helvetica
Monaco
New York
Palatino
Σψμβολ (Symbol)
Times

Figure E-2.   *Font families available with Macintosh System 7*

Additional Fonts for Apple Macintosh System 8 and Higher

In addition to the fonts shown in Figure E-2 for System 7, Macintosh System 8 offers the following fonts; they are displayed in Figure E-3.

Apple Chancery   Hoefler Text   Hoefler Text Ornaments

Skia

Additional Fonts for Apple Macintosh System 8.5 and Higher

In addition to the fonts shown in Figure E-3 for System 8, Macintosh System 8.*x* offers the following fonts; they are displayed in Figure E-4.

Capitals   Charcoal   Gadget

Sand   Techno   Textile

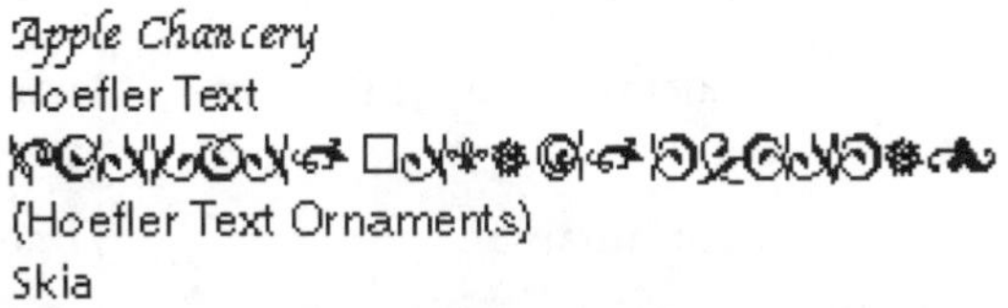

Apple Chancery
Hoefler Text
(Hoefler Text Ornaments)
Skia

Figure E-3.   *Additional font families available with Macintosh System 8*

CAPITALS
Charcoal
Gadget
Sand
Techno
Textile

Figure E-4.   *Additional font families available with Macintosh System 8.5*

Additional Fonts for Apple Macintosh System X

In addition to the fonts shown in Figure E-4 for System 8.5, Macintosh System X offers the following fonts; they are displayed in Figure E-5.

American Typewriter	Andale Mono	Arial
Arial Black	Brush Script	Baskerville
Big Caslon	Comic Sans MS	Copperplate
Courier New	Didot	Georgia
Gill Sans	Futura	Herculanum
Impact	Lucida Grande	Marker Felt
Optima	Osaka	Papyrus
Times New Roman	Trebuchet MS	Verdana
Webdings	Zapf Dingbats	Zapfino

Fonts for UNIX Systems

The following fonts are available for most UNIX systems; they are displayed in Figure E-6.

Charter	Clean	Courier
Fixed	Helvetica	Lucida
Lucidabright	Lucida Typewriter	New Century Schoolbook
Symbol	Terminal	Times
Utopia		

American Typewriter
Andale Mono
Arial
Arial Black
Brush Script
Baskerville
Big Caslon
Comic Sans MS
COPPERPLATE
Courier New
Didot
Georiga
Gill Sans
Futura
HERCULANUM
Impact
Lucida Grande
Marker Felt
Optima
Osaka
Papyrus
Times New Roman
Trebuchet MS
Verdana

Figure E-5. *Additional fonts for Apple Macintosh System X*

Most users may have many other fonts beyond the ones shown in the tables. Users of Microsoft's Office will probably also have access to fonts like Algerian, Book Antiqua, Bookman Old Style, Britannic Bold, Desdemona, Garamond, Century Gothic, Haettenschweiller, and many others. The various browsers are also trying to make new fonts available. Microsoft's Webdings font provides many common icons for use on Web pages viewed in Internet Explore 4.0 or higher. Some of these icons may be useful for navigation, like arrows, while others look like audio or video symbols that could provide an indication of link content.

Charter
Clean
Courier
Fixed
Helvetica
Lucida
Lucidabright
New Century Schoolbook
Σψμβολ (Symbol)
Terminal
Times
Utopia

Figure E-6.   *Font families available on common UNIX systems*

Downloadable Fonts

The best solution for fonts on the Web would be to come up with a cross-platform font that could be downloaded to the browser on-the-fly. Both of the major browser vendors have developed their own versions of downloadable fonts. Microsoft's solution is called OpenType (http://www.microsoft.com/typography). Netscape's solution, called Dynamic Fonts, is based on TrueDoc (http://www.truedoc.com)—but unfortunately, this technology is present only in the 4.*x* generation of the browser and it should be avoided. A cross-platform solution to the font issue using Flash or another binary format is possible but rather involved. Some have tried to address this issue by performing font substitutions on the server side (http://www.em2-solutions.com); but, so far, such an approach is not commonplace. The next section will briefly discuss the only viable downloadable font technology in use at the time of the edition's writing: Microsoft Embedded fonts.

Microsoft's Dynamic Fonts

Microsoft Internet Explorer for Windows provides a fairly robust way to embed fonts in a Web page. To include a font, you must first build the page using the **<font>** element or style sheet rules that set fonts. When creating your page, don't worry about whether or not the end user has the font installed; it will be downloaded. Next, use Microsoft's Web Embedding Fonts Tool or a similar facility to analyze the font usage on the page. The program should create an .eot file that contains the embedded fonts. Then, add the font usage information to the page in the form of cascading style sheets (CSS) style rules, as shown here:

```html
<html>
<head>
<title>Microsoft Font Test</title>
<style type="text/css">
<!--

  @font-face {
    font-family: Ransom;
    font-style:  normal;
    font-weight: normal;
    src: url(fonts/ransom.eot); }
  .special {font-family: Ransom; color: green; font-size: 28pt;}
-->
</style>
</head>
<body>
<font face="Ransom" size="6">Example Ransom Note Font</font><br>
<span class="special">This is also in Ransom</span>
</body>
</html>
```

Notice how it is possible to use both typical style sheet rules like a **class** binding as well as the normal **<font>** tag. A possible rendering of font embedding is shown in Figure E-7.

You must first create a font file and reference it from the file that uses the font. It may be useful to define a font's directory within your Web site to store font files, similar to storing image files for site use.

The use of the **@font-face** acts as a pseudo element that allows you to bring any number of fonts into a page. For more information on embedded fonts under Internet Explorer as well as links to font file creation tools like Web Embedding Font Tool (WEFT), see the Microsoft Typography site (http://www.microsoft.com/typography).

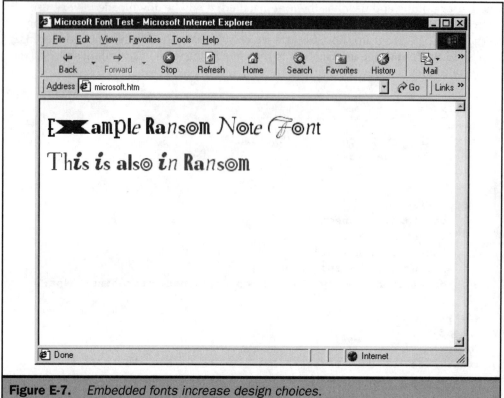

Figure E-7.   *Embedded fonts increase design choices.*

Note   *It is possible to provide links to both Microsoft and Netscape font technology in the same page. This really adds only one line or a few style rules, since the rest of the document would continue to use the same **<font face="">** statements. TrueDoc technology also supports an ActiveX control to allow Internet Explorer users to view their style of embedded fonts. Netscape 6 does not support embedded fonts on any platform, so TrueDoc works only in Netscape 4.x.*

The Complete Reference

Web Design

Appendix F

Color Reference

This appendix provides basic information about the use of colors on the Web, including how to calculate browser-safe colors, adjust unsafe colors, and form hybrid colors. It will also cover the use of color names and their numerical equivalents as used in HTML and CSS, and identify browser support of color names.

Browser-Safe Colors

While 8-bit GIF images support 256 colors, cross-platform issues leave a palette of only 216 colors that are completely safe to use on the Web. This group of Web-safe colors is often called the *browser-safe palette*. It is difficult to present this information visually in a black-and-white book, but the palette can be viewed online at http://www .webdesignref.com/chapter11/designdemos/safepalette.htm. Use of other colors beyond this safe set can lead to poor-looking images when viewed under limited color conditions, such as 8-bit (256-color) VGA. Selecting a set of colors from the safe color palette and mixing them together in a process called *dithering* will approximate colors outside the safe range. This process, which attempts to imitate colors by placing similar colors near them, generally creates irregularities that render the image unappealing.

The selection of the 216 safe colors is fairly obvious if you consider the additive nature of RGB color. Think of a color as being made up of varying amounts of red, green, or blue that could be set by adjusting an imaginary color dial—from the extremes of no color to maximum color saturation. The safe colors suggest six possible intensity settings for each value of red, green, or blue. The settings are 0%, 20%, 40%, 60%, 80%, and 100%. A value of 0%, 0%, 0% on the imaginary color dial would be equivalent to black. A value of 100%, 100%, 100% would indicate pure white, while a value of 100%, 0%, 0% is pure red, and so on. The safe colors are those that have an RGB value set only at one of the safe intensity settings. The hex conversions for saturation are shown in Table F-1.

Setting a safe color is simply a matter of selecting a combination of safe hex values. In this case, #9966FF is a safe hex color; #9370DB is not. Most Web design tools like Macromedia Dreamweaver or HomeSite contain safe color pickers; so do imaging tools like Macromedia Fireworks or recent versions of Adobe PhotoShop. Designers looking for color palettes, including improved color pickers and swatches, should visit http:// www.visibone.com/colorlab/.

Setting an unsafe color to its nearest safe color is fairly easy—just round each particular red, green, or blue value up or down to the nearest safe value. A complete conversion of hex to decimal values is shown in Table F-2. Safe values are indicated in bold.

Although mathematically translating to the closest browser-safe color seems appropriate, the result might not look correct to many people. Consider creating a hybrid color by combining multiple safe colors together. This is done simply by creating a checkerboard effect with a GIF image, in which two or more non-dithering colors are placed side by side to give the appearance of a third color. A variety of PhotoShop plug-ins, such as Colorsafe (http://www.boxtopsoft.com), exist for mixing colors.

Color Intensity	Hex Value	Decimal Value
100%	FF	255
80%	CC	204
60%	99	153
40%	66	102
20%	33	51
0%	00	0

Table F-1. *Color Intensity Conversion Table*

00=00	01=01	02=02	03=03	04=04	05=05
06=06	07=07	08=08	09=09	10=0A	11=0B
12=0C	13=0D	14=0E	15=0F	16=10	17=11
18=12	19=13	20=14	21=15	22=16	23=17
24=18	25=19	26=1A	27=1B	28=1C	29=1D
30=1E	31=1F	32=20	33=21	34=22	35=23
36=24	37=25	38=26	39=27	40=28	41=29
42=2A	43=2B	44=2C	45=2D	46=2E	47=2F
48=30	49=31	50=32	**51=33**	52=34	53=35
54=36	55=37	56=38	57=39	58=3A	59=3B
60=3C	61=3D	62=3E	63=3F	64=40	65=41
66=42	67=43	68=44	69=45	70=46	71=47
72=48	73=49	74=4A	75=4B	76=4C	77=4D
78=4E	79=4F	80=50	81=51	82=52	83=53
84=54	85=55	86=56	87=57	88=58	89=59

Table F-2. *RGB to Hexadecimal Color Conversion Chart*

90=5A	91=5B	92=5C	93=5D	94=5E	95=5F
96=60	97=61	98=62	99=63	100=64	101=65
102=66	103=67	104=68	105=69	106=6A	107=6B
108=6C	109=6D	110=6E	111=6F	112=70	113=71
114=72	115=73	116=74	117=75	118=76	119=77
120=78	121=79	122=7A	123=7B	124=7C	125=7D
126=7E	127=7F	128=80	129=81	130=82	131=83
132=84	133=85	134=86	135=87	136=88	137=89
138=8A	139=8B	140=8C	141=8D	142=8E	143=8F
144=90	145=91	146=92	147=93	148=94	149=95
150=96	151=97	152=98	**153=99**	154=9A	155=9B
156=9C	157=9D	158=9E	159=9F	160=A0	161=A1
162=A2	163=A3	164=A4	165=A5	166=A6	167=A7
168=A8	169=A9	170=AA	171=AB	172=AC	173=AD
174=AE	175=AF	176=B0	177=B1	178=B2	179=B3
180=B4	181=B5	182=B6	183=B7	184=B8	185=B9
186=BA	187=BB	188=BC	189=BD	190=BE	191=BF
192=C0	193=C1	194=C2	195=C3	196=C4	197=C5
198=C6	199=C7	200=C8	201=C9	202=CA	203=CB
204=CC	205=CD	206=CE	207=CF	208=D0	209=D1
210=D2	211=D3	212=D4	213=D5	214=D6	215=D7
216=D8	217=D9	218=DA	219=DB	220=DC	221=DD
222=DE	223=DF	224=E0	225=E1	226=E2	227=E3
228=E4	229=E5	230=E6	231=E7	232=E8	233=E9
234=EA	235=EB	236=EC	237=ED	238=EE	239=EF
240=F0	241=F1	242=F2	243=F3	244=F4	245=F5
246=F6	247=F7	248=F8	249=F9	250=FA	251=FB
252=FC	253=FD	254=FE	**255=FF**		

Table F-2.   *RGB to Hexadecimal Color Conversion Chart* (continued)

Color Names and Numerical Equivalents

Table F-3 lists all the color names commonly supported by the major browsers. The HTML specification defines 16 named colors (aqua, black, blue, fuchsia, gray, green, lime, maroon, navy, olive, purple, red, silver, teal, white, and yellow). Of these colors, only 7 are considered safe in the reproduction sense discussed previously. Many other color names have been introduced by the browser vendors—particularly Netscape—and are in fairly common use. Color names are easier to remember than numerical codes, but they might cause trouble when used with old or uncommon browsers. It is advisable to stick with the hexadecimal approach to colors, since it is generally safer. The corresponding hexadecimal code is shown next to each color name shown in Table F-3, and the code and name are generally interchangeable. Thus, the code **<body bgcolor="lightsteelblue">** would produce the same result as **<body bgcolor="#B0C4DE">** under any browser that supported these color names. Identical colors might be reproducible with different names. For example, "magenta" and "fuchsia" are both equivalent to #FF00FF. Regardless of named color support, keep in mind that not all numeric values are completely browser-safe. Although these names and numbers probably won't be an issue for users with high-resolution monitors and higher degrees of color support, don't forget that these users are not the only people on the Web. Browser-safe colors in Table F-3 appear in bold; RGB equivalents are also included which are useful in graphics programs or CSS rules.

Hexadecimal Code	Name	RGB Equivalent
#F0F8FF	aliceblue	240,248,255
#FAEBD7	antique white	250,235,215
#00FFFF	aqua	0,255,255
#7FFFD4	aquamarine	127,255,212
#F0FFFF	azure	240,255,255
#F5F5DC	beige	245,245,220
#FFE4C4	bisque	255,228,196
#000000	black	0,0,0
#FFEBCD	blanchedalmond	255,235,205
#0000FF	blue	0, 0,255
#8A2BE2	blueviolet	138, 43,226
#A52A2A	brown	165, 42, 42

Table F-3. *Color Names and Their Numerical Equivalents*

Hexadecimal Code	Name	RGB Equivalent
#DEB887	burlywood	222,184,135
#5F9EA0	cadetblue	95,158,160
#7FFF00	chartreuse	127,255, 0
#D2691E	chocolate	210,105, 30
#FF7F50	coral	255,127, 80
#6495ED	cornflowerblue	100,149,237
#FFF8DC	cornsilk	255,248,220
#DC143C	crimson	220,20,60
#00FFFF	cyan	0,255,255
#00008B	darkblue	0,0,139
#008B8B	darkcyan	0,139,139
#B8860B	darkgoldenrod	184,134, 11
#A9A9A9	darkgray	169,169,169
#006400	darkgreen	0,100, 0
#BDB76B	darkkhaki	189,183,107
#8B008B	darkmagenta	139, 0,139
#556B2F	darkolivegreen	85,107, 47
#FF8C00	darkorange	255,140, 0
#9932CC	darkorchid	153, 50,204
#8B0000	darkred	139, 0, 0
#E9967A	darksalmon	233,150,122
#8FBC8F	darkseagreen	143,188,143
#483D8B	darkslateblue	72, 61,139
#2F4F4F	darkslategray	47, 79, 79
#00CED1	darkturquoise	0,206,209
#9400D3	darkviolet	148, 0,211
#FF1493	deeppink	255, 20,147

Table F-3.   *Color Names and Their Numerical Equivalents* (continued)

Hexadecimal Code	Name	RGB Equivalent
#00BFFF	deepskyblue	0,191,255
#696969	dimgray	105,105,105
#1E90FF	dodgerblue	30,144,255
#B22222	firebrick	178, 34, 34
#FFFAF0	floralwhite	255,250,240
#228B22	forestgreen	34,139, 34
#FF00FF	fuchsia	255,0,255
#DCDCDC	gainsboro	220,220,220
#F8F8FF	ghostwhite	248,248,255
#FFD700	gold	255,215, 0
#DAA520	goldenrod	218,165, 32
#808080	gray	127,127,127
#008000	green	0,128,0
#ADFF2F	greenyellow	173,255, 47
#F0FFF0	honeydew	240,255,240
#FF69B4	hotpink	255,105,180
#CD5C5C	indianred	205, 92, 92
#4B0082	indigo	75,0,130
#FFFFF0	ivory	255,255,240
#F0E68C	khaki	240,230,140
#E6E6FA	lavender	230,230,250
#FFF0F5	lavenderblush	255,240,245
#7CFC00	lawngreen	124,252, 0
#FFFACD	lemonchiffon	255,250,205
#ADD8E6	lightblue	173,216,230
#F08080	lightcoral	240,128,128
#E0FFFF	lightcyan	224,255,255

Table F-3.   *Color Names and Their Numerical Equivalents* (continued)

Hexadecimal Code	Name	RGB Equivalent
#FAFAD2	lightgoldenrodyellow	250,250,210
#90EE90	lightgreen	144,238,144
#D3D3D3	lightgray	211,211,211
#FFB6C1	lightpink	255,182,193
#FFA07A	lightsalmon	255,160,122
#20B2AA	lightseagreen	32,178,170
#87CEFA	lightskyblue	135,206,250
#778899	lightslategray	119,136,153
#B0C4DE	lightsteelblue	176,196,222
#FFFFE0	lightyellow	255,255,224
#00FF00	lime	0,255,0
#32CD32	limegreen	50,205, 50
#FAF0E6	linen	250,240,230
#FF00FF	magenta	255, 0,255
#800000	maroon	128,0,0
#66CDAA	mediumaquamarine	102,205,170
#0000CD	mediumblue	0,0,205
#BA55D3	mediumorchid	186, 85,211
#9370DB	mediumpurple	147,112,219
#3CB371	mediumseagreen	60,179,113
#7B68EE	mediumslateblue	123,104,238
#00FA9A	mediumspringgreen	0,250,154
#48D1CC	mediumturquoise	72,209,204
#C71585	mediumvioletred	199, 21,133
#191970	midnightblue	25, 25,112
#F5FFFA	mintcream	245,255,250
#FFE4E1	mistyrose	255,228,225

Table F-3.   *Color Names and Their Numerical Equivalents* (continued)

Hexadecimal Code	Name	RGB Equivalent
#FFE4B5	moccasin	255,228,181
#FFDEAD	navajowhite	255,222,173
#000080	navy	0, 0,128
#9FAFDF	navyblue	159,175,223
#FDF5E6	oldlace	253,245,230
#808000	olive	128,128,0
#6B8E23	olivedrab	107,142, 35
#FFA500	orange	255,165, 0
#FF4500	orangered	255, 69, 0
#DA70D6	orchid	218,112,214
#EEE8AA	palegoldenrod	238,232,170
#98FB98	palegreen	152,251,152
#AFEEEE	paleturquoise	175,238,238
#DB7093	palevioletred	219,112,147
#FFEFD5	papayawhip	255,239,213
#FFDAB9	peachpuff	255,218,185
#CD853F	peru	205,133, 63
#FFC0CB	pink	255,192,203
#DDA0DD	plum	221,160,221
#B0E0E6	powderblue	176,224,230
#800080	purple	128,0,128
#FF0000	red	255, 0, 0
#BC8F8F	rosybrown	188,143,143
#4169E1	royalblue	65,105,225
#8B4513	saddlebrown	139,69,19
#FA8072	salmon	250,128,114
#F4A460	sandybrown	244,164, 96

Table F-3.   *Color Names and Their Numerical Equivalents* (continued)

Hexadecimal Code	Name	RGB Equivalent
#2E8B57	seagreen	46,139, 87
#FFF5EE	seashell	255,245,238
#A0522D	sienna	160, 82, 45
#C0C0C0	silver	192,192,192
#87CEEB	skyblue	135,206,235
#6A5ACD	slateblue	106, 90,205
#708090	slategray	112,128,144
#FFFAFA	snow	255,250,250
#00FF7F	springgreen	0,255,127
#4682B4	steelblue	70,130,180
#D2B48C	tan	210,180,140
#008080	teal	0,128,128
#D8BFD8	thistle	216,191,216
#FF6347	tomato	255, 99, 71
#40E0D0	turquoise	64,224,208
#EE82EE	violet	238,130,238
#F5DEB3	wheat	245,222,179
#FFFFFF	white	255,255,255
#F5F5F5	whitesmoke	245,245,245
#FFFF00	yellow	255,255, 0
#9ACD32	yellowgreen	139,205,50

Table F-3.   *Color Names and Their Numerical Equivalents* (continued)

CSS Color Values

Cascading style sheets (CSS) support the color names and values listed above and also offer a number of other formats not available in HTML.

Three-Digit Hexadecimal Color Values

Under CSS, color values can be defined using three-digit hexadecimal color values, a concise version of the six-digit values just noted. This approach is supported by Internet Explorer 3 and higher and Netscape Navigator 4 and higher.

```
span {font-family: Helvetica; font-size: 14pt; color: #0CF;}
```

RGB Color Values

Under CSS, color values can be defined using RGB values. Colors are defined by the letters *rgb*, followed by three numbers between 0 and 255 that are contained in parentheses, separated by commas, and with no spaces between them. This approach is supported by Internet Explorer 4 and higher and Netscape Navigator 4 and higher.

```
p {color: rgb(204,0,51);}
```

RGB Color Values Using Percentages

Under CSS, RGB color values can also be defined using percentages. The format is the same, except that the numbers are replaced by percentage values between 0% and 100%. This approach is supported by Internet Explorer 4 and higher and Netscape Navigator 4 and higher.

```
p {color: rgb(75%,10%,50%);}
```

Color Practices

Certain limitations of color use on the Web are rapidly being eclipsed by improvements in technology. One thing to consider is whether the 216-color palette actually matters any more. Back in the early days of the Web, most end users had systems that were limited to 8-bit color—the very limitation the 216-color limit was devised to work with. These days, however, monitors with thousands or millions of colors are common, as more and more users gear up their computers for improved gaming or graphics manipulation, and the baseline color capacity of new computer products generally exceeds 8-bit technology. (On the other hand, the rise of wireless handheld devices is bringing the old color issues back into focus in another corner of the Web.)

The bottom line, as always, is to carefully consider who you are trying to reach with your site. If you have a compelling reason to keep your site usable for people with older, more limited systems, do so. More general usability issues, such as concerns about users with poor vision or color blindness, may make the proper contrast of colors more important than aesthetic concerns. For more on these issues, see Chapter 13.

The Complete Reference

Web Design

HTTP

The Hypertext Transfer Protocol (HTTP) is the basic, underlying, application-level protocol used to facilitate the transmission of data to and from a Web server. HTTP provides a simple, fast way to specify the interaction between client and server. The protocol actually defines how a client must ask for data from the server and how the server returns it. HTTP does not specify how the data actually is transferred; that is up to lower-level network protocols such as TCP.

The first version of HTTP, known as version 0.9, was used as early as 1990. HTTP version 1.0, as defined by RFC 1945, is supported by most servers and clients (Web browsers). However, HTTP 1.0 does not properly handle the effects of hierarchical proxies and caching or provide features to facilitate virtual hosts. More important, HTTP 1.0 has significant performance problems due to the opening and closing of many connections for a single Web page. The current version, HTTP 1.1, defined in RFC 2616, solves many of the past problems of the protocol. It has been supported since the 4.x generation Web browsers, and most servers use it as well.

HTTP in Action

The process of a Web browser or other user agent, such as Web spider or Robot, requesting a document from a Web server (more correctly, HTTP server) is simple and has been discussed throughout the book.

First, a user requests a document from a Web server by specifying the URL of the document desired. During this step, a domain name lookup might occur, which translates a machine name such as www.democompany.com to an underlying IP address such as 206.251.142.3. If the domain name lookup fails, an error message such as "No Such Host" or "The server does not have a DNS entry" will be returned. Certain assumptions, such as the default service port to access for HTTP requests (80), also might be made. This is transparent to the user, who simply uses a URL to access a page. Once the server has been located, the browser forms the proper HTTP request and sends the request to the server residing at the address specified by the URL. A typical HTTP request might be

```
HTTP-Method Identifier HTTP-version
<Optional additional request headers>
```

In this example, the HTTP-Method would be **GET** or **POST**. An identifier might correspond to the file desired (for example, /documents/report.htm), and the HTTP-version indicates the dialect of HTTP being used, such as HTTP/1.1.

If a user requests a document with the URL http://www.webdesignref.com/examples/report.htm, the browser might generate a request such as the one shown here to retrieve the object from the server:

```
GET /examples/report.htm HTTP/1.1
If-Modified-Since: Tuesday, 30-Apr-02 01:39:39 GMT;
```

```
Connection: Keep-Alive
User-Agent: Mozilla/4.02 [en] (X11; I; SunOS 5.4 sun4m)
Accept: image/gif, image/x-xbitmap, image/jpeg, image/pjpeg, */*
Accept-Language: en
Accept-Charset: iso-8859-1,*,utf-8
```

People often ask why the complete URL is not shown in the request. It isn't necessary in most cases, except when using a proxy server. The use of a relative URL in the header is adequate. The server knows where it is; it just needs to know what document to get from its own file tree. In the case of using a proxy server, which requests a document on behalf of a browser, a full URL is passed to it that later is made relative by the proxy. Aside from the simple **GET** method, there are various other methods specified in HTTP. Not all are commonly used. Table G-1 provides a summary of the HTTP 1.1 request methods.

Method	Description
GET	Returns the object specified by the identifier. It is also one of the values of the **method** attribute for the **<form>** element.
HEAD	Returns information about the object specified by the identifier, such as last modification data, but does not return the actual object.
OPTIONS	Returns information about the capabilities supported by a server if no location is specified or the possible methods that can be applied to the specified object.
POST	Sends information to the address indicated by the identifier; generally used to transmit information from a form using the **method="POST"** attribute of the **<form>** element to a server-based CGI program.
PUT	Sends data to the server and writes it to the address specified by the identifier, overwriting previous content; in basic form, can be used for file upload.
DELETE	Removes the file specified by the identifier; generally disallowed.
TRACE	Provides diagnostic information by allowing the client to see what is being received on the server.

Table G-1.   *Summary of HTTP 1.1 Request Methods*

It is interesting to note that two of the methods (**GET** and **POST**) supported by HTTP are the values of the **<form>** element's **method** attribute. Recall that this attribute indicates the method in which data is passed from the form to the server-side program. In the case of **GET**, it is passed through the URL because another page is simply being fetched, as a normal **GET** request would do. In the case of a **POST** value, the data of the form is passed behind the scenes to the server program, which should return a result page to the browser as well. As shown by the **<form>** element, it should become clear that HTML and HTTP do interact in more than a casual way.

Within an HTTP request, there are a variety of optional fields for creating a complete request. These are shown in Table G-2.

| Note |

The header information is extremely valuable—you can detect things such as the browser being used, the particular types of images supported by the browser, the language of the browser (such as French, English, or Japanese), and so on.

Field	Description	Example
Accept: *MIME-type/MIME-subtype*	This field indicates the data types accepted by the browser. An entry of */* indicates anything is accepted; however, it is possible to indicate particular content types, such as image/jpeg, so the server can make a decision on what to return. This facility could be used to introduce a form of content negotiation so that a browser could be served only data it understands or prefers, although this approach is not widely understood or implemented.	`Accept: image/gif,` `image/x-xbitmap,` `image/jpeg, image/` `pjpeg, */*`

Table G-2.   *HTTP request headers*

Field	Description	Example

Accept-Charset: *charset*	This field indicates the character set that is accepted by the browser, such as ASCII or foreign character encodings.	`Accept-Charset:`
		`iso-8859-1,*,`
		`utf-8`

Accept-Encoding: *encoding-type*	This field instructs the server on what type of encoding the browser understands. Typically, this field is used to indicate to the server that compressed data can be handled.	`Accept-Encoding:` `x-compress`
Accept-Language: *language*	This field lists the languages preferred by the browser and could be used by the server to pass back the appropriate language data.	`Accept-Language: en`

Authorization: *authorization-scheme authorization-data*	This field typically is used to indicate the userid and encrypted password if the user is returning authorization information.
	
	Generally, the password is transmitted unencrypted, thus the need for security protocols such as SSL.
		`Authorization:`
		`user joeblow:`
		`testpass`

Table G-2.   *HTTP request headers* (continued)

Field	Description	Example
Content-length: *bytes*	This field gives the length in bytes of the message being sent to the server, if any. Remember that the browser can upload or pass data using the **PUT** or **POST** method.	`Content-length: 1805`
Content-type: *MIME-type/MIME-subtype*	This field indicates the MIME-type of a message being sent to a server, if any. The value of this field would be particularly important in the case of file upload.	`Content-type: text/plain`
Date: *date-time*	This field indicates the date and time that a request was made in Greenwich Mean Time (GMT). GMT time is mandatory for time consistency, given the worldwide nature of the Web.	`Date: Thursday, 15-Jan-98 01: 39:39 GMT`
Host	This field indicates the host and port of the server to which the request is being made.	`Host: www. democompany.com`

Table G-2.   *HTTP request headers* (continued)

Field	Description	Example
If-Modified-Since: *date-time*	This field indicates file freshness to improve the efficiency of the **GET** method. When used in conjunction with a **GET** request for a particular file, the requested file is checked to see if it has been modified since the time specified in the field. If the file has not been modified, a "not modified" code (304) is sent to the client so a cached version of the document can be used; otherwise, the file is returned normally.	`If-Modified-Since:` `Thursday,` `15-Jan-98 01:39:` `39 GMT`
If-Match: *"selector-string"*	This field makes a request conditionally only if the items match some selector value passed in. Consider using **POST** only to add data once it has been moved to a file called olddata.	`If-Match:` `"olddata"`

Table G-2. *HTTP request headers* (continued)

Field	Description	Example
If-None-Match: *"selector-string"*	This field does the opposite of If-Match. The method is conditional only if the selector does not match anything. This might be useful for preventing overwrites of existing files.	`If-None-Match: "newfile"`
If-Range: *selector*	If a client has a partial copy of an object in its cache and wishes to have an up-to-date copy of the entire object there, it could use the Range request header with this conditional If-Range modifier to update the file. Modification selection can take place on time as well.	`If-Range: Thursday, 15-Jan-98 01:39: 39 GMT;`
If-Unmodified-Since	This field makes a conditional method. If the requested file has not been modified since the specified time, the server should perform the requested method; otherwise, the method should fail.	`If-Unmodified- Since: Thursday, 15-Jan-98 01:39: 39 GMT`

Table G-2.   *HTTP request headers* (continued)

APPENDIXES

Field	Description	Example
Max-Forwards: *integer*	This field is used with the **TRACE** method to limit the number of proxies or gateways that can forward the request. This would be useful in determining failures if a request moves through many proxies before reaching the final server.	`Max-Forwards: 6`
MIME-version: *version-number*	This field indicates the MIME protocol version, understood by the browser, that the server should use when fulfilling requests.	`MIME-Version: 1.0`
Proxy-Authorization: *authorization information*	This field allows the client to identify itself or the user to a proxy that requires authentication.	`Proxy-Authorization: joeblow: testpass; Realm: All`
Pragma: *server-directive*	This field passes information to a server; for example, this field can be used to inform a caching proxy server to fetch a fresh copy of a page.	`Pragma: no-cache`

Table G-2.   *HTTP request headers* (continued)

Field	Description	Example
Range: *byte-range*	This field requests a particular range of a file, such as a certain number of bytes. The example shows a request for the last 500 bytes of a file.	`Range: bytes=-500`
Referer: *URL*	This field indicates the URL of the document from which the request originates (in other words, the linking document). This value might be empty if the user has entered the URL directly, rather than by following a link.	`Referer: http://www.democompany.com/reports/index.html`
User-Agent: *Agent-code*	This field indicates the type of browser making the request.	`User-Agent: Mozilla/4.0 (compatible; MSIE 5.5; Windows 98)`

Table G-2.   *HTTP request headers* (continued)

Once again, note that all of these request headers seem very familiar. They constitute the same environment variables that you can access from within a CGI program. Now it should be clear how this information is obtained.

After receiving a request, the Web server attempts to process the request. The result of the request is indicated by a server status line that contains a response code; for example, the ever popular "404 Not Found." The server response status line takes this form:

```
HTTP-version Status-code Reason-String
```

For a successful query, a status line might read

```
HTTP/1.0   200   OK
```

whereas in the case of an error, the status line might read

```
HTTP/1.0   404   Not Found
```

The status codes for the emerging HTTP 1.1 standard are shown in Table G-3.

After the status line, the server responds with information about itself and the data being returned. There are various selected response headers, but the most important indicate the type of data in the form of a MIME-type and subtype that will be returned. Like request headers, many of these codes are optional and depend on the status of the request.

Status-Code	Reason-String	Description
Informational Codes (Process Continues After This)		
100	Continue	An interim response issued by the server that indicates the request is in progress but has not been rejected or accepted. This status code is in support of the persistent connection idea introduced in HTTP 1.1
101	Switching Protocols	Can be returned by the server to indicate that a different protocol should be used to improve communication. This could be used to initiate a real-time protocol.
Success Codes (Request Understood and Accepted)		
200	OK	Indicates the successful completion of a request.
201	Created	Indicates the successful completion of a **PUT** request and the creation of the file specified.

Table G-3.   *HTTP 1.1 Status Codes*

Status-Code	Reason-String	Description
202	Accepted	Indicates that the request has been accepted for processing, but that the processing has not been completed and the request might or might not actually finish properly.
203	Non-Authoritative Information	Indicates a successful request, except that returned information, particularly meta-information about a document, comes from a third source and is unverifiable.
204	No Content	Indicates a successful request, but there is no new data to send to the client.
205	Reset Content	Indicates that the client should reset the page that sent the request (potentially for more input). This could be used on a form page that needs consistent refreshing, rather than reloading as might be used in a chat system.

Table G-3.   *HTTP 1.1 Status Codes* (continued)

Status-Code	Reason-String	Description
206	Partial Content	Indicates a successful request for a piece of a larger document or set of documents. This response typically is encountered when media is sent out in a particular order, or byte-served, as with streaming Acrobat files.

Redirection Codes (Further Action Necessary to Complete Request)

300	Multiple Choices	Indicates that there are many possible representations for the requested information, so the client should use the preferred representation, which might be in the form of a closer server or different data format.
301	Moved Permanently	Requested resource has been assigned a new permanent address, and any future references to this resource should be made using one of the returned addresses.
302	Moved Temporarily	Requested resource temporarily resides at a different address. For future requests, the original address should still be used.

Table G-3. *HTTP 1.1 Status Codes* (continued)

Status-Code	Reason-String	Description
303	See Other	Indicates that the requested object can be found at a different address and should be retrieved using a **GET** method on that resource.
304	Not Modified	Issued in response to a conditional **GET**; indicates to the agent to use a local copy from cache or similar action as the request object has not changed.
305	Use Proxy	Indicates that the requested resource must be accessed through the proxy given by the URL in the Location field.

Client Error Codes (Syntax Error or Other Problem Causing Failure)

Status-Code	Reason-String	Description
400	Bad Request	Indicates that the request could not be understood by the server due to malformed syntax.
401	Unauthorized	Request requires user authentication. The authorization has failed for some reason, so this code is returned.
402	Payment Required	Obviously in support of commerce, this code is currently not well defined.

Table G-3.   *HTTP 1.1 Status Codes* (continued)

Status-Code	Reason-String	Description
403	Forbidden	Request is understood but disallowed and should not be reattempted (the 401 code, by contrast, might suggest a reauthentication). A typical response code in response to a query for a directory listing when such requests are disallowed.
404	Not Found	Usually issued in response to a typo by the user or a moved resource, as the server can't find anything that matches the request, nor is there any indication that the requested item has been moved.
405	Method Not Allowed	Issued in response to a method request, such as **GET**, **POST**, or **PUT**, on an object where such a method is not supported. Generally an indication of what methods that are supported will be returned.

Table G-3. *HTTP 1.1 Status Codes* (continued)

Status-Code	Reason-String	Description
406	Not Acceptable	Indicates that the response to the request will not be in one of the content types acceptable by the browser—so why bother doing the request? This is an unlikely response given the */* acceptance issued by most, if not all, browsers.
407	Proxy Authentication Required	Indicates that the proxy server requires some form of authentication to continue. This code is similar to the 401 code.
408	Request Time-out	Indicates that the client did not produce or finish a request within the time that the server was prepared to wait.
409	Conflict	The request could not be completed because of a conflict with the requested resource; for example, the file might be locked.
410	Gone	Indicates that the requested object is no longer available at the server and no forwarding address is known. Search engines might want to add remote references to objects that return this value, since it is a permanent condition.

Table G-3. *HTTP 1.1 Status Codes* (continued)

Status-Code	Reason-String	Description
411	Length Required	Indicates that the server refuses to accept the request without a defined Content-Length. This might happen when a file is posted without a length.
412	Precondition Failed	Indicates that a precondition given in one or more of the request header fields, such as If-Unmodified-Since, evaluated to False.
413	Request Entity Too Large	Indicates that the server is refusing to return data because the object might be too large or the server might be too loaded to handle the request. The server also might provide information indicating when to try again, if possible, but just as well might terminate any open connections.
414	Request-URI Too Large	Indicates that the Uniform Resource Identifier (URI), generally a URL, in the request field is too long for the server to handle. This is unlikely to occur, as browsers probably will not allow such transmissions.

Table G-3.   *HTTP 1.1 Status Codes* (continued)

Status-Code	Reason-String	Description
415	Unsupported Media Type	Indicates the server will not perform the request because the media type specified in the message is not supported. This code might be returned when a server receives a file that it is not configured to accept with the **PUT** method.

Server Error Codes (Server Can't Fulfill a Potentially Valid Request)

Status-Code	Reason-String	Description
500	Internal Server Error	A serious error message indicating that the server encountered an internal error that keeps it from fulfilling the request.
501	Not Implemented	This response is to a request that the server does not support or that might be understood but is not implemented.
502	Bad Gateway	Indicates that the server acting as a proxy encountered an error from some other gateway and is passing the message along.
503	Service Unavailable	Indicates the server currently is overloaded or is undergoing maintenance. Headers can be sent to indicate when the server will be available.

Table G-3. *HTTP 1.1 Status Codes* (continued)

Status-Code	Reason-String	Description
504	Gateway Time-out	Indicates that the server, when acting as a gateway or proxy, encountered too long a delay from an upstream proxy and decided to time out.
505	HTTP Version not supported	Indicates that the server does not support the HTTP version specified in the request.

Table G-3.   *HTTP 1.1 Status Codes* (continued)

Here is an example server response for the request shown earlier:

```
HTTP/1.1 200 OK
Date: Mon, 29 Apr 2002 18:59:54 GMT
Server: Apache/1.3.12 (Unix)
Last-Modified: Fri, 25 Aug 2000 22:19:12 GMT
Accept-Ranges: bytes
Content-Length: 205
Connection: close
Content-Type: text/html

<!DOCTYPE HTML PUBLIC "-//W3C//DTD HTML 4.01 Transitional//EN">
<html>
<head>
<title>Report 1</title>
</head>

<body>
<h1>Report about Important Things</h1>
<hr>
<p>Here is some information about important things. </p>

</body>
</html>
```

A list of the common server response headers for HTTP 1.1, as well as examples of each, can be found in Table G-4.

Response Header	Description	Example
Age	Shows the sender's estimate of the amount of time since the response was generated at the origin server. Age values are nonnegative decimal integers, representing time in seconds.	Age: 10
Content-encoding	Indicates the encoding the data returned is in.	Content-encoding: x-compress
Content-language	Indicates the language used for the data returned by the server.	Content-language: en
Content-length	Indicates the number of bytes returned by the server.	Content-length: 205
Content-range	Indicates the range of the data being sent back by the server.	Content-range: -500
Content-type	This probably is the most important field and indicates what type of content is being returned by the server in the form of a MIME-type.	Content-type: text/html
Expires	Gives the date/time after which the returned data should be considered stale and should not be returned from a cache.	Expires: Thu, 04 Dec 1997 16:00:00 GMT

Table G-4.   *Common HTTP 1.1 Server Response Headers*

Response Header	Description	Example
Last-modified	The Last-modified response-header field is used to indicate the date the content returned was last modified. This can be used by caches to decide to keep local copies of objects.	Last-modified: Thursday, 01-Aug-96 10:09:00 GMT
Location	Used to redirect the browser to another page. Occasionally scripts will use this method for browser redirection based on capability.	Location: http://www.democompany.com/products/index.htm
Proxy-authenticate	Included with a 407 (Proxy Authentication Required) response. The value of the field consists of a challenge that indicates the authentication scheme and parameters applicable to the proxy for the request.	Proxy-authenticate: GreenDecoderRing: 0124.
Public	Lists the set of methods supported by the server. The purpose of this field is strictly to inform the browser of the capabilities of the server when new or unusual methods are encountered.	Public: **OPTIONS, MGET, MHEAD, GET, HEAD**

Table G-4. *Common HTTP 1.1 Server Response Headers* (continued)

Response Header	Description	Example
Retry-after	Can be used in conjunction with a 503 (Service Unavailable) response to indicate how long the service is expected to be unavailable to the requesting client. The value of this field can be either an HTTP date or an integer number of seconds after which to retry.	Retry-after: Fri, 31 Dec 1999 23:59:59 GMT Retry-after: 60
Server	Contains information about the Web software used.	Server: Apache/1.3.12 (Unix)
Warning	Used to carry additional information about the status of a response that might not be found in the status code.	Warning: 10 Response is stale
WWW-authenticate	Included with a 401 (Unauthorized) response message. The field consists of at least one challenge that indicates the authentication scheme and parameters applicable to the request made by the client.	WWW-authenticate: Magic-Key-Challenge= 555121, DecoderRing= Green

Table G-4.   *Common HTTP 1.1 Server Response Headers* (continued)

Note   *The most important header response field is the Content-type field. The MIME-type indicated by this field is a device by which the browser is able to figure out what to do with the data being returned.*

Index

E

I

INTERNATIONAL CONTACT INFORMATION

AUSTRALIA
McGraw-Hill Book Company Australia Pty. Ltd.
TEL +61-2-9415-9899
FAX +61-2-9415-5687
http://www.mcgraw-hill.com.au
books-it_sydney@mcgraw-hill.com

CANADA
McGraw-Hill Ryerson Ltd.
TEL +905-430-5000
FAX +905-430-5020
http://www.mcgrawhill.ca

**GREECE, MIDDLE EAST,
NORTHERN AFRICA**
McGraw-Hill Hellas
TEL +30-1-656-0990-3-4
FAX +30-1-654-5525

MEXICO (Also serving Latin America)
McGraw-Hill Interamericana Editores S.A. de C.V.
TEL +525-117-1583
FAX +525-117-1589
http://www.mcgraw-hill.com.mx
fernando_castellanos@mcgraw-hill.com

SINGAPORE (Serving Asia)
McGraw-Hill Book Company
TEL +65-863-1580
FAX +65-862-3354
http://www.mcgraw-hill.com.sg
mghasia@mcgraw-hill.com

SOUTH AFRICA
McGraw-Hill South Africa
TEL +27-11-622-7512
FAX +27-11-622-9045
robyn_swanepoel@mcgraw-hill.com

**UNITED KINGDOM & EUROPE
(Excluding Southern Europe)**
McGraw-Hill Education Europe
TEL +44-1-628-502500
FAX +44-1-628-770224
http://www.mcgraw-hill.co.uk
computing_neurope@mcgraw-hill.com

ALL OTHER INQUIRIES Contact:
Osborne/McGraw-Hill
TEL +1-510-549-6600
FAX +1-510-883-7600
http://www.osborne.com
omg_international@mcgraw-hill.com